AF182115

Handbook of Positive Body Image and Embodiment

Handbook of Positive Body Image and Embodiment

Constructs, Protective Factors, and Interventions

EDITED BY TRACY L. TYLKA

AND

NIVA PIRAN

OXFORD
UNIVERSITY PRESS

OXFORD
UNIVERSITY PRESS

Oxford University Press is a department of the University of Oxford. It furthers the University's objective of excellence in research, scholarship, and education by publishing worldwide. Oxford is a registered trade mark of Oxford University Press in the UK and certain other countries.

Published in the United States of America by Oxford University Press
198 Madison Avenue, New York, NY 10016, United States of America.

© Oxford University Press 2019

All rights reserved. No part of this publication may be reproduced, stored in a retrieval system, or transmitted, in any form or by any means, without the prior permission in writing of Oxford University Press, or as expressly permitted by law, by license, or under terms agreed with the appropriate reproduction rights organization. Inquiries concerning reproduction outside the scope of the above should be sent to the Rights Department, Oxford University Press, at the address above.

You must not circulate this work in any other form
and you must impose this same condition on any acquirer.

CIP data is on file at the Library of Congress
ISBN 978-0-19-084187-4

In memory of Professor Lina Ricciardelli—

An inspiring scholar, leader, mentor, colleague, and friend.

CONTENTS

SECTION II Cultivating Positive Body Image and Embodiment: Protective Relational, Social, and Other Environmental Factors

LIST OF TABLES AND FIGURES

TABLES

FIGURES

ACKNOWLEDGMENTS

Scholarly work on positive body image and embodiment has burgeoned within the last 15 years, with new insights shaping our understanding of how individuals can positively inhabit their bodies as they engage with the world. Together as co-editors, we set a goal to synthesize and distill this work into a go-to resource for professionals to shape their theory, research, and practice. To achieve this aim, we relied on our colleagues, internationally recognized experts in the body image field. They did not disappoint! Since the inception of this volume, we have felt supported by their enthusiastic responses and willingness to write chapters related to the diverse volume content. They deftly distilled their scientific wisdom into succinct reviews of specific constructs, protective factors, and interventions that address the depth and complexity of positive body image and embodiment. Moreover, they offered innovative insights on how we can carry these constructs, protective factors, and interventions forward in research and practice. We are indebted and grateful to our colleagues who have contributed to this volume.

We also recognize that research and scholarly work involves a larger group of individuals who contribute to progress in the field. We have often commented about the inspiring passion, commitment, and collaboration that we find in the community of scholars in the fields of body image and embodiment. While there are many such individuals—too numerous to discuss in a limited space—we would like to mention two. First, Tom Cash pioneered positive body image research and wisely broadened the study of body image to embodiment, reflected in the journal he founded: *Body Image: An International Journal of Research*. He provided emotional support and guidance throughout the volume. Second, Lina Ricciardelli has served as a "research idol," mentor, colleague, and friend to us and the chapter authors for decades. Sadly, Lina passed away this year (2018) after a long and hard-fought battle with breast cancer. Her passion for body image research, her natural inquisitiveness, her humor, her assertiveness, and her joy were contagious and will carry on in our own work and spirit. Her impact on the body image field, and our hearts, is indelible.

Further, we recognize that in each research and therapy center, there are other academic and administrative staff that make the research possible. Moreover, collectively, the chapters in the book include research done with a very large number of participants, who generously volunteer to take part in the studies. We are therefore grateful to many individuals who have contributed to the work represented in the volume.

In addition, many women were vital in the production of this work. Oxford University Press was an exceptional publisher. We particularly thank Sarah Harrington, Andrea Zekus, and Shelli Stevens, who have provided excellent guidance and support throughout the publication process.

Last, we would like to thank each other. We have determined that we are even better together than apart—a significant interaction if you will—which was a very pleasant (yet logical in hindsight) discovery. Having each other made editing a volume with many chapters not only doable but also enjoyable and gratifying. Our friendship and collaboration will continue well into the future.

CONTRIBUTORS

CO-EDITORS

Tracy L. Tylka, PhD, FAED
Professor of Psychology
The Ohio State University
Editor-in-Chief, *Body Image: An International Journal of Research*

Niva Piran, PhD, CPsych, FAED
Clinical Psychologist
Professor Emerita
University of Toronto

AUTHORS

Jessica M. Alleva, PhD
Assistant Professor
Maastricht University
Associate Editor, *Body Image: An International Journal of Research*

Melissa J. Atkinson, PhD
Lecturer in Psychology
University of Bath

Brooke L. Bennett, MS
PhD Candidate
University of Hawaii at Mānoa

Sofia Berne, PhD
Senior Lecturer
University of Gothenburg

NiCole T. Buchanan, PhD
Associate Professor
Michigan State University

Rachel M. Calogero, PhD, FAED
Associate Professor
Western University
Associate Editor, *Body Image: An International Journal of Research*

Catherine P. Cook-Cottone, PhD, RYT
Professor
State University of New York at Buffalo
Co-Editor-in-Chief, *Eating Disorders: The Journal of Treatment and Prevention*

Sigrún Daníelsdóttir, CandPsych/MSc
Clinical Psychologist
Project Manager for Mental Health Promotion
Directorate of Health
Reykjavik, Iceland

Phillippa C. Diedrichs, PhD, FAED
Associate Professor
University of the West of England

Jessica R. Dupasquier, MA
PhD Candidate, Clinical Psychology Program
University of Waterloo

Debra L. Franko, PhD, FAED
Professor
Northeastern University

Ann Frisén, PhD
Professor
University of Gothenburg

Christy Greenleaf, PhD
Professor
BS Kinesiology Program Director
University of Wisconsin–Milwaukee

Emma Halliwell, PhD
Associate Professor
University of the West of England

Diana Harcourt, PhD
Director, Centre for Appearance Research
Professor
University of the West of England

Beth Hartman McGilley, PhD, FAED, CEDS
Clinical Associate Professor of Psychiatry
University of Kansas School of Medicine

Caitlyn Hauff, PhD
Assistant Professor
University of South Alabama

Mary S. Himmelstein, PhD
Postdoctoral Fellow
University of Connecticut

Kristina Holmqvist Gattario, PhD
Senior Lecturer
University of Gothenburg

Iryna Ivanova, PhD, CPsych
Private Practice
Ottawa, Ontario, Canada

Allison C. Kelly, PhD
Assistant Professor
University of Waterloo

Julie Koven, MSEd, MPhilEd.
Doctoral Student, Counseling Psychology
University of Massachusetts Boston

Andrea LaMarre, PhD
Postdoctoral Fellow
University of Waterloo

Sharon Lamb, PhD, EdD
Professor
University of Massachusetts

Janet D. Latner, PhD
Associate Professor
University of Hawaii at Mānoa

Janet M. Liechty, PhD, LCSW
Associate Professor
University of Illinois at Urbana–Champaign

Alice S. Lowy, MA
PhD Candidate, Counseling Psychology
Northeastern University

Nina Mafrici, PhD
Clinical Psychologist
Broadview Psychology
Toronto, Ontario, Canada

Carolien Martijn, PhD
Associate Professor
Maastricht University

Kathryn E. Miller, MA
PhD Candidate, Clinical Psychology
University of Waterloo

Sarah K. Murnen, PhD
Samuel B. Cummings II Professor of Psychology
Kenyon College
Associate Editor, *Body Image: An International Journal of Research*

Dianne Neumark-Sztainer, PhD, MPH, RD, RYT-500
Professor, Division Head
University of Minnesota

Kelly N. Pedrotty-Stump, MS, RYT
School Counselor
Springfield School District
Exercise Consultant
Renfrew Center of Philadelphia

Rebecca M. Puhl, PhD
Deputy Director
Rudd Center for Food Policy & Obesity
Professor
University of Connecticut
Associate Editor, *Stigma & Health*

Virginia Ramseyer Winter, PhD, MSW
Assistant Professor
University of Missouri

Elyse Resch, MS, RDN, CEDRD, FAND
Nutrition Therapist
Private Practice
Beverly Hills, California, USA

Rachel F. Rodgers, PhD
Associate Professor
Northeastern University
Associate Editor, *Body Image: An International Journal of Research*

Courtney B. Rogers, MA
PhD Candidate, Health Psychology, Clinical Track
University of North Carolina at Charlotte

Emily K. Sandoz, PhD
Emma Louise LeBlanc Burguieres/ BORSF Endowed Professor of Social Sciences
University of Louisiana at Lafayette
Editor, *Journal of Contextual Behavioral Science*

Sonya Satinsky, PhD, MPH
Director, Health Promotion and Prevention Services
Princeton University

Isis H. Settles, PhD
Associate Professor
Michigan State University

Jaclyn A. Siegel, MS
PhD Candidate, Social Psychology
Western University

Linda Smolak, PhD
Professor Emerita
Kenyon College

Emily Squyres, MS
PhD Candidate, Counseling Psychology
Louisiana Tech University

Emily C. Stefano, MS
PhD Candidate, Clinical Psychology
University of Hawaii at Mānoa

Marika Tiggemann, PhD
Matthew Flinders Distinguished Professor
Flinders University

Lianne Trachtenberg, PhD, CPsych (Supervised Practice)
Postdoctoral Fellow
University of Toronto

Kiruthiha Vimalakanthan, MA
PhD Candidate, Clinical Psychology Program
University of Waterloo

Tracey D. Wade, PhD, FAED
Matthew Flinders Distinguished Professor
Flinders University
Associate Editor, *International Journal of Eating Disorders*

Sydney Waring, BA
PhD Candidate, Clinical Psychology Program
University of Waterloo

Jennifer B. Webb, PhD
Associate Professor
University of North Carolina at Charlotte

Simon Wilksch, PhD
Research Fellow in Psychology
Flinders University

Heidi Williamson, DHealth
Senior Research Fellow
University of the West of England

Krystle C. Woods, PhD
Private Practice
River's Bend, PC
Troy, Michigan, USA

Zali Yager, PhD
Senior Lecturer in Health and Physical Education
Victoria University

Focusing on the Positive

An Introduction to the Volume

TRACY L. TYLKA AND NIVA PIRAN

Psychological scholarship concerning the ways individuals live in their bodies has been the focus of a large volume of research to date, related to the close affiliation between ways of inhabiting the body and well-being. For the past five decades, research has concentrated on negative ways individuals live in their bodies and associated clinical challenges, such as eating disorders. In particular, the construct of negative body image has been a major focus of study and publication. Negative body image has been defined as "a persistent report of dissatisfaction, concern, and distress that is related to an aspect of physical appearance" (Thompson, Heinberg, Altabe, & Tantleff-Dunn, 1999, p. 11). That is, negative body image is an *appearance-based construct*, and an important one at that: It has been identified as a risk factor for eating disorders and a target for prevention and clinical interventions (Stice, Marti, & Durant, 2011).

However, the exclusive focus on negative body image introduces limitations to progress in the field of living in the body and related well-being, as Smolak and Cash (2011, p. 472) suggested, "Focusing on positive, adaptive, or healthy body image is essential to the future of the field." Negative body image cannot capture the complex experience of living in the body (Blood, 2005; Piran, 2015, 2016; Tylka & Wood-Barcalow, 2015b), therefore also limiting its ability to predict well-being. For example, a meta-analysis of risk factors to the development of disordered eating patterns revealed that the predictive value of body dissatisfaction, like several other risk factors, ranges between small to moderate, suggesting the importance of other, unexplored variables (Stice, 2002). Further, as has been emphasized by the World Health Organization (Grad, 2002), the reduction of disease does not represent health or well-being.

Within the last 15 years, researchers have expanded the field of scholarship to include *positive* ways of living in the body and their associations with a range of measures of well-being. This research clarifies that positive ways of living in the body are varied and extend far beyond appearance-related concerns, distress, and dissatisfaction (Piran, 2016; Tylka & Wood-Barcalow, 2015b). Further, studies confirmed the importance of assessing positive ways of living in the body above and beyond negative body image. Measures of positive ways of living in the body not only are associated with a range of well-being variables, but also explain a significant portion of the variance on these variables, above and beyond what is explained by measures of body dissatisfaction (Tylka & Wood-Barcalow, 2015b). Furthermore, measuring positive ways of living in the body inherently guides the search for protective factors and sets broader goals for health promotion and therapy interventions (Piran, 2015, 2016, 2017). This includes the prevention and treatment of eating disorders, the development of psychological flexibility, the experience and expression of sexuality, and the fostering of safety and inclusion (e.g., appreciation of size diversity). Overall, then, studying positive ways of inhabiting the body offers a unique perspective that extends far beyond what we know from studying negative body image. So, let us continue to "focus on the positive," which we do in this volume.

The goal of this volume is to share with readers the wealth of research knowledge and innovative possibilities inherent to examining positive ways of living in the body in terms of scholarship, theory, and interventions. More specifically, this 38-chapter volume is the first to broadly explore positive ways of inhabiting the body, which includes body comfort, connection, responsiveness, appreciation, attunement, agency, functionality, desire, self-care, and even safety.

Theory and research on positive ways of inhabiting the body thus far can be divided into two overarching perspectives: *positive body image* (see Tylka & Wood-Barcalow, 2015b) and *positive embodiment* (see Piran, 2016, 2017). The volume first identifies the constructs within these perspectives, then reviews how the environment can nurture these constructs as protective factors for well-being, and last presents interventions for how professionals can cultivate positive body image and positive embodiment within individuals. Thus, this volume is for researchers, practitioners, and theorists at all levels of expertise—from students to seasoned scholars.

This introduction to the volume begins with defining positive body image and embodiment, explicating how they each extend beyond what we know about negative body image, and describing their relationship with each other. It then presents an overview of the three sections of the volume.

POSITIVE BODY IMAGE

Based on the findings of one of the first qualitative studies of positive body image, Wood-Barcalow, Tylka, and Augustus-Horvath (2010, p. 112) defined positive body image as

> an overarching love and respect for the body that allows individuals to (a) appreciate the unique beauty of their body and the functions that it performs

for them; (b) accept and even admire their body, including those aspects that are inconsistent with idealized images; (c) feel beautiful, comfortable, confident, and happy with their body, which is often reflected as an outer radiance, or a "glow;" (d) emphasize their body's assets rather than dwell on their imperfections; and (f) interpret incoming information in a body-protective manner whereby most positive information is internalized and most negative information is rejected or reframed.

Most aspects of this definition also emerged in interviews with adolescent girls and boys from Sweden (Frisén & Holmqvist, 2010; Holmqvist & Frisén, 2012); African American girls from the United States (Pope, Corona, & Belgrave, 2014); Aboriginal girls from Canada (McHugh, Coppola, & Sabiston, 2014); and residents with spinal cord injuries from Canada (Bailey, Gammage, van Ingen, & Ditor, 2015), providing important cross validation of the construct.

Relationship with Negative Body Image. As can be seen, Wood-Barcalow et al.'s (2010) definition of positive body image extends beyond the focus on appearance. Empirical research has confirmed that positive body image is not simply the opposite of what we know about negative body image in four ways. First, positive body image is uniquely tied to many aspects of well-being (e.g., disordered eating, intuitive eating, self-esteem, self-compassion) when controlling for negative body image (Alleva, Tylka, & Kroon Van Diest, 2017; Avalos, Tylka, & Wood-Barcalow, 2005; Tylka & Wood-Barcalow, 2015a; see also Chapter 2). Indeed, as the definition implies, positive body image extends beyond favorable appearance evaluation to appreciating how the body feels and functions as well as interpreting information in a body protective manner. Second, individuals may endorse high body appreciation yet remain dissatisfied with their appearance (Tiggemann & McCourt, 2013). Third, the conceptual overlap between measures of positive and negative body image is not large, providing construct differentiation (Tiggemann & McCourt, 2013; Tylka & Wood-Barcalow, 2015a; Webb, Butler-Ajibade, & Robinson, 2014). Fourth, some activities, such as attending a life-drawing course (Swami, 2017), increase body appreciation but have little to no impact on body dissatisfaction.

POSITIVE EMBODIMENT

Piran (2016, 2017; see Chapters 1 and 10) conducted a large-scale, mixed-method research program whereby, during the first phase, girls, young adult women, and older adult women discussed experiences of living in their bodies as they engaged with the world; the inquiries did not focus on appearance or on particular affects associated with the body. During the second phase, emergent constructs were tested quantitatively. A multidimensional core construct, the Experience of Embodiment, emerged from the narratives of all age groups, providing important cross validation of the construct. The Experience of Embodiment contains five dimensions that collectively "have not been captured by other constructs"

(Piran, 2017, p. 4). Each dimension ranges from positive to negative. First, body connection and comfort (i.e., comfort, connection, and other positive feelings in the body while engaging with the world, as well as self-talk that helps maintain positive body connection) are positioned opposite to disrupted connection and discomfort. Second, agency and functionality (i.e., acting in the world with agency through physical functionality and voice) are positioned opposite to restricted agency and restraint. Third, experience and expression of desire (i.e., connecting to bodily desires such as appetite and sexual desire and expressing them with agency) are positioned opposite to disrupted connection to desire. Fourth, attuned self-care (i.e., engaging with the world in a meaningful way while being aware of, guided by, and responding to internal cues) is positioned opposite to disrupted attunement, neglect, and self-harm. Fifth, inhabiting the body as a subjective site (i.e., focusing on internal experiences while resisting pressures to self-objectify) is positioned opposite to inhabiting the body as an objectified site.

The Experience of Embodiment construct ranges from positive embodiment, described as, "positive body connection and comfort, embodied agency and passion, and attuned self-care," to negative embodiment, defined as "disrupted body connection and discomfort, restricted agency and passion, and self-neglect or harm" (Piran, 2016, p. 47). The embodiment research program also describes 12 protective and risk factors, sorted into three main categories of experiences in the social environment: physical experiences, exposure to social discourses and expectations, and social power and relational connections with others and with desired communities.

Relationship with Negative Body Image. It is quite clear from Piran's (2016, 2017) work that the Experience of Embodiment extends well beyond negative body image. First, negative embodiment involves disrupted body connection and discomfort, restricted agency, disrupted connection to bodily desires, self-neglect or harm, and self-objectification. This construct therefore describes a much broader experience of disruption in inhabiting the body compared with negative body image. In particular, negative body image can be seen as an example of negative body connection and discomfort, the first dimension of negative embodiment. Second, negative embodiment captures a range of experiences beyond the emphasis on appearance in negative body image measures. Third, negative body image does not recognize the sociocultural power structures that corset certain bodies while liberating other bodies, which is a central feature of understanding negative embodiment (Piran, 2016, 2017).

RELATIONSHIP OF POSITIVE BODY IMAGE AND EMBODIMENT

There are theoretical links between positive body image and positive embodiment. Embodiment is an overarching construct that subsumes both positive body image and negative body image. Both positive body image and embodiment examine individuals' experiences of their bodies as they engage with the world around them. Different measures of positive body image have tapped into different domains of embodiment (see Chapter 1), such that, overall, positive body image includes most of the domains of embodiment, though, to date, the dimension of agency in the world has not yet been assessed by a separate measure of positive body image. Within this context of theoretical overlap, positive body image is distinguished from the Experience of Embodiment in three ways: (a) Embodiment considers concurrently five dimensions of the experience of inhabiting the body as one engages with the world; (b) embodiment encompasses negative dimensions of the lived experience of the body; and (c) embodiment links the quality of embodied experiences to the shaping of the social environment by sociocultural power structures. Nonetheless, the positive body image construct is often incorporated within models that explore how positive body image is impacted by sociocultural power structures (e.g., the acceptance model of intuitive eating; Augustus-Horvath & Tylka, 2011; see also Chapters 2 and 20).

SECTIONS OF THE VOLUME

This edited volume aims to provide a state-of-the-art, comprehensive, research-based resource that addresses the breadth of innovative theoretical concepts and related practice in positive ways of living in the body and sets agendas for further expansion. It achieves this goal in three sections.

Section I

The first section includes nine chapters that introduce constructs that represent positive ways of inhabiting the body, beginning with the more comprehensive Experiences of Embodiment construct. It then reviews the more focused constructs of body appreciation, body flexibility, body image flexibility, broad conceptualization of beauty, mindful attunement, intuitive eating, attuned exercise, and attuned sexuality. For each construct, the extant body of research is cogently and concisely summarized and its measurement carefully explicated. Future directions for research are offered. Readers emerge with an understanding of the present conceptualization of each construct and an awareness of numerous possibilities for its research expansion and clarification.

Section II

Section II includes 15 chapters that delineate protective factors related to external (i.e., relational, social, and other environmental) forces that shape embodiment and explicate how these protective factors can be cultivated. It begins with discussing the three domains of protective factors within Piran's (2016, 2017) developmental theory of embodiment: the physical domain, the mental domain, and the social power and relational connections domain. The section continues with addressing how external factors can shape positive physical experiences that enhance embodied well-being, namely, mindful exercise, connection to sexuality, and safety. Next, this section examines the impact and cultivation of resistance toward adverse constraining social molds and stereotypes on positive body image and embodiment. More specifically, it offers how we can help develop a critical stance toward, and thereby work to prevent, sexual objectification and its internalization (i.e., self-objectification), constructs of femininity among girls and women, feminine "molds" of appearance and comportment among young breast cancer survivors, weight/shape and race-based stereotypes, and idealized media images. Last, this section examines the quality of relational connections and the experience of social power with others in cultivating positive body image and embodiment via protective peer, family, and online environments and among those with visible differences. Readers emerge with (a) an understanding of how they can encourage positive (and counter adverse) social, relational, and other environmental experiences with protective factors and (b) ideas for continued advances in these areas.

Section III

The last section contains 14 chapters, 13 of which examine a range of interventions aimed at promoting positive body image and positive embodiment. Some chapters target change within aspects of the individual via the following approaches: compassion-focused therapy, acceptance and commitment therapy, emotion-focused therapy, mindfulness training, yoga, embodied mindfulness and movement-based approaches, cognitive dissonance, and media literacy. Other chapters target change within the broader social environment, such as feminist and social justice approaches, school-based approaches, public health interventions, and policy-based initiatives. Readers emerge armed with varied approaches to increase positive embodiment and positive body image within their clinical work and public health initiatives while also understanding how existing interventions may be modified to further strengthen their applicability for addressing positive embodiment and positive body image. The 14th chapter provides a conclusion to the book.

The breadth of knowledge represented in this volume relies on the expertise of chapter authors. We asked contributors to go beyond existing knowledge and chart paths for future progress. We are thus indebted to all authors for sharing their expertise, scholarship, and innovative visions.

REFERENCES

Alleva, J. M., Tylka, T. L., & Kroon Van Diest, A. M. (2017). The Functionality Appreciation Scale (FAS): Development and psychometric evaluation in US community women and men. *Body Image*, *23*, 28–44. doi:10.1016/j.bodyim.2017.07.008

Augustus-Horvath, C. L., & Tylka, T. L. (2011). The acceptance model of intuitive eating: A comparison of women in emerging adulthood, early adulthood, and middle adulthood. *Journal of Counseling Psychology, 58*, 110–125. doi:10.1037/a0022129

Avalos, L. C., Tylka, T. L., & Wood-Barcalow, N. (2005). The Body Appreciation Scale: Development and psychometric evaluation. *Body Image, 2*, 285–297. doi:10.1016/j.bodyim.2005.06.002

Bailey, K. A., Gammage, K. L., van Ingen, C., & Ditor, D. S. (2015). "It's all about acceptance": A qualitative study exploring a model of positive body image for people with spinal cord injury. *Body Image, 15*, 24–34. doi:10.1016/j.bodyim.2015.04.010

Blood, S. K. (2005). *Body work: The social construction of women's body image*. Hove, England: Routledge.

Frisén, A., & Holmqvist, K. (2010). What characterizes early adolescents with a positive body image? A qualitative investigation of Swedish girls and boys. *Body Image, 7*, 205–212. doi:10.1016/j.bodyim.2010.04.001

Grad, F. G. (2002). The preamble of the constitution of the World Health Organization. *Bulletin of the World Health Organization, 80*, 981–984. Retrieved from: http://www.who.int/bulletin/archives/80(12)981.pdf

Holmqvist, K., & Frisén, A. (2012). "I bet they aren't that perfect in reality": Appearance ideals viewed from the perspective of adolescents with a positive body image. *Body Image, 9*, 388–395. doi:10.1016/j.bodyim.2012.03.007

McHugh, T. L., Coppola, A. M., & Sabiston, C. M. (2014). "I'm thankful for being Native and my body is part of that": The body pride experiences of young Aboriginal women in Canada. *Body Image, 11*, 318–327. doi:10.1016/j.bodyim.2014.05.004

Piran, N. (2015). New possibilities in the prevention of eating disorders: The introduction of positive body image measures. *Body Image, 14*, 146–157. doi:10.1016/j.bodyim.2015.03.008

Piran, N. (2016). Embodied possibilities and disruptions: The emergence of the Experience of Embodiment construct from qualitative studies with girls and women. *Body Image, 18*, 43–60. doi:10.1016/j.bodyim.2016.04.007

Piran, N. (2017). *Journeys of embodiment at the intersection of body and culture: The developmental theory of embodiment*. San Diego, CA: Elsevier. doi:10.1016/c2015-0-04666-4

Pope, M., Corona, R., & Belgrave, F. Z. (2014). Nobody's perfect: A qualitative examination of African American maternal caregivers' and their adolescent girls' perceptions of body image. *Body Image, 11*, 307–317. doi:10.1016/j.bodyim.2014.04.005

Smolak, L., & Cash, T. F. (2011). Future challenges for body image science, practice, and prevention. In T. F. Cash & L. Smolak (Eds.), *Body image: A handbook of science, practice, and prevention* (2nd ed., pp. 471–478). New York, NY: Guilford Press.

Stice, E. (2002). Risk and maintenance factors for eating pathology: A meta-analytic review. *Psychological Bulletin, 128*, 825–848. doi:10.1037//0033-2909.128.5.825

Stice, E., Marti, C. N., & Durant, S. (2011). Risk factors for onset of eating disorders: Evidence of multiple risk pathways from an 8-year prospective study. *Behavior Research and Therapy, 49*, 622–627. doi:10.1016/j.brat.2011.06.009

Swami, V. (2017). Sketching people: Prospective investigations of the impact of life drawing on body image. *Body Image, 20*, 65–73. doi:10.1016/j.bodyim.2016.12.001

Thompson, J. K., Heinberg, L. J., Altabe, M., & Tantleff-Dunn, S. (1999). *Exacting beauty: Theory, assessment, and treatment of body image disturbance*. Washington, DC: American Psychological Association.

Tiggemann, M., & McCourt, A. (2013). Body appreciation in adult women: Relationships with age and body satisfaction. *Body Image, 10*, 624–627. doi:10.1016/j.bodyim.2013.07.003

Tylka, T. L., & Wood-Barcalow, N. L. (2015a). The Body Appreciation Scale-2: Item refinement and psychometric evaluation. *Body Image, 12*, 53–67. doi:10.1016/j.bodyim.2014.09.006

Tylka, T. L., & Wood-Barcalow, N. L. (2015b). What is and what is not positive body image? Conceptual foundations and construct definition. *Body Image, 14*, 118–129. doi:10.1016/j.bodyim.2015.04.001

Webb, J. B., Butler-Ajibade, P., & Robinson, S. A. (2014). Considering an affect regulation framework for examining the association between body dissatisfaction and positive body image in black older adolescent females: Does body mass index matter? *Body Image, 11*, 426–437. doi:10.1016/j.bodyim.2014.07.002

Wood-Barcalow, N. L., Tylka, T. L., & Augustus-Horvath, C. L. (2010). "But I like my body": Positive body image characteristics and a holistic model for young-adult women. *Body Image, 7*, 106–116. doi:10.1016/j.bodyim.2010.01.001

SECTION I

Identifying Positive Ways of Living in the Body

Intraindividual Constructs

1

The Experience of Embodiment Construct

Reflecting the Quality of Embodied Lives

NIVA PIRAN

Current conceptualizations of the construct of embodiment are anchored in the writings of the French philosophers Merleau-Ponty (1962) and Foucault (1995). Merleau-Ponty viewed embodiment as the "perceptual experience of engagement of the body in the world" (Allan, 2005, p. 175), whereby "perceptual experience" refers not only to sensory perception but also to interpreting and experiencing the world meaningfully. The body according to Merleau-Ponty is therefore both a site of subjectivity and a site that, through occupying a particular and meaningful position in the world, is in ongoing dialogical relationships with the world; it both performs and shapes culturally informed practices, blurring the boundaries between body/culture or inner/outer dualisms (Crossley, 1995). Foucault, in addition, focused on the power social institutions hold over individuals' bodies through widely disseminated social discourses and expectations; as individuals learn, internalize, and act in line with these expectations, they start to inhabit "docile" bodies and embody cultural dictates (see Chapter 10).

While the embodiment construct has been used widely in sociological analyses of the intersection of body and culture, researchers have called for its further study within the domain of psychology and well-being (e.g., Blood, 2005; Fahs, 2015; Katzman & Lee, 1997; Piran, 2002, 2016b; Tolman, Bowman, & Fahs, 2014; Young, 1992). In advocating for the use of the embodiment construct, these researchers highlighted its inner focus on the lived-in experiences of the body (e.g., Blood, 2005; Piran, 2016b; Piran & Teall, 2012a); the breadth of the phenomena it can capture (Blood, 2005; Piran, 2016b; Piran & Teall, 2012a; Young, 1992); and the meaningful dialogical relationships between individuals' embodiment and the social context (Fahs, 2015; Piran, 2002, 2016b; Tolman et al., 2014).

This chapter starts with a description of the Experience of Embodiment (EE) construct that emerged in three interview studies with girls and women, capturing the quality of their embodied lives. It continues with a description of the Experience of Embodiment Scale (EES), grounded in girls' and women's narratives, and ends with identifying future directions for this construct and scale.

THE EXPERIENCE OF EMBODIMENT CONSTRUCT

Grounded in Merleau-Ponty's (1962) conceptualization of embodiment, the first phase of a large-scale, mixed-method research program on embodiment involved 171 qualitative interviews with 69 girls and younger and older women in three different studies (see Piran, 2016b, 2017) about their experiences of living in their bodies as they engaged with the world around them. The studies included a life history study with young women ages 20–27, a 5-year prospective study of repeated interviews with girls ages 9–14 during the first interview, and a life history study with women ages 50–68. Inquiries included questions such as, "How did you feel in your body?" or "What would your body say?" Interviews also focused on points of transition in embodied experiences and on times participants felt best or worst in their bodies.

The analysis of narratives in the transcribed interviews related to the experiences of inhabiting the body, using constructivist grounded theory (Charmaz, 2006), led to the emergence of a multidimensional core construct, called the EE, reflecting the quality of embodied lives (Piran, 2016b, 2017). This construct ranged from positive embodiment, described as "positive body connection and comfort, embodied agency and passion, and attuned self-care," to negative embodiment, defined as "disrupted body connection and discomfort, restricted agency and passion, and self-neglect or harm" (Piran, 2016b, p. 47). In the three qualitative studies, the same five dimensions emerged under the EE core construct, providing important cross validation. Like the EE, each of the five dimensions ranged from positive to negative, such that the overall EE depended on the quality of girls' and women's experiences on each dimension. The five dimensions of the EE were (at the positive end)

(a) *Body connection and comfort*—reflects comfort and other positive feelings in the body while engaging with the world, feeling connection and "at home" in the body, and engaging in positive self-talk to counter adverse social influences.
(b) *Agency and functionality*—describes acting in the world with agency, both through physical functionality and through the power of voice.
(c) *Experience and expression of desire*—reflects connection to bodily desires, both appetite and sexual desire, and expressing them with agency and self-attunement.
(d) *Attuned self-care*—describes engagement with the world while being aware of, guided by, and responding to internal cues, such as bodily,

emotional, and relational needs, as well as the need to engage in meaningful pursuits.

(e) *Inhabiting the body as a subjective site* (resisting objectification)—addresses the focus on subjective embodied experiences, as well as resisting pressures to view one's body as an object to be gazed at or to channel multiple resources into compliance with idealized appearance expectations.

Participants' narratives indicated that positive (or negative) experiences on one dimension tended to co-occur with similarly positive (or negative) experiences on other dimensions. The following are examples of positive embodiment narratives:

> I like movement. I feel really good playing. My body feels like, "You're ruling! Go!" I am the best on my team. . . . I like eating. I like pasta and broccoli. . . . I drink milk for calcium and proteins for muscles. I'll pass on diets. [Alice, 10 years old, Aboriginal, middle class, urban]

> I think of myself as a whole, the mind body all integrated. . . . I feel comfortable in my own skin letting go of what a girl should look like. . . . I am a competitive, assertive person. . . . Well, in terms of hunger appetite, I got it. I love food. I love variety. . . . I describe myself as a very sexual person because I was always very much in touch with the sexual feelings that my body had. . . . I was talking about my body sending me signals so I'm in tune with what's going on. [Jane, mid-20s, white, working class background, rural]

> I am happy in my body. . . . My voice blossomed. . . . I am a sexual, sensual person. . . . I take care of myself and I think I will be able to work for a while. . . . I can wear a lumber jacket if I want, I can still feel sexual, I can still feel good about myself. [Gwen, mid-60s, white, working class background, urban]

Experience of Embodiment varied between participants, and within participants across their life journeys, in relation to their social experience (Piran, 2017). Commonly, childhood was associated with the most positive EE, while adolescence was a time of disrupted EE among all participants. Yet, at least some participants experienced recapturing of a more positive EE during adulthood, sometimes only during older adulthood (Piran, 2016a, 2017).

These findings regarding EE add to the existing body of knowledge in a number of ways and have theoretical, clinical, and research implications. One contribution of the emergent EE construct, anchored in girls' and women's lives, is the breadth of phenomena it captures. The EE construct suggests that the quality of embodied lives relates not only to comfort, joy, and positive connection to one's body, sustained at times through protective self-talk, but also to agency and functionality, connection and expression of bodily desires, attuned self-care, and inhabiting the body with subjective immersion while resisting objectification. The construct, then, integrates domains of experience that have thus far been conceptualized and studied as separate phenomena. It further implies that considering all these dimensions *concurrently* offers a deeper understanding of embodied lives (Piran, 2016a, 2017).

A multidimensional delineation of inhabiting the body with comfort, connection, agency, passion, self-attunement, and immersion in meaningful pursuits highlights positive possibilities for girls and women and broader goals for health promotion and therapy interventions than, for example, lowering body dissatisfaction or the internalization of thinness. A detailed description of embodied well-being also attunes social activists, practitioners, and researchers to the range of losses associated with shifts from embodied well-being. According to Piran (2017, p. 12):

> When disruption occurs to EE, such as the changes seen in adolescence among all research participants, this multi-dimensional construct captures the complex nature of this loss, beyond the previously reported change in body esteem (Mendelson, Mendelson, & White, 2001). In this process of disruption, the body becomes an uncomfortable "other" site—agency is dampened, ownership of desires is challenged, and compromises to self-attunement are frequent. Moreover, the carefree lack of self-consciousness found in early childhood—"I did not care about what I wore or what I looked like"—is lost as well. These compounded losses, associated with inhabiting a docile, feminine body, markedly change the way adolescent girls engage with the world. Further, examining social processes that shape embodiment during adolescence clarifies that in creating docile bodies, all domains of the EE are concurrently targeted.

A number of individual dimensions of EE are related conceptually to other constructs and measures that aim at describing positive ways of inhabiting the body. In particular, a number of constructs relate to the first EE dimension of Body Connection and Comfort, including the Body Appreciation construct and scale (Tylka & Wood-Barcalow, 2015a; see Chapter 2), which assesses appreciation, acceptance, and respect for one's body; the Body Image Flexibility construct (Sandoz, Wilson, Merwin, & Kellum, 2013; see Chapter 4), which assesses the capacity to engage in self-regulatory psychological processing of negative emotions caused by adverse body-anchored social experiences, such that positive connection with the body is maintained; and the Functionality Appreciation Scale (Alleva, Tylka, & Kroon Van Diest, 2017; see Chapter 3), which reflects positive connection to the body through the appreciation of its functionality. The second EE dimension, of acting in the world with Agency and Functionality, is often not addressed in conceptualizations of positive ways of inhabiting the body, likely reflecting widespread negative constructions of women's agency and power (Piran, 2017). The third dimension of EE, Experience and Expression of Desire, is related to the Intuitive Eating construct and scale (Tylka & Kroon Van Diest, 2013; see Chapter 7), which assesses individuals' attunement to their appetites, as well as to measures of positive connection to sexuality, though those measures have not previously been integrated into comprehensive constructs that evaluate the quality of embodied lives. The fourth dimension of EE, Attuned Care, is conceptually related to the Mindful Self-Care Scale (Cook-Cottone & Guyker, 2018; see Chapter 6) and is also reflected in two items of the Body Appreciation Scale. The fifth dimension of Subjective Immersion/Resisting Objectification relates to measures of self-objectification. There is therefore conceptual convergence between existing scales and the dimensions of the EE construct, but these existing scales, either individually or collectively, do not capture the depth of girls' and women's experiences of embodiment.

Further, the breadth of phenomena the EE captures relates also to the continuity of the EE and its core dimensions between positive and negative ways of inhabiting the body. This offers a different perspective from current views of body image that view negative and positive body image as conceptually distinct (Piran, 2016b; Tylka & Wood-Barcalow, 2015b). As the large-scale qualitative research program, anchored in girls' and women's narratives across a very broad age range, indicates, the EE and its five dimensions can capture shifts in ways girls and women live in their bodies over time, moving between positive and negative ways of inhabiting their bodies. Tracing these "body journeys" of girls and women over time can guide the development of comprehensive etiological theories of positive embodiment that include a range of protective factors, as well as of risk factors that should be minimized (Piran, 2010, 2015, 2017). Clinically, in body image interventions, examining the quality of embodied lives over time can help girls and women identify points not only of disruptions, but also of body connection, joy, and agency. Girls and women can then seek to recapture such positive embodied experiences through choosing to engage in particular embodying activities (Piran, 2016a, 2017).

EXPERIENCE OF EMBODIMENT SCALE

The EES is a 34-item, fully structured, measure that assesses EE (Piran & Teall, 2006, 2012b). Constructing a quantitative scale that reflects the quality of embodied lives was one of the goals of the large-scale qualitative research program on embodiment. The first version of the scale (Piran & Teall, 2006) was based on themes that emerged from the qualitative study with young women, and the second version (Piran & Teall, 2012b) included revisions informed by the girls' and older women's studies. The scale is anchored in the lived experiences of girls and women across the life span. Scale items reflect repeated qualitative themes and are worded as closely as possible to participants' narratives. Each item receives a ranking of 1 (*strongly disagree*) to 5 (*strongly agree*), and some items are reversed so that a higher total score reflects positive experiences of embodiment. Of the 34 items of the scale, 32 items in the original scale are gender neutral. The remaining two items have been revised for administration in a gender-neutral form. In particular, the item "I feel dissatisfied, envious and frustrated when I compare my body to other girls/women" has been changed to "I feel dissatisfied, envious and frustrated when I compare my body to others," and the item "I consider myself to be a powerful woman" has been changed to "I consider myself to be a powerful person." Accordingly, the scale has been administered to both adolescent girls and boys and to adult women and men.

Three psychometric studies of the scale with women in Canada, ages 18–55, have been conducted (Teall & Piran, 2017). Exploratory factor analysis revealed a six-factor solution and provided important cross-method cross validation of the five EE dimensions that emerged in the qualitative analysis. However, an additional factor emerged, reflecting the experience of the body as a site that encumbers social adjustment. Teall and Piran (2017) also found that the total scale score has high internal consistency (Cronbach's $\alpha = .91–.94$) and high test–retest reliability ($r = .93$). The six factors, their reliability coefficients, and sample items are described in Table 1.1. Similar rates of internal consistency have

Table 1.1 Factor Names, Cronbach's Alphas, Test–Retest Correlations, and Sample Items of the Six Factors of the Experience of Embodiment Scale

Factor Name	Cronbach's Alpha	Test–Retest Correlations	Sample Items
Factor 1: Body Connection and Comfort (7 items)	.91	.89	I feel in tune with my body.
Factor 2: Freedom from the Body as a Disruptive Site (6 items)	.86	.86	My body reduces my sense of self-worth in the world.[a]
Factor 3: Agency and Functionality (6 items)	.84	.88	I believe in my ability to accomplish what I desire in the world.
Factor 4: Experience and Expression of Desire (4 items)	.78	.82	I express what I want and need sexually.
Factor 5: Attuned Self-Care (7 items)	.79	.83	I put a priority on listening to my body and its needs (e.g., stress, fatigue, hunger).
Factor 6: Inhabiting the Body as a Subjective Site (Resisting Objectification) (4 items)	.75	.82	I care more about how my body feels than about how it looks.

[a]Reverse scoring.

been found as well in the United States (Chmielewski, Tolman, & Bowman, 2018) and among women and men in Sweden (Holmqvist Gattario, Frisén, & Piran, 2018).

The EES is positively associated with general measures of well-being, including self-esteem and life satisfaction among women (Chmielewski et al., 2017; Holmqvist Gattario et al., 2018; Teall & Piran, 2017) and men (Holmqvist Gattario et al., 2018). It is also positively associated with a measure of quality of life among young women survivors of breast cancer (Trachtenberg & Piran, 2017). The EES is similarly positively correlated with measures of body esteem in women (Chmielewski et al., 2017; Holmqvist Gattario et al., 2018; Teall & Piran, 2018) and men (Holmqvist Gattario et al., 2018). Teall and Piran (2017) also reported positive correlations between EES and measures of body attunement, connection, and physical self-worth. The EES is positively associated with measures of sexual assertiveness, sexual self-efficacy, and sexual self-esteem (Chmielewski et al., 2017; Teall & Piran, 2017). The EES is negatively associated with measures of self-objectification and eating restraint and alexithymia (Holmqvist Gattario et al., 2018; Teall & Piran, 2017) among women. Regarding discriminant validity, as hypothesized, the EES was not significantly related to the personal standard subscale of a perfectionism scale (Teall & Piran, 2017).

In terms of group comparisons, Teall and Piran (2017) found no differences on the EES between Asian and white women in Canada. Similarly, Chmielewski et al. (2017) found no differences on the EES between black and white women in the United States. As expected, Holmqvist Gattario et al. (2018) found that men had higher average EES scores compared with women.

To date, the EES has been used as an outcome measure in a completed cognitive dissonance prevention study (Jarman, Treneman-Evans, & Halliwell, 2017) and in two ongoing prevention projects, one with adolescents in Norway and one with adult women in the United States. Jarman et al. (2017) used the Body Connection and Comfort subscale of the EES as part of an outcome evaluation package in a selective trial of a 4-hour cognitive dissonance intervention with 99 girls aged 14–18. They found that the intervention was associated with significant increases in both body connection and comfort and in body appreciation, gains that were maintained at a 3-month follow-up. The Body Connection and Comfort subscale of the EES was positively associated with body appreciation and positive affect and negatively associated with body dissatisfaction, restrained eating, and negative affect.

Research results to date with the EES seem promising in that the scale has good psychometric qualities in terms of reliability and validity. As different research centers are currently using the scale in longitudinal designs and intervention trials with adolescents and adults, as well as women and men of diverse heritages, important research data will likely continue to accumulate about the scale during the next few years. Of particular interest are also studies that examine the EES in relation to specific domains of embodied experiences, such as sexuality (Chmielewski et al., 2017).

A number of suggestions for further research can be highlighted in relation to the EES. First, the research program on embodiment conducted in Canada followed a mixed-method design. In developing the EES, the research program used a sequential model whereby a qualitative inquiry is used to help develop a quantitative measure (Creswell, Plano Clark, Gutmann, & Hanson, 2008; Steckler, McLeroy, Goodman, Bird, & McCormick, 1992). In line with this sequential model, a hypothesis about the multidimensional structure of the EE and its specific emergent dimensions, informed by the qualitative inquiry, was tested through an exploratory factor analysis. While the hypothesis was supported, further quantitative studies are needed that will examine and confirm the factor structure in different samples of adolescents, women, men, and other groups.

An additional question relates to the breadth of the EE construct and the EES. The EES covers six dimensions that reflect embodied well-being, while most measures of positive image address mainly one and, less often, two such dimensions. Further studies can reveal what the possible advantages are of using a broader measure of embodiment. For example, in a multiple regression aimed at predicting life satisfaction, Holmqvist Gattario et al. (2018) found that EES predicted life satisfaction among women, while body esteem did not. This suggests that a broader measure of embodiment, beyond the evaluation of body appearance and weight, can shed light about the general well-being of women. In a similar vein, Teall and Piran (2017) found that the EES explained a larger percentage of the variance, compared with body esteem, of measures that reflect attunement with the body, such as alexithymia and body responsiveness, and even of self-esteem. It will be particularly useful to conduct research that includes the EES and multiple other measures of positive and negative body image in relation to a range of measures of well-being and disruption, all the way from general measures of quality of life and life satisfaction to measures specific to particular domains of embodied distress, such as disordered eating behaviors, self-harm, or engaging in sexual activities without protection or connection to desire. Further inquiries could reveal whether the EES, by virtue of its conceptual breadth and consideration of a continuum between negative and positive embodiment, can uniquely support the development of theories of positive embodiment that include a larger number of protective and risk factors than are currently considered in the body image field (Piran, 2010). For example, the list of protective and risk factors related to negative body image may differ from those related to positive embodiment. In addition, as initial studies suggest, the EES can be used as an outcome measure to intervention studies, both prevention and therapy, that aim at enhanced embodied well-being among youth and adults.

CONCLUSION

Research on the construct of embodiment can provide a new lens on the understanding of embodied well-being and distress and on social experiences that shape them. The large-scale, mixed-method research program on embodiment with girls and younger and older women led to the emergence of the EE construct and to its quantitative operationalization through the EES. The EE construct and EES capture a number of dimensions that, to date, have been conceptualized and measured separately; they also include the spectrum of experiences all the way from negative to positive embodiment. At the same time, each of the emergent dimensions supports current measures that have been developed to assess ways of inhabiting the body, such as body appreciation and attunement. The most lacking dimensions among these is embodied agency. As studies to date suggest, the EES may contribute uniquely to the understanding of embodied lives, to etiological theories of embodied well-being and distress, and to intervention studies. Further research will help establish the relationships between this scale and other positive measures of inhabiting the body.

REFERENCES

Allan, H. T. (2005). Gender and embodiment in nursing: The role of the female chaperone in the infertility clinic. *Nursing Inquiry, 12*, 175–183. doi:10.1111/j.1440-1800.2005.00275.x

Alleva, J. M., Tylka, T. L., & Kroon Van Diest, A. M. (2017). The Functionality Appreciation Scale (FAS): Development and psychometric evaluation in US community women and men. *Body Image, 23*, 28–44. doi:10.1016/j.bodyim.2017.07.008

Blood, S. K. (2005). *Body work: The social construction of women's body image*. Hove, East Sussex, England: Routledge.

Charmaz, K. (2006). *Constructing grounded theory: A practical guide through qualitative analysis*. Thousand Oaks, CA: Sage.

Chmielewski, J. F, Tolman, D. L., & Bowman, C. (2018, March). *Feminists do it better: The role of feminism in Black and White young women's sexual subjectivity and embodiment*, Paper presented at the Association for Women in Psychology Annual Meeting, Philadelphia, PA.

Cook-Cottone, C. P., & Guyker, W. M. (2018). The development and validation of the Mindful Self-Care Scale (MSCS): An assessment of practices that support positive embodiment. *Mindfulness, 9*, 161–175. doi:10.1007/s12671-017-0759-1

Creswell, J. W., Plano Clark, V. L., Gutmann, M. L., & Hanson, W. E. (2008). Advanced mixed methods research designs. In V. L. Plano Clark & J. W. Creswell (Eds.), *The mixed methods reader* (pp. 161–195). Thousand Oaks, CA: Sage.

Crossley, N. (1995). Merleau-Ponty, the elusive body and carnal sociology. *Body and Society, 1*, 43–63. doi:10.1177/1357034X95001001004

Fahs, B. (2015). The body in revolt: The impact and legacy of second wave corporeal embodiment. *Journal of Social Issues, 71*, 386–401. doi:10.1111/josi.12117

Foucault, M. (1995). *Discipline and punish: The birth of the prison* (2nd ed.). New York: Vintage.

Holmqvist Gattario, K., Frisén, A., Piran, N. (2018, June). *Embodiment: Cultural and gender differences and associations with life satisfaction*. Paper presented at the Appearance Matters 8 Conference, Bath, 2018.

Jarman, H., Treneman-Evans, G., & Halliwell, E. (2017). *The feasibility and acceptability of dissonance eating disorder prevention in UK schools*. Manuscript in preparation.

Katzman, M. A., & Lee, S. (1997). Beyond body image: The integration of feminist and transcultural theories in the understanding of self starvation. *International*

Journal of Eating Disorders, *22*, 385–394. doi:10.1002/(sici)1098-108x(199712)22:4<385::aid-eat3>3.0.co;2-i

Mendelson, B. K., Mendelson, M. J., & White, D. R. (2001). Body Esteem Scale for Adolescents and Adults. *Journal of Personality Assessment*, *76*, 90–106. doi:10.1037/t00047-000

Merleau-Ponty, M. (1962). *Phenomenology of perception*. New York, NY: Humanities Press.

Piran, N. (2002). Embodiment: A mosaic of inquiries in the area of body weight and shape preoccupation. In S. Abbey (Ed.), *Ways of knowing in and through the body: Diverse perspectives on embodiment* (pp. 211–214). Welland, ON, Canada: Soleil.

Piran, N. (2010). A feminist perspective on risk factor research and on the prevention of eating disorders. *Eating Disorders*, *18*, 183–198. doi:10.1080/10640261003719435

Piran, N. (2015). New possibilities in the prevention of eating disorders: The introduction of positive body image measures. *Body Image*, *14*, 146–157. doi:10.1016/j.bodyim.2015.03.008

Piran, N. (2016a). Embodied paths in aging: Body journeys towards enhanced agency and self-attunement. *Women & Therapy*, *39*, 186–201. doi:10.1080/02703149.2016.1116853

Piran, N. (2016b). Embodied possibilities and disruptions: The emergence of the Experience of Embodiment construct from qualitative studies with girls and women. *Body Image*, *18*, 43–60. doi:10.1016/j.bodyim.2016.04.007

Piran, N. (2017). *Journeys of embodiment at the intersection of body and culture: The developmental theory of embodiment*. San Diego, CA: Elsevier. doi: 10.1016/c2015-0-04666-4

Piran, N., & Teall, T. L. (2006). *The Embodiment Scales for Women*. Unpublished.

Piran, N., & Teall, T. L. (2012a). The developmental theory of embodiment. In G. McVey, M. P. Levine, N. Piran, & H. B. Ferguson (Eds.), *Preventing eating-related and weight-related disorders: Collaborative research, advocacy, and policy change* (pp. 171–199). Waterloo, ON, Canada: Wilfred Laurier Press.

Piran, N., & Teall, T. L. (2012b). *The Embodiment Scales for Women*. Unpublished.

Sandoz, E. K., Wilson, K. G., Merwin, R. M., & Kellum, K. K. (2013). Assessment of body image flexibility: The Body-Image Acceptance and Action Questionnaire. *Journal of Contextual Behavioral Science*, *2*, 39–48. doi:10.1016/j.jcbs.2013.03.002

Steckler, A., McLeroy, K. R., Goodman, R. M., Bird, S. T., & McCormick, L. (1992). Toward integrating qualitative and quantitative methods: An introduction. *Health Education Quarterly*, *19*, 1–8. doi:10.1177/109019819201900101

Teall, T. L., & Piran, N. (2017). *The Experience of Embodiment Scale: A psychometric evaluation*. Manuscript in preparation.

Tolman, D. L., Bowman, C. P., & Fahs, B. (2014). Sexuality and embodiment. In D. L. Tolman & L. M. Diamond (Eds.), *APA handbook of sexuality and psychology* (Vol. 1, pp. 759–804). Washington, DC: American Psychological Association. doi:10.1037/14193-000

Trachtenberg, L. A., & Piran, N. (2017, June). *Experience of embodiment among young women survivors of breast cancer: Relationship to gender role expectations*. Paper presented at the Canadian Psychological Association Annual Convention, Toronto, Canada.

Tylka, T. L., & Kroon Van Diest, A. M. (2013). The Intuitive Eating Scale-2: Item refinement and psychometric evaluation with college women and men. *Journal of Counseling Psychology*, *60*, 137–153. doi:10.1037/a0030893

Tylka, T. L., & Wood-Barcalow, N. L. (2015a). The Body Appreciation Scale-2: Item refinement and psychometric evaluation. *Body Image, 12*, 53–67. doi:10.1016/j.bodyim.2014.09.006

Tylka, T. L., & Wood-Barcalow, N. L. (2015b). What is and what is not positive body image? Conceptual foundations and construct definition. *Body Image, 14*, 118–129. doi:10.1016/j.bodyim.2015.04.001

Young, L. (1992). Sexual abuse and the problem of embodiment. *Child Abuse and Neglect, 16*, 89–100. doi:10.1016/0145-2134(92)90010-O

2

Body Appreciation

TRACY L. TYLKA

In the relatively young field of positive body image, most research has focused on *body appreciation*, which entails having favorable opinions of the body regardless of actual physical appearance, accepting the body in spite of perceived imperfections, respecting the body by attending to its needs and engaging in healthy behaviors, and protecting the body by rejecting unrealistic appearance ideals found in the media (Avalos, Tylka, & Wood-Barcalow, 2005). Body appreciation has gained and maintained empirical ground due to its comprehensiveness in covering the positive body image construct and its ease of assessment (Tylka, 2011; Tylka & Wood-Barcalow, 2015b).

Regarding its comprehensiveness, body appreciation emerged as a primary theme within each qualitative study that aimed to understand the characteristics and components of positive body image by interviewing those who espouse a positive body image. Across the board, participants emphasized that positive body image involves respecting, honoring, loving, and displaying gratitude toward the features, functionality, and health of the body. For instance, US college women reported that they now appreciate features of their bodies that they disliked or ignored during adolescence and are grateful for the ways their bodies appear and function (Wood-Barcalow, Tylka, & Augustus-Horvath, 2010). Swedish adolescents reported appreciating the functionality and appearances of their bodies, even though they considered their appearance to be "average" (Holmqvist & Frisén, 2012). Aboriginal Canadian girls indicated that they appreciate their Native features and their bodies' ability to engage in the powwow dance, which connects them to their culture (McHugh, Coppola, & Sabiston, 2014). Canadian adults with spinal cord injuries revealed that they acknowledge and appreciate improvements in their health, function, independence, and strength (Bailey, Gammage, van Ingen, & Ditor, 2015).

Regarding its assessment, the psychometric integrity and ease of use has made the original Body Appreciation Scale (BAS; Avalos et al., 2005) and the Body Appreciation Scale-2 (BAS-2; Tylka & Wood-Barcalow, 2015a) a viable choice for scholars who need to assess body appreciation within research, clinical, prevention, and education settings. This chapter covers the BAS, BAS-2, and research on the body appreciation construct, including its links to psychological well-being and physical health, and ends with possible future avenues for research and clinical application.

BODY APPRECIATION SCALE

The original 13-item BAS (Avalos et al., 2005) was designed to measure the extent to which individuals accept, hold favorable opinions toward, and respect their bodies, as well as reject media-promoted appearance ideals as the only form of beauty. Exploratory and confirmatory factor analyses have revealed that the BAS has a unidimensional factor structure in many samples, including US women and men, Spanish adolescents, Austrian community women and men, and Turkish college women; however, a two-dimensional factor structure (a large general body appreciation factor and a smaller body image investment factor) was found in samples from Brazil, Hong Kong, Indonesia, Iran, Malaysia, Poland, South Korea, and Zimbabwe (see Swami, 2018, for a review). Evidence for the original BAS's internal consistency, test–retest reliability (when reported), and construct validity has been upheld across all samples. Because it was the only measure of positive body image available between 2005 and 2015, most research on body appreciation has been based on the original BAS.

Although evidence clearly supports its psychometric properties, two of the original BAS authors—myself and Nichole Wood-Barcalow—revised the original BAS in 2015 for several reasons: (a) Three items produce lower factor loadings (perhaps the reason a two-factor structure was found in some cultures); (b) women and men were required to complete different forms due to gender-specific language within an item; (c) two items were written as though it is normative to see the body as flawed; and (d) two items narrowly conceptualized positive body image as the absence of shape and weight concerns. Thus, we revised, reworded, discarded, or replaced eight original BAS items to resolve these issues and better reflect current knowledge of the positive body image construct. This revised scale, the BAS-2 (Tylka & Wood-Barcalow, 2015a), contains five original BAS items and five new items. Like the BAS, the BAS-2 recognizes that body appreciation involves holding favorable opinions toward one's body, accepting its unique characteristics, respecting it by taking care of its needs, and believing that it is beautiful and valuable despite any perceived inconsistency with media-promoted appearance ideals.

A thorough investigation of the BAS-2's psychometric properties was conducted among several samples of US college and community samples of women and men (Tylka & Wood-Barcalow, 2015a). The BAS-2 conformed to a unidimensional factor structure and demonstrated strong internal consistency ($\alpha = .93–.96$) and stability over a 3-week period ($r = .90$). Measurement invariance analyses revealed that its structure is similar between men and women, as well as college and community samples. It was positively related to self-esteem and proactive coping and inversely associated with body dissatisfaction, internalization of societal appearance ideals, and body surveillance, upholding convergent validity. It accounted for unique variance in adaptive and maladaptive eating behaviors after removing its shared variance with appearance evaluation and body dissatisfaction, supporting incremental validity. It was negligibly related to impression management, demonstrating discriminant validity. Its unidimensional factor structure, measurement invariance (when explored), internal consistency, and construct (mainly convergent) validity also have been upheld across many college or community samples from different geographical locations, such as the Netherlands, France, Spain, Iran, Romania, Poland, Portugal, Iceland, Serbia, Hong Kong, and mainland China (see Swami, 2017, for a review).

Illustrative BAS-2 items include "I respect my body," "I appreciate the different and unique characteristics of my body," "I feel love for my body," "I am attentive to my body's needs," and "I feel like I am beautiful even if I am different from media images of attractive people (e.g., models, actresses/actors)." Its 10 items are rated along a 5-point scale ranging from *never* (scored as 1) to *always* (5) and averaged, with higher scores reflecting greater body appreciation. The BAS-2 has also been modified for children (BAS-2C), with its psychometric properties (internal consistency, test–retest reliability, as well as convergent, incremental, and criterion-related validity) upheld in a sample of girls and boys aged 9–11 (Halliwell, Jarman, Tylka, & Slater, 2017). A validated state version of the BAS-2 (SBAS-2), sensitive to context-specific fluctuations in body appreciation, also exists (Homan, 2016).

RESEARCH ON BODY APPRECIATION

Most research on body appreciation, assessed with either the BAS or BAS-2, has focused on how it is linked in an adaptive direction to psychological well-being and physical health—areas with great clinical, empirical, and theoretical relevance—and therefore is the focus of this section. Unless otherwise noted, study designs are cross-sectional and findings are based on samples from the United States, Canada, the United Kingdom, Australia, or the Netherlands.

Psychological Well-Being

Body appreciation is positively associated with multiple indicators of psychological well-being, such as optimism, self-esteem, proactive coping, positive affect, life satisfaction, subjective happiness, and emotional intelligence (Avalos et al., 2005; Gillen, 2015; Swami, Begum, & Petrides, 2010; Swami, Tran, Stieger, Voracek & the YouBeauty.com Team, 2015; Tylka, Calogero, & Daníelsdóttir, 2015; Tylka & Kroon Van Diest, 2013). Body appreciation is also inversely related to negative affect and depressive symptomatology (Gillen, 2015; Tylka et al., 2015; Tylka & Kroon Van Diest, 2013). The spotlight is next placed on body appreciation's strong links to three indices of psychological well-being: intuitive eating, self-compassion, and state body dissatisfaction.

Intuitive Eating

Intuitive eating is a flexible pattern of eating largely based on internal hunger and satiety cues rather than emotional and situational cues (Tylka & Kroon Van Diest, 2013). Body appreciation has been examined within the acceptance model of intuitive eating (Avalos & Tylka, 2006). According to this model, body acceptance by others encourages individuals to appreciate their bodies and focus less on their appearance, which then facilitates intuitive eating. In two studies, Avalos and Tylka (2006) found that body appreciation mediated the relationship between body acceptance by others and intuitive eating; that is, women who perceive that important others accept their bodies have higher body appreciation, which is in turn associated with higher intuitive eating. These associations were also upheld in samples of men (Kroon Van Diest & Tylka, 2010); adolescent girls (Andrew, Tiggemann, & Clark, 2015a); and women in emerging, early, and middle adulthood (Augustus-Horvath & Tylka, 2011). Andrew, Tiggemann, and Clark (2016c) prospectively examined the acceptance model of intuitive eating among adolescent girls assessed at two time points separated by 1 year. They found that body acceptance by others predicted increased body appreciation, and body appreciation predicted increased intuitive eating over the year. Expanding the model, Tylka and Homan (2015) found that, among physically active college students, the connection between body appreciation and intuitive eating was disrupted the more participants endorsed exercising for appearance reasons (e.g., to lose weight).

Self-Compassion

Self-compassion, or being mindful, kind, and nurturing toward the self during situations that threaten self-adequacy (Neff, 2003), has been found to be associated with, and even increase, body appreciation. Albertson, Neff, and Dill-Shackleford (2015) delivered a 3-week self-compassion meditation training to adult women with existing body image concerns. Women who received this training reported significantly greater gains in body appreciation at postintervention compared to a waitlist control group and maintained these gains at a 3-month follow-up.

Over a 7-day period, Kelly and Stephen (2016) found that college women's day-to-day fluctuations in self-compassion were connected to their day-to-day fluctuations in body appreciation: On days women treated themselves more compassionately than usual, they were more appreciative of their bodies. Self-compassion also was found to preserve women's body appreciation during body-related threats, such as situations that promoted body comparison (Homan & Tylka, 2015) and perceived negative evaluations from others (Marta-Simões, Ferreira, & Mendes, 2016). Andrew, Tiggemann, and Clark (2016b) found that the strong link between self-compassion and body appreciation was mediated by reduced focus on appearance. Thus, being kind and compassionate toward the self may minimize the salience of appearance, which helps women appreciate their bodies even when they do not conform to societal ideals.

State Body Dissatisfaction

Evidence suggests that body appreciation can protect against body dissatisfaction among women when they are exposed to sociocultural appearance ideals (e.g., pictures of glamorized thin models). Halliwell (2013) found that women high in body appreciation did not place increased importance on their appearance discrepancies (i.e., differences between how they would like to look and how they actually look) after viewing thin female models; their appearance discrepancies were similar in size to a control group who did not view thin models. In contrast, women low in body appreciation placed increased importance on their appearance discrepancies after viewing thin female models when compared to the control group. Similarly, Andrew, Tiggemann, and Clark (2015b) revealed that women with low body appreciation experienced increased body dissatisfaction following exposure to thin-ideal advertisements of women, whereas those with high body appreciation did not. This effect remained when controlling for participants' state self-objectification, appearance comparison, and previous media consumption and literacy. These studies suggest that body appreciation can protect against declines in state body dissatisfaction as a result of exposure to the "thin-ideal" body type promoted by the media (Andrew et al., 2015b).

Physical Health

Body appreciation also has been found to be linked to several health-related indices in an adaptive direction. These connections are highlighted next.

Physical Activity

Body appreciation is associated with higher engagement in physical activity; however, Homan and Tylka (2014) found that this relationship was significant only when appearance-related motives for exercise were low. Conversations about weight loss and dieting prompt women to evaluate their appearance, which is linked to lower body appreciation, whereas conversations about exercise have been found to orient women to consider what their bodies can do, which is connected to higher body appreciation (Wasylkiw & Butler, 2014).

Certain types of physical activities are embodying and cultivate an appreciation of body functionality and deemphasize appearance. For instance, women who practice Iyengar and Bikram yoga reported higher body appreciation than women who do not practice yoga, with the yogis' lower self-objectification and higher embodiment accounting for this difference (Mahlo & Tiggemann, 2016). Additionally, female modern dancers (Langdon & Petracca, 2010), street dancers (Swami & Tovée, 2009), belly dancers (Tiggemann, Coutts, & Clark, 2014), and recreational pole dancers (Pellizzer, Tiggemann, & Clark, 2016) had higher body appreciation compared to nondancers. Among belly dancers, Tiggemann et al. (2014) demonstrated that lower self-objectification and higher embodiment accounted for this discrepancy.

Sexual and Reproductive Health

Body appreciation has also been connected to higher sexual functioning and positive reproductive attitudes. For instance, body appreciation was found to be connected to higher sexual arousal, orgasm, and satisfaction among a diverse sample of women, even when controlling for sexual orientation, partner status, and age (Satinsky, Reece, Dennis, Sanders, & Bardzell, 2012). Similarly, body appreciation uniquely contributed to women's higher sexual functioning and satisfaction and lower sexual distress, even when controlling for age and appearance dissatisfaction (Robbins & Reissing, 2018). Body appreciation was further found to weaken age-related changes in sexual satisfaction, leading Robbins and Reissing to suggest that body appreciation may be a promising clinical intervention in the treatment of sexual problems emerging with age. Body appreciation was linked to greater sexual liberalism in women and men when controlling for sexual orientation, relationship status, age, and body mass index (Swami, Weis, Barron, & Furnham, 2017), as well as more positive attitudes for women toward their menstrual cycle (Chrisler, Marván, Gorman, & Rossini, 2015).

Physical Self-Care

Body appreciation has been positively linked to a range of behaviors suggested by medical professionals to help promote physical self-care and avoid disease. For example, higher body appreciation among adolescent girls and college women and men was associated with greater intentions to protect their skin from UV exposure and damage and conduct skin cancer screenings (Andrew et al., 2016a; Gillen, 2015). Body appreciation predicted increased physical activity as well as decreased dieting, alcohol, and cigarette use over a year among adolescent girls (Andrew et al., 2016c). Higher body appreciation among first-year medical students from Romania was connected to their oral health (Dumitrescu, Zetu, Teslaru, Dogaru, & Dogaru, 2008). Furthermore, college students with higher body appreciation reported lower abuse of prescription stimulants for weight loss compared to those with lower body appreciation (Jeffers & Benotsch, 2014). Body appreciation was also found to be inversely linked to disordered eating behaviors and endorsing cosmetic surgery among women and men (Andrew et al., 2016a; Avalos et al., 2005; Gillen, 2015; Swami, 2009; Tylka & Kroon Van Diest, 2013; Tylka & Wood-Barcalow, 2015a). These findings highlight body appreciation as an important variable to target for interventions addressing physical self-care.

RESEARCH AND CLINICAL CONSIDERATIONS

Developments in theory, research, and practice on body appreciation are gaining momentum as scholars are beginning to see the benefits of body appreciation to psychological well-being and physical health in their studies, as reviewed previously, and clinical work. Yet, much work still needs to be done. Where should we direct this work?

A major way to advance body appreciation scholarship is to examine it as (a) a protective factor against ill-being and (b) an enhancement factor for well-being. To pursue body appreciation scholarship in this direction, we must shift from correlational and cross-sectional designs, which most studies of body appreciation are based on, to longitudinal and experimental designs. For instance, we need to investigate body appreciation over years to provide a clearer picture of its development, stability, and transience (Tylka & Kroon Van Diest, 2015). Researchers need to identify which variables predict initial levels of body appreciation, the factors that maintain it, and the factors that preserve it in the face of body image threats. Given the development of the BAS-2C (Halliwell et al., 2017), it is possible to begin these investigations in children as young as age 9. Via ecological momentary assessment (EMA), researchers can investigate fluctuations in state body appreciation as a result of moment-to-moment events to determine what contextual factors threaten or enhance body appreciation and how these contextual factors may interact with other internal trait or state factors (e.g., self-compassion, negative affect) to determine levels of and fluctuations of body appreciation. The recently developed SBAS-2 (Homan, 2016) could aid in these endeavors.

Researchers also need to investigate the interaction of positive body image components. Efforts could be directed toward exploring "upward spirals," or combinations of adaptive variables that trigger self-perpetuating cycles and trajectories of positive psychological growth (Garland et al., 2010). Researchers could use this reciprocal influence longitudinal design to study, for instance, whether initial levels of body appreciation predict subsequent body appreciation through embodied activities (e.g., yoga, belly dance), self-care, and intuitive eating.

We also need to investigate whether existing body image and disordered eating interventions promote body appreciation, as such interventions should increase embodiment as well as decrease disembodiment. Positive body image scales could be incorporated into existing and future interventions to more thoroughly evaluate their efficacy and effectiveness. Halliwell, Jarman, McNamara, Risdon, and Jankowski (2015) included the BAS-2 when examining the impact of a 1-hour cognitive dissonance–based intervention whereby secondary school girls voiced opposition to the thin-ideal body type through various activities. The intervention group reported increased body appreciation from pre- to postintervention, whereas the control group experienced no change.

Integrating the BAS-2 into larger and longer term empirically supported programs such as The Body Project (Stice, Rohde, & Shaw, 2013) seems worthwhile. In future developments and refinements of primary and secondary prevention programs, it would be useful to integrate empirical insights on body appreciation into the activities and use the BAS-2 to evaluate their efficacy and effectiveness. Clinicians can use the BAS-2 at the beginning of therapy, at several midpoints, and at the end of therapy to determine improvements in body image (to increase client self-efficacy) and therapy effectiveness (to increase clients' perceptions of positive outcomes); a collection of these assessments across clients could be analyzed via multilevel modeling to determine the effectiveness of certain interventions, such as compassion-focused therapy or acceptance and commitment therapy.

Last, clinical benefits of having a high level of body appreciation, as opposed to low or average levels, need to be investigated. Extending this thought, we need to understand whether it is feasible for clients with eating disorders or body dysmorphia to aspire to a high level of body appreciation in therapy (and if so, when and for whom in therapy) or, alternatively, aim for a more body neutral perspective.

CONCLUSION

Body appreciation has emerged as the predominant variable in positive body image scholarship due to its prominence as a theme in many qualitative studies of positive body image as well as its user-friendly assessments, the BAS and BAS-2. Via these scales, researchers have found much evidence for their hypotheses that body appreciation is associated with numerous psychological well-being indices and physical health indicators; initial evidence even points to it serving as a protective factor to prevent ill-being and an enhancement factor to promote health and well-being. Yet, many research and clinical advancements in body appreciation await us, with the findings sure to hone our understanding of how to cultivate this construct.

REFERENCES

Albertson, E. R., Neff, K. D., & Dill-Shackleford, K. E. (2015). Self-compassion and body dissatisfaction in women: A randomized controlled trial of a brief meditation intervention. *Mindfulness, 6*, 444–454. doi:10.1007/s12671-014-0277-3

Andrew, R., Tiggemann, M., & Clark, L. (2015a). Predictors of intuitive eating in adolescent girls. *Journal of Adolescent Health, 56*, 209–214. doi:10.1016/j.jadohealth.2014.09.005

Andrew, R., Tiggemann, M., & Clark, L. (2015b). The protective role of body appreciation against media-induced body dissatisfaction. *Body Image, 15*, 98–104. doi:10.10166/j.bodyim.2015.07.005

Andrew, R., Tiggemann, M., & Clark, L. (2016a). Positive body image and young women's health: Implications for sun protection, cancer screening, weight loss and alcohol consumption behaviours. *Journal of Health Psychology, 21*, 28–39. doi:10.1177/1359105314520814

Andrew, R., Tiggemann, M., & Clark, L. (2016b). Predicting body appreciation in young women: An integrated model of positive body image. *Body Image, 18*, 34–42.

Andrew, R., Tiggemann, M., & Clark, L. (2016c). Predictors and health-related outcomes of positive body image in adolescent girls: A prospective study. *Developmental Psychology, 52*, 463–474. doi:10.1037/dev0000095

Augustus-Horvath, C. L., & Tylka, T. L. (2011). The acceptance model of intuitive eating: A comparison of women in emerging adulthood, early adulthood, and middle adulthood. *Journal of Counseling Psychology, 58*, 110–125. doi:10.1037/a0022129

Avalos, L. C., & Tylka, T. L. (2006). Exploring a model of intuitive eating with college women. *Journal of Counseling Psychology*, *53*, 486–497. doi:10.1037/0022-1067.53.4.486

Avalos, L. C., Tylka, T. L., & Wood-Barcalow, N. (2005). The Body Appreciation Scale: Development and psychometric evaluation. *Body Image*, *2*, 285–297. doi:10.1016/j.bodyim.2005.06.002

Bailey, K. A., Gammage, K. L., van Ingen, C., & Ditor, D. S. (2015). "It's all about acceptance": A qualitative study exploring a model of positive body image for people with spinal cord injury. *Body Image*, *15*, 24–34. doi:10.1016/j.bodyim.2015.04.010

Chrisler, J. C., Marván, M. L., Gorman, J. A., & Rossini, M. (2015). Body appreciation and attitudes toward menstruation. *Body Image*, *12*, 78–81. doi:10.1016/j.bodyim.2014.10.003

Dumitrescu, A. L., Zetu, L., Teslaru, S., Dogaru, B. C., & Dogaru, C. D. (2008). Is it an association between body appreciation, self-criticism, oral health status, and oral health-related behaviors? *Romanian Journal of Internal Medicine*, *46*, 343–350.

Garland, E. L., Fredrickson, B., Kring, A. M., Johnson, D. P., Meyer, P. S., & Penn, D. L. (2010). Upward spirals of positive emotions counter downward spirals of negativity: Insights from the broaden-and-build theory and affective neuroscience on the treatment of emotional dysfunctions and deficits in psychopathology. *Clinical Psychology Review*, *30*, 849–864. doi:10.1016/j.cpr.2010.03.002

Gillen, M. M. (2015). Associations between positive body image and indicators of men's and women's mental and physical health. *Body Image*, *13*, 67–74. doi:10.1016/j.bodyim.2015.01.002

Halliwell, E. (2013). The impact of thin idealized media images on body satisfaction: Does body appreciation protect women from negative effects? *Body Image*, *10*, 509–514. doi:10.1016/j.bodyim.2013.07.004

Halliwell, E., Jarman, H., McNamara, A., Risdon, H., & Jankowski, G. (2015). Dissemination of evidence-based body image interventions: A pilot study into the effectiveness of using undergraduate students as interventionists in secondary schools. *Body Image*, *14*, 1–4. doi:10.1016/j.bodyim.2015.02.002

Halliwell, E., Jarman, H., Tylka, T. L., & Slater, A. (2017). Adapting the Body Appreciation Scale-2 for children: A psychometric analysis of the BAS-2C. *Body Image*, *21*, 97–102. doi:10.1016/j.bodyim.2017.03.005

Holmqvist, K., & Frisén, A. (2012). "I bet they aren't that perfect in reality": Appearance ideals viewed from the perspective of adolescents with a positive body image. *Body Image*, *9*, 388–395. doi:10.1016/j.bodyim.2012.03.007

Homan, K. J. (2016). Factor structure and psychometric properties of a state version of the Body Appreciation Scale-2. *Body Image*, *19*, 204–207. doi:10.1016/j.bodyim.2016.10.004

Homan, K. J., & Tylka, T. L. (2014). Appearance-based exercise motivation moderates the relationship between exercise frequency and positive body image. *Body Image*, *11*, 101–108. doi:10.1016/j.bodyim.2014.01.003

Homan, K. J., & Tylka, T. L. (2015). Self-compassion moderates body comparison and appearance self-worth's inverse relationships with body appreciation. *Body Image*, *15*, 1–7. doi:10.1016/j.bodyim.2015.04.007

Jeffers, A. J., & Benotsch, E. G. (2014). Non-medical use of prescription stimulants for weight loss, disordered eating, and body image. *Eating Behaviors*, *15*, 414–418. doi:10.1016/j.eatbeh.2014.04.019

Kelly, A. C., & Stephen, E. (2016). A daily diary study of self-compassion, body image, and eating behavior in female college students. *Body Image, 17*, 152–160. doi:10.1016/j.bodyim.2016.03.006

Kroon Van Diest, A. M., & Tylka, T. L. (2010). The Caregiver Eating Messages Scale: Development and psychometric investigation. *Body Image, 7*, 317–326. doi:10.1016/j.bodyim.2010.06.002

Langdon, S. W., & Petracca, G. (2010). Tiny dancer: Body image and dancer identity in female modern dancers. *Body Image, 7*, 360–363. doi:10.1016/j.bodyim.2010.06.005

Mahlo, L., & Tiggemann, M. (2016). Yoga and positive body image: A test of the embodiment model. *Body Image, 18*, 135–142. doi:10.1016/j.bodyim.2016.06.008

Marta-Simões, J., Ferreira, C., & Mendes, A. L. (2016). Exploring the effect of external shame on body appreciation among Portuguese young adults: The role of self-compassion. *Eating Behaviors, 23*, 174–179. doi:10.1016/j.eatbeh.2016.10.006

McHugh, T. L., Coppola, A. M., & Sabiston, C. M. (2014). "I'm thankful for being Native and my body is part of that": The body pride experiences of young Aboriginal women in Canada. *Body Image, 11*, 318–327. doi:10.1016/j.bodyim.2014.05.004

Neff, K. D. (2003). Self-compassion: An alternative conceptualization of a healthy attitude toward oneself. *Self and Identity, 2*, 85–101. doi:10.1080/15298860309032

Pellizzer, M., Tiggemann, M., & Clark, L. (2016). Enjoyment of sexualization and positive body image in recreational pole dancers and university students. *Sex Roles, 74*, 35–45. doi:10.1017/s11199-015-0562-1

Robbins, A. R., & Reissing, E. D. (2018). Appearance dissatisfaction, body appreciation, and sexual health in women across adulthood. *Archives of Sexual Behavior, 47*, 703–714. doi:10.1017/s10508-017-0982-9

Satinsky, S., Reece, M., Dennis, B., Sanders, S., & Bardzell, S. (2012). An assessment of body appreciation and its relationship to sexual function in women. *Body Image, 9*, 137–144. doi:10.1016/j.bodyim.2011.09.007

Stice, E., Rohde, P., & Shaw, H. (2013). *The Body Project: A dissonance-based eating disorder prevention intervention (Updated ed.). Facilitator guide.* New York, NY: Oxford University Press.

Swami, V. (2009). Body appreciation, media influence, and weight status predict consideration of cosmetic surgery among female undergraduates. *Body Image, 6*, 315–317. doi:10.1016/j.bodyim.2009.07.001

Swami, V. (2018). Considering positive body image through the lens of culture and minority social identities. In C. Markey, E. Daniels, & M. Gillen (Eds.), *The body positive: Understanding and improving body image in science and practice* (pp. 59–91). New York, NY: Cambridge University Press.

Swami, V., Begum, S., & Petrides, K. V. (2010). Associations between trait emotional intelligence, actual-ideal weight discrepancy, and positive body image. *Personality and Individual Differences, 49*, 485–489. doi:10.1016/j.paid.2010.05.009

Swami, V., & Tovée, M. J. (2009). A comparison of actual-ideal weight discrepancy, body appreciation, and media influence between street-dancers and non-dancers. *Body Image, 6*, 304–307. doi:10.1016/j.bodyim.2009.07.006

Swami, V., Tran, U. S., Stieger, S., Voracek, M., & The YouBeauty.com Team. (2015). Associations between women's body image and happiness: Results of the YouBeauty.com Body Image Survey (YBIS). *Journal of Happiness Studies, 16*, 705–718. doi:10.1007/s10902-014-9530-7

Swami, V., Weis, L., Barron, D., & Furnham, A. (2017). Associations between positive body image, sexual liberalism, and unconventional sexual practices in US adults. *Archives of Sexual Behavior, 46*, 2485–2494. doi:10.1017/s10508-016-0924-y

Tiggemann, M., Coutts, E., & Clark, L. (2014). Belly dance as an embodying activity? A test of the embodiment model of positive body image. *Sex Roles, 71*, 197–207. doi:10.1007/s11199-014-0408-2

Tylka, T. L. (2011). Positive psychology perspectives on body image. In T. F. Cash & L. Smolak (Eds.), *Body image: A handbook of science, practice, and prevention* (2nd ed., pp. 56–64). New York, NY: Guilford Press.

Tylka, T. L., Calogero, R. M., & Daníelsdóttir, S. (2015). Is intuitive eating the same as flexible dietary control? Their links to each other and well-being could provide an answer. *Appetite, 95*, 166–175. doi:10.1016/j.appet.2015.07.004

Tylka, T. L., & Homan, K. J. (2015). Exercise motives and positive body image in physically active college women and men: Exploring an expanded acceptance model of intuitive eating. *Body Image, 15*, 90–97. doi:10.1016/j.bodyim.2015.07.003

Tylka, T. L., & Kroon Van Diest, A. M. (2013). The Intuitive Eating Scale-2: Item refinement and psychometric evaluation with college women and men. *Journal of Counseling Psychology, 60*, 137–153. doi:10.1037/a0030893

Tylka, T. L., & Kroon Van Diest, A. M. (2015). Protective factors in the development of eating disorders. In L. Smolak & M. P. Levine (Eds.), *The Wiley-Blackwell handbook of eating disorders* (Vol. 1, pp. 430–444). New York, NY: Wiley.

Tylka, T. L., & Wood-Barcalow, N. L. (2015a). The Body Appreciation Scale: Item refinement and psychometric evaluation. *Body Image, 12*, 53–67. doi:10.1016/j.bodyim.2014.09.006

Tylka, T. L., & Wood-Barcalow, N. L. (2015b). What is and what is not positive body image? Conceptual foundations and construct definition [Special series]. *Body Image, 14*, 118–129. doi:10.1016/j.bodyim.2015.04.001

Wasylkiw, L., & Butler, N. A. (2014). Body talk among undergraduate women: Why conversations about exercise and weight loss differentially predict body appreciation. *Journal of Health Psychology, 19*, 1013–1024. doi:10.1177/1359105313483155

Wood-Barcalow, N. L., Tylka, T. L., & Augustus-Horvath, C. L. (2010). "But I like my body": Positive body image characteristics and a holistic model for young-adult women. *Body Image, 7*, 106–116. doi:10.1016/j.bodyim.2010.01.001

3

Body Functionality

JESSICA M. ALLEVA AND CAROLIEN MARTIJN

Body functionality describes everything that the body can *do* and encompasses functions related to (a) physical capacities (e.g., flexibility), (b) internal processes (e.g., digesting food), (c) bodily senses and perception (e.g., sight), (d) creative endeavors (e.g., playing an instrument), (e) communication with others (e.g., body language), and (f) self-care (e.g., showering; Alleva, Martijn, Van Breukelen, Jansen, & Karos, 2015). To date, the majority of body image research has investigated individuals' thoughts, feelings, perceptions, and behaviors relating to their *physical appearance* only. In fact, the paucity of research focusing on body image as related to body functionality has been identified as one of the main limitations in the field (Cash & Smolak, 2011). Luckily, in recent years, more research has begun to emerge that addresses body image in a broader sense, including a focus on body functionality.

This chapter describes how focusing on body functionality can be beneficial for fostering positive embodiment. We then describe existing and emerging measures for assessing aspects of body functionality and discuss how body functionality can be integrated into intervention efforts. We also highlight potential caveats of focusing on body functionality and identify key directions for research.

BODY FUNCTIONALITY, PHYSICAL ABILITY, AND GENDER

Before continuing, it is important to keep two points in mind. First, the concept of body functionality is not limited to able-bodied individuals. That is, even though body functionality can be limited by various factors (e.g., diseases, acquired injuries, differences in body structure), each body possesses a set of unique functions that is not limited to specific functions or domains of functionality. Second, the majority of body image research—including research on body functionality—has been conducted in women, and research in men is comparatively scarce. Yet, based on the extant research, there is reason to believe that body functionality is gendered. For example, objectification theory proposes that, in Western societies, women are viewed and evaluated based predominantly on the physical appearance of their body; in contrast, men's bodies are valued more for aspects of their functionality (Fredrickson & Roberts, 1997). Similarly, women are more likely to focus on and evaluate their own body based on their physical appearance, whereas men tend to focus on and evaluate their own body based on aspects of their functionality (e.g., Abbott & Barber, 2010; Moradi & Huang, 2008). These findings suggest that men are encouraged to—and do adopt—a more functionality-based orientation toward their body than women. However, it is an unanswered question regarding whether men focus on their body functionality holistically or as limited to those aspects of body functionality that are emphasized by the current male beauty ideal and notions of masculinity (e.g., muscularity).

BODY FUNCTIONALITY AND FOSTERING POSITIVE EMBODIMENT

We propose that focusing on body functionality can be beneficial for fostering positive embodiment. There are at least two key theories that support this proposition. First, objectification theory posits that the experience of self-objectification is central to women's negative relationships with their body (Fredrickson & Roberts, 1997). Importantly, self-objectification describes viewing one's own body as a static object, evaluated predominantly for its physical appearance. Therefore, focusing on what one's body can *do* is antithetical to self-objectification and may discourage women from adopting an objectifying and harmful view of their body. Second, the developmental theory of embodiment (Piran, 2016) proposes that engaging in activities that emphasize body functionality and achieving attunement with the body can lead to a sense of connection between the mind and body that directly promotes positive embodiment. Although these theories were developed in the context of women's experiences, immersion in embodying activities should also foster positive embodiment in men. Moreover, research suggests that men also experience self-objectification, albeit to a lesser degree than women, and that it has similar negative consequences for their body image (Moradi & Huang, 2008). Thus, a more functional body orientation should be beneficial for men as well.

Qualitative and correlational research suggests that focusing on body functionality is related to positive embodiment. For example, Piran's (2016) interviews with girls and women across the life span have shown that narratives of positive embodiment were characterized by joyful experiences of body functionality. Interviews with girls, boys, and women espousing a positive body image have also revealed themes centering on appreciating and caring for the body's functionality (Frisén & Holmqvist, 2010; Wood-Barcalow, Tylka, & Augustus-Horvath, 2010). Moreover, correlational research has shown that exercising for functionality-related reasons and engaging in activities that emphasize body functionality are associated with greater body esteem and lower self-objectification (e.g., Prichard & Tiggemann, 2008). Similarly, conversations about exercise were found to orient women to consider what their bodies can do, which was in turn related to higher body appreciation (Wasylkiw & Butler, 2014).

The first experimental support for the benefit of focusing on body functionality came from research by Alleva and colleagues (Alleva, Martijn, Jansen, & Nederkoorn, 2014). In two studies, undergraduate women and men and 30- to 50-year-old community women were asked to describe in at least 100 words their body functionality, physical appearance, or a control topic. Relative to the comparison groups, male undergraduates and 30- to 50-year-old women who described their body functionality experienced improvements in functionality satisfaction; however, female undergraduates did not experience similar improvements. In a later study, female undergraduates and community women screened for having a negative body image completed a more extensive functionality-focused program (described in material that follows) or an active control program (Alleva et al., 2015). Relative to control, participants in the functionality-focused program experienced improvements in functionality satisfaction, appearance satisfaction, and body appreciation and reductions in self-objectification.

MEASURES CAPTURING ASPECTS OF BODY FUNCTIONALITY

The selection of measures to capture aspects of body functionality is small. Four measures that have been commonly used for this purpose are (a) the Embodied Image Scale (Abbott & Barber, 2010); (b) the Physical Condition subscale of the Body Esteem Scale (Franzoi & Shields, 1984); (c) the Self-Objectification Questionnaire (Noll & Fredrickson, 1998); and (d) the Body Surveillance subscale of the Objectified Body Consciousness Scale (McKinley & Hyde, 1996). Although studies using these measures have advanced research on body functionality, these measures are limited in several different respects. Namely, they do not capture the holistic nature of body functionality, as they narrowly focus on the domains of physical capacities and internal processes. Moreover, many of these measures are limited to able-bodied individuals and capture *evaluations* of body functionality (e.g., functionality satisfaction). Yet, research has suggested that, when it comes to enhancing positive body image and well-being, appreciation for one's body may be more important than the degree of satisfaction with one's body (Wood-Barcalow et al., 2010). None of these measures assesses participants' *appreciation* of the functions that their body does perform, which is a less able-bodied construct and one that is consistent with the literature on positive body image and embodiment.

To address these limitations, Alleva, Tylka, and Kroon Van Diest (2017) created the Functionality Appreciation Scale (FAS). The FAS was developed to assess *functionality appreciation*, defined as appreciating, respecting, and honoring the body for what it is capable of doing. Items were designed to be applicable to diverse body functions, to reflect each individual's unique capabilities, and to be general enough to be relevant across individual identities. Importantly, the FAS was not developed to measure body functioning per se or the appreciation of specific domains of body functionality, but rather the overall appreciation of the body's ability to function *to the extent that it can.*

The final FAS comprised seven items (e.g., "I appreciate my body for what it is capable of doing") that are rated from 1 = *strongly disagree* to 5 = *strongly agree.* Across three studies with US community women and men ($N = 1{,}042$), the FAS demonstrated a unidimensional factor structure and invariance across gender, and the internal consistency, test–retest reliability, criterion-related, and construct (convergent, discriminant, incremental) validity of its scores were upheld. Supporting prior research on the benefits of focusing on body functionality, FAS scores were positively associated with aspects of positive body image and well-being (e.g., broad conceptualizations of beauty, intuitive eating) and inversely associated with aspects of negative body image and ill-being (e.g., self-objectification, depression). The analyses also showed that functionality appreciation is *distinct* from high levels of body appreciation, functionality satisfaction, appearance satisfaction, and self-compassion and from low levels of self-objectification, beauty-ideal internalization, and appearance orientation. Interestingly, overall, FAS scores were relatively high and did not significantly differ according to gender, body mass index, or age, suggesting that individuals may be able to appreciate their body functionality despite cultural pressures to overvalue physical appearance and internalize the "ideal" body.

Collectively, these findings show that functionality appreciation is an adaptive and unique construct that is intricately linked with a healthier body image and well-being. It is hoped that the availability of the FAS will help to facilitate the integration of body functionality in research, clinical, prevention, and educational contexts, enabling more comprehensive investigations of body image beyond the scope of physical appearance.

BODY FUNCTIONALITY AND INTERVENTION EFFORTS

Based on their initial studies, Alleva and colleagues (2015) developed a functionality-focused program designed to improve body image, called *Expand Your Horizon*. This program comprises three writing exercises, delivered online over the course of 1 week. Each writing exercise focuses on two different domains of body functionality (e.g., physical capacities and bodily senses) so that, by the end of the program, participants will have focused on their body functionality in a holistic manner. Specifically, they are asked to describe the functions that their body can perform concerning the respective domains and to reflect on why those functions are personally meaningful to them. In addition, at the start of the first writing exercise, participants receive an introduction to the concept of body functionality and a list of body functions that they can refer to throughout the program should they need inspiration.

Alleva et al.'s (2015) research showed that, compared to an active control program, the Expand Your Horizon program led to increases in functionality satisfaction, appearance satisfaction, and body appreciation and decreases in self-objectification at both post-test and 1-week follow-up. More recently, this research was repeated in a larger sample of women based in the United Kingdom (*N* = 261; Alleva, Diedrichs, et al., 2018). Alleva et al.'s original findings were replicated, showing that focusing on body functionality, compared to participation in an active control program, led to improvements in women's body image at post-test and 1-week follow-up. In addition, these improvements persisted at an additional 1-month follow-up. These findings are noteworthy given that the program takes just 45 minutes to complete and is easy and affordable to disseminate (e.g., delivered online, without an interventionist).

Expand Your Horizon has yet to be tested in men, but we predict that the program could also help them feel more positively about their bodies. As described previously, undergraduate men who wrote just 100 words about their body functionality experienced improvements in functionality satisfaction (Alleva et al., 2014). Considering that men may be socialized to focus on body functionality as limited to their physical capacities (e.g., via the emphasis on muscularity in media imagery), Expand Your Horizon could help them to appreciate their body functionality in a more holistic sense, incorporating other valued domains. Testing Expand Your Horizon in men as well as individuals of various intersecting social identities is an important direction for future research. Additional valuable directions for research on Expand Your Horizon include investigating its even longer term effects and its effects in individuals who may be accustomed to focusing on body functionality in a narrowed sense (e.g., individuals experiencing chronic pain, athletes experiencing an injury); its impact on other variables of interest (e.g., beauty-ideal internalization); and strategies for strengthening the program, such as via "booster" writing sessions, additional targeted questions, or homework activities. It will also be valuable to test alternative modes for delivering the program, for example for individuals who are illiterate or less accustomed to expressing their thoughts and feelings in writing or in settings where written responses are less convenient. Ideas include having individuals describe their body functions out loud, discussing the themes of the program in group format, or even expressing one's body functions visually (e.g., via collages or drawings).

Other interventions that are not necessarily explicitly or exclusively focused on body functionality may foster a functionality-based orientation toward the body as well. For example, physical activity and yoga-based interventions, as well as some forms of dance, might also work to enhance positive body image by helping individuals to shift their attention to the functional aspects of their body (e.g., Mahlo & Tiggemann, 2016; Martin & Lichtenberger, 2002; Tiggemann, Coutts, & Clark, 2014). Some cognitive behavioral programs have also encouraged individuals to eschew an appearance-focused view of their body in favor of a functional view. For instance, during mirror exposure exercises, individuals may be asked to describe their body in nonappearance terms, such as by commenting on their emotional or behavioral characteristics (e.g., Becker, Ciao, & Smith,

2008). Likewise, in Cash's (2008) *Body Image Workbook*, individuals are asked to engage in body experiences that foster feelings of mastery or pleasure and are not appearance focused.

Any intervention or activity that is approached with an adaptive functionality-focused mindset could potentially foster positive embodiment (Halliwell, 2015). For instance, acceptance and commitment therapy (see also Chapter 27) helps individuals to lead a life that aligns with their values. For individuals with body concerns, practitioners could guide them to identify how their body functions help them to actualize those values. Concerning day-to-day activities, individuals could learn to be mindful of the various roles played by their body functionality. For instance, at ballet class, a student might focus on the strength of his or her body and its ability to express emotions through movement, rather than focusing on body weight. Or, when with friends and family, an individual might focus on the functions of the body that allow him or her to connect with others, such as via shared laughter or an embrace. Future research could investigate these and other possibilities concerning integrating the functionality-based approach within intervention programs and daily life. Importantly, it will be valuable to incorporate both appearance and functionality-related elements into intervention programs to comprehensively and perhaps more effectively enhance positive embodiment.

POTENTIAL CAVEATS OF FOCUSING ON BODY FUNCTIONALITY

Mounting evidence suggests that focusing on body functionality can foster positive embodiment. However, this may not always be the case. In recent years, the beauty ideal for women has shifted toward an emphasis on being not only thin but also toned and fit (Tiggemann & Zaccardo, 2015). As a result, physical appearance and body functionality can be conflated with one another: An apparent focus on one's body functionality (e.g., lean muscularity) may in fact reflect higher levels of beauty-ideal internalization and appearance concerns. A similar conundrum may arise for men, as the male beauty ideal emphasizes an unrealistic standard for muscularity and low body fat. Indeed, research has shown that exposure to images of female and male models who reflect the "fit ideal" leads to worsened body image in women and men (e.g., Galioto & Crowther, 2013; Tiggemann & Zaccardo, 2015). Research by Mulgrew and Tiggemann (2018) has even shown that the impact of exposure to fit-ideal imagery is more harmful to women than exposure to traditional thin-ideal imagery. Having participants focus on the health and fitness of the models in the fit-ideal imagery exacerbated effects.

This research highlights important differences between focusing on (a) body functionality *holistically* versus narrowly via aesthetic depictions of specific body functions and (b) the functionality of one's *own* body versus another person's body. The latter perspectives may enhance overvaluation of appearance, beauty-ideal internalization, and upward social comparisons, as well as narrow individuals' conceptions of body functionality. A narrowed conceptualization of body functionality may also be deleterious to individuals who experience functional limitations. Future research should test these predictions concerning the impact of these different perspectives. Researchers should also be mindful of how these differences could affect the results of their investigations. For example, when designing functionality-focused programs, it may be important to have participants focus on their *own* body functionality and to include media literacy components that challenge the notion of whether the fit ideal reflects body functionality in a holistic and adaptive sense. For individuals who experience functional limitations, it may be important to help them focus on the functions that their body can perform *despite* experiencing chronic pain or other challenges.

CONCLUSION AND FUTURE DIRECTIONS

The amount of research on body functionality has increased in recent years, and the emerging evidence suggests that focusing on body functionality fosters positive embodiment. We expect continued research growth in this promising area, aided by the psychometrically sound FAS and novel functionality-based interventions. We end by offering areas that, if researched, are next steps to extend what we know about body functionality.

1. What underlying mechanisms explain the benefits of focusing on body functionality?
2. In what ways can individuals learn to focus on their body functionality, aside from completing guided writing exercises and engaging in physical activity?
3. What might more elaborate and extensive functionality-focused body image interventions look like? What combinations of techniques work best, and for whom?
4. What target groups may especially profit from interventions focusing on body functionality?
5. How do individuals' experiences of their body functionality develop across the life span?
6. How do individuals' experiences regarding body functionality vary across intersecting identities, such as gender, sexual orientation, culture, and profession?
7. How do experiences concerning body functionality and physical appearance influence one another (e.g., does functionality appreciation reduce overvaluation of physical appearance)?
8. Can a functional body orientation prevent the development of disrupted embodiment, including disordered eating cognitions and behaviors?
9. Can a functional body orientation increase engagement in self-care behaviors?

10. How can media encourage a focus on body functionality without equating body functionality with physical appearance and narrow beauty ideals?

REFERENCES

Abbott, B. D., & Barber, B. L. (2010). Embodied image: Gender differences in functional and aesthetic body image among Australian adolescents. *Body Image, 7*, 22–31. doi:10.1016/j.bodyim.2009.10.004

Alleva, J. M., Diedrichs, P. C., Halliwell, E., Martijn, C., Stuijfzand, B. G., Treneman-Evans, G., & Rumsey, N. (2018). A randomised-controlled trial investigating potential underlying mechanisms of a functionality-based approach to improving women's body image. *Body Image, 25*, 85–96. doi:10.1016/j.bodyim.2018.02.009

Alleva, J. M., Martijn, C., Jansen, A., & Nederkoorn, C. (2014). Body language: Affecting body satisfaction by describing the body in functionality terms. *Psychology of Women Quarterly, 38*, 181–196. doi:10.1177/0361684313507897

Alleva, J. M., Martijn, C., van Breukelen, G. J. P., Jansen, A., & Karos, K. (2015). Expand Your Horizon: A programme that improves body image and reduces self-objectification by training women to focus on body functionality. *Body Image, 15*, 81–89. doi:10.1016/j.bodyim.2015.07.001

Alleva, J. M., Tylka, T. L., & Kroon Van Diest, A. M. (2017). The Functionality Appreciation Scale (FAS): Development and psychometric evaluation in US community women and men. *Body Image, 23*, 28–44. doi:10.1016/j.bodyim.2017.07.008

Becker, C. B., Ciao, A. C., & Smith, L. M. (2008). Moving from efficacy to effectiveness in eating disorders prevention: The sorority body image program. *Cognitive and Behavioral Practice, 15*, 18–27. doi:1077-7229/07/018-027$1.00/0

Cash, T. F. (2008). *The body image workbook: An eight-step program for learning to like your looks* (2nd ed.). Oakland, CA: New Harbinger.

Cash, T. F., & Smolak, L. (2011). Future challenges for body image science, practice, and prevention. In T. F. Cash & L. Smolak (Eds.), *Body image: A handbook of science, practice, and prevention* (pp. 471–478). New York, NY: Guilford Press.

Franzoi, S. L., & Shields, S. A. (1984). The Body Esteem Scale: Multidimensional structure and sex differences in a college population. *Journal of Personality Assessment, 48*, 173–178. doi:10.1207/s15327752jpa4802_12

Fredrickson, B. L., & Roberts, T.-A. (1997). Objectification theory: Toward understanding women's lived experiences and mental health risks. *Psychology of Women Quarterly, 21*, 173–206. doi:10.1111/j.1471-6402.1997.tb00108.x

Frisén, A., & Holmqvist, K. (2010). What characterizes adolescents with a positive body image? A qualitative investigation of Swedish girls and boys. *Body Image, 7*, 205–212. doi:10.1016/j.bodyim.2010.04.001

Galioto, R., & Crowther, J. H. (2013). The effects of exposure to slender and muscular images on male body dissatisfaction. *Body Image, 10*, 566–573. doi:10.1016/j.bodyim.2013.07.009

Halliwell, E. (2015). Future directions for positive body image research. *Body Image, 14*, 177–189. doi:10.1016/j.bodyim.2015.03.003

Mahlo, L., & Tiggemann, M. (2016). Yoga and positive body image: A test of the embodiment model. *Body Image, 18*, 135–142. doi:10.1016/j.bodyim.2016.06.008

Martin, K. A., & Lichtenberger, C. M. (2002). Fitness enhancement and changes in body image. In T. F. Cash & T. Pruzinsky (Eds.), *Body image: A handbook of theory, research, and clinical practice* (pp. 414–421). New York, NY: Guilford Press.

McKinley, N. M., & Hyde, J. S. (1996). The Objectified Body Consciousness Scale: Development and validation. *Psychology of Women Quarterly, 20*, 181–215. doi:10.1111/j.1471-6402.1996.tb00467.x

Moradi, B., & Huang, Y. P. (2008). Objectification theory and psychology of women: A decade of advances and future directions. *Psychology of Women Quarterly, 32*, 377–398. doi:10.1111/j.1471-6402.2008.00452.x

Mulgrew, K. E., & Tiggemann, M. (2018). Form or function: Does focusing on body functionality protect women from body dissatisfaction when viewing media images? *Journal of Health Psychology, 23*, 84–94. doi:10.1177/1359105316655471

Noll, S. M., & Fredrickson, B. L. (1998). A mediational model linking self-objectification, body shame, and disordered eating. *Psychology of Women Quarterly, 22*, 623–636. doi:10.1111/j.1471-6402.1998.tb00181.x

Piran, N. (2016). Embodied possibilities and disruptions: The emergence of the Experience of Embodiment construct from qualitative studies with girls and women. *Body Image, 18*, 43–60. doi:10.1016/j.bodyim.2016.04.007

Prichard, I., & Tiggemann, M. (2008). Relations among exercise type, self-objectification, and body image in the fitness centre environment: The role of reasons for exercise. *Psychology of Sport and Exercise, 9*, 855–866. doi:10.1016/j.psychsport.2007.10.005

Tiggemann, M., Coutts, E., & Clark, L. (2014). Belly dance as an embodying activity? A test of the embodiment model of positive body image positive body image. *Sex Roles, 71*, 197–207. doi:10.1007/s11199-014-0408-2

Tiggemann, M., & Zaccardo, M. (2015). "Exercise to be fit, not skinny": The effect of fitspiration imagery on women's body image. *Body Image, 15*, 61–67. doi:10.1016/j.bodyim.2015.06.003

Wasylkiw, L., & Butler, N. A. (2014). Body talk among undergraduate women: Why conversations about exercise and weight loss differentially predict body appreciation. *Journal of Health Psychology, 19*, 1013–1024. doi:10.1177/1359105313483155

Wood-Barcalow, N. L., Tylka, T. L., & Augustus-Horvath, C. L. (2010). "But I Like My Body": Positive body image characteristics and a holistic model for young-adult women. *Body Image, 7*, 106–116. doi:10.1016/j.bodyim.2010.01.001

4

Body Image Flexibility

EMILY K. SANDOZ, JENNIFER B. WEBB,
COURTNEY B. ROGERS, AND EMILY SQUYRES ■

Positive body image and embodiment include favorable body-related perceptions, thoughts, and feelings *as well as* adaptive responses to the body and body-related experiences (Piran, 2015). Fitting into the last part of this definition, *body image flexibility* (Sandoz, Wilson, Merwin, & Kellum, 2013) involves awareness and acceptance of sensations, perceptions, feelings, thoughts, and beliefs that comprise the body experience in any one moment while engaging in effective action in valued life domains. Body image *in*flexibility is conceptualized as the opposite: attempts to change or delay aspects of the body experience that ultimately disrupt valued action. In this chapter, we present a thorough review of the body image flexibility construct, including its assessment, relationships to well-being as demonstrated in both research and practice, and future directions for research.

Body image flexibility is rooted in *psychological flexibility*, a model of psychological health and well-being that emphasizes awareness and openness toward ongoing experiences to allow for action toward chosen values, even in times of great discomfort or distress (Bond et al., 2011). Emerging from the contextual behavioral science tradition (see Hayes, Barnes-Holmes, & Wilson, 2012) and posited as fundamental to human functioning (Kashdan & Rottenberg, 2010), psychological flexibility is the primary treatment target of acceptance and commitment therapy (ACT; Hayes, Strosahl, & Wilson, 1999; see also Chapter 27). ACT aims to foster body image flexibility via six interdependent skills: (a) *present moment awareness* (noticing the ongoing, complex, and dynamic body experience); (b) *experiential acceptance* (practicing openness toward the body experience, especially when it is unwanted or painful); (c) *cognitive defusion* (observing cognitive components of the body experience, such as thoughts, memories, and rules, without them dominating attention or behavior); (d) *self-as-context* (experiencing the self as inclusive of and more than the immediate body experience); (e) *valuing* (choosing a purpose or meaning to guide action, especially when the body experience is unwanted or painful); and (f) *committed action* (engaging in values-consistent behavior, even when it results in increased contact with unwanted or painful aspects of the body experience).

ASSESSMENT OF BODY IMAGE FLEXIBILITY

Body image flexibility is assessed using the Body Image—Acceptance and Action Questionnaire (BI-AAQ; Sandoz et al., 2013). The BI-AAQ was developed by incorporating content relevant to body weight and shape into 46 items from the three published versions of the Acceptance and Action Questionnaire (AAQ; Bond & Bunce, 2003; Bond et al., 2011; Hayes et al., 2004) and the original item pools from which AAQ items were selected. The original 46 items contained items worded in the direction of both flexibility (e.g., "How I feel about my body has very little to do with the daily choices I make") and inflexibility (e.g., "Worrying about my weight makes it difficult for me to live a life that I value"; Sandoz, 2010). Respondents (comprising a sample of undergraduate men and women) rated their level of agreement with each statement on a 7-point scale ranging from 1 (*never true*) to 7 (*always true*). Items worded for inflexibility were then reverse scored. The item selection process used a conservative cutoff, retaining only items with factor loadings above .60. The 12 items retained were all worded in the direction of inflexibility, a fact that prompted questions regarding validity (e.g., Webb, Wood-Barcalow, & Tylka, 2015). Recall, however, that body image flexibility and inflexibility were originally proposed to describe opposite ends of a unitary construct. Therefore, having items worded in the direction of inflexibility and reverse scored may not be problematic. Indeed, data from the initial principal factor analysis (Sandoz, 2010) revealed that many of the original items worded in the direction of flexibility loaded on the single retained factor, signifying that flexibility and inflexibility are not distinct, but opposite ends of the same factor.

Data in the original psychometric article supported the internal consistency (e.g., $\alpha = .92–.93$); 3-week stability ($r = .80$); construct validity (via relationships with psychological flexibility, low body dissatisfaction, low disordered eating); and incremental validity (via its unique associations with disordered eating above and beyond body dissatisfaction) of BI-AAQ scores with US undergraduate women and men (Sandoz et al., 2013). Additional studies have supported the reliability and validity of its scores with US undergraduate women and men (Timko, Juarascio, Martin, Faherty, & Kalodner, 2014); US clinical eating disorder samples (Lee, Smith, Twohig, Lensegrav-Benson, & Quakenbush-Roberts, 2017); Portuguese clinical eating disorder and community samples (Ferreira, Pinto-Gouveia, & Duarte, 2011); Brazilian clinical eating disorder and community samples (Lucena-Santos, Carvalho, da Silva Oliveira, & Pinto-Gouveia, 2017); Persian undergraduate samples (Izaadi, Karimi, & Rahmani, 2013); and Hispanic undergraduate samples (Kurz, Flynn, & Bordieri, 2016). Illustrative BI-AAQ items include "Worrying about my weight makes it difficult for me to live a life that I value," "I shut down when I feel bad about my body shape or weight," "To control my life, I need to control my weight," and "When I start thinking about the size and shape of my body, it's hard to do anything else." All 12 BI-AAQ items are included in the work of Sandoz et al. (2013).

RESEARCH ON BODY IMAGE FLEXIBILITY

Body image flexibility is related in an adaptive manner to numerous indices of psychological well-being and psychological suffering. The majority of the research on body image flexibility has been conducted with samples of college or community US women; unless otherwise noted, the studies that follow are based on these samples.

Body image flexibility is positively associated with other components of positive body image, such as body appreciation (e.g., Webb, Butler-Ajibade, & Robinson, 2014); body compassion (Altman, Linfield, Salmon, & Beacham, 2017); and taking care of the body's energy needs via intuitive eating (Webb & Hardin, 2016). Additionally, body image flexibility is positively associated with general psychological strengths, such as psychological flexibility (e.g., Sandoz et al., 2013); distress tolerance (Schoenefeld & Webb, 2013); self-compassion (e.g., Kelly, Vimalakanthan, & Miller, 2014, Canadian sample); and mindfulness (e.g., Moore, Masuda, Hill, & Goodnight, 2014). Body image flexibility is also linked to how individuals regulate the experience of body image–related distress. For example, body image flexibility is inversely related to maladaptive coping with body image, including appearance fixing and body avoidant behaviors (Mancuso, 2016).

Body image flexibility is inversely associated with several aspects of negative body image, such as body dissatisfaction (e.g., Kelly et al., 2014; Lee et al., 2017); body shame (Portuguese sample, Duarte & Pinto-Gouveia, 2016; Webb & Hardin, 2016); drive for thinness (Portuguese sample of men and women, Ferreira et al., 2011); eating and weight concerns (Sandoz et al., 2013); thin-ideal internalization (Timko et al., 2014); internalized weight bias (Webb & Hardin, 2016); and disordered eating cognitions (US men and women, Wendell, Masuda, & Le, 2012). This pattern is reflected further in negative associations between body image flexibility and perfectionism (Ferreira, Trindade, & Martinho, 2015) and general psychological distress (Duarte & Pinto-Gouveia, 2016; Ferreira et al., 2011) in Portuguese samples.

Several studies have supported body image flexibility as a protective factor against disordered eating. Specifically, disordered eating can function as a means of temporarily disrupting unwanted body experiences, such as those brought on by body-related threats and body dissatisfaction. Individual differences in body image flexibility thus have the potential to intensify or mitigate the association between body dissatisfaction and disordered eating. Indeed, body image flexibility is inversely related to eating pathology, in terms of both diagnostic status (Ferreira et al., 2011) and self-reported dysfunctional eating behavior in female and male samples (e.g., Butryn et al., 2013; Masuda, Hill, Tully, & Garcia, 2015).

Further body image flexibility weakened the association between body dissatisfaction and disordered eating in both Portuguese (Ferreira et al., 2011) and US samples (Sandoz et al., 2013) and between dysfunctional eating-related beliefs and disordered eating in US women (Moore et al., 2014).

Research has focused on evaluating body image flexibility within body image- and eating-related process models. Although these models have only been evaluated using cross-sectional designs, they serve as the necessary preliminary groundwork for establishing potential mechanisms of change. Indeed, body image flexibility has been revealed as a potential mechanism of change within this research. For example, body image flexibility partially accounted for the inverse associations between three measures of body dissatisfaction and body appreciation, suggesting that it may be the negative impact of dissatisfaction on flexibility that subsequently limits appreciation (Webb, 2015). Similarly, low body image inflexibility fully accounted for the contribution of favorable appearance evaluations to low rates of appearance fixing in an Australian sample, an experientially avoidant approach to regulating body image–related stress (Mancuso, 2016). Together, these findings suggest that body image flexibility may be an important therapeutic target for minimizing avoidant ways of regulating body image–related distress and simultaneously strengthening positive interactions with the body.

Wendell et al. (2012), in a sample of US men and women, were the first to demonstrate that the relationship between disordered eating cognitions and disordered eating symptomatology is, in part, attributable to low body image flexibility. In another study, low body image flexibility partially mediated the positive association between drive for thinness and symptoms of bulimia (Timko et al., 2014). A related model demonstrated mediating effects of low body image flexibility on the positive relationships between body dissatisfaction and unfavorable appearance comparisons and between body dissatisfaction and an inflexible eating style (Portuguese sample of men and women, Ferreira et al., 2015). Similarly, the associations between self-criticism and drive for thinness with binge eating pathology were partially attributed to low levels of body image flexibility (Lucena-Santos et al., 2017). Further, low body image flexibility and body shame accounted for the links between body image–related victimization (i.e., bullying or teasing due to one's physical appearance) and binge eating severity (Portuguese sample, Duarte & Pinto-Gouveia, 2016). Collectively, these results support body image flexibility as a viable strategy for responding to various dimensions of body image disturbance in a way that reduces maladaptive eating patterns.

Body image flexibility has also been shown to be an intervening variable in models predicting intuitive eating behavior among US college women. For instance, Schoenefeld and Webb (2013) demonstrated that self-compassion's positive association with intuitive eating was fully explained by body image flexibility. Similarly, Webb and Hardin (2016) found that body image flexibility was superior to both self-compassion and body shame in accounting for the inverse relationship between internalized weight bias and intuitive eating. Taken together, these findings suggest that body image flexibility may more readily support intuitive eating than general adaptive self-regulation and negative body image.

BODY IMAGE FLEXIBILITY IN INTERVENTION RESEARCH

If, as the cross-sectional literature suggests, body image flexibility is an important aspect of positive body image and embodiment specifically, and of psychological well-being in general, then targeting body image flexibility should theoretically result in improved body- and eating-related well-being. In support, emerging scholarship demonstrated that changes in body image flexibility during eating disorder treatment tend to accompany treatment success.

Various studies detailing the successful treatment of disordered eating with ACT support the role of body image flexibility in recovery. Individuals in these studies exhibited treatment-resistant anorexia nervosa (Berman, Boutelle, & Crow, 2009); binge eating disorder (Hill, Masuda, Melcher, Morgan, & Twohig, 2015); problematic emotional eating (Hill, Masuda, Moore, & Twohig, 2015); and purging behaviors (Masuda, Ng, Moore, Felix, & Drake, 2016). At the conclusion of treatment, individuals across studies demonstrated increased levels of body image flexibility corresponding with treatment progress and reduced disordered eating.

Body image flexibility may be a useful target for low-intensity interventions for disordered eating. Duarte, Pinto-Gouveia, and Stubbs (2017) examined the efficacy of a brief mindfulness and compassion-based intervention for the treatment of binge eating disorder in a Portuguese community sample that included workshop and self-help components. Participants in the intervention group demonstrated significantly higher levels of body image flexibility following treatment, along with greater reductions in binge eating and other indices of general psychological distress and eating pathology. Results were maintained at a 1-month follow-up.

Body image flexibility may also be a meaningful target for interventions without an eating focus. Berman, Morton, and Hegel (2016) examined the feasibility and outcome of a group intervention that combined elements of Health at Every Size® with ACT to treat depression symptoms in higher weight women. Participants demonstrated significantly higher levels of body image flexibility following the intervention, along with improved depressive symptoms and physiological markers, which were maintained at a 3-month follow-up.

Changes in body image flexibility also seem to correspond with changes in disordered eating symptom intervention programs using approaches such as cognitive behavioral therapy and dialectical behavior therapy. For instance, research has examined body image flexibility in individuals in residential treatment for eating disorders (Bluett et al., 2016; Butryn et al., 2013). Even though body image flexibility was not directly targeted, as treatment progressed and disordered eating improved, body image flexibility also increased. Additionally, participants with lower body image flexibility had more eating disorder symptomatology pretreatment.

FUTURE DIRECTIONS

There are gaps in our current knowledge of body image flexibility that, when addressed, would further advance the research in positive body image and positive embodiment. This includes expansion of populations sampled, assessment approaches used, criterion variables explored, and methodologies employed.

First, future research should examine body image flexibility in diverse samples. Much of the current research base on body image flexibility is based on US women, with a small percentage including men and an even smaller percentage including international samples. Scholars are encouraged to replicate and expand on existing research using samples that are diverse in age, gender, body size and shape, body functioning, ethnicity and country of origin, sexual orientation, and so on. It may be that body image flexibility functions differently in diverse sociocultural groups.

Second, continued scientific progress in this area demands expansion in assessment approaches to allow for further conceptual development. For example, the construct of body image flexibility is not specific to appearance, but no assessment exists that includes flexibility with perceived body functionality. Future efforts to measure body image flexibility might also aim to capture the six facets of the construct described in the psychological flexibility model, which would allow for the model to be examined empirically. Another approach to assessment might involve measuring body image flexibility as a state. For example, a state measure of body image flexibility using experience sampling methods would allow for closer examination of its role over time and in various contexts. It would also be ideal to have measures of body image flexibility that do not rely on self-report, as the demand characteristics are great in noticing and reporting not only body-related distress but also one's reaction to it. To date, there is one known effort to develop a computer-based behavioral measure of body image flexibility (the Body Image Flexibility Assessment Procedure; Sandoz, Auzenne, Williams, Butcher, & Boullion, 2016), which involves training symbolic meaning (i.e., aversive body images or personal values) to arbitrary symbols and assessing adaptive responses to their presentation in different combinations. Developing and validating a measure of body image flexibility appropriate for use with children and adolescents would also be fruitful, given that their psychological flexibility and coping skills in the face of body image–related threats may not be well developed.

Third, in considering body image flexibility as a protective factor, scholars are encouraged to expand the scope of the criterion variables examined to include adaptive eating processes; other health behaviors (e.g., substance use, physical activity); and broader markers of psychosocial and physiological well-being. It is also recommended that scholars consider directly the potential differential effects of sociodemographic (e.g., race/ethnicity, gender, age); recruitment source (e.g., community vs. college/university); and clinical status. Additionally, investigators could evaluate the extent to which body image flexibility protects against the noxious impact of exposure to body image–related threats (e.g., upward appearance comparisons to idealized media images) using experimental designs.

Fourth, with respect to subsequent process models, longitudinal or experimental methodologies should be employed to more accurately assess true mediation. Ideally, it would be worthwhile to directly evaluate body image flexibility as an actual change process in ACT-based or related interventions targeting weight, body image, or eating behavior. It will also remain the task of additional investigations to clarify how body image flexibility may be a useful target in the *prevention* of body image disturbance and disordered eating behavior in a variety of at-risk populations across the life span (e.g., children, adolescents, young adults, women during pregnancy and the postpartum period, women during perimenopause, etc.).

CONCLUSION

Seven years ago, the idea that a person's responses to their body image mattered as much or more as the experiences themselves was not represented in the body image literature, basic or applied. Since 2010, however, body image flexibility has emerged as a unique and important component of positive body image and embodiment. Although the research base still has substantial room to grow, correlation, moderation, mediation, and intervention research all converge to suggest that awareness and acceptance of the dynamic body experience in service of personal values may be critical to fostering a positive relationship with the body and the self. Together, these data challenge scholars to expand the research on body image flexibility to allow for increased understanding of how individuals might best weather the range of difficulties associated with body image–related threats that obstruct embodiment.

REFERENCES

Altman, J. K., Linfield, K., Salmon, P. G., & Beacham, A. O. (2017). The Body Compassion Scale: Development and initial validation. *Journal of Health Psychology*. doi:10.1177/1359105317718924

Berman, M. I., Boutelle, K. N., & Crow, S. J. (2009). A case series investigating acceptance and commitment therapy as a treatment for previously treated, unremitted patients with anorexia nervosa. *European Eating Disorders Review, 17*, 426–434. doi:10.1002/erv.962

Berman, M. I., Morton, S. N., & Hegel, M. T. (2016). Uncontrolled pilot study of an acceptance and commitment therapy and Health at Every Size intervention for obese, depressed women: Accept Yourself! *Psychotherapy, 53*, 462–467. doi:10.1037/pst0000083

Bluett, E. J., Lee, E. B., Simone, M., Lockhart, G., Twohig, M. P., Lensegrav-Benson, T., & Quakenbush-Roberts, B. (2016). The role of body image psychological flexibility on the treatment of eating disorders in a residential facility. *Eating Behaviors, 23*, 150–155. doi:10.1016/j.eatbeh.2016.10.002

Bond, F. W., & Bunce, D. (2003). The role of acceptance and job control in mental health, job satisfaction, and work performance. *Journal of Applied Psychology, 88*, 1057–1067. doi:10.1037/0021-9010.88.6.1057

Bond, F. W., Hayes, S. C., Baer, R. A., Carpenter, K. M., Guenole, N., Orcutt, H. K., . . . Zettle, R. D. (2011). Preliminary psychometric properties of the Acceptance and Action Questionnaire–II: A revised measure of psychological inflexibility and experiential avoidance. *Behavior Therapy, 42*, 676–688. doi:10.1016/j.beth.2011.03.007

Butryn, M. L., Juarascio, A., Shaw, J., Kerrigan, S. G., Clark, V., O'Planick, A. O., & Forman, E. M. (2013). Mindfulness and its relationship with eating disorders symptomatology in women receiving residential treatment. *Eating Behaviors, 14*, 13–16. doi:10.1016/j.eatbeh.2012.10.005

Duarte, C., & Pinto-Gouveia, J. (2016). Body image flexibility mediates the effect of body image-related victimization experiences and shame on binge eating and weight. *Eating Behaviors, 23*, 13–18. doi:10.1016/j.eatbeh.2016.07.005

Duarte, C., Pinto-Gouveia, J., & Stubbs, R. J. (2017). Compassionate attention and regulation of eating behaviour: A pilot study of brief low-intensity intervention for binge eating. *Clinical Psychology and Psychotherapy, 24*, O1437–O1447. doi:10.1002/cpp.2094

Ferreira, C., Pinto-Gouveia, J., & Duarte, C. (2011). The validation of the Body Image Acceptance and Action Questionnaire: Exploring the moderator effect of acceptance on disordered eating. *International Journal of Psychology and Psychological Therapy, 11*, 327–345.

Ferreira, C., Trindade, I. A., & Martinho, A. (2015). Explaining rigid dieting in normal-weight women: The key role of body image inflexibility. *Eating and Weight Disorders: Studies on Anorexia, Bulimia and Obesity, 21*, 49–56. doi:10.1007/s40519-015-0188-x

Hayes, S. C., Barnes-Holmes, D., & Wilson, K. G. (2012). Contextual behavioral science: Creating a science more adequate to the challenge of the human condition. *Journal of Contextual Behavioral Science, 1*, 1–16. doi:10.1016/j.jcbs.2012.09.004

Hayes, S. C., Strosahl, K. D., & Wilson, K. G. (1999). *Acceptance and commitment therapy: An experiential approach to behavior change*. New York, NY: Guilford Press.

Hayes, S. C., Strosahl, K. D., Wilson, K. G., Bissett, R. T., Pistorello, J., Toarmino, D., & Zettle, R. (2004). Measuring experiential avoidance: A preliminary test of a working model. *Psychological Record, 54*, 553–578. doi:10.1007/BF03395492

Hill, M. L., Masuda, A., Melcher, H., Morgan, J. R., & Twohig, M. P. (2015). Acceptance and commitment therapy for women diagnosed with binge eating disorder: A case-series study. *Cognitive and Behavioral Practice, 22*, 367–378. doi:10.1016/j.cbpra.2014.02.005

Hill, M. L., Masuda, A., Moore, M., & Twohig, M. P. (2015). Acceptance and commitment therapy for individuals with problematic emotional eating: A case-series study. *Clinical Case Studies, 14*, 141–154. doi:10.1177/1534650114547429

Izaadi, A., Karimi, J., & Rahmani, M. (2013). Psychometric analysis of Persian version of body image flexibility questionnaire (BI-AAQ) among university students. *Journal of Hayat, 19*, 56–69.

Kashdan, T. B., & Rottenberg, J. (2010). Psychological flexibility as a fundamental aspect of health. *Clinical Psychology Review, 30*, 865–878. doi:10.1016/j.cpr.2010.03.001

Kelly, A. C., Vimalakanthan, K., & Miller, K. E. (2014). Self-compassion moderates the relationship between body mass index and both eating disorder pathology and body image flexibility. *Body Image, 11*, 446–453. doi:10.1016/j.bodyim.2014.07.005

Kurz, A. S., Flynn, M. K., & Bordieri, M. J. (2016). How Bayesian estimation might improve CBS measure development: A case study with body-image flexibility in Hispanic students. *Journal of Contextual Behavioral Science, 5*, 146–153. doi:10.1016/j.jcbs.2016.07.005

Lee, E. B., Smith, B. M., Twohig, M. P., Lensegrav-Benson, T., & Quakenbush-Roberts, B. (2017). Assessment of the Body Image—Acceptance and Action Questionnaire in a female residential eating disorder treatment facility. *Journal of Contextual Behavioral Science, 6*, 21–28. doi:10.1016/j.jcbs.2016.11.004

Lucena-Santos, P., Carvalho, S. A., da Silva Oliveira, M., & Pinto-Gouveia, J. (2017). Body-Image Acceptance and Action Questionnaire: Its deleterious influence on binge eating and psychometric validation. *International Journal of Clinical and Health Psychology, 17*, 151–160. doi:10.1016/j.ijchp.2017.03.001

Mancuso, S. G. (2016). Body image inflexibility mediates the relationship between body image evaluation and maladaptive body image coping strategies. *Body Image, 16*, 28–31. doi:10.1016/j.bodyim.2015.10.003

Masuda, A., Hill, M. L., Tully, E. C., & Garcia, S. E. (2015). The role of disordered eating cognition and body image flexibility in disordered eating behavior in college men. *Journal of Contextual Behavioral Science, 4*, 12–20. doi:10.1016/j.jcbs.2015.01.001

Masuda, A., Ng, S. Y., Moore, M., Felix, I., & Drake, C. E. (2016). Acceptance and commitment therapy as a treatment for a Latina young adult women with purging: A case report. *Practice Innovations, 1*, 20–35. doi:10.1037/pri0000012

Moore, M., Masuda, A., Hill, M. L., & Goodnight, B. L. (2014). Body image flexibility moderates the association between disordered eating cognition and disordered eating behavior in a non-clinical sample of women: A cross-sectional investigation. *Eating Behaviors, 15*, 664–669. doi:10.1016/j.eatbeh.2014.08.021

Piran, N. (2015). New possibilities in the prevention of eating disorders: The introduction of positive body image measures. *Body Image, 14*, 146–157. doi:10.1016/j.bodyim.2015.03.008

Sandoz, E. K. (2010). *Assessment of body image flexibility: The Body-Image Acceptance and Action Questionnaire* (Unpublished doctoral dissertation). University of Mississippi, Oxford.

Sandoz, E. K., Auzenne, J., Williams, N., Butcher, G., & Boullion, G. (2016, June). *The body image flexibility assessment procedure: Development of a behavioral measure of body image flexibility.* Presented at the 14th annual meeting of the Association for Contextual Behavioral Science World Conference, Seattle, WA.

Sandoz, E. K., Wilson, K. G., Merwin, R. M., & Kellum, K. K. (2013). Assessment of body image flexibility: The Body-Image Acceptance and Action Questionnaire. *Journal of Contextual Behavioral Science, 2*, 39–48. doi:10.1016/j.jcbs.2013.03.002

Schoenefeld, S. J., & Webb, J. B. (2013). Self-compassion and intuitive eating in college women: Examining the contributions of distress tolerance and body image acceptance and action. *Eating Behaviors, 14*, 493–496. doi:10.1016/j.eatbeh.2013.09.001

Timko, C. A., Juarascio, A. S., Martin, L. M., Faherty, A., & Kalodner, C. (2014). Body image avoidance: An under-explored yet important factor in the relationship between body image dissatisfaction and disordered eating. *Journal of Contextual Behavioral Science, 3*, 203–211. doi:10.1016/j.jcbs.2014.01.002

Webb, J. B. (2015). Body image flexibility contributes to explaining the link between body dissatisfaction and body appreciation in white college-bound females. *Journal of Contextual Behavioral Science, 4*, 176–183. doi:10.1016/j.jcbs.2015.06.001

Webb, J. B., Butler-Ajibade, P., & Robinson, S. A. (2014). Considering an affect regulation framework for examining the association between body dissatisfaction and positive body image in black older adolescent females: Does body mass index matter? *Body Image, 11*, 426–437. doi:10.1016/j.bodyim.2014.07.002

Webb, J. B., & Hardin, A. S. (2016). An integrative affect regulation process model of internalized weight bias and intuitive eating in college women. *Appetite, 102*, 60–69. doi:10.1016/j.appet.2016.02.024

Webb, J. B., Wood-Barcalow, N. L., & Tylka, T. L. (2015). Assessing positive body image: Contemporary approaches and future directions. *Body Image, 14*, 130–145. doi:10.1016/j.bodyim.2015.03.010

Wendell, J. W., Masuda, A., & Le, J. K. (2012). The role of body image flexibility in the relationship between disordered eating cognitions and disordered eating symptoms among non-clinical college students. *Eating Behaviors, 13*, 240–245. doi:10.1016/j.eatbeh.2012.03.00

5

Broad Conceptualization of Beauty

TRACY L. TYLKA

Western society continuously disseminates an extremely narrow portrayal of beauty for women: To be beautiful, a woman's body should be thin, toned, young, and busty, with body hair removed or at the very least groomed; her skin should be white or light in tone; her hair should be coiffed or long and straight; and she should be clothed and adorned with the latest fashions (Buote, Wilson, Strahan, Gazzola, & Papps, 2011; Piran, 2017). Body image scholars often refer to this narrow portrayal of beauty as "the thin ideal" (Stice, Rohde, & Shaw, 2013), although a more accurate description would be "embodying idealized appearance characteristics for women" (Piran, 2017) or, more concisely, "embodying this ideal." Embodying this ideal blends many privileges associated with being a certain weight, body frame, age, race, ethnicity, gender identity, and social class. Individuals, regardless of their gender, often internalize this ideal—in other words, they adopt this ideal as a yardstick to evaluate girls' and women's beauty—and other appearance characteristics.

Fortunately, internalization of this ideal can be ignored or resisted. To illustrate, many girls and women broadly conceptualize beauty, or perceive many looks, appearances, and body sizes/shapes to be beautiful and draw from inner characteristics when determining beauty (Tylka & Wood-Barcalow, 2015). This chapter covers the broad conceptualization of the beauty construct, including its emergence in qualitative research, its assessment, its links with positive body image and well-being in quantitative research, and its potential value in future body image research and clinical application.

EMERGENCE AS A CONSTRUCT WITHIN QUALITATIVE RESEARCH

Many independent research teams have interviewed adolescents and adult women who personally espouse a positive body image or score highly on measures of body esteem to discuss what having a positive body image means to them. The theme of broadly conceptualizing beauty has emerged within each of these studies. For instance, adolescents from Sweden acknowledged that diverse body sizes are beautiful, and that inner characteristics, such as happiness and self-acceptance, shape their perceptions of beauty (Holmqvist & Frisén, 2012). African American adolescent girls were found to have a flexible and individualized conceptualization of beauty, as they reported that being beautiful means creating a style that makes a personal statement and projects a unique presence (e.g., making "what you've got work for you") rather than adopting narrowly defined societal beauty ideals (Parker et al., 1995, p. 108). Adolescent Aboriginal girls from Canada viewed beauty as originating inward, which then is reflected outward via cultural practices (e.g., powwow dance) and self-care (McHugh, Coppola, & Sabiston, 2014). College women from the United States emphasized that beauty can be defined and expressed in an indefinite number of ways and thus believed that individuals should not be compared in terms of beauty (Wood-Barcalow, Tylka, & Augustus-Horvath, 2010). Canadian adults with spinal cord injuries emphasized that all body shapes and sizes are beautiful, and that beauty encompasses external and internal characteristics that are largely ignored by media (Bailey, Gammage, van Ingen, & Ditor, 2015). Further, many participants in these studies reflected that broadly conceptualizing beauty is not limited to noticing beauty in others but also noticing beauty in their own features that may not align with sociocultural appearance ideals. In sum, individuals with a positive body image perceive a wide range of physical appearances as beautiful, whether these appearances are largely unchangeable (e.g., body shape, weight) or more easily modifiable (e.g., personal style of dress, hairstyle, style accessories), and view positive internal characteristics, such as confidence and self-acceptance, as shaping their perception of women, as well as themselves, as beautiful.

The broadened conceptualization of beauty found in different qualitative studies among women with positive body image suggests the potential usefulness of this construct to research and practice in the body image domain. Including a measure of this construct in research would honor conceptualizations of beauty endorsed by diverse groups of participants who do not subscribe to socially idealized appearance characteristics, as these idealized images privilege few women and exclude most others (Piran, 2017). Including a measure of this construct in practice could help in the development, design, and refinement of interventions to improve positive body image and embodiment, as well as in the prevention or alleviation of restrictive standards of idealized appearance, such as thin-ideal internalization (Piran, 2015). Regarding thin-ideal internalization specifically, researchers have indicated that such internalization is a strong predictor of body image disturbance and eating disorder symptoms (Stice, 2002) and identified it as a main target for dissonance-based eating disorder prevention (Stice et al., 2013). Holding a broad conceptualization of beauty (BCB) may prevent a girl or woman from endorsing thinness as a personal standard. Furthermore, if a girl or woman has already internalized the thin ideal, increasing her BCB may create dissonance, which may lessen her adherence to thinness as a personal standard.

BROAD CONCEPTUALIZATION OF BEAUTY SCALE AND QUANTITATIVE RESEARCH

Given the qualitative findings reviewed, assessing and increasing women's ability to broadly conceptualize beauty could contribute to positive body image and embodiment research and practice. Hence, my student and I developed the Broad Conceptualization of Beauty Scale (BCBS; Tylka & Iannantuono, 2016) to assess the degree to which women consider beauty as inclusive of a wide range of appearance characteristics, as well as of personal qualities. Its items were designed for women respondents only because the social construction of gender involves not only different idealized images for women and men, but also requires stricter adherence to such images by women (Piran, 2017; Wolf, 1991). Further, the term *beauty* may carry different meanings for men in assessing the appearance of other men. Thus, the BCB construct aims at reflecting only girls' and women's experiences.

Prior to psychometric evaluation, we sent our list of potential BCBS items to body image experts, who then reviewed the items for content coverage and clarity. After incorporating their suggested modifications, we evaluated the BCBS's factor structure, finalized items, and examined the reliability and validity of its scores within four samples of adult US community women. These findings are summarized in the remainder of this section, and interested readers can consult Tylka and Iannantuono (2016) for a more thorough description of the analyses.

Exploratory factor analyses with two samples of women revealed that nine items reflecting both external and internal beauty best represented the BCBS's structure, which was unidimensional. Confirmatory factor analyses with two additional samples upheld the BCBS's unidimensional structure and the integrity (i.e., high item-factor loadings) of the nine items. Illustrative BCBS items include, "I think that a wide variety of body shapes are beautiful for women," "I define a woman's beauty differently than how it is portrayed in the media," "Even if a physical feature is not considered attractive by others or by society, I think it can be beautiful," "A woman's confidence level can change my perception of her physical beauty," and "A woman's acceptance of herself can change my perception of her physical beauty." A full list of the nine BCBS items is included in Tylka and Iannantuono (2016); each item is rated along a 7-point scale ranging from *strongly disagree* (scored as 1) to *strongly agree* (7) and averaged, with higher scores indicating a broader conceptualization of beauty.

Estimates revealed that scores on the BCBS were internally consistent ($\alpha = .84$–$.91$) and stable over a 3-week period ($r = .88$). Many additional analyses upheld its convergent, criterion-related, discriminant, and incremental validity, suggesting that the BCBS is a psychometrically sound measure for use with community women. More specifically, the BCBS was positively related to body appreciation, self-compassion, and body image quality of life and inversely related to anti-fat attitudes, body surveillance, thin-ideal internalization, acceptance of cosmetic surgery, and social (body, exercise, and eating) comparisons, supporting its convergent and criterion-related validity. It was unrelated to impression management, narcissism, and hubristic body-related pride (i.e., perceptions that one's appearance is superior to others), illustrating that it does not assess social desirability, conceit, or vanity, upholding its discriminant validity. The BCBS was also (a) inversely associated with anti-fat attitudes after excluding its shared variance with thin-ideal internalization, (b) positively associated with self-compassion after excluding its shared variance with body appreciation, and (c) positively associated with body appreciation and thin-ideal internalization after excluding its shared variance with anti-fat attitudes. These findings suggest that the BCBS is not redundant with low thin-ideal internalization or high body appreciation, upholding its incremental validity. In other words, BCB was revealed to be an adaptive, distinct, and meaningful construct.

The findings mentioned are based on women's perceptions of other women's beauty. Given that women's BCB should extend to themselves as well, we multiplied BCBS total scores with the last item on the Body Appreciation Scale-2 (BAS-2) that assesses self-beauty, that is, Item 10: "I feel like I am beautiful even if I am different from media images of attractive people (e.g., models, actresses/actors)"; thus, perceptions of self-beauty and other-beauty are weighed equally. In the same article (Tylka & Iannantuono, 2016), we found support for this variable's use within positive body image research. Specifically, this variable, which we named BCB (others and self), was positively related to body appreciation, self-compassion, and body image quality of life and inversely related to anti-fat attitudes, body surveillance, thin-ideal internalization, endorsement of cosmetic surgery, and body comparison. It contributed to indices of psychological well-being after excluding its shared variance with body appreciation, indicating that it assesses something different from general body appreciation. These findings suggest that BCB (others and self) is a holistic conceptualization of BCB—extending beyond others to the self—that is not redundant with body appreciation.

FUTURE RESEARCH AND CLINICAL CONSIDERATIONS

Given the strong link between BCB and positive body image (Tylka & Wood-Barcalow, 2015) and that the BCBS has accrued psychometric evidence, it seems valuable and feasible to assess girls' and women's tendency to broadly conceptualize beauty within varied academic/empirical and clinical/educational settings. Broadly conceptualizing beauty, by definition, frees girls and women from rigid appearance standards. Indeed, Tylka and Iannantuono (2016) found that broadly conceptualizing beauty was inversely linked to appearance monitoring (i.e., body surveillance) and many other indices of negative body image. These findings provide evidence that broadly conceptualizing beauty likely does not direct women's attention toward their appearance but instead counters adherence to strict standards of appearance.

Within academic/empirical settings, researchers could explore the BCB among individuals of various developmental stages, cultures, geographic areas, education levels, socioeconomic means, and sexual orientation to determine its applicability and usefulness. Researchers also need to explore BCB as a protective factor for maladaptive outcomes, such as disordered eating and body image disturbance. For example, broadly conceptualizing beauty may protect women from wanting to change their appearance or experiencing heightened body dissatisfaction or negative affect, after viewing thin models. Additionally, researchers could examine whether exposure to family, schools, and peers who reinforce an appreciation of diverse body sizes and appearances protect against future levels of thin-ideal internalization, body image disturbance, or disordered eating.

Within clinical and educational settings, BCBS item content can be used to develop lesson plans and programs aimed at reducing weight stigma within schools, homes, and interpersonal relationships. This would approach body image education from a perspective of diversity, compassion, and acceptance rather than a perspective of pathology and weight bias. Further, integrating BCB within prevention programs potentially could block participants' endorsement of thinness as a personal standard or, if it is already endorsed, create dissonance toward the thin ideal. The BCBS could be integrated into research examining the effectiveness of such prevention programs, as these programs should promote increases in positive body image and embodiment alongside decreases in negative body image (Piran, 2015).

CONCLUSION

Broadly conceptualizing beauty entails perceiving many looks, appearances, and body sizes/shapes as beautiful and drawing from inner characteristics (e.g., confidence, inner strength, self-acceptance) when determining beauty. While broadly conceptualizing beauty can be an important component of positive body image and embodiment, it has been rarely studied. It is my hope that this chapter will direct efforts to explore this key construct by (a) highlighting a valuable and psychometrically sound tool (i.e., the BCBS) to assess this construct and (b) providing recommendations for how it could be used to facilitate research and practice efforts in both understanding and enhancing positive body image and embodiment.

REFERENCES

Bailey, K. A., Gammage, K. L., van Ingen, C., & Ditor, D. S. (2015). "It's all about acceptance": A qualitative study exploring a model of positive body image for people with spinal cord injury. *Body Image, 15*, 24–34. doi:10.1016/j.bodyim.2015.04.010

Buote, V. M., Wilson, A. E., Strahan, E. J., Gazzola, S. B., & Papps, F. (2011). Setting the bar: Divergent sociocultural norms for women's and men's ideal appearance in real-world contexts. *Body Image, 8*, 322–334. doi:10.1016/j.bodyim.2011.06.002

Holmqvist, K., & Frisén, A. (2012). "I bet they aren't that perfect in reality": Appearance ideals viewed from the perspective of adolescents with a positive body image. *Body Image, 9*, 388–395. doi:10.1016/j.bodyim.2012.03.007

McHugh, T. L., Coppola, A. M., & Sabiston, C. M. (2014). "I'm thankful for being Native and my body is part of that": The body pride experiences of young Aboriginal women in Canada. *Body Image, 11*, 318–327. doi:10.1016/j.bodyim.2014.05.004

Parker, S., Nichter, M., Nichter, M., Vuckovic, N., Sims, C., & Ritenbaugh, C. (1995). Body image and weight concerns among African American and white adolescent females: Differences that make a difference. *Human Organization, 54*, 103–114.

Piran, N. (2015). New possibilities in the prevention of eating disorders: The introduction of positive body image measures [Special series]. *Body Image, 14*, 146–157. doi:10.1016/j.bodyim.2015.03.008

Piran, N. (2017). *Journeys of embodiment at the intersection of body and culture: The developmental theory of embodiment*. San Diego, CA: Elsevier. doi:10.1016/C2015-0-04666-4

Stice, E. (2002). Risk and maintenance factors for eating pathology: A meta-analytic review. *Psychological Bulletin, 128*, 825–848. doi:10.1037//0033-2909.128.5.825

Stice, E., Rohde, P., & Shaw, H. (2013). *The Body Project: A dissonance-based eating disorder prevention intervention (Updated ed.). Facilitator guide.* New York, NY: Oxford University Press.

Tylka, T. L., & Iannantuono, A. C. (2016). Perceiving beauty in all women: Psychometric evaluation of the Broad Conceptualization of Beauty Scale. *Body Image, 17*, 67–81. doi:10.1016/j.bodyim.2016.02.005

Tylka, T. L., & Wood-Barcalow, N. L. (2015). What is and what is not positive body image? Conceptual foundations and construct definition [Special series]. *Body Image, 14*, 118–129. doi:10.1016/j.bodyim.2015.04.001

Wood-Barcalow, N. L., Tylka, T. L., & Augustus-Horvath, C. L. (2010). "But I like my body": Positive body image characteristics and a holistic model for young-adult women. *Body Image, 7*, 106–116. doi:10.1016/j.bodyim.2010.01.001

Wolf, N. (1991). *The beauty myth.* New York, NY: Morrow.

6

Mindful Attunement

CATHERINE P. COOK-COTTONE

Positive embodiment can be thought of as having a "pulse," which represents a continuous process of authentic self-awareness (of one's inner experience of self, or internal needs such as bodily, emotional, and relational needs) and authentic self-expression within one's social relationships and environment (outer experiences of self). This pulse is *mindful attunement*. Mindful attunement integrates two components: mindful awareness, or nonjudgmental awareness in the present moment, and attuned action, including healthy, sustainable practices that serve and support positive connections between the inner and outer experiences of self (Cook-Cottone, 2015b, 2016; Koloroutis, 2014). The process is iterative and self-perpetuating, reverberating between actions, feelings, cognitions, and relationships to support well-being (Cook-Cottone, 2016; Siegel, 2009). It is also internalized and embodied over time as we see in other mindfulness practices (e.g., Tang, Hölzel, & Posner, 2015). Aristotle is frequently quoted as saying, "You are what you repeatedly do." Research from the field of mindfulness is aligned with this contention. Over time, mindfulness practice moves us from effortful doing to effortless being (Tang et al., 2015). In this way, the practice *is* you. We *become* the manifestation, or embodiment, of mindful attunement.

To illustrate, Mathilde, or Matty (her preferred name), practices mindful attunement. She experiences fluidity between her inner experience of self and her interactions with others within her close friendship group and community. This was not always true. She went through a period of time in high school in which she thought she had lost a sense of herself. She remembers working really hard to make sure people liked and accepted her, wear the right clothes, and have a date to all the big parties and events. In her high school graduation photo, she is in her gown, and there is a forced smile. Matty recalls that day and remembers hoping that she did not look too big and regretting how much she ate for breakfast. Her smile was forced because she knew she should be enjoying the experience and celebrating her accomplishments instead of thinking about the size and shape of her body and the food she overate.

It was during a college course on women and media that Matty began to get back to a sense of herself. Around the same time, she started going to yoga. Instead of worrying if she had a date, she began organizing events with groups of friends. Over the years, Matty evolved into a mindfully attuned young woman. At 25 years old, she now starts each day meditating for 10 minutes, focusing on her breath and allowing her thoughts to settle. She showers mindfully and dresses for comfort and a bit of style to express who she is, rather than what she thinks others might want to see. She works on mindfulness in her relationships, listening first and speaking with reflection and thoughtfulness. She intentionally chooses friends who inspire her and support her in her endeavors, her authentic expression of self, and self-care. She loves and respects her body and takes good care of it by eating nourishing foods and exercising for health and well-being. People who meet Matty have a sense of who she really is on the inside—a beautiful young woman. They can see that Matty's body image represents more than an *absence* of body dissatisfaction, rumination about the size and shape of her body, and disordered eating. Instead, she has the *presence* of positive embodiment: She is thriving.

Cultivation of positive embodiment through mindful attunement is a salutogenic process, or supportive of health and well-being (Cook-Cottone, 2015a). This is aligned with a growing body of research on flourishing (Seligman, 2011), especially with regard to positive body image (Tylka, 2012; Tylka & Wood-Barcalow, 2015). For example, the Centers for Disease Control and Prevention (CDC) recently released a research-based statement advocating for a focus on actionable practice (e.g., physical activity) and away from a focus on weight, size, and shape (Dollar, Berman, & Adachi-Mejia, 2017). In order to explicate the pathway to positive embodiment, this chapter positions mindful attunement within the attuned representation model of self (ARMS; Cook-Cottone, 2006, 2015a, 2015b, 2017). The Mindful Self-Care Scale (MSCS; Cook-Cottone & Guyker, 2018) is presented as a psychometrically sound tool for the assessment of the aspects of self-care addressing each area of the ARMS through actionable practices. A protocol for a mindful self-care process is explicated. Last, this chapter proposes future directions for research on mindful attunement.

THE ATTUNED REPRESENTATION MODEL OF SELF

The ARMS illustrates and explicates the role of mindful attunement (Figure 6.1). The self is a construction, a representation of the needs and relational dynamics of inner and outer experiences (Cook-Cottone, 2006, 2015a). In mindful attunement, we are asked to step deeply and fully into the role of the self with awareness of, and connection to, both our inner and outer worlds (Cook-Cottone, 2015a, 2015b; Koloroutis, 2014).

Within the ARMS framework, mindful attunement is represented as the balance of inner awareness and integration of the internal system (i.e., body, feelings, and thoughts) and an external engagement that honors and represents the inner

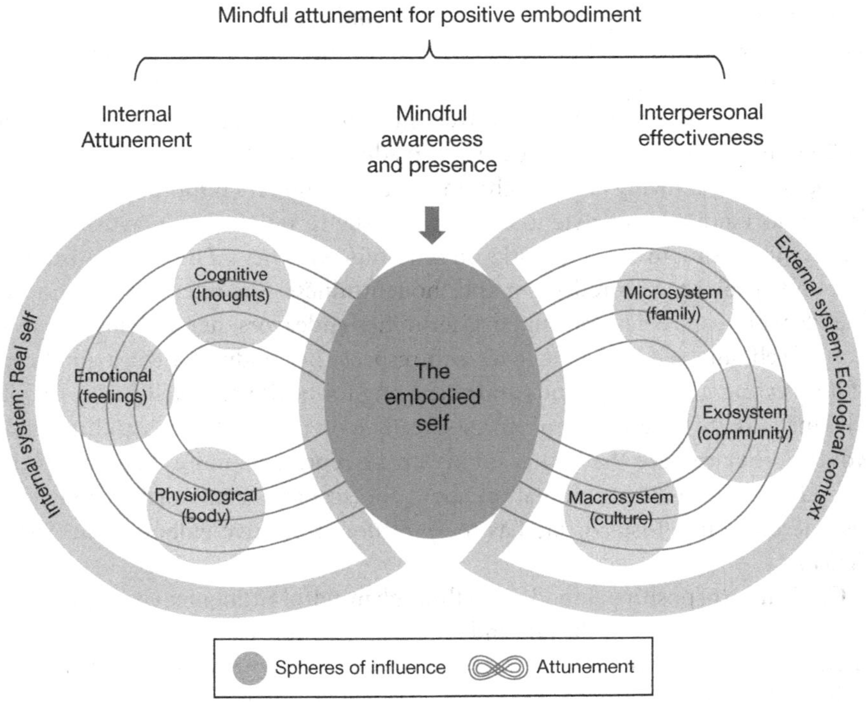

Figure 6.1 The attuned representational model of self (ARMS). Adapted from Cook-Cottone (2006, 2015a, 2017).
This figure has not been used in the form presented in this handbook. The figure was inspired by the author's previous model she published in previous works.

experience and needs of self while negotiating the demands and challenges of the external system (i.e., family, friends, community, and culture; Cook-Cottone, 2006, 2015b, 2017; Figure 6.1). When aligned and integrated, internal experiences of self can be described as internal attunement or self-attunement (Koloroutis, 2014; Siegel, 2012). When the self is functioning within the external system in promotion of individual well-being and in support of mission or purpose, the process can be described as interpersonal effectiveness (Cook-Cottone, 2017; Cook-Cottone & Guyker, 2018; Linehan, 1993). In the center, the representation, or manifestation, of self is experienced as an embodiment of the ongoing behavioral patterns that create and maintain mindful attunement with an individual's life in support of both internal attunement and interpersonal effectiveness (Cook-Cottone, 2015a, 2015b; Piran, 2016).

Critically, within the ARMS framework, effective functioning of the self goes beyond seeing the self as a subject or an object (Cook-Cottone, 2015a). Effective functioning is the creation of *self as witness* who sees the whole (i.e., inner and outer) experience of the self and mindfully selects thoughts and behaviors that help maintain balance, equilibrium, and attunement within the body physiologically, emotionally, and cognitively, as well as within the context of family, community, and culture (Cook-Cottone, 2015a, 2015b; Seligman, 2011). In mindfulness practices, the observer, or witness simply notices the thoughts, feelings, and sensations as they arise and pass (i.e., impermanence); views them without judgment (i.e., nonjudgment); and understands that they will not be a lasting part of the self (i.e., Cook-Cottone, 2015b; Grabovac, Lau, & Willett, 2011). There is no need to be reactive, and with the time and space offered through the process of deeply witnessing, the individual has the opportunity to choose the intentional and effective actions or inactions that service well-being and, potentially, a greater sense of purpose. Referring to Matty, she is mindfully attuned by being aware of and in touch with her emotions. Conscious of the effects of her actions on both herself and others, she expresses her emotions to others in a healthy, assertive way when boundaries are crossed. In this respect, she embodies self-validation, self-protection, and voice. In turn, others have an opportunity to respond positively to Matty, thereby attenuating her negative affect.

As a result of the interactions of complex genetic, biological, familial, interpersonal, socioeconomic, and cultural influences, it can be challenging for some to experience and sustain mindful attunement (Cook-Cottone, 2015a, 2015b). Further, there is risk. Conflict, struggle, and disorder can manifest in the absence of mindful attunement (Cook-Cottone, 2015b). Internally and externally, difficulty with one aspect of the ARMS framework can affect one's internal experience of well-being (Cook-Cottone, 2015a). When there is a lack of mindful attunement, it can be easy for individuals to function on automatic pilot (Koloroutis, 2014). Here, it is easy to be reactive, miss important signals from the physical or emotional self, misread someone's intentions, and have little access to genuine feelings of embodied joy, meaning, and purpose. For instance, individuals vulnerable to experiences of negative body image and disordered eating are reported to have genetic, biological, and psychological factors that place them at risk for struggle with their relationship with their bodies (Cook-Cottone, 2015b; Keel & Forney, 2013). Indeed, those who struggle with body image and eating issues may lack an accurate or valid sense of themselves in terms of both their physical body and a cohesive, functional personality identity (Chernin, 1985).

To illustrate, Sarah, a freshman in college, is struggling with body dissatisfaction and eating disorder symptoms. She comes from a family that displays several risk factors. First, there is a family history of substance abuse and disordered eating. Second, Sarah's mom battles with her weight and has been on a diet for as long as Sarah can recall, even though she sees her mom as healthy. Third, Sarah's father often insists that Sarah should "dress like a girl" and reminds her to "not put on the freshman 15 pounds." He is glad she is going to college because he believes it is the best place to meet potential partners for marriage. Sarah's dad lacks interest in her dream to be an engineer, only considering the field to be a good choice because of the male-to-female ratio that will be in her favor. Further, both parents lack a mindful awareness of their emotions and often drink alcohol to destress and handle emotions. Sarah struggles to stay connected with her inner experience of self as her parents both reinforce her attention to appearance, weight, and shape. She restricts food, and then if she overeats, she purges. She runs and goes to exercise classes to burn calories, hating every minute of the workouts. Her emotions are either absent or, when negative, overwhelming. Sarah either gives in to her friends by doing things she does not want to do or waits until she is so annoyed that she explodes with anger. Often, she feels lost in either her own thoughts and emotions or what she should do for those that are close to her in her life. She often wonders who she really is and what she truly wants in life.

The ARMS model helps explicate the balance that must be maintained in order to embody a healthy self and maintain mindful attunement (Cook-Cottone, 2015b). Through cultivation of mindful awareness and intentional action, steps can be taken within the internal or external aspects of self to create and maintain mindful attunement (Cook-Cottone, 2015a). For Sarah, it would likely be a long, yet fruitful, path that begins with a sense of discontent with the way things are and an interest in living her life in a more mindful and embodied manner. Her struggles with body image and eating may lead her to a body image group in which she can learn more about the cultural and familial influences in her life (e.g., media portrayals of women and gender stereotypes). As her awareness increases, she may seek individual counseling to address her mood instability, interpersonal boundaries, and familial challenges. In this way, she can begin to move away from body dissatisfaction and toward a more positive relationship with her body that includes the practices that promote positive body image and embodiment.

MINDFUL SELF-CARE AS AN ACTIONABLE PATHWAY TO POSITIVE EMBODIMENT

To develop a positive experience of and relationship with the body, individuals must learn to be with, and in, their bodies in a healthy and effective way (Cook-Cottone, 2015a, 2015b; Piran, 2016). Mindful self-care offers a pathway to mindful attunement that can be achieved in concrete, actionable steps. Rooted in mindfulness-based stress reduction (MBSR; Kabat-Zinn, 2003) and dialectic behavioral therapy (DBT; Linehan, 1993), mindful self-care is a methodology for cultivating mindful attunement among the internal aspects of self, within the context of external challenges (Cook-Cottone & Guyker, 2018). Completely aligned with mindful attunement, mindful self-care is "an iterative process that involves (a) mindful awareness and assessment of one's internal needs and external demands and (b) intentional engagement in specific practices of self-care to address the needs and demands in a manner that serves one's well-being and personal effectiveness" (Cook-Cottone & Guyker, 2018, p. 161).

More specifically, mindful self-care is a set of regularly performed behaviors that operationalize what it means to take care of and appreciate the self (Cook-Cottone, 2015a, 2015b, 2016; Cook-Cottone & Guyker, 2018). It is actionable, accessible, and practiced with an attitude of compassion and loving-kindness (Cook-Cottone, 2015a). From this perspective, mindful self-care supports and cultivates self-regulation, body appreciation, and positive embodiment (Cook-Cottone, 2015a; Cook-Cottone & Guyker, 2018; Piran, 2016; Tylka, 2012). Ultimately, practicing self-care is a top-down, bottom-up, and integrative approach to positive embodiment that can deeply shift how an individual thinks about, appreciates, and experiences their body (Andrew, Tiggemann, & Clark, 2016; Cook-Cottone, 2016; Gillen, 2015; Piran, 2016).

Through ongoing engagement in mindful self-care, mindful attunement is internalized and embodied over time—moving us from effortful doing to effortless being—as in other mindfulness practices (e.g., Tang et al., 2015). To illustrate, Jayla struggled with negative body image. Taller and more muscular than many of her friends, she felt that she was too big. To avoid what she called the limelight, she often resigned herself to the back row in a group presentation and the supportive role of tree or snowflake in a school production. She did not see herself as the right shape or size to lead. In young adulthood, she began taking yoga within a yoga community that embraced all shapes and sizes. To her happy surprise, this yoga community had national trainers of all sizes and shapes who were held in very high esteem. With these positive role models and the diversity within the community, Jayla practiced yoga daily. Over time, her body judgment dropped. She began to truly appreciate her body for its functions, for its strength and flexibility, for the way it felt when she breathed deeply, and for the release she felt in the final resting pose at the end of each class. She loved making mistakes in class as her mistakes taught her how to better connect with her body and breathe. She spent so much time with and in her body, the dichotomy of "me versus my body" began to slowly fade. Her body was becoming her sanctuary. Jayla began to fancy the thought of teaching yoga and maybe one day leading a yoga training. She had shifted toward positive embodiment and an experience of positive body image. Now, if someone were to ask Jayla if she was beautiful, she would speak from the mindset of an individual with positive body image: "I am a person of beauty, embodying acts of self-care, radiating loving-kindness and compassion for self and others, grateful for my personal vulnerabilities and challenges as teachers and sources of empathy and connection, and honoring my body and mind for their support and for serving my higher sense of purpose." Jayla's experience was much like a participant interviewed in a mixed-methods study of positive body image among young adult college women: "I'm treating my body with love. My body treats me back with love. It's just like this bond" (Wood-Barcalow, Tylka, & Augustus-Horvath, 2010, p. 110).

MINDFUL SELF-CARE SCALE

The MSCS is a new tool for assessing the aspects of self-care within the ARMS through actionable practices (see Cook-Cottone & Guyker, 2018, for all scale items). Prior to psychometric evaluation, my colleague and I sent the potential list of items to body image and embodiment experts, who then reviewed the items for content coverage and clarity. The 5-point item response scale reflects the frequency of behavior (how much or how often) within the past week (7 days): *never* (*0 days*) scored as 1, *rarely* (*1 day*) scored as 2, *sometimes* (*2 to 3 days*) scored as 3, *often* (*4 to 5 days*) scored as 4, and *regularly*

(*6 to 7 days*) scored as 5, with one reverse scored item. After incorporating their suggested modifications, we evaluated the MSCS's factor structure and examined the internal consistency and validity of its scores with two samples of US community women and men. In the first sample ($N = 448$), participants ranged in age from 18 to 71 (sample mean age [M_{age}] = 33.5, standard deviation [SD] = 11.7), with most identifying as white (90.0%) and women (79.7%). Similarly, in the second sample ($N = 452$), participants ranged in age from 18 to 78 (M_{age} = 34.0, SD = 11.7), with most identifying as white (70.8%) and women (69.7%). Exploratory and confirmatory factor analyses, conducted with the first and second sample, respectively, revealed that six factors best represented the MSCS: Two reflected practices that nurture the internal self (i.e., Physical Self-Care and Self-Compassion/Purpose), two reflected practice that nurtures the external self (i.e., Supportive Relationships, Supportive Structure), and two were integration practices of the internal and external self (i.e., Mindful Awareness, Mindful Relaxation). Cronbach's coefficient alpha was .89 for the total 33-item MSCS (men = .87, women = .89).

More specifically, Physical Self-Care (eight items, $\alpha = .69$) involves taking care of the physical self through adequate water and food intake, exercise, and other physical practices that support physical well-being (e.g., "I ate a variety of nutritious foods," "I took part in sports, dance, or other physical activities"). Self-Compassion involves treating yourself as a loving friend may treat you (e.g., "I kindly acknowledged my own challenges and difficulties"), and Purpose relates to a sense of meaning, spirituality, or greater purpose in life (e.g., "I experienced meaning and/or a larger purpose in my private/personal life"). Together, they form one subscale (six items, $\alpha = .83$). Self-Compassion/Purpose is believed to be a form of mindful grit that helps get us through the hard times and setbacks (Cook-Cottone & Guyker, 2018).

Supportive Relationships (five items, $\alpha = .86$) assesses social support (e.g., "I felt I had someone who would listen to me if I became upset"); respect of boundaries (e.g., "I felt confident that people in my life would respect my choice if I said, 'no' "); and time spent with supportive people (e.g., "I spent time with people who are good to me"). Supportive Structure (four items, $\alpha = .77$) assesses the maintenance of a manageable and balanced schedule (e.g., "I maintained a balance between the demands of others and what is important to me"); comfortable living space (e.g., "I maintained a comfortable and pleasing living environment"); and organized workspace (i.e., "I kept my work/school area organized to support my work/school tasks").

Mindful Awareness (four items, $\alpha = .92$) assesses calm awareness of thoughts, feelings, and the body as well as the intentionality (e.g., "I carefully selected which of my thoughts and feelings I used to guide my actions"). Mindful Relaxation (six items, $\alpha = .77$) assesses a variety of relaxation strategies, including intellectual approaches (e.g., "I did something intellectual [using my mind] to help me relax"); interpersonal (e.g., "I did something interpersonal to relax"); and use of the senses (e.g., "I listened to relax [e.g., listened to music, a podcast, radio show, rainforest sounds]").

Initial validation research (Cook-Cottone & Guyker, 2018) supported the MSCS as situated within the ARMS theoretical model. Although there is more to be assessed in terms of the psychometrics of the scale, preliminary data show positive correlations with body esteem for both women and men. Among men, aspects of mindful self-care were positively associated with perceived physical attractiveness, satisfaction with upper body strength, and perceived physical condition. Among women, aspects of mindful self-care were positively associated with perceived sexual attractiveness, satisfaction with weight, and perceived physical condition. For both men and women, mindful self-care was inversely associated with disordered eating attitudes and behaviors with one exception: The MSCS Physical Self-Care subscale showed negligible yet positive associations with overall disordered eating ($r = .16, p < .01$) and dieting ($r = .18, p < .01$). This counterintuitive finding is likely related to the structure and self-discipline inherent in taking good physical care of yourself, a quality that may share variance with some aspects of food restriction to a small degree.

The potential for using the MSCS, in both research and clinical settings, is broad. For example, a preliminary study by an external team at the Mayo Clinic found the MSCS accounted for 16% of family medical residents' reported wellness indictors (i.e., residents' perceived sense of professional accomplishment and mood in the past week). This research highlights the potential of mindful self-care to increase inner well-being as well as effectiveness in the external domain. The MSCS can be used to facilitate the mindful self-care process in clinical settings, which involves four steps: (a) mindful awareness of self-care as essential to well-being, (b) assessment of self-care domains, (c) assessment-driven self-care goal setting, and (d) engagement in self-care behaviors. This self-reflective process promotes a sense of self-clarity that facilitates adjustments in intentions and actions (Koloroutis, 2014). The process is iterative and requires assessment, action, and reassessment. Clinicians should note that the MSCS was not designed to be inclusive of all self-care behaviors. The current version is brief, allowing for a quick review of the domains of practice highly relevant to mindful attunement in both clients' inner and outer experiences of self. Within therapy, there is always room for exploring new ways to engage in mindful self-care and to be positively embodied.

FUTURE DIRECTIONS

The MSCS serves as a potentially effective way to assess mindful attunement through evaluation of a set of actionable practices that can be easily learned and applied. First, researchers should continue to psychometrically evaluate the scale including test–retest reliability, convergent and discriminant validity, and criterion-related (e.g., predictive) validity with diverse samples. Potential variables to explore alongside the MSCS are behaviors contrary to self-care, such as substance use, self-harm, and burnout. Once the MSCS is more comprehensively validated, it will be interesting to explore mindful self-care as a mechanism of change in the pathway to positive embodiment, such as body responsiveness, body image flexibility, sexual decision-making, intuitive eating, and body appreciation. Reciprocal influence longitudinal designs could examine "upward spirals" in which, for instance, initial levels of mindful self-care promote positive body image, which then promotes additional self-care. Because mindful self-care is actionable, it may be easily accessible for children, and researchers could examine whether it is protective against the development of certain psychological disorders. Important issues related to diverse samples, such as the mechanisms of self-care among individuals of various social identities (e.g., race, class, age, body size), clinical samples, and helping professionals, should be explored. Overall, the MSCS offers a broad range of interesting research opportunities in the domain of positive embodiment.

CONCLUSION

Mindful attunement integrates mindful awareness and attuned action, which includes healthy, sustainable practices that serve and support positive connections between the inner and outer experiences of self. It is a practice that is internalized and embodied over time. This chapter grounded mindful attunement within the context of the ARMS framework, and the MSCS was presented as a tool for the assessment of the aspects of self-care addressing each area of the ARMS through actionable practices. The protocol for a mindful self-care process, which can be useful in therapy, was detailed. It is a relatively simple, although perhaps not easy, pathway filled with awareness, practice, and persistence that moves us from actionable self-care practices to the experience of mindful attunement and positive embodiment. As the case examples in the chapter demonstrate, we *become* the manifestation, or embodiment, of mindful attunement.

REFERENCES

Andrew, R., Tiggemann, M., & Clark, L. (2016). Positive body image and young women's health: Implications for sun protection, cancer screening, weight loss and alcohol consumption behaviours. *Journal of Health Psychology, 21*, 28–39. doi:10.1016/j.jadohealth.2014.09.005

Chernin, K. (1985). *The hungry self: Women, eating, and identity.* New York, NY: Harper and Row.

Cook-Cottone, C. (2006). The attuned representation model for the primary prevention of eating disorders: An overview for school psychologists. *Psychology in the Schools, 43*, 223–230. doi:10.1002/pits.20139

Cook-Cottone, C. P. (2015a). Incorporating positive body image into the treatment of eating disorders: A model of attunement and mindful self-care. *Body Image, 14*, 158–167. doi:10.1016/j.bodyim.2015.03.004

Cook-Cottone, C. P. (2015b). *Mindfulness and yoga for self-regulation: A primer for mental health professionals*. New York, NY: Springer.

Cook-Cottone, C. P. (2016). Embodied self-regulation and mindful self-care in the prevention of eating disorders. *Eating Disorders: Journal of Treatment and Prevention*, *24*, 98–105. doi:10.1080/10640266.2015.1118954

Cook-Cottone, C. P. (2017). *Mindfulness and yoga in schools: A guide for teachers and practitioners*. New York, NY: Springer.

Cook-Cottone, C. P., & Guyker, W. M. (2018). The development and validation of the Mindful Self-Care Scale (MSCS): An assessment of practices that support positive embodiment. *Mindfulness*, *9*, 161–175. doi:10.1007/s12671-017-0759-1

Dollar, E., Berman, M., & Adachi-Mejia, A. M. (2017). Do no harm: Moving beyond weight loss to emphasize physical activity at every size. *Prevention of Chronic Disease*, *14*, *E34*. doi:10.5888/pcd14.170006

Gillen, M. M. (2015). Associations between positive body image and indicators of men's and women's mental and physical health. *Body Image*, *13*, 67–74. doi:10.1016/j.bodyim.2015.01.002

Grabovac, A. D., Lau, M. A., & Willett, B. R. (2011). Mechanisms of mindfulness: A Buddhist psychological model. *Mindfulness*, *2*, 154–166. doi:10.1007/s12671-011-0054-5

Kabat-Zinn, J. (2003). Mindfulness-based interventions in context: Past, present, and future. *Clinical Psychology: Science and Practice*, *10*, 144–156. doi:10.1093/clipsy.bpg016

Keel, P. K., & Forney, K. J. (2013). Psychosocial risk factors for eating disorders. *International Journal of Eating Disorders*, *46*, 433–439. doi:10.1002/eat.22094

Koloroutis, M. (2014). The therapeutic use of self: Developing three capacities for a more mindful practice. *Creative Nursing*, *20*, 77–85.

Linehan, M. (1993). *Cognitive-behavioral treatment of borderline personality disorder*. New York, NY: Guilford Press.

Piran, N. (2016). Embodied possibilities and disruptions: The emergence of the experience of embodiment construct from qualitative studies with girls and women. *Body Image*, *18*, 43–60. doi:10.1016/j.bodyim.2016.04.007

Seligman, M. E. P. (2011). *Flourish: A visionary new understanding of happiness and well-being*. New York, NY: Simon & Schuster.

Siegel, D. J. (2009). Mindful awareness, mindsight, and neural integration. *The Humanistic Psychologist*, *37*, 137–158.

Siegel, D. J. (2012). *The developing mind: How relationships and the brain interact to shape who we are* (2nd ed.). New York, NY: Guilford Press.

Tang, Y. Y., Hölzel, B. K., & Posner, M. I. (2015). The neuroscience of mindfulness meditation. *Nature Reviews Neuroscience*, *16*, 213–225. doi:10.1038/nrn3916

Tylka, T. L. (2012). Positive psychology perspectives on body image. In T. F. Cash (Ed.), *Encyclopedia of body image and human appearance* (Vol. 2, pp. 657–663). San Diego, CA: Academic Press.

Tylka, T. L., & Wood-Barcalow, N. L. (2015). What is and what is not positive body image? Conceptual foundations and construct definition. *Body Image*, *14*, 118–129. doi:10.1016/j.bodyim.2015.04.001

Wood-Barcalow, N. L., Tylka, T. L., & Augustus-Horvath, C. L. (2010). "But I like my body": Positive body image characteristics and a holistic model for young adult women. *Body Image*, *7*, 106–116. doi:10.1016/j.bodyim.2010.01.001

7

Intuitive Eating

ELYSE RESCH AND TRACY L. TYLKA

Disembodiment—or being disconnected from how the body is feeling and functioning—can manifest as maladaptive eating, such as restrained eating, emotional eating, situational eating, overeating, and binge eating. There are benefits to being connected to, trusting in, and responding to the body's internal hunger and satiety cues, a process of embodiment referred to as *intuitive eating* (Tribole & Resch, 1995, 2012; Tylka, 2006). Intuitive eating is grounded in the belief that most people are born with the wisdom for knowing what, when, and how much to eat; infants know when they are hungry, cry to let their caregivers know that it is time for feeding to begin, and turn their head away from the breast or bottle when satiety cues are felt (Tribole & Resch, 2012). Yet, over time, many children learn to replace these internal hunger and satiety cues with external cues when they are taught rules regarding the *quantity* of food to eat (e.g., portion sizes, calorie limits), the *quality* of food to eat (e.g., only prescribed "healthy" foods are acceptable), and *when* they should eat, prompting disembodiment. In this chapter, we present the foundational intuitive eating principles and intuitive eating assessment and research and end with offering avenues for empirical and clinical consideration.

PRINCIPLES OF INTUITIVE EATING

How can we restore eating-related embodiment for those who are disconnected from their internal hunger and satiety cues? Ten principles of intuitive eating were proposed by Tribole and Resch (1995, 2012) to achieve this goal:

Rejecting the diet mentality (1) and *challenging the food police* (2) help individuals understand, resist, and challenge external influences that often become internalized prescriptive and proscriptive thoughts (e.g., "You shouldn't eat that!"). These thoughts, in turn, sabotage intuitive eating.

Making peace with food (3) can neutralize emotional reactions to food. Therefore, instead of making food more powerful than it is (e.g., being obsessed with eating only "good" foods and feeling guilty if consuming "bad" foods, two emotions that are linked to overeating), food becomes neutral.

This neutrality facilitates *coping with emotions without using food* (4), as food becomes a source of sustenance rather than a coping mechanism to deal with stress, loneliness, boredom, and anxiety.

Honoring your hunger (5) and *feeling your fullness* (6) direct individuals to attend to their internal hunger and satiety cues and eat in step with these cues; through this process, individuals can *discover the satisfaction* (7) of savoring food, eating to fuel the body, and eating without deprivation.

Respecting your body (8) and *exercising to feel the difference* (9) can promote body appreciation and embodiment via engaging in joyful physical activities.

After these nine principles are in place, gentle nutrition can be implemented. *Gentle nutrition* (10) involves being mindful of the body's need for increased energy and health and thus choosing foods that help the body function well while eating in a flexible, rather than restrictive, manner.

Being committed to self-compassion, remaining attuned to internal hunger and satiety cues, and practicing autonomy and assertiveness in response to external eating cues are fundamental throughout this process.

INTUITIVE EATING SCALE, ORIGINAL AND REVISED

Tylka (2006) aimed to develop a scale that could be used to add to the scientific literature on intuitive eating. To achieve this goal, she clustered the principles of intuitive eating into three broader domains. *Unconditional permission to eat* (UPE) reflects the willingness to eat when hungry and refusal to label certain foods as forbidden. *Eating for physical rather than emotional reasons* (EPR) represents eating when physically hungry instead of coping with emotional distress, such as anxiety, loneliness, and boredom. Last, *reliance on hunger and satiety cues* (RHSC) reflects trust in internal hunger and satiety cues and reliance on these cues to guide eating behavior. She then developed items for each of these domains and examined the Intuitive Eating Scale (IES) with college women to investigate its psychometric properties. Exploratory and confirmatory factor analyses upheld its three-factor higher order structure. Internal consistency was supported, with Cronbach's alpha estimates ranging from .85 to .88 for the overall IES score and between .72 and .89 for its three subscales. It was stable over a 3-week period, with estimates for the total score ($r = .90$) and subscale scores ($r = .74$–$.88$) upholding test–retest reliability. It yielded evidence of construct validity via its inverse associations with disordered eating and body image disturbance, positive associations with well-being, and negligible association with social desirability.

Tylka and Kroon Van Diest (2013) updated the original IES by adding items to assess gentle nutrition, which was left out of the original IES, and replacing negatively worded items (which assess the absence of intuitive eating) with positively worded items (which assess the presence of intuitive eating). They then examined its psychometric properties in samples of college women and men. Exploratory and second-order confirmatory factor analyses upheld its hypothesized four-factor higher order structure: the original three factors and Body–Food Choice Congruence (B-FCC), the gentle nutrition factor. Its factor structure was invariant across gender. Illustrative IES-2 items include "If I am craving a certain food, I allow myself to have it" (UPE), "I find other ways to cope with stress and anxiety than by eating" (EPR), "I trust my body to tell me when to eat" (RHSC)," and "I mostly eat foods that make my body perform efficiently (well)" (B-FCC). The item response scale is identical to the original IES: Items are rated along a 5-point scale ranging from *strongly disagree* (scored as 1) to *strongly agree* (5) and averaged, with higher scores reflecting greater intuitive eating. For those who would like to use the IES-2, we recommend the item order specified online (https://u.osu.edu/tracyltylka/scales-developed/) rather than the article by Tylka and Kroon Van Diest (2013). The item order on the website keeps subscale items together, making it easier for participants to complete and researchers to score.

Psychometric data support the IES-2. In the original psychometric article (Tylka & Kroon Van Diest, 2013), internal consistency was supported (Cronbach's α = .87–.89 for the total scale score and .81–.93 for subscale scores) as well as its stability over a 3-week period (r = .88, .92 for the total score and .75–.92 for subscale scores). It was positively related to body appreciation and well-being, inversely related to disordered eating and body image disturbance, and negligibly related to social desirability, upholding construct validity.

To date, the IES-2 has been translated into German (van Dyck, Herbert, Happ, Kleveman, & Vögele, 2016); French (Camilleri et al., 2015); French Canadian (Carbonneau et al., 2016); Turkish (Bas et al., 2017); and Portuguese (Duarte, Pinto Gouveia, & Mendes, 2016), with other translation and validation projects under way. Its four-factor structure was upheld among the German, French Canadian, Turkish, and Portuguese samples. However, a three-factor, 18-item IES-2 emerged with the French sample (i.e., the B-FCC subscale and two UPE items were dropped). Internal consistency, test–retest reliability, and construct (mainly convergent) validity have been supported among all samples. A version for adolescents exists (Dockendorff, Petrie, Greenleaf, & Martin, 2012); however, it is based on Tylka's (2006) original IES rather than the IES-2 and thus does not have the benefits of the revised version. Furthermore, the factor structure of this version was slightly different from the original IES. Specifically, among middle school girls and boys, the RHSC factor was divided into two factors: Awareness of Internal Cues and Trust in Internal Cues (Dockendorff et al., 2012). Four original IES items were dropped due to poor item–factor loadings. Its internal consistency and convergent validity were upheld; however, the alpha for awareness of internal cues was .65, falling below the .70 cutoff of acceptability.

RESEARCH ON INTUITIVE EATING

Three clear findings emerged from intuitive eating research. Overall, findings emphasized the usefulness of intuitive eating as a unique construct to promote well-being and health.

Intuitive Eating Is a *Unique* Construct

Intuitive eating is distinct from other eating behaviors studied in the literature, and it is more than the absence of disordered eating. For example, in college and community samples, intuitive eating was linked to well-being after its shared variance with eating disorder symptomatology was extracted (Carbonneau et al., 2016; Tylka & Kroon Van Diest, 2013; Tylka & Wilcox, 2006). Similarly, in community adults, intuitive eating was related to many indices of well-being after its shared variance with flexible and rigid dietary restraint was removed (Linardon & Mitchell, 2017; Tylka, Calogero, & Daníelsdóttir, 2015). It appears that there are two overarching eating behaviors: internally driven eating (the adaptive form, where intuitive eating falls) and externally determined eating (the maladaptive form, determined by external cues, dieting rules, and disordered eating attitudes and behaviors).

Intuitive Eating Is an *Adaptive* Way of Eating and Living

Intuitive eating is linked to numerous indices of psychological well-being and physical health. This research represents different sample types (adolescents, college students, and adult community members) from various geographic areas mainly representative of Western culture (United States, Australia, Canada, the United Kingdom, France, Germany, Portugal, Netherlands, and Turkey).

Psychological Well-Being

Intuitive eating is positively associated with variables representative of psychological flourishing, including self-compassion, mindfulness, emotional awareness, distress tolerance, life satisfaction, positive affect, self-esteem, proactive coping, optimism, unconditional self-regard, psychological hardiness, and social problem-solving (Dockendorff et al., 2012; Kelly & Stephen, 2016; Sairanen et al., 2015; Schoenefeld & Webb, 2013; Shouse & Nilsson, 2011; Tylka, 2006; Tylka & Wilcox, 2006; Tylka & Wood-Barcalow, 2015; Webb & Hardin, 2016). Additionally, intuitive eating is inversely related to variables representative of psychological distress, such as negative affect, depression, anxiety and stress, dichotomous thinking, and self-silencing (Dockendorff et al., 2012; Duarte et al., 2016; Linardon & Mitchell, 2017; Shouse & Nilsson, 2011; Tylka et al., 2015).

Intuitive eating is also positively linked to body appreciation and body image flexibility (Avalos & Tylka, 2006; Bas et al., 2017; Duarte et al., 2016; Kelly, Miller, & Stephen, 2016; Linardon & Mitchell, 2017; Schoenefeld & Webb, 2013; Tylka et al., 2015; Tylka & Wood-Barcalow, 2015; Webb & Hardin, 2016). Much research supports its inverse relationships with thin-ideal internalization, problems in awareness of appetite and emotions, body dissatisfaction, body shame, body surveillance, internalized weight bias, weight/shape evaluation and concerns, weight preoccupation, body checking, and perceived sociocultural pressures to be thin (Bas et al., 2017; Dockendorff et al., 2012; Duarte et al., 2016; Linardon & Mitchell, 2017; Smith & Hawks, 2006; Tylka, 2006; Tylka et al., 2015; Tylka & Wood-Barcalow, 2015; van Dyck et al., 2016; Webb & Hardin, 2016).

Intuitive eating is linked in positive ways to the eating experience. Specifically, higher intuitive eating scores are associated with experiencing greater enjoyment and pleasure of food, being relaxed and comfortable while eating, eating a wide variety of food, tolerating hunger until the next available meal or snack, being mindful when eating, and choosing foods that are nutritious (Smith & Hawks, 2006; Tylka, Eneli, Kroon Van Diest, & Lumeng, 2013). Intuitive eating may serve as a protective factor for eating disorders (Tylka & Kroon Van Diest, 2015), as it is linked to lower binge eating, bulimic symptoms, drive for thinness, rigid dietary restraint, external (i.e., situational) eating, emotional eating, food preoccupation, and food anxieties (Bas et al., 2017; Carbonneau et al., 2016; Denny, Loth, Eisenberg, & Neumark-Sztainer, 2013; Duarte et al., 2016; Linardon & Mitchell, 2017; Smith & Hawks, 2006; Tylka, 2006; Tylka et al., 2015; Tylka & Wood-Barcalow, 2015; van Dyck et al., 2016). Importantly, depression was linked to binge eating only when intuitive eating was low, suggesting that intuitive eating may protect against binge eating when depressive symptoms are experienced (Duarte et al., 2016).

Physical Health

Intuitive eating is also associated with adaptive physical health indicators, such as lower triglycerides, higher high-density lipoprotein (HDL) cholesterol, and improved cardiovascular risk (Hawks et al., 2005). In a study including 31,955 women and 9,581 men, the intuitive eating dimensions of EPR and RHSC were associated with healthier dietary intakes (Camilleri et al., 2016a). In adolescents with Type 1 diabetes mellitus, intuitive eating (overall scores and EPR) was strongly related to better glycemic control (Wheeler et al., 2016). In women, intuitive eating (overall scores as well as EPR and RHSC) was positively related to women's interoceptive sensitivity as measured by a validated heartbeat perception task (Herbert, Blechert, Hautzinger, Matthias, & Herbert, 2013).

Intuitive Eating–Based Interventions Promote Well-Being and Health

Interventions, such as Health at Every Size® (HAES), teach intuitive eating skills as well as emphasize well-being in lieu of weight loss, challenge weight stigma, and champion access to healthcare for all body sizes. To illustrate the positive impacts of these interventions on well-being, we highlight select within-program effects from randomized, controlled studies. A 6-month HAES-based intervention decreased total cholesterol, low-density lipoprotein (LDL) cholesterol, triglycerides, and systolic blood pressure at a 1- and 2-year follow-up as well as decreased physical hunger, disinhibited eating, bulimic symptomatology, drive for thinness, body dissatisfaction, poor interoceptive awareness, and depression at a 2-year follow-up among middle-aged women with high body mass index (BMI; Bacon et al., 2002; Bacon, Stern, Van Loan, & Keim, 2005).

Another 6-month HAES-based intervention improved total and LDL cholesterol, physical activity, fruit and vegetable intake, self-esteem, and quality of life from baseline to a 2-year follow-up among women with high BMI (Mensinger, Calogero, Stranges, & Tylka, 2016). A 13-week HAES-based intervention revealed that diet quality improved from baseline to postintervention (Carbonneau et al., 2017). Women who received a 10-week intuitive eating-specific intervention reported lower disordered eating and body dissatisfaction and higher body appreciation and mindfulness at a 10-week follow-up (Bush, Rossy, Mintz, & Schopp, 2014).

Middle-aged women with high BMI who completed an intuitive eating web-based program increased their intuitive eating, psychological flexibility, and general mental health, as well as decreased their binge eating from baseline to postintervention in a pilot single-arm study (Boucher et al., 2016). At a 3-month follow up, improvements in intuitive eating and psychological flexibility were maintained, and there were further improvements in binge eating and general mental health.

CLINICAL CONSIDERATIONS AND FUTURE RESEARCH

Situating intuitive eating within theoretical models and testing them empirically has yielded insight that would be helpful to clinicians and could be used to guide future research.

The Foundation for Intuitive Eating Is Grounded in Body Acceptance

The acceptance model of intuitive eating (Avalos & Tylka, 2006) has confirmed via many samples that the foundation for intuitive eating is body acceptance—of self and others. Indeed, body acceptance by others may encourage individuals to retain focus on their internal hunger and satiety cues in lieu of replacing them with external cues as they search for acceptance they have not yet received. In two studies, Avalos and Tylka (2006) found that women who perceive that important others accept their bodies have higher body appreciation, which in turn is linked to higher intuitive eating. Andrew, Tiggemann, and Clark (2016) revealed that body acceptance by others predicted increased body appreciation, and body appreciation predicted increased intuitive eating over a 1-year period among adolescent girls. Next, we need to know whether the acceptance model of intuitive eating can be applied to youth of all genders and ethnically diverse samples using longitudinal designs. Extending investigations beyond a 1-year period and earlier in development are also worthwhile.

Trust in the Body's Cues Is Important

Intuitive eating skills reach far beyond helping individuals become aware of their internal hunger and satiety cues. Another essential ingredient to eating intuitively is valuing, trusting in, and responding to these cues (interoceptive responsiveness). Oswald, Chapman, and Wilson (2017) found that interoceptive responsiveness accounted for the relationship between body appreciation and intuitive eating, concluding that valuing and appraising bodily sensations are just as important as detecting internal cues. Next, we need to know the best ways to increase interoceptive responsiveness. How can we help individuals trust their internal cues amid cultural messages that bodies cannot be trusted? This knowledge could enhance the effectiveness of intuitive eating interventions.

Intuitive Eating May Be Sabotaged for Some Individuals

Much research has shown that intuitive eating is higher for those with lower BMI and boys/men (Bas et al., 2017; Camilleri et al., 2016b; Carbonneau et al., 2016; Denny et al., 2013; Dockendorff et al., 2012; Duarte et al., 2016; Hawks et al., 2005; Herbert et al., 2013; Linardon & Mitchell, 2017; Madden, Leong, Gray, & Horwath, 2012; Schoenefeld & Webb, 2013; Smith & Hawks, 2006; Tylka et al., 2015; Tylka & Kroon Van Diest, 2013; Tylka & Wood-Barcalow, 2015; Webb & Hardin, 2016). While it is easy to interpret the inverse relationship between intuitive eating and BMI as "intuitive eating will lead to weight loss," causal interpretations must be avoided. It is equally plausible that individuals who are not fat are more likely to be "left alone"—not pressured to diet—whereas those considered fat are exposed to more pressure to lose weight and diet. Weight control attempts sway individuals away from intuitive eating (as they have more difficulty detecting and trusting internal hunger and satiety cues due to externally focused eating) and toward binge eating (Leong, Gray, Haszard, & Horwath, 2016). Similarly, the argument that "boys/men are more natural intuitive eaters" may be due to the fact that girls and women are incessantly pressured to achieve the unrealistic "thin ideal" (see Chapter 14). Attempts to achieve this ideal require intentionally suppressing appetite and disconnecting from inner cues. Next, we need to develop interventions targeting vulnerable groups who are likely to learn from an early age that they cannot trust their internal hunger and satiety cues. Also, we need to know how best to preserve the natural tendency to eat intuitively in the face of cultural pressures to diet.

Intuitive Eating Is Nurtured via an Autonomy-Supportive Environment

Autonomy-supportive environments allow intrinsic motivation to flourish and external motives to be internalized in an adaptive way. In turn, intrinsic motivation and adaptive internalizations facilitate self-initiation and choice and promote higher psychological well-being. Conversely, controlling social environments pressure individuals to think, feel, and behave in certain ways. Carbonneau, Carbonneau, Cantin, and Gagnon-Girouard (2015) found that partners' autonomy-supportive style was positively associated with women's autonomous eating regulation, which was positively linked to intuitive eating. Mothers' and partners' controlling style was positively associated with women's controlled eating regulation (i.e., eating restraint), which was inversely linked to intuitive eating. Next, we need to know the best ways to encourage autonomy-supportive environments and whether these interventions specifically preserve intuitive eating.

Intuitive Eating Is Intricately Connected to Self-Compassion

Self-compassion is needed to remain mindful and kind to oneself during difficult emotions and thoughts, which ebb and flow throughout life. Schoenefeld and Webb (2013) found that having self-compassion toward difficult internal experiences related to the body (e.g., felt shame due to body image threats) was linked to higher intuitive eating. They concluded that intuitive eating could be viewed as "valued action," or acting in accordance with one's adaptive goals and values, even while experiencing negative thoughts and feelings about one's body. In a 7-day study, Kelly and Stephen (2016) found that women ate more intuitively on days when they treated themselves more self-compassionately than usual. On days when they were less self-compassionate than usual, their interactions with body-focused others (e.g., those who comment frequently about weight) were linked to lower intuitive eating (Kelly et al., 2016). Next, we need to know the best interventions for helping women identify when heightened self-compassion is needed and ways to increase it in the moment. Investigations of whether moment-to-moment fluctuations in self-compassion affect intuitive eating in varied situations, such as exposure to appearance-focused media discussing the "new diet," are also needed.

Intuitive Eating Can Be Taught, Even Among People with Eating Disorders

A 2-year pilot, single-arm intervention study evaluated the effectiveness of an intuitive eating program for patients in an eating disorder treatment center (Richards, Crowton, Berrett, Smith, & Passmore, 2017). Patients developed the skills of intuitive eating, and the ability to eat intuitively was linked to positive treatment outcomes for each diagnostic category. The authors discussed how to implement intuitive eating safely and effectively in inpatient and residential treatment programs. Also, interventions teaching intuitive eating skills have been shown to improve intuitive eating while decreasing disordered eating from baseline to a 10-week (Bush et al., 2014), a 1-year (Carbonneau et al., 2017), and a 2-year (Mensinger et al., 2016) follow-up among adult women, many with high BMI. Next, we need to know whether integrating intuitive eating skills in treatment aids in disordered eating remission and enhances well-being and body appreciation post-treatment.

Unconditional Permission to Eat Is Not Positively Associated with Overeating

Due to the diet mentality, individuals may fear that granting themselves UPE will prompt overeating. There is no evidence to support this relationship. In fact, UPE is *inversely* associated with emotional eating (Tylka & Kroon Van Diest, 2013) and unrelated to uncontrolled eating (Camilleri et al., 2015). While UPE was found to be associated with lower fruit, vegetable, and whole-grain intake (Camilleri et al., 2016a), this intuitive eating component honors making peace with all foods, which is needed to reduce food preoccupation (Tylka et al., 2015). Further, UPE may not be associated with lower consumption of healthy foods over time. To illustrate, the association between UPE and diet quality was negative at baseline but was positive and marginally significant at the end of a 13-week HAES-based intervention (Carbonneau et al., 2017). Next, we need longitudinal evidence that UPE, as well as the other intuitive eating dimensions, is linked to health and well-being indicators in the long term.

CONCLUSION

Intuitive eating is a behavioral manifestation of embodiment, as it entails remaining connected to internal hunger and satiety cues and trusting these cues to direct when, what, and how much to eat. Research has revealed that it is adaptive for psychological well-being and physical health, with evidence that intuitive eating–based interventions enhance these areas. As such, intuitive eating is extremely relevant to clinical practice among individuals who have a difficult time trusting their bodies and engage in disordered eating. Research on how to sustain individuals' natural tendency to eat intuitively, as well as cultivate it as individuals develop across time, is needed in the face of cultural pressures to engage in restrained, externally regulated, and disembodied eating practices.

REFERENCES

Andrew, R., Tiggemann, M., & Clark, L. (2016). Predictors and health-related outcomes of positive body image in adolescent girls: A prospective study. *Developmental Psychology, 52*, 463–474. doi:10.1037/dev0000095

Avalos, L. C., & Tylka, T. L. (2006). Exploring a model of intuitive eating with college women. *Journal of Counseling Psychology, 53*, 486–497. doi:10.1037/0022-1067.53.4.486

Bacon, L., Keim, N. L., Van Loan, M. D., Derricote, M., Gale, B., Kazaks, A., & Stern, J. S. (2002). Evaluating a "non-diet" wellness intervention for improvement of metabolic fitness, psychological well-being and eating and activity behaviors. *International Journal of Obesity, 26*, 854–865. doi:10.1038/sj.ijo.0802012

Bacon, L., Stern, J. S., Van Loan, M. D., & Keim, N. L. (2005). Size acceptance and intuitive eating improve health for obese, female chronic dieters. *Journal of the American Dietetic Association, 105*, 929–936. doi:10.1016/j.jada.2005.03.011

Bas, M., Karaca, K. E., Saglam, D., Aritici, G., Cengiz, E., Köksal, S., & Buyukkaragoz, A. H. (2017). Turkish version of the Intuitive Eating Scale-2: Validity and reliability among university students. *Appetite, 114*, 391–397. doi:10.1016/j.appet.207.04.017

Boucher, S., Edwards, O., Gray, A., Nada-Raja, S., Lillis, J., Tylka, T. L., & Horwath, C. C. (2016). Teaching intuitive eating and acceptance and commitment therapy skills via a web-based intervention: A pilot single-arm intervention study. *JMIR Research Protocols, 5*, e180. doi:10.2196/resprot.5861

Bush, H. E., Rossy, L., Mintz, L. B., & Schopp, L. (2014). Eat for life: A work site feasibility study of a novel mindfulness-based intuitive eating intervention. *American Journal of Health Promotion, 28*, 380–388. doi:10.4278/ajhp.120404-QUAN-186

Camilleri, G. M., Méjean, C., Bellisle, F., Andreeva, V. A., Kesse-Guyot, E., Hercberg, S., & Péneau, S. (2016a). Intuitive eating dimensions were differently associated with food intake in the general population-based NutriNet-Santé study. *Journal of Nutrition, 147*, 61–69. doi:10.3945/jn.116.234088

Camilleri, G. M., Méjean, C., Bellisle, F., Andreeva, V. A., Kesse-Guyot, E., Hercberg, S., & Péneau, S. (2016b). Intuitive eating is inversely associated with body weight status in the general population-based NutriNet-Santé study. *Obesity, 24*, 1154–1161. doi:10.1002/oby.21440

Camilleri, G. M., Méjean, C., Bellisle, F., Andreeva, V. A., Sautron, V., Hercberg, S., & Péneau, S. (2015). Cross-cultural validity of the Intuitive Eating Scale-2. Psychometric evaluation in a sample of the general French population. *Appetite, 84*, 34–42. doi:10.1016/j.appet.2014.09.009

Carbonneau, E., Bégin, C., Lemieux, S., Mongeau, L., Paquette, M.-C., Turcotte, M., . . . Provencher, V. (2017). A Health at Every Size intervention improves intuitive eating and diet quality in Canadian women. *Clinical Nutrition, 36*, 747–754. doi:10.1016/j.clnu.2016.06.008

Carbonneau, N., Carbonneau, E., Cantin, M., & Gagnon-Girouard, M.-P. (2015). Examining women's perceptions of their mother's and romantic partner's interpersonal styles for a better understanding of their eating regulation and intuitive eating. *Appetite, 92*, 156–166. doi:10.1016/j.appet.2015.05.020

Carbonneau, E., Carbonneau, N., Lamarche, B., Provencher, V., Bégin, C., Bradette-Laplante, M., . . . Lemieux, S. (2016). Validation of a French-Canadian adaptation of the Intuitive Eating Scale-2 for the adult population. *Appetite, 105*, 37–45. doi:10.1016/j.appet.2016.05.001

Denny, K. N., Loth, K., Eisenberg, M. E., & Neumark-Sztainer, D. (2013). Intuitive eating in young adults. Who is doing it, and how is it related to disordered eating behaviors? *Appetite, 60*, 13–19. doi:10.1016/j.appet.2012.09.029

Dockendorff, S. A., Petrie, T. A., Greenleaf, C. A., & Martin, S. (2012). Intuitive Eating Scale: An examination among early adolescents. *Journal of Counseling Psychology, 59*, 604–611. doi:10.1037/a0029962

Duarte, C., Pinto Gouveia, J., & Mendes, A. (2016). Psychometric properties of the Intuitive Eating Scale-2 and association with binge eating symptoms in a Portuguese community sample. *International Journal of Psychology and Psychological Therapy, 16*, 329–341.

Hawks, S., Madanat, H., Hawks, J., & Harris, A. (2005). The relationship between intuitive eating and health indicators among college women. *American Journal of Health Education, 36*, 331–336. doi:10.1080/19325937.2005.10608206

Herbert, B. M., Blechert, J., Hautzinger, M., Matthias, E., & Herbert, C. (2013). Intuitive eating is associated with interoceptive sensitivity. Effects on body mass index. *Appetite, 70*, 22–30. doi:10.1016/j.appet.2013.06.082

Kelly, A. C., Miller, K. E., & Stephen, E. (2016). The benefits of being self-compassionate on days when interactions with body-focused others are frequent. *Body Image, 19*, 195–203. doi:10.1016/j.bodyim.2016.10.005

Kelly, A. C., & Stephen, E. (2016). A daily diary study of self-compassion, body image, and eating behavior in female college students. *Body Image, 17*, 152–160. doi:10.1016/j.bodyim.2016.03.006

Leong, S. L., Gray, A., Haszard, J., & Horwath, C. (2016). Weight-control methods, 3-year weight change, and eating behaviors: A prospective nationwide study of middle-aged New Zealand women. *Journal of the Academy of Nutrition and Dietetics, 116*, 1276–1284. doi:10.1016/j.jand.2016.02.021

Linardon, J., & Mitchell, S. (2017). Rigid dietary control, flexible dietary control, and intuitive eating: Evidence for their differential relationship to disordered eating and body image concerns. *Eating Behaviors, 26*, 16–22. doi:10.1016/j.eatbeh.2017.01.008

Madden, C. E. L., Leong, S. L., Gray, A., & Horwath, C. C. (2012). Eating in response to hunger and satiety signals is related to BMI in a nationwide sample of 1,601 mid-age New Zealand women. *Public Health Nutrition, 15*, 2272–2279. doi:10.1017/S1368980012000882

Mensinger, J. L., Calogero, R. M., Stranges, S., & Tylka, T. L. (2016). A weight-neutral versus weight-loss approach for health promotion in women with high BMI: A randomized-controlled trial. *Appetite, 105*, 364–374. doi:10.1016/j.appet.2016.06.006

Oswald, A., Chapman, J., & Wilson, C. (2017). Do interoceptive awareness and interoceptive responsiveness mediate the relationship between body appreciation and intuitive eating in young women? *Appetite, 109*, 66–72. doi:10.1016/j.appet.2016.11.019

Richards, P. S., Crowton, S., Berrett, M. E., Smith, M. H., & Passmore, K. (2017). Can patients with eating disorders learn to eat intuitively? A 2-year pilot study. *Eating Disorders, 25*, 99–113. doi:10.1080/10640266.2017.1279907

Sairanen, E., Tolvanen, A., Karhunen, L., Kolehmainen, M., Järvelä, E., Kolehmainen, M., . . . Lappalainen, R. (2015). Psychological flexibility and mindfulness explain intuitive eating in overweight adults. *Behavior Modification, 39*, 557–579. doi:10.1177/0145445515576402

Schoenefeld, S. J., & Webb, J. B. (2013). Self-compassion and intuitive eating in college women: Examining the contributions of distress tolerance and body image acceptance and action. *Eating Behaviors, 14*, 493–496. doi:10.1016/j.eatbeh.2013.09.001

Shouse, S. H., & Nilsson, J. (2011). Self-silencing, emotional awareness, and eating behaviors in college women. *Psychology of Women Quarterly, 35*, 451–457. doi:10.1177/0361684310388785

Smith, T., & Hawks, S. R. (2006). Intuitive eating, diet composition, and the meaning of food in healthy weight promotion. *American Journal of Health Education, 37*, 130–136.

Tribole, E., & Resch, O. (1995). *Intuitive eating*. New York, NY: St. Martin's Griffin.

Tribole, E., & Resch, E. (2012). *Intuitive eating: A revolutionary program that works* (3rd ed.). New York, NY: St. Martin's Press.

Tylka, T. L., Eneli, I. U., Kroon Van Diest, A. M., & Lumeng, J. C. (2013). Which adaptive maternal eating behaviors predict child feeding practices? An examination with mothers of 2-to5-year-old children. *Eating Behaviors, 14*, 57–63. doi:10.1016/j.eatbeh.2012.10.014

Tylka, T. L. (2006). Development and psychometric evaluation of a measure of intuitive eating. *Journal of Counseling Psychology, 53*, 226–240. doi:10.1037/0022-0167.53.2.226

Tylka, T. L., Calogero, R. M., & Daníelsdóttir, S. (2015). Is intuitive eating the same as flexible dietary control? Their links to each other and well-being could provide an answer. *Appetite, 95*, 166–175. doi:10.1016/j.appet.2015.07.004

Tylka, T. L., & Kroon Van Diest, A. M. (2013). The Intuitive Eating Scale-2: Item refinement and psychometric evaluation with college women and men. *Journal of Counseling Psychology, 60*, 137–153. doi:10.1037/a0030893

Tylka, T. L., & Kroon Van Diest, A. M. (2015). Protective factors in the development of eating disorders. In L. Smolak & M. P. Levine (Eds.), *The Wiley-Blackwell handbook of eating disorders* (Vol. 1, pp. 430–444). New York, NY: Wiley.

Tylka, T. L., & Wilcox, J. A. (2006). Are intuitive eating and eating disorder symptomatology opposite poles of the same construct? *Journal of Counseling Psychology, 53*, 474–485. doi:10.1037/0022-0167.53.4.474

Tylka, T. L., & Wood-Barcalow, N. L. (2015). The Body Appreciation Scale: Item refinement and psychometric evaluation. *Body Image, 12*, 53–67. doi:10.1016/j.bodyim.2014.09.006

van Dyck, Z., Herbert, B. M., Happ, C., Kleveman, G. V., & Vögele, C. (2016). German version of the Intuitive Eating Scale: Psychometric evaluation and application to an eating disordered population. *Appetite, 105*, 798–807. doi:10.1016/j.appet.2016.07.019

Webb, J. B., & Hardin, A. S. (2016). An integrative affect regulation process model of internalized weight bias and intuitive eating in college women. *Appetite, 102*, 60–69. doi:10.1016/j.appet.2016.02.024

Wheeler, B. J., Lawrence, J., Chae, M., Paterson, H., Gray, A. R., Healey, D., . . . Taylor, B. J. (2016). Intuitive eating is associated with glycaemic control in adolescents with Type 1 diabetes mellitus. *Appetite, 96*, 160–165. doi:10.1016/j.appet.2015.09.016

8

Attunement with Exercise (AWE)

RACHEL M. CALOGERO, TRACY L. TYLKA, BETH HARTMAN MCGILLEY, AND KELLY N. PEDROTTY-STUMP ■

Engagement in physical exercise constitutes a fundamental embodied practice, but exercise itself does not automatically foster positive embodiment simply by being "in" our bodies when we exercise. Rather, people living in cultures that perpetuate body shaming and valorize bodily discipline and control are more likely to be disconnected and unresponsive to bodily needs (Piran, 2017). Drawing from theories of embodiment and mindfulness and our own clinical work with women with eating disorders, we developed the concept of attunement with exercise (AWE) to represent physical activity experiences that reflect being in the body and caring for the body. In this chapter, we describe our conceptual model of AWE, its measurement, and its development within clinical and community samples of women and men. We provide empirical evidence for the role of attuned exercise in cultivating positive embodiment and operating as a protective factor against disordered eating, self-objectification, and negative embodiment more generally. We close with suggestions and strategies for becoming more attuned with exercise to foster this embodied practice.

ATTUNEMENT WITH EXERCISE—WORKING WITH THE CONCEPT

Our conceptualization of AWE has developed over a period of many years and derives from our work with women with eating disorders to address their dysfunctional exercise attitudes and behaviors. We begin with an articulation of dysfunctional exercise in order to contrast it fully with attuned exercise. We use the term *dysfunctional exercise* to cover the range of terms, labels, and definitions that have been used to describe problematic exercise attitudes and behaviors in the literature (Calogero & Pedrotty-Stump, 2010). A sizable research literature has linked dysfunctional exercise to the etiology, maintenance, and relapse of eating disorders. Dysfunctional exercise often precedes the onset of eating pathology, predicts longer periods of hospitalization and quicker time to relapse after discharge from treatment, and is often one of the last symptoms to subside for patients with eating disorders (for review, see Calogero & Pedrotty-Stump, 2010). Other research has further implicated dysfunctional exercise in the suicidal behavior of women with eating disorders (primarily bulimia nervosa) and college-based samples of women (Smith et al., 2013). Notably, this association was observed after controlling for other eating disorder behaviors, underscoring the unique significance of dysfunctional exercise for mental health.

Drawing from direct experience with women with eating disorders, we observed that dysfunctional exercise encompasses wider patterns of attitudes and behaviors around physical activity than typically assessed in the literature. Dysfunctional exercise can include a variety of characteristics and qualities that indicate an underlying problematic practice beyond frequency and intensity-based descriptions of activity. We define dysfunctional exercise as a *matter of quality* and not quantity and consider the variety of contexts in which exercise may reflect a disembodied exercise mindset (Calogero & Pedrotty, 2003, 2004a, 2004b, 2007; Calogero & Pedrotty-Stump, 2010; de la Torre, 1995; Mond & Calogero, 2009; Pedrotty & Calogero, 2002, 2003, 2009, 2010). These qualities of dysfunctional exercise are especially important to assess because they reflect a core disembodiment of self during and through exercise.

Consistent with this broadened definition, dysfunctional exercise includes exercising in the absence of adequate hydration or nourishment, for permission to eat, in unsafe environmental conditions, when injured or in pain, and to self-punish or self-harm. When exercise is dysfunctional, people ignore bodily signals telling them when to stop (or whether to even start), do not take adequate rest and recovery periods from exercise, do not take pleasure from the exercise experience, and rarely feel they have exercised enough. Exercise avoidance is also a pattern of dysfunctional exercise when motivated by mental and emotional anguish and negative experiences associated with it. For example, research has shown that individuals who experience frequent negative thoughts and feelings about exercise, but who do not actually exercise, report lower self-esteem, more depression, and more disordered eating compared to individuals who engage in frequent exercise without the accompanying negative thoughts and feelings (Ackard, Brehm, & Steffen, 2002).

Dysfunctional exercise can also be signified by holding the identity of exerciser as most important to self-concept and identity, being guided by the belief that there is one correct or perfect way to exercise, and prioritizing of exercise over everything else, especially time spent on relationships with family, friends, and one's wider social network. Patterns of dysfunctional exercise tend to be characterized by feelings of shame, guilt, general negative affect, and habitual comparisons with others around exercise. And finally, dysfunctional exercise is characterized by the pursuit of weight loss and weight control as the sole or primary purpose of exercise. This particular quality of dysfunctional exercise is more likely to be missed as a cause for concern because of the culturally sanctioned duty to control weight

(Rich & Evans, 2005). In the pursuit of contemporary fitness, thinness, and beauty standards (Calogero, Boroughs, & Thompson, 2007), exercise for weight loss is not only normalized, but encouraged. Yet, this feature of dysfunctional exercise, along with feelings of intense guilt when exercise is missed, most clearly distinguishes the exercise behavior of eating disorder patients from non-clinical community samples of women (Mond & Calogero, 2009). Appearance-based motives signify the rigid outcome-orientation of dysfunctional exercise, which is an idea we return to further in the chapter.

Implemented in 2001, the first and last author of this chapter developed and facilitated an experiential, psychoeducational exercise program for women with eating disorders during their residential treatment stay with the specific purpose of replacing dysfunctional exercise with more attuned exercise. This program consisted of weekly sessions focused on the creation of new experiential associations with exercise through bodily awareness and connection in safe internal and external environmental conditions to facilitate treatment and recovery (Calogero, 2016; Calogero & Pedrotty, 2004a, 2004b, 2016; Calogero, Tylka, & Pedrotty-Stump, 2016; Pedrotty & Calogero, 2002, 2003, 2009, 2010). We used every opportunity to debunk women's exercise myths and misconceptions (Robison, 2000). In particular, we would share scientific data to address the misconception that the primary purpose of exercise is for weight loss and should be driven by weight loss goals. The deeply entrenched belief that exercise is for weight loss rests, in part, on the distinct outcome orientation of dysfunctional exercise (Calogero & Pedrotty, 2007), whereby weight- and appearance-based goals orient exercise attitudes and behaviors away from the experience of bodily awareness, care, and connection and toward external measurements and evaluations of the body and performance. These myths and misconceptions are informed and driven by deeply entrenched attitudes of weight stigma on the part of professionals and the lay public, which we also actively countered with scientific data (Calogero, Tylka, Mensinger, Meadows, & Daníelsdóttir, 2018; Tylka et al., 2014).

Challenging the outcome orientation is critical to foster attuned exercise. Homan and Tylka (2014) found that appearance-based motives fully nullified the adaptive connection between physical activity and positive body image, providing evidence that focusing on these sorts of goals and outcomes disrupts embodiment. An outcome orientation directs attention toward external appearance and the evaluations of others to determine what should be gained, lost, corrected, quieted, or undone through exercise. Indeed, this orientation may explain why many people display considerable dependence on often arbitrary and regularly shifting guidelines and prescriptions for exercise (Corbin, LeMasurier, & Franks, 2002). A chronic externally-directed focus (e.g., media, other people who exercise, personal trainers, health professionals) supplants an internally-directed focus on how our bodies feel and what they require. This reliance on others also relinquishes one's personal and social power, further disconnecting them from their own bodies, fostering mistrust of their own bodies' preferences and needs related to exercise, and thereby deepening negative embodiment. Certainly, there are fitness professionals who consider individual needs and promote attuned exercise, but many people do not have direct or safe access to these resources or have the means to assess their quality (Estabrooks, Lee, & Gyuresik, 2003; Wilson, Kirtland, Ainsworth, & Addy, 2004).

Under this guiding framework for what constitutes dysfunctional exercise, we supervised and guided exercise activities during each exercise session with the aim of cultivating an attuned approach to exercise by centering their moment-by-moment experience during exercise and then processing that experience after the activity (Calogero & Pedrotty, 2004b). The activities included stretching, alignment and posture, yoga, strength training, balance, outdoor activities, and recreational games. Through these experiences, we encouraged patients to expand their practice and process of exercise, by reflecting on what *counts* as exercise, to discover physical activities that bring joy and rejuvenation, and to do so without compromising safety and self-care. Specific details of the program can be found elsewhere (Calogero & Pedrotty, 2004b; Calogero & Pedrotty-Stump, 2010).

To meet our aim, we based the design of the program on three essential building blocks of attuned exercise that corresponded with the three levels of the program (Calogero et al., 2016; Figure 8.1). Level 1 is *safety* and focuses on being safe during exercise. This level is centered primarily on factors associated with physical safety: fueling and hydrating the body appropriately for activity (internal environment) as well as the social context in which activity is undertaken (external environment). This level also focuses on reconnecting to internal signals during exercise by incorporating yoga and other guided physical activities to cultivate greater attunement with self through exercise. Level 2 is *process* and builds on the first level to focus on mindful awareness and staying present during exercise instead of making comparisons, negative self-judgments, and bodily disconnection. This level underscores the purpose of exercise for the sake of attunement and connection and to practice reliance on internal cues instead of external sources to guide activities. This level also focuses on balance, flexibility, and variety to

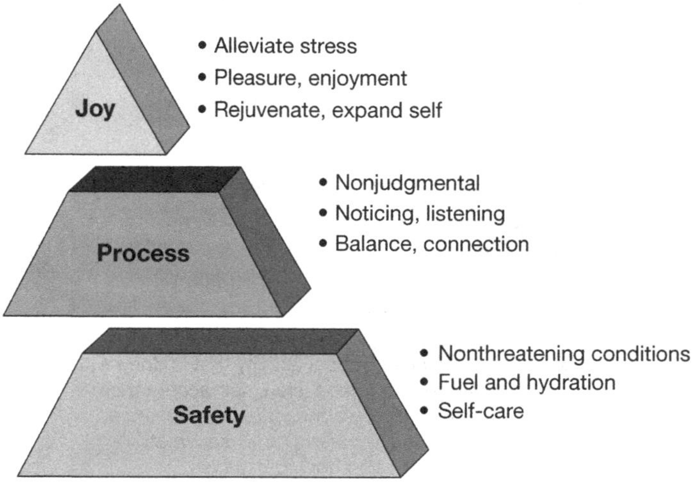

Figure 8.1 Three building blocks of attunement with exercise (AWE).

support the self through exercise. Level 3 is *joy* and builds on the previous two levels to focus on the experience of pleasure and enjoyment through physical activity. This level centers on identifying activities that bring joy instead of pain and/or dread and that align with unique interests and strengths, instead of being dictated by arbitrary standards and external sources. This level also focuses on finding activities that rejuvenate the body and mind instead of exhausting and depleting them. An empirical test of the effectiveness of the exercise program found significant reductions in dysfunctional exercise attitudes and behaviors, without negatively affecting weight gain, among women who participated in the program compared to those who did not (Calogero & Pedrotty, 2004a, 2004b).

Our concept of AWE emerged out of these firsthand accounts and observations of women's disembodiment, and specifically that dysfunctional exercise was both a reflection of their disembodiment and a creator of it. Drawing from our own clinical experiences and theories of mindfulness (Siegel, 2007) and embodiment (Piran, 2016, 2017), we conceptualized AWE along a continuum that ranges from *less attunement with* exercise to *more attunement with* exercise and applies to any physical activity (Figure 8.2). Attuned exercise reflects mindful attention, self-compassion, self-acceptance, joyful moments, and becoming more connected and present in the body. As a reflection of positive embodiment, attuned exercise requires a foundation of physical and psychological *safety* on which people can focus on the *process* of becoming more aware, connected, and responsive to one's body and come to experience *joy* through physical activity.

Over the years, we have assessed individual differences in AWE in clinical and community samples of women and men (Calogero & Mensinger, 2015; Calogero et al., 2010). Most recently, we have developed the Attunement with Exercise Scale (AWE Scale), which assesses the extent to which people engage in exercise that is oriented around themes of self-care (vs. self-harm), process (vs. outcome), balance (vs. imbalance), and rejuvenation (vs. control). We demonstrated its factor structure, internal consistency, and validity (construct, criterion related, and incremental) for assessing attuned exercise and predicting more positive embodiment

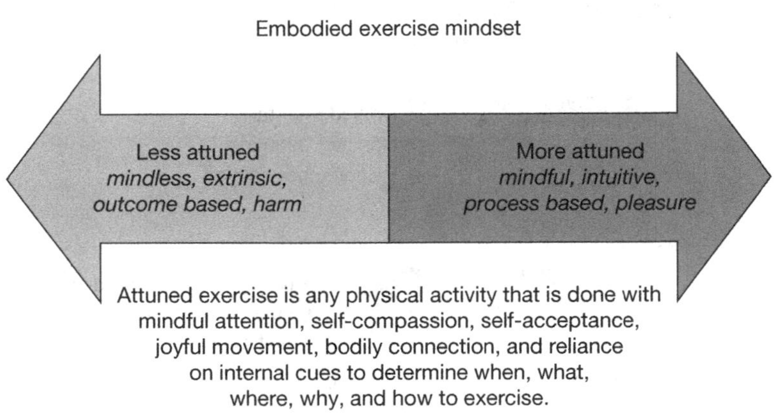

Figure 8.2 Attuned exercise continuum.

and less negative embodiment in community and college samples of women and men (Calogero, Tylka, Hartman McGilley, & Pedrotty-Stump, 2018). More specifically, the AWE total scale and subscales are positively associated with indicators of positive embodiment, including intuitive eating, broader conceptualizations of beauty, body pride, body responsiveness, body appreciation, self-compassion, trait mindfulness, and exercising for the purposes of joy and revitalization. The AWE total scale and subscales are inversely associated with indicators of negative embodiment, including disordered eating, comparisons with others in the domains of body, eating, and exercise; body shame and guilt; self-surveillance; compulsive commitment to exercise; exercise dependence; defining oneself as an exerciser; and exercising for the purpose of appearance management and weight loss. The AWE total scale and subscales explained unique variance in disordered eating beyond body mass index, body dissatisfaction, interceptive deficits, thin-ideal internalization, exercise frequency, and commitment to exercise.

Evidence has also supported the central role of attuned exercise (as assessed with the AWE Scale) within a theoretical model. In community samples of women and men, previous experiences of weight-based and appearance teasing predicted less attuned exercise and more exercise addiction, with lower attuned exercise mediating the link between teasing experiences and exercise addiction (Calogero, Tylka, Hartman McGilley, et al., 2018). These findings further underscore body acceptance (environments free of weight-based and appearance teasing; see Chapter 20) as a foundation for attuned exercise. Collectively, research based on the AWE Scale has revealed that directing attention toward exercise as embodied practice is critical for attaining psychological and physical wellness and balance and stands in direct contrast to dysfunctional exercise.

CULTIVATING AWE AS AN EMBODIED PRACTICE

Yoga is a particularly powerful tool for cultivating AWE (Calogero, 2011; Costin & Kelly, 2016; see also Chapter 30), and with education and guidance, yoga communities can harness this holistic method to help promote positive embodiment for those with, and at risk for, eating disorders (Cook-Cottone & Douglass, 2017; Ressler, Kleinman, & Mott, 2010). The aim of yoga is to fully experience the present moment, encouraging attunement to internal sensations versus external stimuli. Yoga serves as a metaphor for life in many different ways. A yoga practice can be created to include poses (or asanas) that address particular psychological or emotional challenges. Some asanas emphasize balance or flexibility, whereas others may focus on openness and trust or on acceptance. We know from research on mindfulness-based practices that responsiveness to bodily needs and self-care can be improved through greater attention and awareness without increasing reactivity to stress and other triggers (Siegel, 2007; Wall, 2005). In addition, mindfulness practices decrease cortisol levels, thereby changing the neurophysiology of the body to facilitate healing (e.g., Monnazzi, Leri, Guizzardi, Mattioli, & Patacchioli, 2002; Schell, Allolio, & Schonecke, 1994; West, Otte, Geher, Johnson,

& Mohr, 2004). Thus, as an experiential mindfulness practice, yoga teaches specific tools to facilitate healing and attunement.

Daubenmier (2005) found that regular yoga participants had significantly greater body awareness, body responsiveness, and body satisfaction and less self-objectification compared to nonyoga participants. Dale et al. (2009) observed significant improvements in psychological well-being and mood and less negative emotionality after an intensive 6-day yoga workshop among a sample of women with histories of eating disorders, and these effects were maintained up to 1 month following the workshop. A recent population-based longitudinal study of young adults also found higher body satisfaction among those adults who practiced yoga on a weekly basis (Neumark-Sztainer, MacLehose, Watts, Pacanowski, & Eisenberg, 2018).

Consistent with the findings from our non-randomized trial of the exercise program delivered during residential eating disorders treatment (Calogero & Pedrotty, 2004b), one randomized controlled clinical trial found that incorporating individualized yoga as an adjunctive therapy in eating disorder outpatient treatment significantly reduced eating disorder pathology compared to a no yoga control group and did not interfere with weight gain/maintenance (Carei, Fyfe-Johnson, Breuner, & Brown, 2010). While one study did not find any significant post-intervention differences in eating disorder pathology among a yoga intervention group compared to a control group (Mitchell, Mazzeo, Rausch, & Cooke, 2007), it is important to note that this study investigated a brief yoga intervention among women largely new to yoga, whereas the studies that have demonstrated positive effects included participants familiar with yoga. However, none of these studies examined the effect of yoga on fostering attuned exercise and reducing dysfunctional exercise per se. Therefore, the effectiveness of yoga for cultivating attuned exercise cannot be inferred from these findings alone.

Although yoga may most closely exemplify the qualities of attuned exercise, the idea of cultivating AWE applies to all types of physical activity. The principles and techniques that characterize yoga (and mindful awareness more generally) could be—and we would argue should be—applied to any exercise activity (Calogero & Pedrotty, 2007). In so doing, we recognize that attuned exercise is influenced by historical, physical, environmental, emotional, social, cognitive, and cultural contexts; therefore, we must attend to all of these facets of embodiment in the cultivation of attuned exercise. Importantly, we should practice more attuned exercise to enhance the mind–body connection and coordination, alleviate mental and physical stress, and experience enjoyment, pleasure, and rejuvenation in and through our bodies (Calogero & Pedrotty-Stump, 2010, 2016; McGilley, 2014).

CONCLUSION

Attunement with exercise represents a key phenomenological shift in how people move and feel in their bodies. The concepts and findings reviewed here underscore the capacity for attuned exercise to cultivate embodiment, tuning in our internal needs and tuning out external concerns and anticipated outcomes. We use the term *exercise* intentionally, perhaps subversively, to reclaim exercise as an embodied practice at its core. Adopting mindful-based practices alongside the standard exercise approach keeps dysfunctional exercise practices rooted in place: The practice and process of exercise itself needs to change. Although the development of AWE was borne out of our work with women with eating disorders, dysfunctional exercise is not unique to this population, and the cultivation of AWE has the potential to benefit everyone.

REFERENCES

Ackard, D. M., Brehm, B. J., & Steffen, J. J. (2002). Exercise and eating disorders in college-aged women: Profiling excessive exercisers. *Eating Disorders, 10*, 31–47. doi:10.1080/106402602753573540

Calogero, R. M. (2011). Sensing the body: Why mindfulness practices help. In A. Lui & J. Banker (Eds.), *Restoring our bodies, reclaiming our lives: Guidance and reflections on recovery from eating disorders* (pp. 108–114). Boston, MA: Trumpeter Books.

Calogero, R. M. (2016, April). *Exercise and eating disorders: Cultivating an intuitive approach.* Paper presented at INSIDE Research Group, University of Luxembourg, Luxembourg City.

Calogero, R. M., Boroughs, M., & Thompson, J. K. (2007). The impact of Western beauty ideals on the lives of women and men: A sociocultural perspective. In V. Swami & A. Furnham (Eds.), *Body beautiful: Evolutionary and sociocultural perspectives* (pp. 259–298). New York: Palgrave Macmillan.

Calogero, R. M., & Mensinger, J. (2015, November). *Development and validity of the Experiential Exercise Scale: A new tool for measuring process vs. outcome-driven exercise.* Poster presented at the Renfrew Center Foundation Annual Conference, Philadelphia, PA.

Calogero, R. M., & Pedrotty, K. N. (2003, April). *Targeting exercise abuse in women with eating disorders: A test of an innovative treatment program.* Paper presented at the International Conference on Eating Disorders, Denver, CO.

Calogero, R. M., & Pedrotty, K. N. (2004a, April). *The practice and process of healthy exercise: Identifying and treating exercise issues in women with eating disorders.* Paper presented at the International Conference on Eating Disorders, Orlando, FL.

Calogero, R. M., & Pedrotty, K. N. (2004b). The practice and process of healthy exercise: An investigation of the treatment of exercise abuse in women with eating disorders. *Eating Disorders, 12*, 273–291. doi:10.1080/10640260490521352

Calogero, R. M., & Pedrotty, K. N. (2007). Daily practices for mindful exercise. In L. L'Abate, D. Embry, & M. Baggett (Eds.), *Handbook of low-cost preventive interventions for physical and mental health: Theory, research, and practice* (pp. 141–160). New York, NY: Springer-Verlag.

Calogero, R. M., Pedrotty, K. N., Menzel, J., Thompson, J. K., Wood, K., & Levine, M. P. (2010, June). *Mindful exercise: A new tool in health promotion and eating disorders prevention?* Paper presented at the International Conference on Eating Disorders, Salzburg, Austria.

Calogero, R. M., & Pedrotty-Stump, K. N. (2010). Incorporating exercise into the treatment and recovery of eating disorders: Cultivating a mindful approach. In M. Maine, D. Bunnell, & B. H. McGilley (Eds.), *Treatment of eating disorders: Bridging the research-practice gap* (pp. 425–441). New York, NY: Elsevier.

Calogero, R. M., & Pedrotty-Stump. K. N. (2016, May). Cultivating mindful exercise: Implications for eating disorders prevention and treatment. In T. L. Tylka & N. Piran (Chairs), *Using positive ways of inhabiting the body to facilitate eating disorder prevention and treatment*. Symposium presented at the International Conference on Eating Disorders, San Francisco, CA.

Calogero, R. M., Tylka, T. L., Hartman McGilley, B., & Pedrotty-Stump, K. N. (2018). *Attunement with Exercise (AWE): Scale development and validation*. Manuscript in preparation.

Calogero, R. M., Tylka, T. L., Mensinger, J. L., Meadows, A., & Daníelsdóttir, S. (2018). Recognizing fat as fundamental right: A weight-inclusive approach to size acceptance and healing from sizeism. *Women & Therapy*. doi:10.1080/02703149.2018.1524067

Calogero, R. M., Tylka, T. L., & Pedrotty-Stump, K. N. (2016). The role of attuned exercise in positive body image. A theoretical, empirical, and practical case. In E. Halliwell & D. Harcourt (Chairs), *Examining positive body image through development transitions, the experience of visible differences, and engaging in mindful exercise*. Symposium presented at Appearance Matters 7 Conference, London.

Carei, T. R., Fyfe-Johnson, A. L., Breuner, C. C., & Brown, M. A. (2010). Randomized controlled clinical trial of yoga in the treatment of eating disorders. *Journal of Adolescent Health, 46*, 346–351. doi:10.1016/j.adohealth.2009.08.007

Cook-Cottone, C., & Douglass, L. L. (2017). Yoga communities and eating disorders: Creating safe space for positive embodiment. *International Journal of Yoga Therapy*. Advance online publication. doi:10.17761/IJYT2017_Methods_Cook-Cottone

Corbin, C. B., LeMasurier, G., & Franks, B. D. (2002). Making sense of multiple physical activity recommendations. *President's Council on Physical Fitness and Sports Research Digest, 3*, 1–8.

Costin, C., & Kelly, J. (2016). *Yoga and eating disorders: Ancient healing for modern illness*. New York, NY: Taylor & Francis.

Dale, L. P., Mattison, A. M., Greening, K., Galen, G., Neace, W. P., & Matacin, M. L. (2009). Yoga workshop impacts psychological functioning and mood of women with self-reported history of eating disorders. *Eating Disorders, 17*, 422–434. doi:10.1080/10640260903210222

Daubenmier, J. J. (2005). The relationship of yoga, body awareness, and body responsiveness to self-objectification and disordered eating. *Psychology of Women Quarterly, 29*, 207–219. doi:10.1111/j.1471-6402.2005.00183.x

de la Torre, J. (1995). Mens sana in corpore sano, or exercise abuse? Clinical considerations. *Bulletin of the Menninger Clinic, 59*, 15–31.

Estabrooks, P. A., Lee, R., & Gyuresik, N. (2003). Resources for physical activity participation: Does availability and accessibility differ by neighborhood socioeconomic status? *Annals of Behavioral Medicine, 25*, 100–104. doi:10.1207/S15324796ABM2502_05

Homan, K. J., & Tylka, T. L. (2014). Appearance-based exercise motivation moderates the relationship between exercise frequency and positive body image. *Body Image, 11*, 101–108. doi:10.1016/j.bodyim.2014.01.003

McGilley, B. (2014, April 30). Intuitive exercise. *Eating Disorders Resource Catalogue.* https://www.edcatalogue.com/intuitive-exercise/

Mitchell, K. S., Mazzeo, S. E., Rausch, S. M., & Cooke, K. L. (2007). Innovative interventions for disordered eating: Evaluating dissonance-based and yoga interventions. *International Journal of Eating Disorders, 40,* 120–128. doi:10.1002/eat.20282

Mond, J. M., & Calogero, R. M. (2009). Excessive exercise in eating disorder patients and in healthy women. *Australian and New Zealand Journal of Psychiatry, 43,* 227–234. doi:1080/00048670802653323

Monnazzi, P., Leri, O., Guizzardi, L., Mattioli, D., & Patacchioli, F. R. (2002). Antistress effect of yoga-type breathing: Modification of salivary cortisol, heart rate and blood pressure following a step-climbing exercise. *Stress & Health, 18,* 195–200. doi:10.1002/smi.938

Neumark-Sztainer, D., MacLehose, R. F., Watts, A. W., Pacanowski, C. R., & Eisenberg, M. E. (2018). Yoga and body image: Findings from a large population-based study of young adults. *Body Image, 24,* 69–75. doi:10.1016/j.bodyim.2017.12.003

Pedrotty, K. N., & Calogero, R. M. (2002, November). *Healing the mental and physical body through exercise: Evaluation of a model for the treatment of eating disorders.* Paper presented at the Renfrew Center Foundation, Philadelphia.

Pedrotty, K. N., & Calogero, R. M. (2003, November). *Challenge the mindset, reduce the abuse: An approach for treating exercise issues in women with eating disorders.* Paper presented at the Renfrew Center Conference for Professionals, Philadelphia.

Pedrotty, K. N., & Calogero, R. M. (2009, November). *Treating exercise issues in eating disorder clients: A mindful approach.* Paper presented at the Renfrew Center Foundation Conference for Professionals, Philadelphia, PA.

Pedrotty, K. N., & Calogero, R. M. (2010, November). *Walking a fine line: Exercise and eating disorders.* Paper presented at the Renfrew Center Foundation Conference for Professionals, Philadelphia, PA.

Piran, N. (2016). Embodied possibilities and disruptions: The emergence of the Experience of Embodiment construct from qualitative studies with girls and women. *Body Image, 18,* 43–60. doi:10.1016/j.bodyim.2016.04.007

Piran, N. (2017). *Journeys of embodiment at the intersection of body and culture: The developmental theory of embodiment.* San Diego, CA: Academic Press. doi:10.1016/c2015-0-04666-4

Ressler, A., Kleinman, S., & Mott, E. (2010). The use of holistic methods to integrate the shattered self. In M. Maine, D. Bunnell, & B. H. McGilley (Eds.), *Treatment of eating disorders: Bridging the research-practice gap* (pp. 405–423). New York, NY: Elsevier.

Rich, E., & Evans, J. (2005). "Fat ethics"—The obesity discourse and body politics. *Social Theory & Health, 3,* 341–358. doi:10.1057/palgrave.sth.8700057

Robison, J. I. (2000, September/October). Do we really need to exercise and eat low fat to get into heaven? *Healthy Weight Journal,* pp. 74–75.

Schell, F. J., Allolio, B., & Schonecke, O. W. (1994). Physiological and psychological effects of Hatha-Yoga exercise in healthy women. *International Journal of Psychosomatics, 41,* 46–52.

Siegel, D. J. (2007). Mindfulness training and neural integration: Differentiation of distinct streams of awareness and the cultivation of well-being. *Social Cognitive and Affective Neuroscience, 2,* 259–263. doi:10.1093/scan/nsm034

Smith, A. R., Fink, E. L., Anestis, M. D., Ribeiro, J. D., Gordo, K. H., Davis, H., . . . Joiner, T. E. (2013). Exercise caution: Over-exercise is associated with suicidality among individuals with disordered eating. *Psychiatry Research, 206*, 246–255.

Tylka, T. L., Annunziato, R., Burgard, D., Danielsdottir, S., Shuman, E., Davis, C., & Calogero, R. M. (2014). The weight-inclusive vs. weight-normative approach to health: Evaluating the evidence for prioritizing well-being over weight. *Journal of Obesity*, 2014, Article ID 983495, http://dx.doi.org/10.1155/2014/983495

Wall, R. B. (2005). Tai chi and mindfulness-based stress reduction in a Boston public middle school. *Journal of Pediatric Health Care, 19*, 230–237. doi:10.1016/j.pedhc.2005.02.006

West, J., Otte, C., Geher, K., Johnson, J., & Mohr, D. C. (2004). Effects of Hatha yoga and African dance on perceived stress, affect, and salivary cortisol. *Annals of Behavioral Medicine, 28*, 114–118. doi:10.1207/s15324796abm2802_6

Wilson, D. K., Kirtland, K. A., Ainsworth, B. E., & Addy, C. L. (2004). Socioeconomic status and perceptions of access and safety for physical activity. *Annuals of Behavioral Medicine, 28*, 20–28. doi:10.1207/s15324796abm2801_4

9

Attuned Sexuality

SONYA SATINSKY AND VIRGINIA RAMSEYER WINTER ■

We define *attuned sexuality* as an ideal state where an individual's sexual self-concept and experiences encompass desired levels of sexual connection, desire, self-concept, functioning, and expression. Building on Piran's (2016) conceptualization of positive embodiment, attuned sexuality includes not only positive body image, but also positively constructed notions of sexual agency and function, access to one's sexual desires, use of protective strategies to protect and nurture one's body, and the ability to tune mindfully into bodily pleasures in sexual contexts (Figure 9.1). As such, attuned sexuality cannot be understood outside of the context of interpersonal relationships, desirability politics, and partner skill and attention to one's body and pleasure. Comparable to other aspects of positive embodiment, attuned sexuality as a construct is highly influenced by cultural context, power dynamics, and sociodemographics.

In this chapter, we assess the state of the literature on components of attuned sexuality, offering views across multiple disciplines and concluding with potential future directions for theorization and assessment of this construct and its utilization in applied settings. We begin by stating that the construct of attuned sexuality has not yet been comprehensively conceptualized or assessed in existing literature. Instead, we proffer that different components have been explored, with various degrees of evidence as well as attention paid to diverse populations. We enumerate these constructs and existing evidence in the discussion that follows: body image, both negatively and positively conceptualized and frequently studied in relationship to various protective and risky sexual behaviors and outcomes; sexual agency and function; access to sexual desires; and mindfulness of bodily pleasures related to sexuality. We argue that the exploration of the intersections of these aspects of embodiment have yet to be captured in quantitative social science literatures. Further exploration must also involve the lived experiences and perspectives of those not regularly included in these discussions: individuals with disabilities, fat people, individuals who are gender nonconforming and transgender, people

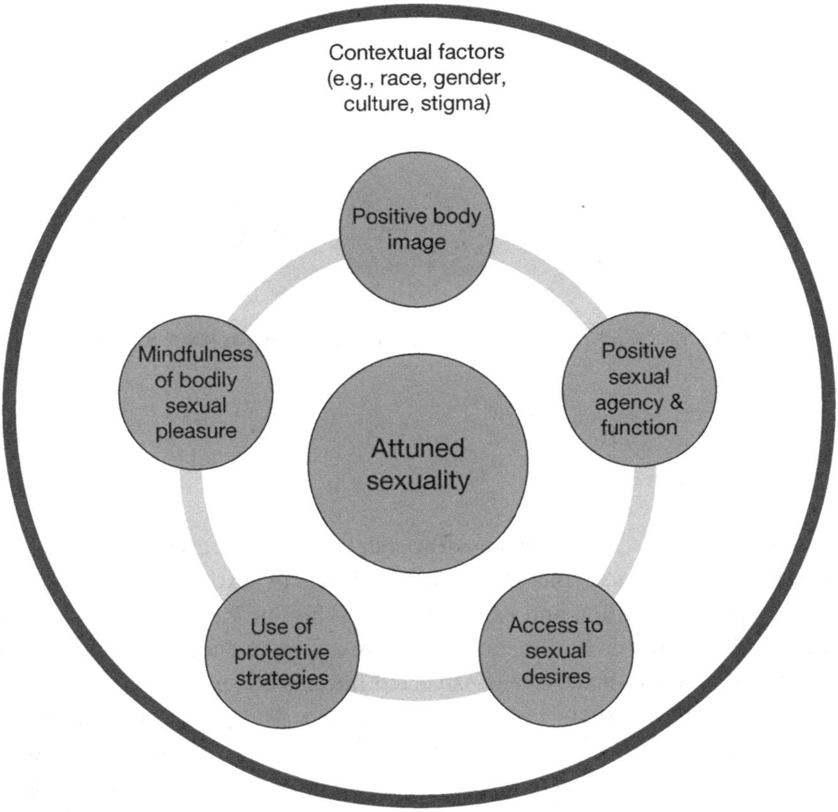

Figure 9.1 Attuned sexuality.

of color, populations who are of varying ages, and the multiple overlapping intersections of each of these identities.

NEGATIVE BODY IMAGE AND DISRUPTED SEXUAL ATTUNEMENT

The vast body of social scientific knowledge connecting body image to sexuality has focused on the negative side of these constructs and has principally focused on the sexual experiences of young, white, heterosexual, cisgender women (see Woertman & van den Brink, 2012). This literature links negative body image constructs with the following sexuality-related outcomes in women: (a) engagement in sexual behaviors that could increase women's risk for sexually transmitted/HIV infection or unintended pregnancy (e.g., Gillen, Lefkowitz, & Shearer, 2006); (b) lower levels of sexual desire and arousability (e.g., Sanchez & Kiefer, 2007); (c) less frequent sexual initiation or sexual avoidance (e.g., Cash, Maikkula, & Yamamiya, 2004); (d) decreased pleasure, orgasm, and sexual satisfaction (e.g., Quinn-Nilas, Benson, Milhausen, Buchholz, & Goncalves, 2016);

and (e) cognitive distraction or dissociation pulling attention away from the sexual encounter (e.g., Carvalheira, Price, & Neves, 2017).

Although the most robust findings are among cisgender women, some research has been conducted among sexual minority populations. Peplau et al. (2009) found that nearly half (42%) of the gay men in their study reported that their body image had a negative impact on their sex lives, while smaller proportions of lesbian women (27%) reported the same. Blashill et al. (2016) reported that body dissatisfaction predicted elevated sexual anxiety and lower sexual self-efficacy among the sexual minority men in their study. However, Meanley, Hickok, Johns, Pingel, and Bauermeister (2014) did not find a relationship between body dissatisfaction and unprotected sexual behavior.

OBJECTIFICATION THEORY

The primary explanatory theory for the connection between the various constructs measuring body image and sexuality is objectification theory (Fredrickson & Roberts, 1997). Objectification theory in its original conceptualization focused primarily on the experiences of cisgender women; it posits that the sociocultural contexts cisgender women live and interact within treat them primarily as bodies for surveillance or consumption by others. This objectification, which has been found to be frequent (Holland, Koval, Stratemeyer, Thomson, & Haslam, 2017), becomes internalized, which then leads to body surveillance (i.e., habitual body monitoring), subsequently resulting in decreased attention to internal body states such as physical pleasure and desire and increased body-based anxiety and shame. This decreased attunement is then proposed to be connected to sexual dysfunction, depression, and eating disorders. Indeed, research has supported the links from the objectification theory constructs of body surveillance, body shame, and appearance anxiety to sexuality and sexual health-related outcomes (e.g., lower sexual self-esteem, less sexual satisfaction, lower condom use self-efficacy, and lower perceived control over sexual activity; Calogero & Thompson, 2009; Claudat & Warren, 2014; Parent & Moradi, 2014; Robbins & Reissing, 2018b). Findings such as these emphasize the importance of attending to body image, appearance anxiety, and depression when working clinically with women reporting concerns with their sexual functioning (Vencill, Tebbe, & Garos, 2015). Incorporating body appreciation and the quality of the sexual relationship within the objectification theory framework, Ramseyer Winter (2017) found that this expanded model provided a more holistic view of attuned sexuality than originally theorized.

POSITIVE BODY IMAGE AND SEXUAL ATTUNEMENT

Recent years have seen an increase in research around body appreciation as an index of positive body image (Tylka & Wood-Barcalow, 2015). Body appreciation, in line with Piran's (2016) concept of the body as a comfortable "home," reflects holding favorable attitudes toward the body regardless of actual physical appearance, accepting the body in spite of perceived imperfections, respecting the body by attending to its needs and engaging in healthy behaviors, and protecting the body by rejecting unrealistic appearance ideals (Tylka & Wood-Barcalow, 2015; see also Chapter 2). Higher body appreciation is related to greater comfort communicating about sex (Ramseyer Winter, Gillen, & Kennedy, 2016); being more likely to utilize contraception (Ramseyer Winter & Ruhr, 2016); engaging in additional preventive sexual health behaviors (Ramseyer Winter, 2017); and having higher levels of sexual function (Robbins & Reissing, 2018a; Satinsky, Reece, Dennis, Sanders, & Bardzell, 2012), particularly in the realms of arousal, orgasm, and satisfaction (Satinsky et al., 2012). Though the salience of bodily experiences may be particularly high among gender-nonconforming and transgender individuals and communities, no research was uncovered that specifically spoke to the potential connections between body image, gender presentation, and sexual behavior or outcomes.

POSITIVE SEXUAL AGENCY, FUNCTION, AND DESIRE

Piran (2016, p. 49) described agency and functionality as "acting in and on the world with agency, both physically and through the power of voice." Sexual agency therefore can include not only proactively engaging in wanted and desired sexual experiences but also affirmatively and verbally consenting in partnered sexual situations (Satinsky & Jozkowski, 2015). In order to do so, given the social nature of bodies and sexuality, agency needs to take into account not only internal perceptions, feelings, and somatic responses, but also the dynamic social world in which these internal feelings are shaped (Peterson, 2010).

Sexual subjectivity, or the understanding of the self as a sexual being (Zimmer-Gembeck & French, 2016), may be a way of looking at the positive sexual agency component of attuned sexuality. Building on the qualitative work of Martin (1996) and Tolman (2002), the Female Sexual Subjectivity Inventory (Horne & Zimmer-Gembeck, 2006) and the Male Sexual Subjectivity Inventory (Zimmer-Gembeck & French, 2016) were developed. Sexual subjectivity, as measured in these scales, includes sexual body esteem; entitlement to sexual desire and pleasure (from self, from partner, and self-efficacy); and sexual self-reflection. Research using these scales has indicated that, compared to their male counterparts, young adult women report lower entitlement to self-sexual pleasure, lower self-efficacy in achieving sexual pleasure, and higher entitlement to sexual pleasure from a partner, whereas multiple aspects of general and sexual well-being were significantly associated with elements of sexual subjectivity among both men and women (Zimmer-Gembeck & French, 2016). Further, for women, higher sexual subjectivity was positively related to greater sexual experience (Zimmer-Gembeck, Ducat, & Boislard-Pepin, 2011), and higher entitlement to pleasure was linked to affirmative verbal consent to oral sex, as a function of increased self-efficacy in achieving sexual pleasure; therefore, a woman's belief that her partner will be responsive influences her ability to communicate what she is interested in sexually (Satinsky & Jozkowski, 2015). As both scales assume a gender binary for utilization, it is unclear how sexual subjectivity is conceptualized and what its correlates may be among individuals who are gender nonconforming, transgender, or nonbinary.

Tolman (2002) argued that "sexual subjectivity is a necessary component of [sexual] agency" (quoted in Tolman, 2012, p. 750) but is not necessarily sufficient for a fully fledged and developed agentic self. As multiple feminist theorists (Bay-Cheng, 2012; Lamb & Peterson, 2012; Peterson & Lamb, 2012; Tolman, 2012) argued in an issue of *Sex Roles* devoted to conceptualizing sexual empowerment and agency among young women, true agency requires not only exploration of individualized and internalized feelings as measured by sexual subjectivity but also an understanding and deconstruction of the dynamic social forces, such as sexism, racism, and objectification, that undermine the development of an attuned sexual self that is able to act in and on the social world.

Conceptualizations of individual and collective empowerment, sexual subjectivity, and sexual agency all have implications for an individual's ability to consent to interpersonal sexual experiences, ask for protection in the form of condoms, and express sexual desire. Feminist philosopher Elizabeth Grosz (1994) posited, "It is only the sensory, perceiving object, the corporeal subject, who is capable of initiating sexual desire, responding to and proliferating desire" (p. 109). Therefore, experiencing embodied sexual agency may be an essential correlate to exploring fully embodied access to sexual desires. Sexual desire is conceptually complex and has been explicated in some depth in other arenas (see Brotto & Smith, 2014). Unfortunately, desire is largely absent in the discourse of young women's sexuality (Tolman, 2012). In fact, Tolman argues that embodied desire often presents as a dilemma for adolescent girls, which is problematic as developing desire is an ongoing process through adulthood (see also Piran, 2017).

In addition to being aware of one's desires, one must be able to communicate these to sexual partner(s). Higher levels of body appreciation have been associated with more comfort communicating about sex among young women (Ramseyer Winter et al., 2016), but this has only been explored in one study and does not address communication about desire specifically. As such, desire continues to be underrepresented in this discourse.

MINDFULNESS OF BODILY SEXUAL PLEASURE

Mindful attention to bodily sexual pleasure can be disrupted by body surveillance and shame (e.g., Sanchez & Kiefer, 2007). Cognitive distraction, or the inability to concentrate on the sexual experience due to worrying about or monitoring appearance, has been extensively documented in the literature among primarily cisgender women (e.g., Meana & Nunnink, 2006).

Sexual and relationship therapists have long promoted "sensate focus" as a tool within sex therapy (Weiner & Avery-Clark, 2014). Masters and Johnson found that those who focused on tactile sensations, who focused on their own experiences rather than their partner's, and who redirected their attention back to sensations when they became distracted moved more easily throughout the sexual response cycle (Weiner & Avery-Clark, 2014).

Subsequently, clinicians and researchers have moved beyond the specific mode of sensate focus to promote mindfulness more broadly within sexual contexts (e.g., Brotto & Goldmeier, 2015). Researchers have found positive relationships between mindfulness and various aspects of sexual functioning both among college women (Fink, Foran, Sweeney, & O'Hea, 2009) and mixed-gender samples (Dunkley, Goldsmith, & Gorzalka, 2015). Interventions promoting the use of mindfulness strategies have thus emerged as an antidote to disruptions in mindful sexual experiences, although these interventions have been conducted only with groups of cisgender women. Specifically, Brotto, Basson, and Luria (2008) conducted three-session mindfulness groups with women with problems with desire/interest disorders or sexual arousal disorders; their initial findings underscored the need for longer mindfulness training. Subsequent studies have found significant improvements in female sexual function using an 8-week model (Paterson, Handy, & Brotto, 2017). Similarly, Silverstein, Brown, Roth, and Britton (2011) found that college women who received meditation training in a 12-week course more quickly registered their physiological responses to sexual stimuli, an outcome congruent with mindful attention to bodily sexual pleasure. Thus, mindfulness practices may offer an intervention method to counter self-objectification and cognitive distraction, but need further study with diverse groups.

CONCLUSION: IMPLICATIONS FOR SEXUALITY EDUCATION, INTERVENTION, AND FUTURE RESEARCH

Given that the overarching multicomponent construct of attuned sexuality is newly conceptualized, there are significant steps and various areas of exploration for those who would like to extend the current research landscape. We detail some in the material that follows.

Sexuality Education

The various components comprising attuned sexuality (Figure 9.1) should be incorporated into sexuality education from a young age. This could include, for example, the discourse around puberty and menstruation. Discussing menstruation as a natural process, as opposed to a scary, disgusting event (Roberts, 2004), could lead to girls who are more attuned to their bodily changes through puberty and may ultimately have an impact on their sexual decision-making (Schooler, Ward, Merriwether, & Caruthers, 2005). Adopting an attuned sexuality framework for formal sexuality education could be reflected in the National Sexuality Education Standards (Future of Sex Education Initiative, 2012).

Qualitative and Quantitative Comprehensive Assessment

Each component that comprises attuned sexuality is complex and nuanced. At the time this chapter was written, there were no social scientific assessments of all of the constituent parts of attuned sexuality. Using attuned sexuality as a comprehensive framework for both qualitative and quantitative research and practice may yield more robust findings about the interconnections of the construct's elements among diverse populations (gender, age, ethnicity).

Additional Populations

It is notable that the intersection of body image with sexuality is underexplored among heterosexual cisgender men. Though it is assumed that in a culture of sexual objectification women would be more likely to have negative experiences of their bodies, which subsequently impacts their sexuality and vice versa in dynamic ways, heterosexually identified men do not escape cultures of objectification (Parent & Moradi, 2011). More important still, the ways in which the social pressure to be objectifiers might impact men is undertheorized. In the few studies conducted with heterosexual men, as in women, body satisfaction is reciprocal with sexual satisfaction and sexual self-caretaking (Schooler & Ward, 2006), and higher levels of sexual satisfaction were connected to higher levels of body satisfaction in the context of partnered relationships (Goins, Markey, & Gillen, 2012).

As with much social science research, the voices and experiences of various groups are underrepresented: gender-nonconforming and transgender individuals; Latinx, black, Asian, and biracial individuals; fat and higher weight individuals; those living with disabilities; and so on. Given that the experiences of those within these categories may vary just as much as those across categories, it behooves researchers to be explicit about working with these communities in both clinical and research capacities to understand how living within cultures that support racism, sizeism, transphobia, and so on contributes to the dynamics of attuned sexuality/disrupted attunement.

Temporality and Fluidity

Given the contextual nature of positive and negative body image (Cash, Fleming, Alindogan, Steadman, & Whitehead, 2002), as well as the social construction of attuned sexual bodies (Tolman, Bowman, & Fahs, 2014), attuned sexuality should be studied across sexual contexts and partners, as well as at the trait level. This attention to temporality and fluidity may require more complex research designs and attention to event-level data collection.

Expanding the Lens

Attuned sexuality is an ideal state; given that we do not live in an ideal world, we should expect that there will always be room for positive movement toward achieving a truly attuned experience and sense of a sexual self. However, the onus for this improvement does not solely lie on those who experience deficiencies in one or more attunement elements. Instead, we as clinicians and researchers should continue to train our eyes on culture-level messages, such as those that increase objectification or that interfere with an attuned and embodied sexuality (Satinsky & Jozkowski, 2015). Individual-level interventions may have implications for those individuals involved, but do not impact a larger culture that moves us away from an agentic and embodied sexuality.

REFERENCES

Bay-Cheng, L. Y. (2012). Recovering empowerment: De-personalizing and re-politicizing adolescent female sexuality. *Sex Roles, 66*, 713–717. doi:10.1007/s11199-011-0070-x

Blashill, A. J., Tomassilli, J., Biello, K., O'Cleirigh, C., Safren, S. A., & Mayer, K. H. (2016). Body dissatisfaction among sexual minority men: Psychological and sexual health outcomes. *Archives of Sexual Behavior, 45*, 1241–1247. doi:10.1007/s10508-015-0683-1

Brotto, L. A., Basson, R., & Luria, M. (2008). A mindfulness-based group psychoeducational intervention targeting sexual arousal disorder in women. *Journal of Sexual Medicine, 5*, 1646–1659. doi:10.1111/j.1743-6109.2008.00850.x

Brotto, L. A., & Goldmeier, D. (2015). Mindfulness interventions for treating sexual dysfunctions: The gentle science of finding focus in a multitask world. *Journal of Sexual Medicine, 12*, 1687–1689. doi:10.1111/jsm.12941

Brotto, L. A., & Smith, K. B. (2014). Sexual desire and pleasure. In D. L. Tolman & L. M. Diamond (Eds.), *APA handbook of sexuality and psychology, Vol. 1, person-based approaches* (pp. 205–244). Washington, DC: American Psychological Association.

Calogero, R. M., & Thompson, J. K. (2009). Sexual self-esteem in American and British college women: Relations with self-objectification and eating problems. *Sex Roles, 60*, 160–173. doi:10.1007/s11199-008-9517-0

Carvalheira, A., Price, C., & Neves, C. F. (2017). Body awareness and bodily dissociation among those with and without sexual difficulties: Differentiation using the Scale of Body Connection. *Journal of Sex and Marital Therapy, 43*, 801–810. doi:10.1080/0092623.X.2017.1299823

Cash, T. F., Fleming, E. C., Alindogan, J., Steadman, L., & Whitehead, A. (2002). Beyond body image as a trait: The development and validation of the Body Image States Scale. *Eating Disorders, 10*, 103–113. doi:10.1080/10640260290081678

Cash, T. F., Maikkula, C. L., & Yamamiya, Y. (2004). "Baring the body in the bedroom": Body image, sexual self-schemas, and sexual functioning among college women and men. *Electronic Journal of Human Sexuality, 7*, 1–9.

Claudat, K., & Warren, C. S. (2014). Self-objectification, body self-consciousness during sexual activities, and sexual satisfaction in college women. *Body Image, 11*, 509–515. doi:10.1016/j.bodyim.2014.07.006

Dunkley, C. R., Goldsmith, K. M., & Gorzalka, B. B. (2015). The potential role of mindfulness in protecting against sexual insecurities. *Canadian Journal of Human Sexuality, 24*, 92–103.

Fink, S., Foran, K. A., Sweeney, A. C., & O'Hea, E. L. (2009). Sexual body esteem and mindfulness in college women. *Body Image, 6*, 326–329. doi:10.1016/bodyim.2009.07.003

Fredrickson, B. L., & Roberts, T. A. (1997). Objectification theory: Towards understanding women's lived experiences and mental health risks. *Psychology of Women Quarterly, 21*, 173–206. doi:10.1111/j.1471-6402.1997.tb00108.x

Future of Sex Education Initiative. (2012). National Sexuality Education Standards: Core content and skills, K–12 [a special publication of the *Journal of School Health*]. Retrieved from http://www.futureofsexed.org/documents/josh-fose-standards-web.pdf

Gillen, M. M., Lefkowitz, E. S., & Shearer, C. L. (2006). Does body image play a role in risky sexual behavior and attitudes? *Journal of Youth and Adolescence, 35*, 243–255. doi:10.1007/s10964-005-9005-6

Goins, L. B., Markey, C. N., & Gillen, M. M. (2012). Understanding men's body image in the context of their romantic relationships. *American Journal of Men's Health, 6*, 240–248. doi:10.1177/1557988311431007

Grosz, E. A. (1994). *Volatile bodies: Toward a corporeal feminism*. Bloomington: Indiana University Press.

Holland, E., Koval, P., Stratemeyer, M., Thomson, F., & Haslam, N. (2017). Sexual objectification in women's daily lives: A smartphone ecological momentary assessment study. *British Journal of Social Psychology, 56*, 314–333. doi:10.1111/bjso.12152

Horne, S., & Zimmer-Gembeck, M. J. (2006). The Female Sexual Subjectivity Inventory: Development and validation of a multidimensional inventory for late adolescents and emerging adults. *Psychology of Women Quarterly, 30*, 125–138. doi:10.1111/j.1471-6402.2006.00276.x

Lamb, S., & Peterson, Z. D. (2012). Adolescent girls' sexual empowerment: Two feminists explore the concept. *Sex Roles, 66*, 703–712. doi:10.1007/s11199-011-9995-3

Martin, K. A. (1996). *Puberty, sexuality, and the self: Girls and boys at adolescence.* New York, NY: Routledge.

Meana, M., & Nunnink, S. E. (2006). Gender differences in the content of cognitive distraction during sex. *Journal of Sex Research, 43*, 59–67. doi:10.1080/00224490609552299

Meanley, S., Hickok, A., Johns, M. M., Pingel, E. S., & Bauermeister, J. A. (2014). Body mass index, body esteem, and unprotected receptive anal intercourse among young men who have sex with men who seek partners online. *Archives of Sexual Behavior, 43*, 735–744. doi:10.1007/s10508-013-0159-0

Parent, M. C., & Moradi, B. (2011). His biceps become him: A test of objectification theory's application to drive for muscularity and propensity for steroid use in college men. *Journal of Counseling Psychology, 58*, 246–256. doi:10.1037/a0021398

Parent, M. C., & Moradi, B. (2014). Self-objectification and condom use self-efficacy in women university students. *Archives of Sexual Behavior, 44*, 971–981. doi:10.1007/s10508-014-0384-1

Paterson, L. Q. P., Handy, A. B., & Brotto, L. A. (2017). A pilot study of eight-session mindfulness-based cognitive therapy adapted for women's sexual interest/arousal disorder. *Journal of Sex Research, 54*, 850–861. doi:10.1080/00224499.2016.1208800

Peplau, L. A., Frederick, D. A., Yee, C., Maisel, N., Lever, J., & Ghavami, N. (2009). Body image satisfaction in heterosexual, gay, and lesbian adults. *Archives of Sexual Behavior, 38*, 713–725. doi:10.1007/s10508-008-9378-1

Peterson, Z. D. (2010). What is sexual empowerment? A multidimensional and process-oriented approach to adolescent girls' sexual empowerment. *Sex Roles, 62*, 307–313. doi:10.1007/s11199-009-9725-2

Peterson, Z. D., & Lamb, S. (2012). The political context for personal empowerment: Continuing the conversation. *Sex Roles, 66*, 758–763. doi:10.1007/s11199-012-0150-6

Piran, N. (2016). Embodied possibilities and disruptions: The emergence of the Experience of Embodiment construct from qualitative studies with girls and women. *Body Image, 18*, 43–60. doi:10.1016/j.bodyim.2016.04.007

Piran, N. (2017). *Journeys of embodiment at the intersection of body and culture: The developmental theory of embodiment.* San Diego, CA: Elsevier. doi:10.1016/c2015-0-04666-4

Quinn-Nilas, C., Benson, L., Milhausen, R. R., Buchholz, A. C., & Goncalves, M. (2016). The relationship between body image and domains of sexual functioning among heterosexual, emerging adult women. *Journal of Sexual Medicine, 4*, e182–e189. doi:10.1016/j.esxm.2016.02.004

Ramseyer Winter, V. (2017). Toward a relational understanding of objectification, body image, and preventive sexual health. *Journal of Sex Research, 54*, 341–350. doi:10.1080/00224499.2016.1190807

Ramseyer Winter, V., Gillen, M. M., & Kennedy, A. K. (2016). Associations between body appreciation and comfort communicating about sex: A brief report. *Health Communication, 33*, 359–362. doi:10.1080/10410236.2016.1255845

Ramseyer Winter, V., & Ruhr, L. R. (2016). Body appreciation and contraceptive use among college women: A brief report. *International Journal of Sexual Health, 29*, 168–172. doi:10.1080/19317611.2016.1259707

Robbins, A. R., & Reissing, E. D. (2018a). Appearance dissatisfaction, body appreciation, and sexual health in women across adulthood. *Archives of Sexual Behavior, 47*, 703–714.

Robbins, A.-R., & Reissing, E. D. (2018b). Out of "objectification limelight"? The contribution of body appreciation to sexual adjustment in midlife women. *Journal of Sex Research, 55*, 758–771. doi:10.1080/00224499.2017.1372352

Roberts, T. A. (2004). Female trouble: The menstrual self-evaluation scale and women's self-objectification. *Psychology of Women Quarterly, 28*, 22–26. doi:10.1111/j.1471-6402.2004.00119.x

Sanchez, D., & Kiefer, A. (2007). Body concerns in and out of the bedroom: Implications for sexual pleasure and problems. *Archives of Sexual Behavior, 36*, 808–820. doi:10.1007/s10508-007.9205-0

Satinsky, S., & Jozkowski, K. N. (2015). Female sexual subjectivity and verbal consent to receiving oral sex. *Journal of Sex and Marital Therapy, 41*, 413–426. doi:10.1080/0092623x.2014.918065

Satinsky, S., Reece, M., Dennis, B., Sanders, S., & Bardzell, S. (2012). An assessment of body appreciation and its relationship to sexual function in women. *Body Image, 9*, 137–144. doi:10.1016/j.bodyim.2011.09.007

Schooler, D., & Ward, L. M. (2006). Average Joes: Men's relationships with media, real bodies, and sexuality. *Psychology of Men & Masculinity, 7*, 27–41. doi:10.1037/1524-9220.7.1.27

Schooler, D., Ward, L., Merriwether, A., & Caruthers, A. (2005). Cycles of shame: Menstrual shame, body shame, and sexual decision-making. *Journal of Sex Research, 42*, 324–334. doi:10.1080/00224490509552288

Silverstein, R. G., Brown, A.-C. H., Roth, H. D., & Britton, W. B. (2011). Effects of mindfulness training on body awareness to sexual stimuli: Implications for female sexual dysfunction. *Psychosomatic Medicine, 73*, 817–825. doi:10.1097/psy.0b013e318234e628

Tolman, D. L. (2002). *Dilemmas of desire: Teenage girls talk about sexuality*. Cambridge, MA: Harvard University Press.

Tolman, D. L. (2012). Female adolescents, sexual empowerment and desire: A missing discourse of gender inequity. *Sex Roles, 66*, 746–757. doi:10.1007/s11199-012-0122-x

Tolman, D. L., Bowman, C. P., & Fahs, B. (2014). *Sexuality and embodiment*. In D. L. Tolman & L. M. Diamond (Eds.), *APA handbook of sexuality and psychology, Vol. 1, person-based approaches* (pp. 759–784). Washington, DC: American Psychological Association.

Tylka, T. L., & Wood-Barcalow, N. L. (2015). The Body Appreciation Scale: Item refinement and psychometric evaluation. *Body Image, 12*, 53–67. doi:10.1016/j.bodyim.2014.09.006

Vencill, J. A., Tebbe, E. A., & Garos, S. (2015). It's not the size of the boat or the motion of the ocean: The role of self-objectification, appearance anxiety, and depression in female sexual functioning. *Psychology of Women Quarterly, 39*, 471–483. doi:10.1177/0361684315587703

Weiner, L., & Avery-Clark, C. (2014). Sensate focus: Clarifying the Masters and Johnson's model. *Sexual and Relationship Therapy, 29*, 307–319. doi:10.1080/14681994.2014.892920

Woertman, L., & van den Brink, F. (2012). Body image and female sexual functioning and behavior: A review. *Journal of Sex Research, 49*, 184–211. doi:10.1080/00224499.2012.658586

Zimmer-Gembeck, M. J., Ducat, W. H., & Boislard-Pepin, M. A. (2011). A prospective study of young females' sexual subjectivity: Associations with age, sexual behavior, and dating. *Archives of Sexual Behavior, 40*, 927–938. doi:10.1007/s10508-011-9751-3

Zimmer-Gembeck, M. J., & French, J. (2016). Associations of sexual subjectivity with global and sexual well-being: A new measure for young males and comparison to females. *Archives of Sexual Behavior, 45*, 315–327. doi:10.1007/s10508-014-0387-y

SECTION II

Cultivating Positive Body Image and Embodiment

Protective Relational, Social, and Other Environmental Factors

10

The Developmental Theory of Embodiment

Protective Social Factors that Enhance Positive Embodiment

NIVA PIRAN ■

> Within a period of 5 years or so (ages 8–13), associated with puberty, the social environment of girls changes such that they become acculturated to inhabit their bodies with diminished agency, disrupted connection to desire, reduced self-attunement, and greater self-objectification. These compounded losses undermine girls' ability to act in the world with power.
>
> —Piran, 2017a, p. 261

This excerpt from a book about the developmental theory of embodiment (DTE) highlights the focus of this theory on social factors that shape the quality of girls' and women's embodied lives and on the production of "docile," disempowered bodies. Indeed, the meeting place of body and culture has been identified as a problematic intersection for girls and women of diverse backgrounds (e.g., Conboy, Medina, & Stanbury, 1997). A theory that examines the social forces that discipline the bodies of diverse girls and women may be particularly important at a time when prevalent ideologies that purport to espouse equity contrast with challenging realities in the embodied lives of diverse girls and women (Bordo, 1989). Such a theory may have an even greater impact if it includes protective social factors that can guide constructive social transformations.

All conceptualizations of health/illness, etiological theories, and related research methodology are couched within particular domains of knowledge, values, and ideologies. The chapter, therefore, starts by situating the DTE in relation to the topics of embodiment, risk and protective factors, and research methodology. It then continues with a description of the theory and its implications to practice and ends with ideas about future research.

THE DEVELOPMENTAL THEORY OF EMBODIMENT: BACKGROUND INFORMATION

The DTE aims to predict the quality of embodied lives. The focus on embodiment, defined by Merleau-Ponty (1962) as the "perceptual experience of engagement of the body in the world" (Allan, 2005, p. 175), denotes the body as a center of subjectivity and, concurrently, a site that performs and shapes culturally informed practices (Piran, 2016b; see Chapter 1). The phenomenological field of embodiment therefore rejects dualistic divisions, such as body–mind, body–culture, or inner–outer. Further, the societal "hold" on individuals' bodies has been a major focus of scholarly writings on embodiment, in particular Foucault's (1995) description of the role that individuals' self-surveillance of their own compliance with social expectations has in maintaining societal structures of power. Couching a theory, such as the DTE, within the embodiment frame therefore inherently involves a socially critical perspective and an allegiance with the goals of social justice.

The focus on social structures of power and their shaping of individuals' ways of inhabiting their bodies aligns as well with the multilevel model of causality central to public health perspectives (e.g., McKinlay & Marceau, 1999). According to this model, at the highest level are risk and protective factors that relate to social structures and position, such as gender, social class, age, and ethnicity/race. In turn, these factors shape all lower level risk and protective factors associated with environmental influences (e.g., neighborhoods, schools), lifestyle choices (e.g., nutrition, exercise), and intraindividual (e.g., personality) factors. As McKinlay and Marceau described, "Risk factors and risky behaviors are obviously manifested in individuals, but they are generated and reinforced within an ecosocial context and they are strongly related to social position" (p. 297). For these reasons, these authors proposed that low-level risk factors might actually be *epiphenomena* of higher level factors. The DTE aims to examine gender and other dimensions of social location as "lived" experiences, shaping multiple layers of the social environment, and not merely as "demographic" variables (Piran, 2010).

Yet, inquiries about social experiences should also include a search for protective factors alongside risk factors. Seligman and Csikszentmihalyi (2000) stressed the role of a science of positive psychology in illuminating the factors that allow individuals, communities, and societies to flourish. To date, research in the area of body image development has focused on risk factors (Piran, McVey, & Levine, 2014). The DTE has aimed to address both protective and risk factors.

Embodiment captures a breadth of experiences (e.g., Conboy et al., 1997). One area of interest within the domain of embodiment relates to girls' and women's *quality of embodied lives*. For example, Bordo (1989) problematized the "conviction of lack, insufficiency, of never being good enough. At the farthest extremes, the practices of femininity may lead us to utter demoralization, debilitation, and death" (Bordo, 1989, p. 14). Bartky (1988), similarly highlighted difficulties in "feminine" embodiment, in particular women moving in the public sphere while restricting the use of physical space and their self-objectification. Impett, Schooler, and Tolman (2006) similarly stated that "femininity includes dissociating from one's body, that is losing awareness of one's own desires and hungers" (p. 133). Piran and Teall (2012) highlighted the importance of examining the shared state of disrupted embodiment that underlies different behavioral expressions, such as disordered eating, self-harm, or sexual involvement without desire or negotiating for protection.

The quality of embodied lives is at the heart of the DTE in that the theory aims to predict the breadth of embodied experiences, all the way from positive to negative embodiment. The first phase of the research program on embodiment involved a large-scale, mixed-method research program that led to the emergence of the multidimensional Experience of Embodiment construct, which reflects girls' and women's quality of embodied lives (Piran, 2016b; see Chapter 1). The five dimensions of the Experience of Embodiment construct include body connection and comfort, agency and functionality, experience and expression of desire, attuned self-care, and inhabiting the body as a subjective site (resisting objectification). Negative body image and disordered eating patterns are aspects of a negative Experience of Embodiment.

The mixed-method research program that led to the emergence of the DTE involved multiple studies (see Piran & Teall, 2012). Guiding principles across all studies involved a critical lens toward the social experiences of girls and women, the value placed on participants' voicing of experiences and reflections, and the use of quantitative measures that are anchored in girls' and women's narratives. The final stage in developing the DTE included three qualitative studies involving 171 interviews with 69 girls and younger and older women in three different studies about their experiences of living in their bodies and the social experiences associated with these experiences. These qualitative studies included a 5-year prospective study with girls, ages 9–14 during the first interview, and life history studies with younger and older women. The emergent theoretical structures have been operationalized into quantitative scales in order to provide cross-method cross validation of the DTE in three quantitative studies. Overall, the DTE is based on four qualitative studies, of which one followed a prospective design, and six quantitative cross-sectional studies.

THE DEVELOPMENTAL THEORY OF EMBODIMENT: KEY PROTECTIVE FACTORS

The DTE examines the relationship between social processes and girls' and women's embodied experiences. Anchored in the narratives of girls and younger

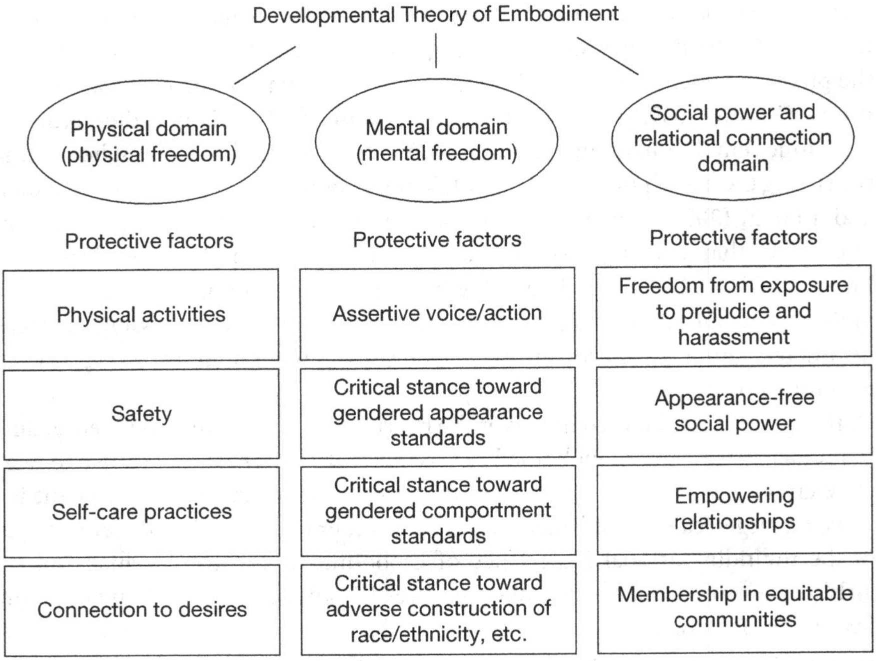

Figure 10.1 An illustration of the developmental theory of embodiment (Piran, 2017a) protective dimension (risk dimension is not portrayed). Adapted from Piran (2015). Reprinted with permission from Elsevier Publishing © 2015.

and older women and tested using cross-sectional quantitative designs, it provides a critical look at social structures and mores. Such a critical look at the social environment can guide social transformations, as well as health promotion and therapy interventions.

According to the DTE, social experiences shape girls' and women's quality of embodied lives via three core pathways: the *physical* domain, the *mental* domain of social discourses and expectations, and the *social power and relational connections* domain. Each of these domains includes protective (and risk) factors: physical freedom (vs. corseting), mental freedom (vs. corseting also), and social power and relational connections (vs. disempowerment and disconnection). This chapter focuses on protective factors in each of the three domains (Figure 10.1) that enhance positive embodiment, defined as "positive body connection and comfort, embodied agency and passion, and attuned self-care" (Piran, 2016b, p. 47).

Physical Domain

Physical experiences are powerful in shaping embodiment. Detailed age-related research (Piran, 2017a) clarified that, at puberty in particular, physical freedom becomes compromised. However, girls who are supported in holding on to their physical freedom during adolescence are more likely to describe positive embodiment throughout their adult journeys. Importantly, we find that recapturing physical freedom can take place at any time, even during older adulthood (Piran, 2002, 2016a).

Protective Factors in the Physical Domain

Four categories of protective factors fall under the physical freedom domain (Piran, 2002, 2017a; Piran & Teall, 2012; Figure 10.1).

Freedom in Physical Engagement and Movement

The freedom in physical engagement and movement category includes engagement in immersed and joyful physical activities. In order to enhance positive embodiment, these activities should be nonobjectifying, nonsexualizing, and nonappearance or weight related. In contrast, activities that are motivated by a discourse of body deficiency often remain dominated by this discourse. This category also includes the freedom to move freely in the private and public spheres (including nature sites), as well as the freedom to take physical space in the world through unrestricted movement and actual physical size. These experiences enhance a positive and joyful connection to the body as well as physical agency and functionality.

Safety for the Body Territory

Physical safety keeps the body a site of respectful ownership, positive connection and emotions, agency, and attunement. This category includes safety from bodily violations, which may range from unwanted sexual attention to sexual coercion, rape, and other physical violations. Violations to the body territory disrupt connection to the body and prompt a host of negative emotions. Violations also compromise experiences of desires, body attunement, and agency. Even common sexual harassment is not benign and, like all forms of violations, communicates to girls and women their disenfranchised position in the world. This category also includes safety from coercive body alterations and practices with which girls and women of diverse backgrounds are expected to comply.

Care of the Body

This category includes exposure to social experiences that teach, support, and model attuned self-care of the body. Such social experiences encourage connection to the body as a worthy site and enhance responding to its desires and attunement to its needs.

Freedom of Desire

The category of freedom of desire includes experiences that validate desire and encourage attuned, assertive, and joyful responses to appetite and sexual desire. Such experiences enhance body connection, embodied agency, and attunement to bodily needs.

Enhancing Physical Freedom Toward Positive Embodiment

In line with the DTE, positive embodiment could be facilitated through social transformations and interventions that aim at enhancing physical freedom, in particular: engagement in joyful physical activities, safety from violations and forced compliance with body alterations, opportunities and role modeling in practicing attuned self-care, and support for pleasurable and attuned expressions of desire (for a detailed discussion, see Piran, 2017a). These changes involve major social and organizational transformations, as the corseting of physical freedom is an expression of gender (and other) inequity and a way to maintain an oppressive social status quo. For example, increasing girls' joyful engagement in physical activities would require a major shift in the allocation of resources to girls' and women's sports (e.g., funds, physical sites, representation of women in leadership positions in sports organizations) at all levels of competitiveness (from Olympic competitions to recreational) and at all levels of the social environment (from sports organizations to families). Policies and norms regarding girls' clothing and sport uniforms need to change (e.g., compare uniforms for men and women in beach volleyball). Norms related to the masculinization of sports need to shift in the media as well as in schools and among peers. Similarly, enhancing girls' and women's safety from sexual violations involves multiple systemic changes around the world, involving the law, policies, and norms, as well as public education, consciousness raising, and activism (see, e.g., Buchwald, Fletcher, & Roth, 1993).

Toward health promotion, it is important to address challenges to self-attunement among girls and women because the social environment tends be primarily attuned to the needs of privileged members of society. For example, the pervasive social expectations that girls and women take care of others while silencing their own needs and the inequity in carrying out domestic chores need to be countered. Parents have an important role in supporting girls' attunement to their bodies and needs as they go through puberty and encounter pressures regarding appearance and sexual activities. It is so helpful for girls to have significant women who role model embodying self-attunement (Piran, 2017a). Health promotion activities such as yoga that enhance self-attunement can be helpful (see Chapter 28).

A positive connection to bodily desires is another important protective factor. Positive connection to appetite and eating is learned within the family (see Chapters 7 and 22) and advocated by organizations such as Health at Every Size® (see Chapter 27). It is important that adults in girls' lives support their positive connection to appetite throughout puberty and beyond and counter social pressures that disrupt such healthy connection (Piran, 2017a; see Chapter 7). Connection to sexual desire also enhances positive embodiment. Considering the multiple societal influences that disrupt connection to sexual desire (Impett et al., 2006; Piran, 2017a; see also Chapter 12), supportive and validating relational connections and forums are needed to provide girls and women with opportunities to examine their own sexual desires, the spectrum of desired sexual activities, as well as sexual boundaries and rights (see Chapter 9).

Mental Domain

Mental freedom relates to "engaging with the world meaningfully and passionately, as well as holding a critical stance towards, and experiencing freedom from, constraining social discourses that regulate embodied lives of individuals of different social locations" (Piran, 2017a, p. 21). In line with this view, social discourses that aim to maintain the social status quo act as mental corsets, encouraging compliance with constraining socially constructed molds related to one's social location. Consequently, they limit individuals' possibilities of engaging fully with the world and restricting agency and self-attunement. Girls and women of diverse locations who are supported and validated in maintaining an assertive voice and a resistant and critical stance toward oppressive discourses act in the world with embodied agency, positive connection, and self-attunement.

Protective Factors in the Mental Domain

According to the DTE, mental freedom involves a general assertiveness/resistance factor, as well as specific resistant factors that counter different oppressive social discourses.

A General Resistant Factor

Hierarchical social structures validate the voices, worldviews, and lived knowledge of socially privileged individuals, while silencing the voices and knowledge of the disenfranchised (e.g., Freire, 1993). Maintaining one's voice while holding a less privileged position involves important mental freedom to act in the world with embodied agency. Girls and women who hold on to their assertive voice often describe having been supported in holding views that are different from people around them or in acting in line with what they believe in and are passionate about (Piran, 2016b, 2017a).

Resistance to the Gender-Based, Appearance-Related Discourse Cluster "Body as a Deficient Object"

A critical stance toward the gender-based, appearance-related discourse cluster "body as a deficient object" involves resisting both self-objectification and viewing one's body as inherently deficient—common experiences for women within a patriarchal world (Piran, 2017a). A critical perspective toward this discourse cluster allows for engaging with embodied agency in the world, rather than focusing on forced body alterations motivated by shame, as 15-year-old Jessica, a white girl from a working class background, described: "It's good to know you have people who don't think that you should change everything about you. . . . Cause if you're changing everything about yourself, it's probably hard to be happy cause you've got really nothing to work with" (Piran, 2017a, pp. 166–167).

Resistance to the Gender-Based, Comportment-Related Discourse Cluster "Woman as Docile"

A critical stance toward the gender-based, comportment-related discourse cluster "woman as docile" involves resistance to acting demure, nice, or submissive; being other-attuned; curtailing engagement in passionate and "nonfeminine" activities (such as sports); being a sexual object without owning desire with agency; or prioritizing sexualized relationships with men over other relational connections. A critical perspective toward this discourse cluster allows for engaging with embodied agency and passion in the world, as Jane, a white woman in her 20s from a working class background described: "I was always fairly aggressive-assertive. . . . It has a fairly negative connotation in society for women but we should get rid of that. You can get so much further in life having your opinion heard" (Piran, 2017a, p. 228).

Resistance to Ethnicity-/Race-Based Discourse Cluster

Participants in our studies from African-Canadian, Caribbean-Canadian, and Aboriginal Heritages, referred to encountering demeaning social discourses that presented them as primitive, animalistic, scary, or hyper-sexual. The African American sociologist Patricia Hill Collins (2000) coined the term *controlling images* to refer to images developed by dominant groups to suppress subordinate group members' hopes, actions, and possibilities. Maintaining a critical stance toward such constructions supports embodied well-being, as Claire, a woman in her 20s from a Caribbean Canadian heritage and a working class background, described the development of her critical stance and related academic project at the intersection of gender and race: "There is a privilege of gaze. . . . It is masculine, patriarchal, and ethnic. . . . I am doing this project . . . so I could work through all these norms and wanting to know how it has taken a toll as you get older" (Piran, 2017a, p. 225).

Enhancing Mental Freedom Toward Positive Embodiment

Mental freedom from oppressive social constructions enhances embodied agency in the world. Explicating and naming oppressive discourses is the first step in countering them. Different processes can help in explicating and resisting oppressive discourses. The articulation of costs associated with compliance with oppressive discourses can introduce a shift in girls' and women's embodied awareness, as Kyra, a 12-year-old white girl, described: "I need to be perfect for him! But I am sick and tired of trying to be perfect" (Piran, 2017a, p. 109). A second process that can raise resistant awareness is the critical understanding of the way in which oppressive discourses maintain relational and societal power inequities, as described by Ashley, 16-year-old girl from an African Canadian heritage, regarding the "slutty" presentation of black women in music videos: "Music videos are unbelievably sexist. . . . And it's hurting African American women as well as guys. Calling girls sluts, it's just keeping the word out there" (Piran, 2017a, p. 163).

Different relational forums can help foster critical awareness about adverse social constructions. In critical group discussions, negative constructions and labels can shift from an individual source of distress to an external social issue that needs to be resisted. Catherine MacKinnon (1989, p. 101) described this process as consciousness raising that "socializes women's knowing. It produces an analysis of woman's world which is . . . collective and critical." A shared group stance opposing oppressive social stereotypes is a powerful tool against negative internalizations. School-based programs, such as media literacy (see Chapter 32) and cognitive dissonance programs (see Chapter 30), have been effective in reducing the internalization of the thin ideal discourse. The media need to take a greater role in countering, rather than transmitting, oppressive stereotypes.

Social Power and Relational Connections Domain

Girls' and women's experiences of social power and relational connections to others relate to their experiences of embodiment.

Protective Factors in the Social Power and Relational Connections Domain

Four categories of protective factors fall under the social power and relational connections domain (Piran, 2002, 2017a; Piran & Teall, 2012; Figure 10.1).

Freedom from Prejudice and Harassment

The category of freedom from prejudice and harassment relates to the body as a site of social capital influenced by intersecting dimensions of social privilege and disenfranchisement (Bourdieu, 1984). Inhabiting privileged bodies involves access to valued resources (e.g., education, employment, chosen social connections) as well as freedom from body-based harassment, both experiences that are associated with embodied well-being. However, girls and women, and more so girls and women whose social location is less privileged related to their race, ethnicity, immigration, health, or other factors, commonly experience body-based prejudice and harassment (e.g., Bucchianeri, Eisenberg, Wall, Piran, & Neumark-Sztainer, 2014).

Freedom from Appearance-Based Social Power

Having access to sources of social power that are unrelated to appearance frees girls and women to act in the world powerfully, passionately, and with self-attunement. Relying on appearance for social power diverts the allocation of personal resources to body alterations, perpetuates the demoted status of women as objects of gaze, and, at the same time, keeps one's hold on power tenuous because idealized appearance is concurrently unachievable and demeaned (Piran, 2017a).

Empowering Relationships

Empowering relational connections provide essential validation of a girl's or a woman's worth, wishes, meaningful pursuits, critical reflections about her social environment, and encouragement in the pursuit of social justice. Validation through these connections encourages acting in the world with embodied agency. It is particularly powerful when the individual(s) providing such empowerment shares dimensions of social location with the girl or woman (e.g., gender, race/

ethnicity, sexual orientation) and provides a source of pride and strength in one's social location.

Membership in Equitable Communities

The DTE emphasizes the value of being part of, and accepted by, at least one social system where equity is practiced along different dimensions of social location, such as gender, ability, or ethnic/racial heritage. While equity is central to the experience of embodied worth, experiences of inequity are detrimental to embodied well-being.

Enhancing Social Power and Relational Connections Toward Positive Embodiment

There are multiple pathways to enhancing social power and relational connections, all the way from large-scale systemic changes to changes in the immediate social environment and in individuals' resistant stance toward experiences of inequity and disconnection. Regarding the freedom from body-based prejudicial treatment and harassment, systemic interventions that enhance equitable access to resources, such as free and accessible sites of physical activities or educational opportunities, are important. Conscious-raising interventions among gatekeepers of social resources regarding the adverse impact of prejudicial ideologies are needed; for example, guidance counselors in schools may steer girls away from the sciences and math. Consciousness-raising programs about the body as a receptacle of societal prejudices, supplemented by implemented and well-advertised policies, can help curtail body-based harassment.

The reliance on appearance as a source of social power is taught early in girls' lives and is reinforced within patriarchal systems. Families and other social systems should not associate social power with specific appearance characteristics, but rather enhance individuals' engagement in meaningful pursuits and unique contributions. We find that students are keen to discuss issues of appearance, body, and social power, including the fickle nature of appearance-based social power (Piran, 2001, 2017a). Further, school-based prevention programs that emphasize activism and empowerment have been associated with higher body esteem (see Chapters 21 and 31).

Empowering relationships are very important to embodied well-being, including close familial relationships, mentors at school and in the community, and even other, less immediate, role models with whom individuals share important dimensions of social location. Maximizing such opportunities in the life of youth can contribute to their embodied well-being. In a similar vein, one cannot overemphasize the value of being an equitable member in relational communities. Families are one such setting; parents can be invited to examine the differential treatment of gender at home or of other sources of inequity, such as weight or skin color. Membership in social groups, school clubs, or community-based organizations that can offer such experience heightens embodied well-being. School-based programs that aim at establishing norms of equity and social justice can similarly contribute to providing students with a school environment where students living in diverse bodies can flourish (Piran, 2001, 2017a).

CONCLUSION AND FUTURE DIRECTIONS

The DTE is an integrated social theory that aims to predict, through the delineation of both protective and risk factors, the quality of embodied lives among girls and women across the life span. The research-based theory, anchored in girls' and women's narratives and a number of quantitative studies, addresses a broader spectrum of protective and risk factors than have been included to date in social models aimed at explaining the development of negative body esteem or disordered eating patterns. While we have used quantitative research designs, such as structural equation modeling (e.g., Piran & Thompson, 2008) to test the theory with existing measures, we also developed quantitative measures to assess each of the proposed protective and risk factors (Piran, 2017b). Using these measures, we found that they all correlated with measures of body esteem and embodiment at the moderate or strong levels (Piran, 2017b), and that, together, in multiple regressions, they explained about 56% of the variance on a measure of embodiment (Teall & Piran, 2015). While a qualitative prospective study has informed the development of the theory, the DTE needs to be further tested utilizing quantitative longitudinal designs. Further, based on an early participatory action project with girls and boys (Piran, 2001) and on clinical work, we hypothesize that boys' and men's embodiment is also shaped by physical experiences (e.g., physical activities, safety), constraining gender and other molds, and embodied social power. However, this hypothesis needs to be studied as well. Overall, as an integrated social theory of embodiment, the DTE illuminates the complex relationships between social structures and individuals' embodied experiences. This deepened understanding has implications for a range of health promotion interventions and for therapy.

REFERENCES

Allan, H. T. (2005). Gender and embodiment in nursing: The role of the female chaperone in the infertility clinic. *Nursing Inquiry, 12*, 175–183. doi:10.1111/j.1440-1800.2005.00275.x

Bartky, S. L. (1988). Foucault, femininity and the modernization of patriarchal power. In I. Diamond & L. Quinby (Eds.), *Feminism and Foucault: Reflections on resistance* (pp. 61–86). Boston, MA: Northeastern University.

Bordo, S. (1989). The body and the reproduction of femininity: A feminist appropriation of Foucault. In A. M. Jaggar & S. R. Bordo (Eds.) *Gender/body/knowledge* (pp. 13–33). New Brunswick, NJ: Rutgers University Press.

Bourdieu, P. (1984). *Distinction: A social critique of the judgment of taste*. Cambridge, MA: Harvard University Press.

Bucchianeri, M. M., Eisenberg, M. E., Wall, M. M., Piran, N., & Neumark-Sztainer, D. (2014). Multiple types of harassment: Associations with emotional well-being and unhealthy behaviors in adolescents. *Journal of Adolescent Health, 54*, 724–729. doi:10.1016/j.jadohealth.2013.10.205

Buchwald, E., Fletcher, P. R., & Roth, M. (1993). *Transforming a rape culture.* Minneapolis, MN: Milkweed Editions.

Conboy, K., Medina, N., & Stanbury, S. (1997). *Female embodiment and feminist theory.* New York, NY: Columbia University Press.

Foucault, M. (1995). *Discipline and punish: The birth of the prison* (2nd ed.). New York, NY: Vintage.

Freire, P. (1993). *Pedagogy of the oppressed.* New York, NY: Continuum.

Hill Collins, P. (2000). *Black feminist thought: Knowledge, consciousness, and the politics of empowerment* (2nd ed.). New York, NY: Routledge.

Impett, E. A., Schooler, D., & Tolman, D. L. (2006). To be seen and not heard: Femininity ideology and adolescent girls' sexual health. *Archives of Sexual Behavior, 35*, 129–142. doi:10.1007/s10508-005-9016-0

MacKinnon, C. A. (1989). *Towards a feminist theory of the state.* Cambridge, MA: Harvard University Press.

McKinlay, J. B., & Marceau, L. D. (1999). A tale of 3 tails. *American Journal of Public Health, 89*, 295–298. doi:10.2105/AJPH.89.3.295

Merleau-Ponty, M. (1962). *Phenomenology of perception.* New York, NY: Humanities Press.

Piran, N. (2001). Re-inhabiting the body from the inside out: Girls transform their school environment. In D. L. Tolman & M. Brydon-Miller (Eds.), *From subjects to subjectivities: A handbook of interpretive and participatory methods* (pp. 218–238). New York: New York University Press.

Piran, N. (2002). Embodiment: A mosaic of inquiries in the area of body weight and shape preoccupation. In S. Abbey (Ed.), *Ways of knowing in and through the body: Diverse perspectives on embodiment* (pp. 211–214). Welland, ON, Canada: Soleil.

Piran, N. (2010). A feminist perspective on risk factor research and on the prevention of eating disorders. *Eating Disorders, 18*, 183–198. doi:10.1080/10640261003719435

Piran, N. (2015). New possibilities in the prevention of eating disorders: The introduction of positive body image measures. *Body Image, 14*, 146–157. doi:10.1016/j.bodyim.2015.03.008

Piran, N. (2016a). Embodied paths in aging: Body journeys towards enhanced agency and self-attunement. *Women & Therapy, 39*, 186–201. doi:10.1080/02703149.2016.1116853

Piran, N. (2016b). Embodied possibilities and disruptions: The emergence of the Experience of Embodiment construct from qualitative studies with girls and women. *Body Image, 18*, 43–60. doi:10.1016/j.bodyim.2016.04.007

Piran, N. (2017a). *Journeys of embodiment at the intersection of body and culture: The developmental theory of embodiment.* San Diego, CA: Elsevier. doi: 10.1016/c2015-0-04666-4

Piran, N. (2017b, August). *Protective factors that enhance positive embodiment: A mixed-method inquiry.* Paper presented at the American Psychological Association Annual Convention, Washington, DC.

Piran, N., McVey, G. L., & Levine, M. P. (2014). Eating disorders in adolescence. In T. P. Gullotta & M. Bloom (Eds.), *The encyclopedia of primary prevention and health promotion* (2nd ed., Vol. 3, pp. 1134–1147). New York, NY: Springer.

Piran, N., & Teall, T. L. (2012). The developmental theory of embodiment. In G. McVey, M. P. Levine, N. Piran, & H. B. Ferguson (Eds.), *Preventing eating-related and weight-related disorders: Collaborative research, advocacy, and policy change* (pp. 171–199). Waterloo, ON, Canada: Wilfred Laurier Press.

Piran, N., & Thompson, S. (2008). A study of the adverse social experiences model to the development of eating disorders. *International Journal of Health Promotion and Education, 46*, 65–71. doi:10.1080/14635240.2008.10708131

Seligman, M. E. P., & Csikszentmihalyi, M. (2000). Positive psychology: An introduction. *American Psychologist, 55*, 5–14. doi:10.1037//0003-066X.55.1.5

Teall, T., & Piran, N. (2015, August). *Embodiment scales for women: A psychometric study of the Experience of Embodiment Scale.* Poster presented at the American Psychological Association Annual Convention, Toronto.

11

Environments that Cultivate Positive Embodiment Through Mindful Movement

CHRISTY GREENLEAF AND CAITLYN HAUFF ■

Our bodies are meant to move as a means of enjoyment and utility; yet, the hyperfocus on healthism, competitive outcomes, and appearance has driven an externalized and detached relationship with our bodies and movement. Rather than moving for feelings of joy, connection, contemplation, autonomy, and empowerment, we are taught to exercise for a specific number of minutes at a prescribed intensity and duration regardless of the experience and to train our bodies to outperform and outshine others. Moreover, the prescribed nature of movement so prevalent in fitness, public health, and sport places a central focus on the body as an object to be maintained, improved, treated, and competed. At the same time, there is great potential to reenvision and re-create spaces (e.g., physical, social, digital) to promote and facilitate mindful physical movement that supports positive embodiment.

Embodiment, as conceptualized by Piran (2016), is a meaningful experience and consequence of physical activity, exercise, and sport engagement. In this chapter, we reflect on and advocate for the power and possibility of embodiment through mindful movement. Specifically, we consider the ways in which both traditional exercise and sport environments, such as athletic departments and fitness facilities, as well as nontraditional environments, including green and mind–body spaces, can support and facilitate mindful movement experiences. Finally, we explore social and online media spaces as opportunities for cultivating embodiment via physical activity. These physical, social, and digital environments, in which we live and move, are powerful conduits for embodiment and mindful movement.

PROMOTING EMBODIED EXPERIENCES IN TRADITIONAL ATHLETIC AND EXERCISE ENVIRONMENTS

Traditional sport and exercise spaces, such as athletic departments, fitness centers, weight rooms, and swimming pools, often focus on the body as an outcome or product of movement. Sports, for example, emphasize competitive outcomes (i.e., winning), sometimes at all/any costs, along with athlete conformity and compliance to coach instructions and directions (Connor, 2009). Fitness environments commonly emphasize and capitalize on improved appearance/attractiveness via weight or fat loss and increased musculature (Dworkin & Wachs, 2009) and place the body on display. Nonetheless, traditional movement spaces can provide individuals with many opportunities for developing and practicing embodiment via autonomy, resilience, intuitive body awareness, and self-respect and care.

Competitive Sport Environments

Competitive sport provides the opportunity for athletes to be empowered in the pursuit of achievement; to appreciate the functionality, power, and performance of their bodies; to see value in body diversity; and to find joy in the physical movement of their bodies (Lunde & Holmqvist Gattario, 2017). Indeed, sport participation is associated with positive body image (e.g., Greenleaf, Boyer, & Petrie, 2009); instrumentality (Greenleaf et al., 2009; Parsons & Betz, 2001); and other positive psychological characteristics related to embodiment (Eime, Young, Harvey, Charity, & Payne, 2013). Body functionality is certainly of value within the sport environment via required fitness, skill, and performance; to be effective in promoting and supporting embodying experiences within such environments, purposeful and planned steps can be taken to prioritize function over appearance, value body diversity and self-care, and encourage mindfulness.

Sport environments, even those that emphasize aesthetics or utilize weight classes, can provide embodying spaces and experiences. For example, providing athletes with practice and performance attire options that vary in the degree to which physique is revealed can contribute to feelings of autonomy and could reduce feelings of objectification associated with revealing attire (Greenleaf, 2002; Steinfeldt, Zakrajsek, Bodey, Middendorf, & Martin, 2013). Athletes indicate that sport offers great opportunity for varied body shapes and sizes because of multiple demands of different sports and positions, yet find it frustrating when coaches give preference to less skilled athletes with preferred body shapes over more skilled athletes with less preferred physiques (Coppola, Ward, & Freysinger, 2014; Lunde & Holmqvist Gattario, 2017). There is a missed opportunity to endorse body diversity when coaches overlook performance for appearance; awareness of this and action to avoid it can be a powerful endorsement of the value of function and skill over appearance. Athletes in weight class sports (e.g., wrestling, powerlifting, etc.) can be appropriately placed in weight classes that allow for healthful eating and exercise behaviors, thereby prioritizing the value of self-care and body respect. These types of actions within traditional sport environments require strong and purposeful leadership.

Sport leaders play an important role in creating spaces that promote embodiment. Coaches influence many aspects of athletes' sense of self, including body image and satisfaction, competence and autonomy, and resilience (e.g., Appleton & Duda, 2016; Muscat & Long, 2008; White & Bennie, 2015). Coach comments about athletes' weight, body shape, and eating behaviors, as well as coaches' own exercise and eating behaviors, contribute to the extent to which sporting spaces support embodiment and mindful movement (e.g., Coppola et al., 2014). When coaches focus on process, experience, and health, rather than outcome and weight, body awareness and respect are supported and valued. Coaches and administrators can take action to cultivate embodying experiences. For example, they can do this by creating and implementing policies for athletes to be weighed only by sports medicine personnel and only for medical/health reasons; avoiding participation in fat talk and body shaming; giving athletes a voice by purposefully including them in team discussions and decision-making; and providing safe psychological and social spaces in which athletes can seek support. These types of sport leader actions create caring climates (see Fry & Gano-Overway, 2010) that can contribute to empowering experiences within sport.

Mindfulness training, along with meditation, is growing in popularity within sport domains as practices to improve athletic performance, reduce stress and anxiety, and enhance life satisfaction, well-being, and flow (e.g., Kaufman, Glass, & Arnkoff, 2009). Flow is an intrinsically rewarding state during which one feels that their skills are sufficient to successfully meet the challenges at hand; the individual is completely absorbed in an activity with clear focus and a sense of control and is self-aware without feeling self-conscious (Jackson & Csikszentmihalyi, 1999). Facilitating flow and mindfulness in sport is a realistic and attainable strategy for creating embodying experiences in traditional sport spaces. Athletic department leadership can provide system-level endorsement of embodiment and mindfulness among coaches, athletes, administrative staff, and sports medicine staff by providing mindfulness education and training, along with role modeling self-awareness and respect, resilience, and empowering others.

Exercise and Fitness Environments

Traditional exercise and fitness spaces, such as community recreation centers and commercial gyms, can also facilitate embodiment via mindful movement. The physical and social environments within such spaces typically recognize and reward an ultralean physique that is unrealistic and unattainable for most people (Frew & McGillivray, 2005) and is often achieved via unhealthy body management practices, such as restrictive eating and excessive exercise (Goodwin, Haycraft, & Meyer, 2014; Jeffers & Benotsch, 2014). However, exercise and fitness spaces can also promote self-care, body respect, instrumentality, and resilience.

Physical spaces can be created or modified so that exercising bodies of all shapes, sizes, and skill levels are respected, rather than objectified. Mirrors can be removed or limited and equipment arranged so that there are places to exercise where one's body is not on display. Equipment can be spaced appropriately to allow for comfortable and accessible movement between equipment as well as ease getting on and off equipment, thus creating spaces that value body diversity (Pickett & Cunningham, 2017). Advertising, imagery, and marketing within exercise and fitness spaces can reinforce concepts of embodiment by representing health not as a "look" or particular physique, but as actions that align with self-care, body awareness, and intrinsic motivation. For example, exercise and fitness spaces can promote inclusivity by avoiding the promotion of unrealistic body ideals and expectations and depicting people with a variety of physiques as competent and fit in their advertising.

The social climate within physical exercise and fitness spaces can also play an important role in cultivating embodying and mindful movement. Like athletic coaches, fitness leaders and personal trainers are powerful in their influence and can impact how exercisers experience the space (Brown & Fry, 2011). Focusing on function, strength, and personal improvement, along with helping exercisers develop body awareness and respect to avoid injury, can facilitate exercisers' enjoyment and feelings of competence (Brown & Fry, 2011). Leaders and trainers can provide educational information so that exercisers are knowledgeable and gain feelings of autonomy. Moreover, mindfulness can be integrated into traditional aspects of exercise and fitness routines by having exercisers use a nonjudgmental approach to identify exercise intensity, self-awareness for body alignment during activity, and meditative breathing during cool-down exercises (La Forge, 2016).

This approach to mindful exercise is similar to the concept of intuitive exercise (Reel, Galli, Miyairi, Voelker, & Greenleaf, 2016), which involves an internally regulated approach to exercise. An individual engaged in intuitive exercise uses a flexible approach to exercise (i.e., duration, type of exercise, intensity), relying on how the body feels rather than external cues, such as time or energy expenditure. Exercise and fitness environments can promote intuitive exercise by providing and encouraging multiple modes of activity (Sylvester et al., 2014) and educating personal trainers to teach clients how to listen to their bodies' internal cues of energy or fatigue. Using an intuitive exercise and mindful movement approach within exercise and fitness environments may challenge dominant practices (e.g., adhering to physical activity guidelines); however, the potential benefits to psychological and physical health are great.

INNOVATIVE AND CREATIVE MOVEMENT SPACES

The spaces in which people move are varied and include unique environments, such as functional fitness facilities and green spaces, as well as creative environments, including Zumba, belly dancing, and yoga studies. These movement environments are innovative spaces that provide opportunities for individuals to move and experience their bodies in a way they might not in more traditional forms of sport and exercise. Whether an individual connects to their experience and body by feeling the rhythm of the music or lifting heavy weight, these nontraditional spaces offer outlets for positive embodiment experiences.

Dance

Dance has served as a form of self-expression for thousands of years (Hill, Sandford, & Enright, 2016) and is associated with a number of positive body outcomes, including body appreciation and intuitive eating (Moe, 2012; Tiggemann, Coutts, & Clark, 2014). Dance, in its varied forms and styles, has the capability of producing physical and psychological empowerment (Moe, 2012). Tiggemann and colleagues (2014) proposed that belly dancing, for example, is a style of dance that encompasses the major elements of positive embodiment. Belly dancing requires an individual to be physically skilled, flexible, strong, and in tune with breathing and movements of specific muscles. It elicits a mind–body experience allowing dancers to reconnect with their bodies and experience a new appreciation for their body's uniqueness and beauty (Moe, 2012). While many think of belly dancing as an objectifying experience due to its seemingly sexual nature, belly dancing has a positive relationship with body appreciation and reduced feelings of self-objectification through the focus on the internal experiences of the body (Moe, 2012; Tiggemann et al., 2014). Belly dancers report finding their experiences fun and empowering (Moe, 2012; Tiggemann et al., 2014).

Zumba can also promote embodying exercise experiences. It incorporates a variety of dance styles (i.e., hip hop, ballet, jazz, etc.) and has grown to incorporate fitness elements such as squats, kicks, and punches. Zumba is popular because of the upbeat and energized music and instructors and the emphasis on fun and personal exploration, versus technique and perfect execution of movement. Women explain that Zumba allows them to appreciate their body movements and provides a safe space for expressing themselves (Nieri & Hughes, 2016). Individuals participating in Zumba are instructed to move in a way that is comfortable and are encouraged add their own flair to the routine. Zumba can provide a low-pressure environment that allows for individuality, independence, self-expression, exploration, and expansion of skill and capability and connection with others.

The mindful approaches to body movement promoted by Zumba and belly dancing could be expanded to other dance disciplines, particularly those that traditionally have emphasized an ultrathin ideal. For instance, by allowing individuals to choose their own music or to create movement sequences, dance becomes a place for self-expression and connection. Additionally, by helping individuals focus on the strength and power of the body elicited by dance, as opposed to fitting into an aesthetically pleasing ideal, dance environments can promote an appreciation for the functionality of the body. Dance leaders, including company owners, directors, and instructors, directly shape the cultural climate of their studios and the experiences of dancers. Steps that can be taken to create dance environments that support embodiment include employing instructors with high skill and varied body shapes and sizes, training staff on self-care and injury prevention, and implementing policies to discourage body shaming.

Yoga

Yoga, another form of movement that produces a powerful mind–body experience, focuses on stretching, flexibility, balancing, and awareness of breath (Mahlo & Tiggemann, 2016). La Forge (2016) discussed yoga in terms of stimulating muscle sense or the ability to create a powerful cognitive and kinesthetic experience through nonjudgmental internal mental focus on the self. It cultivates a space of mindfulness, as participants are challenged to remain in tune with their bodies in an accepting and nonjudgmental manner. The awareness of both physical and mental states fosters a deep mind–body connection, promotes appreciation of functionality and capabilities, and fosters positive body image (Mahlo & Tiggemann, 2016). Compared to individuals who do not practice yoga, individuals who practice yoga report lower levels of self-objectification and higher levels of embodiment (Mahlo & Tiggemann, 2016).

Yoga serves as an embodying activity because it encourages those who practice to focus on internal states (i.e., body as a process) as opposed to an outsider's perspective (i.e., body as an object). Because instructors encourage participants to engage and respond to their bodies, participants are able to block out external factors, such as mirrors and physique-revealing clothing, that often are distractions and barriers to positive exercise experiences in more traditional environments (Mahlo & Tiggemann, 2016). The focus on posture, breath, and being present allows individuals to turn inward and connect with their body and breath. Additionally, honoring one's self is often at the center of yoga practice, thus promoting value in self-care and respect, which are essential characteristics of embodying experiences.

Functional Fitness

Functional fitness environments might not initially be thought of as spaces in which individuals have embodying experiences, yet there are many ways in which such environments can promote instrumentality, personal achievement, resilience, and social support. Functional fitness typically involves a mixture of high-intensity interval training, plyometrics, Olympic weightlifting, powerlifting, and gymnastics and has been criticized because of concerns regarding participant injury rates and the social environment, which some have considered cult-like (e.g., Dawson, 2017). While functional fitness programs do have some critics, these programs focus on strength and conditioning and provide a shared workout routine that participants modify to match their skill level.

Functional fitness facilities can promote embodiment by ensuring that fitness leaders/instructors are knowledgeable about safe exercise progressions and communicate that information to participants. Such environments can be positive, as they provide opportunity for individuals to strive to surpass their own performance standards, while being motivated and supported by other members to push beyond their previous limits (Dawson, 2017). The focus on body functionality at the center of most functional fitness programs clearly highlights the value of personal capability (Alleva, Martijn, Van Breukelen, Jansen, & Karos, 2015) and the body as a process rather than an outcome or object (Mulgrew & Tiggemann, 2018). Thus, individuals engaging in functional fitness programs may have embodying experiences as they become familiar with and expand the capabilities of their bodies. Such environments can cultivate embodiment by valuing and embracing participants of varying body shapes and sizes, educating participants on how to appropriately modify activities and work through safe progressions, and providing supportive social environments that encourage self-care and resilience.

Green Exercise

Green exercise refers to activity that takes place in nature (e.g., in a local park, nature trail, or river walkway; Barton & Pretty, 2010; Gladwell, Brown, Wood, Sandercock, & Barton, 2013). Exercising in green spaces is associated with enhanced body esteem and mood (Barton & Pretty, 2010), as well as mindfulness and psychological well-being (Swami, Barron, Weis, & Furnham, 2016). Green exercise is also thought to increase enjoyment of activity, as individuals can escape from everyday realities and distractions of life and focus on their internal emotions and cognitions (Gladwell et al., 2013; Swami et al., 2016). This, in a sense, stimulates a deeper mind–body connection that might not be experienced in a fitness center environment where distractions are present. For example, green spaces can prompt individuals to disconnect from technology and focus intentionally on the activity. Green spaces provide opportunities for individuals to connect with nature in a way that promotes a shift in focus from self-interest (i.e., appearance) to a better understanding of how they fit into and can contribute to something beyond themselves (Gladwell et al., 2013; Swami et al., 2016). Indeed, when strong connections with nature are formed, individuals tend to report higher levels of happiness and greater life satisfaction (Gladwell et al., 2013). Thus, green spaces provide ideal environments in which people can connect with nature and themselves free from distraction and social comparison.

SOCIAL MEDIA SPACES

Social media platforms, such as Facebook, Pinterest, and Snapchat, are commonly used to construct public fitness, exercise, and athletic personas. Both traditional and nontraditional exercisers, athletes, and dancers craft posts and display photos of themselves engaging in a variety of activities (Gonzales & Hancock, 2011; Hauff, 2016a, 2016b) that can serve to demonstrate competence and seek feedback (Perloff, 2014). Moreover, social media provides an environment for like-minded individuals to group together, interact, and share and affirm their experiences (Toma & Hancock, 2013). Additionally, social media is a tool for gaining information about exercises and activities for varied body shapes and sizes (Hauff, 2016b).

Being part of a community of similar others allows one to feel connected and comfortable (Teodoro & Naaman, 2013). While "likes" and comments have the capability of boosting self-confidence, a lack of acknowledgment for successes (in terms of likes) can just as easily deflate confidence and self-esteem. Social media users can promote embodying movement experiences by engaging in supportive behaviors, such as leaving positive commentary for others, providing motivational quotes that focus on process rather than outcome, and promoting body appreciation messages. It is also important to provide support for self-care, such as taking time off because of injury or illness. Social media are commonly used to promote successes, but by talking about struggles and challenges, users might better connect with others who have experienced similar challenges and build solidarity in body appreciation and respect.

Recently, social media communities have launched body-positive campaigns that promote body acceptance and encourage embodied movement for people of all body shapes and sizes. These body-positive advocates use social media as a tool to spread their message of body acceptance to diverse audiences. For example, Taryn Brumfitt, the founder of the Body Image Movement, has shared her story of body loathing to body loving through her book and documentary, *Embrace*. Additionally, Twitter users have found themselves utilizing the hashtags #honoryourcurves, #effyourbeautystandards, #healthateverysize, and #loveyourbody (to name a few) in order to spread a message of body positivity across the web. Many individuals have also turned to blogs as a means to share positive embodiment with others. Ragen Chastain, a fat activist, runs a successful blog called "Dances with Fat." Her tagline is "Life, Liberty, and the Pursuit of Happiness Are Not Size Dependent." Messages from such advocacy platforms create online communities that celebrate the capabilities and experiences of individuals regardless of size. Moreover, these types of social media campaigns clearly promote the right of people of all shapes and sizes to fully embrace moving their bodies, not in pursuit of weight loss, but in pursuit of joy, expression, freedom, creativity, accomplishment, stress relief, and the like.

CONCLUSION

It is imperative that we continue to find ways to facilitate and create embodying exercise experiences that promote mindful movement, a connection to the self, and a feeling of self-worth and self-satisfaction within traditional and nontraditional movement spaces, as well as within social and digital media spaces. As research in this area continues to evolve, La Forge (2016) recommended incorporating mind–body philosophies into movement practices in order to create embodying experiences; for example, focusing on the process to remain present; being aware of body, mind, and breath; and embracing and enjoying creative movement. Physical, social, and digital spaces can promote these philosophies when leaders take an intentional approach to creating spaces and programs that encourage and facilitate embodying movement experiences. The ultimate goal is for people to feel comfortable in their own bodies, confident in their ability to take on and accomplish their goals, secure in the value of caring for themselves, and empowered to live active lives.

REFERENCES

Alleva, J., Martijn, C., Van Breukelen, G., Jansen, A., & Karos, K. (2015). Expand Your Horizon: A programme that improves body image and reduces self-objectification by training women to focus on body functionality. *Body Image, 15*, 81–89. doi:10.1016/j.bodyim.2015.07.001

Appleton, P. R., & Duda, J. L. (2016). Examining the interactive effects of coach-created empowering and disempowering climate dimensions on athletes' health and functioning. *Psychology of Sport and Exercise, 26*, 61–70. doi:10.1016/j.psychsport.2016.06.007

Barton, J., & Pretty, J. (2010). What is the best dose of nature and green exercise for improving mental health? A multi-study analysis. *Environmental Science and Technology, 44*, 3947–3955. doi:10.1021/es903183r

Brown, T. C., & Fry, M. D. (2011). Helping members commit to exercise: Specific strategies to impact the climate at fitness centers. *Journal of Sport Psychology in Action, 2*, 70–80. doi:10.1080/21520704.2011.582803

Connor, J. (2009). The athlete as widget: How exploitation explains elite sport. *Sport in Society, 12*, 1369–1377. doi:10.1080/17430430903204900

Coppola, A. M., Ward, R. M., & Freysinger, V. J. (2014). Coaches' communication of sport body image: Experiences of female athletes. *Journal of Applied Sport Psychology, 26*, 1–16. doi:10.1080/10413200.2013.766650

Dawson, M. C. (2017). CrossFit: Fitness cult or reinventive institution? *International Review for the Sociology of Sport, 52*, 361–379. doi:10.1177/ 1012690215591793

Dworkin, S. L., & Wachs, F. L. (2009). *Body panic: Gender, health, and the selling of fitness*. New York, NY: New York University Press.

Eime, R. M., Young, J. A., Harvey, J. T., Charity, M. J., & Payne, W. R. (2013). A systematic review of the psychological and social benefits of participation in sport for adults: Informing development of a conceptual model of health through sport. *International Journal of Behavioral Nutrition and Physical Activity, 10*, 135. doi:10.1186/1479-5868-10-135

Frew, M., & McGillivray, D. (2005). Health clubs and body politics: Aesthetics and the quest for physical capital. *Leisure Studies, 24*, 161–175. doi:10.1080/0261436042000300432

Fry, M. D., & Gano-Overway, L. A. (2010). Exploring the contribution of the caring climate to the youth sport experience. *Journal of Applied Sport Psychology, 22*, 294–304. doi:10.1080/10413201003776352

Gladwell, V., Brown, D., Wood, C., Sandercock, G., & Barton, J. (2013). The great outdoors: How a green environment can benefit all. *Extreme Physiology and Medicine, 2*, 1–7. doi:10.1186/2046-7648-2-3

Gonzales, A. L., & Hancock, J. T. (2011). Mirror, mirror on my Facebook wall: Effects of exposure to Facebook on self-esteem. *Cyberpsychology, Behavior, and Social Networking, 14*, 79–83. doi:10.1089/cyber.2009.0411

Goodwin, H., Haycraft, E., & Meyer, C. (2014). Sociocultural risk factors for compulsive exercise: A prospective study of adolescents. *European Eating Disorders Review, 22*, 360–365. doi:10.1002/erv.2309

Greenleaf, C. (2002). Athletic body image: Exploratory interviews with former competitive female athletes. *Women in Sport and Physical Activity Journal, 11*, 63–88. doi:10.1123/wspaj.11.1.63

Greenleaf, C., Boyer, E. M., & Petrie, T. A. (2009). High school sport participation and subsequent psychological well-being and physical activity: The mediating influences of body image, physical competence, and instrumentality. *Sex Roles, 61*, 714–726. doi:10.1007/s11199-009-9671-z

Hauff, C. R. (2016a). Dress to impress or dress to sweat? Examining the perceptions of exercise apparel through the eyes of active women. *Women in Sport and Physical Activity Journal, 24*, 99–109. doi:10.1123/wspaj.2015-0015

Hauff, C. R. (2016b). *Hashtagging your health: Using psychosocial variables and social media use to understand impression management and exercise behaviors in women* (Unpublished doctoral dissertation). University of Wisconsin, Milwaukee.

Hill, J., Sandford, R., & Enright, E. (2016). "It has really amazed me what my body can now do": Boundary work and the construction of a body-positive dance community. *Sport and Society, 19*, 667–679. doi:10.1080/17430437.2015.1073946

Jackson, S. A., & Csikszentmihalyi, M. (1999). *Flow in sports*. Champaign, IL: Human Kinetics.

Jeffers, A. J., & Benotsch, E. G. (2014). Non-medical use of prescription stimulants for weight loss, disordered eating, and body image. *Eating Behaviors, 15*, 414–418. 10.1016/j.eatbeh.2014.04.019

Kaufman, K. A., Glass, C. R., & Arnkoff, D. B. (2009). Evaluation of mindful sport performance enhancement (MSPE): A new approach to promote flow in athletes. *Journal of Clinical Sport Psychology, 3*, 334–356. doi:10.1123/jcsp.3.4.334

La Forge, R. (2016). Mind-body (mindful) exercise in practice. *ACSM's Health & Fitness Journal, 20*, 6–8. 10.1249/FIT.0000000000000212

Lunde, C., & Holmqvist Gattario, K. (2017). Performance or appearance? Young female sport participants' body negotiations. *Body Image, 21*, 81–89. doi:10.1016/j.bodyim.2017.03.001

Mahlo, L., & Tiggemann, M. (2016). Yoga and positive body image: A test of the embodiment model. *Body Image, 18*, 135–142. doi:10.1016/j.bodyim.2016.06.008

Moe, A. (2012). Beyond the belly: An appraisal of Middle Eastern dance (aka belly dance) as leisure. *Journal of Leisure Research, 44*, 201–233.

Mulgrew, K., & Tiggemann, M. (2018). Form or function: Does focusing on body functionality protect women from body dissatisfaction when viewing media images? *Journal of Health Psychology, 23*, 84–94. doi:10.1177/1359105316655471

Muscat, A. C., & Long, B. C. (2008). Critical comments about body shape and weight: Disordered eating of female athletes and sport participants. *Journal of Applied Sport Psychology, 20*, 1–24. 10.1080/10413200701784833

Nieri, T., & Hughes, E. (2016). All about having fun: Women's experience of Zumba fitness. *Sociology of Sport Journal, 33*, 1–33. 10.1123/ssj.2015-0071

Parsons, E. M., & Betz, N. E. (2001). The relationship of participation in sports and physical activity to body objectification, instrumentality, and locus of control among young women. *Psychology of Women Quarterly, 25*, 209–222. doi:10.1111/1471-6402.00022

Perloff, R. (2014). Social media effects on young women's body image concerns: Theoretical perspectives and an agenda for research. *Sex Roles, 71*, 363–377. doi:10.1007/s11199-014-0384-6

Pickett, A. C., & Cunningham, G. B. (2017). Physical activity for every body: A model for managing weight stigma and creating body-inclusive spaces. *Quest, 69*, 19–36. doi:10.1080/00336297.2016.1145129

Piran, N. (2016). Embodied possibilities and disruptions: The emergence of the experience of embodiment construct from qualitative studies with girls and women. *Body Image, 18*, 43–60. doi:10.1016/j.bodyim.2016.04.007

Reel, J. J., Galli, N., Miyairi, M., Voelker, D., & Greenleaf, C. (2016). Development and validation of the Intuitive Exercise Scale. *Eating Behaviors, 22*, 129–132. doi:10.1016/j.eatbeh.2016.06.013

Steinfeldt, J. A., Zakrajsek, R. A., Bodey, K. J., Middendorf, K. G., & Martin, S. B. (2013). Role of uniforms in the body image of female college volleyball players. *The Counseling Psychologist, 41*, 791–819. doi:10.1177/0011000012457218

Swami, V., Barron, D., Weis, L., & Furnham, A. (2016). Bodies in nature: Associations between exposure to nature, connectedness to nature, and body image in US adults. *Body Image, 18*, 153–161. doi:10.1016/j.bodyim.2016.07.002

Sylvester, B. D., Standage, M., Dowd, A. J., Martin, L. J., Sweet, S. N., & Beauchamp, M. R. (2014). Perceived variety, psychological needs satisfaction and exercise-related well-being. *Psychology & Health, 29*, 1044–1061. doi:10.1080/08870446.2014.907900

Tiggemann, M., Coutts, E., & Clark, L. (2014). Belly dance as an embodying activity? A test of the embodiment model of positive body image. *Sex Roles, 71*, 197–207. doi:10.1007/s11199-014-0408-2

Teodoro, R., & Naaman, M. (2013). Fitter with Twitter: Understanding personal health and fitness activity in social media. In E. Kiciman, N. B. Ellison, B. Hogan, P. Resnick & I. Soboroff (Eds.), *International conference on web and social media* (pp. 1–10). Palo Alto, CA: Association for the Advancement Artificial Intelligence Press.

Toma, C., & Hancock, J. (2013). Self-affirmation underlies Facebook use. *Personality and Social Psychology Bulletin, 39*, 321–331. doi:10.1177/0146167212474694

White, R. L., & Bennie, A. (2015). Resilience in youth sport: A qualitative investigation of gymnastics coach and athlete perceptions. *International Journal of Sports Science & Coaching, 10*, 379–393. doi:10.1260/1747-9541.10.2-3.379

12

Adolescent Female Desire

Influences on the Construction of Agency and Desire

SHARON LAMB AND JULIE KOVEN ■

The development of healthy female sexuality is a complex and multidimensional process. In understanding female adolescent sexual development, we must understand both the suppression and the celebration of female desire in its historical and structural contexts. Feminist theorists have long studied the suppression of desire and connected that desire to both subjectivity and agency. However, desire remains an elusive concept, sometimes referring to a person "connecting to" what kinds of acts or treatment she wants during sex; sometimes referring to the pleasure she has during sex; sometimes referring to embodied sexual feelings that she is able to feel as a sexual person; sometimes the word *desire* is used to simply mean agency; and sometimes all of these things at once. In this chapter, we review the history of desire and sexual freedom, look at three historical and institutional influences over adolescent sexual desire (gender inequality, education, and the media) and then interrogate the idea of sexual agency to understand how adolescents and young women conceive of sexual agency today in a neoliberal context. We do not claim these are the most important or only institutional influences but do believe the discourses and ideologies girls are exposed to and interact with in these three areas determine what kind of agency they can develop or perceive that they can develop.

GENDER INEQUALITY AND PATRIARCHY

Any history of adolescent female sexuality must examine the gender hierarchy and how women have been treated across time. Depending on their race, sexuality, ability, socioeconomic class, and other intersecting identities, women have been denied qualities of being human such as subjectivity, autonomy, and creativity (Hill Collins, 2004). Despite strides made by women in different waves, gender inequality and discrimination persist in healthcare, education, and political representation and are evidenced by the global wage gap (International Trade Union Confederation [ITUC], 2009; United Nations Development Programme [UNDP], 2016). These values not only infiltrate our public spaces but also define women's sexual relationships. Sexual socialization is dominated by institutionalized heterosexuality, or heteronormativity, which reproduces gender inequalities in heterosexual relationships and marginalizes LGBTQ (lesbian, gay, bisexual, transgender, queer/questioning) individuals (Holland, Ramazanoglu, Sharpe, & Thomson, 2004; Jackson, 2006; Tolman, 2006). Sexualization narratives in schools and homes perpetuate white, middle-class heterosexuality and shame girls who act with agency (Renold & Ringrose 2011; Ringrose & Renold, 2012). With regard to what is made normative regarding sexuality, adolescent girls participate in a culture that sexually socializes them toward pleasing their partners and anticipating social advantages for doing so and rejection for failing to (Burns, Futch, & Tolman, 2011; Tolman, 2002). Additionally, black girls and other girls of color often face harsher bullying, violence, and disciplinary interventions in schools because they are seen as being loud and unruly instead of as feminine and passive (Crenshaw, Ocen, & Nanda, 2015).

Bay-Cheng and Eliseo-Arras (2008) have drawn attention to the way in which gender norms, such as female sexual passivity, contribute to the subordination of women's sexual interests and the practice of engaging in unwanted sex for male pleasure. This gender inequality that persists is the background for how adolescent girls negotiate their sexual development, how they find sexual subjectivity, and how the culture perceives their agency. At the same time, critics highlight that this concern about girls' sexuality has become somewhat of a moral panic perpetuated by those who questions girls' ability to make their own choices and thoughtfully reflect on media influences (Egan & Hawkes, 2008; Gill, 2012; Lamb 2010). We are currently in a period of girl activism that serves as a resistance to the power structures beholden to patriarchy. Building on the activism of prior generations, girls are coming together in groups such as the SPARK Movement, which works with and inspires girls to combat racism and gender inequality and also advocates for girls' sexuality, empowerment, and well-being (SPARK Movement, n.d.). In her book *Powered by Girl*, Lyn Mikel Brown (2016) draws on the importance of connecting young activists to older women so that their activism is also informed by history.

EDUCATION AND SEX EDUCATION

The educational system is still one in which girls suffer discrimination, particularly girls of color (Crenshaw et al., 2015). While the 2008 report, "Where the Girls Are," on gender inequity in education showed girls outperforming boys in multiple areas at school, this advantage was not shown in SAT scores and was less distinct among children of color (Corbett, Hill, & Rose, 2008). The "Black Girls

Matter" report indicates that black girls are particularly vulnerable to discrimination in the educational system (Crenshaw et al., 2015). Further, the American Association of University Women (AAUW), which originally put out the report "Hostile Hallways," reconfirmed in 2011 that girls still experience sexual harassment to a frightening degree, and yet it is normalized as just part of the school day for most (Hill, 2011). Additionally, the National Women's Law Center (2017) noted that since the 2016 election, there has been more overall harassment of girls in schools, with LGBTQ girls also reporting higher rates. Sexual harassment in schools provides a certain kind of sex education and reconfirms a hidden curriculum that teaches girls that no matter how they attempt to achieve and move ahead through schooling, they must remember that they are also sexual objects.

Sex education in the United States has reflected the suppression of female sexuality, prescribing heteronormative relationships and stereotypical gender roles. Feminist psychologists first became aware of this issue with Michelle Fine's (1988) piece "The Missing Discourse of Desire," and this discussion continues today. Instead of feeling entitled to autonomy and pleasure, girls can be terrorized by discourses of harm, disease, and victimization (Fine & McClelland, 2006). Use of gender stereotypes that perpetuate traditional gender roles and power relations supports the double standard and overall gender inequality in sexual and romantic relationships (Lamb, Graling, & Lustig, 2011; Szirom, 2017). In sex education curricula, girls who express themselves sexually are at risk of being denigrated as sluts and may be seen as less desirable future partners. This is particularly true for girls of color (Bay-Cheng, 2015; Fields, 2005, 2008). Sex education curricula vary greatly across the states in the United States. While many states integrate health information within broader sex education, others provide more limited programming focusing on risk and promoting abstinence (Guttmacher Institute, 2017). Sex education has the potential to help girls and boys develop positive and healthy sexualities (Lamb, 2010), but only 28 US states and the District of Columbia require the teaching of healthy sexuality, including skills to make healthy decisions, communicate with partners and family, and avoid sexual coercion (Guttmacher Institute, 2017).

Sex education also fails to address female pleasure. While male pleasure is taught as a part of the reproductive process, including the need for an erection and ejaculation, female pleasure has been absent (Fine, 1988). Girls are instead taught to avoid coercion, protect themselves against disease, and defend themselves against victimization (Lamb, 2010). This focus on the negative aspects of sexuality does nothing to prepare adolescent girls to have mutually satisfying relationships and experience sexual freedom and agency.

MEDIA INFLUENCES

As a platform for cultural values, various forms of media are laden with sexualized content that depicts girls and women as sexual objects and encourages them to perform as such in their sexual encounters and relationships (American

Psychological Association, Task Force on the Sexualization of Girls, 2007; Collins, Martino, & Shaw, 2011; Gill, 2008). Additionally, these forms of media convey societal expectations for gender-typed behavior and encourage girls to judge their social worth based on their appearance (Gunter, 2012; Halliwell & Diedrichs, 2012; Mischner, van Schie, & Engels, 2013).

As highlighted in the American Psychological Association, Task Force on the Sexualization of Girls' 2007 report and more recent studies, research has shown that mainstream media (such as television, movies, and music) disproportionately sexually objectify women through images, lyrics, and other content. Findings indicate that women and female artists are consistently shown in more sexual ways than men and male artists (Aubrey & Frisby, 2011; Frisby & Aubrey, 2012; Wallis, 2011; Ward, Reed, Trinh, & Foust, 2013). Research has explored how exposure to sexually objectifying media is linked to internalization of cultural beauty standards, self-objectification, body shaming, appearance anxiety, body dissatisfaction, and disordered eating (Krawczyk & Thompson, 2015; for a review, see Moradi & Huang, 2008). Additionally, this exposure is indirectly associated with low self-esteem, depressed mood, trauma symptoms, and depression (Miles-McLean et al., 2015; Nadal & Haynes, 2012; Szymanski & Henning, 2007).

Additionally, studies have shown that college students, and presumably adolescents, use Internet-based sexually explicit material (SEM), or pornography, at rates ranging from 56% to 86% of young men and 31% to 50% of young women (Braun-Courville & Rojas, 2009; Carroll et al., 2008; Goodson, McCormick, & Evans, 2001; Morgan 2011). The majority of pornography has been found to show themes of male dominance of women and physical aggression toward women (Foubert, Brosi, & Bannon, 2011; Peter & Valkenburg, 2010). While many may view pornography for titillation or entertainment, it can be a source of sex education. Using pornography as educational material is problematic in that it inaccurately depicts the human form as nondisabled, flawless, confident, and always orgasmic. It fails to consider the complexities of relationships, emotions, and bodily functioning (Allen, 2006). Further, viewing pornography can have negative effects on adolescents' self-concept, body image, social development, and attitudes about sex; some of these attitudes include unrealistic beliefs about sex, attitudes of male domination and female submission, and the belief that women are sexual objects (Owens, Behun, Manning, & Reid, 2012). Exposure to online pornography is also associated with decreased satisfaction in adolescents' sex lives and sexual expression (Peter & Valkenburg, 2009).

Media as a whole have the potential to support sexuality development in youth (Gill, 2012). While some critics voice all-encompassing concerns about the perils of media, others (e.g., Gill, 2012) recognize that media are not homogeneous and monolithic, but diverse in form and representation of girls and women. Gill also asserted that "girls are increasingly involved as active producers, not merely consumers" (p. 738) and discussed girls' use of online forums and video diaries to share their experiences of media, the culture of sexualization, and how it makes them feel. Ringrose and Renold (2012) challenged these notions as well, citing numerous ways girls use digital media to engage in activism around sexuality, from reclaiming the word *slut* on social media to fighting back against sexual violence and "blaming the victim" discourses on Twitter and other sites.

CHALLENGES IN THE PATHS TOWARD ADOLESCENT SEXUAL AGENCY AND EMPOWERMENT

Sexual desire and sexual agency are concepts that appear to be deeply connected. To desire is to become a subject, to have wants, to have entitlements, and to feel oneself as an actor. However, it is important not to simplify the constructs of sexual agency or choice. While sexual agency can mean the undoing of objectification and the ownership of one's subjective voice, it can also be used to support self-objectification. For example, this occurred with the rallying cry of "girl power," which was also co-opted for commercial ends where girls who self-sexualized were envisioned as agentic via the magical words *girl power* (Attwood, 2007; Gill, 2008; Lamb & Brown, 2006; Lamb & Peterson, 2012; Peterson & Lamb, 2012). Also, the idea of an authentic voice has been challenged and replaced with the idea of shifting and multiple voices (Crenshaw, 1991; Ludvig, 2006). Similar challenges can be voiced about embodiment, and in particular embodied sexual pleasure, when it is viewed as a sensate authentic experience (Tolman, 2012; Tolman, Bowman, & Fahs, 2014) instead of more critically as a socially constructed experience that involves learned "performative" practices that maintain the status quo (Jackson & Scott, 2001). That is, what is felt to be "embodied" might not express agency at all. Or, the agency it expresses (one tied to getting to know one's body through awareness practices like yoga) is such an individualized one that it can never really work to undo the greater oppressive contexts. It is similar to lighting candles and taking a warm bath to fight stress caused by oppression, poverty, and lack of resources (Becker, 2013). Feminist scholars are therefore challenged in that goals of interventions toward sexual agency, choice, and embodiment may actually reinforce inequitable power structures.

CONCLUSION

Girls today are attempting to address forces that challenge their sexual agency and rights and to raise awareness about inequality. Within the context of social inequity and institutional heterosexuality, experiences of subjectivity, autonomy, and creativity associated with the ownership of sexual desire are disrupted. Adolescents' progress toward comfort with their own desires is therefore *intertwined with feminist pursuits toward equity along all dimensions of social location*. In this regard, there seems to sometimes be a disconnection between long-standing feminists and those young women have yet to understand the complicated links between oppression, objectification, and sexual desire. Raising consciousness among adolescents about the expressions of power and power inequity in the sexual domain may support the development of alternative sexual discourses in youth and enlist young women toward broader feminist causes. For example, Bay-Cheng and Eliseo-Arras's work (2008) regarding gender norms of expected female sexual passivity and its impact on girls' sexual behavior can guide one such area of consciousness raising. Activism is another answer; currently, some girls engage in activism in the sexual domain protesting slut shaming, body shaming, and sexual violence (Brown, 2016; Valenti, 2012). Making critical perspectives *normative among peers* can be powerful in opening opportunities for shifts in the practice of desire.

Schools are currently complicit in conveying multiple adverse messages to girls regarding their place in the world, especially to girls of color. Pervasive and unchanged rates of sexual harassment continue to transmit to girls their disenfranchised place in the world. Yet, many schools do not combat such harassment through education and policy implementation. Such systemic changes are vital.

Further, sex education should be offered in all schools and include the examination of power, relational connection, intimacy, safety, and desire. Currently, in particular, there is rarely discussion of female desire or male emotion or an ethic of mutuality as a basis for "good" sex (Lamb, 2010). But, there are examples of this kind of sex and relationship education that hold promise (see Lamb & Randazzo, 2016).

Finally, as an institution, the media have to be a target of change and corralled into support for positive sexual development and challenges to objectification. Public health campaigns initiated by governmental bodies, industries, or foundations can be pivotal in changing the sexualized objectification of women, as can news sources. Encouraging and supporting the new generation of critical media by young women can lead to the transformation of messages regarding youth and sexuality.

In the end, activism around these concerns has the potential to show girls and help them to discover for themselves what it means to have a healthy, relational sexual life. This would be one in which they know their rights, make choices in their own best interest, and focus on developing the kinds of relationships that will give them satisfaction in a number of positive ways.

REFERENCES

Allen, L. (2006). "Looking at the real thing": Young men, pornography and sexuality education. *Discourse: Studies in the Cultural Politics of Education, 27*, 69–83.

American Psychological Association, Task Force on the Sexualization of Girls. (2007). *Report of the APA task force on the sexualization of girls.* Washington, DC: American Psychological Association. Retrieved from https://www.apa.org/pi/women/programs/girls/index.aspx

Attwood, F. (2007). Sluts and riot grrrls: Female identity and sexual agency. *Journal of Gender Studies, 16*, 233–247. doi:10.1080/09589230701562921

Aubrey, J., & Frisby, C. (2011). Sexual objectification in music videos: A content analysis comparing gender and genre. *Mass Communication & Society, 14*, 475–501. doi:10.1080/15205436.2010.513468

Bay-Cheng, L. Y. (2015). The agency line: A neoliberal metric for appraising young women's sexuality. *Sex Roles, 73*, 279–291. doi:10.1007/s11199-015-0452-6

Bay-Cheng, L. Y., & Eliseo-Arras, R. K. (2008). The making of unwanted sex: Gendered and neoliberal norms in college women's unwanted sexual experiences. *Journal of Sex Research, 45*, 386–397. doi:10.1080/00224490802398381

Becker, D. (2013). *One nation under stress: The trouble with stress as an idea*. New York, NY: Oxford University Press.

Braun-Courville, D., & Rojas, M. (2009). Exposure to sexually explicit web sites and adolescent sexual attitudes and behaviors. *Journal of Adolescent Health, 45*, 156–162. doi:10.1016/j.jadohealth.2008.12.004

Brown, L. M. (2016). *Powered by girl.* Boston, MA: Beacon Press.

Burns, A., Futch, V., & Tolman, D. (2011). "It's like doing homework": Academic achievement discourse in adolescent girls' fellatio narratives. *Sexuality Research and Social Policy, 8*, 239–251. doi:10.1007/s13178-011-0062-1.

Carroll, J. S., Padilla-Walker, L. M., Nelson, L. J., Olson, C. D., Barry, C. M., & Madsen, S. D. (2008). Generation XXX: Pornography acceptance and use among emerging adults. *Journal of Adolescent Research, 23*, 6–30. doi:10.1177/0743558407306348

Collins, R. L., Martino, S. C., & Shaw, R. (2011). *Influence of new media on adolescent sexual health: Evidence and other opportunities* (Working Paper WR-761). Retrieved from Office of the Assistant Secretary for Planning and Evaluation website: http://aspe.hhs.gov/hsp/11/AdolescentSexualActivity/NewMediaLitRev/

Corbett, C., Hill, C., & Rose, A. S. (2008). *Where the girls are: The facts about gender equity in education.* Retrieved from http://www.aauw.org/research/where-the-girls-are/

Crenshaw, K. (1991). Mapping the margins: Intersectionality, identity politics, and violence against women of color. *Stanford Law Review, 43*, 1241–1299.

Crenshaw, K., Ocen, P., & Nanda, J. (2015). *Black girls matter: Pushed out, overpoliced and underprotected.* Report issued by the African American Policy Forum (AAPF) and Columbia Law School's Center for Intersectionality and Social Policy Studies. Retrieved from https://www.atlanticphilanthropies.org/wp-content/uploads/2015/09/BlackGirlsMatter_Report.pdf

Egan, R., & Hawkes, G. (2008). Endangered girls and incendiary objects: Unpacking the discourse on sexualization. *Sexuality & Culture, 12*, 291–311. doi:10.1007/s12119-008-9036-8.

Fields, J. (2005). "Children having children": Race, innocence, and sexuality education. *Social Problems, 52*, 549–571. doi:10.1525/sp.2005.52.4.549

Fields, J. (2008). *Risky lessons: Sex education and social inequality*. Piscataway, NJ: Rutgers University Press.

Fine, M. (1988). Sexuality, schooling, and adolescent females: The missing discourse of desire. *Harvard Educational Review, 58*, 29–53. doi:10.17763/haer.58.1.u0468k1v2n2n8242

Fine, M., & McClelland, S. I. (2006). Sexuality education and desire: Still missing after all these years. *Harvard Educational Review, 76*, 297–338. doi:10.17763/haer.76.3.w5042g23122n6703

Foubert, J. D., Brosi, M. W., & Bannon, R. S. (2011). Pornography viewing among fraternity men: Effects on bystander intervention, rape myth acceptance and behavioral intent to commit sexual assault. *Sexual Addiction & Compulsivity, 18*, 212–231. doi:10.1080/10720162.2011.625552

Frisby, C. M., & Aubrey, J. S. (2012): Race and genre in the use of sexual objectification in female artists' music videos. *Howard Journal of Communications, 23*, 66–87. doi:10.1080/10646175.2012.641880

Gill, R. (2008). Empowerment/sexism: Figuring female agency in contemporary advertising. *Feminism & Psychology, 18*(1), 35–60. doi:10.1177/0959353507084950

Gill, R. (2012). Media, empowerment, and "sexualization of culture" debates. *Sex Roles, 66*(11–12), 736–745. doi:10.1007/s11199-011-0107-1

Goodson, P., McCormick, D., & Evans, A. (2001). Searching for sexually explicit material on the Internet: An exploratory study of college students' behavior and attitudes. *Archives of Sexual Behavior, 30*, 101–117.

Gunter, B. (2012). The role of the media. In N. Rumsey & D. Harcourt (Eds.), *The Oxford handbook of the psychology of appearance* (pp. 455–467). New York, NY: Oxford University Press.

Guttmacher Institute. (2017). *Sex and HIV education*. Retrieved from https://www.guttmacher.org/state-policy/explore/sex-and-hiv-education

Halliwell, E., & Diedrichs, P. C. (2012). Influence of the media. In N. Rumsey & D. Harcourt (Eds.), *The Oxford handbook of the psychology of appearance* (pp. 217–238). New York, NY: Oxford University Press.

Hill, C. (2011). Crossing the Line: Sexual Harassment at School. Retrieved from the American Association of University Women website: http://www.aauw.org/resource/crossing-the-line-sexual-harassment-at-school/

Hill Collins, P. (2004). *Black sexual politics: African Americans, gender, and the new racism*. New York, NY: Routledge.

Holland, J., Ramazanoglu, C., Sharpe, S., & Thomson, R. (2004). *The male in the head: Young people, heterosexuality, and power* (2nd ed.). London, England: Tufnell Press.

International Trade Union Confederation (ITUC). (2009). *Gender (in)equality in the labour market: An overview of global trends and developments 2009*. Retrieved from http://www.ituc-csi.org/IMG/pdf/GAP-09_EN.pdf

Jackson, S. [Stevi]. (2006). Gender, sexuality and heterosexuality: The complexity (and limits) of heteronormativity. *Feminist Theory, 7*, 105–121. doi:10.1177/1464700106061462.

Jackson, S., & Scott, S. (2001). Embodying orgasm: Gendered power relations and sexual pleasure. *Women and Therapy, 24*, 99–110. doi:10.1300/j015v24n01_13

Krawczyk, R., & Thompson, J. K. (2015). The effects of advertisements that sexually objectify women on state body dissatisfaction and judgments of women: The moderating roles of gender and internalization. *Body Image, 15*, 109–119. doi:10.1016/j.bodyim.2015.08.001

Lamb, S. (2010). Feminist ideals of healthy female adolescent sexuality: A critique. *Sex Roles, 62*, 294–306. doi:10.1007/s11199-009-9698-1

Lamb, S., & Brown, L. M. (2006). *Packaging girlhood: Rescuing our daughters from marketer's schemes*. New York, NY: St. Martin's Press.

Lamb, S., Graling, K., & Lustig, K. (2011). Stereotypes in four current AOUM curricula: Good girls, good boys, and the new gender equality. *American Journal of Sexuality Education, 6*, 360–380.

Lamb, S., & Peterson, Z. (2012). Adolescent girls' sexual empowerment: Two feminists explore the concept. *Sex Roles, 66*, 703–712. doi:10.1007/s11199-011-9995-3

Lamb, S., & Randazzo, R. (2016). From I to we: Sex education as a form of civics education in a neoliberal context. *Curriculum Inquiry, 46*, 148–167. doi:10.1080/03626784.2016.1144465

Ludvig, A. (2006). Differences between women? Intersecting voices in a female narrative. *European Journal of Women's Studies 13*, 245–258. doi:10.1177/1350506806065755

Miles-McLean, H., Liss, M., Erchull, M. J., Robertson, C. M., Hagerman, C., Gnoleba, M. A., & Papp, L. J. (2015). "Stop looking at me!" Interpersonal sexual objectification as a source of insidious trauma. *Psychology of Women Quarterly, 39*, 363–374. doi:10.1177/0361684314561018

Mischner, I. H. S., van Schie, H. T., & Engels, R. C. M. E. (2013). Breaking the circle: Challenging Western sociocultural norms for appearance influences young women's attention to appearance-related media. *Body Image, 10*, 316–325. doi:10.1016/j.bodyim.2013.02.005

Moradi, B., & Huang, Y. P. (2008). Objectification theory and psychology of women: A decade of advances and future directions. *Psychology of Women Quarterly, 32*, 377–398. doi:10.1111/j.1471-6402.2008.00452.x

Morgan, E. M. (2011). Associations between young adults' use of sexually explicit material and their sexual preferences, behaviors, and satisfaction. *Journal of Sex Research, 48*, 520–530. doi:10.1080/00224499.2010.543960

Nadal, K. L., & Haynes, K. (2012). The effects of sexism, gender microaggressions, and other forms of discrimination on women's mental health and development. In P. K. Lundberg-Love, K. L. Nadal, & M. A. Paludi (Eds.), *Women and mental disorders* (pp. 87–101). Santa Barbara, CA: Praeger.

National Women's Law Center (NWLC). (2017). *Stopping school pushout: Overview and key findings*. Retrieved from https://nwlc.org/resources/stopping-school-pushout-overview-and-key-findings/

Owens, E. W., Behun, R. J., Manning, J. C., & Reid, R. C. (2012). The impact of Internet pornography on adolescents: A review of the research. *Sexual Addiction & Compulsivity, 19*, 99–122. doi:10.1080/10720162.2012.660431

Peter, J., & Valkenburg, P. M. (2009). Adolescents' exposure to sexually explicit Internet material and sexual satisfaction: A longitudinal study. *Human Communication Research, 35*, 171–194. doi:10.1111/j.1468-2958.2009.01343.x

Peter, J., & Valkenburg, P. M. (2010). Processes underlying the effects of adolescents' use of sexually explicit internet material: The role of perceived realism. *Communication Research, 37*, 375–399. doi:10.1177/0093650210362464

Peterson, Z., & Lamb, S. (2012). The political context for personal empowerment: Continuing the conversation. *Sex Roles, 66*, 758–763. doi.org/10.1007/s11199-012-0150-6

Renold, E., & Ringrose, J. (2011). Schizoid subjectivities? Re-theorizing teen girls' sexual cultures in an era of "sexualization." *Journal of Sociology 47*, 389–409. doi:10.1177/1440783311420792

Ringrose, J., & Reynod, E. (2012). Slut-shaming, girl power and "sexualisation": Thinking through the politics of the International SlutWalks with teen girls. *Gender and Education*, *24*, 333–343. doi:10.1080/09540253.2011.645023

SPARK Movement. (n.d.). *Research blog*. Retrieved from http://www.sparkmovement.org/category/research-blog/

Szirom, T. (2017). *Teaching gender? Sex education and sexual stereotypes*. London, England: Routledge.

Szymanski, D. M., & Henning, S. L. (2007). The role of self-objectification in women's depression: A test of objectification theory. *Sex Roles*, *56*, 45–53. doi:10.1007/s11199-006-9147-3

Tolman, D. L. (2002). *Dilemma of desire: Teenage girls and sexuality*. Cambridge, MA: Harvard University Press.

Tolman, D. L. (2006). In a different position: Conceptualizing female adolescent sexuality development within compulsory heterosexuality. *New Directions for Child and Adolescent Development*, *2006*, 71–89. doi:10.1002/cd.163

Tolman, D. L. (2012). Female adolescents, sexual empowerment and desire: A missing discourse of gender inequity, *Sex Roles*, *66*, 746–757. doi:10.1007/s11199-012-0122-x

Tolman, D. L., Bowman, C. P., & Fahs, B. (2014). Sexuality and embodiment. In D. L. Tolman & L. M. Diamond (Eds.), *APA handbook of sexuality and psychology* (Vol. 1, pp. 759–804). Washington, DC: American Psychological Association.

United Nations Development Programme (UNDP). (2016). *2016 human development report*. Retrieved from http://hdr.undp.org/en/2016-report

Valenti, J. (2012, August 2). The upside of ugly. *The Nation*. Retrieved from https://www.thenation.com/blog/169208/upside-ugly

Wallis, C. (2011). Performing gender: A content analysis of gender display in music videos. *Sex Roles*, *64*, 160–172. doi:10.1007/s11199-010-9814-2

Ward, L. M., Reed, L., Trinh, S., & Foust, M. (2013). Sexuality and entertainment media. In D. L. Tolman & L. M. Diamond (Eds.), *APA handbook of sexuality and psychology, Vol. 2: Contextual approaches* (pp. 373–423). Washington, DC: American Psychological Association.

13

Personal Safety as Bedrock and Safeguard for Positive Embodiment

RACHEL M. CALOGERO, TRACY L. TYLKA, AND JACLYN A. SIEGEL ■

Personal safety is an issue of importance to everyone. For women, there is a real threat in the air when it comes to feeling and being safe in the world. In this chapter, we consider personal safety to be a pillar of positive embodiment, without which girls and women cannot fully be "at home" in their bodies. We explore the absence of personal safety for girls and women in any environment where sexual objectification is pervasive and gender inequality remains entrenched. We give particular focus to the fact that being female-bodied in these environmental contexts subjects all women to greater risks of sexual harm—a markedly different experience from that of most men—and how it engages women in vigilant policing of their safety that fragments their consciousness, restricts their movement, and serves as an obstacle to positive embodiment. We close by considering ways of claiming space in the world and the imperative for cultivating women's safety through social activism and embodied social change.

THE SAFETY THREAT OF SEXUAL OBJECTIFICATION

In order to understand women's sense of personal safety and security in the world, or lack thereof, we focus necessarily on a primary source of threat to their personal safety: actual and implied instances of sexual violence. Clear gender differences have been documented regarding who is most likely to victimize and be victimized by sexual violence (Benoit, Shumka, & Vallance, 2010). On average, women as a social group report more threats to personal safety and feeling less safe than men as a social group (Allik & Kearns, 2017). This pattern is consonant with the fact that in nearly all incidents of sexual violence, the perpetrators are male and the victims are female. Women are more likely than men to experience contact sexual violence, sexual coercion, noncontact sexual harassment, and stalking victimization (Smith et al., 2017). The Uniform Reporting Survey of Canada in 2011 found that women were 11 times more likely than men to be a victim of a sexual offense (Sinha, 2013). National and international reports showed approximately 1 in 5 US women reported being raped in their lifetime (Tjaden & Thoennes, 2000), and more than 1 in 4 women on US college campuses have experienced rape or attempted rape (Fisher, Cullen, & Turner, 2000). Nearly half of all female victims of rape first experienced sexual assault when they were 17 or younger, and 1 in every 9 girls experience sexual abuse or assault from an adult before the age of 18 (Finkelhor, Shattuck, Turner, & Hamby, 2014). Globally, women are more likely than men to be the victims of intimate partner violence and rape (World Health Organization, 2016). In sum, gender is a fundamental determinant of sexual violence, and being female-bodied markedly and uniquely increases a person's risk for sexual harm.

Given these objectively higher rates of sexual violence that women have either witnessed or directly experienced, it is unsurprising gender differences exist in fear of crime and concerns about safety (Harris & Miller, 2000). Women's sense of their personal safety is cultivated in an environment characterized by *sexual terrorism*, whereby the omnipresent threat and perpetration of violence against girls and women by boys and men keeps them in a state of fear (Kissling, 1991; Sheffield, 1987; Yodanis, 2004) and alert to their more vulnerable status. Dynamics of sexual terrorism are on display quite prominently in early adolescence, with boys engaged in unwanted sexualized contact and publicly humiliating treatment (e.g., slut shaming) toward girls, especially when boys' overtures have been rebuffed, thereby enforcing the gender order and male entitlement to women's bodies "through symbolic or physical violence" (Pascoe, 2011, p. 114).

The unique role of sexual violence in women's safety concerns was further underscored in a recent study among black women and men who live in low-income, high-crime urban neighborhoods in the United States, finding that perceptions of sexual violence resulted in differential perceptions of safety among women and men, whereas other types of violence (i.e., fighting with a weapon, gang fights, and robbery or mugging) did not (Hoffman, Mair, Hunter, Prince, & Tebes, 2018). That is, women who reported higher perceptions of sexual violence also reported less perceived safety, whereas men's perceived safety did not significantly vary by perceptions of sexual violence. It follows from these insights and observations that women's fear of sexual assault casts a shadow over perceptions of other nonsexual crimes and physical harm happening to them (Ferraro, 1996; Fisher & Sloan, 2003; Schafer, Huebner, & Bynum, 2006).

The potential for sexual violence always exists in contexts of sexual objectification. Sexual violence constitutes the extreme end of a wider spectrum of sexually objectifying treatment of women. Girls and women encounter myriad forms of interpersonal sexual objectification in their everyday lives, such as sexualized gazing and leering, (unsolicited and often public) sexualized comments and calls, sexual groping, harassment, and stalking, and sexual assault and rape (American Psychological Association, 2010; Davidson & Gervais, 2015; Fredrickson & Roberts, 1997; Roberts, Calogero, & Gervais, 2018). Underscoring this reality, a series of daily diary studies revealed that 94% of undergraduate women encounter some form of sexually objectifying treatment at least once during a semester, and these encounters were unique predictors of daily sexism for women, whereas men reported markedly fewer instances of sexual objectification (Swim, Hyers, Cohen, & Ferguson, 2001).

Unwanted sexual attention by men is a common theme connecting the various forms of interpersonal sexual objectification. In particular, public stranger harassment is prevalent and pervasive (Gardner, 1995). Nine of 10 Canadian women have reported an experience of stranger harassment at least once in their lives (Lenton, Smith, Fox, & Morra, 1999). In a national representative sample of Canadian women, over 80% reported experiences of harassment by a male stranger in public (Macmillan, Nierobisz, & Welsh, 2000). In a sample of women aged 18 to 34 living in London, 43% reported encounters of stranger harassment during the previous year (YouGov, 2012). Among a sample of US college women, over 40% reported experiencing unwanted sexual attention from strangers at least once a month (Fairchild & Rudman, 2008). In an Australian sample, women reported an average of one encounter of stranger harassment every 2 days over a 7-day period (Holland, Koval, Stratemeyer, Thomson, & Haslam, 2017).

In a recent study, experiences of stranger harassment and self-objectification were uniquely linked to women's perceived likelihood of rape and intimate partner violence happening to them (and unrelated to perceived likelihood of burglary or human trafficking happening to them), the former reflecting two gender crimes whereby women are disproportionately the victims of blatant sexual and physical harm and men the perpetrators (Donnelly & Calogero, 2018). Research has shown that the anticipation of sexually motivated bodily harm affects women across multiple spheres of daily living, serving as a continual source of anxiety for many of them (Gordon & Riger, 1991; Yodanis, 2004). These divergent experiences with safety anxiety and vigilance in the context of sexual objectification represents a fundamental distinction between women and men as gendered social groups (Kaschak, 1992). Indeed, it may be the threat of sexual violence in the context of sexual objectification that effectively socializes girls and women to experience their bodies as belonging less to them and more to others (Davidson & Gervais, 2015; Fredrickson & Roberts, 1997). Therefore, in addition to adopting a view of oneself as an object of sexual desire, women come to view themselves as targets of sexual violence as a result of being sexually objectified, thus setting the stage for experiences of negative embodiment.

PERCEIVED SAFETY AND DISRUPTIONS TO POSITIVE EMBODIMENT

An accumulation of evidence has demonstrated the disruptive nature of sexual objectification for women's sense of safety and security in the world. This threat to personal safety has a number of downstream consequences for women's positive embodiment. Notably, a heightened vigilance around personal safety creates markedly different subjective experiences for women as a group compared to men as a group. When asked to describe what they do on any given day to maintain their personal safety, women list multiple strategies (e.g., checking back seat of car, keeping keys between fingers, pretending to talk on cell phone) for keeping themselves safe, whereas men list noticeably fewer strategies (Fredrickson & Roberts, 1997). To be clear, men also experience sexual objectification and threats to their personal safety, but research has shown that women employ specific strategies and remain vigilant of their surroundings because of safety concerns to a much greater degree than men do (Fisher, Sloan, & Wilkins, 1995).

The restriction of voluntary movement—the ability to engage freely in the world without safety concerns—is a particular way in which women's agency and functionality become policed and constrained, reflecting sexual terrorism (Hickman & Muehlenhard, 1997). Fairchild and Rudman (2008) provided quantitative evidence for an association between women's experiences of sexual objectification and their modes of voluntary movement. Specifically, in a sample of predominantly white female US college students, women's experiences of stranger harassment predicted more fear of rape, perceived risk of rape, and self-objectification, with the last measured as a composite of self-surveillance and body shame. By far the most commonly reported coping strategy used in the face of stranger harassment was a passive response (e.g., "I pretended nothing was happening"), which strengthened the positive link between stranger harassment and self-objectification for those women. Further statistical modeling of these associations revealed that fear of rape mediated the association between stranger harassment and voluntary restriction of their movement in terms of how, when, and where women travel to avoid the threat of sexual violence.

Other research has linked women's experiences of sexual objectification more directly to psychological distress (i.e., depression, anxiety, stress) through their fear of crime and safety concerns. In one study, researchers found significant positive associations between interpersonal sexual objectification experiences and perceived risk and fear of crime in black and white women, and the relationship between sexual objectification and fear of crime was fully explained by their perceptions of an overall greater perceived risk of crime (Watson, Marszalek, Dispenza, & Davids, 2015). On further analysis, they observed that women's fear of crime had distinct relations with sexual objectification and psychological distress for black and white women. Specifically, perceived risk of crime fully mediated the relationship between sexual objectification experiences and psychological distress for black women only, suggesting that black women's lived encounters of sexual objectification and crime creates a different sociocultural experience for these women that may produce a larger effect on their overall psychological well-being compared to the experience of white women (Watson, Robinson, Dispenza, & Nazari, 2012).

Authors of another study narrowed their investigation to women's generalized anxiety in the context of street harassment experiences and safety concerns (Davidson, Butchko, Robbins, Sherd, & Gervais, 2016). In a sample of predominantly white US college women, the authors found higher levels of street harassment predicted less perceived safety in both busy and isolated public settings, yet it was only for the more secluded public spaces (e.g., walking alone at night, walking alone in a parking garage, and using public transportation at night) where perceptions of safety served as an indirect link between experiences of street harassment and higher general anxiety. Thus, lower levels of perceived safety in isolated public settings (but not busy public settings) partly explained the positive association between experiences of street harassment and general anxiety in predominantly white US college women, highlighting another disruptive effect of eroded personal safety on women's positive embodiment.

In a set of studies, we examined personal safety anxiety specifically and directly in conjunction with experiences of sexual objectification and associated downstream effects on women's subjectivity and mental health (Calogero, Tylka, Pina, & Siegel, 2018). Given the threat and uncontrollable nature of sexually objectifying experiences encountered in everyday life, objectification theory posits that women experience a merging of hyperawareness and anxiety around physical appearance *and* personal safety (Fredrickson & Roberts, 1997; Roberts et al., 2018). We tested the idea that personal safety anxiety is a subjective experience that occurs for women in relation to their experiences of sexual objectification and operates as another mediating mechanism between sexual objectification and mental health outcomes (Calogero et al., 2018). Across five studies and 1,280 participants, we validated a new measure of personal safety anxiety and tested the theoretically proposed role of this construct within objectification theory. We observed a common and undeniable pattern for women whereby personal safety anxiety was manifest alongside experiences of sexual and self-objectification, and it predicted more fear of rape, perceived likelihood of rape, and heightened vigilance and policing of their personal safety (e.g., planned route with safety in mind, avoid going out at night alone), whereas these patterns were not observed for men.

In a comprehensive test of the multiple subjective (i.e., appearance anxiety, body shame, interceptive awareness, flow) and mental health (i.e., depression, sexual dysfunction, disordered eating) experiences associated with sexual and self-objectification in objectification theory, we also found that personal safety anxiety predicted higher levels of self-objectification, safety vigilance, body shame, and appearance anxiety (Calogero et al., 2018). Notably, personal safety anxiety connected sexual objectification and self-objectification to safety vigilance, as well as connected sexual objectification to appearance anxiety, thus lending further support to the idea that women's appearance concerns in the context of sexual objectification are fused with concerns about their personal safety. We also observed an indirect effect of personal safety anxiety on symptoms of disordered eating via safety vigilance. Disordered eating is one of the clearest manifestations of a disconnection between the mind and body, as well as an attempt to control and discipline the body, and therefore represents some of the most troubling features of negative embodiment (Cook-Cottone, 2006). Our research provided further evidence that personal safety anxiety and corresponding safety vigilance are disruptive to positive embodiment in a profound way through women's attempts to control, reduce, and deny their physical presence and taking up space in the world (Calogero et al., 2018).

CLAIMING AND CULTIVATING PERSONAL SAFETY

Piran (2016) identified five core dimensions of the experience of embodiment. We argue that personal safety is the bedrock on which these experiences of embodiment can be realized. Women must feel and be safe in order to inhabit their bodies as a subjective site and resist objectification without retribution, fully experience and express their desires, and foster bodily connection and comfort, agency and functionality, and attuned self-care. In a qualitative analysis of the significance and meaning of safety for women, participants described their experience of a feminist women-only safe space as a "freeing" environment because it allowed women to express themselves cognitively, emotionally, and intellectually and be all they can be (Lewis, Sharp, Remnant, & Redpath, 2015)—safety from misogyny in all its forms "creates conditions for women to be fully human" (p. 9). In other words, personal safety would allow for a host of embodied possibilities (Piran, 2016).

There are no simple remedies to the sexual objectification of women and the threat to personal safety implied or enacted in these encounters. Yet, this social reality for women constitutes a form of everyday discrimination and oppression, which is multiplied for women across mutually constitutive categories of race, class, and sexuality (Shields, 2008). We agree with objectification theorists who posit that being female-bodied creates a nearly universal experience with sexual objectification for girls and women regardless of race, ethnicity, religion, economic status, cultural background, and sexual orientation (Fredrickson & Roberts, 1997). Even so, research on women's safety-related attitudes and behaviors has relied predominantly on the experiences of cisgender and white young women to inform our understanding of safety concerns, creating a critical knowledge gap in the literature that we need to close. In the discussion that follows, we identify three needed shifts in any cultural landscape to move us closer toward a safe reality for women.

One effort to claim and cultivate personal safety for women would involve the creation of more feminist women-only safe spaces (Lewis et al., 2015). These spaces enable women to build solidarity with other women and counter hostility toward each other. We wish to point out that the onus on women to protect themselves from harm is at once empowering (women can keep themselves safe) and disempowering (women are to blame if they cannot keep themselves safe) and continues to reinforce the normativity of rape culture and unsafe spaces for girls and women (Ullman, 2007). Indeed, a second effort would involve stopping the cultural shame and guilt game, whereby women feel ashamed for being made to feel unsafe, vulnerable, and responsible for the sexual violence committed against them by boys and men (Weiss, 2010). This internalized shame and guilt can be paralyzing for individual women and stall social change (Calogero, 2013, 2017; Watson & Grotewiel, 2016). For this shift to be realized, a third effort is needed to detox masculinity and redistribute social power along gender lines, as boys and men are an integral part of the solution (Addis & Cohane, 2005; Drury & Kaiser, 2014; Foubert, 2005; Vandello, Bosson, Cohen, Burnaford, & Weaver, 2008; see also Chapter 14).

CONCLUSION

On the whole, we leave readers with a troubling conclusion. The erosion of personal safety creates more opportunities for negative embodiment in women, which means in sexually objectifying environments, many women ironically may self-objectify and court treatment as a sexual object under the illusion that paternalistic protection and sexual dependency might insure their safety against sexual violence (Calogero & Jost, 2011). These psychological processes require further empirical investigation, but one thing is clear: The effects of the omnipresent threat of sexual objectification are deeply insidious. Personal safety and freedom from sexual harm must be claimed and cultivated in order for women to be free in the world. We must put an end to the threats to safety from sexual objectification in order for women to realize embodied social justice.

REFERENCES

Addis, M. E., & Cohane, G. H. (2005). Social scientific paradigms of masculinity and their implications for research and practice in men's mental health. *Journal of Clinical Psychology*, *61*, 633–647. doi:10.1002/jclp.20099

Allik, M., & Kearns, A. (2017). "There goes the fear": Feelings of safety at home and in the neighborhood: The role of personal, social, and service factors. *Journal of Community Psychology*, *45*, 543–563. doi:10.1002/jcop.21875

American Psychological Association, Task Force on the Sexualization of Girls. (2010). *Report of the APA Task Force on the Sexualization of Girls*. Retrieved from https://www.apa.org/pi/women/programs/girls/report.aspx

Benoit, C., Shumka, L., & Vallance, K. (2010). *Violence as a determinant of girls' and women's health* (Research Brief #1). Women's Health Research Network. Retrieved from https://www.uvic.ca/research/centres/youthsociety/assets/docs/resources/violence-determinant-girls-womens-health.pdf

Calogero, R. M. (2013). Objects don't object: Evidence that self-objectification disrupts women's social activism. *Psychological Science, 24*, 312–318. doi:10.1177/0956797612452574

Calogero, R. M. (2017). Political consciousness and gender collective action: A case and place for self-objectification. In A. L. Bos & M. C. Schneider (Eds.), *The political psychology of women in US politics* (pp. 93–110). New York, NY: Routledge.

Calogero, R. M., & Jost, J. T. (2011). Self-subjugation among women: Sexist ideology, self-objectification, and the buffering function of the need to avoid closure. *Journal of Personality and Social Psychology, 100*, 11–228.

Calogero, R. M., Tylka, T. L., Pina, A., & Siegel, J. (2018). *Smile pretty and watch your back: Personal safety anxiety and vigilance in objectification theory*. Manuscript under review.

Cook-Cottone, C. (2006). The attuned representation model for the primary prevention of eating disorders: An overview for school psychologists. *Psychology in the Schools, 43*, 223–230. doi:10.1002/pits.20139

Davidson, M. M., Butchko, M. S., Robbins, K., Sherd, L. W., & Gervais, S. J. (2016). The mediating role of perceived safety on street harassment and anxiety. *Psychology of Violence, 6*, 553–561. doi:10.1037/e505232016-001

Davidson, M. M., & Gervais, S. J. (2015). Violence against women through the lens of objectification theory. *Violence Against Women, 21*, 330–354. doi:10.1177/1077801214568031

Donnelly, L. C., & Calogero, R. M. (2018). The role of stranger harassment experiences in college women's perceived possibility of gender crimes happening to them. *Journal of Applied Social Psychology, 48*, 165–173. doi:10.1111/jasp.12497

Drury, B. J., & Kaiser, C. R. (2014). Allies against sexism: The role of men in confronting sexism. *Journal of Social Issues, 70*, 637–652.

Fairchild, K., & Rudman, L. A. (2008). Everyday stranger harassment and women's objectification. *Social Justice Research, 21*, 338–357. doi:10.1007/s11211-008-0073-0

Ferraro, K. F. (1996). Women's fear of victimization: Shadow of sexual assault? *Social Forces, 75*, 667–690. doi:10.2307/2580418

Finkelhor, D., Shattuck, A., Turner, H. A., & Hamby, S. L. (2014). The lifetime prevalence of child sexual abuse and sexual assault assessed in late adolescence. *Journal of Adolescent Health, 55*, 329–333. doi:10.1016/j.jadohealth.2013.12.026

Fisher, B. S., Cullen, F. T., & Turner, M. (2000). *The sexual victimization of college women*. Washington, DC: US Department of Justice.

Fisher, B. S., & Sloan, J. J. (2003). Unraveling the fear of victimization among college women: Is the "shadow of sexual assault hypothesis" supported? *Justice Quarterly, 20*, 633–659. doi:10.1080/07418820300095641

Fisher, B. S., Sloan, J. J., & Wilkins, D. L. (1995). Fear and perceived risk of victimization in an urban university setting. In B. S. Fisher & J. J. Sloan (Eds.), *Campus crime: Legal, social and policy perspectives* (pp. 179–209). Springfield, IL: Thomas.

Foubert, J. D. (2005). *The Men's Program: A peer education guide to rape prevention* (3rd ed.). New York, NY: Routledge.

Fredrickson, B. L., & Roberts, T.-A. (1997). Objectification theory: Toward understanding women's lived experiences and mental health risks. *Psychology of Women Quarterly, 21*, 173–206. doi:10.1111/j.1471-6402.1997.tb00108.x

Gardner, C. G. (1995). *Passing by: Gender and public harassment*. Berkeley, CA: University of California Press.

Gordon, M. T., & Riger, S. (1991). *The female fear: The social cost of rape*. Chicago: University of Illinois Press.

Harris, M. B., & Miller, K. (2000). Gender and perceptions of danger. *Sex Roles, 43*, 843–863. doi:10.1023/A:1011036905770

Hickman, S. E., & Muehlenhard, C. L. (1997). College women's fears and precautionary behaviors relating to acquaintance rape and stranger rape. *Psychology of Women Quarterly, 21*, 527–547. doi:10.1111/j.1471-6402.1997.tb00129.x

Hoffman, E. E., Mair, T. T. M., Hunter, B. A., Prince, D. M., & Tebes, J. K. (2018). Neighborhood sexual violence moderates women's perceived safety in urban neighborhoods. *Journal of Community Psychology, 46*, 79–94. doi:10.1002/jcop.21917

Holland, E., Koval, P., Stratemeyer, M., Thomson, F., & Haslam, N. (2017). Sexual objectification in women's daily lives: A smartphone ecological momentary assessment study. *British Journal of Social Psychology, 56*, 314–333. doi:10.1111/bjso.12152

Kaschak, E. (1992). *Engendered lives: A new psychology of women's experience*. New York, NY: Basic Books.

Kissling, E. A. (1991). Street harassment: The language of sexual terrorism. *Discourse & Society, 2*, 451–460. doi:10.1177/0957926591002004006

Lenton, R., Smith, M. D., Fox, J., & Morra, N. (1999). Sexual harassment in public places: Experiences of Canadian women. *Canadian Review of Sociology, 36*, 517–540. doi:10.1111/j.1755-618X.1999.tb00962.x

Lewis, R., Sharp, E., Remnant, J., & Redpath, R. (2015). "Safe spaces": Experiences of feminist women-only space. *Sociological Research Online, 20*, 9. doi:10.5153/sro.3781

Macmillan, R., Nierobisz, A., & Welsh, S. (2000). Experiencing the streets: Harassment and perceptions of safety among women. *Journal of Research in Crime and Delinquency, 37*, 306–322. doi:10.1177/0022427800037003003

Pascoe, C. J. (2011). *Dude, you're a fag: Masculinity and sexuality in high school*. Berkeley: University of California Press.

Piran, N. (2016). Embodied possibilities and disruptions: The emergence of the experience of embodiment construct from qualitative studies with girls and women. *Body Image, 18*, 43–60. doi:10.1016/j.bodyim.2016.04.007

Roberts, T.-A., Calogero, R. M., & Gervais, S. (2018). Objectification theory: Continuing contributions to feminist psychology. In C. Travis & J. White (Eds.), *APA handbook of the psychology of women, Vol. 1: History, theory, and battlegrounds* (pp. 249–272). Washington, DC: American Psychological Association.

Schafer, J. A., Huebner, B. M., & Bynum, T. S. (2006). Fear of crime and criminal victimization: Gender-based contrasts. *Journal of Criminal Justice, 34*, 285–301. doi:10.1016/j.jcrimjus.2006.03.003

Sheffield, C. J. (1987). Sexual terrorism: The social control of women. In B. B. Hess & M. M. Ferree (Eds.), *Analyzing gender: A handbook of social science research* (pp. 171–189). Thousand Oaks, CA: Sage.

Sinha, M. (Ed.). (2013). *Measuring violence against women: Statistical trends*. Canadian Centre for Justice Statistics Profile Series, no. 85-002-X. Retrieved from http://www.statcan.gc.ca/pub/85-002-x/2013001/article/11766-eng.pdf

Smith, S. G., Chen, J., Basile, K. C., Gilbert, L. K., Merrick, M. T., Patel, N., . . . Jain, A. (2017, April). *The National Intimate Partner and Sexual Violence Survey: 2010–2012 State Report*. Retrieved January 8, 2018, from https://www.cdc.gov/violenceprevention/nisvs/index.html

Swim, J. K., Hyers, L. L., Cohen, L. L., & Ferguson, M. J. (2001). Everyday sexism: Evidence for its incidence, nature, and psychological impact from three daily diary studies. *Journal of Social Issues*, *57*, 31–53. doi:10.1111/0022-4537.00200

Tjaden, P., & Thoennes, N. (2000). *Extent, nature, and consequences of intimate partner violence: Findings from the National Violence Against Women Survey*. Washington, DC: US Department of Justice. Retrieved February 7, 2018, from https://www.ncjrs.gov/pdffiles1/nij/181867.pdf

Ullman, S. E. (2007). A 10-year update of "review and critique of empirical studies of rape avoidance." *Criminal Justice and Behavior*, *34*, 411–429. doi:10.1177/0093854806297117

Vandello, J. A., Bosson, J. K., Cohen, D., Burnaford, R. M., & Weaver, J. (2008). Precarious manhood. *Journal of Personality and Social Psychology*, *95*, 1325–1339. doi:10.1037/a0012453

Watson, L. B., & Grotewiel, M. (2016). The protective role of commitment to social change in the relationship between women's experiences and self-silencing. *Sex Roles*, *75*, 249–250. doi:10.1007/s11199-016-0594-1

Watson, L. B., Marszalek, J. M., Dispenza, F., & Davids, C. M. (2015). Understanding the relationships among white and African American women's sexual objectification experiences, physical safety anxiety, and psychological distress. *Sex Roles*, *72*, 91–104. doi:10.1007/s11199-014-0444-y

Watson, L. B., Robinson, D., Dispenza, F., & Nazari, N. (2012). African American women's sexual objectification experiences: A qualitative study. *Psychology of Women Quarterly*, *36*, 458–475. doi:10.1177/036168431244724

Weiss, K. G. (2010). Too ashamed to report: Deconstructing the shame of sexual victimization. *Feminist Criminology*, *53*, 286–310. doi:10.1177/1557085110376343

World Health Organization. (2016). *Violence against women fact sheet*. Retrieved July 11, 2017, from www.who.int/mediacentre/factsheets/fs239/en/

Yodanis, C. L. (2004). Gender inequality, violence against women, and fear: A cross-national test of the feminist theory of violence against women. *Journal of Interpersonal Violence*, *19*, 655–675. doi:10.1177/088626050426368

YouGov. (2012, May 25). *Sexual harassment in the capital*. Retrieved from https://yougov.co.uk/news/2012/05/25/sexual-harassment-capital

14

Promoting a Resistant Stance Toward Objectification

TRACY L. TYLKA AND RACHEL M. CALOGERO ■

Individuals who are positively embodied experience agency and functionality in the world, are attuned with their body's needs while engaging in the world, experience and express their desires, and inhabit their body as a subjective site (Piran, 2016, 2017). A destructive force that usurps positive embodiment is *objectification*, or the fragmentation of others or oneself into a collection of body parts or sexual functions for scrutiny or gratification (Bartky, 1990).

When objectified, a person is no longer perceived as whole and integrated, but instead fragmented, lacking in depth and unique subjectivity (Piran, 2016, 2017). When objectification is directed at another, it is often sexual, whereby the person being viewed is perceived to be worthwhile only to the extent that person can sexually gratify the observer. When objectification is directed inward, the person self-objectifies, or adopts an observer's perspective of their self as a sexual object (Fredrickson & Roberts, 1997), scrutinizing their appearance and sexiness to determine how to make it coincide with what is desired by others. Sexual objectification and self-objectification are associated with many forms of disrupted embodiment, including body shame, disordered eating, depression, and sexual dysfunction (Tiggemann & Williams, 2012); less social agency (Calogero, 2013); more negative self-evaluations (Calogero, 2004); poorer health and well-being at work (Chan, Lam, Chow, & Cheung, 2008); and reduced performance on cognitive tasks (Gervais, Vescio, & Allen, 2011).

In this chapter, we discuss a two-prong approach to promote a resistant stance toward objectification: (a) delegitimize the system of sexual objectification and (b) arm individuals with skills to resist self-objectification. Although men, especially gay men, can be objectified, girls and women are targeted as objects of sexual objectification more frequently, more severely, and across life domains (Fredrickson & Roberts, 1997); thus, we focus on women's experiences.

DELEGITIMIZE THE SYSTEM OF SEXUAL OBJECTIFICATION

Everyday environments present recurrent opportunities for girls and women to encounter varying degrees and forms of sexual objectification (Fredrickson & Roberts, 1997), such as being gazed or leered at, hearing or seeing comments about their bodies, being whistled or honked at, being sent unsolicited naked photos, being pressured to send naked photos, witnessing another take photos of their bodies without permission, and being sexually harassed/assaulted (Calogero & Tylka, 2014). This rampant exposure to women being sexually objectified encourages boys and men to devalue girls and women, which undermines interpersonal intimacy and satisfaction, well-being, and health for all involved (Zurbriggen, Ramsey, & Jaworski, 2011). Yet, men *and* women at times justify and promote its occurrence. Why?

The reason is that sexual objectification is a system: a structured set of social arrangements that prescribe specific, interdependent roles and behaviors to men and women that reinforce the gender hierarchy (see Calogero & Tylka, 2014). Sexual objectification signals women's decorative, subordinate, and disadvantaged status, positioning them to be the target of evaluation and sexual consumption. Women cannot simply "opt out" of this system because it is interwoven into the wider social landscape that they navigate every day; thus, women are dependent on this system and less able to escape it (Kay & Friesen, 2011). Further, men and women inadvertently protect those who objectify and assault women by debasing the victim (Loughnan et al., 2010; Loughnan, Pina, Vasquez, & Puvia, 2013) or, at the very least, serving as a passive bystander due to fear—a realistic fear that reporting or confronting it will damage their careers or social standing, jeopardize their safety, and diminish their power (Banyard, Plante, & Moynihan, 2004; Foubert, Langhinrichsen-Rohling, Brasfield, & Hill, 2010; Swim & Hyers, 1999). As such, a fundamental tendency to defend and support this system keeps it in place.

To disrupt the system of sexual objectification, harmful consequences of sexually objectifying practices must be acknowledged and commitment to reducing these practices endorsed. Yet, challenging this system is threatening, as it goes against deeply entrenched cultural patterns that expect—and reward—women for being available for sexual objectification. According to system justification theory, people are generally motivated to defend, bolster, and justify those systems that they participate in when they are threatened, making change unlikely (Jost et al., 2012). The reasons for justifying sexual objectification include cultural myths that sexual objectification is "natural," women should be flattered by and enjoy the sexual attention, and many (if not all) forms of sexual objectification are innocuous; these reasons legitimize sexual objectification and reduce distress over it (Calogero & Tylka, 2014). These cultural myths permeate through media, interpersonal encounters, and the wider cultural context—which *normalize* and *protect* them. These myths are also intertwined with compulsory heterosexual masculinity and femininity. Women learn that their value is highly dependent on the degree to which they complement and compliment men through their sexual availability, bolstering their investment in a system that subordinates them. So, how do we as scholars, activists, clinicians, and researchers devoted to positive embodiment help others acknowledge the harms of sexual objectification and address how to reduce sexual objectification when doing so elicits defense of this system?

Reframe Sexual Objectification as a Threat to a Broader System

One answer may lie in framing the reduction of sexual objectification as both necessary and in line with societal values and goals. In other words, the cultural practices of sexual objectification are positioned as the threat to another system: the betterment of the broader society.

In order to disrupt support for the system of sexual objectification and activate *system-sanctioned change* (Feygina, Jost, & Goldsmith, 2010), we need to (a) defuse or redirect the threat; (b) increase awareness that sexual objectification is already happening and how we can resist contributing to it; (c) help people perceive that their outcomes are not dependent on sexual objectification being sustained; and (d) encourage people to feel that they do not need to rely on sexual objectification to feel personal control (Kay & Friesen, 2011). Feygina et al. used the principles of system-sanctioned change in enlisting support for environmentalism by linking this value to patriotism and to preserving the country's natural resources. Thus, the resistance to pro-environmental behavior was framed as the threat to the American way of life. People thus became motivated to defend environmentalism, instead of sanctioning values that supported the status quo of disregard toward the natural environment. In a parallel way, framing the rejection of sexual objectification as pivotal for the betterment of society might sanction a system shift and provide a new path to delegitimizing the system of sexual objectification. We now detail how Kay and Friesen's recommendations can be applied toward this goal.

Ways to Reframe Sexual Objectification as a Threat to a Broader System

Redirect the Threat

Instead of the threat being *to* sexual objectification, which leads to rationalizations in support of sexual objectification (e.g., "It's natural for men to desire women"), the threat *is* sexual objectification (e.g., "Treating anyone as a sexual object threatens their personal safety and denies their personhood, thereby stripping away basic freedoms"), which leads to its rejection. For example, instead of silencing those targeted by sexually objectifying practices (threat *to* sexual objectification), we can hold those who sexually objectify accountable and encourage bystanders of sexual objectification to come forward and not let it linger in silence (threat *is* sexual objectification). Further, we could bring more attention to the ways in which sexualized portrayals of adolescent girls in the media, or the clothing sold for toddlers with slogans such as "Future Porn Star," promote sexual interest in children. Given that "freedom" and "protection of innocent childhood" are in line with societal values and goals, system-sanctioned change may take place (Calogero & Tylka, 2014).

Redirecting the threat may be extremely difficult, and it will not likely be effective with everyone. The senate race in Alabama during the 2017 special election provides a case in point. During that race, allegations surfaced that the Republican nominee, Roy Moore, pursued or sexually assaulted high school girls while he was in his 30s. Moore denied the allegations. While many, including some Republicans, called for Moore to drop out of the race and indicated that they believed the allegations (threat *is* sexual objectification), some continued to defend or minimize his alleged actions or discredit the women who came forward (threat *to* sexual objectification). On November 14, 2017, Meghan McCain, a conservative author and former Fox News host tweeted, "Those of you who have the audacity to demand I defend Roy Moore for the sake of his senate seat—your soul may be for sale, but mine is not." Perhaps having people verbalize their opposition to sexual objectification will crystalize their commitment to rejecting this system. This strategy, which calls on the principles of cognitive dissonance to create attitudinal change (Festinger, 1957; Stice, Shaw, Becker, & Rohde, 2008), has been shown to be effective in other domains, such as lowering women's endorsement of the thin-ideal body type, which predicts lower eating disorder behaviors, attitudes, and risk factors (see Chapter 33).

Frame Sexual Objectification as Already Happening and Offer Ways We Can Challenge It

Sexual objectification has been happening throughout "herstory." Countless women have come forward with their stories, yet these stories often get minimized, covered up, and swept under the rug. We as scholars and activists can use our power to emphasize the prevalence of the various types of sexual objectification (e.g., through media interviews, blogs) and encourage speaking out about it, not only by those who have been targeted, but also by all members of society. We need to ensure that individuals coming forward are protected from harm.

Currently, the #MeToo movement provides hope that people are becoming aware of sexual objectification and are committed to reducing it. Blogger and advocate Tarana Burke started the "Me Too" movement 10 years ago in order to enhance awareness and advocacy about sexual violence. Individuals who have been sexually objectified, harassed, and assaulted wrote Me Too on their MySpace page and, if they so wished, told their stories. This movement gave those who were harassed a voice, strength, and collective power to work toward eradicating sexual harassment. Recently, the movement resurfaced as the #MeToo campaign following a *New York Times* exposé revealing decades of sexual assault allegations against Hollywood producer Harvey Weinstein. Female actors began to speak out widely about being sexually harassed during their long-standing careers, naming their assailants and those who protected them. On October 15, 2017, Alyssa Milano retweeted, "Suggested by a friend: 'If all the women who have been sexually harassed or assaulted wrote 'Me too.' as a status, we might give people a sense of the magnitude of the problem." Milano's call to action transformed into a social media movement on Twitter, Facebook, and Instagram, resulting in an estimated 12 million people indicating #MeToo by October 17, 2017, with even more coming forward in the days and weeks that followed. Directors, actors, comedians, news personalities, chief executive officers, coaches, trainers, and politicians were identified as assailants, with negative consequences imposed on many.

Some men also posted #YesIhave, #ItWasMe, and #IHearYou on social media to challenge sexual objectification. These men indicated how they have contributed to harassment and rape culture and pledged to uphold better boundaries for themselves, respect the boundaries of women, and raise awareness of the problem of men sexually objectifying women. For example, one man wrote, "I was 'that guy' who would undermine the claims of survivors," "I was lighthearted about the consequences of rape," and "I didn't change because I'm smart. I didn't change because I'm a nice guy. I didn't change because I am a 'liberal.' I didn't change because I know survivors. I changed because people spoke out. I changed because I was proven wrong. I changed because I was challenged to learn. I changed because all my friends changed. Most importantly, I changed because of your persistence" (Pallin, 2017).

These movements challenge participation in sexual objectification because they do not rationalize it, and they discourage people from adopting the mindset that they simply need to make the best out of a bad situation; rather, they instill hope that their situation can change. The long-term impact of these movements on curtailing sexual harassment has yet to be determined, and some backlash is expected. Given the initial favorable reaction, however, providing and nurturing public outlets for coming forward, discussing personal accounts of objectifying experiences, and challenging objectification, seems a worthwhile investment.

Another way to challenge participation in sexual objectification is by educating and promoting *radical consent*, whereby all adults involved in a sexual activity agree to a coercion-free situation. However, the potential for coercion exists when power is unequal. In such conditions, no one is placed in a situation where they would be too uncomfortable to say no (e.g., having power over women's careers and asking them if it is okay to masturbate in front of them, as in the case of Louis C.K., or to engage in sexual acts with them, as in the case of Matt Lauer) or could not say no (e.g., those under the legal age, intoxicated, incapacitated). These instances reflect an abuse of power. Silence is not taken as a yes, but the other's boundaries are respected by holding back and asking permission. Consent should be provided for each part of the encounter, rather than be seen as a blanket yes for all sexual activities or for future sexual encounters; it can further be revoked at any point without explanation. In court, prosecutors should not ask victims about the number of times, and how clearly, they said no, but instead ask perpetrators how many times they asked for and honored a yes response. Prosecutors should also consider the power perpetrators have over victims.

Help People (and Businesses) Perceive that Their Outcomes Are Not Dependent on Sexual Objectification Being Sustained

Individuals' emotional, social, and sexual well-being are not dependent on sexual objectification being sustained. In fact, sexual objectification *reduces* various forms of well-being. For example, exposure to sexually objectified imagery, such as pornography and sexualized (e.g., thin-ideal) media images, has adverse consequences for viewers' well-being. A three-wave panel survey among Dutch adolescents revealed that exposure to pornography consistently reduced sexual satisfaction, which then prompted greater reliance on pornography, creating a downward spiral of sexual satisfaction (Peter & Valkenburg, 2009). Compared to a control group, men and women who viewed pornography for 6 weeks reported less satisfaction with their intimate partner's affection, physical appearance, sexual curiosity, and sexual performance (Zillmann & Bryant, 1988). Exposure to sexualized female thin-ideal images has deleterious effects on body satisfaction and cognitive functioning (i.e., greater appearance schema activation) for adolescent girls and boys (Hargreaves & Tiggemann, 2002) and women and men (Aubrey & Taylor, 2009; Baker & Blanchard, 2017; Krawczyk & Thompson, 2015). Men exposed to female thin-ideal ads reported lower romantic confidence, lower body confidence, and higher appearance anxiety than men who viewed ads with male models or ads with neutral content (Aubrey & Taylor, 2009).

For businesses, profit and product popularity are not dependent on perpetuating sexual objectification. First, objectified imagery may not be more appealing to consumers or sell more products, countering the belief that "sex sells." Researchers are beginning to address this area. For example, one characteristic of many sexually objectified images is the "thin ideal" (Krawczyk & Thompson, 2015). Diedrichs and Lee (2011) investigated whether "average"-size models would promote positive body image and appeal to women and men consumers in Australia. They compared thin and average-size models in advertisements for clothing and beauty products and investigated their advertising appeal and effect on body image. Both women and men reacted as positively to advertisements for clothing and beauty products featuring average-size models as they did to those featuring thin models and a no model, product-only comparison group. These findings suggest that average-size models provide a marketable alternative to current sexualized imagery, appealing to both women and men consumers. As a bonus, exposure to average-size models prompted a more positive body image among women than exposure to thin models. Similar findings have been reported in the United Kingdom (e.g., Halliwell & Dittmar, 2004). This area begs additional research (e.g., expanding beyond thin-ideal imagery), which has tremendous potential to shape public health and policy.

Encourage People to Understand that They Do Not Need to Rely on Sexual Objectification to Feel Personal Control

Traditional masculinity scripts, such as ones that breed sexual objectification (e.g., playboy, power over women, dominance, violence, pursuit of status), provide men with a sense of control in the form of *power over* others. In contrast, we need to work to replace traditional masculinity scripts with a strengths-based version of "positive masculinity" that encompasses compassion, empathy, and resilience (Englar-Carlson & Kiselica, 2013), facilitating personal control in a way that would promote power *with* others. In other words, positive masculinity improves the lives of men and those around them and resists (as opposed to defends) the system of sexual objectification.

Countering sexual objectification can be further reinforced by redefining masculinity. We suggest that, in line with Englar-Carlson and Kiselica's (2013) description of three characteristics of positive masculinity (i.e., group orientation, male ways of caring, and male courage), men can disrupt the system of sexual objectification. First, boys and men are oriented toward banding together in groups to achieve a common purpose, which provides identity and community. Second, men are socialized to care for their loved ones and show high action empathy (i.e., the ability to act based on how they see things from a loved one's perspective). Third, men express their courage by taking sensible risks without being reckless. Thus, men could gather in structured groups to fight violence against women and practice ways to challenge sexualized violence (e.g., rape jokes, rape myth acceptance) in everyday life.

The Men's Program (Foubert & Perry, 2007) takes this approach and thus serves as an excellent framework to implement positive masculinity in the fight against sexualized violence. Specifically, this program increases men's understanding of sexual violence and its relevance to them and motivation to act against it. This method is undertaken by (a) using same-age male group facilitators who present facts about sexual violence to increase transferability of information; (b) showing a video of a male-on-male rape to discuss rape myths and evoke empathy toward women; (c) emphasizing that sexualized violence is likely to impact a girl/woman that they love; (d) discussing why it is important for men to act and how they should act in support of loved ones who are assaulted; (e) increasing action empathy by inspiring men to act to ensure women are not sexually assaulted; and (f) articulating ways that they can contribute to a culture that does not support sexualized violence (e.g., confronting rape jokes, challenging sexist behavior). This program is also structured to minimize men's defensiveness by assuming that they want to help stop sexualized violence, rather than positioning them as potential perpetrators of this violence. Because these strength-based qualities are embedded in masculinity, it is less likely to evoke a defense of sexual objectification. In comparison to control groups, college men taking The Men's Program have reported increased understanding of how rape may feel, resistance to telling rape jokes, willingness to help a survivor and intervene as bystanders in potentially dangerous situations, efficacy to help survivors seek assistance, and intolerance of rape myths (Foubert & Perry, 2007; Langhinrichsen-Rohling, Foubert, Brasfield, Hill, & Shelley-Tremblay, 2011).

To help women feel that they do not need to rely on sexual objectification to feel personal control, we need to target and dismantle "raunch culture," which teaches and encourages girls and women to sexually objectify themselves to please boys and men (Levy, 2005). However, raunch culture is not an "individual problem with women." Instead, it is a manifestation of patriarchy: Women's reduced status positions them to gain power through their identification with men who sexually objectify women. Thus, ending raunch culture will likely entail leadership that promotes social justice; educating individuals on privilege, oppression, and social justice; adopting an intersectional approach by seeing how systems of privilege and oppression are intertwined; and evoking empathic action toward oppressed groups. In cultures where *all* women within all social locations are fundamentally respected, women have the power and personal control to present themselves as empowered, capable individuals independent of the male gaze.

ARM WOMEN WITH SKILLS TO RESIST SELF-OBJECTIFICATION

Extracting perceptions of control gained from participating in or defending the system of sexual objectification is a societal intervention that must be addressed at the cultural level. Nevertheless, until this cultural-level work is complete, we must also work at the individual level to prevent self-objectification (e.g., treating oneself as an instrument for others' sexual pleasure, habitual focus on appearance, internalizing the thin ideal). The need to act at an individual level is illustrated by findings that women with high levels of thin-ideal internalization are more negatively impacted from exposure to sexually objectifying images than women with low levels of thin-ideal internalization (e.g., Krawczyk & Thompson, 2015). When women strive toward an idealized appearance to gain power and status and are reinforced for their attempts (e.g., "You lost weight; you look hot!"), they are less likely to challenge sexual objectification because they view it as fair and necessary (Calogero, 2013). Thus, we need to help girls and women identify sexual objectification as a threat to themselves and society (e.g., the rampant sexualization of girls) and minimize their self-objectification. Providing girls and women with specific actions that can be taken in the face of sexual objectification is necessary to instill a greater sense of personal control over these largely uncontrolled and uncontrollable situations.

Develop a Contextualization Schema

We can actively help girls and women first articulate and discuss the ill effects of sexual objectification and then develop a schema to contextualize it. Equipped with these skills, they are less likely to self-objectify and more likely to pinpoint instances in which sexual objectification is harmful. Specifically, developing a *contextualization schema* entails a girl or woman placing appropriate blame on the threatening cultural conditions that facilitate sexual objectification rather than internalizing instances of sexual objectification and blaming herself (Tylka & Augustus-Horvath, 2011). When facing a sexually objectifying situation, she is then more likely to acknowledge that her discomfort is due to the person (or media) objectification of her or other girls or women, rather than indicating her low worth. Through exposure to the contextualization schema, a girl or woman can learn to identify the myriad sexually objectifying situations and develop scripts for how to handle such encounters. Developing a contextualization schema is a form of system-sanctioned change, in that the threat is placed on sexual objectification itself and the societal conditions in which it is rooted. Sexual objectification is positioned as the problem undermining health, well-being, and safety. Useful interventions include cognitive dissonance (see Chapter 33), media literacy (Chapter 34), and feminist/social justice–informed approaches (Chapter 35).

Cultivate an Embodied Identity

Once a contexualization schema is constructed, we could work to replace an appearance-focused objectified identity with an embodied identity that includes a focus on competence, bodily functionality, body appreciation, passion, individuality, achievement, and sexual desire and pleasure (see Chapters 1–3, 9; Piran, 2016, 2017). An embodied identity will also entail helping girls and women cope with appearance-related threats and pursue valued, embodied action while processing their emotional response to these threats (i.e., body image flexibility; see Chapter 4). By shifting investment away from appearance and toward abilities, aspirations, and achievements, girls and women should come to view themselves as less dependent on sexual objectification to define their value and self-worth.

Overall, an embodied identity will provide girls and women with options for how to be more attuned to their wishes, meaningful passions, and agency within a cultural context that narrowly defines and packages the female body and behavior. These adjustments and expansions are critical for reducing not only self-objectification but also women's perceived dependence on the system of sexual objectification and the perceived lack of control over such circumstances. Interventions that will aid in the development of an embodied identity include self-compassion, acceptance and commitment therapy, weight-inclusive approaches, yoga, mindfulness training, embodied mindfulness, cognitive dissonance, feminist/social justice, and media literacy (see Chapters 25–34).

CONCLUSION

Positive embodiment is disrupted by sexual and self-objectification. We offer a two-prong approach for challenging the system of sexual objectification by delegitimizing sexual objectification at the societal level and cultivating resistance toward it at the individual level. Drawing from a range of feminist, social, and psychological theories and practices, we identify the common defense of sexual objectification as a critical target for social change. The recent upsurge in public challenges to sexual objectification underscores the power of delegitimizing sexual objectification in dismantling this system. In so doing, more women and men may be able to realize more fully their embodied identities within the context of social justice for all.

REFERENCES

Aubrey, J. S., & Taylor, L. D. (2009). The role of lad magazines in priming men's chronic and temporary appearance-related schemata: An investigation of longitudinal and experimental findings. *Human Communication Research, 35*, 28–58. doi:10.1111/j.1468-2958.2008.01337.x

Baker, A., & Blanchard, C. (2017). The effects of female "thin ideal" media on men's appearance schema, cognitive performance, and self-evaluations: A self-determination theory approach. *Body Image, 22*, 103–113. doi:10.1016/j.bodyim.2017.06.006

Banyard, V. L., Plante, E. G., & Moynihan, M. M. (2004). Bystander education: Bringing a broader community perspective to sexual violence prevention. *Journal of Community Psychology, 32*, 61–79. doi:10.1002/jcop.10078

Bartky, S. (1990). *Femininity and domination.* New York, NY: Routledge.

Calogero, R. M. (2004). A test of objectification theory: Effect of the male gaze on appearance concerns in college women. *Psychology of Women Quarterly, 28*, 16–21. doi:10.1111/j.1471-6402.2004.00118.x

Calogero, R. M. (2013). Objects don't object: Evidence that self-objectification disrupts women's social activism. *Psychological Science, 24*, 312–318. doi:10.1177/0956797612452574

Calogero, R. M., & Tylka, T. L. (2014). Sanctioning resistance to sexual objectification: An integrative system justification perspective. *Journal of Social Issues, 70*, 763–778. doi:10.1111/josi.12090

Chan, D. K.-S., Lam, C. B., Chow, S. Y., & Cheung, S. F. (2008). Examining the job-related, psychological, and physical outcomes of workplace sexual harassment: A meta-analytic review. *Psychology of Women Quarterly, 32*, 362–376. doi:10.1111/j.1471-6402.2008.00451.x

Diedrichs, P. C., & Lee, C. (2011). Waif goodbye! Average-size female models promote positive body image and appeal to consumers. *Psychology & Health, 26*, 1273–1291. doi:10.1080/08870446.2010.515308

Englar-Carlson, M., & Kiselica, M. S. (2013). Affirming the strengths in men: A positive masculinity approach to assisting male clients. *Journal of Counseling & Development, 91*, 399–409. doi:10.1002/j.1556-6676.2013.00111.x

Festinger, L. (1957). *A theory of cognitive dissonance.* Palo Alto, CA: Stanford University Press.

Feygina, I., Jost, J. T., & Goldsmith, R. (2010). System justification, the denial of global warming, and the possibility of "system-sanctioned change." *Personality and Social Psychology Bulletin, 36*, 326–338. doi:10.1177/0146167209351435

Foubert, J. D., Langhinrichsen-Rohling, J., Brasfield, H., & Hill, B. (2010). Effects of a rape awareness program on college women: Increasing bystander efficacy and willingness to intervene. *Journal of Community Psychology, 38*, 813–827. doi:1002/jcop.20397

Foubert, J. D., & Perry, B. C. (2007). Creating lasting attitude and behavior change in fraternity members and male student athletes. *Violence Against Women, 13*, 70–86. doi:10.1177/1077801206295125

Fredrickson, B. L., & Roberts, T.-A. (1997). Objectification theory: Towards understanding women's lived experience and mental health risks. *Psychology of Women Quarterly, 21*, 173–206. doi:10.1111/j.1471-6402.1997.tb00108.x

Gervais, S. J., Vescio, T. K., & Allen, J. (2011). When what you see is what you get: The consequences of the objectifying gaze for women and men. *Psychology of Women Quarterly, 35*, 5–17. doi:10.1177/0361684310386121

Halliwell, E., & Dittmar, H. (2004). Does size matter? The impact of model's body size on women's body-focused anxiety and advertising effectiveness. *Journal of Social and Clinical Psychology, 23*, 104–122. doi:10.1521/jscp.23.1.104.26989

Hargreaves, D., & Tiggemann, M. (2002). The effect of television commercials on mood and body dissatisfaction: The role of appearance-schema activation. *Journal of Social and Clinical Psychology, 21*, 287–308. doi:10.1521/jscp.21.3.287.22532

Jost, J. T., Chaikalis-Petritsis, V., Abrams, D., Sidanius, J., van der Toorn, J., & Bratt, C. (2012). Why men (and women) do and don't rebel: Effects of system justification in willingness to protest. *Personality and Social Psychology Bulletin, 38*, 197–208. doi:10.1177/0146167211422544

Kay, A. C., & Friesen, J. (2011). On social stability and social change: Understanding when system justification does and does not occur. *Current Directions in Psychological Science, 20*, 360–364. doi:10.1177/0963721411422059

Krawczyk, R., & Thompson, J. K. (2015). The effects of advertisements that sexually objectify women on state body dissatisfaction and judgments of women: The moderating roles of gender and internalization. *Body Image, 15*, 109–119. doi:10.1016/j.bodyim.2015.08.001

Langhinrichsen-Rohling, J., Foubert, J. D., Brasfield, H. M., Hill, B., & Shelley-Tremblay, S. (2011). The Men's Program: Does it impact college men's self-reported bystander efficacy and willingness to intervene? *Violence Against Women, 17*, 743–759. doi:10.1177/1077801211409728

Levy, A. (2005). *Female chauvinist pigs: Women and the rise of raunch culture*. New York, NY: Free Press.

Loughnan, S., Haslam, N., Murnane, T., Vaes, J., Reynolds, C., & Suitner, C. (2010). Objectification leads to depersonalization: The denial of mind and moral concern to objectified others. *European Journal of Social Psychology, 40*, 709–717. doi:10.1002/ejsp.755

Loughnan, S., Pina, A., Vasquez, E. A., & Puvia, E. (2013). Sexual objectification increases rape victim blame and decreases perceived suffering. *Psychology of Women Quarterly, 37*, 455–461. doi:10.1177/0361684313485718

Pallin, Z. (2017, October 16). Re: #itwasme #ihearyou [Facebook comment]. Retrieved from https://www.facebook.com/zpallin?fref=search

Peter, J., & Valkenburg, P. M. (2009). Adolescents' exposure to sexually explicit Internet material and sexual satisfaction: A longitudinal study. *Human Communication Research, 35*, 171–194. doi:10.1111/j.1468-2958.2009.01343.x

Piran, N. (2016). Embodied possibilities and disruptions: The emergence of the experience of embodiment construct from qualitative studies with girls and women. *Body Image, 18*, 43–60. doi:10.1016.j.bodyim.2016.04.007

Piran, N. (2017). *Journeys of embodiment at the intersection of body and culture: The developmental theory of embodiment*. San Diego, CA: Elsevier Press. doi:10.1016/c2015-0-04666-4

Stice, E., Shaw, H., Becker, C. B., & Rohde, P. (2008). Dissonance-based interventions for the prevention of eating disorders: Using persuasion principles to promote health. *Prevention Science*, *9*, 114–128. doi:10.1007/s11121-008-0093-x

Swim, J. K., & Hyers, L. L. (1999). Excuse me—what did you say?! Women's public and private responses to sexist remarks. *Journal of Experimental Social Psychology*, *35*, 68–88. doi:10.1006/jesp.1998.1370

Tiggemann, M., & Williams, E. (2012). The role of self-objectification in disordered eating, depressed mood, and sexual functioning among women: A comprehensive test of objectification theory. *Psychology of Women Quarterly*, *36*, 66–75. doi:10.1177/0361684311420250

Tylka, T. L., & Augustus-Horvath, C. L. (2011). Fighting self-objectification in prevention and intervention contexts. In R. M. Calogero, S. Tantleff-Dunn, & J. K. Thompson (Eds.), *Self-objectification in women: Causes, consequences, and counteractions* (pp. 187–214). Washington, DC: American Psychological Association.

Zillmann, D., & Byrant, J. (1988). Pornography's impact on sexual satisfaction. *Journal of Applied Social Psychology*, *18*, 438–453. doi:10.1111/j.1559-1816.1988.tb00027.x

Zurbriggen, E. L., Ramsey, L. R., & Jaworski, B. K. (2011). Self- and partner-objectification in romantic relationships: Associations with media consumption and relationship satisfaction. *Sex Roles*, *64*, 449–462. doi: 10.1007/s11199-011-9933-4

15

Negotiating Gender Roles to Enact Body Appreciation and Positive Embodiment

SARAH K. MURNEN AND LINDA SMOLAK ■

It is an integral part of women's gender role in Western cultures to care about physical appearance and to specifically value thinness (Mahalik et al., 2005). For men, physical appearance is not central to gendered expectations, but muscularity might help men enact stereotypic masculine roles related to dominance (Mahalik et al., 2003). To the extent that gender roles encourage a preoccupation with a socially defined body form over function, appreciation of one's body and embodiment are compromised. In this chapter, we consider how gender role expectations might influence both women's and men's body attitudes and experiences and how these expectations can be negotiated, resisted, and changed to promote positive body image and embodiment.

Considered a central component of positive body image, body appreciation reflects acceptance and respect for the body, an inclination to reject unrealistic appearance ideals, having a broad definition of attractiveness, and believing that inner positivity influences one's outer demeanor (Avalos, Tylka, & Wood-Barcalow, 2005; Tylka & Wood-Barcalow, 2015; see also Chapter 2). Body appreciation is not solely the opposite of body dissatisfaction, as indicated by findings that age was correlated positively with body appreciation but not with body dissatisfaction among women (Tiggemann & McCourt, 2013), and that body appreciation predicted unique variability in women's and men's well-being after accounting for body dissatisfaction (Tylka & Wood-Barcalow, 2015). Although there is some research linking gendered roles and experiences with body appreciation (e.g., Swami & Abbasnejad, 2010), for this review we also draw on the more extensive literature linking gendered experiences with body dissatisfaction.

Much research shows that body dissatisfaction is a gendered experience. In a recent meta-analysis examining body dissatisfaction across time, it was found that women and girls reported higher rates of body dissatisfaction related to weight and shape at all time periods compared to men and boys, who in turn had higher scores on drive for muscularity (Karazsia, Murnen, & Tylka, 2017). Body appreciation also appears to be gendered. In Tylka's (2013) study of more than 900 college students, men showed greater body appreciation than women on all items except two that assessed self-care of the body. In most studies where the genders have been compared, men's total scores have been higher, as reviewed by Tiggemann (2015). This difference can be explained in part by gender role expectations and gender-related experiences associated with the body.

GENDER ROLE EXPECTATIONS

Although gender roles have changed in American culture since the second wave of the women's movement (especially for girls and women), traditional gender role expectations persist to some degree (Twenge, 2009). Feminine stereotyped traits are associated with communality and expressiveness, while masculine traits are associated with agency and industriousness (and power) (Rudman, Moss-Racusin, Phelan, & Nauts, 2012). According to social role theory, biological differences between women and men helped produce gender-segregated roles, which encourage gendered behaviors (Wood & Eagly, 2013). Mahalik and colleagues defined contemporary gender role norms for both women (Mahalik et al., 2005) and men (Mahalik et al., 2003). While some norms for women, like *valuing thinness*, directly predict body concerns, norms for men relate less directly to men's body issues, as we discuss further in this chapter.

While some gender-stereotyped traits developed through the gendered division of labor, others likely arose from the fact that unlike other groups that differ in status, women and men often want to form relationships with one another. Heterosexual interdependence exists along with male dominance (Rudman & Glick, 2008), putting women in a position where they might invest in a sexual object role to secure male attention and protection (Murnen & Smolak, 2013). There is much evidence that women are portrayed as sex objects in popular culture to a greater extent than men, and that people are more likely to be confronted with images of the body ideal for women than men on a daily basis (e.g., Buote, Wilson, Strahan, Gazzola, & Papps, 2011). There is concern that even girls are being sexualized in the culture, with evidence of sexualized clothing for girls (Goodin, Van DenBurg, Murnen, & Smolak, 2011) and sexualized female dolls (Boyd & Murnen, 2017).

FEMININITY AND SELF-OBJECTIFICATION

In Western cultures, feminine traits and roles are associated with an objectified view of the body that compromises body appreciation and empowerment. Objectification theory (Fredrickson & Roberts, 1997) predicts that the ubiquitous sexual objectification of women in society can influence women's feelings about their bodies. Women often internalize societal objectification, leading to self-objectification, a tendency to habitually surveil one's own body to see if it meets cultural standards. Viewing the body as an object threatens the ability to appreciate the body as functional, essential for experiencing body appreciation and embodiment. While it is harmful to engage in self-objectification, it is also normative, and it likely perpetuates women's lower status (Murnen & Smolak, 2015). Calogero, Tylka, Donnelly, McGetrick, and Leger (2017) found that women invested in beauty ideals were more likely to report self-objectification and were more accepting of the gender status quo. Swami and Abbasnejad (2010) found that endorsing feminine-stereotyped images and activities and the idea of female purity were negatively related to body appreciation among women.

Men are less likely to experience sexual objectification and self-objectification compared to women (Calogero & Thompson, 2010), perhaps because they are stereotyped as sexual actors rather than sexual objects in the "heterosexual script" (Kim et al., 2007). However, when men do experience objectification, the correlates are similar (Calogero & Thompson, 2010). Male gay culture is particularly likely to emphasize the importance of physical appearance for men (Jankowski, Fawkner, Slater, & Tiggemann, 2014), and in a meta-analytic review, it was found that gay men experienced less body satisfaction than heterosexual men (Morrison, Morrison, & Sager, 2004).

MASCULINITY AND BODY FUNCTIONALITY

The feminine-stereotyped experience that seems most problematic is a strong focus on appearance for self-definition, which encourages self-objectification (Calogero et al., 2017). Further, the proscription of instrumentality for girls and women (Rudman et al., 2012) is problematic, as masculine-stereotyped traits promote a more functional view of the body. Among both women and men, possessing feminine-stereotyped expressive traits related negatively to body appreciation, while possessing masculine-stereotyped instrumental traits was positively related to body appreciation (Swami, Hadji-Michael, & Furnham, 2008).

Piran (Piran, 2017; Piran & Teall, 2012) proposed in her developmental theory of embodiment that experiences of physical freedom, mental freedom, and social power, as people "engage with their body in the world," promote positive embodiment. Particular masculinity-oriented, gender-related attitudes and experiences might encourage physical freedom and a sense of embodiment. For example, masculine gender roles and experiences are associated with athletic participation.

Sport is still stereotyped as more masculine than feminine (Daniels & Lavoi, 2013), and engagement in physical activities for body functionality is more associated with boys than girls (Tatangelo & Ricciardelli, 2013).

When girls and women do participate in sport it can be associated with better body satisfaction, depending on the nature of the sport in which they participate. In a meta-analysis, it was found that female athletes in stereotyped feminine sports like gymnastics were at greater risk for body image concerns, which was not true for girls and women in endurance sports like swimming (Varnes et al., 2013). Those who engage in sport for appearance motives rather than for body functionality motives report more self-objectification (Slater & Tiggemann, 2011), which can compromise empowerment and embodiment (Piran, 2016).

Further, the stereotype that sports are masculine can affect girls' and women's experiences with sport. In focus groups of Australian high school girls, dropping out of sport was linked with perceptions that it was not feminine and not "cool" (Slater & Tiggemann, 2010). Girls have been found to experience more sport-related teasing than boys, which was related to self-objectification and body shame (Slater & Tiggemann, 2011). In focus group studies, it was found that Division I women athletes sometimes felt there was a conflict between definitions of femininity and their muscular physiques, but they still valued the functioning of their athletic bodies and felt a sense of empowerment (Krane, Choi, Baird, Aimar, & Kauer, 2004). Similarly, Swedish young women athletes expressed tension between objectified versus functional views of their bodies; however, they reported more experiences of disempowerment than empowerment (Lunde & Holmqvist Gattario, 2017).

Masculinity is encouraged more in men than women, and among men masculinity is positively linked with drive for muscularity (Griffiths, Murray, & Touyz, 2015). In a study of men in four Western cultures (Australia, the United Kingdom, the United States, and Sweden) subscribing to the masculine playboy norm was related to drive for muscularity, and in three of the four countries the masculine winning norm was correlated with muscularity concerns (Holmqvist Gattario et al., 2015). Smolak and Murnen (2008) found that the masculine norms of disdain for homosexuals and winning showed direct relationships to drive for muscularity in college men. In a study of Division II football players, drive for muscularity was associated with the norm of winning (Steinfeldt, Gilchrist, Halterman, Gomory, & Steinfeldt, 2011).

The relationship between winning and drive for muscularity might be more functional than pathological, but this hypothesis should be tested in future research. However, the association of drive for muscularity with sexism (playboy) and heterosexism (disdain for homosexuals) is troubling. It is consistent with the finding that drive for muscularity was correlated with objectification of women, sexism, and hostility toward women (Swami & Voracek, 2013), suggesting that muscularity might be a means for men to try to preserve dominance over women and gay men under changing societal conditions. In support of this idea, other researchers have found that men and boys who experience gender role conflict have higher drive for muscularity (McCreary, Saucier, & Courtenay, 2005; Smolak & Stein, 2006).

Relating this research to body appreciation, we argue that high drive for muscularity is at least somewhat unhealthy and is not likely to support body appreciation. A high drive for muscularity is associated with problematic behaviors like steroid use and excessive exercise (Murnen & Karazsia, 2017). Further, health attitudes and behaviors in men are related to masculine roles, according to a recent meta-analysis in which conformity to masculine norms was related to mental health indices such as body dissatisfaction and substance abuse (Wong, Ho, Wang, & Miller, 2017). In future research relating masculine role norms to body appreciation, it will be helpful to examine individual norms and to differentiate between different aspects of body appreciation and embodiment. While appreciation of body functionality might be promoted by masculinity traits and roles to some degree, self-care of the body probably is not (see Tylka, 2013). There is also concern that to the extent that men overidentify with extreme forms of masculinity, they will likely engage in greater sexual objectification of women, which compromises women's body empowerment.

NEGOTIATING GENDER ROLES, BODY APPRECIATION, AND EMBODIMENT

In addition to women athletes, there are other groups of women who manage to experience better body outcomes, partially as a result of atypical experience with gender roles. For example, in a meta-analytic review of research relating feminist identity to body dissatisfaction, Murnen and Smolak (2009) found a negative association between a synthesized feminist identity and body shame, as well as between feminist identity and internalization of the media ideal. Feminist attitudes might allow one to critique the unrealistic ideal and offer some protection against the most serious body concerns. Some research has found that lesbian women have better body satisfaction than heterosexual women (Morrison et al., 2004). Tiggemann (2015) predicted that both feminist women and lesbian women will likely experience relatively high body appreciation due to more approval of women's body diversity.

The sparse research that has been conducted suggests that African and Hispanic cultural identities are more strongly associated with body positivity in women (Tiggemann, 2015). A broader conceptualization of beauty in these groups and identification with non-Western cultural ideals might be protective. This research is consistent with a meta-analysis of body dissatisfaction by ethnicity that showed African American women to be more satisfied with their bodies than Caucasian women, which may be related to African American women's greater gender role flexibility (Grabe & Hyde, 2006). Future research might examine whether certain groups experience a greater sense of instrumentality and less focus on appearance for self-worth that promotes body appreciation. The extent to which being able to recognize and critique racism or heterosexism might allow one greater ability to critique unrealistic body ideals; this prediction should also be studied further.

There is not much research examining men's negotiation of gender roles to enact body empowerment, perhaps because men's body appreciation is not as greatly compromised as women's. However, we encourage greater body-related self-care for men and discourage overidentification with muscularity and extreme forms of masculinity. A study of messages in men's magazines found that there were more messages promoting "hypermasculine" values (acceptance of violence and dominance over women) in publications geared toward men of lower (compared to higher) socioeconomic status (Vokey, Bruce, & Tysiaczny, 2013). Minority groups might turn to the power promised by hypermasculinity and extreme muscularity if other sources of power are not available to them in society. The intersection of sexuality, social class, and race with men's masculinity, embodiment, and empowerment should be studied further.

CHANGING GENDERED ROLES TO PROMOTE BODY APPRECIATION AND POSITIVE EMBODIMENT

If gendered social roles are at the root of gendered experiences with body appreciation, we need to encourage ways to resist and challenge these roles. An implication of social role theory is that change needs to happen at the societal level for resulting change at the individual level. Feminism has been the key tool for societal change related to gender, resulting in some dramatic change in women's roles, but the change has not gone far enough. Some theorists suggest we live in a "half-changed" world in that men's roles have not changed to the degree that women's roles have (Anderson, 2014). Research showed that many people still agree with attitudes indicative of modern and benevolent sexism, and that some believe we are "postfeminist" (no longer in need of feminism) because some societal change has occurred (Anderson, 2014). Persisting gender inequalities still need feminist attention (see Chapter 35), ideally using an approach that reflects appreciation of intersectionality. Further, sexism is supported by interlocking societal forces that sometimes take subtle or disguised forms of influence, as we discuss in the material that follows.

Consistent with a feminist approach, we need to change particular gendered roles to change the balance of gendered power. For example, we need to encourage greater male caretaking, which could result in more balance in work and family roles for both genders and in the creation of more empathy in men (antithetical to hypermasculinity). This effort would need to start in childhood with parenting and education that discourages gender-stereotyped behaviors related to power. Even the toys that children play with can promote gendered roles. Play with nonobjectified dolls and stuffed animals encourages empathy, while play with aggressive video games in which women are sexually objectified does not (Murnen, 2018). The workplace could encourage more balance in work and family roles for both women and men. Some of the most gender egalitarian countries (e.g.,

Scandinavian countries) legislate long parental leaves for fathers, encouraging male caretaking.

We also need to bolster women's instrumental societal roles through encouraging female leadership, equal pay, and harsh treatment of sexual violence against women. The ubiquitous treatment of women as sexual objects threatens women's empowerment (Murnen & Smolak, 2015). Since at least the 1970s, feminists such as Jean Kilbourne in her *Killing Us Softly* series (jeankilbourne.com) have brought attention to the issue of the objectification of women in advertisements. Such efforts might be responsible for the stalling of drive for thinness concerns among women in the 1990s that Karazsia and colleagues found (2017), but it does not mean that objectification of women has ended. There has been increased sexualization of women in the culture (Murnen & Smolak, 2013), and this sexualization is sold to women as a source of power (Smolak, Murnen, & Myers, 2014), making it difficult to combat. Recent research suggests that female self-sexualization is not likely empowering as it incites self-objectification (e.g., Halliwell, Malson, & Tischner, 2011).

Further, both women and men are increasingly encouraged to buy commercial products to manipulate their bodies, which threatens body appreciation (Murnen & Karazsia, 2017; Murnen & Smolak, 2015). When Ashikali and Dittmar (2012) primed women participants with materialistic slogans, they experienced heightened perceptions of the importance of appearance to their self-concept. The commercial culture in which we live benefits from people's body dissatisfaction with the sale of products designed to "help." So, along with feminism we need a strong critique of consumerism and media messages. Media literacy efforts have helped, but education needs to keep up with changing societal messages and modes of communication, such as new uses and forms of social media that might threaten body appreciation and embodiment.

Along with societal critique, we need to render people less vulnerable to commercial pressures. We need promotion of children's body appreciation from parents, peers, and educators. Adolescent girls who perceived that their bodies are accepted by others showed increases in body appreciation across time (Andrew, Tiggemann, & Clark, 2016). More critique of heterosexuality might help promote body appreciation, as gendered sexual roles are intertwined with gendered body ideals (Boyd & Murnen, 2017). The critique that has emerged from sexual minority individuals fighting for equal rights might serve to loosen up gendered expectations for all and encourage a greater appreciation for body diversity.

Gender polarization and gendered body experiences are also encouraged by our current gendered notion of sport, which is problematic because sport can encourage embodiment to its participants provided it does not encourage self-objectification. Legislation in various countries (e.g., Title IX in the United States) has helped increase the participation of girls and women in sport, but as indicated previously, some sport-related experiences reinforce female self-objectification. We need more women involved at the highest level of sport, and more media coverage of women athletes, helping to celebrate women athletes as functionally empowered actors rather than objects. We should also change women's sports uniforms that encourage objectification and train coaches to promote body appreciation in their players. Finally, we need to promote embodying activities that do not involve competition and high levels of skill. If all children practiced yoga or t'ai chi on a daily basis in their schools in a nonobjectifying environment that treated all genders with respect, it might go a long way to encourage embodiment.

CONCLUSION

The experience of body appreciation is gendered. Femininity can promote an unhealthy focus on appearance and self-objectification, which affects women to a greater degree than men. Masculinity is associated with encouragement of body instrumentality for both women and men that supports body appreciation, but extreme levels of masculinity and a high drive for muscularity likely compromise men's body-related self-care and are associated with the treatment of women as sexual objects. Change in gender role expectations is difficult because gendered roles result from, and help support, a gender unequal society. Nevertheless, feminism, the encouragement of caretaking in men, the bolstering of instrumental traits and roles in women, and other societal-level actions can upset the current gender power imbalance to promote individuals' embodiment and positive body image.

REFERENCES

Anderson, K. J. (2014). *Modern misogyny: Anti-feminism in a post-feminist era.* New York, NY: Oxford University Press.

Andrew, R., Tiggemann, M., & Clark, L. (2016). Predictors and health-related outcomes of positive body image in adolescent girls: A prospective study. *Developmental Psychology, 52*, 463–474. doi:10.1037/dev0000095

Ashikali, E.-M., & Dittmar, H. (2012). The effect of priming materialism on women's responses to thin-ideal media. *British Journal of Social Psychology, 51*, 514–533. doi:10.1111/j.2044-8309.2011.02020.x

Avalos, L., Tylka, T. L., & Wood-Barcalow, N. (2005). The Body Appreciation Scale: Development and psychometric evaluation. *Body Image, 2*, 285–297. doi:10.1016/j.bodyim.2005.06.002

Boyd, H., & Murnen, S. K. (2017). Thin and sexy versus muscular and dominant: Prevalence of gendered body ideals in popular dolls and action figures. *Body Image, 21*, 90–96. doi:10.1016/j.bodyim.2017.03.003

Buote, V. M., Wilson, A. E., Strahan, E. J., Gazzola, S. B., & Papps, F. (2011). Setting the bar: Divergent sociocultural norms for women's and men's ideal appearance in real-world contexts. *Body Image, 8*, 322–334. doi:10.1016/j.bodyim.2011.06.002

Calogero, R. M., & Thompson, J. K. (2010). Gender and body image. In J. C. Chrisler & D. R. McCreary (Eds.), *Handbook of gender research in psychology: Gender research in social and applied psychology* (Vol. 2, pp. 153–184). New York, NY: Springer.

Calogero, R. M., Tylka, T. L., Donnelly, L. C., McGetrick, A., & Leger, A. M. (2017). Trappings of femininity: A test of the "beauty as currency" hypothesis in shaping college women's gender activism. *Body Image, 21*, 66–70. doi:10.1016/j.bodyim.2017.02.008

Daniels, E. A., & Lavoi, N. M. (2013). Athletics as solution and problem: Sport participation for girls and the sexualization of female athletes. In E. Zurbriggen & T.-A. Roberts (Eds.), *The sexualization of girls and girlhood* (pp. 63–83). New York, NY: Oxford University Press.

Fredrickson, B. L., & Roberts, T.-A. (1997). Objectification theory: Toward understanding women's lived experiences and mental health risks. *Psychology of Women Quarterly, 21*, 173–206. doi:10/1111/j.1471-6402.1997.tb00108x

Goodin, S. M., Van DenBurg, A., Murnen, S. K., & Smolak, L. (2011). "Putting on" sexiness: A content analysis of the presence of sexualizing characteristics in girls' clothing. *Sex Roles, 65*, 1–12. doi:10.1007/s11199-011-9966-8

Grabe, S., & Hyde, J. S. (2006). Ethnicity and body dissatisfaction among women in the United States: A meta-analysis. *Psychological Bulletin, 132*, 622–640. doi:10.1037/0033-2909.132.4.622

Griffiths, S., Murray, S. B., & Touyz, S. B. (2015). Extending the masculinity hypothesis: An investigation of gender role conformity, body dissatisfaction, and disordered eating in young heterosexual men. *Psychology of Men and Masculinity, 16*, 108–114. doi:10.1037/a0035958

Halliwell, E., Malson, H., & Tischner, I. (2011). Are contemporary media images which seem to display women as sexually empowered actually harmful to women? *Psychology of Women Quarterly, 35*, 38–45. doi:10.1037/t13685-000

Holmqvist Gattario, K., Frisén, A., Fuller-Tyszkiewicz, M., Ricciardelli, L. A., Diedrichs, P. C., Yager, Z., . . . Smolak, L. (2015). How is men's conformity to masculine norms related to their body image? Masculinity and muscularity across Western countries. *Psychology of Men and Masculinity, 16*, 337–347. doi:10.1037/a0038494

Jankowski, G. S., Fawkner, H., Slater, A., & Tiggemann, M. (2014). "Appearance potent"? A content analysis of UK gay and straight men's magazines. *Body Image, 11*, 474–481. doi:10.1016/j.bodyim.2014.07.010

JeanKilbourne.Com. Home page. Retrieved from: http://www.jeankilbourne.com/films

Karazsia, B. T., Murnen, S. K., & Tylka, T. L. (2017). Is body dissatisfaction changing across time? A cross-temporal meta-analysis. *Psychological Bulletin, 143*, 293–320. doi:10.1037/bul0000081

Kim, J. L., Sorsoli, C. L., Collins, K., Zylbergold, B. A., Schooler, D., & Tolman, D. (2007). From sex to sexuality: Exposing the heterosexual script on primetime network television. *Journal of Sex Research, 44*, 245–157. doi:10.1080/00224490701263660

Krane, V., Choi, P. Y. L., Baird, S. M., Aimar, C. M., & Kauer, K. H. (2004). Living the paradox: Female athletes negotiate femininity and muscularity. *Sex Roles, 50*, 315–329. doi:10.1023/B:SERS.0000018888.48437.4f

Lunde, C., & Holmqvist Gattario, K. (2017). Performance or appearance? Young female sport participants' body negotiations. *Body Image, 21*, 81–89. doi:10.1016/j.bodyim.2017.03.001

Mahalik, J. R., Locke, B. D., Ludlow, L. H., Diemer, M. A., Scott, R. P. J., Gottfried, M., & Freitas, G. (2003). Development of the Conformity to Masculine Norms Inventory. *Psychology of Men and Masculinity, 4*, 3–25. doi:10.1037/1524-9220.4.1.3

Mahalik, J. R., Mooray, E. B., Coonerty-Femiano, A., Ludlow, L. H., Slattery, S. M., & Smiler, A. (2005). Development of the Conformity to Feminine Norms Inventory. *Sex Roles*, 52, 417–435. doi:10.1007/s11199-005-3709-7

McCreary, D. R., Saucier, D. M., & Courtenay, W. H. (2005). The drive for muscularity and masculinity: Testing the associations among gender-role traits, behaviors, attitudes, and conflict. *Psychology of Men and Masculinity*, *6*, 83–94. doi:10.1037/1524-9220.6.2.83

Media Education Foundation. (n.d.). Home page. Retrieved from http://www.mediaed.org

Morrison, M. A., Morrison, T. G., & Sager, C.-L. (2004). Does body satisfaction differ between gay men and lesbian women and heterosexual men and women? A meta-analytic review. *Body Image*, *1*, 127–138. doi:10.1016/j.bodyim.2004.01.002

Murnen, S. K. (2018). Fashion or action? Gender stereotyped toys and social behavior. In E. Weisgram & L. M. Dinella (Eds.), *Gender-typing of children's toys* (pp. 189–212). Washington, DC: American Psychological Association.

Murnen, S. K., & Karazsia, B. (2017). A review of research on men's body image and drive for muscularity. In Y. J. Wong & R. Levant (Eds.), *Psychology of men and masculinities* (pp. 229–257). Washington, DC: American Psychological Association.

Murnen, S. K., & Smolak, L. (2009). Are feminist women protected from body image problems? A meta-analytic review of relevant research. *Sex Roles*, *60*, 186–197. doi:10.1007/s11199-008-9523-2

Murnen, S. K., & Smolak, L. (2013). "I'd rather be a famous fashion model than a famous scientist." The rewards and costs of internalizing sexualization. In E. Zurbriggen & T.-A. Roberts (Eds.), *The sexualization of girls and girlhood* (pp. 235–256). New York, NY: Oxford.

Murnen, S. K., & Smolak, L. (2015). Gender and eating disorders. In L. Smolak & M. P. Levine (Eds.), *The Wiley handbook of eating disorders* (Vol. 1, pp. 352–366). Oxford, England: Wiley-Blackwell.

Piran, N. (2016). Embodied possibilities and disruptions: The emergence of the Experience of Embodiment construct from qualitative studies with girls and women. *Body Image*, *18*, 43–60. doi:10.1016/j.bodyim.2016.04.007

Piran, N. (2017). *Journeys of embodiment at the intersection of body and culture: The developmental theory of embodiment.* San Diego, CA: Elsevier. doi:10.1016/c2015-0-04666-4

Piran, N., & Teall, T. (2012). The developmental theory of embodiment. In G. McVey, M. Levine, N. Piran, & H. B. Ferguson (Eds.), *Preventing eating-related and weight-related disorders: Collaborative research, advocacy, and policy change* (pp. 169–198). Waterloo, ON, Canada: Laurier.

Rudman, L. A., & Glick, P. (2008). *The social psychology of gender: How power and intimacy shape gender relations.* New York, NY: Guilford Press.

Rudman, L. A., Moss-Racusin, C. A., Phelan, J. E., & Nauts, S. (2012). Status incongruity and backlash effects: Defending the gender hierarchy motivates prejudice towards female leaders. *Journal of Experimental Social Psychology*, *48*, 165–179. doi:10.1016/j-jesp.2011.10.008

Slater, A., & Tiggemann, M. (2010). "Uncool to do sport": A focus group study of adolescent girls' reasons for withdrawing from physical activity. *Psychology of Sport and Exercise*, *11*, 619–626. doi:10.1016/j.psychsport.2010.07.006

Slater, A., & Tiggemann, M. (2011). Gender differences in adolescent sport participation, teasing, self-objectification and body image concerns. *Journal of Adolescence, 34*, 455–463. doi:10.1016/j.adolescence.2010.06.007

Smolak, L., & Murnen, S. K. (2008). Drive for leanness: Assessment and relationship to gender, gender role and objectification. *Body Image, 5*, 251–260. doi:10.1016/j.bodyim.2008.03.004

Smolak, L., Murnen, S. K., & Myers, T. (2014). Sexualizing the self: What college women and men think about and do to be "sexy." *Psychology of Women Quarterly, 38*, 379–397. doi:10.1177/0361684314524168

Smolak, L., & Stein, J. A. (2006). The relationship of drive for muscularity to sociocultural factors, self-esteem, physical attributes gender role, and social comparison in middle school boys. *Body Image, 3*, 121–129. doi:10.1016/j.bodyim.2006.03.002

Steinfeldt, J. A., Gilchrist, G. A., Halterman, A. W., Gomory, A., & Steinfeldt, M. C. (2011). Drive for muscularity and conformity to masculine norms among college football players. *Psychology of Men and Masculinity, 12*, 324–338. doi:10.1037/a0024839

Swami, V., & Abbasnejad, A. (2010). Associations between femininity ideology and body appreciation among British female undergraduates. *Personality and Individual Differences, 48*, 685–687. doi:10.1016/j.paid.2009.12.017

Swami, V., Hadji-Michael, M., & Furnham, A. (2008). Personality and individual difference correlates of positive body image. *Body Image, 5*, 322–325. doi:10.1016/j.bodyim.2008.03.007

Swami, V., & Voracek, M. (2013). Associations among men's sexist attitudes, objectification of women, and their own drive for muscularity. *Psychology of Men and Masculinity, 14*, 168–174. doi:10.1037/a0028437

Tatangelo, G. L., & Ricciardelli, L. A. (2013). A qualitative study of preadolescent boys' and girls' body image: Gendered ideals and sociocultural influences. *Body Image, 10*, 591–598. doi:10.1016/j.bodyim.2013.07.006

Tiggemann, M. (2015). Considerations of positive body image across various social identities and special populations. *Body Image, 14*, 168–176. doi:10/1016/j.bodyim.2015.03.002

Tiggemann, M., & McCourt, A. (2013). Body appreciation in adult women: Relationships with age and body satisfaction. *Body Image, 10*, 624–627. doi:10.1016/j.bodyim.2013.07.003

Twenge, J. M. (2009). Status and gender: The paradox of progress in an age of narcissism. *Sex Roles, 61*, 338–340. doi:10.1007/s11199-009-9617-5.

Tylka, T. L. (2013). Evidence for the Body Appreciation Scale's measurement equivalence/invariance between US college women and men. *Body Image, 10*, 415–418. doi:10.1016/j.bodyim.2013.02.006

Tylka, T. L., & Wood-Barcalow, N. L. (2015). The Body Appreciation Scale-2: Item refinement and psychometric evaluation. *Body Image, 12*, 53–67. doi:10.1016/j.bodyim.2014.09.006

Varnes, J. R., Stellefson, M. L., Janelle, C. M., Dorman, S. M., Dodd, V., & Miller, M. D. (2013). A systematic review of studies comparing body image concerns among female college athletes and non-athletes, 1997–2012. *Body Image, 10*, 421–432. doi:10.1016/j.bodyim.2013.06.001

Vokey, M., Bruce, T., & Tysiaczny, C. (2013). An analysis of hyper-masculinity in magazine advertisements. *Sex Roles, 68*, 562–576. doi:10.1007/s11199-013-0268-1

Wong, Y. J., Ho, M.-H. R., Wang, S-Y., & Miller, I. S. K. (2017). Meta-analyses of the relationship between conformity to masculine norms and mental-health related outcomes. *Journal of Counseling Psychology*, *64*, 80–93. doi:10.1037/cou0000176

Wood, W., & Eagly, A. H. (2013). Biology or culture alone cannot account for human sex differences and similarities. *Psychological Inquiry*, *24*, 241–247. doi:10.1080/1047840X.2013.815034

16

Resisting Restrictive Feminine Molds and Promoting Embodied Well-Being Among Breast Cancer Survivors

LIANNE TRACHTENBERG AND NIVA PIRAN ■

Young women cancer survivors face challenges to their embodied experiences. The most difficult challenge relates to dealing with a life-threatening condition and facing one's mortality (e.g., Rubin & Tanenbaum, 2011). In addition, after being diagnosed and treated for breast cancer, having physically endured possibly disfiguring breast surgery, hair loss, and hormonal changes (including premature menopause and, sometimes, infertility), women take on the challenging task of reconnecting to their altered bodies and gender-related identity, which may no longer fit with their precancer selves. Studies consistently suggest that negative body image following breast cancer treatment is associated with mental health challenges (e.g., Falk Dahl, Reinertsen, Nesvold, Fosså, & Dahl, 2010). Toward enhanced well-being, processes of reinhabiting the body positively and of renegotiating one's embodied identity can take place. While researchers document differential outcomes among young breast cancer survivors' psychosocial well-being and embodiment, studies have only recently started to explore the factors that may account for such differences (e.g., Boquiren, Esplen, Wong, Toner, & Warner, 2013). As Boquiren et al. suggested, gender role socialization is one factor that has been highlighted as shaping the embodied experiences of young breast cancer survivors.

Gender role socialization involves learned pressures to comply with gender-related role expectations. A well-researched aspect of gender role socialization among women involves the emphasis on appearance and self-objectification, or viewing one's body as an outsider would (e.g., Cash & Smolak, 2011). However, in addition, gender role socialization for women includes a broader range of behavioral patterns, such as passivity or care of others (see Chapter 15). Overall, research to date suggests that resistance to gender socialization is associated with lower levels of body satisfaction and disordered eating patterns (e.g., Murnen & Smolak, 2009), as well as positive embodiment (Piran, 2017). Resistance to constraining gender socialization may have a particular role in enhancing psychosocial adjustment, as well as positive body image and embodiment, among breast cancer survivors and survivors of other health challenges whereby the illness and its treatment challenge the experience of the body (Cash & Smolak, 2011). The chapter describes quantitative and qualitative research findings about gender socialization and well-being among breast cancer survivors and continues with directions for additional research and implication for practice.

GENDER ROLE SOCIALIZATION AMONG BREAST CANCER SURVIVORS AND EMBODIED WELL-BEING

A number of studies examined gender role socialization in relation to embodied well-being among women breast cancer survivors. One studied factor of gender socialization involves the valuing of appearance (e.g., Carver et al., 1998; Moreira & Canavarro, 2010; Moreira, Silva, & Canavarro, 2010). These authors found that women with higher concerns about appearance reported greater mental distress, body dissatisfaction, and poorer quality of life postsurgery and treatment for breast cancer. In a different study that explored body image in a group of women who were 67 years or older (average age = 73.7 years), Figueiredo, Cullen, Hwang, Rowland, and Mandelblatt (2004) found that, among older women survivors of breast cancer, those who desired and received breast reconstruction had a more positive body image and mental health 2 years postsurgery, compared with women who desired reconstruction and did not have the surgery. These studies suggest that appearance concerns affect well-being among breast cancer survivors.

More recently, studies have expanded the lens through which the impact of gender role socialization on breast cancer survivors' embodied well-being has been explored, beyond an exclusive focus on appearance. Boquiren et al. (2013) used the Gender Role Socialization Scale (Toner et al., 2012) to assess the impact of gender socialization on body surveillance, body shame, body dissatisfaction, and quality of life for women who have undergone treatment for breast cancer. The Gender Role Socialization Scale includes items related to appearance, such as "I cannot feel good about myself unless I am physically attractive," as well as items related to other social expectations of women, such as "I feel that I am not allowed to ask that my own needs be met." Among 150, mainly white, women (average age = 49.5 years), Boquiren et al. found that greater internalization of traditional gender role socialization correlated positively with body surveillance and shame, as well as with body dissatisfaction and quality of life. Further, a path analysis revealed that endorsement of traditional gender roles contributed directly to body dissatisfaction as well as indirectly through contributing to increased body shame and self-surveillance.

Trachtenberg and Piran (2017), using a broader range of gender role measures, explored the relationship between gender role internalization and young (average age = 39.5 years) breast cancer survivors' embodiment and quality of life. In addition to the gender role measure used by Boquiren et al. (2013), they used the Silencing the Self Scale (Jack & Dill, 1992), a scale that assesses the tendency to silence one's needs in intimate relationships, and a measure that assesses women's resistance to, or compliance with, appearance and comportment "femininity"-related expectations, the Mental Freedom Scale (Piran & Teall, 2012; see Chapter 10). The Experience of Embodiment Scale (Piran & Teall, 2012; see Chapter 1) provided the assessment of the quality of embodied lives, such that higher scores indicated positive embodiment. The 113, mostly white (62.8%) women received their diagnosis, on average, at the age of 36.25 (standard deviation [*SD*] = 5.89), and most were diagnosed with Stage III (31.9%) or Stage II (31.0%) cancers, completed a mastectomy (57%), and received a combination of chemotherapy (85%), radiation therapy (80%), and hormone therapy (66%). The pattern of results indicated significant associations between gender role socialization and embodiment, such that positive embodiment correlated negatively with all measures that assessed compliance with restrictive measures of "femininity" and positively with mental freedom, indicating resistance to femininity stereotypes. As expected, the reverse pattern was found for challenges to the quality of life. A simultaneous entry multiple regression revealed that scores on the four measures of gender role socialization predicted 47% of the scores on the Experience of Embodiment Scale, whereby self-surveillance, body shame, and mental freedom were significant predictors of embodiment. The study replicated and expanded on the Boquiren et al. (2013) study by including a measure of positive embodiment and a broader range of gender socialization measures, all indicating that compliance with gender role socialization disrupted embodiment and quality of life among breast cancer survivors, while resistance enhanced embodiment and quality of life.

This pattern of results is not unique to women with breast cancer. Research with healthy women similarly indicated the disruptive effects of traditional role socialization on their body and self-image and depression (Moradi & Huang, 2008), embodiment (Teall & Piran, 2015), and disordered eating (Morrison & Sheahan, 2009; Murnen & Smolak, 1997, 2009; Piran & Cormier, 2005). However, in light of the challenges encountered by women who are dealing with breast cancer, it is important to consider the added toll of contending with the multiplicity of social expectations associated with femininity. For example, a strong focus on maintaining appearance standards that approximate idealized, objectified, and sexualized images of women (in terms of weight, hair, and breasts) can become oppressive and discouraging (Helms, O'Hea, & Corso, 2008; Lemieux, Maunsell, & Provencher, 2008). In a similar vein, idealized constructions of women as selfless caretakers, functioning perfectly at work and home, can stand in the way of much needed self-care and disrupt self-esteem (Boquiren et al., 2013). Further, the qualities of power and agency, attuned self-care, and the pursuit of own passions, often discouraged among girls and women (Piran, 2017), could be important in asserting needs and choices related to treatment and healing. These processes are important to understand as they have implications for providing health promotion interventions with women survivors of breast cancer. In particular, a critical look at the shaping of one's internalized gender role expectations and the examination of possibilities inherent in changing and acting differently in the world can build other sources of social power.

Qualitative studies can further deepen the understanding of processes of resistance to gender role socialization that are associated with positive embodiment and well-being among breast cancer survivors. In an interview study with 12 young (average age = 37.2 years) breast cancer survivors (Trachtenberg & Piran, 2017), internalization versus rejection of gender-related expectations was one of six core categories that emerged in participants' narratives about their self and body experiences. Other categories included loss and adversity, life goals and meaning, social power and the body, as well as body and relational connections. Considering internalization versus rejection of gender-related expectations, overall, women who described shifts toward greater freedom from varied gender-related social expectations also described greater embodied well-being.

Participants in Trachtenberg and Piran's (2017) study who described finding constructive ways of coping with the cancer diagnosis reported resistance to precancer gender-related expectations in three main areas. One important area included a shift from inhabiting the body as an object to be gazed at to inhabiting the body as a site of greater subjective attunement, valued functionality, and wisdom. A second shift involved letting go of the exclusive other-oriented care and the incessant performance expectations in the domestic sphere (often in addition to the work sphere) and refocusing on own needs and passions. A third important shift took place in the domain of voice and power, namely, shifting from being submissive or demure to negotiating needs with agency. All three themes are reflected, for example, in the following narratives of Sabrina (research name), a woman in her early 40s who emigrated from the Middle East to Canada and was partnered with children. She described her resolve to "be a fighter and do stuff that's good for me."

> [A shift from an objectified to an attuned and functional way of inhabiting the body] There are more important things in life than worrying how your body is. As you get older, you're not going to have the body of a model. You get wrinkles, your hair is getting grey and you kind of come to the conclusion that that's okay. . . . I am more aware of my needs. If I need to take a nap, I'll go take a nap, the laundry can wait. If I'm super tired and I can't cook okay, guys we're getting pizza. Always self-care is the most important thing. . . . I am into dragon boating now; that is important for me.
>
> [A shift from other- to self-care] Being a woman means you're nurturing, you're patient, you're always doing things for other people, meaning, my kids

> and my family. I always didn't take care of myself. It has always been drilled into me that you're second as a woman. I think that's one of the biggest things that change in me since having the diagnosis: I'm doing more stuff for myself.
>
> [A shift from submission to acting with agency] I stand up and say, "OK. I want to do this for myself." I go to practice [dragon boats] and in my culture that's like a big no-no. So if there is a family party that night when I go for practice, "sorry, can't make the party."

In contrast, trying to hold on to traditional gender roles, and facing rigid social systems, was often associated with feelings of failure and depression, as the narratives of Nikola (research name), a woman in her early 40s who emigrated from Eastern Europe to Canada and was partnered with no children, indicated.

> [Continued self-objectification] Prior to cancer I was you know a young, beautiful, slim woman traveling the world. I always had men compliment me on my looks and suddenly now I felt like I just, overnight I aged, I am no longer sexy, I have one breast, I put on weight through all the treatments. My hair is like a boy buzz cut and I feel so unfeminine. Losing the breast is difficult for me. What kind of bride will I be where I have to wear a certain dress because I have a breast prosthesis? At home in the bedroom I would not have sex unless I have lingerie on, I always have the breast prosthesis. It terrifies me because I don't want my partner to see me that way.
>
> [Continued centrality of other and domestic care] I feel like I failed because my house isn't clean and my bathroom isn't spotless and there are dishes in the sink. And it drives me crazy, but I can't do it anymore because I'm so tired. It's been a failure for me that I can't have the same beautiful home like I used to. I grew up where my mom did everything and my dad didn't do much. So I was like that with [my partner]. I just felt that's sort of my job so I always did everything for him.
>
> [Continued submission] His [partner] question was, "What's to eat?" I'm like, "Well why can't you cook something?" "Well, you do it better," you know what I mean? I really need a lot more, but we're struggling and I feel like a failure.

The findings of this qualitative study therefore supported the findings of quantitative studies, linking resistance to traditional gender role for women and embodied well-being.

CONCLUSIONS AND IMPLICATIONS

Studies conducted to date with women survivors of breast cancer suggest that constraining molds of femininity interfere with internal attunement to self-care and meaningful pursuits required to deal with a cancer diagnosis and its treatment. Further research is needed in the broad domain of women's health challenges and the impact of gender socialization on processes of recovery. Prospective designs, either qualitative or quantitative, can shed light on shifts in internalized gender molds and embodied well-being. Quantitative studies can be enriched by utilizing a range of measures of gender socialization, as well as a range of measures of embodied well-being, including positive ways of inhabiting the body (e.g., see Section I). Qualitative inquiries can further clarify the processes of change and their relationship to well-being. Group-based participatory action research paradigms (Brydon-Miller, 1997), encouraging group members' critical knowledge construction about learned roles and their impact on their lives, as well as processes of change, may be particularly illuminating. Further, research is needed with groups of participants who are diverse in their social locations in terms of social class, ethnicity/race, sexual orientation, and gender identities.

Women could benefit from health promotion interventions that support them in feeling greater freedom from restrictive learned gender roles and expectations. Gender roles and expectations are learned since childhood and continue to be perpetuated throughout women's lives; it is therefore important to make these internalizations explicit and name them to develop the critical awareness needed to reduce compliance with unrealistic feminine molds. Validating the challenges and strengths required in altering gender roles and related discourses is an important step in maintaining a resistant stance and sustaining positive embodied well-being (Piran, 2016, 2017). As Piran (2017) described, women are rarely exposed to other women who can model inhabiting the body with attuned care or to protective messages that safeguard women's well-being in their caretaking role. Positive role modeling and the reinforcement of norms of attuned self-care can be important components in interventions that aim at shifting women's ways of inhabiting their bodies. Paradigms that emphasize empowerment and agency can work as well to counter restrictive gender role socialization. Providing and suggesting alternative ways of connecting to the body, in particular through engagement in immersed and joyful physical activities (in tune with one's physical state), such as yoga, hiking in nature, dancing, or mindful breathing meditation, can help resist self-objectification. Such activities can enhance attunement to the body and connection with its functionality. It is important to recognize that women survivors of breast cancer face objectification pressures, such as choosing breast reconstruction, applying makeup and wearing wigs, also by health professionals and the larger able-bodied culture (e.g., Rubin & Tanenbaum, 2011). Critical awareness and education regarding the negative impact of perpetuated adverse social pressures in the life of breast cancer survivors is vital.

REFERENCES

Boquiren, V. M., Esplen, M. J., Wong, J., Toner, B., & Warner, E. (2013). Exploring the influence of gender-role socialization and objectified body consciousness on body image disturbance in breast cancer survivors, *Psycho-Oncology, 22*, 2177–2185. doi:10.1002/pon.3271

Brydon-Miller, M. (1997). Participatory action research: Psychology and social change. *Journal of Social Issues, 53*, 657–666. doi:10.1111/j.1540-4560.1997.tb02454.x

Carver, C. S., Pozo-Kaderman, C., Price, A. A., Noriega, V., Harris, S. D., Derhagopian, R. P., . . . Moffatt, F. L., Jr. (1998). Concern about aspects of body image and adjustment to early stage breast cancer. *Psychosomatic Medicine, 60*, 168–174. doi:10.1097/00006842-199803000-00010

Cash, T. F., & Smolak, L. (Eds.). (2011). *Body image: A handbook of science, practice, and prevention* (2nd ed.). New York, NY: Guilford Press.

Falk Dahl, C. A., Reinertsen, K. V., Nesvold, I., Fosså, S. D., & Dahl, A. A. (2010). A study of body image in long-term breast cancer survivors. *Cancer, 116*, 3549–3557. doi:10.1002/cncr.25251

Figueiredo, M. I., Cullen, J., Hwang, Y. T., Rowland, J. H., & Mandelblatt, J. S. (2004). Breast cancer treatment in older women: Does getting what you want improve your long-term body image and mental health? *Journal of Clinical Oncology, 22*, 4002–4009. doi:10.1200/JCO.2004.07.030

Helms, R. L., O'Hea, E. L., & Corso, M. (2008). Body image issues in women with breast cancer. *Psychology, Health & Medicine, 13*, 313–325. doi:10.1080/13548500701405509

Jack, D. C., & Dill, D. (1992). The Silencing the Self Scale. *Psychology of Women Quarterly, 16*, 97–106. doi:10.1111/j.1471-6402.1992.tb00242.x

Lemieux, J., Maunsell, E., & Provencher, L. (2008). Chemotherapy-induced alopecia and effects on quality of life among women with breast cancer: A literature review. *Psycho-Oncology, 17*, 317–328. doi:10.1002/pon.1245

Moradi, B., & Huang, Y. (2008). Objectification theory and psychology of women: A decade of advances and future directions. *Psychology of Women Quarterly, 32*, 377–398. doi:10.1111/j.1471-6402.2008.00452.x

Moreira, H., & Canavarro, M. C. (2010). A longitudinal study about the body image and psychosocial adjustment of breast cancer patients during the course of the disease. *European Journal of Oncology Nursing, 14*, 263–270. doi:10.1016/j.ejon.2010.04.001

Moreira, H., Silva, S., & Canavarro, M. C. (2010). The role of appearance investment in the adjustment of women with breast cancer. *Psycho-Oncology, 19*, 959–966. doi:10.1002/pon.1647

Morrison, T. G., & Sheahan, E. E. (2009). Gender-related discourses as mediators in the association between internalization of the thin-body ideal and indicants of body dissatisfaction and disordered eating. *Psychology of Women Quarterly, 33*, 374–383. doi:10.1111/j.1471-6402.2009.01515.x

Murnen, S. K., & Smolak, L. (1997). Femininity, masculinity, and disordered eating: A meta-analytic review. *International Journal of Eating Disorders, 22*, 231–242. doi:10.1002/(sici)1098-108x(199711)22:3<231::aid-eat2>3.0.co;2-o

Murnen, S. K., & Smolak, L. (2009). Are feminist women protected from body image problems? A meta-analytic review of relevant research. *Sex Roles, 60*, 186–197. doi:10.1007/s11199-008-9523-2

Piran, N. (2016). Embodied paths in aging: Body journeys towards enhanced agency and self-attunement. *Women & Therapy, 39*, 186–201. doi:10.1080/02703149.2016.1116853

Piran, N. (2017). *Journeys of embodiment at the intersection of body and culture: The developmental theory of embodiment*. San Diego, CA: Elsevier. doi:10.1016/c2015-0-04666-4

Piran, N., & Cormier, H. C. (2005). The social construction of women and disordered eating patterns. *Journal of Counseling Psychology, 52*, 549–558. doi:10.1037/0022-0167.52.4.549

Piran, N., & Teall, T. (2012). The developmental theory of embodiment. In G. McVey, M. Levine, N. Piran, & B. Ferguson (Eds.), *Preventing eating-related and weight-related disorders: Collaborative research, advocacy, and policy change* (pp. 169–198). Waterloo, ON, Canada: Wilfred Laurier University Press.

Rubin, L. R., & Tanenbaum, M. (2011). "Does that make me a woman?" Breast cancer, mastectomy, and breast reconstruction decisions among sexual minority women. *Psychology of Women Quarterly, 35*, 401–414. doi:10.1177/0361684310395606

Teall, T., & Piran, N. (2015, August). *Embodiment scales for women: A psychometric study of the Experience of Embodiment Scale.* Poster presented at the American Psychological Association annual convention, Toronto, ON, Canada.

Toner, B., Tang, T., Ali, A., Akman, D., Stuckless, N., Esplen, M. J., . . . Ross, L. (2012). Developing a gender role socialization scale. In J. L. Oliffe & L. Greaves (Eds.), *Designing and conducting gender, sex, and health research* (pp. 189–200). Thousand Oaks, CA: Sage. doi:10.4135/9781452230610.n11

Trachtenberg, L., & Piran, N. (2017, June). *Experience of embodiment among young women survivors of breast cancer: Relationship to gender role expectations.* Paper presented at the Canadian Psychological Association annual convention, Toronto, ON, Canada.

17

Promoting a Resistant Stance Toward Weight Stigma

BROOKE L. BENNETT, EMILY C. STEFANO, AND JANET D. LATNER ■

Weight stigma (i.e., weight bias, fat prejudice) is broadly defined as negative attitudes, stereotypes, or beliefs about individuals perceived as fat (Puhl & Brownell, 2003a; Puhl & Heuer, 2009). Being fat is considered a deviant and devalued social identity (Degher & Hughes, 1999), and fat people have often been the target of weight-based discrimination at both the interpersonal and the institutional levels (Puhl & Brownell, 2003a). It is important to clarify our use of the term *fat*. We use fat as a descriptor, much like we use "tall" and "thin" to describe a person; that is, if we shun the use of the word *fat*, we validate and perpetuate weight stigma.

Weight stigmatization and discrimination are pervasive, reaching nearly every facet of life. Sources of stigma and weight-based discrimination can include teachers, students, friends, family (Puhl & Heuer, 2010), and healthcare providers—even those specializing in the treatment of obesity and eating disorders (Puhl, Latner, King, & Luedicke, 2014; Schwartz, Chambliss, Brownell, Blair, & Billington, 2003). Indeed, physicians provide less and lower quality healthcare to fat people (Bertakis & Azari, 2005), which could result in avoidance of healthcare settings and routine care, mistrust of doctors, and poorer treatment adherence (Puhl & Heuer, 2009). Numerous health consequences, such as increased risk for heart disease (Puhl & Suh, 2015), symptoms of psychological distress (Wott & Carels, 2010), and lower health-related quality of life (Latner, Barile, Durso, & O'Brien, 2014) likely result from the chronic stress associated with continuous exposure to weight-based discrimination (Sikorski, Luppa, Luck, & Riedel-Heller, 2015; Tomiyama, 2014). Furthermore, weight stigma can be internalized; that is, many fat individuals accept weight-related prejudices and stereotypes as true about themselves (Durso & Latner, 2008). This weight bias internalization is associated with numerous negative psychological indices, such as low self-esteem, emotional dysregulation, disordered eating, poor body image, exercise avoidance, and continued weight gain (Puhl, Moss Racusin, & Schwartz, 2007). Due to the multiple problems with weight stigma, weight-based discrimination, and weight bias internalization, developing a resistant stance against weight stigma is imperative. This chapter considers societal and individual ways to do this.

SOCIETAL SOLUTIONS FOR A SOCIETAL PROBLEM

As a societal problem, weight stigma requires societal-level solutions. Despite its pervasiveness and well-documented harmful effects, weight stigma has historically been ignored and unchallenged, with little consideration as a major societal problem. There are few, if any, legal protections or sanctions against weight-based discrimination, leaving those who encounter weight bias continually vulnerable to its harmful ramifications. Major shifts in public health and public policy approaches are needed to eradicate the weight stigma embedded within institutions and interpersonal interactions (see also Chapters 36 and 37). Placing the burden of responsibility on the individual to change their weight, or accept or cope with stigma, potentially sidesteps the larger human rights issue.

We believe that the first step is to educate the public to create awareness of the problem. Education is needed in schools, health professional training programs, continuing education programs, and the media, not only presenting a diversity of body sizes and shapes but also specifically promoting awareness of the widespread problem of weight bias. This is distinct from and at odds with public health education campaigns stemming from the "war on obesity," which feeds weight stigma. Education campaigns must emphasize the unacceptability of bullying or discrimination due to a person's weight. Schools should encourage potential witnesses of these actions to report them, as they should in the case of bullying and discrimination more generally.

Further, we assert that these educational initiatives should come from diverse sources. Schoolteachers should be educated about weight stigma and dedicate time to addressing it within units on discrimination or in health classes. Educating health professionals is also imperative, given the high rates of bias displayed among health professionals and obesity specialists. Treating fat individuals in nonbiased ways should be taught in early stages of health training programs, such as nursing school, medical school, psychology programs, physical therapy programs, and other health fields. Bias prevention involving 6 weeks of intensive education on nonpersonal causes for weight status has proven effective for pre–health service professionals (O'Brien, Puhl, Latner, Mir, & Hunter, 2010), suggesting that such educational programs may take time and resources. Continuing education programs teaching unbiased attitudes should be required for professionals.

Learners in educational programs should also be assigned to carefully examine and challenge their own biases and beliefs. This can be done with implicit bias measures (e.g., implicit association tests) and formal assessment measures, as well as through careful introspection about whether possible stereotypes or negative attributions are taking place during real-time interactions with fat people. Learners should be taught to acknowledge their own biases and prejudices and actively replace them with more reasonable and compassionate alternatives. During interactions with others, it may also be helpful for learners to recognize and understand the effects that stigma can have on others (as well as on the self). Ideally, such educational initiatives should begin at young ages, as an early prevention measure against the development of initial weight-based discrimination. Providing awareness of weight stigma among physical and mental health care professionals is particularly important, given the weight-based discrimination prevalent in these professions (Puhl et al., 2014; Schwartz et al., 2003).

In the mass media, "counteradvertising" campaigns, like the type launched against tobacco use (see http://countertobacco.org/), could be implemented to warn people about the dangerous effects of weight bias. Media literacy programs should be developed, tested, and disseminated to counteract weight bias depicted in the media (see Chapter 34). Legislation should put regulations into place prohibiting antifat media representations (see Chapter 37), which could target the weight loss industry in particular. However, given how widely weight stigma is propagated by the weight loss industry, short of dismantling much of the industry, it might be difficult or impossible to reverse the harmful trends the industry has put in motion.

Initiatives to prevent weight bias should use evidence-based methods for stigma reduction, such as those most often researched: controllability, empathy, and social consensus interventions (Daníelsdóttir, O'Brien, & Ciao, 2010; Lee, Ata, & Brannick, 2014). Because perceived controllability of stigmatized characteristics is associated with greater discrimination (Crocker, Major, & Steele, 1998) (e.g., those who believe that weight is controllable are more likely to discriminate based on weight); controllability has been one of the most often manipulated variables in stigma-reduction studies. For example, studies have provided information and instruction presenting an uncontrollable model of weight (e.g., focusing on genetic, biological, and environmental causes) to one group and a controllable model of weight (e.g., focusing on diet and exercise-related causes) to another group and compared participants' weight stigma thereafter (e.g., O'Brien et al., 2010). However, results on this approach and others were mixed, with some showing effective stigma reduction and some showing null effects (Lee et al., 2014). There is substantial room in the field for the development of new interventions and theories to guide them, such as intergroup contact theory. The results of a large-scale meta-analysis suggested the importance of intergroup contact, in that positive experiences with members of the stigmatized group are reliably effective means of reducing other forms of prejudice (Pettigrew & Tropp, 2006).

A harder line needs to be taken with respect to legal penalties for weight-based discrimination and bullying. Local, state, and national governments need to pass and enforce laws protecting fat people as a group. Support for anti–weight prejudice legislation does exist and is strongest for antibullying legislation in schools (Puhl, Latner, O'Brien, Luedicke, Daníelsdóttir, et al., 2015; Puhl, Latner, O'Brien,

Luedicke, Forhan, et al., 2015). Similar to tobacco control, one strategy is to start with particular locations in which bullying and discrimination are strictly not tolerated, such as schools and workplaces. Being fat should be categorized as a protected group, such as racial, religious, and sexual minorities. It is important to note that classifying obesity as a "disease" would not aid this endeavor because higher weight often does not represent compromised health. Increasing use of the judiciary system to enforce such legislation would inevitably increase public compliance with such regulations.

The aforementioned interventions likely produce an interactive effect and reinforce one another (Institute of Medicine, 2000). Thus, it is essential that society invest public health resources in multiple solutions to dismantle weight stigma.

RESISTANCE ORGANIZATIONS

As documentation of the negative consequences associated with experiencing weight stigma has increased, so has the realization of the need for appropriate organizations. On a societal level, two major organizations are leading the charge to resist and fight weight-related stigma. The first is the National Association to Advance Fat Acceptance (NAAFA), described as "an all-volunteer, civil rights organization" (NAAFA, 2016). NAAFA aims to "eliminate discrimination based on body size and provide fat people with the tools for self-empowerment through advocacy, public education, and support" (NAAFA, 2016). The second organization is Health at Every Size (HAES®; see also Chapter 28). The mission of HAES is to advance social justice, maintain an inclusive and respectful community, and support compassionate care and self-care for people of all sizes (HAES, 2017). It advocates respect, critical awareness, and compassion as core components. These movements have picked up momentum recently through greater press exposure, which has also brought much debate about their stances and approaches (Michael, 2011).

INDIVIDUAL-LEVEL PROTECTIVE FACTORS FOR WEIGHT PREJUDICE

While researchers, clinicians, and other professionals continue to advocate for, and work toward, eradicating weight stigma on a societal level, it is crucial not to overlook interventions at the individual level. One key area of focus should be the prevention or alleviation of weight bias internalization due to its many negative psychological effects (Latner et al., 2014). Indeed, a non–weight-focused, HAES-based "healthy living program" was only effective in promoting physical activity and adaptive eating if the participants (middle-age women with high body mass index) had low levels of weight bias internalization (Mensinger, Calogero, & Tylka, 2016; Mensinger & Meadows, 2017). Preventing weight bias internalization may be improved through the bolstering of protective factors, which interrupt the pathway between experiencing weight prejudice and the subsequent negative outcomes.

Protective Factors

One potential protective factor is positive self-concept for physical appearance. Body dissatisfaction has been found to be both predictive of, and positively correlated with, weight bias internalization (Durso & Latner, 2008). Positive self-concept for physical appearance prevented the development of depressive symptoms after the experience of weight-based victimization or bullying in a sample of children (Adams & Bukowski, 2008). Positive overall self-image may be an additional protective factor. For example, self-esteem is inversely related to weight bias internalization (Durso & Latner, 2008).

Body image flexibility and self-compassion are two other potential protective factors. Body image flexibility is defined as a process "reflecting the willingness to approach aversive body image-related internal content with mindful acceptance in order to continue to move in valued life direction" (Webb & Hardin, 2016, p. 66). Webb and Hardin created an integrative affective model that explained the effects of weight bias internalization in the domain of eating behavior. Body image flexibility and, to a lesser extent, self-compassion partially mediated the relationship between adhering to internalized weight-stigmatizing beliefs and the likelihood of practicing intuitive eating in a sample of college women after controlling for body mass index. Therefore, reported low body image flexibility and low self-compassion partially explained the inverse association found between internalized weight bias and intuitive eating. Notably, body image flexibility was identified as the most robust protective factor relative to the other two affective regulation strategies included in the study (self-compassion and body shame; Webb & Hardin, 2016).

In addition to contributing to the inverse relationship between weight bias internalization and intuitive eating, self-compassion was found to be linked to a variety of well-being outcomes. Notably, self-compassion reduced the contribution of weight bias internalization to psychological and physical health outcomes (e.g., depression, somatic symptoms, quality of life) by one third among German community adults (Hilbert et al., 2015). Self-compassion can be enhanced through therapy (see Chapters 25 and 27) and is a potential variable for exploration in treating weight bias internalization. Preliminary research has found that interventions designed to specifically target self-acceptance among fat individuals have demonstrated efficacy in improving quality of life and distress tolerance (Lillis, Hayes, Bunting, & Masuda, 2009).

Yet, it is likely difficult for fat individuals to be satisfied with their bodies and have a favorable self-image while embedded in a culture of weight stigma—one that criticizes their body type and assigns negative self-characteristics to being fat—making societal reform imperative. Future research needs to investigate whether certain variables disrupt the pathway between experiencing weight stigma and experiencing its negative outcomes.

Coping with Stigma

Coping skills may be key to lessening the deleterious effects of weight stigma. Two strategies identified by Puhl and Brownell (2003b) have been relatively well established as adaptive in coping with weight stigma across situations. The first is *self-protection*, which contains a variety of mechanisms used to protect an individual's self-esteem from the impact of prejudice, such as positive self-talk and filtering out negative remarks (Puhl & Brownell, 2006). This coping skill may be similar to protective filtering (Wood-Barcalow, Tylka, & Augustus-Horvath, 2010) and positive rational acceptance (Cash, Santos, & Williams, 2005). Protective filtering serves to safeguard positive body image by guiding individuals toward accepting information that is consistent with positive body image while rejecting body image threats (e.g., weight stigma) that endanger it. Positive rational acceptance includes positive self-care or rational self-talk about one's appearance (e.g., remind self of good qualities, emphasize other important qualities than appearance) while being mindful during body image threats. The second strategy is *social activism*. People may participate in social activism through public protests, joining an advocacy group such as NAAFA, or helping educate the public about weight stigma. Confronting those who stigmatize and communal coping can also be effective coping strategies (Dickins, Thomas, King, Lewis, & Holland, 2011). Communal coping involves group communication about weight stigma and collaboration to produce strategies to confront it, which has become particularly relevant with the expansion of social media and online communities. Future research should focus on developing interventions or training programs that teach and bolster adaptive coping skills for individuals facing weight stigma.

TREATMENT AND PREVENTION IMPLICATIONS

Weight stigma and its effects have implications for mental and physical health providers. The first implication involves providing consumers with a safe place to share their lived experiences. Providers should validate consumers' accounts of facing weight-based prejudice, discrimination, or stigmatization. Healthcare providers must further examine and process their own beliefs and biases to ensure that they will not perpetrate weight stigma or shame. Shared health information should be free of negative weight-based stereotypes, and the focus should be on fostering healthy behaviors rather than weight loss. Moreover, educators, caregivers, and therapists need to carefully avoid the use of blaming language and convey respect and acceptance.

Professionals can also take steps to make their offices a more weight-inclusive place (Calogero, Tylka, Mensinger, Meadows, & Daníelsdóttir, in press; Tylka et al., 2014). For example, they can ensure that medical offices have appropriate supplies for health consumers across the weight spectrum and seating areas that accommodate large bodies. Further, providers can conduct trainings to inform other healthcare professionals about the ramifications of weight bias. Informing families about the adverse impact of weight-stigmatizing comments could be useful as well. Interested readers may want to consult the work of Calogero et al. (in press), who described practical strategies for therapists to challenge their own weight stigma and provide an accepting environment for individuals of all sizes.

For providers hoping to help consumers alleviate the adverse effects of experiencing weight prejudice, there are additional treatment implications. Fostering in individuals the development of protective factors (e.g., body satisfaction and appreciation, a positive self-image, protective filtering, self-compassion) may reduce the likelihood that weight bias will be internalized. Thus, treatment programs should focus on developing and strengthening protective factors, similar to what is done in HAES-based programs (see Mensinger et al., 2016).

Treatment providers could also enhance consumers' coping skills through enhancing social activism and self-protection. Acceptance and mindfulness training have demonstrated success in reducing psychological distress, improving quality of life, and improving weight stigma (Lillis et al., 2009). The fact that weight stigma and weight bias internalization occur at a young age (Puhl & Latner, 2007) underscores the importance of prevention programs that can help individuals develop coping strategies and inner resources early in life.

CONCLUSION AND FUTURE DIRECTIONS

Resistance to weight stigma needs to occur, first and foremost, at the societal level. Although multiple potential strategies exist, few have yet been implemented or tested. Resistance strategies at the individual level are also needed to protect people from the harms caused by this widespread societal problem. To develop a resistant stance toward weight stigma, both societally and individually, research is needed to guide public health interventions, to determine the best theories on which to base programs to prevent weight stigma, and to understand the best methods for spreading positive representations of people of all sizes and coping strategies for dealing with widespread weight bias.

Additional research is needed to examine the potential effects of participation in HAES and NAAFA groups, including their possible positive impact on coping and protection from the harmful impact of stigma. Facilitating positive intergroup contact might be one potential method for weight stigma reduction, and this could be a promising avenue for future research. For example, studies could facilitate positive social interactions with people of different weight levels and examine potential effects on weight stigma. However, societal change should not wait until all these data are in; changes need to be implemented immediately, as weight stigma is costly in terms of compromised psychological well-being and physical health for those targeted. Indeed, when dealing with important, widespread public health issues like weight stigma, "the lack of definitive science should never paralyze action" (Institute of Medicine, 2000, p. 36).

REFERENCES

Adams, R. E., & Bukowski, W. M. (2008). Peer victimization as a predictor of depression and body mass index in obese and non-obese adolescents. *Journal of Child Psychology and Psychiatry, 49*, 858–866. doi:10.1111/j.1469-7610.2008.01886.x

Bertakis, K. D., & Azari, R. (2008). The impact of obesity on primary care visits. *Obesity Research, 13*, 1615–1622. doi:10.1038/oby.2005.198

Calogero, R. M., Tylka, T. L., Mensinger, J. L., Meadows, A., & Daníelsdóttir, S. (in press). Recognizing fat as a fundamental right: A weight inclusive approach to size acceptance and healing from sizeism. *Women and Therapy*.

Cash, T. F., Santos, M. T., & Williams, E. F. (2005). Coping with body-image threats and challenges: Validation of the Body Image Coping Strategies Inventory. *Journal of Psychosomatic Research, 58*, 191–199. doi:10.1016/j.jpsychores.2004.07.008

Crocker, J., Major, B., & Steele, C. (1998). Social stigma. In D. T. Gilbert, S. T. Fiske, & G. Lindzey (Eds.), *Handbook of social psychology* (4th ed., Vol. 2, pp. 504–554). Boston, MA: McGraw-Hill.

Daníelsdóttir, S., O'Brien, K. S., & Ciao, A. (2010). Anti-fat prejudice reduction: A review of published studies. *Obesity Facts, 3*, 47–58. doi:10.1159/000277067

Degher, D., & Hughes, G. (1999). The adoption and management of a "fat" identity. In J. Sobal & D. Maurer (Eds.), *Interpreting weight: The social management of fatness and thinness* (pp. 11–27). New York, NY: Transaction. doi:10.5860/choice.37-3383

Dickins, M., Thomas, S. L., King, B., Lewis, S., & Holland, K. (2011). The role of the Fatosphere in fat adults' responses to obesity stigma: A model of empowerment without a focus on weight loss. *Qualitative Health Research, 21*, 1679–1691. doi:10.1177/1049732311417728

Durso, L. E., & Latner, J. D. (2008). Understanding self-directed stigma: Development of the Weight Bias Internalization Scale. *Obesity, 16*, S80–S86. doi:10.1038/oby.2008.448.

Health at Every Size. (2017). Home page. Retrieved from https://haescommunity.com/

Hilbert, A., Braehler, E., Schmidt, R., Löwe, B., Häuser, W., & Zenger, M. (2015). Self-compassion as a resource in the self-stigma process of overweight and obese individuals. *Obesity Facts, 8*, 293–301. doi:10.1159/000438681

Institute of Medicine. (2000). *Promoting health: Intervention strategies from social and behavioral research*. Washington, DC: National Academies Press. doi:10.17226/9939

Latner, J. D., Barile, J., Durso, L. E., & O'Brien, K. S. (2014). Weight and health-related quality of life: The moderating role of weight discrimination and internalized weight bias. *Eating Behaviors, 15*, 586–590. doi:10.1016/j.eatbeh.2014.08.014

Lee, M., Ata, R. N., & Brannick, M. T. (2014). Malleability of weight-biased attitudes and beliefs: A meta-analysis of weight bias reduction interventions. *Body Image, 11*, 251–259. doi:10.1016/j.bodyim.2014.03.003

Lillis, J., Hayes, S. C., Bunting, K., & Masuda, A. (2009). Teaching acceptance and mindfulness to improve the lives of the obese: A preliminary test of a theoretical model. *Annals of Behavioral Medicine, 37*, 58–69. doi:10.1007/s12160-009-9083-x

Mensinger, J. L., Calogero, R. M., & Tylka, T. L. (2016). Internalized weight stigma moderates eating behavior outcomes in women with high BMI participating in a healthy living program. *Attitude, 102*, 32–43. doi:10.1016/j.appet.2016.01.033

Mensinger, J. L., & Meadows, A. (2017). Internalized weight stigma mediates and moderates physical activity outcomes during a healthy living program for women with high body mass index. *Psychology of Sport and Exercise, 30*, 64–72. doi:10.1016/j.psychsport.2017.01.010

Michael, R. (2011, March 9). Health at Every Size? *New York Times.* Retrieved from https://6thfloor.blogs.nytimes.com/2011/03/09/health-at-every-size/

National Association to Advance Fat People. (2016). *About us.* Retrieved from https://www.naafaonline.com/dev2/about/index.html

O'Brien, K. S., Puhl, R. M., Latner, J. D., Mir, A. S., & Hunter, J. A. (2010). Reducing anti-fat prejudice in pre-service health students: A randomized trial. *Obesity, 18*, 2138–2144. doi:10.1038/oby.2010.79

Pettigrew, T. F., & Tropp, L. R. (2006). A meta-analytic test of intergroup contact theory. *Journal of Personality and Social Psychology, 90*, 751–783. doi:10.1037/0022-3514.90.5.751

Puhl, R. M., & Brownell, K. D. (2003a). Psychosocial origins of obesity stigma: Toward changing a powerful and pervasive bias. *Obesity Reviews, 4*, 213–227. doi:10.1046/j.1467-789x.2003.00122.x

Puhl, R. M., & Brownell, K. D. (2003b). Ways of coping with obesity stigma: Review and conceptual analysis. *Eating Behaviors, 4*, 53–78. doi:10.1016/s1471-0153(02)00096-x

Puhl, R. M., & Brownell, K. D. (2006). Confronting and coping with weight stigma: An investigation of overweight and obese adults. *Obesity, 14*, 1802–1815. doi:10.1038/oby.2006.208

Puhl, R. M., & Heuer, C. A. (2009). The stigma of obesity: A review and update. *Obesity, 17*, 941–964. doi:10.1038/oby.2008.636

Puhl, R. M., & Heuer, C. A. (2010). Obesity stigma: Important considerations for public health. *American Journal of Public Health, 100*, 1019–1028. doi:10.2105/ajph.2009.159491

Puhl, R. M., & Latner, J. D. (2007). Stigma, obesity, and the health of the nation's children. *Psychological Bulletin, 133*, 557–580. doi:10.1037/0033-2909.133.4.557

Puhl, R. M., Latner, J. D., King, K. M., & Luedicke, J. (2014). Weight bias among professionals treating eating disorders: Attitudes about treatment and perceived patient outcomes. *International Journal of Eating Disorders, 47*, 65–75. doi:10.1002/eat.22186

Puhl, R. M., Latner, J. D., O'Brien, K. S., Luedicke, J., Daníelsdóttir, S., & Forhan, M. (2015). Potential policies and laws to prohibit weight discrimination: Public views from four countries. *Milbank Quarterly, 9*, 691–731. doi:10.1111/1468-0009.12162

Puhl, R. M., Latner, J. D., O'Brien, K. S., Luedicke, J., Forhan, M., & Daníelsdóttir, S. (2015). Cross-national perspectives about weight-based bullying in youth: Nature, extent, and remedies. *Pediatric Obesity, 11*, 241–250. doi:10.1111/ijpo.12051

Puhl, R. M., Moss Racusin, C. A., & Schwartz, M. B. (2007). Internalization of weight bias: Implications for binge eating and emotional well-being. *Obesity, 15*, 19–23. doi:10.1038/oby.2007.521

Puhl, R. M., & Suh, Y. (2015). Health consequences of weight stigma: Implications for obesity prevention and treatment. *Current Obesity Reports, 4*, 182–190. doi:10.1007/s13679-015-0153-z

Schwartz, M. B., Chambliss, H. O. N., Brownell, K. D., Blair, S. N., & Billington, C. (2003). Weight bias among health professionals specializing in obesity. *Obesity Research, 11*, 1033–1039. doi:10.1038/oby.2003.142

Sikorski, C., Luppa, M., Luck, T., & Riedel-Heller, S. G. (2015). Weight stigma "gets under the skin"—evidence for an adapted psychological mediation framework—a systematic review. *Obesity, 23*, 266–276. doi:10.1002/oby.20952

Tomiyama, A. J. (2014). Weight stigma is stressful. A review of evidence for the cyclic obesity/weight-based stigma model. *Appetite, 82*, 8–15. doi:10.1016/j.appet.2014.06.108

Tylka, T. L., Annunziato, R. A., Burgard, D., Daníelsdóttir, S., Shuman, E., Davis, C., & Calogero, R. M. (2014). The weight-inclusive versus weight-normative approach to health: Evaluating the evidence for prioritizing well-being over weight loss. *Journal of Obesity, 2014*, 1–18. doi:10.1155/2014/983495

Webb, J. B., & Hardin, A. S. (2016). An integrative affect regulation process model of internalized weight bias and intuitive eating in college women. *Appetite, 102*, 60–69. doi:10.1016/j.appet.2016.02.0240195-6663

Wood-Barcalow, N. L., Tylka, T. L., & Augustus-Horvath, C. L. (2010). "But I like my body": Positive body image characteristics and a holistic model for young-adult women. *Body Image, 7*, 106–116. doi:10.1016/j.bodyim.2010.01.001

Wott, C. B., & Carels, R. A. (2010). Overt weight stigma, psychological distress and weight loss treatment outcomes. *Journal of Health Psychology, 15*, 608–614. doi:10.1177/1359105309355339

18

Black Women's Positive Embodiment in the Face of Race × Gender Oppression

NICOLE T. BUCHANAN, ISIS H. SETTLES,
AND KRYSTLE C. WOODS ■

Black women's bodies are often glamorized and fetishized, but Black women's relationships with their bodies are rarely theoretically or empirically examined. Although heralded as having an idealized view of their bodies and comfort with their sexuality (Capodilupo & Kim, 2014), for many Black women their relationship with their physique is complicated and nuanced by narratives of race, gender, and their intersection. Given this reality, positive embodiment is a hard-won battle for those Black women who achieve it, and their efforts are repeatedly challenged by mainstream cultural narratives that view their bodies as deviant and lacking value (Beauboeuf-Lafontant, 2009).

FROM THE "HOTTENTOT VENUS" TO SERENA WILLIAMS

Saartjie (Sarah) Baartman (1789–1815) was forcibly brought to London in 1810 and made to perform in public and private shows where voyeurs were allowed to gawk and fondle her at will (Crais & Scully, 2010). Ms. Baartman was a member of the Khoisan tribes from South Africa, who commonly evidenced steatopygia, resulting in substantial layers of adipose tissue to build in the buttocks, hips, and thighs (Magak & Okombo, 2014). Dubbed the "Hottentot Venus," she was put on display throughout London and Ireland because her enlarged buttocks and genitals were eroticized, fetishized, and simultaneously denounced as grotesque. Five years later, Ms. Baartman died, potentially from a combination of alcohol addiction, syphilis, and pneumonia. Georges Cuvier then pickled her genitals and buttocks and placed them on display with her brain, skeleton, and a plaster cast of her body in the Paris Museum of Man. Her dissected body and cast remained on public display until 1974, and her dissected body and cast were not returned to her homeland until 2002, when South Africa's president, Nelson Mandela, requested their return (Crais & Scully, 2010; Parkinson, 2016).

Tennis phenom Serena Williams is known for her unprecedented number of world championships, unbridled strength, and unsurpassed serve speed (estimated at over 130 miles per hour). In tennis, she is unmistakable, tall (5 feet, 9 inches; 155 pounds), with a muscular physique that is without rival among women or men in the sport. Serena's body has garnered attention because of her hourglass figure, with an undeniably small waist juxtaposed against her curved chest and hips. She admits to having struggled with negative body esteem for many years, stemming from the belief that her body is too muscular, too strong, and too masculine (Williams, 2016). These negative feelings about her body were fueled by media coverage that both criticized her muscularity and power and sexualized and objectified her hourglass figure. In fact, other tennis competitors openly mock her. During a tennis exhibition match, Caroline Wozniacki stopped the tournament to caricaturize Serena Williams by placing towels in her shirt and tennis skirt to create an exaggerated chest and bottom, then continued the match dressed in this manner. She had also done this during a previous match and a month prior; Novak Djokovic and Andy Roddick had done the same. None of these players were sanctioned for their behavior. In fact, each garnered laughter from onlookers as they mocked Serena Williams's body and later defended their behavior. Although there were those who denounced the behavior as simultaneously racist and sexist, the vast majority of media coverage supported their assertions that it was nothing more than a harmless joke, not worthy of punishment or sanctions.

Although separated by two centuries, the experiences of both Saartjie (Sarah) Baartman and Serena Williams demonstrate the complicated ways in which Black women's bodies have been objectified, hypersexualized, and simultaneously critiqued as deviant. Moreover, both women were subjected to humiliating displays of public objectification. Although often less public, many Black girls and women also experience sexual objectification that is uniquely raced and gendered. In this chapter, we examine race–gender stereotypes, victimization, and prejudice and their influence on Black women's embodiment, highlighting sources of strength and resistance that promote positive embodiment in the face of derogation.

POSITIVE EMBODIMENT, INTERSECTIONALITY, AND MULTIPLE JEOPARDY

Embodiment is a multidimensional construct that holistically accounts for relationships between the self and the body. Piran (2016) identified core facets of embodiment, each of which could be experienced positively or negatively. For example, comfort and connection with one's body could range from feeling oneness with one's body to feeling ashamed and wanting to control, restrict, and change it. Agency and functionality reflect the extent to which one feels free to use the body for self-expression and voice. Embodiment further encompasses the ability to experience and express desire, to be attuned and responsive to internal body cues, and to experience the resistance or incorporation of social expectations regarding body appearance and use. Embodiment is influenced by objectification: Being routinely sexualized and treated as a sexual object erodes embodiment (Fredrickson & Roberts, 1997; Moradi & Huang, 2008). Women may internalize these views and link their self-worth to their appearance (self-objectification), which is in turn associated with distorted body image, body shame, and disordered eating (Forbes, Jobe, & Revak, 2006; Lindberg, Hyde, & McKinley, 2006). In a society where sexualization of women is pervasive, objectification is thought to be universal, but important differences in embodiment and women's relationships with their bodies have been documented across ethnic groups.

Intersectionality theory (Crenshaw, 1991) can help to explain Black women's experience of embodiment, as it emerged from Black feminist analyses of race and gender as inextricably intertwined and essential for understanding the nature and consequences of Black women's victimization and oppression. Intersectionality theory posits that social identities are interdependent, making the meaning of one identity dependent on the other identities one holds (Cole, 2009; Settles & Buchanan, 2014). Importantly, intersectionality theory also attends to differential power and one's position within social hierarchies, which reflect the social context and one's status as simultaneously privileged and marginalized (Warner, Settles, & Shields, 2018). Finally, intersectionality theory compliments theories of multiple jeopardy and multiple disadvantage (Beale, 1970; King, 1988), which assert that holding multiple marginalized identities increases one's risk for accrued disadvantages over time, polyvictimization, and subsequent psychological and physical harm.

Thus, intersectionality theory suggests that the experiences of victimization, bias, prejudice, and their consequences will differ as a result of one's specific intersecting identities. For example, Black women experience gendered forms of racial victimization, such as racialized sexual harassment, which draws on sexualized stereotypes specific to Black women (Buchanan, 2005; Buchanan & Ormerod, 2002; Buchanan & West, 2009). Experiencing victimization based on multiple social identities is associated with greater distress and psychological harm (Buchanan & Fitzgerald, 2008; Settles & Buchanan, 2014). Specifically, racialized sexual harassment is often more damaging than experiencing a single form of harassment (Woods, Buchanan, & Settles, 2009) and is associated with unhealthy coping responses that further harm Black women's psychological well-being (Szymanski & Lewis, 2016). In turn, this may impact one's embodied sense of self, body image, and eating behaviors.

BODY SIZE, SATISFACTION, AND WELL-BEING

Despite associations between early menarche, weight gain, and body dissatisfaction across many groups, Black adolescent girls and women on average show greater satisfaction with their bodies than their White peers (Chithambo & Huey, 2013). Even after controlling for socioeconomic status and body mass index, 7th- to 12th-grade Black girls reported the highest body satisfaction when compared across six ethnic groups, were the most likely to report wanting to gain rather than lose weight, and endorsed the belief that extra body fat denotes health and makes them feel more feminine (Neumark-Sztainer et al., 2002). Consistent with this finding, Black women reported an ideal body size significantly larger than that reported by White women and described being curvaceous positively. In fact, a study of Black college-bound girls found no association between body mass index and body indicators, such as dissatisfaction and disordered eating (Webb, Butler-Ajibade, & Robinson, 2014).

Black women, on average, appear to have generally positive body image (i.e., body appreciation). Qualitative interviews with college women and experts on body image revealed that positive body image is not merely the absence of negative body image (Wood-Barcalow, Tylka, & Augustus-Horvath, 2010). Instead, positive body image reflects love and respect for one's body, as evidenced by accepting and holding favorable opinions of one's body, attending to body needs and engaging in healthy behaviors, and guarding against harmful images and portrayals of the body, especially those that contribute to an unrealistic thin ideal. Compared across studies, Black women report higher levels of positive body image and body acceptance compared to White peers (Cotter, Kelly, Mitchell, & Mazzeo, 2015) and significantly less discrepancy between their perceived body and their ideal body (Webb et al., 2014).

Black girls are also less likely than White girls to internalize media depictions of idealized thin body images and do not expect that their peers or potential partners would value such images (Chithambo & Huey, 2013). In contrast, despite acknowledging that the images were unrealistic, White adolescent girls believed family, friends, and future partners would use such idealized images to judge them. Consistent with this finding, Black men and boys reported appreciation for larger female body sizes compared to White counterparts (Chithambo & Huey, 2013). Taken together, these studies suggest that ethno-specific social norms do shape how Black girls and women evaluate their bodies, with thinness being less important to self-perceptions of their attractiveness.

Despite well-documented links between negative embodiment and depression among White women (e.g., Richard, Rohrmann, Lohse, & Eichholzer, 2016), body image, body satisfaction, and disordered eating do not appear to confer the same mental health risks for Black women (Bisaga et al., 2005). Unless categorized as obese, even when their body mass indices are significantly higher than White peers, Black women report less body dissatisfaction, dieting, and disordered eating than White adolescent girls, and no association exists between their body size and level of depression (Bisaga et al., 2005; Witherspoon, Latta, Wang, &

Black, 2013). Black girls are also at significantly lower risk for other indices of eating pathology, such as attempting to lose weight, binge eating, and extreme weight control behaviors, such as purging and the use of diet pills (Neumark-Sztainer et al., 2002). In sum, race appears to moderate the relationship between several risk factors for disordered eating and body dissatisfaction and common mental health outcomes, such as depression.

SKIN TONE, HAIR TEXTURE, AND RACIAL PROTOTYPICALITY

Although typically discussed in the context of body shape and size, Black women's embodiment is interconnected with colorism (prejudice based on the color of one's skin), hair texture, and racial prototypicality or the extent to which one's features (e.g., nose and lips) are more stereotypically African or European. Centuries of racial oppression in the United States have shifted women's beauty standards toward a "White ideal" characterized by a preference for light skin, wavy or straight hair, narrow noses, and small lips (Russell, Wilson, & Hall, 2013). These characteristics predict how Black women are perceived and treated by in-group and out-group members (Adams, Kurtz-Costes, & Hoffman, 2016; Hagiwara, Kashy, & Cesario, 2012), with consequent effects on self-esteem and mental health that are evident by preschool and persist through adolescence and early adulthood (Adams et al., 2016; Breland-Noble, 2013; Mucherah & Frazier, 2013).

Historically, popular culture images portrayed dark-skinned women as masculine, obese, and unattractive. In contemporary times, magazine and television advertisements are still significantly more likely to feature light-skinned Black women, reflecting the belief that light skin is a prerequisite for beauty (Breland-Noble, 2013). Similarly, when darker skinned women are portrayed in the media, they continue to be caricaturized as obese, unattractive, and masculine. When cast as beautiful, dark-skinned women are far more likely to have long, straight hair, narrow noses, and small to medium-size lips. The persistent message is that, even for Black women, beauty is defined by prototypical Whiteness, whether evidenced by skin tone, hair texture, facial features, or some combination of the three.

CULTURAL INFLUENCES ON EMBODIMENT

Given their high rates of sexual victimization, their historical and contemporary objectification, and standards of beauty that glorify a White ideal, the relatively low levels of negative embodiment reported by Black adolescent girls and women, as demonstrated by their high levels of body satisfaction and low levels of disordered attitudes and behaviors, is surprising. However, Black culture may serve as a protective factor that shields Black girls and women, even when overweight, from body dissatisfaction, disordered eating, and negative mental health correlates.

One such protective cultural factor is the Strong Black Women archetype, which despite being associated with some problematic coping behaviors (Beauboeuf-Lafontant, 2009), stereotypes Black women as having unwavering strength despite hardship, promotes emotional and physical strength, and encourages physical capability to use one's body to achieve goals (Donovan & West, 2015). Commonly held beliefs about women's attractiveness among Black people correspond with this archetype, as they often embrace a larger, stronger version of femininity. Seeing one's body as physically capable and embracing a broad view of what types of bodies are attractive for women are both common in Black culture and likely contribute to Black women's positive embodiment.

FUTURE DIRECTIONS

Greater research focus is needed that incorporates positive body image and embodiment indices (Piran, 2015), factors that promote positive embodiment, particularly cultural factors that may buffer the relationships between negative experiences related to the body (e.g., prejudice, discrimination, and harassment) and disrupted or negative embodiment. For example, studies have identified that a strong positive racial identity is protective against some negative mental health outcomes following negative race-related events (Brondolo, Brady, Pencille, Beatty, & Contrada, 2009), but this relationship has received little attention regarding outcomes related to facets of embodiment (exceptions include Cotter et al., 2015; Watson, Ancis, White, & Nazari, 2013). Given the nature of experiences such as racialized sexual harassment (Buchanan & Ormerod, 2002), examining intersecting identities such as Black women's identities as simultaneously Black and female and their positive perception of this intersecting identity may specifically buffer against negative embodiment. Examining raced-gendered norms, such as the Strong Black Woman archetype and its connection to embodiment will provide a strong contribution to the literature to date.

Continuing to monitor these trends over time will be critical in future research given that cultural differences regarding body satisfaction may be less relevant in years to come. As people of color continue to integrate mainstream culture, Black girls and women may begin to increasingly identify with Western standards of beauty. Notably, assimilation to and identification with mainstream culture has increased rates of eating disorder symptoms among women of color (Bisaga et al., 2005). Similarly, although Black girls and women have traditionally shunned the thin ideal in media images, Black–White differences in endorsement of the thin ideal are narrowing as Black girls show increased vulnerability to the thin ideal (Snapp, 2009), corresponding with media images of Black women moving toward a "fit-and-skinny" ideal (Capodilupo & Kim, 2014). It is also possible that images of Black beauty will morph toward an unreasonable set of expectations for most Black women (e.g., discordant waist–hip proportions) that are not focused on thinness, but nevertheless distort Black women's body satisfaction and positive embodiment (Capodilupo, 2015).

Finally, the research literature to date demonstrates that Black girls and women on average appear to be protected from the thin ideal, buffering their positive embodiment and well-being. However, the literature is largely silent regarding those Black girls and women who do struggle with negative embodiment, despite evidence that heavier Black girls appear to experience the largest negative shifts on indicators of body dissatisfaction and appreciation (Webb et al., 2014). To date, there are few published studies focused on eating pathology among Black women. When examined specifically, studies have often focused on overeating among Black women (e.g., Lydecker & Grilo, 2016; Udo et al., 2016), not maladaptive efforts to achieve an unattainable body ideal. Moreover, none addressed clinical levels of eating pathology in this population. These research and practice biases have been described as "scientific weightism" by Calogero, Tylka, and Mensinger (2016), who noted that not only are research foci biased by race, but also some have argued against positive body promotion with Black women for fear of discouraging efforts to reduce their body weight. Without increased focus on their specific needs, not only do we run the risk of failing to identify risk factors among Black girls and women; we also may fail to identify and promote protective factors that encourage positive embodiment.

CONCLUSION

Positive embodiment has persevered for many Black girls and women despite race and gender derogation. Nevertheless, the future is unclear as Black cultural images of women move toward less naturally attainable bodies, even if not a thin ideal. The findings presented here may shift as Black women identify more with mainstream culture. Although focused on the experiences of Black women, this chapter may be relevant to women from other ethnocultural and racial groups that embrace larger body shapes and sizes as well. The specific manifestations may be similar or different as a result of their unique racial–gendered cultural gender role norms, historical and contemporary experiences of objectification, specific race–gender stereotypes, and the ways each may hamper or promote positive embodiment.

REFERENCES

Adams, E. A., Kurtz-Costes, B. E., & Hoffman, A. J. (2016). Skin tone bias among African Americans: Antecedents and consequences across the life span. *Developmental Review, 40*, 93–116. doi:10.1016/j.dr.2016.03.002

Beale, F. (1970). Double jeopardy: To be Black and female. In T. C. Bambara (Ed.), *The Black woman: An anthology* (pp. 90–100). New York, NY: New American Library.

Beauboeuf-Lafontant, T. (2009). *Behind the mask of the strong Black woman: Voice and the embodiment of a costly performance*. Philadelphia, PA: Temple University Press.

Bisaga, K., Whitaker, A., Davies, M., Chuang, S., Feldman, J., & Walsh, B. T. (2005). Eating disorder and depressive symptoms in urban high school girls from different ethnic backgrounds. *Journal of Developmental and Behavioral Pediatrics, 26*, 257–266. doi:10.1097/00004703-200508000-00001

Breland-Noble, A. M. (2013). The impact of skin color on mental and behavioral health in African American and Latina adolescent girls: A review of the literature. In R. E. Hall (Ed.), *The melanin millennium* (pp. 219–229). Amsterdam, the Netherlands: Springer.

Brondolo, E., Brady, V. H., Pencille, M., Beatty, D., & Contrada, R. J. (2009). Coping with racism: A selective review of the literature and a theoretical and methodological critique. *Journal of Behavioral Medicine, 32*, 64–88. doi:10.1007/s10865-008-9193-0

Buchanan, N. T. (2005). The nexus of race and gender domination: The racialized sexual harassment of African American women. In P. Morgan & J. Gruber (Eds.), *In the company of men: Re-discovering the links between sexual harassment and male domination* (pp. 294–320). Boston, MA: Northeastern University Press.

Buchanan, N. T., & Fitzgerald, L. F. (2008). The effects of racial and sexual harassment on work and the psychological well-being of African American women. *Journal of Occupational Health Psychology, 13*, 137–151. doi:10.1037/1076-8998.13.2.137

Buchanan, N. T., & Ormerod, A. J. (2002). Racialized sexual harassment in the lives of African American women. *Women & Therapy, 25*, 107–124. doi:10.1300/J015v25 n03_08

Buchanan, N. T., & West, C. M. (2009). Sexual harassment in the lives of women of color. In H. Landrine & N. F. Russo (Eds.), *Handbook of diversity in feminist psychology: Theory, research, and practice* (pp. 449–476). New York, NY: Springer.

Calogero, R. M., Tylka, T. L., & Mensinger, J. (2016). Scientific weightism: A view of mainstream weight stigma research through a feminist lens. In T.-A. Roberts, N. Curtin, L. E. Duncan, & L. Cortina (Eds.), *Feminist perspectives on building a better psychological science of gender* (pp. 9–28). Basel, Switzerland: Springer.

Capodilupo, C. M. (2015). One size does not fit all: Using variables other than the thin ideal to understand Black women's body image. *Cultural Diversity and Ethnic Minority Psychology, 21*, 268–278. doi:10.1037/a0037649

Capodilupo, C. M., & Kim, S. (2014). Gender and race matter: The importance of considering intersections in Black women's body image. *Journal of Counseling Psychology, 61*, 37–49. doi:10.1037/a0034597

Chithambo, T. P., & Huey, S. J. (2013). Black/white differences in perceived weight and attractiveness among overweight women. *Journal of Obesity, 2013*, 1–4. doi:10.1155/2013/320326

Cole, E. R. (2009). Intersectionality and research in psychology. *American Psychologist, 64*, 170–180. doi:10.1037/a0014564

Cotter, E. W., Kelly, N. R., Mitchell, K. S., & Mazzeo, S. E. (2015). An investigation of body appreciation, ethnic identity, and eating disorder symptoms in Black women. *Journal of Black Psychology, 41*, 3–25. doi:10.1177/0095798413502671

Crais, C., & Scully, P. (2010). *Sara Baartman and the Hottentot Venus: A ghost story and a biography.* Princeton, NJ: Princeton University Press.

Crenshaw, K. (1991). Mapping the margins: Intersectionality, identity politics, and violence against women of color. *Stanford Law Review, 43*, 1241–1299. doi:10.2307/1229039

Donovan, R. A., & West, L. M. (2015). Stress and mental health: Moderating role of the strong Black woman stereotype. *Journal of Black Psychology, 41*, 384–396. doi:10.1177/0095798414543014

Forbes, G. B., Jobe, R. L., & Revak, J. A. (2006). Relationships between dissatisfaction with specific body characteristics and the Sociocultural Attitudes Toward Appearance Questionnaire-3 and Objectified Body Consciousness Scale. *Body Image, 3*, 295–300. doi:10.1016/j.bodyim.2006.07.003

Fredrickson, B. L., & Roberts, T. (1997). Objectification theory: Toward understanding women's lived experiences and mental health risks. *Psychology of Women Quarterly, 21*, 173–206. doi:10.1111/j.1471-6402.1997.tb00108.x

Hagiwara, N., Kashy, D. A., & Cesario, J. (2012). The independent effects of skin tone and facial features on Whites' affective reactions to Blacks. *Journal of Experimental Social Psychology, 48*, 892–898. doi:10.1016/j.jesp.2012.02.001.

King, D. K. (1988). Multiple jeopardy, multiple consciousness: The context of Black feminist ideology. *Signs, 14*, 42–72. doi:10.1086/494491

Lindberg, S. M., Hyde, J. S., & McKinley, N. M. (2006). A measure of objectified body consciousness for preadolescent and adolescent youth. *Psychology of Women Quarterly, 30*, 65–76. doi:10.1111/j.1471-6402.2006.00263.x

Lydecker, J. A., & Grilo, C. M. (2016). Different yet similar: Examining race and ethnicity in treatment-seeking adults with binge eating disorder. *Journal of Consulting and Clinical Psychology, 84*, 88–94. doi:10.1037/ccp0000048

Magak, K., & Okombo, L. (2014). Portraits of an African Aphrodite: The woman's body as social text in popular Luo music. *International Journal of Science, Commerce, and Humanities, 2*, 171–181.

Moradi, B., & Huang, Y. (2008). Objectification theory and psychology of women: A decade of advances and future directions. *Psychology of Women Quarterly, 32*, 377–398. doi:10.1111/j.1471-6402.2008.00452.x

Mucherah, W., & Frazier, A. D. (2013). How deep is skin deep? The relationship between skin tone satisfaction, estimation of body image, and self-esteem in women of African descent. *Journal of Applied Social Psychology, 43*, 1177–1184. doi:10.1111/jasp.12081.

Neumark-Sztainer, D., Croll, J., Story, M., Hannan, P. J., French, S. A., & Perry, C. (2002). Ethnic/racial differences in weight-related concerns and behaviors among adolescent girls and boys: Findings from Project EAT. *Journal of Psychosomatic Research, 53*, 963–974. doi:10.1016/S0022-3999(02)00486-5

Parkinson, J. (2016, January 7). The significance of Sarah Baartman. *BBC News Magazine.* Retrieved from http://www.bbc.com/news/magazine-35240987

Piran, N. (2015). New possibilities in the prevention of eating disorders: The introduction of positive body image measures. *Body Image, 14*, 146–157. doi:10.1016/j.bodyim.2015.03.008

Piran, N. (2016). Embodied possibilities and disruptions: The emergence of the Experience of Embodiment construct from qualitative studies with girls and women. *Body Image, 18*, 43–60. doi:10.1016/j.bodyim.2016.04.007.

Richard, A., Rohrmann, S., Lohse, T., & Eichholzer, M. (2016). Is body weight dissatisfaction a predictor of depression independent of body mass index, sex and age? Results of a cross-sectional study. *BMC Public Health, 16*, 863–871. doi:10.1186/s12889-016-3497-8

Russell, K. Y., Wilson, M., & Hall, R. E. (2013). *The color complex (revised): The politics of skin color in a new millennium*. New York, NY: Random House.

Settles, I. H., & Buchanan, N. T. (2014). Intersectionality: Multiple categories of identity and difference. In V. Benet-Martinez & Y. Hong (Eds.), *The Oxford handbook of multicultural identity* (pp. 160–180). New York, NY: Oxford University Press.

Snapp, S. (2009). Internalization of the thin ideal among low-income ethnic minority adolescent girls. *Body Image, 6*, 311–314. doi:10.1016/j.bodyim.2009.05.005

Szymanski, D. M., & Lewis, J. A. (2016). Gendered racism, coping, identity centrality, and African American college women's psychological distress. *Psychology of Women Quarterly, 40*, 229–243. doi:10.1177/0361684315616113

Udo, T., White, M. A., Lydecker, J. L., Barnes, R. D., Genao, I., Garcia, R., . . ., & Grilo, C. M. (2016). Biopsychosocial correlates of binge eating disorder in Caucasian and African American women with obesity in primary care settings. *European Eating Disorders Review, 24*, 181–186. doi:10.1002/erv.2417

Warner, L. R., Settles, I. H., & Shields, S. A. (2018). Intersectionality theory in the psychology of women. In C. B. Travis, J. W. White, A. Rutherford, W. S. Williams, S. L. Cook, & K. F. Wyche (Eds.), *APA handbooks in psychology series: APA handbook of the psychology of women: History, theory, and battlegrounds* (pp. 521–539). Washington, DC: American Psychological Association.

Watson, L. B., Ancis, J. R., White, D. N., & Nazari, N. (2013). Racial identity buffers African American women from body image problems and disordered eating. *Psychology of Women Quarterly, 37*, 337–350. doi:10.1177/0361684312474799

Webb, J. B., Butler-Ajibade, P., & Robinson, S. A. (2014). Considering an affect regulation framework for examining the association between body dissatisfaction and positive body image in Black older adolescent females: Does body mass index matter? *Body Image, 11*, 426–437. doi:10.1016/j.bodyim.2014.07.002

Williams, S. (2016, December 18). *The undefeated in-depth: Serena with Common* (Common, ESPN) [Video file]. Retrieved from http://theundefeated.com/features/serena-williams-sits-down-with-common-to-talk-about-race-and-identity/

Witherspoon, D., Latta, L., Wang, Y., & Black, M. M. (2013). Do depression, self-esteem, body-esteem, and eating attitudes vary by BMI among African American adolescents? *Journal of Pediatric Psychology, 38*, 1112–1120. doi:10.1093/jpepsy/jst055

Wood-Barcalow, N. L., Tylka, T. L., & Augustus-Horvath, C. L. (2010). "But I like my body": Positive body image characteristics and a holistic model for young-adult women. *Body Image, 7*, 106–116. doi:10.1016/j.bodyim.2010.01.001

Woods, K. C., Buchanan, N. T., & Settles, I. H. (2009). Sexual harassment across the color line: Experiences and outcomes of cross- vs. intra-racial sexual harassment among Black women. *Cultural Diversity and Ethnic Minority Psychology, 15*, 67–76. doi:10.1037/a0013541

19

Promoting a Resistant Stance Toward Media Images

JANET M. LIECHTY ■

To be nobody-but-yourself—in a world which is doing its best, night and day, to make you everybody else—means to fight the hardest battle which any human being can fight; and never stop fighting.

—E. E. CUMMINGS

No one can make you feel inferior without your consent.

—ELEANOR ROOSEVELT

Mass media images both reflect and transmit sociocultural norms and stereotypes about the body, such as weight and shape ideals, appearance standards, and gender expression. While body image is a multidimensional construct with many determinants (Cash & Smolak, 2011), it is well established that media consumption is a potent source of influence on young people's body image, thoughts, and behaviors (Bandura, 2001; Levine & Murnen, 2015). Meta-analyses have demonstrated that media exposure adversely impacts body image, increases women's risk for internalizing the thin ideal (Grabe, Ward, & Hyde, 2008), and increases men's body dissatisfaction, depressive symptoms, and pressure to conform to muscularity ideals (Barlett, Vowels, & Saucier, 2008). Because mass media images and messages are manifestations of sociocultural values and ideals, they can serve as focal points for discussion, critique, and analysis and potentially as levers for consciousness-raising and social change. This chapter discusses media exposure and its effects among children and adolescents, explores the meaning of resilience and metaphor of resistance to adverse media effects, and considers research on the role of positive emotion in cultivating resilience and of rest as essential to resistance. Strategies for fostering resilience and implications for practice, parenting, and advocacy are discussed.

MEDIA EXPOSURE AND EFFECTS

Mass media exposure is inescapable in the digital age. In the most recent national survey of media consumption among US youth, those aged 8–18 spent an average of 7 hours and 38 minutes per day on entertainment media, amounting to more than 53 hours per week (Kaiser Family Foundation [KFF], 2010). Seventy-one percent had TVs in their bedrooms, and nearly half (45%) reported that a TV is on "most of the time" at home (KFF, 2010). Additionally, advertising heavily targets children and youth (Jenkin, Madhvani, Signal, & Bowers, 2014). The KFF estimated that, on average, youth ages 8–12 are exposed to 229 hours of TV advertising per year (30,155 ads), and by age 17, a typical US child has been exposed to 2,866 hours of ads on TV, or nearly 400,000 ads (KFF, 2010). In the same study, a content analysis of ads running on children's programs found that 50% of all advertising time was for packaged food and beverages, and only 15% of ads depicted body competence (i.e., bodies engaging in physical activity or active lifestyles). There were a small number of public service announcements (PSAs) that promoted healthy nutrition or fitness, but these were relatively insignificant: Children ages 2–7 viewed 52 times more product ads than PSAs, and teenagers viewed 260 times more product ads than PSAs (KFF, 2010).

Media are one of three primary conveyers of sociocultural influence on body image and eating behavior posited in the widely studied tripartite influence model, along with parents and peers (Thompson, Heinberg, Altabe, & Tantleff-Dunn, 1999). In the tripartite influence model, media messages lead to body dissatisfaction through increased thin-ideal internalization and increased social comparison, mechanisms that have garnered robust empirical support (Grabe et al., 2008). In turn, body dissatisfaction can lead to disordered eating (e.g., restriction, bulimic symptoms) and lower global psychological functioning (Thompson et al., 1999).

Media exposure and food and beverage marketing to youth are also associated with child health indicators such as poor sleep and consumption of sugar-sweetened beverages (Kenney & Gortmaker, 2017; Zhang, Wu, Zhou, Lu, & Mao, 2016). Fast food and low-nutrient, high-energy foods are heavily marketed to young children (Kenney & Gortmaker, 2017), but concerns extend beyond caloric intake. Food ads, ostensibly about food, can activate deeply ingrained cognitive schemas that reinforce societal body shape and appearance norms; gender stereotypes; weight bias; emotional and moral overtones to eating (e.g., "guilty pleasures," food as reward, food to make you happy); poor diet; and exaggerated claims (Batada, Seitz, Wootan, & Story, 2008; Roberts & Pettigrew, 2007). Like the fashion and cosmetics industries, food ads prey on body dissatisfaction and insecurities to sell the latest fads in fat-free, sugar-free, low carbohydrate, and/or low-calorie products. By the time viewers reach adolescence, the happy cartoon ads that sold them low-nutrient, sugary foods as young children fade oddly into ads featuring airbrushed ultrathin models selling "slimming foods," diet beverages, and the cult of thinness.

These contradictory messages, in media and our society, are a perfect storm for disembodiment: perpetual body dissatisfaction, body shame, dieting, body self-surveillance, and disconnection from actual body cues of hunger and satiety. In short, it is profitable. Consumers pay not only in dollars but also in self-esteem and body confidence. Concerns about media exposure may differ in emphasis, ranging from body image to nutritional quality, but the toxic messages are the same: body objectification, body inadequacy, and disruption of intuitive, enjoyable relations among body, food, and self.

One of the more troubling aspects of mass media is the sexualization of young girls (American Psychological Association, 2007; Slater & Tiggemann, 2016; Smolak & Murnen, 2011). Objectification theory (Calogero, Tantleff-Dunn, & Thompson, 2011; Fredrickson & Roberts, 1997) describes how early and repeated exposure to sexually objectifying media and other cultural practices socializes girls and women to view and experience themselves "from the outside," thus internalizing the male gaze in a process of self-objectification that leads to self-surveillance, body shame, and mental health problems (Calogero et al., 2011; see also Chapter 14). These societal socialization processes raise questions about individual susceptibility, resistance to self-objectification, and resilience.

RESISTANCE AND RESILIENCE

A growing body of research focuses on protective factors that promote resistance and resilience in the face of widespread media exposure. This strengths-based approach highlights individuals' agentic role. Children and youth and their caregivers are not passive recipients of media messages, but in fact actors who make choices (conscious and unconscious) about what, when, and how much media to view and how they will interpret the information (Bandura, 2001). Despite near-universal exposure to harmful media, why do some develop body dissatisfaction and eating problems while others do not? There are promising indications that the cultivation of positive body image and positive embodiment are fundamental protective factors (Halliwell, 2013; Levine & Smolak, 2016; Piran, 2015, 2016; Tylka & Kroon Van Diest, 2015).

The concepts of resistance to and resilience against constricting media images are often invoked together, though their meanings differ. *Resilience* is defined as the capacity to recover from adversity, to adapt successfully and "bounce back" after setbacks, trauma, or threat (Masten et al., 1999; Rutter, 1987). Resilience has been studied extensively as part of a risk, resilience, and protective factors framework (Fraser, Richman, & Galinsky, 1999; Masten et al., 1999; Rutter, 1987) and specifically in the context of body image (Choate, 2005; Snapp, Hensley-Choate, & Ryu, 2012) and disordered eating (Levine & Smolak, 2006). Resilience has been operationalized as a formal construct with standardized measures for use in various contexts (for a review of measures, see Ahern, Kiehl, Sole, Byers, & Lou Sole, 2006).

In contrast, the concept of resistance draws on roots from multiple fields of study, and its definition is nuanced depending on context. Its meaning is best understood when paired with something that warrants resisting or rejecting (e.g., "resistance to infection," "resistance to media influence," "resistance to peer pressure"). The term has origins in biology in the context of resistance to pathogens; in feminist discourses in the context of resisting forces of oppression such as patriarchy and objectification; and in the field of marketing in the context of cognitive resistance to persuasion (or influence) as described in inoculation theory (Banas & Rains, 2010).

Each perspective is potentially relevant to its usage in the body image literature, but to date, a synthesized understanding of resistance has not yet been formally operationalized. Without the clarity of a formal construct and validated measures, we must ask: What aspects of media messages need resisting? A resistant stance to harmful media images and messages could include *resistance* to body objectification, to the thin ideal and other hegemonic appearance norms, to weight bias and stigma, and to restrictive gender expression, as well as *resistance to the influence (persuasion)* from media images and messages, families, and peers that can activate oppressive cognitive schemas and negative affective states leading to body dissatisfaction and disruption of positive embodiment. Resistance to harmful media effects on body image can refer to the capacity to identify and critique marketing tactics, to filter out harmful body messages or counter them with body protective messages, or to generate self-acceptance and compassion when social comparisons are activated. These skills are consistent with characteristics of body appreciation, as measured by the Body Appreciation Scale (BAS; Avalos, Tylka, & Wood-Barcalow, 2005) and the BAS-2 (Tylka & Wood-Barcalow, 2015a), such as the BAS-2 item, "I feel like I am beautiful even if I am different from media images of attractive people (e.g., models, actresses/actors)."

Formal interventions have been developed to help young people build resistance to harmful media images, such as programs based on media literacy (Levine, 2016; Levine & Murnen, 2015; McLean, Paxton, & Wertheim, 2016; Wilksch & Wade, 2015) and cognitive dissonance (Becker, Smith, & Ciao, 2006; Stice, Rohde, Shaw, & Gau, 2011; see also Chapters 33 and 34). Empirically informed theoretical formulations of positive body image and embodiment (Cook-Cottone, 2015; Piran, 2015, 2016; Tylka, 2011; Tylka & Kroon Van Diest, 2015; Tylka & Wood-Barcalow, 2015b) present new possibilities and frameworks for identifying the factors in existing programs that lead to *resistance* to media's adverse effects (Andrew, Tiggemann, & Clark, 2016; Piran, 2015), as well as relational contexts such as the family in which to promote and develop these factors (Hart, Damiano, & Paxton, 2016; Liechty, Clarke, Birky, & Harrison, 2016, Piran, 2017). Positive body image and embodiment can be conceptualized as predictors of resistance to thin-ideal internalization (Andrew, Tiggemann, & Clark, 2015), as outcomes of reduced media consumption and social comparison (Andrew et al., 2016), or as protective factors against harmful media effects (Halliwell, 2013; Levine & Smolak, 2016). Though further prospective studies are needed, together these findings and theories suggest that positive body image and self-efficacy to resist harmful media images may be bidirectional and mutually reinforcing, a potential upward spiral.

POSITIVE EMOTIONS, RESISTANCE, AND RESILIENCE

The concept of upward spirals of positive emotions, a process that broadens thinking and builds personal resources that enhance future well-being, is described in the broaden-and-build theory of positive emotions (Fredrickson, 2001, 2004) and has relevance for positive body image and embodiment. Empirical studies have shown that positive emotions have important functions for learning and well-being; they (a) broaden thinking and attention, (b) undo the effects of negative emotions, (c) enhance psychological resilience, (d) build enduring personal resources, (e) activate upward spirals of well-being, and (f) contribute to human flourishing (Fredrickson, 2004). These functions have resonance with many of the dimensions of positive body image and embodiment, such as broadened conceptualization of beauty, body image flexibility, and body appreciation and gratitude; as well as with the dimensions of freedom and power (as enduring personal resources) outlined in the developmental theory of embodiment (Piran, 2015, 2016, 2017; see also Chapters 1, 2, 4, 5, and 10).

These areas of theoretical convergence, and the mounting evidence that positive emotions are modifiable and can be cultivated to enhance a wide range of outcomes (Seligman, 2012; Taylor, Lyubomirsky, & Stein, 2017), suggest the importance of assessing positive emotions. To date, little research has assessed the distinct role of positive emotions in studies on positive body image and embodiment or tested it as an active ingredient in media literacy or cognitive dissonance interventions. Perhaps the positive emotions that are cultivated as by-products of positive body image and embodiment (e.g., appreciation, gratitude, confidence) are active ingredients that enhance capacity to counteract media pressures, thus fostering self-efficacy, building enduring personal resources, and prompting an upward spiral. In contrast, negative emotion in relation to one's body may narrow and constrict one's bodily experience, and leave one mired in a downward spiral of body dissatisfaction, negative affect, and unhealthful dieting, thus weakening resistance to adverse media messages. Fostering positive embodiment through cultivation of positive emotions about the body in early family life, school cultures, and other relational contexts may be potent, nonspecific protective factors that help lay a foundation for resilience throughout development (Davis & Suveg, 2014; Layous, Chancellor, & Lyubomirsky, 2014) and against effects of harmful media images.

RESISTANCE AS METAPHOR

All language is symbolic and has its roots in physical experience (Lakoff, 2006). We "feel burdened," "try to hold on," "see the light at the end of the tunnel," and "move through the day" on schedule. As metaphor, the term *resistance* connotes physical struggle, standing firm against unwanted external pressure or force (Resistance, 2017). The language of resistance suggests there is a central dominating force, and the "resistor" is struggling against it to avoid being co-opted or suppressed. The metaphor of *resistance* is both empowering and limiting. There is strong agentic potential in the metaphor, but it evokes a cognitive frame of oppression; ideally, we want to create and evoke new cognitive frames, not only resist harmful ones. Cognitive frames can be deeply ingrained and function as filtering devices that limit what we can see, understand, and imagine (Lakoff, 2006). Hence, resistance may be an apt metaphor to describe acts of nonconformity and protest against harmful media messages, but it may not be the most useful metaphor to inspire new cognitive frames in which positive embodiment, acts of body appreciation and love, and quiet attention to body signals that lead to body–mind–spirit attunement can flourish.

What new metaphors and cognitive frames that resonate with core human values (Lakoff, 2006) might be possible? The burgeoning field of positive body image and embodiment has potential to offer alternative and compelling new cognitive frames, metaphors, and terminology to the literature and to society. Already, the field of positive body image has generated terms such as body appreciation, embodiment, body attunement, and body confidence and detected *protective filtering* of media as a cognitive device that helps individuals counteract harmful societal messages (Wood-Barcalow, Tylka, & Augustus-Horvath, 2010). Cognitive science shows that, to the extent that new narratives and cognitive frames are fleshed out in public and professional discourses, strengthened through repetition and media, and resonant with core human values, individuals in society will be increasingly able to think about themselves, their bodies, and representations of themselves in new ways (Lakoff, 2006).

BEYOND RESISTANCE: RECLAIMING REST AND RECOVERY

A component of resilience that is often missing from narratives of resistance and from the literature on negative body image prevention is the essential notion of rest and recovery (Egan, Clarkson, & Hirt, 2015). During regular periods of rest, individuals can recover and "recharge" after responding to daily insults and threats to embodiment, so they can be fully rested and ready to return to active resistance mode when needed. Resisting societal stereotypes, harmful media, and oppressive cognitive frames can be exhausting. Cultivating resilience and capacity for resistance requires skill in self-care and conscious strategies for relaxation and recovery, such as mindfulness. Positive emotions have been shown to promote restoration after negative emotional arousal as well as recovery following cardiovascular challenge tasks (Seligman, 2012). Other factors that increase capacity for restoration include sleep, diet, exercise, laughter, and coping strategies (see also Chapter 6 on mindful attunement).

RECOMMENDATIONS AND IMPLICATIONS

The previous discussion leads to several recommendations for practice and to implications for research, described next.

Reduce Media Exposure and Make a Family Media Use Plan

The American Academy of Pediatrics (AAP) discourages media use before age 2, noting links to sleep and behavior problems (AAP, 2016b). For children ages 2–5, the AAP recommends that screen use be limited to 1 hour per day of "high-quality programming" during which parents co-view, discuss, and help children understand what they are viewing (AAP, 2016b). For youth ages 6–18, AAP now recommends that families develop an individualized "family media plan" (see https://www.healthychildren.org/English/media/Pages/default.aspx) based on child age, sleep needs, and other activities (AAP, 2017) that emphasizes family rules for media use, such as media-free times during meals and homework and avoiding TVs in bedrooms (AAP, 2016a).

Cultivate Rest and Recovery

Pay greater attention to the overall nonspecific emotional climate factors that affect children's susceptibility and resilience against harmful mass media influence. In addition to skills of resistance, young people need to learn skills to relax, to take restorative breaks, to generate positive emotion, to reconnect to what matters most to them, and to slow down and listen mindfully to the wisdom of their bodies. Children and adolescents need respite from high external demands and spaces where they can be themselves, free from performance and appearance pressures and at home in their bodies as agentic subjects not objects. To be rested and resilient, they also need sleep, good nutrition, regular activity/exercise, friendship, regular doses of nature, and skills to cultivate positive emotions.

Cultivate Positive Emotions

Learn strategies and practices that have been shown to increase positive emotions and increase well-being. Many such strategies have been adapted for children and adolescents, such as practicing kindness and generosity, keeping a gratitude journal or "counting blessings" each day, identifying signature strengths and virtues, writing a gratitude letter or affirmation to give to someone, and verbalizing positive or pleasurable moments of the day (Davis & Suveg, 2014; Layous et al., 2014). Positive emotions broaden and build cognitive and mental freedom, hence cultivating embodiment, and can contribute to restoration and recovery following negative emotional arousal (Egan et al., 2015; Fredrickson, 2004) and psychological resilience against mental distress (Davis & Suveg, 2014; Layous et al., 2014).

Cultivate a Protective Filter

Talk with children and adolescents about media messages in ways that help them build and maintain a protective filter. Protective filtering allows us to confront and reject rather than absorb harmful messages about the body by refocusing attention on body functionality and self-care (Wood-Barcalow et al., 2010). To foster protective filtering, we could promote media literacy (e.g., questioning sociocultural appearance ideals and the agenda of businesses to profit from body dissatisfaction), minimize the importance of striving toward these ideals, emphasize the body as more than appearance, and model/practice how to filter body-related threats in real time (e.g., "I need to go up a size in clothing. Not a big deal—it just means my body is changing. Bodies continue to change throughout life. My body is still fabulous."). Verbalizing protective filtering processes helps activate and strengthen cognitive frames that are resistant to body objectification and thin-ideal internalization.

Cultivate a Broad Conceptualization of Beauty

Celebrate diversity, individual style, and authenticity as aspects of inner and outer beauty. Seek exposure to racially and ethnically diverse images and representations of beauty in books, magazines, art, music, and other media; learn to appreciate the uniqueness of each body shape, size, ability, skin, and hair. Expanding our notions of physical attractiveness and incorporating attributes of personal style and character in the definition of beauty create more freedom to be oneself and counteract the narrowly constructed appearance ideals so prevalent in mass media.

Examine Reciprocal Effects Between Positive Emotions and Positive Body Image and Embodiment

The potential role of positive emotions in the cultivation of positive body image and positive embodiment warrants further study. For example, to what extent are measures of positive body image and embodiment associated with positive emotions or, more broadly, with the other dimensions of well-being, such as engagement, caring connection to others, meaning and purpose in life, and skill mastery or accomplishments (Seligman, 2012)? Does positive embodiment contribute independently to overall well-being, and if so, might this fundamental aspect of experience constitute a previously overlooked dimension of well-being? Would the effectiveness of prevention programs be enhanced if we augmented them with specific exercises to cultivate positive emotions?

Advocate for Better Protection of Children Against Advertising

Children under the age of 8 do not yet have the cognitive capacity to differentiate advertising from programming or engage in critical thinking and other skills of media literacy and have been described as "defenseless" against advertising (Strasburger, Jordan, & Donnerstein, 2010). Some experts have urged parents, schools, and policymakers to engage in activism to enhance restrictions to protect children from the harms of advertising and to promote media's pro-social potential (AAP, 2017; Strasburger et al., 2010). The United States and other nations have already embraced restrictions on advertising tobacco and alcohol to children and are considering others. Advocacy organizations such as the Campaign for a Commercial-Free Childhood (http://www.commercialfreechildhood.org/) aim to inspire families to unplug, "reclaim childhood from corporate marketing," and end sexualization of children in the media.

CONCLUSION

Media exposure is ubiquitous and inescapable and can be highly consequential for health, body image, diet and activity, and well-being. Learning to directly resist and refute unwanted influences through critical awareness, protective filtering, activism, and advocacy are essential skills. In addition, promoting nonspecific protective factors early in life, such as cultivating positive emotions and self-compassion, may help build a strong foundation of enduring personal resources that will enhance resistance and resilience against harmful media messages and potentially unleash upward spirals of positive embodiment and well-being.

REFERENCES

Ahern, N., Kiehl, E., Sole, M., Byers, J., & Lou Sole, M. (2006). A review of instruments measuring resilience. *Issues in Comprehensive Pediatric Nursing, 29*, 103–125. doi:10.1080/01460860600677643

American Academy of Pediatrics. (2016a). Media use in school-aged children and adolescents. *Pediatrics, 138*, 1–8. doi:10.1542/peds.2016-2592

American Academy of Pediatrics. (2016b). Media and young minds. *Pediatrics, 138*, 1–8. doi:10.1542/peds.2016-2591

American Academy of Pediatrics. (2017). *Media and children communication toolkit.* Retrieved from https://www.aap.org/en-us/advocacy-and-policy/aap-health-initiatives/Pages/Media-and-Children.aspx

American Psychological Association, Task Force on the Sexualization of Girls. (2007). *Report of the APA Task Force on the Sexualization of Girls.* Retrieved from http://www.apa.org/pi/women/programs/girls/report.aspx

Andrew, R., Tiggemann, M., & Clark, L. (2015). The protective role of body appreciation against media-induced body dissatisfaction. *Body Image, 15*, 98–104. doi:10.10166/j.bodyim.2015.07.005

Andrew, R., Tiggemann, M., & Clark, L. (2016). Predicting body appreciation in young women: An integrated model of positive body image. *Body Image, 18*, 34–42. doi:10.1016/j.bodyim.2016.04.003

Avalos, L., Tylka, T. L., & Wood-Barcalow, N. (2005). The Body Appreciation Scale: Development and psychometric evaluation. *Body Image, 2*, 285–297. doi:10.1016/j.bodyim.2005.06.002

Banas, J. A., & Rains, S. A. (2010). A meta-analysis of research on inoculation theory. *Communication Monographs, 77*, 281–311. doi:10.1080/03637751003758193

Bandura, A. (2001). Social cognitive theory of mass communication. *Media Psychology, 3*, 265–299. doi:10.1207/S1532785XMEP0303_03

Barlett, C. P., Vowels, C. L., & Saucier, D. A. (2008). Meta-analyses of the effects of media images on men's body-image concerns. *Journal of Social and Clinical Psychology, 27*, 279–310. doi:10.1521/jscp.2008.27.3.279

Batada, A., Seitz, M. D., Wootan, M. G., & Story, M. (2008). Nine out of 10 food advertisements shown during Saturday morning children's television programming are for foods high in fat, sodium, or added sugars, or low in nutrients. *Journal of the American Dietetic Association, 108*, 673–678. doi:10.1016/j.jada.2008.01.015

Becker, C. B., Smith, L. M., & Ciao, A. C. (2006). Peer-facilitated eating disorder prevention: A randomized effectiveness trial of cognitive dissonance and media advocacy. *Journal of Counseling Psychology, 53*, 550–555. doi:10.1037/0022-0167.53.4.550

Calogero, R. M., Tantleff-Dunn, S., & Thompson, J. K. (2011). *Self-objectification in women.* Washington, DC: American Psychological Association.

Cash, T. F., & Smolak, L. (2011). *Body image: A handbook of science, practice, and prevention* (2nd ed.). New York, NY: Guilford Press.

Choate, L. H. (2005). Toward a theoretical model of women's body image resilience. *Journal of Counseling & Development, 83*, 320–330. doi:10.1002/j.1556-6678.2005.tb00350

Cook-Cottone, C. P. (2015). Incorporating positive body image into the treatment of eating disorders: A model for attunement and mindful self-care. *Body Image, 14*, 158–167. doi:10.1016/j.bodyim.2015.03.004

Davis, M., & Suveg, C. (2014). Focusing on the positive: A review of the role of child positive affect in developmental psychopathology. *Clinical Child and Family Psychology Review, 17*, 97–124. doi:10.1007/s10567-013-0162-y

Egan, P. M., Clarkson, J. J., & Hirt, E. R. (2015). Revisiting the restorative effects of positive mood: An expectancy-based approach to self-control restoration. *Journal of Experimental Social Psychology, 57*, 87–99. doi:10.1016/j.jesp.2014.11.006

Fraser, M., Richman, J., & Galinsky, M. (1999). Risk, protection, and resilience: Toward a conceptual framework for social work practice. *Social Work Research, 23*, 131–143. doi:10.1093/swr/23.3.131

Fredrickson, B. L. (2001). The role of positive emotions in positive psychology: The broaden-and-build theory of positive emotions. *American Psychologist, 56*, 218–226. doi:10.1037/0003-066X.56.3.218

Fredrickson, B. L. (2004). The broaden-and-build theory of positive emotions. *Philosophical Transactions of the Royal Society B: Biological Sciences, 359*, 1367–1378. doi:10.1098/rstb.2004.1512

Fredrickson, B. L., & Roberts, T. A. (1997). Objectification theory: Toward understanding women's lived experiences and mental health risks. *Psychology of Women Quarterly, 21*, 173–206. doi:10.1111/j.1471-6402.1997.tb00108.x

Grabe, S., Ward, L. M., & Hyde, J. S. (2008). The role of the media in body image concerns among women: A meta-analysis of experimental and correlational studies. *Psychological Bulletin, 134*, 460–476. doi:10.1037/0033-2909.134.3.460

Halliwell, E. (2013). The impact of thin idealized media images on body satisfaction: Does body appreciation protect women from negative effects? *Body Image, 10*, 509–514. doi:10.1016/j.bodyim.2013.07.004

Hart, L. M., Damiano, S. R., & Paxton, S. J. (2016). Confident body, confident child: A randomized controlled trial evaluation of a parenting resource for promoting healthy body image and eating patterns in 2- to 6-year old children. *International Journal of Eating Disorders, 49*, 458–472. doi:10.1002/eat.22494

Jenkin, G., Madhvani, N., Signal, L., & Bowers, S. (2014). A systematic review of persuasive marketing techniques to promote food to children on television. *Obesity Reviews, 15*, 281–293. doi:10.1111/obr.12141

Kaiser Family Foundation. (2010). *Generation M2: Media in the lives of 8- to 18-year-olds*. Retrieved from https://www.kff.org/other/report/generation-m2-media-in-the-lives-of-8-to-18-year-olds/

Kenney, E. L., & Gortmaker, S. L. (2017). U.S. adolescents' television, computer, videogame, smartphone, and tablet use: Associations with sugary drinks, sleep, physical activity, and obesity. *Journal of Pediatrics, 182*, 144–149. doi:10.1016/j.jpeds.2016.11.015

Lakoff, G. (2006). *Whose freedom? The battle over America's most important idea*. New York, NY: Farrar, Straus and Giroux.

Layous, K., Chancellor, J., & Lyubomirsky, S. (2014). Positive activities as protective factors against mental health conditions. *Journal of Abnormal Psychology, 123*, 3–12. doi:10.1037/a0034709

Levine, M. P. (2016). Media literacy approaches to prevention. In T. Wade (Ed.), *Encyclopedia of feeding and eating disorders* (pp. 1–6). Singapore: Springer.

Levine, M. P., & Murnen, S. K. (2015). Media and eating disorders. In L. Smolak & M. P. Levine (Eds.), *Wiley handbook of eating disorders* (pp. 379–393). Oxford, England: Wiley.

Levine, M. P., & Smolak, L. (2006). *The prevention of eating problems and eating disorders: Theory, research, and practice*. Mahwah, NJ: Earlbaum.

Levine, M. P., & Smolak, L. (2016). The role of protective factors in the prevention of negative body image and disordered eating. *Eating Disorders, 24*, 39–46. doi:10.1080/10640266.2015.1113826

Liechty, J. M., Clarke, S., Birky, J. P., & Harrison, K. (2016). Perceptions of early body image socialization in families: Exploring knowledge, beliefs, and strategies among mothers of preschoolers. *Body Image*, *19*, 68–78. doi:10.1016/j.bodyim.2016.08.010

Masten, A., Gest, S., Tellegen, A., Garmezy, N., Ramirez, M., & Hubbard, J. O. N. (1999). Competence in the context of adversity: Pathways to resilience and maladaptation from childhood to late adolescence. *Development and Psychopathology*, *11*, 143–169. doi:10.1017/s0954579499001996

McLean, S. A., Paxton, S. J., & Wertheim, E. H. (2016). Does media literacy mitigate risk for reduced body satisfaction following exposure to thin-ideal media? *Journal of Youth and Adolescence*, *45*, 1678–1695. doi:10.1007/s10964-016-0440-3

Piran, N. (2015). New possibilities in the prevention of eating disorders: The introduction of positive body image measures. *Body Image*, *14*, 146–157. doi:10.1016/j.bodyim.2015.03.008

Piran, N. (2016). Embodied possibilities and disruptions: The emergence of the Experience of Embodiment construct from qualitative studies with girls and women. *Body Image*, *18*, 43–60. doi:10.1016/j.bodyim.2016.04.007

Piran, N. (2017). *Journeys of embodiment at the intersection of body and culture: The developmental theory of embodiment*. San Diego, CA: Elsevier Press. doi:10.1016/c2015-0-04666-4

Resistance. (2017). In Oxford English dictionary online. Retrieved from http://www.oed.com/

Roberts, M., & Pettigrew, S. (2007). A thematic content analysis of children's food advertising. *International Journal of Advertising*, *26*, 357–367. doi:10.1080/02650487.2007.11073018

Rutter, M. (1987). Psychosocial resilience and protective mechanisms. *American Journal of Orthopsychiatry*, *57*, 316–331. doi:10.1111/j.1939-0025.1987.tb03541.x

Seligman, M. E. (2012). *Flourish: A visionary new understanding of happiness and well-being*. New York, NY: Simon and Schuster.

Slater, A., & Tiggemann, M. (2016). Little girls in a grown up world: Exposure to sexualized media, internalization of sexualization messages, and body image in 6–9 year-old girls. *Body Image*, *18*, 19–22. doi:10.1016/j.bodyim.2016.04.004

Smolak, L., & Murnen, S. K. (2011). The sexualization of girls and women as a primary antecedent of self-objectification. In R. M. Calogero, S. Tantleff-Dunn, & J. K. Thompson (Eds.), *Self-objectification in women: Causes, consequences, and counteractions* (pp. 53–75). Washington, DC: American Psychological Association.

Snapp, S., Hensley-Choate, L., & Ryu, E. (2012). A body image resilience model for first-year college women. *Sex Roles*, *67*, 211–221. doi:10.1007/s11199-012-0163-1

Stice, E., Rohde, P., Shaw, H., & Gau, J. (2011). An effectiveness trial of a selected dissonance-based eating disorder prevention program for female high school students: Long-term effects. *Journal of Consulting and Clinical Psychology*, *79*, 500–508. doi:10.1037/a0024351

Strasburger, V. C., Jordan, A. B., & Donnerstein, E. (2010). Health effects of media on children and adolescents. *Pediatrics*, *125*, 756–767. doi:10.1542/peds.2009-2563

Taylor, C. T., Lyubomirsky, S., & Stein, M. B. (2017). Upregulating the positive affect system in anxiety and depression: Outcomes of a positive activity intervention. *Depression and Anxiety*, *34*, 267–280. doi:/10.1002/da.22593

Thompson, J. K., Heinberg, L. J., Altabe, M., & Tantleff-Dunn, S. (1999). *Exacting beauty: Theory, assessment, and treatment of body image disturbance*. Washington, DC: American Psychological Association.

Tylka, T. L. (2011). Positive psychology perspectives on body image. In T. F. Cash & L. Smolak (Eds.), *Body image: A handbook of science, practice, and prevention* (2nd ed., pp. 56–64). New York, NY: Guilford Press.

Tylka, T. L., & Kroon Van Diest, A. M. (2015). Protective factors. In L. Smolak & M. P. Levine (Eds.), *The Wiley handbook of eating disorders* (Vol. 1, pp. 430–444). West Sussex, England: Wiley.

Tylka, T. L., & Wood-Barcalow, N. L. (2015a). The Body Appreciation Scale-2: Item refinement and psychometric evaluation. *Body Image, 12*, 53–67. doi:10.1016/j.bodyim.2014.09.006

Tylka, T. L., & Wood-Barcalow, N. L. (2015b). What is and what is not positive body image? Conceptual foundations and construct definition. *Body Image, 14*, 118–129. doi:10.1016/j.bodyim.2015.04.001

Wilksch, S., & Wade, T. D. (2015). Media literacy in the prevention of eating disorders. In L. Smolak & M. P. Levine (Eds.), *The Wiley handbook of eating disorders* (Vol. 1, pp. 610–624). West Sussex, England: Wiley.

Wood-Barcalow, N. L., Tylka, T. L., & Augustus-Horvath, C. L. (2010). "But I like my body": Positive body image characteristics and a holistic model for young-adult women. *Body Image, 7*, 106–116. doi:10.1016/j.bodyim.2010.01.001

Zhang, G., Wu, L., Zhou, L., Lu, W., & Mao, C. (2016). Television watching and risk of childhood obesity: A meta-analysis. *European Journal of Public Health, 26*, 13–18. doi:10.1093/eurpub/ckv213

20

Relationships that Cultivate Positive Body Image Through Body Acceptance

MARIKA TIGGEMANN ■

As positive body image is so strongly connected to overall psychological well-being, the identification of factors that promote its development becomes a critical task. The identification of such predictors is important for both the theoretical conceptualization of positive body image and for locating potential points for intervention. One such factor is perceived body acceptance from important others in one's life (Tylka, 2011, 2012).

This chapter reviews existing research and theory on body acceptance by others as an interpersonal factor promoting positive body image. It then considers a variety of different contexts and relationships that might cultivate positive body image through body acceptance. In particular, a developmental perspective is taken in considering the manifestations of body acceptance by others through childhood, adolescence, and adulthood. In addition, the available measure of body acceptance by others is reviewed. This is followed by a discussion of implications for preventive and treatment interventions. Finally, limitations and future research directions are identified.

THEORY AND RESEARCH

Unconditional body acceptance by significant others has emerged as a major theme in qualitative accounts given by adult women and adolescents with positive body image (Frisén & Holmqvist, 2010; Wood-Barcalow, Tylka, & Augustus-Horvath, 2010). Respondents reported that their family and friends generally accept and like their body and are not critical of it. Any conversations on appearance typically center not on the body itself, but on modifiable aspects, such as clothes and hairstyle. In addition, individuals felt loved and valued for their authentic inner qualities rather than external appearance (Tylka, 2012).

Accordingly, body acceptance by others has become an important variable in theoretical accounts of the development of positive body image and adaptive eating. In particular, Tylka and colleagues proposed the acceptance model of intuitive eating (Avalos & Tylka, 2006). The acceptance model postulates that women who perceive that their bodies are accepted by others will be able to resist adopting an observer's perspective of their bodies and will feel more accepting, respectful, and appreciative of their own bodies. Such positive body image will, in turn, be associated with healthier and more internally responsive eating patterns. The acceptance model has now been cross-sectionally supported in samples of undergraduate women (Andrew, Tiggemann, & Clark, 2016a; Avalos & Tylka, 2006); college athletes (Oh, Wiseman, Hendrickson, Phillips, & Hayden, 2012); physically active college students (Tylka & Homan, 2015); and young and middle-age adult women (Augustus-Horvath & Tylka, 2011). In each case, body acceptance by significant others has predicted body appreciation, both directly and indirectly, via reduced self-objectification. Some other studies have also shown a positive relationship between body acceptance by others and positive body image (Homan & Cavanaugh, 2013; Kroon Van Diest & Tylka, 2010; Swami, Weis, Barron, & Furnham, 2017).

The acceptance model has also been shown to hold in a sample of adolescent girls (Andrew, Tiggemann, & Clark, 2015). Here, positive body image was associated with perceived acceptance of the body by family and friends. The study also identified reduced social comparison as an additional mechanism linking body acceptance by others to positive body image. This makes sense as girls whose bodies are accepted and appreciated by others and by themselves should have little need to make peer or media comparisons on the basis of appearance, otherwise very common among adolescent girls.

In the only longitudinal study to date, Andrew, Tiggemann, and Clark (2016b) showed that girls who initially felt more body acceptance from their family and friends expressed greater appreciation for their body 1 year later. Interestingly, there was also evidence for some reverse causation, indicating that the relationship between perceived body acceptance by others and body appreciation was bidirectional. It seems likely that girls with greater body appreciation may surround themselves with peers who are also body positive and who communicate body acceptance.

Nearly all the research examining the relationship between body acceptance by others and positive body image has been conducted with white women (mostly college students) in the United States or Australia. In the first test of the acceptance model to include men (Tylka & Homan, 2015), the model fit as well for physically active college men as for physically active college women. Two other studies have found the relationship between body acceptance from others and body appreciation to be similar for men and women (Kroon Van Diest & Tylka, 2010; Swami et al., 2017). In the only study to report on ethnicity, Avalos and Tylka

(2006) reported similar size correlations between body acceptance by others and body appreciation for a small sample of African American female students as for their European American counterparts. Future research should confirm these relationships in other demographic groups.

The reported correlations in the studies mentioned ranged from .35 to .69, with a mean well above .50, denoting a large effect size. Further, in studies that have included a wider range of predictors, such as media consumption and sports participation (Andrew et al., 2016a, 2016b), perceived body acceptance by family and friends has emerged as the most robust predictor of positive body image.

MEASURE OF BODY ACCEPTANCE BY OTHERS

Avalos and Tylka (2006) developed the Body Acceptance by Others Scale (BAOS) to measure an individual's feelings of acceptance of their body shape and weight by important others and society. The scale consists of 10 items. There are two main stems: "I've felt acceptance from ____ regarding my body shape and/or weight" and "______ has/have sent me the message that my body shape and weight are fine." Participants rate these two items on a 5-point scale (1 = *never*, 5 = *always*) for five different potential sources: friends, family, people whom they have dated/partners, society, and media. Items are averaged to produce a score between 1 and 5, with higher scores reflecting greater perceived acceptance of body shape and weight. Avalos and Tylka (2006) demonstrated the scale to have good psychometric properties: internal consistency ($\alpha = .91$), test–retest reliability over a 3-week period ($r = .85$), and construct validity in its pattern of correlations with other related constructs.

A few studies have adapted the measure to focus on interpersonal relationships, in particular, family and friends (Andrew et al., 2015, 2016a, 2016b). Oh et al. (2012) showed that body acceptance from two additional sources, namely, coaches/trainers and teammates, was important for their sample of female college athletes. These variants have produced acceptable internal reliabilities; thus, it seems the measure can be used flexibly as befits the sample. Indeed, there are a variety of other interpersonal sources that may be of relevance for different individuals or groups. These include doctors and other health professionals, ministers of religion, and teachers and mentors.

As yet, the measure has not been validated in ethnically diverse samples. It is also limited in that it refers explicitly to body shape and weight, the most salient attributes for women in Western societies. However, these may not be the most important dimensions for men or particular cultural groups. Finally, the measure is clearly one of perceived, rather than actual, body acceptance by others. While women's perceptions and interpretations of their social environment will be most important in shaping their relationship to their body (Avalos & Tylka, 2006), research could usefully determine the role of actual body acceptance.

RELATIONSHIPS IN DEVELOPMENTAL CONTEXTS

Which relationships matter? Sources of acceptance and support are likely to alter throughout development. For children, the most obvious support will be from their family. Just as mothers and fathers can communicate aspects of negative body image to their children, so can they communicate acceptance and positive attitudes to the body. Such influence may be direct or indirect. The wider family environment (e.g., older brothers who do/do not tease a girl on the basis of appearance and older sisters who do/do not model age-inappropriate or sexualized behaviors) is also likely to be influential.

In adolescence, allegiances shift from family to friends. Indeed, relationships with friends become of the utmost importance. Accordingly, friendship groups tend to be similar in body image attitudes (Paxton, Schutz, Wertheim, & Muir, 1999). In particular, the extent to which teens engage in appearance conversations, including "fat talk," and immerse themselves in "an appearance culture" (Jones, Vigfusdottir, & Lee, 2004) will impede any developing sense of embodiment. In later adolescence and into adulthood, body acceptance by romantic and sexual partners may become a crucial environmental support for developing a strong sexual identity and sense of embodiment. In addition, experiences like childbirth that focus on functionality may lead women to be able to appreciate and celebrate their bodies. This is consistent with the small amount of evidence showing that positive body image tends to increase with age across the female life span (Tiggemann, 2015).

Thus, it is likely that women will encounter relationships important for positive body image throughout the life span. Nevertheless, there is some suggestion that early family relationships might be particularly influential and have an impact beyond childhood. Adult women's current perceptions of body acceptance by others, positive body image, and adaptive eating have been shown to be positively related to unconditional acceptance from the most important person in their life while growing up (Avalos & Tylka, 2006) and negatively related to restrictive or critical messages around eating while growing up (Iannantuono & Tylka, 2012; Kroon Van Diest & Tylka, 2010). This is not to say that body attitudes cannot change. Indeed, many of the respondents in Wood-Barcalow et al.'s (2010) qualitative study reported that they had once had a negative body image but had transitioned to a positive body image by consciously gathering around themselves people who offered support and body acceptance, associating with friends who were not focused on body and weight issues, and modeling women who were proud of their body.

In this, the communication of body acceptance by others may be more subtle than the communication of body unacceptance, which often consists of overt pressures to lose weight or change appearance. Women may not be directly complimented about their appearance but instead receive messages that their body is acceptable and fine as is because of general unconditional support and a lack of appearance-related talk among their family and friends or because their partner caresses their body in loving manner (Augustus-Horvath & Tylka, 2011; Tylka & Wood-Barcalow, 2015).

OTHER ENVIRONMENTAL CONTEXTS

It is likely that perceived body acceptance by others will differ across cultural contexts. A few studies have shown that men in Western cultures generally experience greater body acceptance from others than do women (Swami et al., 2017; Tylka & Homan, 2015), consistent with the general observation that body appreciation is higher for men than for women (Tiggemann, 2015). In addition, it seems that African and Hispanic cultural identification may promote positive body image (Tylka, 2012). While the most salient aspect is likely the endorsement of a broader conceptualization of beauty beyond the narrow Western ideal, an integral part of the explanation may lie in living in a culture where others are accepting of one's body. Thus, members may routinely experience body acceptance on a daily basis from their family, friends, and partners in a way that is rare for most women in Western cultures. The link between a broader conceptualization of beauty at the cultural level and body acceptance at the interpersonal level remains to be demonstrated.

This reasoning might also apply to embodying activities (those that are "in" the body), like belly dancing and yoga, which have been linked to positive body image (Mahlo & Tiggemann, 2016; Tiggemann, Coutts, & Clark, 2014). In addition to providing women an opportunity to reconnect with their bodies in an enjoyable and unselfconscious way, these activities most often take place in a female social context, giving rise to a sense of support, social connectedness, and community among women. Further, the context is one in which acceptance and even celebration of bodies of whatever shape and size is virtually integral to the experience; thus, this interpersonal aspect may also contribute to the resultant positive body image.

It seems likely, then, that perceptions of body acceptance from others may be an influential factor in many other as yet untested contexts (e.g., among feminist friendship groups or in lesbian relationships). Thus, it is possible that the role of relationships may be much larger than we might have thought. Each day, women likely move in and out of a series of interpersonal environmental contexts that have the power to reinforce or undermine their sense of embodiment and positive body image.

IMPLICATIONS FOR PREVENTION, HEALTH PROMOTION, AND TREATMENT

Across the board, perceived body acceptance by others matters; this seems particularly crucial in childhood. Accordingly, parents and other caregivers and educators of young children need to be educated to give body positive and accepting messages. In particular, well-meaning parents who may be concerned about their child's weight need to understand that restrictive messages and practices around eating can be very damaging. Appearance should not be a focus, as even compliments can lead to a focus on appearance at the expense of other characteristics (Augustus-Horvath & Tylka, 2011; Calogero, Herbozo, & Thompson, 2009). Instead, the focus should be on internal qualities, and the body should be celebrated in un–self-conscious activities like dancing by parent and child alike.

Likewise, adolescent girls need to be educated to be compassionate and accepting in their peer groups and not to engage in fat talk and derogation on the basis of appearance. Similarly, romantic and sexual partners should be encouraged not to criticize their partner's appearance. In this, counselors and therapists working with women with negative body image or disordered eating may have a role in discussing with their client's families or partner just how important communication of body acceptance is.

More generally, girls and women (with and without body image concerns) should be advised to seek others who have positive body image in both their romantic relationships and friendship groups and to avoid those who do not accept their body or are critical of their appearance. They should cultivate and nurture relationships that are body affirming and provide body acceptance. Women seeking new sources of support should consider embarking on a non–appearance-focused group activity (e.g., belly dancing, yoga) in a supportive environment that promotes a sense of community and exudes positive body acceptance.

In addition, interventions could incorporate training for women and girls on unhelpful thinking styles and challenging thoughts. In particular, women could be trained in the "protective filtering" (Wood-Barcalow et al., 2010) that has been shown to be important for positive body image in qualitative studies (Frisén & Holmqvist, 2010; Wood-Barcalow et al., 2010) in order that unhelpful appearance messages from peers or family (or media) can be consciously filtered out.

LIMITATIONS AND FUTURE RESEARCH DIRECTIONS

Most of the work on body acceptance by others has focused on young, white, college women. Now, we need research to investigate the role of interpersonal relationships in other more diverse groups across age, gender, ethnicity, and sexual orientation. In particular, here it has been suggested that cultural values of body acceptance may play a significant role in the observed higher levels of body appreciation in some cultural groups, as well as in participants of activities that take place in an accepting social environment.

Given that perceived body acceptance by others has been shown to be important, more research is required on its precursors. This is particularly important for the development of positive body image in children. The available evidence suggests an unconditionally accepting and supportive family environment that focuses on inner strengths and body functionality rather than appearance is key. The specific characteristics and behaviors of such families could be analyzed in more detail. Likewise, the specific relational processes by which women and girls transition from negative to positive body image warrant more investigation to point the way for future interventions. As the communication of body acceptance is often subtle, implicit, and indirect, this requires careful analysis.

Although there exists a validated measure of body acceptance by others (BAOS; Avalos & Tylka, 2006), there remain a number of challenges in the measurement of body acceptance by others. In particular, the measure requires psychometric evaluation in more diverse groups for whom the dimensions assessed and sources of support in the existing measure may not necessarily be the most salient. It would also be useful to see how perceptions of body acceptance match actual body acceptance as reported by independent or multiple informants.

One important methodological limitation of the existing body of research on body acceptance by others is that the research is largely correlational and cross sectional in design. Thus, it is impossible to come to any definitive causal conclusions. The one existing prospective study (Andrew et al., 2016b) showed that the relationship between perceived body acceptance by others and positive body image in adolescent girls was bidirectional, although this may well differ at different time points in the life span. Nevertheless, it is consistent with the conceptualization of positive body image as a reciprocal process (Tylka, 2011, 2012; Wood-Barcalow et al., 2010). Positive body image is both shaped by and shapes the social environment in a number of possible ways. In particular, people with positive body image choose to surround themselves and connect with others who are accepting of their bodies. They also actively seek to encourage others to be more positive toward their bodies. In addition, people with positive body image may perceive others to be relatively more accepting, in that they may be better at filtering out negative or ambiguous comments. Finally, people with positive body image may actually elicit greater body acceptance from others. Thus, the interplay between perceptions of body acceptance from others and positive body image may be both complex and highly dynamic, working together in an "upward spiral" (Tylka & Wood-Barcalow, 2015). Although this presents a methodological challenge, sophisticated longitudinal and experimental research designs are required to better tease out these complexities.

Finally, one contemporary trend that has not been addressed as a source of perceived body acceptance from peers is social media. Many women and girls are increasingly putting their faith and their idea of their own beauty in the number of "likes" or followers they have on photo-based platforms like Instagram (Chua & Chang, 2016). Even if positive, such indicators are highly conditional, and it is difficult to see how girls can ever experience a sense of body acceptance from peers under these conditions. Future research should explicitly address the implications of positioning social media as a potent source of objective and perceived peer body acceptance.

CONCLUSION

Perceived body acceptance by others has been shown to be critically important in promoting positive body image in a variety of contexts. It is to date the most robustly demonstrated predictor of positive body image and adaptive eating. Women and girls need nurturing and supportive relationships where body acceptance is communicated at all ages. In this way, they can begin to learn to appreciate, respect, and honor their own bodies so that they can live fully embodied lives.

REFERENCES

Andrew, R., Tiggemann, M., & Clark, L. (2015). Predictors of intuitive eating in adolescent girls. *Journal of Adolescent Health, 56*, 209–214. doi:10.1016/j.jadohealth.2014.09.005

Andrew, R., Tiggemann, M., & Clark, L. (2016a). Predicting body appreciation in young women: An integrated model of positive body image. *Body Image, 18*, 34–42. doi:10.1016/j.bodyim.2016.04.003

Andrew, R., Tiggemann, M., & Clark, L. (2016b). Predictors and health-related outcomes of positive body image in adolescent girls: A prospective study. *Developmental Psychology, 52*, 463–474. doi:10.1037/dev0000095

Augustus-Horvath, C. L., & Tylka, T. L. (2011). The acceptance model of intuitive eating: A comparison of women in emerging adulthood, early adulthood, and middle adulthood. *Journal of Counseling Psychology, 58*, 110–125. doi:10.1037/a0022129

Avalos, L. C., & Tylka, T. L. (2006). Exploring a model of intuitive eating with college women. *Journal of Counseling Psychology, 53*, 486–497. doi:10.1037/0022-1067.53.4.486

Calogero, R. M., Herbozo, S., & Thompson, J. K. (2009). Complimentary weightism: The potential costs of appearance-related commentary for women's self-objectification. *Psychology of Women Quarterly, 33*, 120–132. doi:10.1111/j.1471-6402.2008.01479.x

Chua, T. H. H., & Chang, L. (2016). Follow me and like my beautiful selfies: Singapore teenage girls' engagement in self-presentation and peer comparison on social media. *Computers in Human Behavior, 55*, 190–197. doi:10.1016/j.chb.2015.09.011

Frisén, A., & Holmqvist, K. (2010). What characterizes early adolescents with a positive body image? A qualitative investigation of Swedish girls and boys. *Body Image, 7*, 205–212. doi:10.1016/j.bodyim.2010.04.001

Homan, K. J., & Cavanaugh, B. N. (2013). Perceived relationship with God fosters positive body image in college women. *Journal of Health Psychology, 18*, 1529–1539. doi:10.1080/13674676.2015.1075481

Iannantuono, A. C., & Tylka, T. L. (2012). Interpersonal and intrapersonal links to body appreciation in college women: An exploratory model. *Body Image, 9*, 227–235. doi:10.1016/j.bodyim.2012.01.004

Jones, D. C., Vigfusdottir, T. H., & Lee, Y. (2004). Body image and the appearance culture among adolescent girls and boys: An examination of friend conversations, peer criticism, appearance magazines, and the internalization of appearance ideals. *Journal of Adolescent Research, 19*, 323–339. doi:10.1177/0743558403258847

Kroon Van Diest, A. M., & Tylka, T. L. (2010). The Caregiver Eating Messages Scale: Development and psychometric investigation. *Body Image, 7*, 317–326. doi:10.1016/j.bodyim.2010.06.002

Mahlo, L., & Tiggemann, M. (2016). Yoga and positive body image: A test of the embodiment model. *Body Image, 18*, 135–142. doi:10.1016/j.bodyim.2016.06.008

Oh, K. H., Wiseman, M. C., Hendrickson, J., Phillips, J. C., & Hayden, E. W. (2012). Testing the acceptance model of intuitive eating with college women athletes. *Psychology of Women Quarterly, 36*, 88–98. doi:10.1177/0361684311433282

Paxton, S. J., Schutz, H. K., Wertheim, E. H., & Muir, S. L. (1999). Friendship clique and peer influences on body image concerns, dietary restraint, extreme weight-loss behaviors, and binge eating in adolescent girls. *Journal of Abnormal Psychology, 108*, 255–266. doi:10.1037//0021-843x.108.2.255

Swami, V., Weis, L., Barron, D., & Furnham, A. (2017). Associations between positive body image, sexual liberalism, and unconventional sexual practices in US adults. *Archives of Sexual Behavior, 46*, 285–2494. doi:10.1017/s10508-016-0924-y

Tiggemann, M. (2015). Considerations of positive body image across various social identities and special populations. *Body Image, 14*, 168–176. doi:10.1016/j.bodyim.2015.03.002

Tiggemann, M., Coutts, E., & Clark, L. (2014). Belly dance as an embodying activity? A test of the embodiment model of positive body image. *Sex Roles, 71*, 197–207. doi:10.1007/s11199-014-0408-2

Tylka, T. L. (2011). Positive psychology perspectives on body image. In T. F. Cash & L. Smolak (Eds.), *Body image: A handbook of science, practice, and prevention* (2nd ed., pp. 56–64). New York, NY: Guilford Press.

Tylka, T. L. (2012). Positive psychology perspectives on body image. In T. F. Cash (Ed.), *Encyclopedia of body image and appearance* (Vol. 2, pp. 657–663). London, England: Elsevier.

Tylka, T. L., & Homan, K. J. (2015). Exercise motives and positive body image in physically active college women and men: Exploring an expanded acceptance model of intuitive eating. *Body Image, 15*, 90–97. doi:10.1016/j.bodyim.2015.07.003

Tylka, T. L., & Wood-Barcalow, N. L. (2015). What is and what is not positive body image? Conceptual foundations and construct definition. *Body Image, 14*, 118–129. doi:10.1016/j.bodyim.2015.04.001

Wood-Barcalow, N. L., Tylka, T. L., & Augustus-Horvath, C. L. (2010). "But I like my body": Positive body image characteristics and a holistic model for young-adult women. *Body Image, 7*, 106–116. doi:10.1016/j.bodyim.2010.01.001

21

Cultivating Positive Embodiment Through Peer Connections

NINA MAFRICI AND NIVA PIRAN

Peers represent important transmitters of weight- and body-related norms and ideals. The internalization of these norms and ideals through various peer processes has a profound influence on the way girls and women inhabit their bodies throughout development. A plethora of research exists on the peer processes that disrupt girls' and women's connection to their bodies, particularly during the period of adolescence, when concerns for peer acceptance are especially heightened and revolve around complying with appearance norms. However, there exists a growing body of literature on the protective peer influences that support girls and women in distancing themselves from dominant appearance norms and facilitate enhanced comfort in, and connection to, their bodies. Understanding the specific peer processes that foster positive body image and embodiment is essential to the development of prevention interventions.

This chapter begins with a review of peer norms that influence girls' and women's body experiences. The chapter continues with a brief review of the impact of peer teasing and harassment on body image, including interventions aimed at supporting peer groups in actively resisting and protecting against teasing and harassment. This is followed by a summary of the impact of social power on body experiences within the peer environment, as well as initiatives emphasizing activism and empowerment to support embodiment. The chapter concludes with a discussion of implications for research and for clinical and prevention initiatives.

PEER NORMS

Quantitative and qualitative studies have consistently confirmed the relationship between peer groups that promote stringent appearance-based norms on girls' and women's internalization of the thin ideal (e.g., Mafrici, 2014; Piran, 2017; VanHuysse, Burt, O'Connor, Thompson, & Klump, 2016); body dissatisfaction; and engagement in weight-control practices (e.g., Gerner & Wilson, 2005; Mafrici, 2014; Paxton, Schutz, Wertheim, & Muir, 1999; Piran, 2017). From a positive embodiment standpoint, however, a growing body of literature has demonstrated the importance of norms pertaining to (a) body acceptance, (b) distancing from appearance-based comments and comparisons, and (c) alternative norms that foster resiliency from dominant peer appearance pressures and enhance comfort and connection to one's body.

Body Acceptance

Across both adolescent and adult populations, several qualitative studies have revealed the impact of peer acceptance on girls' and women's own enhanced comfort and satisfaction in their bodies, as well as their overall body esteem (e.g., Frisén & Holmqvist, 2010; Mafrici, 2014; Mizevich, 2012; Piran, 2017; Wood-Barcalow, Tylka, & Augustus-Horvath, 2010). Specifically, in two Canadian studies employing life history interviews with adult women, acceptance by one's peer group demonstrated a protective influence against reported pressures to conform or comply with dominant norms of thinness in their social environments throughout adolescence and adulthood (Mafrici, 2014; Mizevich, 2012). Further, Piran's (2017) extensive qualitative research with 69 Canadian girls and women has highlighted the importance of empowering relational connections within the peer environment throughout development, contributing to positive embodiment. In particular, these empowering connections facilitated a shared confidence and pride in one another's bodies, as well as a rejection of societal prejudices and protection from adverse treatment (e.g., body-based teasing and harassment). Additionally, from Wood-Barcalow and colleagues' (2010) interview study with 15 college women classified as having "positive body image" emerged a holistic model of body image fluidity that highlighted the positive impact of women who surrounded themselves with individuals who promoted body acceptance, resulting in decreased investment in body change strategies and increased body esteem. Although qualitative studies shedding light on body acceptance norms have been limited to female samples, one Swedish interview revealed the importance of body acceptance by peers on heightened body esteem and adolescent girls' and boys' own acceptance of their perceived body imperfections (Frisén & Holmqvist, 2010).

A number of quantitative studies examining the construct of body acceptance as a protective factor for girls and women have corroborated the existing qualitative findings. For instance, Avalos and Tylka's (2006) acceptance model of intuitive eating, which proposes that acceptance of one's body by others translates into reduced self-objectification and greater appreciation of one's own body, has been supported by several cross-sectional studies with young adult and middle-aged women (e.g., Andrew, Tiggemann, & Clark, 2015; Augustus-Horvath & Tylka,

2011; Avalos & Tylka, 2006; see Chapters 7 and 20). The acceptance model has been supported by two studies involving adolescent populations. First, Andrew and colleagues' (2015) study with 400 adolescent girls demonstrated the relationship between perceived acceptance by peers and family reduced social comparisons, greater intuitive eating, and positive body image. Extending their research prospectively, the researchers also showed that adolescent girls' perception of their body acceptance by peers and family was related to greater appreciation toward their body over a 1-year period (Andrew, Tiggemann, & Clark, 2016).

Appearance-Based Comments and Comparisons

Norms pertaining to bodies and appearances are actively reinforced within the peer environment through direct comments that serve to heighten body comparisons (e.g., "fat talk"; Mafrici, 2014; Nichter, 2000; Paxton et al., 1999; Piran, 2017). The prevalence of appearance dialogue and comparisons within the peer environment, particularly in adolescence, has led to what Jones and Crawford (2006) have termed a highly rigid *peer appearance culture*. The disruptive effects of this appearance culture, and the conversations and comparisons that circulate it, have been examined extensively in both quantitative and qualitative studies. Across these studies, results have shown that girls and women engage in greater appearance conversations and comparisons with their female peers in relation to their male peers (Clark & Tiggemann, 2007; Jones & Crawford, 2006; Myers & Crowther, 2009), resulting in heightened internalization of the thin ideal and greater disordered eating (Nichter, 2000; Paxton et al., 1999; Shomaker & Furman, 2007). Additionally, Myers and Crowther's (2009) extensive meta-analysis from 156 studies examining social comparison further revealed that comparing oneself unfavorably to others also predicted greater dissatisfaction with one's overall appearance.

Further, in the last several years, researchers have explored the growing popularity of engagement in appearance comparisons with peers across social networking sites (SNSs; see Chapter 23). For instance, Chua and Chang's (2016) study with teenage girls in Singapore revealed the importance of virtual comparisons in laying the foundation for peer standards of beauty and girls' own carefully curated self-presentations to conform to these standards. Quantitative studies on young adult women's engagement with SNSs has also shown the link between appearance-focused social media accounts (e.g., Facebook, Instagram) and higher thin-ideal internalization, body surveillance, drive for thinness, and body dissatisfaction (Cohen, Newton-John, & Slater, 2017; Howard, Heron, MacIntyre, Myers, & Everhart, 2017).

Quantitative research on the positive impact of appearance messages and comparisons is limited, given that studies that have examined positive messaging (e.g., compliments regarding bodies) have revealed an equally detrimental impact. For instance, among a sample of 220 ethnically diverse college women, Calogero, Herbozo, and Thompson (2009) discovered that women reported higher body surveillance and body dissatisfaction in association with feeling good about receiving appearance compliments. Importantly, a select number of studies have demonstrated shifts in the peer environment, where peers actively resisted or challenged messaging about appearances and weight control practices. Exploring the socioenvironmental factors of body satisfaction in adolescent American girls, Kelly and colleagues' (Kelly, Wall, Eisenberg, Story, & Neumark-Sztainer, 2004) qualitative study uncovered that girls with higher body satisfaction were part of peer groups emphasizing healthy values pertaining to their bodies and actively discouraged dieting. Further, Mafrici's (2014) life history study with women revealed the importance of being surrounded by peers in adolescence and adulthood who modeled comfort in their appetite and enjoyment of food, fostering girls' and women's connection to their bodies and ability to respond to their appetite in an embodied way.

A few intervention-based studies have lent further support to the importance of active resistance to harmful peer messaging about appearances and the value peers place on qualities other than appearances. Piran's (1999, 2001) participatory action research project in a large Canadian ballet school highlighted the significant positive shift in peer norms in an environment that maintains a widespread promotion of unhealthy body pressures. Based on their own reflections of the problematic norms of the school, students initiated changes that included no evaluative appearance comments and no teasing or harassment pertaining to weight, gender, or other appearance/body-related domains. These initiatives, together with other systemic changes, were associated with a significant reduction in disordered eating within the school during a 15-year period. Additionally, Wade, Davidson, and O'Dea's (2003) controlled evaluation of a school-based media literacy program for Grade 8 students showcased the positive impact of the program for girls' and boys' favorable view of their friendships as accepting, close, and trustworthy, as well as the reduced importance of weight within their peer networks.

Alternative Norms

Research on peer contexts emphasizing alternative body norms has similarly demonstrated the positive impact of membership in peer groups that promote diversity in physical appearances. For instance, qualitative studies have highlighted the significance of identifying with "alternative subcultures" that distance from peers who adopt dominant norms of femininity (e.g., Currie, Kelly, & Pomerantz, 2006; Mizevich, 2012; Piran, 1999, 2017). For instance, in her life history study on Canadian women's resiliency to social pressures of thinness, Mizevich (2012) discovered that women who identified with peer groups that embodied norms outside traditional femininity (e.g., nerds, tomboys, Goths) were more resistant to internalizing and adopting dominant appearance-based norms. Similarly, in a qualitative study on empowerment among adolescent girls from Vancouver, Currie and colleagues (2006) found that girls who actively positioned themselves against "emphasized femininity" were better able to resist pressures associated with appearance conformity in their peer environments. Lending support for these qualitative findings are the results from Murnen and Smolak's (2009) meta-analysis of 26 studies that explored the impact of a feminist identity on women's body experiences. Their collective findings revealed that adopting a feminist identity that resists oppressive norms for thinness was associated with a reduced drive for thinness, although effect sizes remained small.

TEASING AND HARASSMENT

Appearance-related teasing and harassment within the peer environment is a significant contributor to experiences of body shame and self-surveillance, placing individuals at an increased risk for body dissatisfaction and disordered eating (Lieberman, Gavin, Bukowski, & White, 2001; Lindberg, Grabe, & Hyde, 2007). Menzel and colleagues' (2010) meta-analysis demonstrated significant relationships between appearance-related teasing and body dissatisfaction, dietary restraint, and bulimic behaviors. However, a number of other studies have extended the exploration of peer teasing to include harassment across other pertinent domains, such as gender, ethnicity, race, and social class, which have all supported the conclusion that any violations of body ownership or prejudicial treatments can have an adverse impact on body experiences and the development of eating disorders (e.g., Bucchianeri, Eisenberg, Wall, Piran, & Neumark-Sztainer, 2014; Harned & Fitzgerald, 2002; Larkin & Rice, 2005; Piran, 2017; Piran & Thompson, 2008; Reddy & Crowther, 2007).

Interventions aimed at controlling teasing and harassment in the peer environment, while limited, have shown promising results. Haines and colleagues' (Haines, Neumark-Sztainer, Perry, Hannan, & Levine, 2006) Very Important Kids program demonstrated the effectiveness of a multilevel school intervention designed to reduce teasing in elementary school children in Minnesota. Piran's (1999, 2001) ballet school prevention program similarly suggested the contribution of students' initiatives to cease body-based teasing, supplemented by similar school policies, to a more constructive school environment.

SOCIAL POWER WITHIN PEER GROUPS

Particularly during adolescence, when concerns for peer acceptance are heightened, adherence to appearance norms plays a critical role for the establishment and maintenance of social power within the peer environment. A prospective study with girls (Piran, 2017) and retrospective life history interviews with young women (Mafrici, 2014; Piran, 2017) have demonstrated the attempts girls and women make to alter their bodies as a means to restore social power in inequitable peer environments, related not only to the thin-ideal body but also to other domains of social location, including ethnicity, race, sexual identity, and social class.

However, there exists an increasing body of literature on the impact of constructs like activism and empowerment as positive determinants of social power within the peer environment. Several qualitative studies, for instance, have highlighted the significance of empowering relationships that emphasize acceptance, equality, and loyalty on women's experiences of positive embodiment and ability to resist dominant peer appearance conformity (e.g., Currie et al., 2006; Mafrici, 2014; Mizevich, 2012; Piran, 2017).

Most important, social power must be determined by values and activities separate from physical appearances. The developmental theory of embodiment (Piran, 2017) proposes the importance of developing peer social justice values that critically examine and challenge the promotion and internalization of appearance-based social power related to gender, ethnicity, race, sexual identity, and social class and encourage a dialogue that promotes social equity and enhances relational connections. Several school-based prevention programs, such as GO GIRLS! Media Literacy, Activism, and Advocacy Project (Piran, Levine, & Irving, 2000); Girls on the Go! (Tirlea, Truby, & Haines, 2016); and REbel (Breithaupt, Eickman, Byrne, & Fischer, 2017), which emphasize activism, empowerment, and equitable relational connections, have demonstrated promising results that include higher body satisfaction and self-esteem and reduced internalization of the thin ideal. Research has also highlighted the importance of girls' and women's active leadership in these programs, contributing to their own heightened agency and reduced dietary restraint and body dissatisfaction (Becker, Bull, Smith, & Ciao, 2008).

CONCLUSION AND IMPLICATIONS FOR PREVENTION

Given the prominent role of appearance-based norms, body comparisons, and teasing and harassment within peer environments, the research stresses the importance of early school-based interventions that educate students on social discourses pertaining to appearances, the body, and femininity, while actively supporting girls in positioning themselves against preoccupation with adherence to idealized and harmful ways of inhabiting their bodies. Further, research suggests the potential contribution of developing supportive spaces for students to challenge oppressive attitudes and behaviors and, together with school authorities, develop guidelines and parameters that promote safe, harassment-free environments. From a clinical perspective, it is essential that individuals working with young girls and women with disordered eating and body image difficulties conceptualize their challenges in relation to the interaction among multiple social processes that have impacted their ability to live in their bodies in a connected way. Group programs have a particularly unique and beneficial role in this regard, providing both the space to raise awareness into peer processes, as well as to foster supportive relational connections, among girls themselves. Further study of peer-based prevention strategies can contribute not only to the growing science of prevention interventions but also to the deepened understanding of the impact of constructive peer processes to positive body image and embodiment.

REFERENCES

Andrew, R., Tiggemann, M., & Clark, L. (2015). Predictors of intuitive eating in adolescent girls. *Journal of Adolescent Health, 56*, 209–214. doi:10.1016/j.jadohealth.2014.09.005

Andrew, R., Tiggemann, M., & Clark, L. (2016). Predictors and health-related outcomes of positive body image in adolescent girls: A prospective study. *Developmental Psychology, 52*, 463–474. doi:10.1037/dev0000095

Augustus-Horvath, C. L., & Tylka, T. L. (2011). The acceptance model of intuitive eating: A comparison of women in emerging adulthood, early adulthood, and middle adulthood. *Journal of Counseling Psychology, 58*, 110–125. doi:10.1037/a0022129

Avalos, L. C., & Tylka, T. L. (2006). Exploring a model of intuitive eating with college women. *Journal of Counseling Psychology, 53*, 486–497. doi:10.1037/0022-1067.53.4.486

Becker, C. B., Bull, S., Smith, L. M., & Ciao, A. C. (2008). Effects of being a peer-leader in an eating disorder prevention program: Can we further reduce eating disorder risk factors? *Eating Disorders, 16*, 444–459. doi:10.1080/10640260802371595

Breithaupt, L., Eickman, L., Byrne, E., & Fischer, S. (2017). Enhancing empowerment in eating disorder prevention: Another examination of the REbeL peer education model. *Eating Behaviors, 25*, 38–41. doi:10.1016/j.eatbeh.2016.05.003

Bucchianeri, M. M., Eisenberg, M. E., Wall, M. M., Piran, N., & Neumark-Sztainer, D. (2014). Multiple types of harassment: Associations with emotional well-being and unhealthy behaviors in adolescents. *Journal of Adolescent Health, 54*, 724–729. doi:10.1016/j.jadolhealth.2013.10.205

Calogero, R. M., Herbozo, S., & Thompson, J. K. (2009). Complimentary weightism: The potential costs of appearance-related commentary for women's self-objectification. *Psychology of Women Quarterly, 33*, 120–132. doi:10.1111/j.1471-6402.2008.01479.x

Chua, T. H. H., & Chang, L. (2016). Follow me and like my beautiful selfies: Singapore teenage girls' engagement in self-presentation and peer comparison on social media. *Computers in Human Behavior, 55*, 190–197. doi:10.1016/j.chb.2015.09.011

Clark, L., & Tiggemann, M. (2007). Sociocultural influences and body image in 9- to 12-year-old girls: The role of appearance schemas. *Journal of Clinical Child and Adolescent Psychology, 36*, 76–86. doi:10.1080/15374410709336570

Cohen, R., Newton-John, T., & Slater, A. (2017). The relationship between Facebook and Instagram appearance-focused activities and body image concerns in young women. *Body Image, 23*, 183–187. doi:10.1016/j.bodyim.2017.10.002

Currie, D. H., Kelly, D. M., & Pomerantz, S. (2006). "The geeks shall inherit the earth": Girls' agency, subjectivity and empowerment. *Journal of Youth Studies, 9*, 419–436. doi:10.1080/13676260600914416

Frisén, A., & Holmqvist, K. (2010). What characterizes early adolescents with a positive body image? A qualitative investigation of Swedish girls and boys. *Body Image, 7*, 205–212. doi:10.1016/j.bodyim.2010.04.001

Gerner, B., & Wilson, P. (2005). The relationship between friendship factors and adolescent girls' body image concern, body dissatisfaction, and restrained eating. *International Journal of Eating Disorders, 37*, 313–320. doi:10.1002/eat.20094

Haines, J., Neumark-Sztainer, D., Perry, C. L., Hannan, P. J., & Levine, M. P. (2006). VIK (Very Important Kids): A school-based program designed to reduce teasing and unhealthy weight-control behaviors. *Health Education Research, 21*, 884–895. doi:10.1093/her/cyl123

Harned, M. S., & Fitzgerald, L. F. (2002). Understanding a link between sexual harassment and eating disorder symptoms: A mediational analysis. *Journal of Consulting and Clinical Psychology, 70*, 1170–1181. doi:10.1037//0022-006x.70.5.1170

Howard, L. M., Heron, K. E., MacIntyre, T. I., Myers, T. A., & Everhart, R. S. (2017). Is use of social networking sites associated with young women's body dissatisfaction and disordered eating? A look at black–white racial differences. *Body Image, 23*, 109–113. doi.org/10.1016/j.bodyim.2017.08.008

Jones, D. C., & Crawford, J. K. (2006). The peer appearance culture during adolescence: Gender and body mass variations. *Journal of Youth and Adolescence, 2*, 257–269. doi:10/1007/s10964-005-9006-5

Kelly, A. M., Wall, M., Eisenberg, M., Story, M., & Neumark-Sztainer, D. (2004). High body satisfaction in adolescent girls: Associations with demographics, socio-environmental, personal and behavioral factors. *Journal of Adolescent Health, 34*, 129–135. doi:10.1016/j.jadohealth.2003.11.003

Larkin, J., & Rice, C. (2005). Beyond "healthy eating" and "healthy weights": Harassment and the health curriculum in middle schools. *Body Image, 2*, 219–232. doi:10.1016/j.bodyim.2005.07.001

Lieberman, M., Gavin, L., Bukowski, W. M., & White, D. R. (2001). Interpersonal influence and disordered eating behaviors in adolescent girls: The role of peer modeling, social reinforcement and body-related teasing. *Eating Behaviors, 2*, 215–236. doi:10.1016/S1471-0153(01)00030-7

Lindberg, S. M., Grabe, S., & Hyde, J. S. (2007). Gender, pubertal development, and peer sexual harassment predict objectified body consciousness in early adolescence. *Journal of Research on Adolescence, 17*, 723–742. doi:10.1111/j.1532-7795.2007.00544.x

Mafrici, N. M. (2014, January). *The influence of peer relationships on women's lived body experiences across the lifespan* (Doctoral thesis, University of Toronto, ON, Canada). Retrieved from https://tspace.library.utoronto.ca/handle/1807/43656

Menzel, J. E., Schaefer, L. M., Burke, N. L., Mayhew, L. L., Brannick, T. J., & Thompson, J. K. (2010). Appearance-related teasing, body dissatisfaction, and disordered eating: A meta-analysis. *Body Image, 7*, 261–270. doi:10.1016/j.bodyim.2010.05.004

Mizevich, J. (2012). *Resilient women: Resisting the pressure to be thin* (Thesis, University of Toronto, ON, Canada). ProQuest Dissertations and Theses. Retrieved from https://tspace.library.utoronto.ca/bitstream/1807/34813/1/Mizevich_Jane_201211_PhD_thesis.pdf

Murnen, S. K., & Smolak, L. (2009). Are feminist women protected from body image problems? A meta-analytic review of relevant research. *Sex Roles, 60*, 186–197. doi:10.1007/s11199-008-9523-2

Myers, T. A., & Crowther, J. H. (2009). Social comparison as a predictor of body dissatisfaction: A meta-analytic review of relevant research. *Journal of Abnormal Psychology*, 118, 683–698. doi.org/10.1037/a0016763

Nichter, M. (2000). *Fat talk: What girls and their parents say about dieting.* Cambridge, MA: Harvard University Press.

Paxton, S. J., Schutz, H. K., Wertheim, E. H., & Muir, S. L. (1999). Friendship clique and peer influences on body image concerns, dietary restraint, extreme weight-loss behaviors, and binge eating in adolescent girls. *Journal of Abnormal Psychology, 108,* 255–266. doi:10.1007/s11199-004-0722-1

Piran, N. (1999). Eating disorders: A trial of prevention in a high risk school setting. *Journal of Primary Prevention, 20,* 75–90. doi:10.1023/A:1021358519832

Piran, N. (2001). Re-inhabiting the body from the inside out: Girls transform their school environment. In D. L. Tolman & M. Brydon-Miller (Eds.), *From subjects to subjectivities: A handbook of interpretive and participatory methods* (pp. 218–238). New York, NY: New York University Press.

Piran, N. (2017). *Journeys of embodiment at the intersection of body and culture: The developmental theory of embodiment.* San Diego, CA: Elsevier. doi:10.1016/c2015-0-04666-4

Piran, N., Levine, M. P., & Irving, L. M. (2000). GO GIRLS! Media literacy, activism, and advocacy project. *Healthy Weight Journal, 14,* 89–90.

Piran, N., & Thompson, S. (2008). A study of the adverse social experiences model to the development of eating disorders. *International Journal of Health Promotion and Education, 46,* 65–71. doi:10.1080/14635240.2008.10708131

Reddy, S. D., & Crowther, J. H. (2007). Teasing, acculturation, and cultural conflict: Psychosocial correlates of body image and eating attitudes among South Asian women. *Cultural Diversity and Ethnic Minority Psychology, 13,* 45–53. doi:10.1037/1099-9809.13.1.45

Shomaker, L. B., & Furman, W. (2007). Same-sex peer influences on young women's body image: An experimental manipulation. *Journal of Social and Clinical Psychology, 26,* 871–895. doi:10.1521/jscp.2007.26.8.871

Tirlea, L., Truby, H., & Haines, T. P. (2016). Pragmatic, randomized controlled trials of the Girls on the Go! program to improve self-esteem in girls. *American Journal of Health Promotion, 30,* 231–241. doi:10.1177/0890117116639572

VanHuysse, J. L., Burt, S. A., O'Connor, S. M., Thompson, J. K., & Klump, K. L. (2016). Socialization and selection effects in the association between weight conscious peer groups and thin-ideal internalization: A co-twin control study. *Body Image, 17,* 1–9. doi:10.1016/j.bodyim.2016.01.005

Wade, T. D., Davidson, S., & O'Dea, J. A. (2003). A preliminary controlled evaluation of a school-based media literacy program and self-esteem program for reducing eating disorder risk factors. *International Journal of Eating Disorders, 33,* 371–383. doi:10.1002/eat.10136

Wood-Barcalow, N. L., Tylka, T. L., & Augustus-Horvath, C. L. (2010). "But I like my body": Positive body image characteristics and a holistic model for young-adult women. *Body Image, 7,* 106–116. doi:10.1016/j.bodyim.2010.01.001

22

Cultivating Positive Embodiment Through The Family Environments

TRACY L. TYLKA ■

Families represent an early and key socialization agent for children, and it is largely through families that children first learn how to inhabit their bodies and engage their bodies in the world (Wood-Barcalow, Tylka, & Augustus-Horvath, 2010), a process referred to as *embodiment* (Piran, 2016, 2017). Embodiment is intricately connected to intrapersonal and interpersonal health and well-being (Piran, 2017); therefore, we want our children to be positively embodied. However, families may be confused about how to effectively guide their children toward positive embodiment. As professionals, we can help families understand embodiment and how to structure the family environment to cultivate it. For example, clinicians often include a client's family as a source of support within eating disorder treatment, with the family helping the client follow treatment plans aimed at restoring embodiment (Hill, Peck, Wierenga, & Kaye, 2016). Moreover, certain universal eating disorder prevention efforts assist families in promoting embodiment in young children (Hart, Damiano, & Paxton, 2016).

Patriarchal cultural norms tend to preserve boys' and men's positive embodiment while systematically dismantling it for girls and women (Pipher, 1994; Piran, 2017). Thus, to date, most theory and research on building embodiment has targeted girls and women. Piran (2016) offered a comprehensive conceptualization of girls' and women's embodiment rooted in decades of research. To arrive at this conceptualization, she interviewed three generations of 171 girls and women (ages 9–68) to understand how they inhabit their bodies from their earliest memories to the present. Her research revealed five interconnected experiences of embodiment, represented as dimensions ranging from positive to negative: body connection and comfort; agency and functionality; experience and expression of desire; attuned self-care; and inhabiting the body as a subjective (vs. an objectified) site. This chapter explicates how families can cultivate girls' positive embodiment within each of Piran's (2016) five dimensions.

BODY CONNECTION AND COMFORT

The body connection and comfort dimension describes the quality of girls' and women's connection with their bodies as they engage with the world (Piran, 2016). Girls and women with positive embodiment described experiences of "comfort," "feeling at one," and "at home" in their bodies. They used positive self-talk that countered adverse social experiences, such as body image threats (e.g., exposure to idealized media images) and social injustice.

Fostering Body Connection

First, families can cultivate body connection by creating an environment that accepts children's body type, size, and weight. Specifically, fixed aspects of appearance and body size are minimized, internal qualities (e.g., personality) are emphasized, and beauty is broadly defined (Wood-Barcalow et al., 2010). Indeed, body acceptance by family and friends was associated with higher levels of body appreciation (a manifestation of body connection and comfort) 1 year later among adolescent girls (Andrew, Tiggemann, & Clark, 2016). Clearly, family members should avoid appearance-related criticisms and teasing, as these comments prompt children to feel that their bodies are a source of shame and humiliation rather than a source of connection, joy, and interaction with the world (Neumark-Sztainer, 2005). Also, less intuitively, family members should avoid appearance-related "compliments" (e.g., "You're so pretty!"), as these well-intentioned compliments are linked to higher body surveillance and body dissatisfaction (Calogero, Herbozo, & Thompson, 2009). Parents should also focus on promoting healthy behaviors (e.g., physical activity) rather than weight control or weight loss (Neumark-Sztainer, 2005).

Second, families can practice mind–body connection activities such as yoga (see Chapter 30). In supportive environments (e.g., those that do not focus on appearance, weight, or size), yoga helps link the body, mind, and emotions in a compassionate, positive, and embodied manner, promoting a greater sense of body connection, and can be adapted to meet different physical needs, skill levels, and body size (Cook-Cottone & Douglass, 2017). Practicing yoga reduced body surveillance and improved physical self-worth from pre- to post-intervention in adolescent girls and boys when compared to a physical education-only control group (Cox, Ullrich-French, Howe, & Cole, 2017). Among young adults, yoga practice is associated with higher body appreciation, with greater embodiment and reduced self-objectification accounting for this association (Mahlo & Tiggemann, 2016). To expose children to yoga, families could practice yoga together (providing opportunities for children to model parents and older siblings), watch and practice a kids' yoga video together, or sign children up for kids' yoga lessons provided by many yoga studios and YMCAs.

Fostering Positive Body Expression

It is important that families engage in positive and self-accepting body talk rather than fat talk, as children are likely to model the types of discourse that they hear. Positive and self-accepting body talk may be expressed as, "My body is fine as it is," "I really like how my body helps me play soccer," and "All bodies are beautiful." Conversely, fat talk may include variants of, "I'm so fat," "Ugh! I gained weight and look so bad," "I need to diet," "She gained weight and looks bad," and "She lost weight and looks so good!" It is critical that families do not portray fat as "bad," as it perpetuates weight stigma, which children can internalize and, consequently, experience negative body image (see Chapter 17). Parents can intercept when they hear fat talk within their family or a child's peer group and help turn the conversation into self-accepting and positive body talk, modeling it for children.

Families also can encourage positive body expression by supporting their child's style preferences (e.g., of clothes, hair, accessories) that reflect their personality and body comfort. In a classic study, African American girls described beauty as "making what you got work for you in your own way" and "putting it together," or creating a style that fits their personality and projects a unique presence (Parker et al., 1995, pp. 108–109). Their white counterparts, who had a less positive body image, tended to report that beauty is "making yourself look as close as possible to an ideal body shape and face."

AGENCY AND FUNCTIONALITY

Another dimension of positive embodiment is acting in and on the world with agency—both physically and through the power of voice (Piran, 2016). According to Pipher (1994), girls are often happy and free, but culture takes away their voice in adolescence: "Vibrant, confident girls become shy, doubting young women. Girls stop thinking, 'Who am I? What do I want' and start thinking, 'What must I do to please others?'" (p. 22).

Girls enter a patriarchal world in which they are pressured to be feminine in their relationships (by suppressing anger, always "being nice," and avoiding conflict) and display femininity through their bodies (by conforming to societal standards of beauty via monitoring their appearance) (Tolman & Porche, 2000). To align themselves with these cultural expectations, girls and women often silence their own voice, experiences, and actions while tending to the needs and desires of others. For example, they may defer to boys and men on daily activities (e.g., where to go to eat) or conform to their spouse's political beliefs. Additionally, focusing on appearance diminishes girls' and women's ability to see their bodies as functional. How can families preserve, cultivate, and restore girls' voice and body functionality?

Preserving, Cultivating, and Restoring Voice

Self-silencing is rooted in the feminine gender role, as the feminine voice is relational, dependent, and considerate of others and characterized by a moral obligation to maintain harmony within a network of relationships (Smolak, 2010). Yet, self-silencing detaches girls from their inner experiences and undermines their authentic connections within relationships, creating disembodiment (Impett, Schooler, & Tolman, 2006). Girls learn from a very early age to self-silence, and the message to do so is deeply rooted in culture; an example is in Walt Disney's *A Little Mermaid.* Ariel, the mermaid, relinquishes her voice to the witch, Ursula, in exchange for legs so she can attract her human male love interest—and this is celebrated. To help preserve, cultivate, and restore girls' voice, parents need to be able to (a) identify aspects of the feminine gender role present in media and interpersonal interactions; (b) deconstruct gender roles within the family, media, and culture; and (c) be committed to helping their daughters preserve, cultivate, and restore their voice.

Professionals need to work with families to help them understand the ubiquity of gender roles and how they are deleterious for girls and boys. They are not innocent messages, but instructions for how girls should behave as women and how boys should behave as men. Once they notice gendered messages, they can discuss and deconstruct them with children. For example, when watching *A Little Mermaid*, parents could point out the importance of retaining one's voice, address that it is important not to relinquish their power within relationships because their opinions and expressions are what makes them who they are, and discuss how children can challenge gendered expectations for behavior; in these ways, parents can foster media literacy. Parents can help girls identify powerful women who defied gender stereotypes and used their voice to help change society for the better. Parents can also expose children to constructing their own media that empower girls and women (see Kearney, 2006); that way, girls practice agency in constructing a world that represents their standpoint rather than one constricted by gender roles. Parents can read books such as *Wonder Girls: Changing Our World* (Gianturco & Sangster, 2017) with their children to ignite social interest and action. This particular book presents the stories of 90 young female activists transforming the world around them using their intelligence, passion, determination, creativity, and dreams to tackle issues such as enhancing education, health, equality, and the environment.

Parents can be cognizant to attend to girls' voice instead of stifling it. For example, when girls challenge, parents can say, "You disagree with me about that. What makes you come to your conclusion?" Parents can give girls a voice in their afterschool activities and allow them to pursue activities that provide the opportunity to master challenges; boost self-efficacy, resilience, and self-esteem; and affirm their intrinsic value rather than their appearance. Furthermore, to promote girls' voice within their relationships, professionals can help parents incorporate specific interpersonal effectiveness skills from dialectic behavioral therapy (DBT; Linehan, 2015), such as DEAR MAN (i.e., asking directly for what you want or need or saying no by **D**escribing the situation, **E**xpressing an opinion/feeling, **A**sserting what you need or saying "no," **R**einforcing the person ahead of time, staying **M**indful of what you need/want in spite of the other person's behavior, **A**ppearing confident, and **N**egotiating).

Preserving, Cultivating, and Restoring Body Functionality

Families help girls develop and maintain a sense of physical competence and confidence via emphasizing the functionality of their bodies. Engagement in nonelite and nonlean sports (i.e., sports that are not Division I and do not require a lean body to be competitive) may provide girls with a sense of pride that is separate from appearance and help them focus on what their body can do rather than how it looks or being "the best" at a sport (Smolak, Murnen, & Ruble, 2000).

Alleva, Martijn, van Breukelen, Jansen, and Karos (2015) developed the Expand Your Horizon program, which consists of three online writing exercises in which participants describe the functions that their body can perform (physical capabilities, internal bodily processes, body senses and perceptions, creative endeavors, communication with others, and self-care) and reflect on why these functions are personally meaningful to them. Compared to an active control program, Expand Your Horizon increased women's functionality satisfaction, appearance satisfaction, and body appreciation and decreased self-objectification at post-test and a 1-week follow-up (Alleva et al., 2015). Given that this intervention is simple and inexpensive and takes just 45 minutes to complete, it would be worthwhile for researchers to tailor it to children and examine its effectiveness. If shown to be effective, it may be a tool for families to increase children's functionality appreciation.

Menstruation is an aspect of girls' and women's body functionality that is derided and degraded by society, prompting girls to conceal evidence that they are on their periods and experience self-loathing, disgust, and shame with their body's natural functions (Roberts & Waters, 2004). To promote positive embodied menstruation in girls, parents can first explore the ways in which they have internalized cultural messages of menstruation and make a commitment to discussing menstruation in a positive, embodied way with their daughters and sons (e.g., "It's a forerunner to being able to carry a child"). Second, parents can point out to children the messages inherent in the images and advertisements that depict feminine hygiene products (e.g., to "hide" their bleeding), which place the problem on how society reacts to menstruation rather than menstruation itself. Third, parents can engage in broader educational efforts to reduce secrecy, ignorance, and stigma about menstruation. Doing so challenges the cultural resistance to define women according to their functionality and agency, rather than their appearance.

EXPERIENCE AND EXPRESSION OF DESIRE

The experience and expression of desire dimension represents girls' and women's embodied connection to appetite and sexuality, in terms of both experiencing these desires and responding to them in attuned and self-caring ways (Piran, 2016).

Enhancing the Pleasures of Eating

Diet culture diminishes the pleasures of eating with prescriptive behaviors, such as calorie counting and restricting calorie-dense foods, which is linked to greater food preoccupation, less pleasure when eating, and poorer well-being (Tylka, Calogero, & Daníelsdóttir, 2015). In contrast, *intuitive eating*—an eating style characterized by following internal hunger and satiety cues to guide when, what, and how much to eat—is linked to lower food preoccupation, more pleasure when eating, and greater well-being (see Chapter 7; Tylka, Calogero, et al., 2015; Tylka, Eneli, Kroon Van Diest, & Lumeng, 2013). Parents can guide their children toward intuitive eating by honoring their children's hunger and satiety cues during feeding times, eating intuitively themselves, not commenting critically when their children are eating, and structuring family meals.

Satter (2008) offered an approach that reflects these recommendations by encouraging a "division of responsibility" between parents and children. Parents determine when children should eat (three meals and two snacks); what foods should be presented (based on nutritional value, variety, cost, and family food preferences); and where to eat (a distraction-free, conflict-free environment with family present). In contrast, children determine how much to eat. Parents are instructed not to comment on children's food intake or encourage children to start/stop eating. Only water is provided in between meals and snacks to ensure that children come to the table hungry. This approach offers the structure children need (e.g., predictability of food presentation and consumption if so desired) in an environment that facilitates mindful eating while respecting hunger and satiety cues. Other resources for parents include the book *Intuitive Eating* (Tribole & Resch, 2012) and the *Intuitive Eating Workbook* (Tribole & Resch, 2017).

Indeed, research has supported the benefits of intuitive eating and structured family meals. Mothers who eat intuitively reported lower restriction of their young child's food intake when concerned about their child's weight (Tylka, Lumeng, & Eneli, 2015). Intuitive eating among early adolescents was positively linked to life satisfaction and positive affect and inversely linked to body dissatisfaction, negative affect, pressure to be thin, and thin-ideal internalization (Dockendorff, Petrie, Greenleaf, & Martin, 2012). In a 5-year longitudinal population-based study, family meal frequency in adolescence predicted higher intakes of fruits, vegetables, and key nutrients and lower intake of soft drinks (Larson, Neumark-Sztainer, Hannan, & Story, 2007) and lower disordered eating behaviors, such as self-induced vomiting, binge eating, fasting, skipping meals, smoking to control appetite, chronic dieting, and use of laxatives, diet pills, and diuretics (Neumark-Sztainer, Eisenberg, Fulkerson, Story, & Larson, 2008) in young adulthood.

Sexual Desire

There is disagreement among scholars about whether expressions of sexual desire among adolescent girls are in line with their own experienced desire and reflect agency in desire or, rather, a result of acting out cultural expectations to be sexual objects for boys and men (Lamb & Peterson, 2012). Images of female sexual empowerment are often highly sexually objectified. Girls may be proud of their ability to perform sexual acts that please others, but do not describe their desire, pleasure, or satisfaction in an embodied way (Tolman, 2012).

For parents, then, it may be difficult to know how to cultivate healthy sexuality in their daughters. Parents can encourage *attuned sexuality* (see Chapter 9) with their daughters by nurturing their positive body image (e.g., respect for their bodies and treating them with kindness); helping them assert their sexual agency (e.g., insisting on condom use; setting boundaries in relationships); providing access to contraception, human papillomavirus (HPV) vaccines, and gynecological care; and characterizing the body and sexuality as a source of pleasure rather being "dirty" or a source of shame. Importantly, parents also need to be active at the cultural level to dismantle institutional heteronormativity and the structures that keep it in place. Parents and their daughters could become involved in non–school-centered sex education efforts (e.g., Planned Parenthood's "Ask the Experts"; https://www.plannedparenthood.org/learn/teens/ask-experts/) and media literacy/activism, such as SPARK (Sexualization Protest: Action, Resistance, Knowledge; see http://www.sparkmovement.org), an intergenerational, community-based, girl-fueled movement that engages girls in becoming activists to challenge sexualization.

ATTUNED SELF-CARE

The attuned self-care dimension reflects the connection to internal needs and engagement in self-care as one engages with the world (Piran, 2016). Internal needs include bodily, emotional, and relational needs and the need to engage in meaningful pursuits. Previously reviewed strategies parents can use to promote agency within relationships (e.g., DEAR MAN, attuned sexuality) and mindful connection to the self (e.g., yoga, intuitive eating) can also nurture attuned self-care.

As a framework for self-care, Cook-Cottone and Guyker (2018) promoted six domains of actionable practices that support positive embodiment and overall well-being: physical care, supportive relationships, mindful awareness, self-compassion and purpose, mindful relaxation, and supportive structure. These practices promote a strong body and a strong mind, which then facilitate strong relationships and a strong presence in the world. Parents can structure the family environment to facilitate children's self-care by (a) engaging in regular physical activity as a family and types of activities their child enjoys while underscoring body functionality rather than weight control; (b) emphasizing hydration and nutrition following Satter's (2008) model; (c) ensuring adequate time for sleep and rest/relaxation; (d) promoting and modeling activities that facilitate mindful awareness (e.g., meditation, yoga); (e) seeking medical, dental, and vision treatment; (f) ensuring an organized environment and schedule; and (g) providing outlets for spiritual connection and transcendence, such as nature. Indeed, these activities have been associated with positive body image and embodiment (for a review, see Chapters 1 and 2).

Emotion regulation, self-compassion, mindfulness, and effective relationships are essential for self-care (Cook-Cottone & Guyker, 2018). Parents can expose children to the many DBT skills that build emotion regulation, distress tolerance, mindfulness, and interpersonal effectiveness (see Linehan, 2015). Self-compassion is extremely beneficial for children, as self-acceptance and self-kindness may help buffer rejection, the ability to frame their distress as common may help provide a sense of other-connectedness that helps buffer their negative affect and facilitate empathy, and mindfulness may help buffer rumination. Families appear to play a critical role in fostering their children's well-being through teaching self-compassion. In a sample of adolescents, higher maternal support, more positive family functioning, and secure attachment were linked to higher self-compassion, and self-compassion mediated the relationship between these family characteristics and well-being (Neff & McGehee, 2010).

INHABITING THE BODY AS A SUBJECTIVE (VERSUS AN OBJECTIFIED) SITE

The dimension of inhabiting the body as a subjective site emphasizes inner characteristics, such as personality, pleasure, comfort, health, and intellect, while also protesting, resisting, and defying normative pressures to self-objectify (Piran, 2016). First, families can build these inner characteristics via providing girls with a sense of unconditional body acceptance. Research has shown that perceived body acceptance by family members and friends is linked to adolescent girls' lower body surveillance and higher body appreciation over a 1-year period (Andrew et al., 2016). Additionally, high body appreciation buffered girls' body satisfaction after viewing thin-ideal media (Andrew, Tiggemann, & Clark, 2015). By providing body acceptance and building body appreciation, families can offset self-objectification and the effects of sexualized imagery on their daughters.

Second, due to the pervasive sexualization of the female body and cultural pressures to self-objectify, inhabiting the body as a subjective site requires media literacy and social activism, which parents can encourage in children. According to the American Psychological Association (APA) Task Force on the Sexualization of Girls (2010), families can help children interpret sexualized images and messages in ways that mitigate or prevent harm. For example, girls' coviewing and active discussions with parents about sexualized messages and content may decrease the adverse impact of viewing sexualized images (APA, Task Force on the Sexualization of Girls, 2010). After identifying sexually objectifying content, family members can help children form a schema to contextualize it (see Chapter 14). This *contextualization schema* entails placing appropriate blame on society for sexually objectifying content rather than internalizing sexualized content as aspirational for themselves. When we help children articulate sexual objectification and its ill effects and develop a schema to contextualize it as a societal problem, then they may be more likely to pinpoint instances in which sexual objectification is harmful and less likely to self-objectify. Consequently, when confronted with sexually objectifying content that arouses discomfort, children can acknowledge that their discomfort is due to this content (e.g., "manufacturers use sex to sell products") rather than a personal fault (e.g., "I need to look like that model"). Family members can also help children build a *protective filter* (see Wood-Barcalow et al., 2010), which "filters in" content that maintains a positive body image (e.g., positive comments about intellect and functionality) and blocks content that is inconsistent with having a positive body image (e.g., pressures to lose weight or appear "sexy" for others) from affecting the self.

CONCLUSION

Being immersed in a patriarchal culture crafts disembodiment among girls, stripping away or preventing the formation of their body comfort, agency and functionality, connection to desire, attuned self-care, and subjective sense of self (Piran, 2017). This process is reflective of the *null environment* (Freeman, 1979), which suggests environments that claim to be "hands off" and not treat girls and boys differently indeed pose greater harm to girls because the gendered norms that provide greater power to boys and men implicitly shape these environments. Consequently, boys' power protects their embodiment, and if girls do not receive alternative and subversive ways of processing the world, they are more likely to internalize cultural messages that they should be sexual objects rather than agentic individuals. Thus, to position girls toward positive embodiment, families need to refuse to be "null" and instead play a critical role in identifying, challenging, and offsetting misogynistic messages.

REFERENCES

Alleva, J. M., Martijn, C., van Breukelen, G. J. P., Jansen, A., & Karos, K. (2015). Expand Your Horizon: A programme that improves body image and reduces self-objectification by training women to focus on body functionality. *Body Image, 15*, 81–89. doi:10.1016/j.bodyim.2015.07.001

American Psychological Association, Task Force on the Sexualization of Girls. (2010). *Report of the APA Task Force on the Sexualization of Girls*. Retrieved from https://www.apa.org/pi/women/programs/girls/report-full.pdf

Andrew, R., Tiggemann, M., & Clark, L. (2015). The protective role of body appreciation against media-induced body dissatisfaction. *Body Image*, *15*, 98–104. doi:10.10166/j.bodyim.2015.07.005

Andrew, R., Tiggemann, M., & Clark, L. (2016). Predictors and health-related outcomes of positive body image in adolescent girls: A prospective study. *Developmental Psychology*, *52*, 463–474. doi:10.1037/dev0000095

Calogero, R. M., Herbozo, S., & Thompson, J. K. (2009). Complimentary weightism: The potential costs of appearance-related commentary or women's self-objectification. *Psychology of Women Quarterly*, *33*, 120–132. doi:10.1111/j.1471-6402.2008.01479.x

Cook-Cottone, C. P., & Douglass, L. L. (2017). Yoga communities and eating disorders: Creating safe space for positive embodiment. *International Journal of Yoga Therapy*. Advance online publication. doi:10.17761/ijyt2017_methods_cook-cottone_epub

Cook-Cottone, C. P., & Guyker, W. M. (2018). The development and validation of the Mindful Self-Care Scale (MSCS): An assessment of practices that support positive embodiment. *Mindfulness*, *9*, 161–175. doi:10.1007/s12671-017-0759-1

Cox, A. E., Ullrich-French, S., Howe, H. S., & Cole, A. N. (2017). A pilot yoga physical education curriculum to promote positive body image. *Body Image*, *23*, 1–8. doi:10.1016/j.bodyim.2017.07.007

Dockendorff, S. A., Petrie, T. A., Greenleaf, C. A., & Martin, S. (2012). Intuitive Eating Scale: An examination among early adolescents. *Journal of Counseling Psychology*, *59*, 604–611. doi:10.1037/a0029962

Freeman, J. (1979). How to discriminate among women without really trying. In J. Freeman (Ed.), *Women: A feminist perspective* (2nd ed., pp. 194–208). Palo Alto, CA: Mayfield.

Gianturco, P., & Sangster, A. (2017). *Wonder girls: Changing our world*. Brooklyn, NY: powerHouse Books.

Hart, L. M., Damiano, S. R., & Paxton, S. J. (2016). Confident Body, Confident Child: A randomized controlled trial evaluation of a parenting resource for promoting healthy body image and eating patterns in 2- to 6-year old children. *International Journal of Eating Disorders*, *49*, 458–472. doi:10.1002/eat.22494

Hill, L., Peck, S. K., Wierenga, C. E., & Kaye, W. H. (2016). Applying neurobiology to the treatment of adults with anorexia nervosa. *Journal of Eating Disorders*, *4*, 31. doi:10.1186/s40337-016-0119-x

Impett, E. A., Schooler, D., & Tolman, D. L. (2006). To be seen and not heard: Femininity ideology and adolescent girls' sexual health. *Archives of Sexual Behavior*, *35*, 131–144. doi:10.1007/s10508-005-9016-0

Kearney, M. C. (2006). *Girls make media*. New York, NY: Oxford University Press.

Lamb, S., & Peterson, Z. D. (2012). Adolescent girls' sexual empowerment: Two feminists explore the concept. *Sex Roles*, *66*, 1–10. doi:10.1007/s11199-011-9995-3

Larson, N. I, Neumark-Sztainer, D., Hannan, P. J., & Story, M. (2007). Family meals during adolescence are associated with higher diet quality and healthful meal patterns during young adulthood. *Journal of the American Dietetic Association*, *107*, 1502–1510. doi:10.1016/j.jada.2007.06.012

Linehan, M. M. (2015). *DBT® skills training manual* (2nd ed.). New York, NY: Guilford Press.

Mahlo, L., & Tiggemann, M. (2016). Yoga and positive body image: A test of the embodiment model. *Body Image*, *18*, 135–142. doi:10.1016/j.bodyim.2016.06.008

Neff, K. D., & McGehee, P. (2010). Self-compassion and psychological resilience among adolescents and young adults. *Self and Identity, 9*, 225–240. doi:10.1080/15298860902979307

Neumark-Sztainer, D. (2005). Preventing the broad spectrum of weight-related problems: Working with parents to help teens achieve a healthy weight and a positive body image. *Journal of Nutrition Education and Behavior, 37*, S133–S139.

Neumark-Sztainer, D., Eisenberg, M. E., Fulkerson, J. A., Story, M., & Larson, N. I. (2008). Family meals and disordered eating in adolescents: Longitudinal findings from Project EAT. *Archives of Pediatrics and Adolescent Medicine, 162*, 17–22. doi:10.1001/archpediatrics.2007.9

Parker, S., Nichter, M., Nichter, M., Vuckovic, N., Sims, C., & Ritenbaugh, C. (1995). Body image and weight concerns among African American and white adolescent females: Differences that make a difference. *Human Organization, 54*, 103–114.

Pipher, M. (1994). *Reviving Ophelia: Saving the selves of adolescent girls.* New York, NY: Random House.

Piran, N. (2016). Embodied possibilities and disruptions: The emergence of the experience of embodiment construct from qualitative studies with girls and women. *Body Image, 18*, 43–60. doi:10.1016.j.bodyim.2016.04.007

Piran, N. (2017). *Journeys of embodiment at the intersection of body and culture: The developmental theory of embodiment.* San Diego, CA: Elsevier. doi:10.1016/c2015-0-04666-4

Roberts, T.-A., & Waters, P. L. (2004). Self-objectification and that "not so fresh feeling": Feminist therapeutic interventions for healthy female embodiment. *Women & Therapy, 27*, 5–21. doi:10.1300/J015v27n03_02

Satter, E. (2008). *Secrets of feeding a healthy family: How to eat, how to raise good eaters, how to cook* (2nd ed.). Madison, WI: Kelcy Press.

Smolak, L. (2010). Gender as culture: The meanings of self-silencing in women and men. In D. C. Jack & A. Ali (Eds.), *Silencing the self across cultures: Depression and gender in the social world* (pp. 129–145). New York, NY: Oxford University Press.

Smolak, L., Murnen, S. K., & Ruble, A. E. (2000). Female athletes and eating problems: A meta-analysis. *International Journal of Eating Disorders, 27*, 371–380. doi:10.1002/(sici)1098-108x(200005)27:4<371::aid-eat1>3.0.co;2-y

Tolman, D. L. (2012). Female adolescents, sexual empowerment and desire: A missing discourse of gender inequity. *Sex Roles, 66*, 746–757. doi:101007/s11199-012-0122-x

Tolman, D. L., & Porche, M. V. (2000). The Adolescent Femininity Ideology Scale: Development and validation of a new measure for girls. *Psychology of Women Quarterly, 24*, 365–376. doi:10.1111/j.1471-6402.2000.tb00219.x

Tribole, E., & Resch, E. (2012). *Intuitive eating: A revolutionary program that works* (3rd ed.). New York, NY: St. Martin's Press.

Tribole, E., & Resch, E. (2017). *The intuitive eating workbook: Ten principles for nourishing a healthy relationship with food.* Oakland, CA: New Harbinger.

Tylka, T. L., Calogero, R. M., & Daníelsdóttir, S. (2015). Is intuitive eating the same as flexible dietary control? Their links to each other and well-being could provide an answer. *Appetite, 95*, 166–175. doi:10.1016/j.appet.2015.07.004

Tylka, T. L., Eneli, I. U., Kroon Van Diest, A. M., & Lumeng, J. C. (2013). Which adaptive maternal eating behaviors predict child feeding practices? An examination with mothers of 2- to 5-year-old children. *Eating Behaviors, 14*, 57–63. doi:10.1016/j.eatbeh.2012.10.014

Tylka, T. L., Lumeng, J. C., & Eneli, I. U. (2015). Maternal intuitive eating as a moderator of the association between concern about child weight and restrictive child feeding. *Appetite, 95*, 158–165. doi:10.1016/j.appet.2015.06.023

Wood-Barcalow, N. L., Tylka, T. L., & Augustus-Horvath, C. L. (2010). "But I Like My Body": Positive body image characteristics and a holistic model for young-adult women. *Body Image, 7*, 106–116. doi:10.1016/j.bodyim.2010.01.001

23

Acceptance, Activism, and Freedom from Bullying

The Online Context

ANN FRISÉN, KRISTINA HOLMQVIST GATTARIO, AND SOFIA BERNE ■

The contexts in which we live our everyday lives play a major role in shaping the way we experience our bodies. Today, a substantial part of many people's everyday lives takes place online. Online contexts can be distinguished from other everyday contexts with regard to the conditions for identity explorations, self-presentations, and social interactions (Wängqvist & Frisén, 2016). Online, people interact in ways that were not possible earlier, such as by uploading and sharing texts and photos on social networking sites (SNSs). People also receive and make positive and negative appearance-related comments based on the texts and photos that are published online. Like offline contexts, online contexts are filled with stereotypical messages related to people's bodies and appearance. Therefore, the Internet and especially SNSs provide potent contexts for the formation of individuals' views of their bodies and appearance. In relation to this, research has found that more frequent exposure to the Internet, especially SNSs, is associated with poorer body image (Fardouly & Vartanian, 2016). However, it is not the use of the Internet per se that influences peoples' body image negatively, but what people experience on the Internet. For instance, research has found that extensive use of specific SNSs as well as being the victim of appearance-related cyberbullying are experiences that are associated with poorer body esteem (Frisén, Berne, & Lunde, 2013). However, little is known about the positive role that involvement in online contexts may play in body-related experiences.

First, this chapter covers appearance-related cyberbullying and elaborates on what can be done about this growing problem. The second part covers the positive aspects of body image–defining experiences online, for instance, body acceptance and body activism movements. Throughout the chapter, as much as possible, we use Swedish examples. The motive for this choice is that previously published examples of positive online activities in relation to body and appearance have often been from the United States and examples from other parts of the world have been lacking.

APPEARANCE-RELATED CYBERBULLYING: WHAT CAN BE DONE TO COUNTERACT IT?

Here, we explore young people's perceptions of appearance-related cyberbullying and how they think it can be stopped. The adolescents' perspectives on these matters are illustrated through focus group data that have not previously been presented elsewhere.

Victims' Appearance as the Main Target in Cyberbullying

Cyberbullying occurs through modern information and communication technology, especially through the Internet and mobile phones. It can, for example, involve nasty or offensive text messages or unfriendly information such as photos, videos, and text on SNSs, uploaded by the perpetrator. Cybervictims often report that they are being bullied because of their appearance (Mishna, Cook, Gadalla, Daciuk, & Solomon, 2010), and they also tend to experience poorer body esteem (Frisén et al., 2013; Landstedt & Persson, 2014; Shemesh & Heiman, 2016). Thus, in order to make the online context a more positive arena for body image and beyond, appearance-related cyberbullying needs to be stopped. This section therefore presents a focus group study of adolescents' perceptions of appearance-related cyberbullying and what they believe can be done to stop it. To our knowledge, there is no other qualitative investigation of appearance-related cyberbullying among adolescents, which is why this part of the chapter largely focuses on presenting the results from that specific focus group study. It should be noted that we start with some results from the focus group study that have previously been published (see Berne, Frisén, & Kling, 2014) and then continue with new findings that are presented for the first time.

Adolescents' Perceptions of Appearance-Related Cyberbullying

The adolescents in Berne et al.'s (2014) focus group study stated that being the target of appearance-related cyberbullying is common, especially for girls. Appearance-related cyberbullying was also considered to be a potent strategy when attempting to hurt girls, as they more often than boys are socialized to value themselves in terms of their appearance. Girls reported that they often received comments about being fat, while boys more frequently received comments on having or not having a muscular body. According to the adolescents, an important reason for engaging in appearance-related cyberbullying was to attain higher social status in the peer group. The study also showed that the girls and boys reacted differently when they were targets of appearance-related cyberbullying. Boys tended to act out or take no offense, while girls experienced poor self-esteem and feelings of depression. These findings align with previous studies (Frisén et al., 2013; Landstedt & Persson, 2014; Shemesh & Heiman, 2016) to indicate that being bullied over one's appearance online is associated with several negative consequences, including poorer body esteem. Thus, in order to make the online context an arena for positive body image–defining experiences, appearance-related cyberbullying needs to be stopped.

Adolescents' Views of How to Deal with Appearance-Related Cyberbullying

A thematic analysis was conducted on sections of the focus group material (see description of sample and method in Berne et al., 2014) where the adolescents shared their thoughts regarding what they would do to stop appearance-related cyberbullying. The analysis revealed two themes and two subthemes. The first theme was *Take a stand against appearance-related cyberbullying*. This theme was divided into two subthemes *Confronting the bully* and *Supporting the victim*. The second theme was *Technical solutions*.

Take a Stand Against Appearance-Related Cyberbullying

Many adolescents expressed that they would take a stand against appearance-related cyberbullying. First, many adolescents expressed that one way to stop appearance-related cyberbullying is to confront the bully online. For example, the adolescents suggested that if they read a negative comment directed at a victim's appearance, they could write a comment to the bully and question his or her action. This way to confront the bully is exemplified by the following statement of one of the boys: "You write back to the person who has written the negative comment—Stop, it's not fair." Furthermore, the adolescents explained that it might be more effective if several people jointly agreed to do this in order to make a bigger impression on the bully. However, it is important to point out that this activity may have the opposite effect than what was intended. We found in another focus group study with adolescents that sometimes confronting the bully can get out of hand, especially online, so that the parties involved retaliate against each other, neither wanting to give in, creating an escalating circle of aggression (Frisén & Berne, 2016). Future research could therefore benefit from focusing on how peers can defend a targeted friend online without it backfiring at them.

Second, focus group participants suggested ways to show support to a victim of appearance-related cyberbullying, for instance by writing supportive comments and giving many "likes." As one girl put it: "You can say 'It's not true and you look nice' and just say supportive things." Interestingly, a study among Irish adolescents found that strong friendship dynamics partially mediated the relationship between cyberbullying (overall, not only appearance related) and perceptions of feeling too fat, for both boys and girls (Kenny, Sullivan, Callaghan, Molcho, & Kelly, 2017). The authors suggested that it is possible that the cybervictims had received negative comments about their appearance and friends had supported the cybervictim by providing appearance reassurance during or subsequent to the cyberbullying situation. This finding indicates that positive peer relationships might have the potential to reduce the risk of body dissatisfaction among cybervictims.

Technical Solutions

Many adolescents also considered technical solutions against appearance-related cyberbullying, such as removing the bully from their friend list, blocking the sender, and reporting the incident to the provider of the service. Previous research has shown that it is helpful for adolescents to use technical solutions to deal with other types of cyberbullying (Raskauskas & Huynh, 2015), and this may also apply to appearance-related cyberbullying.

ACCEPTANCE AND ACTIVISM IN THE ONLINE CONTEXT

Next, we focus on ways to promote acceptance and positive body image in the online context. More specifically, we discuss how the online context, especially SNSs, may constitute an arena for exploration of alternative ideals, resistant communications, and body activism.

SNSs as Context for Exploration of Alternative Ideals and Resistant Communications

Before we elaborate on the positive aspects of SNSs, it should be noted that *overall* usage of SNSs is associated with negative body image and related adverse constructs (e.g., self-objectification, thin-ideal internalization, and disordered eating) (see Holland & Tiggemann, 2016, for a review). One possible explanatory factor is that individuals who engage in SNSs are also exposed to appearance-related cybervictimization. However, the online appearance culture per se is also suggested to have adverse effects on body image in that it encourages appearance-based social comparisons, which result in more negative body image (Holland & Tiggemann, 2016).

However, almost no studies have examined SNS usage and *positive* body image. This omission is significant because positive body image is not the opposite of negative body image but rather is a multifaceted construct distinct from low levels of negative body image (Tylka & Wood-Barcalow, 2015). Therefore, we cannot rely on the literature on SNS usage and negative body image to draw conclusions about how SNS usage relates to positive body image. Unfortunately, to date we have only found two studies that have investigated SNS usage in relation to a specific component of positive body image: body appreciation (Andrew, Tiggemann, & Clark, 2016; Lunde, 2013). Andrew and colleagues (2016) found that greater usage of appearance-related media (including SNSs) was associated with less body appreciation in young women. Lunde (2013) investigated adolescent girls' and boys' reading of fashion blogs (which can be categorized as appearance-related online media) and found no relationship between the extent to which they read these blogs and body appreciation. These discrepant findings indicate that more research is needed to understand the potential associations between SNSs and positive body image.

On a broader note, some researchers have emphasized that usage of SNSs, although being a context in which appearance is central, can promote other aspects of positive development, which may extend to body image and embodiment. For instance, a systematic review of research of online communication and adolescents' well-being identified several benefits of using SNS, including increased self-esteem, perceived social support, increased social capital, safe identity experimentation, and increased opportunity for self-disclosure (Best, Manktelow, & Taylor, 2014). While the authors did not specifically investigate the role of body image in relation to these benefits, several are linked to positive body image and embodiment through processes of improved self-image, social belonging, and feelings of agency (Piran, 2016). Consistent with these ideas, Gyberg and Lunde (2015) conducted an in-depth examination of the contents of adolescent girls' blog posts and suggested that this regular uploading of diary-style content and photos may provide girls with a sense of control over their own bodies and their presented selves. Even the specific acts of taking selfies, which are frequent components of adolescents' blogging, have been proposed as possibly promoting positive youth development. Indeed, some researchers suggested that taking selfies can be understood as a healthy expression of self-exploration, in which individuals, young women especially, are allowed to take space, embrace their femininity and sexuality, try different roles, and actually boost their self-esteem (e.g., Murray, 2015). In addition, it is notable that recent popular media have interpreted selfies as current "works of art" (BBC, 2017). Still, other researchers problematized the fact that many individuals present an idealized image of themselves in these photos (Toma & Hancock, 2010), and findings suggest that individuals who highly engage in manipulation of, and investment in, their selfies tend to experience more body dissatisfaction (McLean, Paxton, Wertheim, & Masters, 2015).

Future research will need to look further into SNS usage and the specific acts of blogging and taking selfies and how, when, and for whom these behaviors promote a positive body image. For instance, it may be that taking selfies that counteract stereotypical ideals (for instance, that are natural and unaltered) is less problematic for body image. Also, the organization Endangered Bodies, through its initiative Shape Your Culture (http://www.shapeyourculture.org.uk), has introduced the concept of "no-body selfies" as a positive way of challenging current ideals. No-body selfies are images of people that feature things that they feel describe them in that moment. Whereas traditional selfies present how we look from day to day, "no-body selfies may be about books we love, shoes we keep, things that we think 'say' things about us. A no-body selfie, is a step away from worry about how we look in a picture on the surface, it's a different way of describing ourselves to the world." (http://www.shapeyourculture.org.uk/?udt_portfolio=taking-a-no-body-selfie-2). Taking a no-body selfie can also be considered a form of online body activism.

Online Body Activism

With the proliferation of the Internet, the engagement in different types of activism has been made more accessible as any person with an online connection has the opportunity to start a thought-provoking blog, an online petition, or a social media protest, to give a few examples. Activism acts such as these have the potential to reach and engage thousands, or even millions, of people and thereby serve as an important step to achieve social and political change concerning important issues. Body activism is a growing phenomenon that typically includes efforts to encounter and change prevailing stereotypical appearance ideals and counteract objectified perspectives of the body. SNSs have become a powerful context where acts of body activism can take place through blogs, photos, online videos, and so on. In Sweden, body activists Natashja Blomberg (@ladydahmers) and Ebba Nilsson (@babe_ebba) publish powerful, nonnormative self-portraits and anecdotes and have become some of the most well-known Swedish activists, with many thousands of followers. A recent post by Natashja (http://ladydahmer.nu/) told of an experience she had on the crowded shuttle one morning when a man gave her his seat, probably thinking she was pregnant (though she is not). She wrote:

> What if this was a few years ago? I would have probably been washed by feelings of shame and humiliation. . . . [And now I thought] Yes! And I happily sat down. I bulged my belly and breathed heavily. . . . I got to sit down on the shuttle! (http://ladydahmer.nu/2017/march/fordelar-med-att-vara-tjock.html)

Another story of body activism pertains to 32-year-old Lina Ehrin, until then unknown, who in 2012 happened to flash her natural, unshaved axillary hair on national TV as the camera filmed the audience at the Swedish Eurovision song contest, where Lina appeared cheering for the winner with her arms raised. As many viewers expressed their disgust on SNSs, the Facebook riot *Ta håret tillbaka* ("Reclaim the Hair") encouraged thousands of Swedes to show their support for Lina and all women's right to decide on how to treat their own bodies by uploading photos of themselves flashing their axillary hair.

This is a powerful example of how social media activism can engage many people to fight in favor of nonnormative bodies to be present in the media. However, while researchers (e.g., Thompson & Heinberg, 1999) emphasize the potential of social activism to take control over media messages telling us to be skinny, fit, tanned, shaved, and so on, there is a dearth of studies conducted on body activism and its possible consequences for body image and embodiment. The few studies available have focused specifically on fat activism.

Fat Activism

Because activism is about changing stereotypical appearance ideals and overweight and obese individuals are strongly excluded from these ideals and stigmatized, a frequent type of body activism is fat activism. Central components of fat activism are fashion blogs and web magazines, in which women of size, referred to as "fatshionistas," illustrate practices of dressing up in fashionable clothes—hence taking space in a marketplace (the fashion industry) that tends to exclude and condemn fat people (Gurrieri & Cherrier, 2013).

While fat activism is a widespread phenomenon, we have only been able to find two studies that have examined it. In a netnographic study, Gurrieri and Cherrier (2013) analyzed the blog posts of five female fatshionistas in the Australian fat activism movement. Similarly, Afful and Ricciardelli (2015) analyzed the blog posts of four Canadian female fat acceptance bloggers. A common theme in the two studies was that the blog posts involved the process of "coming out as fat," that is, leaving feelings of shame and self-loathing behind and beginning to accept and embrace one's fat body. This, in turn, provided license to adorn and decorate the body, which was emphasized in blog activities using phrases such as "outfit of the day." Also, the practice of flaunting fat was a way for the women to reclaim their own body by affirming its visibility (i.e., I'm not ashamed of my body—I will not hide it). For the participating women, the fatshionista or fat acceptance community provided them with an alternative space of values, beliefs, lifestyles, and practices that disrupted thin normativity and gave them a sense of belonging.

How Can Online Body Activism Promote Positive Body Image in Its Followers?

If one of the motives of body activism is to reach large-scale social change, one may also discuss the potential positive effects on the many people that follow the activists' updates. To our knowledge, this has not been studied. We encourage research within this domain, with suggested avenues for future research presented next.

There are many possible ways in which taking part in activist material may enhance one's body image. For instance, engaging with body activist material can generate critical thinking and discussions about current ideals (i.e., media literacy), which is a strength that has been shown to protect body image (Mclean, Paxton, & Wertheim, 2016). Also, viewing people with nonnormative appearances appreciate their bodies and expose them publicly may encourage others to do the same. From a macrostructural perspective, online body activism increases the variety of body types visible in the media, which ultimately may help to change people's representations of beauty to include a wider range of sizes and appearances. One of the characteristics of positive body image is having a broad conceptualization of beauty (Tylka & Wood-Barcalow, 2015), and a broad conceptualization of beauty is connected to higher body appreciation, self-compassion, and body image quality of life as well as lower body surveillance, lower thin-ideal internalization, body comparison, and antifat attitudes (Tylka & Iannantuono, 2016; see also Chapter 5). Therefore, adopting a wider definition of beauty may help to promote positive body image in those who engage with activist material.

A discussable feature of the body activism movement, and the fat activism movement in particular, is that although the movement strives to change stereotypical ideals, they still revolve around appearance in many ways (e.g., selfies, fashion, flaunting fat). This is a paradox that was also raised by one of the fatshionistas in Gurrieri and Cherrier's (2013) study, who said that by participating in the study she realized just how much she still plays along with stereotypical beauty norms of always wearing something new, something fancy, and something that pushes boundaries. This paradox makes us wonder: Could body activism also be about *not* focusing on appearance, and how could such activism be expressed?

One possible way to think about this question is for activism to emphasize body functionality instead of appearance, as a functional perspective on the body has been found to promote positive body image in an experimental context (Alleva, Martijn, Van Breukelen, Jansen, & Karos, 2015). A recent study investigated the effects on women's body image of viewing two functionality-focused media campaigns: This Girl Can (Sport England, 2015) and #jointhemovement (Mulgrew, McCulloch, Farren, Prichard, & Lim, 2017; Queensland Government, 2016). These campaigns have been promoted online and show a diverse range of women with different body shapes and abilities demonstrating realistic depictions of exercise (e.g., body jiggling/sweating) in a nonobjectified manner. Results showed that both campaigns improved women's appearance satisfaction and exercise intent, but only the This Girl Can campaign improved women's functionality satisfaction (Mulgrew et al., 2017). Unfortunately, the positive effects were not maintained after the women viewed idealized media images or at follow-up 1 week later.

Another example of online body activism emphasizing body functionality in a somewhat different way is Swedish video blogger and comedienne Clara Henriksson, who, by herself (as opposed to large-scale media campaigns), critically and humorously discusses women's menstruation. For instance, in one of her videos, she argues that the Swedish government should subsidize sanitary protection for women in the name of gender equality (https://www.youtube.com/watch?v=NvCzWRCIPYE). Indeed, research has demonstrated an association between negative attitudes toward one's menstruation and self-objectification (Grose & Grabe, 2014), so online activism aimed at changing the stigma around menstruation may well be one way to enhance women's positive embodiment (Piran, 2016).

CONCLUSION

Like traditional media, it is arguably the case that social media are permeated by negative appearance-related messages affecting its users. This chapter highlighted strategies for adolescents to counteract appearance-related cyberbullying via taking a stand against the bully, offering support to the victim, and seeking technical solutions. Yet, a notable difference between traditional and social media is that traditional media feature models and celebrities, who represent the appearance culture and a profitable beauty industry, whereas social media include this aspect but are also shaped by their users as they feature the users themselves, their lives, and their pursuits. These conditions make some of the SNS contexts more malleable, less dependent on profit, and a more fertile ground for individual exploration of alternative ideals as well initiatives leading to large-scale social changes when it comes to appearance norms. This chapter presented different positive initiatives online, such as body acceptance and body activism movements, which may promote positive body image and embodiment. Diverse acts of online body activism are increasingly common, but to date, little empirical research has investigated this movement in relation to body image. Future research may investigate the specific contents and meanings of this growing movement, who engages in it, and if (and how) engaging in it may promote positive body image and embodiment.

REFERENCES

Afful, A. A., & Ricciardelli, R. (2015). Shaping the online fat acceptance movement: Talking about body image and beauty standards. *Journal of Gender Studies*, *24*, 453–472. doi:10.1080/09589236.2015.1028523

Alleva, J. M., Martijn, C., Van Breukelen, G. J. P., Jansen, A., & Karos, K. (2015). Expand Your Horizon: A programme that improves body image and reduces self-objectification by training women to focus on body functionality. *Body Image*, *15*, 81–89. doi:10.1016/j.bodyim.2015.07.001

Andrew, R., Tiggemann, M., & Clark, L. (2016). Predicting body appreciation in young women: An integrated model of positive body image. *Body Image*, *18*, 34–42. doi:10.1016/j.bodyim.2016.04.003

Berne, S., Frisén, A., & Kling, J. (2014). Appearance-related cyberbullying: A qualitative investigation of characteristics, content, reasons, and effects. *Body Image*, *11*, 527–533. doi:10.1016/j.bodyim.2014.08.006

BBC. (2017, March 31). Selfies get the art treatment. *Newsbeat*. Retrieved from http://www.bbc.co.uk/newsbeat/article/39459441/selfies-get-the-art-treatment

Best, P., Manktelow, R., & Taylor, B. (2014). Online communication, social media and adolescent wellbeing: A systematic narrative review. *Children and Youth Services Review*, *41*, 27–36. doi:10.1016/j.childyouth.2014.03.001

Fardouly, J., & Vartanian, L. R. (2016). Social media and body image concerns: Current research and future directions. *Current Opinion in Psychology*, *9*, 1–5. doi:10.1016/j.copsyc.2015.09.005

Frisén, A., & Berne, S. (2016). *Nätmobbning: Handbok för skolan*. Stockholm, Sweden: Natur & Kultur.

Frisén, A., Berne, S., & Lunde, C. (2013). Cybervictimization and body esteem: Experiences of Swedish children and adolescents. *European Journal of Developmental Psychology*, *11*, 331–343. doi:10.1080/17405629.2013.825604

Grose, R. G., & Grabe, S. (2014). Sociocultural attitudes surrounding menstruation and alternative menstrual products: The explanatory role of self-objectification. *Health Care for Women International, 35*, 677–694. doi:10.1080/07399332.2014.888721

Gurrieri, L., & Cherrier, H. (2013). Queering beauty: Fatshionistas in the fatosphere. *Qualitative Market Research: An International Journal, 16*, 276–295. doi:10.1108/13522751311326107

Gyberg, F., & Lunde, C. (2015). A revealing generation? Exploring the blogging of adolescent girls in Sweden. *Nordic Psychology, 67*, 46–64. doi:10.1080/19012276.2014.997782

Holland, G., & Tiggemann, M. (2016). A systematic review of the impact of the use of social networking sites on body image and disordered eating outcomes. *Body Image, 17*, 100–110. doi:10.1016/j.bodyim.2016.02.008

Kenny, U., Sullivan, L., Callaghan, M., Molcho, M., & Kelly, C. (2017). The relationship between cyberbullying and friendship dynamics on adolescent body dissatisfaction: A cross-sectional study. *Jornal of Health Psychology, 23*, 629–639. doi:10.1177/1359105316684939

Landstedt, E., & Persson, S. (2014). Bullying, cyberbullying, and mental health in young people. *Scandinavian Journal of Public Health, 42*, 393–399. doi:10.1177/1403494814525004

Lunde, C. (2013). Acceptance of cosmetic surgery, body appreciation, body ideal internalization, and fashion blog reading among late adolescents in Sweden. *Body Image, 10*, 632–635. doi:10.1016/j.bodyim.2013.06.007

Mishna, F., Cook, C., Gadalla, T., Daciuk, J., & Solomon, S. (2010). Cyber bullying behaviors among middle and high school students. *American Journal of Orthopsychiatry, 80*, 362–374. doi:10.1111/j.1939-0025.2010.01040.x

McLean, S. A., Paxton, S. J., & Wertheim, E. H. (2016). The role of media literacy in body dissatisfaction and disordered eating: A systematic review. *Body Image, 19*, 9–23. doi:10.1016/j.bodyim.2016.08.002

McLean, S. A., Paxton, S. J., Wertheim, E. H., & Masters, J. (2015). Photoshopping the selfie: Self photo editing and photo investment are associated with body dissatisfaction in adolescent girls. *International Journal of Eating Disorders, 48*, 1132–1140. doi:10.1002/eat.22449

Mulgrew, K. E., McCulloch, K., Farren, E., Prichard, I., & Lim, M. S. C. (2018). *This girl can #jointhemovement: Effectiveness of functionality-focused campaigns for women's body satisfaction and exercise intent. Body Image, 24,* 26–35.

Murray, D. C. (2015). Notes to self: The visual culture of selfies in the age of social media. *Consumption Markets and Culture, 18*, 490–516. doi:10.1080/10253866.2015.1052967

Piran, N. (2016). Embodied possibilities and disruptions: The emergence of the Experience of Embodiment construct from qualitative studies with girls and women. *Body Image, 18*, 43–60. doi:10.1016/j.bodyim.2016.04.007

Queensland Government. (2016). Start playing, stay playing. Retrieved from https://www.qld.gov.au/recreation/health/women-girls/

Raskauskas, J., & Huynh, A. (2015). The process of coping with cyberbullying: A systematic review. *Aggression and Violent Behavior, 23*, 118–125. doi:10.1016/j.avb.2015.05.019

Shemesh, D. O., & Heiman, T. (2016). Cyberbullying victimization in adolescents as related to body esteem, social support, and social self-efficacy. *Journal of Genetic Psychology, 178*, 28–43. doi:10.1080/00221325.2016.1195331

Sport England. (2015). This girl can. Retrieved from http://www.sportengland.org/our-work/national-work/this-girl-can/

Thompson, J. K., & Heinberg, L. J. (1999). The media's influence on body image disturbance and eating disorders: We've reviled them, now can we rehabilitate them? *Journal of Social Issues, 55*, 339–353. doi:10.1111/0022-4537.00119

Toma, C. L., & Hancock, J. T. (2010). Looks and lies: The role of physical attractiveness in online dating self-presentation and deception. *Communication Research, 37*, 335–351. doi:10.1177/0093650209356437

Tylka, T. L., & Iannantuono, A. C. (2016). Perceiving beauty in all women: Psychometric evaluation of the Broad Conceptualization of Beauty Scale. *Body Image, 17*, 67–81. doi:10.1016/j.bodyim.2016.02.005

Tylka, T. L., & Wood-Barcalow, N. L. (2015). What is and what is not positive body image? Conceptual foundations and construct definition. *Body Image, 14*, 118–129. doi:10.1016/j.bodyim.2015.04.001

Wängqvist, M., & Frisén, A. (2016). Who am I online? Understanding the meaning of online contexts for identity development. *Adolescent Research Review, 1*, 139–151. doi:10.1007/s40894-016-0025-0

24

Positive Body Image in People Living with Visible Differences

DIANA HARCOURT AND HEIDI WILLIAMSON ■

We use the term *visible difference* to refer to an appearance that deviates from "the norm," including, for example, congenital conditions (i.e., those present at birth, such as craniofacial conditions, including cleft lip and/or palate); and acquired differences, including skin conditions such as acne and psoriasis and the consequences of medical treatment (e.g., chemotherapy-induced hair loss [alopecia] due to cancer treatment) or injuries (e.g., scarring from burn injuries).

Appearing visibly different precipitates distinct social and personal challenges, and there is no doubt that these can have an enduring and negative impact on the psychological and social well-being of many, but this is by no means the complete picture. Increasingly, although still tentatively, the field is beginning to shift its research focus beyond the necessary work of highlighting the support needs of those who are struggling, to examining and learning from the experiences of those who not only manage these challenges but also experience positive embodiment as a result. This work is an important step toward developing a more balanced and complete understanding of the impact of a visible difference and, in turn, developing interventions to exploit this perspective, but there is still much more to be done. In this chapter, we discuss and share evidence illustrating examples of positive embodiment associated with a visible difference, we summarize common interventions currently advocated to promote adjustment to a visible difference, we suggest how these could be developed to encourage positive embodiment, and finally we provide directions for further research.

Accurate figures for the incidence of visible difference are hard to establish, but it has been estimated that, in the United Kingdom alone, more than a million people live with an appearance that is in some way "different" (https://www.changingfaces.org.uk). Most research in this field has focused on identifying the unique challenges and resultant difficulties facing this group, with the aim of targeting these trials and tribulations to alleviate distress. Challenges typically center on ongoing/painful treatment; dealing with the inquisitiveness and reactions of others; managing potential experiences of social discrimination and prejudice from strangers, peers, employers, and family (in the form of unwanted attention, abusive behavior, and negative appearance-based judgments); and overcoming concerns around initiating and maintaining intimate relationships (summarized by Rumsey & Harcourt, 2004). A study (the largest to date) by Rumsey et al. of 1,265 adults with a range of visible differences suggested that 30–50%, at some point across their life span, struggle with these challenges and report psychological difficulties that indicate poor adjustment, including social anxiety, avoidance, shame, and depressive symptoms (reported in full as an appendix in Clarke, Thompson, Jenkinson, Rumsey, & Newell, 2014).

ADJUSTMENT TO VISIBLE DIFFERENCE

A wide range of psychosocial factors and dynamic processes influence adjustment to visible difference (see Clarke et al., 2014; Moss & Rosser, 2012). Some of these were the focus of Rumsey et al.'s study with 1,265 adults referenced previously (reported in Clarke et al., 2014). More specifically, while demographics (age and gender) and the nature of the visible difference (e.g., type, severity, or whether it was present at birth or acquired at a later date) were influential, their contribution was relatively small in comparison to disposition, appearance-specific cognitions, and social factors. These psychosocial variables include levels of optimism and the degree to which individuals value and invest in appearance, fear being judged negatively by others, and feel socially supported and accepted despite their appearance. This study added to a body of evidence showing that adjustment to visible difference is associated with psychosocial factors that are amenable to change, rather than biological factors.

Rumsey et al.'s study, reported in Clarke et al. (2014), demonstrated that many adults with visible difference successfully manage the challenges they face. Yet, much of the work in this field is predominantly negative and potentially pathologizing. A more balanced, holistic approach toward understanding the challenges and support needs of this group would be invaluable in increasing our understanding of adjustment more fully and could, potentially, inform interventions for those who are negatively affected.

While our understanding of positive body image has developed considerably in recent years, there remains a dearth of rigorous research exploring the facets of positive body image among people with visible differences. Halliwell (2015) and Tiggemann (2015) have both highlighted the need for research that explores positive body image among individuals who have a visible difference. Positive body image is not simply the opposite of poor adjustment (i.e., it is not just the absence of difficulties and distress) or the inverse of poor body image (Bailey, Gammage, van Ingen, & Ditor, 2015; Tylka & Wood-Barcalow, 2015; see also Chapter 2); it encompasses positive gains and outcomes, such as holding favorable opinions of the body as well as respecting and feeling gratitude toward the body regardless of its appearance.

POSITIVE OUTCOMES ASSOCIATED WITH VISIBLE DIFFERENCE

Most of the limited existing research in this field has examined positive aspects of visible difference among samples of individuals with *specific* conditions or injuries, such as psoriasis (Fortune, Richards, Griffiths, & Main, 2005); Moebius syndrome (i.e., a neurological disorder primarily affecting the muscles that control facial expression and eye movement; Meyerson, 2001); and burn scarring. The last has arguably received the most attention in terms of positive outcomes, with studies and review articles identifying positive growth among some patients (see, e.g., Martin, Byrnes, McGarry, Rea, & Wood, 2017; L. M. McLean et al., 2015). However, both Egan, Harcourt, Rumsey, and The Appearance Research Collaboration (2011) and Thompson and Broom (2009) identified similarities in positive consequences and adjustment across participants with *various* disfiguring conditions, supporting previous research that has repeatedly found more similarities than differences in the experiences of people living with a range of visible differences.

Too often, studies focus on those with or without visible differences and treat them as two distinct groups, rarely acknowledging the potential overlaps and similarities between them, and assume the cause of appearance-related concerns are due to weight and shape (in body image research) or altered appearance (in visible difference research). Yet, a person with a burn could be unperturbed by the scars but bothered by other aspects of his or her appearance. Often, published research fails to consider whether participants in body image research might have a visible difference of some sort because this information is rarely gathered.

Despite these limitations, a small body of qualitative research has emerged that tentatively indicates the nature of positive outcomes as a consequence of unusual or altered looks. For example, Strauss and Fenson (2005) examined literary writings as primary sources of data to explore how adults with craniofacial conditions believed they had benefited from their experience. Notably, individuals attributed increased learning about others and themselves to their unique experience and recognized they had benefited from diverting energy and attention from appearance to other meaningful aspects of their lives. Similarly, a study with six young women whose appearance had been altered by cancer treatment described how participants experienced a positive shift in views about and expectations of their appearance, as well as the value they put on it: expressing increased satisfaction with their own appearance and a decrease in its importance (Wallace, Harcourt, Rumsey, & Foot, 2007). Participants in a study of 12 adults with a variety of disfiguring conditions who self-identified as well adjusted also described having an outlook on life that involved placing less importance on appearance (Egan et al., 2011).

A study of positive body image in college women who had an illness that affected their appearance (e.g., cancer) described how the participants' diagnosis had prompted them to become more respectful and caring of their body, as opposed to a previous emphasis on its appearance (Wood-Barcalow, Tylka, & Augustus-Horvath, 2010). Moreover, even when participants focused on their appearance, they were more appreciative. For example, one participant in Wood-Barcalow et al.'s (2010) study appreciated her hair because she anticipated losing it to chemotherapy. She declared, "Turns out it's not such a pain. It's naturally curly. It takes me hours to do it. But it's still my hair and I love it" (pp. 109–110). Likewise, some participants in Egan et al.'s (2011) study of adults with a range of disfigurements discussed valuing and caring for parts of their body that were unaffected by the visible difference. For example, a 45-year-old male interviewee who had the skin condition psoriasis stated, "It's encouraged me to put a bit of a higher priority on trying to take care of whatever physical assets I've got. . . . I try and keep fit and everything, I run a lot. I think I probably . . . having kept all my hair . . . probably err try and look after the things that are alright, you know" (Egan et al., 2011, p. 744).

Whereas previous research into the many conditions and traumatic injuries that shift a person's appearance further away from societal ideals typically reported negative outcomes, including poorer body image, Bailey et al.'s (2015) study exploring participants' experiences of spinal cord injury suggests a more complex picture. Body acceptance (and not dwelling on any limitations) was central to their experiences, influenced by factors including body appreciation, respect, and gratitude, and not focusing on physical appearance. Importantly, recognizing improvements in physical function and becoming more independent were significant in determining positive body image, as were having a broad conceptualization of what constituted beauty and being supported by others who were accepting of the participant's appearance and had a positive body image themselves. These findings resemble Rumsey et al.'s finding (reported in Clarke et al., 2014) that social acceptance is a key factor in adjustment. In an analysis of online blogs written by 10 people with burn scarring, Garbett, Harcourt, and Buchanan (2017) also reported the importance of appreciating the body's ability rather than focusing on its imperfections. For example, a woman with scars over 80% of her body said, "I have skin! That is good enough for me. I don't care what condition it's in—I have it." These findings reflect the gratitude for body functionality reported in earlier positive body image studies (e.g., Holmqvist & Frisén, 2012; Wood-Barcalow et al., 2010).

The findings from these studies dispel assumptions that people with an appearance that does not meet societal norms cannot value, appreciate, and love their bodies. Indeed, Tylka and Wood-Barcalow (2015) have previously stated that having a positive body image does not mean having a "perfect body," and Tiggemann (2015) referred to feeling comfortable with one's body, regardless of any "flaws." Clearly, positive body image can be important for people who have a visible difference, but as yet, this has not been considered in larger scale, quantitative research.

To our knowledge, the only study to date (Halliwell, Jarman, Tylka, Slater, & Harcourt, 2016) that has tested a model of positive body image among people with visible differences involved 375 women aged between 18 and 76 years, of whom 153 self-reported having a visible difference (19% congenital conditions, 28% acquired during childhood, and 53% acquired since adulthood). This study found that the acceptance model of positive body image and intuitive eating (Augustus-Horvath & Tylka, 2011; see also Chapters 2 and 7) was a good fit for both groups of women (those with and without a visible difference), with body acceptance by others contributing to positive body image and intuitive eating. The results also suggested that psychological inflexibility (i.e., a tendency to avoid emotions and not living with mindful awareness or in the service of chosen values) could be a useful addition to the model and a risk factor worthy of being targeted by interventions. However, the women disclosing visible differences reported significantly less favorable scores on measures of body appreciation, body surveillance, and body acceptance by others. These findings have implications for the development of interventions, suggesting that existing positive body image interventions could be beneficial but may need to be adapted to meet the additional, specific needs of people with visible differences. For example, we recommend (a) including strategies to build resilience to social stigma and promote social acceptance by family and peers in order to encourage investment in multiple self-concept domains, thereby putting appearance in its place; and (b) guidance on building an actionable, values-based approach to life. Because family members are likely to play a key role in each of these areas, research into parental and partner interventions to promote positive body image among both themselves and those with a visible difference is an area ripe for investigation and development.

INTERVENTIONS

To date, the majority of interventions to support those negatively affected by visible difference tend to center on cognitive behavioral therapy (CBT) and social interaction skills training (see Jenkinson, Williamson, Byron-Daniel, & Moss, 2015; Muftin & Thompson, 2013; and Norman & Moss, 2015, for systematic reviews of available support), and more recently research has begun exploring the suitability of acceptance and commitment therapy (ACT) for this population (Zucchelli et al., 2018). As yet, we are not aware of positive body image interventions developed or tested specifically with people with visible differences, despite the growing interest in positive body image more generally. The exploration of collective and unique factors of positive body image among people with and without a visible difference may inform the future development of interventions to support those who are affected by appearance-related concerns.

Interestingly, Lewis-Smith, Harcourt, and Diedrichs (2018) found that the body image intervention Set Your Body Free (S. A. McLean, Paxton, & Wertheim, 2011), which was originally developed for women in midlife but adapted in response to a survey of 169 women who had been treated for breast cancer, was acceptable and feasible to this group, and preliminary findings indicated potential improvements in body appreciation. This manualized intervention consists of seven weekly small-group sessions, facilitated by a clinical psychologist and a peer who had been diagnosed and treated for breast cancer in the past. It includes psychoeducation about the nature and causes of appearance-related anxiety and teaches cognitive behavioral strategies to manage negative appearance-related thoughts, promote acceptance of postsurgical appearance change, and manage anxiety around intimacy and disclosing an altered appearance to others. Further testing is needed to establish the effectiveness of this adapted intervention, but preliminary findings suggest that body appreciation can be improved among people struggling to adapt to an altered appearance.

LOOKING FORWARD

Given the relative dearth of research in this field, there are a wealth of possibilities for future studies that could have direct implications for the provision of care and support for people with visible differences. For example, the limited research to date has focused on adults; we still need to understand the predictors and consequences of positive body image among children and young people with visible differences. Likewise, there is a need to explore these issues among people from a variety of cultural backgrounds and lived experiences to consider how intersections of identity contribute to embodied experience (Tiggemann, 2015). Longitudinal research would also be useful to examine whether positive body image among people with visible differences is stable or fluctuating and which factors and processes might influence it at different times. Cohort studies, such as the cleft lip/palate cohort established by the Cleft Collective in the United Kingdom (Stock et al., 2016), would offer opportunities to examine the longitudinal profile and determinants of positive body image. Further research in this field could go some way toward balancing the current dominant focus on negative aspects of visible difference and challenging common assumptions that visible differences are necessarily a negative experience.

CONCLUSION

Greater consideration of positive body image among people living with visible differences is needed. This could offer exciting, novel perspectives that could usefully inform the future development of support and interventions and, importantly, challenge assumptions about the inevitability of negative body image among people whose appearance is in any way different or unusual.

REFERENCES

Augustus-Horvath, C. L., & Tylka, T. L. (2011). The acceptance model of intuitive eating: A comparison of women in emerging adulthood, early adulthood, and middle adulthood. *Journal of Counseling Psychology, 58*, 110–125. doi:10.1037/a0022129

Bailey, K. A., Gammage, K. L., van Ingen, C., & Ditor, D. S. (2015). "It's all about acceptance": A qualitative study exploring a model of positive body image for people with spinal cord injury. *Body Image, 15*, 24–34. doi:10.1016/j.bodyim.2015.04.010

Clarke, A., Thompson, A. R., Jenkinson, E., Rumsey, N., & Newell, R. (2014). *CBT for appearance anxiety: Psychosocial interventions for anxiety due to visible difference.* Oxford, England: Wiley.

Egan, K., Harcourt, D., Rumsey, N., & The Appearance Research Collaboration. (2011). A qualitative study of the experiences of people who identify themselves as having adjusted positively to a visible difference. *Journal of Health Psychology, 16*, 739–749. doi:10.1177/1359105310390246

Fortune, D., Richards, H., Griffiths, C., & Main, C. (2005). Adversarial growth in patients undergoing treatment for psoriasis: A prospective study of the ability of patients to construe benefits from negative events. *Psychology, Health & Medicine, 10*, 44–56. doi:10.1080/13548500512331315352

Garbett, K., Harcourt, D., & Buchanan, H. (2017). Using online blogs to explore positive outcomes after burn injuries. *Journal of Health Psychology, 22*, 1755–1766. doi:10.1177/1359105316638549

Halliwell, E. (2015). Future directions for positive body image research. *Body Image, 14*, 177–189. doi:10.1016/j.bodyim.2015.03.003

Halliwell, E., Jarman, H., Tylka, T., Slater, A., & Harcourt, D. (2016, June). *Examining the acceptance model of positive body image and intuitive eating among women with and without a visible difference.* Symposium presented at Appearance Matters 7, London, England.

Holmqvist, K., & Frisén, A. (2012). "I bet they aren't that perfect in reality": Appearance ideals viewed from the perspective of adolescents with a positive body image. *Body Image, 9*, 388–395. doi:10.1016/j.bodyim.2012.03.007

Jenkinson, E., Williamson, H., Byron-Daniel, J., & Moss, T. P. (2015). Systematic review: Psychosocial interventions for children and young people with visible differences resulting from appearance altering conditions, injury, or treatment effects. *Journal of Pediatric Psychology, 40*, 1017–1033. doi:10.1093/jpepsy/jsv048

Lewis-Smith, H., Diedrichs, P. C., & Harcourt, D. (2018). A pilot study of a body image intervention for breast cancer survivors. *Body Image, 27*, 21–31. doi:10.1016/j.bodyim.2018.08.006

Martin, L., Byrnes, M., McGarry, S., Rea, S., & Wood, F. (2017). Posttraumatic growth after burn injury in adults: An integrative literature review. *Burns, 43*, 459–470. doi:10.1016/j.burns.2016.09.021

McLean, L. M., Rogers, V., Kornhaber, R., Proctor, M. T., Kwiet, J., Streimer, J., & Vandervord, J. (2015). The patient-body relationship and the "lived experience" of a facial burn injury: A phenomenological inquiry of early psychosocial adjustment. *Journal of Multidisciplinary Healthcare, 8*, 377–387. doi:10.2147/jmdh.s89375

McLean, S. A., Paxton, S. J., & Wertheim, E. H. (2011). A body image and disordered eating intervention for women in midlife: A randomized controlled trial. *Journal of Consulting and Clinical Psychology, 79*, 751–758. doi:10.1016/j.ypsy.2012.06.045

Meyerson, M. D. (2001). Resiliency and success in adults with Moebius syndrome. *The Cleft Palate-Craniofacial Journal, 38*, 231–235. doi:10.1597/1545-1569(2001)038<0231:rasiaw>2.0.co;2

Moss, T., & Rosser, B. (2012). Adult psychosocial adjustment to visible differences: Physical and psychological predictors of variation. In N. Rumsey & D. Harcourt (Eds.), *The Oxford handbook of the psychology of appearance* (pp. 273–295). Oxford, England: Oxford University Press. doi:10.1093/oxfordhb/9780199580521.013.0022

Muftin, Z., & Thompson, A. R. (2013). A systematic review of self-help for disfigurement: Effectiveness, usability, and acceptability. *Body Image, 10*, 442–450. doi:10.1016/j.bodyim.2013.07.005

Norman, A., & Moss, T. P. (2015). Psychosocial interventions for adults with visible differences: A systematic review. *PeerJ, 2*, e870. doi:10.7717/peerj.870

Rumsey, N., & Harcourt, D. (2004). Body image and disfigurement: Issues and interventions. *Body Image, 1*, 83–97. doi:10.1016/s1740-1445(03)00005-6

Stock, N. M., Humphries, K., St. Pourcain, B., Bailey, M., Persson, M., Ho, K., . . . Sandy, J. (2016). Opportunities and challenges in establishing a cohort study: An example from cleft lip/palate research in the UK. *Cleft Palate-Craniofacial Journal, 53*, 317–325. doi:10.1597/14-306

Strauss, R. P., & Fenson, C. (2005). Experiencing the "good life": Literary views of craniofacial conditions and quality of life. *The Cleft Palate-Craniofacial Journal, 42*, 14–18. doi:10.1597/03-097.1.1

Thompson, A., & Broom, L. (2009). Positively managing intrusive reactions to disfigurement: An interpretative phenomenological analysis of naturalistic coping. *Diversity in Health and Care, 6*, 171–180.

Tiggemann, M. (2015). Considerations of positive body image across various social identities and special populations. *Body Image, 14*, 168–176. doi:10.1016/j.bodyim.2015.03.002

Tylka, T. L., & Wood-Barcalow, N. L. (2015). What is and what is not positive body image? Conceptual foundations and construct definition. *Body Image, 14*, 118–129. doi:10.1016/j.bodyim.2015.04.001

Wallace, M., Harcourt, D., Rumsey, N., & Foot, A. (2007). Managing appearance changes resulting from cancer treatment: resilience in adolescent females. *Psycho-Oncology, 16*, 1019–1027. doi:10.1002/pon.1176

Wood-Barcalow, N. L., Tylka, T. L., & Augustus-Horvath, C. L. (2010). "But I like my body": Positive body image characteristics and a holistic model for young-adult women. *Body Image, 7*, 106–116. doi:10.1016/j.bodyim.2010.01.001

Zucchelli, F., Donnelly, O., Williamson, H., & Hooper, N. (2018). Acceptance and commitment therapy for people experiencing appearance-related distress associated with a visible difference: Rationale and review of relevant research. *Journal of Cognitive Psychotherapy, 32*, 171–183. ISSN 0889-8391

SECTION III

Enhancing Positive Body Image and Embodiment

Interventions

25

Compassion-Based Interventions to Facilitate Positive Body Image and Embodiment

ALLISON C. KELLY, KATHRYN E. MILLER, KIRUTHIHA VIMALAKANTHAN, JESSICA R. DUPASQUIER, AND SYDNEY WARING ■

Body image is one of many life domains in which interest in the cultivation of compassion, in particular self-compassion, has grown tremendously over recent years. Across definitions, compassion is thought to involve noticing suffering *and* wanting to alleviate it (Gilbert, 2010; Strauss et al., 2016). *Self-compassion* is essentially compassion for one's own suffering and involves responding to personal distress with self-kindness rather than self-judgment, viewing one's struggles as part of the human condition instead of as unique to oneself, and noticing one's negative feelings in a mindful, observer-like way rather than becoming overwhelmed by them (Neff, 2003). A growing body of research now shows that self-compassion protects against eating pathology and body dissatisfaction and is associated with intuitive eating (see Chapter 7) and positive body image (see review by Braun, Park, & Gorin, 2016). Two primary compassion-based interventions have been applied to the realm of body image and eating: compassion-focused therapy (CFT; Gilbert, 2005; Goss & Allan, 2012) and self-compassion meditations from Neff and Germer's (2013) Mindful Self-Compassion program.

COMPASSION-FOCUSED THERAPY

Compassion-focused therapy is a transdiagnostic psychotherapeutic approach that was developed for individuals who struggle with high levels of shame and self-criticism (Gilbert & Irons, 2005). It grew partly out of the observation that these individuals often fail to respond to traditional cognitive interventions, reporting that although they understand the logic of an alternative thought such as "I am not to blame," they are unable to feel reassured by such a thought (Gilbert, 2010). Gilbert (2005) proposed that this difficulty feeling reassured often stems from a relative lack of warmth from caregivers early in life: Without memories of having been soothed by others, it is very difficult to self-soothe. CFT helps individuals develop a caring and compassionate orientation toward their struggles to better regulate their feelings of distress.

Theoretical Model Behind CFT

The tripartite model of affect regulation that underpins CFT provides a useful lens to understand positive and negative forms of body image. Supported by research in affective neuroscience (Depue & Morrone-Strupinsky, 2005; LeDoux, 1998), the theory postulates that there are at least three interacting but distinct affect regulatory systems. The first system is the threat system, which produces various forms of negative affect in response to cues of physical or interpersonal danger. It also triggers behaviors aimed at removing the source(s) of threat (LeDoux, 1998). In the body image domain, criticism or teasing from others about one's appearance acts as an input to the threat system. These experiences lead to feelings of shame and anxiety and behaviors such as hiding or trying to alter one's body to reduce the sense of feeling threatened. Importantly, in humans, the threat system can activate in response to internally generated cues of danger, such as self-criticizing one's appearance or imagining that others are judging one's body negatively (Gilbert, 2005, 2010). The threat system is therefore likely to be active when individuals experience negative body image, that is, when they feel dissatisfied with, critical toward, or ashamed of their bodies.

The two other affect regulatory systems produce distinct types of positive affect that might help to explain and distinguish between various forms of positive body image. The first system, referred to as the drive system, promotes high-arousal positive emotions such as pride, excitement, and vitality; it also stimulates striving-like behaviors (Depue & Morrone-Strupinsky, 2005). This system activates in response to signs of achievement and success, such as winning some sort of overt or covert competition. In humans, the drive system also activates in response to imagined success and achievement, for example, thinking that others see you as attractive. Therefore, in the body image domain, inputs to the drive system might include losing more weight than a fellow dieter, receiving a compliment for one's appearance, or assessing oneself as more attractive than a peer. In addition to stimulating activated forms of positive affect, these experiences might act as a source of motivation, for example, promoting dieting and exercise behaviors to maintain positive feelings about the self. Goss and Allan (2009) theorized that this system is overactive in individuals with anorexia nervosa (AN), who often feel proud of their weight control successes and become motivated to escalate their weight control efforts. Therefore, the drive system likely promotes a type of positive body image that is evaluation based and contingent on seeing oneself—or being seen by others—as successful in achieving certain standards of beauty and weight control.

The other positive affect system is the soothing system, and this likely underpins more acceptance-based forms of positive body image such as body image flexibility, defined as accepting one's appearance shortcomings without letting them interfere with desired life pursuits (see Chapter 4), and body appreciation, which refers to valuing and respecting one's body for its unique characteristics and the functions it serves (see Chapter 2). The soothing system produces lower arousal positive emotions, such as feelings of reassurance, calmness, and contentedness (Gilbert, 2005, 2010). This system is thought to activate in response to cues that one is safe and can rest, without needing to strive or compete. *Inter*personal inputs to the soothing system include cues of acceptance, warmth, and care from others, whereas *intra*personal inputs might include images and memories of others as compassionate, as well as self-compassionate feelings and self-talk (Gilbert, 2005). Therefore, treating one's body in a kind and caring way (e.g., providing it with the nutrients it needs rather than eating restrictively, allowing oneself a day off from exercise, and being compassionate toward one's body image struggles) should stimulate the soothing system. The soothing system produces a sense that "I am okay as I am," whether or not one is meeting standards of beauty or outperforming others in attractiveness.

CFT-Based Interventions

Although not specifically developed to promote positive body image, the CFT approach has been adapted for individuals who have eating disorders and thus have extreme forms of body dissatisfaction (Gale, Gilbert, Read, & Goss, 2014; Goss & Allan, 2012). A clinician working from a CFT perspective generally spends time with the client formulating his or her difficulties by making use of the tripartite model of affect regulation reviewed previously (Goss & Allan, 2012). Special attention is paid to the client's tendencies to self-criticize and to understand the developmental origins of this self-criticism as well as its past and current functions (Gale et al., 2014; Gilbert & Irons, 2005). In the CFT model, self-criticism is understood as a self-protective way of coping with a sense of threat. As applied to body image, for example, someone who was teased for her appearance might come to view her body in a judgmental way, which would serve the purpose of motivating her to alter her body to prevent continued criticism from others. The CFT clinician helps clients recognize these initially adaptive functions of their self-criticism while also coming to understand the negative consequences the self-criticism may be having now, for example, a harsh, relentless focus on undereating, an inability to feel accepting of one's body, and perpetual feelings of shame. CFT does not view self-criticism as simply negative thoughts but instead sees it as a harsh, dominant mentality that habitually becomes activated in relation to oneself. Therefore, instead of challenging the self-criticism as in standard cognitive interventions, the

CFT therapist helps the client develop compassion for this "critical self" and the fears that drive it (Gilbert, 2005, 2010).

It is important to recognize, however, that self-critical individuals will often feel afraid of having compassion for themselves and opening themselves up to receiving compassion from others (Gilbert, McEwan, Matos, & Rivis, 2011). They worry, for example, that they are undeserving of compassion or that having or allowing compassion for self will lead to a drop in personal standards. Individuals with eating disorders have elevated fears of self-compassion, and these fears contribute to the severity and persistence of their symptoms (Kelly, Carter, Zuroff, & Borairi, 2013; Kelly, Vimalakanthan, & Carter, 2014). Therefore, a key part of CFT is compassionately exploring these fears with clients while also helping them to experiment with facing their fears of compassion through compassionate mind-training exercises.

Compassionate mind-training exercises help individuals adopt a more compassionate stance toward themselves and others (Gilbert & Irons, 2005). Mindfulness and breathing are used to slow the sympathetic nervous system and activate the parasympathetic nervous system to reduce threatened feelings (Gilbert, 2010). CFT also makes use of imageries in which one vividly brings to mind images of compassion, for example, an image of a compassionate other, focusing on how his or her presence makes you feel. Increasingly, CFT focuses on helping individuals cultivate their "compassionate self"—the part of self that is wise, compassionate, and courageous—and does this through imagery (i.e., imagining one's ideal compassionate self), chair work (i.e., having the client move to a different "compassionate" chair and respond to the critical and criticized self from there), letter writing, and thought records (Gilbert, 2010).

In self-compassionate letter writing, the client writes him- or herself a letter from the perspective of his or her caring, compassionate part of self. For example: "I'm sorry to hear how much you're struggling with your body image these days. It's really hard to feel so preoccupied with one's body because there's no escaping it, so it's understandable that these feelings are getting in the way of school. Try and remind yourself that lots of people struggle with their body image and that these difficult feelings come and go." CFT also makes use of thought records, but rather than challenging self-critical thoughts with logic (i.e., evidence for and against the negative thoughts), the therapist guides the client to shift into his or her compassionate self mindset and to respond to the self-criticism from this perspective (Gilbert, 2010; Gilbert & Irons, 2005). For example, in response to the thought, "I'm fat and ugly," a client would cultivate the "compassionate self" to evoke feelings of warmth and care and might say, "It is really hard to feel this way. I will try to be more caring toward myself, and encourage myself to eat if I'm hungry, even if a part of me wants to restrict my eating." The motivational and emotional place from which this statement originates is central as this will be more powerful at shifting affect than the content of the statement itself. Finally, as evident from this last example, CFT encourages clients to make behavior changes that, while difficult and scary, are important for long-term well-being. Cultivating the compassionate self helps to bring the courage needed for these actions.

In sum, compassionate mind-training activities help clients learn how to shift into a compassionate mindset and to really "feel for" themselves, rather than working with their struggles from a purely cognitive perspective. By enacting this shift in mindsets, clients are able to activate their soothing system and feel reassured, which can help them better regulate body image distress and also experience more acceptance-based forms of positive body image. In this sense, compassionate mind-training exercises can be seen as cultivating positive embodiment. Individuals are training themselves to strengthen their compassionate perspective vis-à-vis themselves and their struggles and to inhabit their bodies from this compassionate place.

Empirical Research on CFT

Studies testing the theoretical model behind CFT have generally supported its key tenets, showing that individuals with eating disorders who have greater capacities for self-compassion or who experience gains in self-compassion through treatment have better outcomes in terms of overall symptoms and body image concerns (Kelly, Carter, & Borairi, 2014; Kelly et al., 2013). Gale and colleagues (2014) conducted the first and largest CFT treatment outcome study in eating disorders. This was an effectiveness study of 99 outpatients (95 females) at an eating disorders program who received a 20-week, group-based treatment consisting of psychoeducation and cognitive behavioral therapy (CBT) combined with CFT-based psychoeducation and intervention. Previously, this center had relied almost exclusively on CBT, so the integration of CFT was new. The authors found that across patients, there were improvements over time in eating disorder symptoms, including weight and shape concerns, and overall well-being. These effects were most pronounced among patients with bulimia nervosa (BN), who also had the highest recovery rate at 73% by the end of the 20 weeks, as compared to 21% of those with AN and 30% of those with an eating disorder not otherwise specified (EDNOS). This study showed promising results regarding the integration of CFT and CBT for improving symptoms, body image concerns, and well-being among individuals with an eating disorder. However, there was no comparison group, and the study design makes it difficult to know how much, if at all, the addition of CFT to the treatment accounted for patient outcomes.

Kelly, Wisniewski, Martin-Wagar, and Hoffmann (2017) conducted a pilot randomized controlled trial (RCT) in a sample of 22 female outpatients with a variety of eating disorders. They were randomly assigned to 12 weeks of an empirically supported treatment as usual (TAU), involving weekly individual therapy (CBT and dialectical behavioral therapy) or TAU plus a weekly CFT group. Participants in CFT plus TAU had greater increases in self-compassion and larger decreases in fears of becoming self-compassionate, fears of receiving compassion, and global eating pathology as measured by the Eating Disorder Examination Questionnaire (EDE-Q) composite of weight concerns, shape concerns, eating concerns, and dietary restraint. Mean EDE-Q Global scores post-CFT resembled those seen in community samples, suggesting clinically significant improvements took place. The CFT group also demonstrated high acceptability and feasibility; it had an average "usefulness" rating of 88% and retained 82% of participants (vs. 72% in TAU alone). The study had a small sample and did not control for the additional therapy time and group support in the CFT condition. Nevertheless, the design made it possible to isolate the incremental gains associated with adding CFT to TAU.

Kelly and Carter (2015) conducted a brief RCT of a CFT-based self-help intervention for individuals with binge eating disorder (BED). Forty-one individuals (34 females) were randomly assigned to 3 weeks of a CFT-based self-compassion training intervention, CBT-based behavioral strategies intervention, or a wait-list control condition. In the two intervention conditions, participants were asked to plan and monitor their eating and were educated about the importance of regular, flexible eating during the day. In the self-compassion condition, participants were asked to respond to urges to binge with a self-compassionate inner dialogue, whereas those in the behavioral strategies condition were asked to engage in an activity that was incompatible with binge eating. Both treatments reduced binge eating more than the control condition, but the self-compassion condition was most effective at increasing self-compassion and also at reducing global eating pathology and weight concerns as measured by the EDE-Q. These results support the relative efficacy of CFT-based self-help interventions for individuals with BED, but the small sample size and brief intervention period make replication necessary.

Another study examined whether a CFT-based intervention would promote greater motivation for treatment among individuals with AN who commonly deny the seriousness of their illness. Kelly and Waring (2018) randomly assigned 40 women who met research criteria for AN, but who were not yet receiving specialized treatment, to 2 weeks of a wait-list control group or a CFT intervention that involved writing oneself a daily self-compassionate letter about one's struggles. Over the 2 weeks, participants in the CFT-based intervention experienced greater decreases in fears of self-compassion, fears of receiving compassion, and global and body shame, as well as greater increases in self-compassion and autonomous motivation to seek treatment for their eating and body image problems (Kelly & Waring 20178. These preliminary findings suggest that among women with restrictive eating disorders, brief CFT-inspired interventions may help to reduce some of the negative experiences of self that perpetuate eating disorder symptoms, while promoting attitudes that are more positive that might facilitate treatment seeking.

Three studies examined structured group treatments that integrated elements from CFT with mindfulness (see Chapter 29) and acceptance and commitment therapy (see Chapter 27), where approximately two to three treatment sessions were compassion focused. Pinto-Gouveia et al. (2017) studied 36 overweight and obese women with BED and found that those who received 12 sessions of this BEfree group treatment experienced improvements in binge eating, body image flexibility, and other indicators of psychological functioning, whereas the wait-list control group experienced no such gains. Palmeira, Pinto-Gouveia, and Cunha (2017b) studied a similar 12-session treatment, Kg-Free, which was adapted for overweight and obese individuals *without* binge eating. Among 59 women, adding Kg-Free to TAU improved outcomes such as weight self-stigma (i.e., a sense that one is stigmatized for one's weight); weight-related experiential avoidance (i.e., avoiding thoughts and feelings about one's weight); health-related quality of life; exercise; and body mass index more than a TAU-only condition. They also found that 53 women who completed Kg-Free had improved health and psychological functioning, including lowered shame and self-judgment and greater quality of life, mindfulness, and self-compassion, at 3-month follow-up (Palmeira, Pinto-Gouveia, & Cunha, 2017a). These studies add to the growing literature supporting the applicability of CFT to individuals with eating, weight, and body image difficulties, although the specific contribution of CFT to the treatments is unknown.

A final study investigated a CFT-inspired intervention for body image, but one in which the focus was on increasing compassionate feelings toward *others* (Vimalakanthan, Kelly, & Trac, 2018). This study recruited 119 women who endorsed making frequent appearance-based social comparisons. Participants were taught one of three self-help strategies in the lab and were instructed to practice their assigned strategy every time they made an unfavorable appearance comparison over the subsequent 48-hour period. The compassion condition guided participants to shift their mindset to a caregiving one and to generate well wishes and feelings of warmth toward their comparison target. The competition condition asked participants to identify nonappearance domains in which they were superior to their comparison target (e.g., intelligence, personality). Finally, the control condition asked participants to distract themselves by counting backward from 50 in threes. Findings revealed that participants across conditions showed decreases in body dissatisfaction, restrained eating, and body, eating, and exercise comparisons; however, those who were higher in social comparison orientation (i.e., who were generally more focused on comparing themselves to others) fared best in the compassion intervention (Vimalakanthan et al., 2018). These results suggest that adopting a compassionate attitude toward individuals who normally threaten one's body image may have important benefits for young women who are highly comparison oriented. Findings are the first to suggest that in the body image and eating domain, there are internal benefits to practicing outward compassion.

Summary and Future Research

Preliminary research on CFT-based interventions for eating disorders and body image suggests that these interventions are beneficial. They have been found to reduce eating pathology, body dissatisfaction, and other negative internal processes that may undermine positive embodiment. These include shame, self-judgment, fears of compassion, weight-related self-stigma, and weight-related experiential avoidance. CFT-based interventions have also been found to increase general positive psychological functioning and variables that should theoretically be associated with greater positive embodiment, including self-compassion, mindfulness, well-being, and in one study (Pinto-Gouveia et al., 2017), body image flexibility. There is nevertheless a need for more empirical research on CFT-based interventions and for continued investigations into their impact on positive body image variables. Only two studies to date have included males (Gale et al., 2014; Kelly & Carter, 2015), and most have not followed up with participants after the intervention period. The field would therefore benefit from longer studies in larger, more diverse samples. Although CFT is not meant to be a stand-alone treatment (Gilbert & Irons, 2005), it may be useful for future studies to more systematically isolate the effects of CFT interventions on body image outcomes.

SELF-COMPASSION MEDITATIONS

Two published studies (Albertson, Neff, & Dill-Shackleford, 2015; Toole & Craighead, 2016) have examined the efficacy of self-compassion meditation interventions for body image based on Neff and Germer's (2013) Mindful Self-Compassion program. In this program, loving-kindness meditations, which involve directing compassion and well wishes toward others and self (Salzberg, 2002), are adapted to specifically target self-compassion. In both published studies, the authors investigated the impact of three 20-minute self-compassion meditations: (a) compassionate body scan, which involves slowly scanning each body part from toe to head with compassionate awareness; (b) affectionate breathing, which involves mindfully breathing in affection and kindness for self and breathing out affection and kindness for others; and (c) self-compassion/loving kindness, which involves bringing to mind a source of inadequacy or suffering and then repeating various compassionate and self-compassionate statements (e.g., "May I be safe," "May we all be happy") (for audio files, see https://www.self-compassion.org).

Albertson et al. (2015) tested the impact of these meditations in a 3-week online study of women aged 18 to 60 who identified as having body image concerns. Nearly 500 women were recruited from the Internet and were randomly assigned to the intervention condition or a wait-list control condition. Those in the intervention condition were asked to perform alternating versions of the above-mentioned meditations daily for 3 weeks. Attrition in this study was high at nearly 50%, but this rate did not differ between the two groups. Study completers in the meditation group, compared to those in the control group, experienced greater decreases in body dissatisfaction, body shame, and appearance-contingent self-worth and greater increases in body appreciation, with some evidence that gains were sustained 3 months later (Albertson et al., 2015). Notably, increases in self-compassion over the study were positively associated with improvements in all other outcomes. Furthermore, the number of days per week that participants reported meditating positively predicted the increase in body appreciation they experienced. The authors suggested that frequent meditation might have promoted a kinder, more compassionate awareness of one's body and thereby facilitated body appreciation (Albertson et al., 2015).

Toole and Craighead (2016) conducted a similarly designed study but sought to overcome Albertson et al.'s (2015) high dropout rate by reducing the intervention period from 1 weeks to 1 week and by including in-lab sessions. Participants were 80 college women who endorsed body image concerns. In their first lab visit, participants assigned to the intervention condition practiced their first assigned meditation and were then instructed to meditate daily for a week. The wait-list control condition received the same in-lab session 1 week later. Attrition in this study was low, at 4.6%. Both conditions showed improvements in body shame, body dissatisfaction, and self-compassion over the study week. However, body appreciation, body surveillance, and appearance-contingent self-worth all improved more in the meditation condition than the control condition. Two subgroups emerged in the intervention condition: those who did not meditate after the in-lab session (57.3%) and those who did (mean [*M*] = 4.53 days; standard deviation [*SD*] = 1.74). Interestingly, though, these subgroups did not differ in how useful they perceived the intervention to be or in the gains they experienced over the week (Toole & Craighead, 2016).

Toole and Craighead's (2016) results suggest there may be no more body image value to meditating once versus daily over a week's time. This finding parallels Albertson et al.'s (2015) finding that most outcomes, except body appreciation, were unrelated to participants' time spent meditating. Future research should further examine how frequently body-concerned individuals need to meditate to experience gains and whether this differs for negative versus positive body image outcomes. It is also surprising that although the meditation condition was more effective at improving certain outcomes in Toole and Craighead's (2016) study, other outcomes improved equally across both the intervention and wait-list conditions. Perhaps the face-to-face contact participants had with the research team and the short 1-week wait in this study made control participants more engaged and hopeful, contributing to improved body image and self-compassion. Future research should compare this meditation intervention to another active intervention to determine the former's specific effects on body image. Of note, body appreciation improved more in the meditation intervention than the control condition in both studies, which supports the idea that cultivating self-compassion can lead to greater respect for one's body, an important element of positive embodiment. Together, results from these studies offer preliminary support for the use of self-compassion–based meditations as a means of improving women's body image.

CONCLUSION

Compassion-based interventions typically aim to increase individuals' ability to treat themselves with compassion in the face of personal distress. As this relates to body image, these interventions focus on both alleviating the high levels of shame and self-criticism associated with pathological body image dissatisfaction and increasing feelings of acceptance and kindness toward the self in the face of body image distress. Two primary compassion-based interventions, CFT and self-compassion meditations, have garnered growing empirical support for their effectiveness in reducing maladaptive body image processes (i.e., self-criticism, body dissatisfaction, eating pathology, appearance comparisons) and promoting certain positive processes (i.e., body appreciation, body image flexibility). It will nevertheless be important for researchers to further substantiate the benefits of compassion interventions on positive body image outcomes. Additional future steps will be to test compassion-based interventions in larger and more diverse samples, to use longitudinal designs to test retention of treatment effects, and to understand the mechanisms by which improved capacities for self-compassion and compassion for others may lead to greater positive embodiment and positive body orientation.

REFERENCES

Albertson, E. R., Neff, K. D., & Dill-Shackleford, K. E. (2015). Self-compassion and body dissatisfaction in women: A randomized controlled trial of a brief meditation intervention. *Mindfulness*, *6*, 444–454. doi:10.1007/s12671-014-0277-3

Braun, T. D., Park, C. L., & Gorin, A. (2016). Self-compassion, body image, and disordered eating: A review of the literature. *Body Image*, *17*, 117–131. doi:10.1016/j.bodyim.2016.03.003

Depue, R. A., & Morrone-Strupinsky, J. V. (2005). A neurobehavioral model of affiliative bonding: Implications for conceptualizing a human trait of affiliation. *Behavioral Brain Science*, *28*, 313–350. doi:10.1016/j.bodyim.2016.03.003

Gale, C., Gilbert, P., Read, N., & Goss, K. (2014). An evaluation of the impact of introducing compassion focused therapy to a standard treatment programme for people with eating disorders. *Clinical Psychology & Psychotherapy*, *21*, 1–12. doi:10.1002/cpp.1806

Gilbert, P. (2005). Compassion and cruelty: A biopsychosocial approach. In P. Gilbert (Ed.), *Compassion: Conceptualisations, research, and use in psychotherapy* (pp. 1–74). London, England: Routledge.

Gilbert, P. (2010). *Compassion focused therapy: Distinctive features*. London, England: Routledge.

Gilbert, P., McEwan, K., Matos, M., & Rivis, A. (2011). Fears of compassion: Development of three self-report measures. *Psychology and Psychotherapy: Theory, Research and Practice*, *84*, 239–255. doi:10.1348/147608310X526511

Gilbert, P., & Irons, C. (2005). Focused therapies and compassionate mind training for shame and self-attacking. In P. Gilbert (Ed.), *Compassion: Conceptualisations, research and use in psychotherapy* (pp. 263–325). Hove, England: Routledge.

Goss, K., & Allan, S. (2009). Shame, pride and eating disorders. *Clinical Psychology & Psychotherapy*, *16*, 303–316. doi:10.1002/cpp.627

Goss, K., & Allan, S. (2012). An introduction to compassion-focused therapy for eating disorders (CFT-E). In J. R. E. Fox & K. P. Goss (Eds.), *Eating and its disorders* (pp. 303–314). Chichester, England: Wiley.

Kelly, A. C., & Waring, S. V. (2018). A feasibility study of a 2-week self-compassionate letter-writing intervention for nontreatment seeking individuals with typical and atypical anorexia nervosa. *International Journal of Eating Disorders.* doi: 10.1002/eat.22930.

Kelly, A. C., & Carter, J. C. (2015). Self-compassion training for binge eating disorder: A pilot randomized controlled trial. *Psychology and Psychotherapy: Theory, Research and Practice, 88,* 285–303. doi:10.1111/papt.12044

Kelly, A. C., Carter, J. C., & Borairi, S. (2014). Are improvements in shame and self-compassion early in eating disorders treatment associated with better patient outcomes? *International Journal of Eating Disorders, 47,* 54–64. doi:10.1002/eat.22196

Kelly, A. C., Carter, J. C., Zuroff, D. C., & Borairi, S. (2013). Self-compassion and fear of self-compassion interact to predict response to eating disorders treatment: A preliminary investigation. *Psychotherapy Research, 23,* 252–264. doi:10.1080/10503307.2012.717310

Kelly, A. C., Vimalakanthan, K., & Carter, J. C. (2014). Understanding the roles of self-esteem, self-compassion, and fear of self-compassion in eating disorder pathology: An examination of female students and eating disorder patients. *Eating Behaviors, 15,* 388–391. doi:10.1016/j.eatbeh.2014.04.008

Kelly, A. C., Wisniewski, L., Martin-Wagar, C., & Hoffman, E. (2017). Group-based compassion-focused therapy as an adjunct to outpatient treatment for eating disorders: A pilot randomized controlled trial. *Clinical Psychology & Psychotherapy, 24,* 475–487. doi:10.1002/cpp.2018

LeDoux, J. (1998). *The emotional brain.* London, England: Weidenfeld and Nicolson.

Neff, K. D. (2003). Self-compassion: An alternative conceptualization of a healthy attitude toward oneself. *Self and Identity, 2,* 85–101. doi:10.1080/15298860390129863

Neff, K. D., & Germer, C. K. (2013). A pilot study and randomized controlled trial of the mindful self-compassion program. *Journal of Clinical Psychology, 69,* 28–44. doi:10.1002/jclp.21923

Palmeira, L., Cunha, M., & Pinto-Gouveia, J. (2017a). Processes of change in quality of life, weight self-stigma, body mass index and emotional eating after an acceptance-, mindfulness-and compassion-based group intervention (Kg-Free) for women with overweight and obesity. *Journal of Health Psychology,* Jan 1, 1359105316686668. E-pub ahead of print. doi:10.1177/1359105316686668

Palmeira, L., Pinto-Gouveia, J., & Cunha, M. (2017b). Exploring the efficacy of an acceptance, mindfulness and compassionate-based group intervention for women struggling with their weight (Kg-Free): A randomized controlled trial. *Appetite, 112,* 107–116. doi:10.1016/j.appet.2017.01.027

Pinto-Gouveia, J., Carvalho, S. A., Palmeira, L., Castilho, P., Duarte, C., Ferreira, C., . . . Costa, J. (2017). BEfree: A new psychological program for binge eating that integrates psychoeducation, mindfulness, and compassion. *Clinical Psychology & Psychotherapy, 24,* 1090–1098. doi:10.1002/cpp.2072

Salzberg, S. (2002). *Lovingkindness: The revolutionary art of happiness.* Boston, MA: Shambhala.

Strauss, C., Taylor, B. L., Gu, J., Kuyken, W., Baer, R., Jones, F., & Cavanagh, K. (2016). What is compassion and how can we measure it? A review of definitions and measures. *Clinical Psychology Review*, *47*, 15–27. doi:10.1016/j.cpr.2016.05.004

Toole, A. M., & Craighead, L. W. (2016). Brief self-compassion meditation training for body image distress in young adult women. *Body Image*, *19*, 104–112. doi:10.1016/j.bodyim.2016.09.001

Vimalakanthan, K., Kelly, A. C., & Trac, S. (2018). From competition to compassion: A caregiving approach to intervening with appearance comparisons. *Body Image*, *25*, 148–162. doi:10.1016/j.bodyim.2018.03.003

26

Emotion-Focused Therapy to Facilitate Positive Body Image and Embodiment

IRYNA IVANOVA ■

Emotion-focused therapy (EFT) is an empirically supported, experiential approach for depression (Watson, Gordon, Stermac, Kalogerakos, & Steckley, 2003); trauma (Paivio, Jarry, Chagigiorgis, Hall, & Ralston, 2010); and couples in distress (Johnson, Hunsley, Greenberg, & Schindler, 1999). Over the past 5–10 years, EFT has begun to be recognized as a promising approach to treating eating disorders (EDs) and improving body image in adolescents and adults (Dolhanty & Greenberg, 2007; Lafrance Robinson, Dolhanty, & Greenberg, 2015). EFT has been indicated due to the reported difficulties in emotion regulation in individuals with ED symptoms and related body image disturbances (Dolhanty & Greenberg, 2007). Enhancing the capacity to regulate emotions could reduce the reliance on disordered eating patterns and body preoccupation as a way of coping with unpleasant feelings and facilitate a more positive way to inhabit the body and relate to one's emotions. This chapter begins with an overview of emotion regulation and dysregulation and highlights possible links between emotion regulation deficits, negative body image, and disordered eating. The subsequent section provides a brief description of EFT and its application to the treatment of EDs and body dissatisfaction and suggests ways EFT can enhance positive embodiment. Outcome evaluation of research on EFT with EDs is then described. The final section provides suggestions for future research to advance the application of EFT in reducing disordered eating and enhancing more attuned and compassionate ways to inhabit the body.

EMOTION REGULATION, BODY IMAGE, AND EATING DISORDERS

Effective emotion regulation is fundamental to well-being (Watson, 2011). Emotion regulation involves the capacity to be aware, label, modulate, and reflect on emotions in order to meet one's needs and goals (Elliott, Watson, Goldman, & Greenberg, 2004; Gratz & Roemer, 2004). When emotion regulation is adaptive, individuals are aware of their inner experience and bodily signals, or their felt sense. They can further understand their emotions, symbolize them, and put them into words. In addition, individuals are able to accept and tolerate their emotions and modulate their arousal in flexible ways in order to meet their needs and pursue meaningful activities. Finally, adaptive emotion regulation involves the ability either to inhibit or to enable the expression of emotion in order to produce the desired effect on others (Gratz & Roemer, 2004).

Early attachment experiences play a crucial role in the development of emotion regulation capacities (Gross, 2014). Attuned caregivers provide comfort and soothing to their children in various ways, such as by speaking in a calming tone, giving a hug, or helping children express in words what they are feeling. They promote the expression of emotion through playful activities or by modeling emotional expression. Children who are well cared for learn to associate particular bodily signals with the communication of needs and therefore as guides for action (Greenberg, 2011). These learned experiences are internalized, enabling individuals to attune to their emotional and bodily experiences in self-soothing and self-enhancing ways.

According to emotion theory, *emotion schemes* govern much of individuals' experiences and are central to emotion regulation. Emotion schemes are complex cognitive–affective structures that are formed during early childhood and help individuals anticipate future outcomes (Elliott et al., 2004). When an adaptive emotion scheme is activated, a self-enhancing action tendency follows. For example, individuals who feel sad at a loss will be guided by bodily sensations, associated needs, and memories to seek solace and will experience a sense of comfort when a loved one consoles them. This complex emotion scheme therefore results in adaptive regulation of emotions by meeting individuals' needs for comfort and solace, often without cognitive awareness.

Emotion dysregulation can arise due to a combination of familial, social, and biological factors (Gross, 2014). According to EFT, repeated neglect, maltreatment, or abuse can lead individuals to develop a rigid response to their inner and outer experiences, resulting in maladaptive emotion schemes and emotional dysregulation (Elliott et al., 2004). Impaired capacity to regulate emotions involves poor emotional awareness (due to biological predisposition or fears of negative affect), lack of symbolic differentiation of emotion, and emotional under- or overarousal. Finally, the inability to accept, tolerate, inhibit, or express emotion appropriately can be problematic, leaving individuals with unresolved distress and feelings of ineffectiveness. For example, rather than feeling sadness at a loss, the individual may feel maladaptive fear or shame. In this case, connection to bodily sensations is disrupted, symbolic meaning-making processes of the experienced emotion are adversely affected, and associated action tendencies are impaired. Further, past images or memories of being rejected or ridiculed for feeling sad may be evoked and may lead some individuals to withdraw from others and resort to engaging in varied maladaptive behaviors (e.g., binge eating or starvation) as a way to self-soothe or numb out. Repeated activation of the maladaptive schemes disrupts attunement to self and the body and impairs self-regulation (Greenberg, 2011).

Impaired emotion regulation is empirically supported in the literature as a transdiagnostic risk and/or maintenance factor in many mental health conditions (e.g., depression, anxiety, trauma, substance use, borderline personality disorder) (Aldao, Nolen-Hoeksema, & Schweizer, 2010; Ehring & Quack, 2010; Svaldi, Griepenstroh, Tuschen-Caffier, & Ehring, 2012) and is prevalent in individuals with disrupted eating patterns and body image, as well as clinical levels of an ED (Lavender et al., 2015; Nowakowski, McFarlane, & Cassin, 2013; Oldershaw, Lavender, Sallis, Stahl, & Schmidt, 2015). A number of authors described ways in which EDs and body preoccupation could provide a way to cope with dysregulated emotions. Polivy and Herman (2002) proposed that negative affect typically precedes binge eating, and purging provides a relief from the affective discomfort; however, the guilt and shame associated with these behaviors tend to perpetuate the disruptive cycle. Heatherton and Baumeister (1991) similarly proposed that binge eating symptoms provide a way to escape aversive emotional states through focusing on the control of eating and body shape. Haynos and Fruzzetti (2011) suggested that individuals with anorexia nervosa were brought up in an invalidating environment, leading to dysregulation in response to emotional or bodily stimulation; symptoms of anorexia could therefore be a way of gaining emotional control. In particular, starvation could numb one's feelings, excessive exercise could provide a means to escape distress, binge eating could be soothing, and purging could provide emotional relief (Dolhanty & Greenberg, 2007). As EDs and body preoccupation become entrenched ways of coping, they, in turn, reinforce the lack of self-efficacy in coping with emotions.

Research indicates that ED subtypes are equally affected by a range of emotion regulation problems (Brockmeyer et al., 2014). Individuals with anorexia, bulimia, or binge eating disorder have significant problems regulating affective states and a limited repertoire of adaptive emotion regulation skills, and they tend to rely more on maladaptive strategies when compared to healthy controls (Brockmeyer et al., 2014; Oldershaw et al., 2015; Svaldi et al., 2012). They have higher levels of negative affect, reduced self-awareness, nonacceptance and suppression of emotions, difficulties with distress tolerance, rumination, and a poor ability to control behavior when emotionally distressed, when compared to those without EDs.

Poor awareness, understanding, and communication of emotions are commonly found in individuals with alexithymia (Nowakowski et al., 2013). Alexithymia refers to difficulties in identifying and distinguishing emotions from physical reactions, putting emotions into words, and communicating them to others. A review of experimental studies comparing adolescents and adults with clinical EDs (e.g., anorexia, bulimia, and binge eating disorder), subclinical eating disturbances, and healthy controls demonstrated that affected individuals have difficulties identifying and communicating emotions to others (Nowakowski et al., 2013). Given that alexithymia and emotion regulation difficulties are empirically linked to clinical and subclinical EDs, therapeutic approaches that focus on enhancing emotional awareness and regulation capacities are highly suitable. EFT is an approach that aims to enhance both emotional awareness and regulation, transform maladaptive emotion schemes, and help individuals create more empowering self-narratives, hence leading to an embodied sense of self and well-being (Elliott et al., 2004).

EFT AND ITS APPLICATION TO TREATMENT OF EATING DISORDERS AND NEGATIVE BODY IMAGE

Emotion-focused therapy is a process–experiential approach that emphasizes personal growth over dysfunction (Watson, 2011), helping to promote adaptive processing of emotions through an empathic therapeutic relationship and experiential therapy tasks (Elliott et al., 2004). EFT therapists use a variety of empathic reflections to access, deepen, contain, and reflect clients' emotional experiences. Several therapeutic tasks that are utilized throughout the treatment are described in the material that follows, including focusing on an unclear felt sense, two-chair dialogues for self-interruptive and self-critical splits, and empty-chair dialogues for unfinished business with a significant other. Evocative unfolding of a puzzling reaction is another therapeutic task that helps clients reflect on confusing to them reaction/overreaction in order to arrive at a new meaning about themselves and/or others (Elliott et al., 2004). Throughout therapy, EFT therapists remain attuned to moment-to-moment emotional processing in order to maintain alliance and identify appropriate interventions to enhance clients' self-attunement and differentiation.

Emotion-Focused Therapy: Brief Overview

According to EFT, there are three types of emotions: *primary adaptive, secondary,* and *maladaptive* (Greenberg, 2011). Assessing the quality of emotion helps an EFT therapist identify markers for intervention. *Primary adaptive emotions* are initial reactions to situations, such as joy at a pleasant surprise or fear at being threatened. *Secondary emotions* are "reactions to reactions" that arise when the primary emotion is deemed unacceptable (i.e., guilt in response to pleasure or reactive anger when feeling afraid) or is undifferentiated, such as feeling "bad" and "overwhelmed." *Maladaptive* emotions are typically recurring, stuck, and stale feelings that do not easily change with experience (i.e., core sense of shame or deep sense of unlovability). EFT therapists help clients reflect on, and transform, secondary and maladaptive emotions in order to arrive at primary adaptive ones. It is the ability to be guided by primary adaptive emotions and associated needs that leads to a sense of meaning and well-being (Greenberg, 2011).

Emotion-Focused Therapy and Eating Disorders: Facilitating Positive Ways to Inhabit the Body

Several EFT interventions target emotion dysregulation and maladaptive emotion schemes (e.g., shame, anger) in individuals with EDs, disordered eating, and negative body image (Dolhanty & Greenberg, 2007; Ivanova & Watson, 2014; Wnuk, Greenberg, Dolhanty, 2015). These interventions are well suited to enhancing self-attunement so that clients can be guided by internal cues to meet their physical, emotional, and interpersonal needs, thereby enhancing ways of positively inhabiting the body.

Experiential Focusing on an Unclear Feeling

Intolerable negative affect that is often displaced onto the body obscures primary emotions and leaves clients with vague and overwhelming secondary emotional states that are difficult to modulate. *Focusing* encourages clients to attend to bodily sensed feelings that they have avoided and have not been able to express in words yet, including feeling "numb," and describe them through images. The goal is to help clients describe and make sense of the underlying feelings (e.g., a core fear or hopelessness) and transform them into adaptive responses. Arriving at an adaptive feeling in the validating presence of a therapist leads to an empowered sense of self.

Two-Chair Dialogue for Interruptive Self-Splits

The two-chair dialogue intervention for interruptive self-splits can be used to address the self-interruptive function of disordered eating patterns or body preoccupation (Dolhanty & Greenberg, 2007). In particular, clients enact the "interrupter" of emotions facing an empty chair, with the goal of clarifying the role of the symptoms in shutting down emotions and the impact of this silencing on the experience of the client as a receiver of such messages. Repeated activation of the self-silencing part enables clients to reclaim their voice and express themselves more freely, enhancing agency and therefore embodiment.

Two-Chair Dialogue for Self-Critical Splits

A harsh inner critic is a hallmark of individuals with negative body image and disordered eating, who may berate themselves for not being thin, attractive, lovable, or capable enough (Brennan, Emmerling, & Whelton, 2015). The goal of this two-chair dialogue is to make this critical part explicit and amenable to change. This process often starts with appearance-based self-criticisms and progresses to core maladaptive schemes of worth and lovability (Wnuk et al., 2015). Clients may also find that this critical side has helped them survive an abusive or neglectful environment by disconnecting from the more vulnerable parts of the self (Brennan et al., 2015). Eventually, clients integrate the protective function of the critic, access healthy parts of their identity, and develop more self-accepting, compassionate, and integrated inner dialogues that render disordered eating unnecessary and that help them connect to, and appreciate, their bodies, thereby enhancing positive body image and embodiment.

Empty-Chair Task for Unfinished Business with a Significant Other

As individuals in therapy develop stronger attunement to their emotions and their bodies, they become more aware of the relational interactions with others that contributed to the disembodied relationship to themselves. For example, in relationships with significant others, self-care and the enjoyment of foods may have been criticized, or food may have been used as a reward or for soothing. To facilitate a more nurturing relationship with themselves and their bodies, clients often need to process past relational injuries with significant others. Within therapy, an EFT therapist guides clients to enact and express, via empty-chair dialogue, previously disavowed feelings and unmet needs toward significant others, holding them accountable to traumatic experiences and relieving self-blame. Often, this is associated with a sense of understanding or acceptance of the other person (Paivio et al., 2010). As a result, clients can then develop more accepting and empowering relationships with themselves, their bodies, and those around them.

RESEARCH OUTCOMES WITH EMOTION-FOCUSED THERAPY FOR EATING DISORDERS

Emotion-focused therapy has been found in a randomized, controlled study to have a similar outcome as cognitive behavioral therapy (CBT; Watson et al., 2003) and is considered an empirically supported treatment (American Psychological Association [APA], Society of Clinical Psychology Division 12, 2013) for depression. It has also been found effective in couple therapy (Johnson et al., 1999), and initial studies suggest its possible effectiveness in the treatment of trauma (Paivio et al., 2010).

Outcome evaluation research with EFT, as adapted for EDs treatment by Dolhanty and Greenberg (2007), is at its initial stages. Over the past 5 years, preliminary yet promising research findings have begun to emerge. The findings thus far suggest that EFT effectively addresses a range of ED symptoms (e.g., binge eating, starvation), stabilizes weight, improves emotion regulation capacities, improves body image, increases efficacy, improves interpersonal functioning, and enhances overall quality of life (Brennan et al., 2015; Dolhanty & Greenberg, 2009; Glisenti, Strodl, & King, 2018; Tweed, 2013; Wnuk et al., 2015).

An uncontrolled pilot study examined the outcome of a 16-week, group-based EFT with 12 outpatient women with bulimic symptoms. Significant reductions were found in the frequency of bingeing, as well as on measures of bulimia, body dissatisfaction, depression, interoceptive awareness, ineffectiveness, and general psychopathology (Wnuk et al., 2015). Further, the women reported significant improvements with emotion regulation and greater levels of self-efficacy (Wilson, Fairburn, Agras, Walsh, & Kraemer, 2002). Tweed (2013) compared 32 women with bulimic symptomatology who were randomly assigned to either group EFT or an active treatment control group (combination of motivational enhancement, psychoeducation, and CBT) in an outpatient hospital setting. The results demonstrated that, compared to the control group, EFT was significantly more effective at improving distress tolerance at post-treatment. Follow-up univariate tests showed medium-to-large effect sizes and significant improvements on the following measures at post-treatment in the EFT, but not the control, group: reduced binge frequency and body concerns, improved emotion regulation, and increased self-efficacy, especially in relation to body image. Examining in-session processes in relation to outcome within the same EFT group, Ivanova (2013) found, while controlling for pretreatment scores, that successful resolutions of two- and empty-chair tasks were associated with positive postsession changes. In particular, successful resolution of these tasks predicted nearly 50% of the variance on a measure of emotion regulation, 17% of the variance on a measure of interpersonal insecurity, and 12% of the variance on a measure of general psychological maladjustment at post-treatment.

In a single-subject design involving six women diagnosed with binge-eating disorder, Glisenti et al. (2018) found that 12 individual EFT sessions had either resulted in reliable recovery or significant improvement in binge-eating frequency and EDs psychopathology, emotion-regulation strategies, depression and anxiety symptoms. The frequency of binges decreased from 17 at pretreatment to 2 at post treatment when tested over a 28-day period. Most common improvements were reported in areas of increased awareness and experience of emotions. This suggests that EFT may be helpful in assisting individuals with binge-eating disorders to identify and differentiate confusing emotional states, thereby improving embodiment.

A qualitative study with six women with EDs (anorexia nervosa binge/purge type, bulimia nervosa, and binge eating disorder) who completed 12 weeks of group EFT found that these women reported a better capacity to access and accept previously avoided feelings, especially anger (Brennan et al., 2015). They also reported improved ability to identify needs, such as the need for space to find their own voice, and increased self-compassion. As part of differentiating their own voice from the ED voice, one client challenged the internalized body image standard by stating, "Holding me accountable to some unrealistic image of what a woman 'should' be is not [realistic]!" (Brennan et al., 2015, p. 70). As part of enhanced self-compassion, another woman described becoming "more self-forgiving and gentler in my criticisms" at the end of the group treatment (Brennan et al., 2015, p. 71).

Research with anorexia nervosa, restrictive type, has been limited to two case studies. After 18 months of individual EFT therapy, a woman with anorexia nervosa experienced enhanced interoceptive awareness and reduced alexithymia (Dolhanty & Greenberg, 2009). Therapy transcripts indicated that this client was more able to self-soothe and be self-compassionate, as well as address unfinished business with her mother, transforming maladaptive shame by expressing previously disavowed anger. By the end of the therapy, the client developed a sense of agency in navigating her world, pursuing hobbies, self-care, and socializing. The second case study involved an EFT approach to training parents to support their children diagnosed with ED (Lafrance Robinson et al., 2015). A mother who completed individual EFT therapy reported increased confidence in caring for her adolescent daughter with anorexia nervosa. The authors reported that the greater emotional attunement and validation offered by the mother were associated with greater emotional attunement and weight recovery in the daughter. This case study inspired the development of emotion-focused family therapy for ED and a subsequent evaluation of a 2-day intervention for parents of children with ED (Lafrance Robinson, Dolhanty, Stillar, Henderson, & Mayman, 2016).

Two uncontrolled studies evaluated the outcome of the emotion-focused family therapy 2-day intervention aimed at helping parents of children with an ED to feel more efficacious in supporting them through recovery (Lafrance Robinson et al., 2016; Strahan et al., 2017). The first study consisted of 33 parents, and the second one had 124 parents from eight different sites, including hospital, community clinics, and private practice. At postintervention, participating parents reported higher efficacy in supporting their child's recovery and reduced maladaptive fear and self-blame in the parents postintervention. No evaluation of children's well-being was conducted.

CONCLUSION AND FUTURE DIRECTIONS

Emotion-focused therapy research in the treatment of ED is at its initial stages; nonetheless, it shows some promising results. In particular, a randomized study showed that EFT was effective at reducing binge eating when compared to a combined motivational enhancement and CBT group (Tweed, 2013). Outcome evaluation of EFT among individuals with anorexia needs to follow initial positive case study reports (Dolhanty & Greenberg, 2009). Importantly, outcome evaluation studies of EFT included a range of outcome measures beyond negative body image or general psychopathology, such as emotion regulation and self-efficacy, which may relate to both positive body image and embodiment (Piran, 2016; Tylka & Wood-Barcalow, 2015). For example, following a course of EFT, women became more accepting and proud of their bodies and developed more self-attuned eating patterns (Tweed, 2013). Improvements on emotional regulation and distress tolerance following individual and group EFT, and improvements on alexithymia after individual EFT, suggest that women become more aware and accepting of their emotions and are better able to modulate and utilize them toward pursuing their goals (Gilsenti et al., 2018; Dolhanty & Greenberg, 2009; Tweed, 2013; Wnuk et al., 2015). Qualitative accounts also suggest greater self-attunement, self-compassion, and agency following a course of EFT (Brennan et al., 2015; Dolhanty & Greenberg, 2009).

There are several areas for future advancement. EFT should be further evaluated in randomized, controlled trials against empirically supported treatments (e.g., CBT or interpersonal psychotherapy), with short- and long-term follow-up periods, and among men and women with different ED patterns, disordered eating, body image experiences, and disembodiment. The field will further benefit from mixed-methods research to capture the complexity of mechanisms of change in ED and reflect the positive growth and embodiment that EFT aims to facilitate, rather than focusing on symptom reduction alone. Along the same lines, measures of positive ways of inhabiting the body and positive body image, such as the Experience of Embodiment Scale (Piran & Teall, 2012) and the Body Appreciation Scale-2 (Tylka & Wood-Barcalow, 2015), should be included in future research, particularly given that EFT is a growth-oriented treatment model. The potential of EFT in healing bodily and emotional disruptions is promising. Future advancement in this field will aid greatly in our understanding of transforming body shame into an embodied sense of well-being.

REFERENCES

Aldao, A., Nolen-Hoeksema, S., & Schweizer, S. (2010). Emotion-regulation strategies across psychopathology: A meta-analytic review. *Clinical Psychology Review, 30*, 217–237. doi:10.1016/j.cpr.2009.11.004

American Psychological Association, Society of Clinical Psychology Division 12. (2013). Home page [website on research-supported psychological treatments]. Retrieved from https://www.div12.org/

Brennan, M. A., Emmerling, M. E., & Whelton, W. J. (2015). Emotion-focused group therapy: Addressing self-criticism in the treatment of eating disorders. *Counselling & Psychotherapy Research, 15*, 67–75. doi:10.1002/capr.12012

Brockmeyer, T., Skunde, M., Wu, M., Bresslein, E., Rudofsky, G., Herzog, W., & Friederich, H. (2014). Difficulties in emotion regulation across the spectrum of eating disorders. *Comprehensive Psychiatry, 55*, 565. doi:10.1016/j.comppsych.2013.12.001

Dolhanty, J., & Greenberg, L. S. (2007). Emotion-focused therapy in the treatment of eating disorders. *European Psychotherapy, 7*, 97–116. doi:10.1002/cpp.1861

Dolhanty, J., & Greenberg, L. S. (2009). Emotion-focused therapy in a case of anorexia nervosa. *Clinical Psychology & Psychotherapy, 16*, 366–382. doi:10.1002/cpp.624

Ehring, T., & Quack, D. (2010). Emotion regulation difficulties in trauma survivors: The role of trauma type and PTSD symptom severity. *Behavior Therapy, 41*, 587–598. doi:10.1016/j.beth.2010.04.004

Elliott, R., Watson, J. C., Goldman, R. N., & Greenberg, L. S. (2004). *Learning emotion-focused therapy: The process-experiential approach to change.* Washington, DC: American Psychological Association. doi:10.1037/10725-015

Glisenti, K., Strodl, E., & King, R. (2018). Emotion-focused therapy for binge-eating disorder: A review of six cases. *Clinical Psychology & Psychotherapy, 25*, 1–14. doi:10.1002/cpp.2319

Gratz, K., & Roemer, L., (2004). Multidimensional assessment of emotion regulation and dysregulation: Development, factor structure, and initial validation of the Difficulties in Emotion Regulation Scale. *Journal of Psychopathology and Behavioral Assessment, 26*, 41–54. doi:10.1023/b:joba.0000007455.08539.94

Greenberg, L. S. (2011). Emotion-focused therapy. In J. Carlson & M. Englar-Carlson (Eds.), *Theories of psychotherapy series* (pp. 1–181). Washington, DC: American Psychological Association.

Gross, J. J. (2014). *Handbook of emotion regulation* (2nd ed.). New York, NY: Guilford Press.

Haynos, A. F., & Fruzzetti, A. E. (2011). Anorexia nervosa as a disorder of emotion dysregulation: Evidence and treatment implications. *Clinical Psychology: Science and Practice, 18*, 183–202. doi:10.1111/j.1468-2850.2011.01250.x

Heatherton, T., & Baumeister, R. (1991). Binge eating as escape from self-awareness. *Psychological Bulletin, 110*, 86–108. doi:10.1037//0033-2909.110.1.86

Ivanova, I. (2013). *The "how" of change in emotion-focused group therapy for eating disorders*. University of Toronto, Toronto, Ontario, Canada. Retrieved from https://search-proquest-com.myaccess.library.utoronto.ca/docview/1635317654

Ivanova, I., & Watson, J. (2014). Emotion-focused therapy for eating disorders: Enhancing emotional processing. *Person-Centered & Experiential Psychotherapies, 13*, 278–293. doi:10.1080/14779757.2014.910132

Johnson, S. M., Hunsley, J., Greenberg, L., & Schindler, D. (1999). Emotionally focused couple therapy: Status and challenges. *Clinical Psychology: Science and Practice, 6*, 67–79. doi:10.1093/clipsy.6.1.67

Lafrance Robinson, A., Dolhanty, J., & Greenberg, L. S. (2015). Emotion-focused family therapy for eating disorders in children and adolescents. *Clinical Psychology & Psychotherapy, 22*, 75–82. doi:10.1002/cpp.1861

Lafrance Robinson, A., Dolhanty, J., Stillar, A., Henderson, K., & Mayman, S. (2016). Emotion-focused family therapy for eating disorders across the lifespan: A pilot study of a 2-day transdiagnostic intervention for parents. *Clinical Psychology & Psychotherapy, 23*, 14–23. doi:10.1002/cpp.1933

Lavender, J. M., Wonderlich, S. A., Engel, S. G., Gordon, K. H., Kaye, W. H., & Mitchell, J. E. (2015). Dimensions of emotion dysregulation in anorexia nervosa and bulimia nervosa: A conceptual review of the empirical literature. *Clinical Psychology Review, 40*, 111–122. doi:10.1016/j.cpr.2015.05.010

Nowakowski, M. E., McFarlane, T., & Cassin, S. (2013). Alexithymia and eating disorders: A critical review of the literature. *Journal of Eating Disorders, 1*, 21. doi:10.1186/2050-2974-1-21

Oldershaw, A., Lavender, T., Sallis, H., Stahl, D., & Schmidt, U. (2015). Emotion generation and regulation in anorexia nervosa: A systematic review and meta-analysis of self-report data. *Clinical Psychology Review, 39*, 83–95. doi:10.1016/j.cpr.2015.04.005

Paivio, S. C., Jarry, J. L., Chagigiorgis, H., Hall, I., & Ralston, M. (2010). Efficacy of two versions of emotion-focused therapy for resolving child abuse trauma. *Psychotherapy Research, 20*, 353–366. doi:10.1080/10503300903505274

Piran, N. (2016). Embodied possibilities and disruptions: The emergence of the Experience of Embodiment construct from qualitative studies with girls and women. *Body Image, 18*, 43–60. doi:10.1016/j.bodyim.2016.04.007

Piran, N., & Teall, T. L. (2012). The developmental theory of embodiment. In G. L. McVey, M. P. Levine, N. Piran, & H. B. Ferguson (Eds.), *Preventing eating-related and weight-related disorders: Collaborative research, advocacy, and policy change* (pp. 169–198). Waterloo, ON, Canada: Wilfrid Laurier University Press. doi:10.1037/10403-012

Polivy, J., & Herman, C. P. (2002). Causes of eating disorders. *Annual Review of Psychology, 53*, 187–213. doi:10.1146/annurev.psych.53.100901.135103

Strahan, J. S., Stillar, A., Files, N., Nash, P., Scarborough, J., Connors, S., Gusella, J., . . . Lafrance, A. (2017). Increasing parental self-efficacy with emotion-focused family therapy for eating disorders: a process model, *Person-Centered & Experiential Psychotherapies, 16*(3), 256–269. doi:10.1080/14779757.2017.1330703

Svaldi, J., Griepenstroh, J., Tuschen-Caffier, B., & Ehring, T. (2012). Emotion regulation deficits in eating disorders: A marker of eating pathology or general psychopathology? *Psychiatry Research, 197*, 103–111. doi:10.1016/j.psychres.2011.11.009

Tylka, T. L., & Wood-Barcalow, N. L. (2015). The Body Appreciation Scale-2: Item refinement and psychometric evaluation. *Body Image, 12*, 53–67. doi:10.1016/j.bodyim.2014.09.006

Tweed, S. (2013). *Group-based emotion focused therapy (EFT) for women with binge spectrum eating disorders in an outpatient setting: A preliminary comparison* (Unpublished doctoral dissertation). York University, Toronto, ON, Canada.

Watson, J. C. (2011). The process of growth and transformation: Extending the process model. *Person-Centered & Experiential Psychotherapies, 10*, 11–27. doi:10.1080/14779757.2011.564760

Watson, J. C., Gordon, L. B., Stermac, L., Kalogerakos, F., & Steckley, P. (2003). Comparing the effectiveness of process-experiential with cognitive-behavioral psychotherapy in the treatment of depression. *Journal of Consulting and Clinical Psychology, 71*, 773–781. doi:10.1037/0022-006x.71.4.773

Wilson, G. T., Fairburn, C. G., Agras, W. S., Walsh, B. T., & Kraemer, H. D. (2002). Cognitive behavior therapy for bulimia nervosa: Time course and mechanisms of change. *Journal of Consulting and Clinical Psychology, 70*, 267–274. doi:10.1037//0022006x.70.2.267

Wnuk, S. M., Greenberg, L., & Dolhanty, J. (2015). Emotion-focused group therapy for individuals with symptoms of bulimia nervosa. *Eating Disorders, 23*, 253–261. doi:10.1080/10640266.2014.964612

27

Acceptance and Commitment Therapy to Facilitate Positive Body Image and Embodiment

JENNIFER B. WEBB ■

Acceptance and commitment therapy (ACT; Hayes, Strosahl, & Wilson, 1999) is an empirically based intervention that uses acceptance and mindfulness strategies with commitment and behavior change strategies to increase psychological flexibility, that is, to be present with difficult thoughts and feelings and to move toward valued behavior even in times of discomfort and distress. Recent decades have witnessed tremendous growth in research on the benefits of utilizing ACT for targeting a wide range of psychological and physical health concerns (Powers, Zum Vorde Sive Vording, & Emmelkamp, 2009). Despite this promising evidence base in general, scholarship is only just beginning to tap into the possibilities afforded by applying ACT toward transforming the experience of disrupted embodiment into a more embodied connection to the self (e.g., Manlick, Cochran, & Koon, 2013). Toward this goal, this chapter starts by making theoretical links between the conceptual foundations of ACT and embodiment. Second, a fictional case example is described to illustrate the practical ways in which core ACT strategies may be useful in enhancing experiences of positive embodiment. Third, a brief overview of emergent research that addresses the application of ACT in relation to body image, weight, eating, and physical activity is presented. Last, future research directions are offered, grounded in multicultural and life span perspectives on well-being promotion.

ACT AND EMBODIMENT: AN OPPORTUNITY FOR THEORETICAL INTEGRATION

Acceptance and commitment therapy is representative of the constellation of third-wave behavior therapy approaches that have become popularized among clinical scientists and practitioners alike for their broad spectrum, transdiagnostic appeal (Hayes, Luoma, Bond, Masuda, & Lillis, 2006). This contemporary therapeutic modality blends centuries-old Eastern wisdom (e.g., Buddhist mindfulness philosophy) with Western contextual behavioral scientific principles (Hayes et al., 2006) to conceptualize and optimize human functioning.

Acceptance and commitment therapy is mobilized to strengthen six adaptive self-regulatory competencies that underlie psychological flexibility: *present moment awareness* (noticing the ongoing, complex, and dynamic internal experiences such as thoughts, emotions, and physical sensations as they unfold without judgment); *experiential acceptance* (practicing openness toward internal experiences, especially when they are unwanted or painful); *cognitive defusion* (observing cognitive components of one's experience, such as thoughts, memories, and rules, without them dominating attention or dictating overt behavior); *self-as-context* (engaging the observing self or recognizing the experience of self as a neutral context in which internal experiences unfold distinct from the content or evaluation of one's experiences); *valuing* (choosing a purpose or meaning to guide action, especially when internal experiences are unwanted or painful); and *committed action* (maintaining active engagement in value-consistent behavior, even when this results in increased contact with unwanted or painful aspects of one's internal experiences; Hayes et al., 2006). Bolstering processes inherent in psychological flexibility weakens maladaptive tendencies of psychological *in*flexibility (i.e., dominance of the conceptualized past and feared future, experiential avoidance, cognitive fusion, attachment to the conceptualized self, lack of value clarity and inaction, impulsivity, or avoidance persistence), which gives rise to psychopathology (Hayes et al., 2006). Thus, ACT promotes greater freedom to engage in living with meaning and vitality in accordance with one's most deeply held values.

Psychological flexibility can be directly tied to the dynamic experiences of body image and embodiment as they unfold within individuals in their everyday lives. I label the theoretical construct that represents this integration *embodied flexibility*. Enhanced through ACT interventions, embodied flexibility could shift one's experiences of disrupted embodiment or negative body image to positive embodiment and positive body image, as illustrated in the model presented in Figure 27.1 (see Chapters 1 and 10, as well as Piran, 2016, 2017, for a discussion of embodiment; see Chapters 2 and 7, as well as Tylka & Wood-Barcalow, 2015, for a discussion of positive body image and intuitive eating). In particular, this model suggests that the shift from disconnected embodiment to positive embodiment is mediated through embodied flexibility, facilitated through engagement in ACT-informed interventions. More specifically, this model conceptualizes forms of disconnected embodiment to reflect experiences that are perpetuated

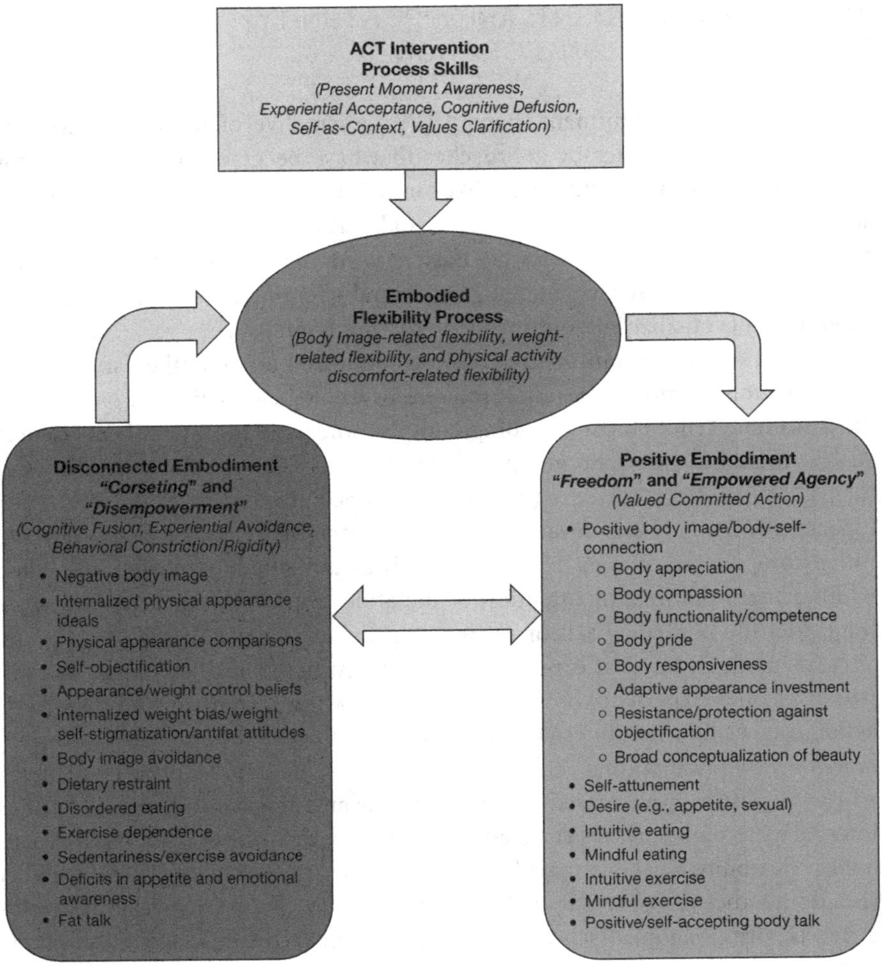

Figure 27.1 An integrative heuristic model of the dynamic interactions between acceptance and commitment therapy and embodiment processes.

by psychological inflexibility processes (e.g., cognitive fusion, disconnection from values, experiential avoidance, ineffective action). Meanwhile, the active implementation of ACT-related psychological flexibility processes (e.g., present moment awareness, experiential acceptance, contact with values, cognitive defusion) as applied to experiences of disconnected embodiment enables individuals to transform these experiences to be more reflective of positive embodiment values and actions in the moment they are occurring (Figure 27.1).

Embodied flexibility is conceptualized and measured with respect to relating more adaptively to the experiences of negative body image (Sandoz, Wilson, Merwin, & Kellum, 2013); problematic weight-related attitudes and feelings (Lillis & Hayes, 2008); and physical activity–related discomfort (Butryn, Forman, Hoffman, Shaw, & Juarascio, 2011) in the service of sustaining engagement in health behaviors consistent with chosen life directions (e.g., dimensions of positive embodiment; Figure 27.1). Conversely, body image inflexibility (Callaghan, Sandoz, Darrow, & Feeney, 2015) and body image–related cognitive fusion (Ferreira, Trindade, Duarte, & Pinto-Gouveia, 2014) involve entanglement with undesired experiences of embodiment that may derail taking effective action in one's life.

APPLYING CORE ACT STRATEGIES TO ENHANCE EMBODIED FLEXIBILITY AND POSITIVE EMBODIMENT: A FICTIONAL CLINICAL VIGNETTE

> Miranda is a 33-year-old, married, higher weight African American woman who is experiencing increasing body dissatisfaction with unusually elevated pregnancy-related weight gain. She believes she is already "as big as a whale" and is a "complete failure" for not maintaining her physician's recommended diet plan and being too exhausted and physically uncomfortable to meet her daily exercise goals. Miranda frequently compares her body to the pregnant models she sees on the covers of *Fit Pregnancy* magazine and on Instagram. Her ability to distinguish between her emotions and true hunger signals has been compromised due to chronic past dieting. As a result of her uncomfortable internal experiences, she recently began consuming large quantities of high-fat snack foods in the evenings while "zoning out" watching Netflix and hiding her intake of several candy bars during her daily lunch breaks at work. At first, Miranda chalked her behavior up to her "overly restrictive" eating plan and allowed herself to give in to "pregnancy-related food cravings" because she was "eating for two." Yet, when confronted by her doctor, she acknowledges that her eating is out of control and that she believes that she is going to be a "horrible mother" because of the eating binges, which "show no concern for the baby growing inside me."

In this example, Miranda is exhibiting several indicators of disrupted embodiment during this transition to motherhood, which reflect limitations in multiple domains of embodied flexibility. In working with Miranda clinically, the following ACT strategies (following from the six core psychological flexibility processes) might be considered to help enhance embodied connection and empowered agency at this critical juncture. For instance, *present moment awareness* techniques such as those that enhance mindfulness skills (e.g., "the mindful mirror"; Pearson, Heffner, & Follette, 2010) would enable her to observe her self-critical thoughts and appearance comparisons with a curious, nonjudgmental awareness. Relatedly, Miranda could learn to mindfully savor and enjoy a piece of chocolate even in the presence of emerging feelings of guilt for having eaten a "forbidden food," knowing that she is capable of intuitively responding to her body's internal hunger and satiety signals, without the need to buy into her automatic thoughts, which rigidly categorize food as good or bad (Tylka & Kroon Van Diest, 2013).

Experiential acceptance strategies could help bolster Miranda's ability to embrace uncomfortable physical sensations (e.g., fatigue, thighs rubbing together, etc.) or unwanted emotions (e.g., body shame) by physicalizing them and then letting them go without becoming overly attached to them or pushing them away. For example, in the "taking it all in" practice, she might imagine that she is holding a negative emotion in her hand, then breathing it into her skin and letting it dissolve (Sandoz & DuFrene, 2013). *Cognitive defusion* exercises (e.g., saying the word *fat* repeatedly so many times or in a silly voice that it loses its meaning) could create space to unhook the power of weight-stigmatizing thoughts and feelings about her body in mindlessly dictating her behavior (e.g., binge eating).

Self-as-context exercises (e.g., the "chessboard metaphor"; Heffner, Sperry, Eifert, & Detweiler, 2002) could connect her to the experience of self that is a constant. Imagining herself from the neutral vantage point of the chessboard, there is no investment in who wins the ongoing war inside her head between the opposing sides of good and bad self-evaluative thoughts (i.e., the black and white chess pieces). Rather, with practice, she may come to realize that this transcendent part of her is unbounded by time or the content of a fixed or conceptualized self.

Helping Miranda *clarify her values* as a mother-to-be through reflective activities (e.g., wondering what life would be like without any concerns over her weight, body, or eating; imagining what would be important as a role model of positive embodiment for her unborn child; Pearson et al., 2010) could help stimulate motivation to prioritize embodied self-attunement, desire, and body–self-connection (Piran, 2016). Finally, her *commitment* to sustaining an embodied connection could be reinforced by keeping her values continuously accessible (e.g., having her smartphone send her encouraging reminders to attend her weekly prenatal yoga class even when feeling somewhat tired or physically uncomfortable knowing that she will likely feel more energized afterwards).

A SNAPSHOT OF THE EVIDENCE BASE

The following sections provide a brief overview of select research examining the application of ACT or its components to improving particular aspects of embodiment. More specifically, attention is primarily reserved for studies targeting the experiences of body image flexibility, stigmatizing weight-related attitudes, adaptive eating, and physical activity, with an emphasis given to research demonstrating benefits to embodied flexibility processes and positive embodiment outcomes (see Manlick et al., 2013, for a review of the treatment of eating disorders using ACT). Unless otherwise noted, all studies were conducted with US samples.

Body Image Flexibility

Early-stage scholarship featuring descriptive case series with clinical and subclinical samples has shown the promise of ACT in enhancing *body image flexibility*, or the awareness and acceptance of sensations, perceptions, feelings, thoughts, and beliefs specific to weight and shape while engaging in effective action in valued life domains (see Chapter 4). Significant immediate and sustained improvements in body image flexibility were demonstrated among ethnically diverse women with eating disorders (Berman, Boutelle, & Crow, 2009; Hill, Masuda, Melcher, Morgan, & Twohig, 2015; Masuda, Ng, Moore, Felix, & Drake, 2016), with sexual minority individuals endorsing problematic emotional eating difficulties (Hill, Masuda, Moore, & Twohig, 2015), and with a middle-aged, ethnically diverse man reporting elevated body image concerns (Altman, Zimmaro, & Woodruff-Borden, 2017). The majority of these ACT-based protocols were typically 10 weeks in duration and delivered in an individualized format.

Recent outcome evaluation studies assessed the impact of ACT in combination with other therapy approaches on body image flexibility. Berman, Morton, and Hegel (2016) found that higher weight women with depression who completed the 11-week, group-based Accept Yourself! program (integrating principles of ACT and Health at Every Size®) reported significant increases in body image flexibility, which were maintained at a 3-month follow-up. Higher weight Portuguese women participating in the 12-session BEfree group (i.e., intervention for binge eating disorder combining elements of mindfulness, self-compassion, and value-based living) evidenced significant reductions on one dimension of body image inflexibility, namely, body image–related cognitive fusion, and these reductions were sustained at 3- and 6-month follow-ups (Pinto-Gouveia et al., 2016).

Weight-Related Attitudes

As an extension of more general body image-related difficulties with embodiment, experts have recognized the additional psychological burden uniquely associated with inhabiting bodies of higher weights (Tylka et al., 2014). Indeed, scholarship confirmed that the health and well-being of higher weight individuals are not only exposed to explicit weight discrimination but also may be adversely affected by *internalized weight stigma* (i.e., adopting societal weight stigma as a belief set to judge oneself and others; Tylka et al., 2014). When considered from an ACT framework, fusion with such self-deprecating thoughts and shameful feelings from internalized weight stigma work to perpetuate experiential avoidance and unworkable action, thus interfering with effective living (Lillis, Hayes, Bunting, & Masuda, 2009). Therefore, a growing body of research has targeted applying ACT in the context of reducing weight self-stigma and enhancing weight-related psychological flexibility among higher weight individuals.

For example, gains in weight-related psychological flexibility were reported among higher weight individuals randomized to a 1-day ACT workshop (Lillis et al., 2009) and mediated reductions in binge eating in this sample (Lillis, Hayes, & Levin, 2011). Research further indicated that ACT-enhanced psychological flexibility regarding problematic weight-related internal experiences was also achievable in more weight-diverse samples (Pearson, Follette, & Hayes, 2012) and among higher weight individuals in ACT-inclusive nonrandomized trials of US (Berman et al., 2016; Niemeier, Leahey, Reed, Brown, & Wing, 2012) and Portuguese (Palmeira, Pinto-Gouveia, & Cunha, 2017) adults. These effects were extended to improvements in internalized weight stigma among higher weight individuals participating in a small open trial of ACT delivered in a 7-week, guided, self-help format (Levin, Potts, Haeger, & Lillis, 2018).

Adaptive Eating Behavior

From an ACT lens, eating disorders and disordered eating are conceptualized as rigid efforts to avoid experiencing painful thoughts and emotions related to the body. Consistent with this psychological inflexibility formulation, there is encouraging preliminary evidence of ACT's utility in reducing these forms of disconnected embodiment predominantly (though not exclusively) in adult female samples (e.g., Hill, Masuda, Melcher, et al., 2015; see Manlick et al., 2013, for a review). Nevertheless, although several of these ACT-informed protocols encourage embodied ways of eating as healthier alternatives (e.g., mindful or intuitive eating), they surprisingly do not typically measure these more adaptive eating processes as actual treatment outcomes. Mindful and intuitive eating are conceptualized here as engaging positive embodiment values (e.g., integrating body–self-connection and appetitive desires; Piran, 2016). The absence of including measures of mindful and intuitive eating assumes that reductions in dysfunctional eating patterns coincide with improvements in healthier approaches to food intake, which may or may not be the case as adaptive eating represents more than the absence of dysfunctional eating attitudes (Tylka & Kroon Van Diest, 2013).

A noteworthy exception is a recent analysis comparing a wait-list control group to a group receiving ACT (delivered via either an 8-week in-person, group-based format or a self-guided, smartphone application); both groups contained higher weight individuals experiencing significant life stress and not necessarily problematic eating behavior (Sairanen et al., 2017). In comparison to the control group, participants randomized to either ACT intervention condition experienced significant improvements in intuitive eating over time. Effects for the total intuitive eating score along with two of its dimensions (i.e., eating for physical rather than emotional reasons, reliance on internal hunger and fullness cues to guide food intake) were mediated by gains in weight-related psychological flexibility (Sairanen et al., 2017).

Physical Activity

Finally, it is worth highlighting the nascent applications of ACT targeting increases in embodied experiences in the domain of physical activity. Scholars position the utility of ACT toward improving engagement in exercise and physical activity as a function of its core processes working to enhance experiential acceptance of the discomfort (e.g., sweating, fatigue, distressing thoughts, emotions, etc.) that may arise with the aim of persisting in values-congruent action within this life domain (Butryn et al., 2011). In this context, research spanning a range of college, community, and clinical samples has documented significant increases in physical activity or acceptance of physical activity–related discomfort following exposure to ACT-related interventions delivered in a variety of formats and intensities.

For instance, undergraduate women who participated in a brief physical activity–focused ACT intervention consisting of two 2-hour group sessions made more visits to the campus athletic center by postassessment than did their counterparts assigned to a psychoeducation control condition, with both groups reporting increases in physical activity–related experiential acceptance (Butryn et al., 2011). Additionally, college women randomized to an eight-session, ACT-based group intervention reported significant immediate and sustained increases in physical activity–related experiential acceptance across the yearlong follow-up relative to the control group (Katterman, Goldstein, Butryn, Forman, & Lowe, 2014). Meanwhile, researchers have further shown improvements in physical activity engagement after exposure to ACT-informed interventions among minimally active Canadian women (e.g., Ivanova, Jensen, Cassoff, Gu, & Knauper, 2015); Australian adults (Moffitt & Mohr, 2015); and US adults (Martin, Galloway-Williams, Cox, & Winett, 2015). Gains in exercise-related experiential acceptance and in objective measures of cardiorespiratory fitness were also observed (Martin et al., 2015). Interventions ranged from ACT applied to a single bout of high-intensity cardiovascular exercise (Ivanova et al., 2015), ACT combined with a 10-week fitness walking program (Martin et al., 2015), and ACT delivered via DVD at home in combination with a 12-week walking program (Moffitt & Mohr, 2015).

CONCLUSION AND FUTURE DIRECTIONS

As illustrated, ACT has promise in promoting embodied flexibility. Strengths of the evidence base include the diversity of intervention delivery methods and dosages, efforts to include culturally diverse samples, and evidence of the acceptability, feasibility, and fidelity to the protocols. This review has also revealed important gaps that invite additional scholarship.

As this body of research is still in its infancy, the majority of studies reviewed were either uncontrolled or involved a wait-list control design. Future research is encouraged to conduct more rigorous, large-scale, randomized, controlled trials and subsequently more pragmatic dissemination trials comparing ACT to other active controls to further strengthen the evidence base. As measures of embodied flexibility are theoretically conceptualized as therapeutic change processes, there is a greater need to more consistently demonstrate this conceptualization in future research involving direct tests of mediation (e.g., Lillis et al., 2011; Sairanen et al., 2017). Additionally, there is limited use of qualitative methods, which could be valuable in not only providing richer assessment of the acceptability of ACT over the course, or at its conclusion, but also enhancing the ways in which it is adapted or modified at the outset. Moreover, most of the current literature tends to rely on self-reported measures of process or change; therefore, developing and including objective measures of these constructs is warranted (e.g., behavioral measures of embodied flexibility processes and positive embodiment outcomes). Relatedly, developing and validating a comprehensive measure of eating-related psychological flexibility beyond regulating food cravings in the service of weight control would be a useful complement to existing measures of mindful and intuitive eating orientations.

As previously noted, the experiences of embodiment and body image are complex, such that both positive and negative forms can co-occur within individuals (Piran, 2016; Webb, 2015). Further, given that low levels of negative or disrupted embodiment (or negative body image) are not necessarily equivalent to positive embodiment (or positive body image), it is critical for scientists to assess both types of experiences simultaneously in future research. From the standpoint of gender diversity, there is limited representation of men and non-*cis* gender individuals and their experiences of body image, embodiment, and disordered eating. Further, some researchers argued that applying the ACT framework to experiences of embodiment in sexual minority men may be particularly well suited given their stigmatized identity coupled with a heightened focus on physical appearance (Walloch, Cerezo, & Heide, 2012).

It will also remain vital for experts to continue to grapple with the instances where the philosophies underlying ACT and embodiment theory may be incompatible with intervention goals. For instance, tension could arise if weight loss or weight loss maintenance is the principal goal of therapy, which could further the maladaptive agendas of control, experiential avoidance, or appearance-focused "corseting" (i.e., stifling experiential freedom and autonomous expression in connection with one's body and how it engages in the world; Lillis & Kendra, 2014; Piran, 2017). Similarly, using ACT to rigidly control food cravings and in turn food choice and consumption would be at odds with the principles of positive embodiment and intuitive eating. Finally, it is exciting to consider the possibilities of extending the application of the model proposed in Figure 27.1 to enhance positive embodiment in a wider range of psychiatric (e.g., trauma-induced sexual dysfunction, self-injury behavior) and medical (e.g., pain intolerance, irritable bowel syndrome, diabetes, infertility, postpartum, etc.) populations.

REFERENCES

Altman, J. K., Zimmaro, L. A., & Woodruff-Borden, J. (2017). Targeting body compassion in the treatment of body dissatisfaction: A case study. *Clinical Case Studies, 16*, 431–445. doi:10.1177/1534650117731155

Berman, M. I., Boutelle, K. N., & Crow, S. J. (2009). A case series investigating acceptance and commitment therapy as a treatment for previously treated, unremitted patients with anorexia nervosa. *European Eating Disorders Review, 17*, 426–434. doi:10.1002/erv.962

Berman, M. I., Morton, S. N., & Hegel, M. T. (2016). Uncontrolled pilot study of an acceptance and commitment therapy and Health at Every Size intervention for obese, depressed women: Accept Yourself! *Psychotherapy*, *53*, 462–467. doi:10.1037/pst0000083

Butryn, M. L., Forman, E., Hoffman, K., Shaw, J., & Juarascio, A. (2011). A pilot study of acceptance and commitment therapy for promotion of physical activity. *Journal of Physical Activity and Health*, *8*, 516–522.

Callaghan, G. M., Sandoz, E. K., Darrow, S. M., & Feeney, T. K. (2015). The Body Image Psychological Inflexibility Scale: Development and psychometric properties. *Psychiatry Research*, *226*, 45–52. doi:10.1016/j.psychres.2014.11.039

Ferreira, C., Trindade, I. A., Duarte, C., & Pinto-Gouveia, J. (2014). Getting entangled with body image: Development and validation of a new measure. *Psychology and Psychotherapy: Theory, Research and Practice*, *88*, 304–316. doi:10.1111/papt.12047

Hayes, S. C., Luoma, J. B., Bond, F. W., Masuda, A., & Lillis, J. (2006). Acceptance and commitment therapy: Model, processes, and outcomes. *Behaviour Research and Therapy*, *44*, 1–25. doi:10.1016/j.brat.2005.06.006

Hayes, S. C., Strosahl, K. D., & Wilson, K. G. (1999). *Acceptance and commitment therapy: An experiential approach to behavior change*. New York, NY: Guilford Press.

Heffner, M., Sperry, J., Eifert, G. H., & Detweiler, M. (2002). Acceptance and commitment therapy in the treatment of an adolescent female with anorexia nervosa: A case example. *Cognitive and Behavioral Practice*, *9*, 232–236. doi:10.1016/s1077-7229(02)80053-0

Hill, M. L., Masuda, A., Melcher, H., Morgan, J. R., & Twohig, M. P. (2015). Acceptance and commitment therapy for women diagnosed with binge eating disorder: A case-series study. *Cognitive and Behavioral Practice*, *22*, 367–378. doi:10.1016/j.cbpra.2014.02.005

Hill, M. L., Masuda, A., Moore, M., & Twohig, M. P. (2015). Acceptance and commitment therapy for individuals with problematic emotional eating: A case-series study. *Clinical Case Studies*, *14*, 141–154. doi:10.1177/1534650114547429

Ivanova, E., Jensen, D., Cassoff, J., Gu, F., & Knauper, B. (2015). Acceptance and commitment therapy improves exercise tolerance in sedentary women. *Medicine and Science in Sports and Exercise*, *47*, 1251–1258. doi:10.1249/MSS.0000000000000536

Katterman, S. N., Goldstein, S. P., Butryn, M. L., Forman, E. M., & Lowe, M. R. (2014). Efficacy of an acceptance-based behavioral intervention for weight gain prevention in young adult women. *Journal of Contextual Behavioral Science*, *3*, 45–50. doi:10.1016/j.jcbs.2013.10.003

Levin, M. E., Potts, S., Haeger, J., & Lillis, J. (2018). Delivering acceptance and commitment therapy for weight self-stigma through guided self-help: Results from an open pilot trial. *Cognitive and Behavioral Practice*, *25*, 87–104. doi:10.1016/j.cbpra.2017.02.002

Lillis, J., & Hayes, S. C. (2008). Measuring avoidance and inflexibility in weight related problems. *International Journal of Behavioral Consultation and Therapy*, *4*, 30–40. doi:10.1037/h0100829

Lillis, J., Hayes, S. C., Bunting, K., & Masuda, A. (2009). Teaching acceptance and mindfulness to improve the lives of the obese: A preliminary test of a theoretical model. *Annals of Behavioral Medicine*, *37*, 58–69. doi:10.1007/s12160-009-9083-x

Lillis, J., Hayes, S. C., & Levin, M. E. (2011). Binge eating and weight control: The role of experiential avoidance. *Behavior Modification*, *35*, 252–264. doi:10.1177/0145445510397178

Lillis, J., & Kendra, K. E. (2014). Acceptance and commitment therapy for weight control: Model, evidence, and future directions. *Journal of Contextual Behavioral Science, 3*, 1–7. doi:10.1016/j.jcbs.2013.11.005

Manlick, C. F., Cochran, S. V., & Koon, J. (2013). Acceptance and commitment therapy for eating disorders: Rationale and literature review. *Journal of Contemporary Psychotherapy, 43*, 115–122. doi:10.1007/s10879-012-9223-7

Martin, E. C., Galloway-Williams, N., Cox, M. G., & Winett, R. A. (2015). Pilot testing of a mindfulness- and acceptance-based intervention for increasing cardiorespiratory fitness in sedentary adults: A feasibility study. *Journal of Contextual Behavioral Science, 4*, 237–245. doi:10.1016/j.jcbs.2015.10.005

Masuda, A., Ng, S. Y., Moore, M., Felix, I., & Drake, C. E. (2016). Acceptance and commitment therapy as a treatment for a Latina young adult women with purging: A case report. *Practice Innovations, 1*, 20–35. doi:10.1037/pri0000012

Moffitt, R., & Mohr, P. (2015). The efficacy of a self-managed acceptance and commitment therapy intervention DVD for physical activity initiation. *British Journal of Health Psychology, 20*, 115–129. doi:10.1111/bjhp.12098

Niemeier, H. M., Leahey, T., Reed, K. P., Brown, R. A., Wing, R. R. (2012). An acceptance-based behavioral intervention for weight loss: A pilot study. *Behavior Therapy, 43*, 427–435. doi:10.1016/j.beth.2011.10.005

Palmeira, L., Pinto-Gouveia, J., & Cunha, M. (2017). Exploring the efficacy of an acceptance, mindfulness and compassionate-based group intervention for women struggling with their weight (Kg-Free): A randomized controlled trial. *Appetite, 112*, 107–116. doi:10.1016/j.appet.2017.01.027

Pearson, A. N., Follette, V. M., & Hayes, S. C. (2012). A pilot study of acceptance and commitment therapy as a workshop intervention for body dissatisfaction and disordered eating attitudes. *Cognitive and Behavioral Practice, 19*, 181–197. doi:10.1016/j.cbpra.2011.03.001

Pearson, A. N., Heffner, M., & Follette, V. M. (2010). *Acceptance and commitment therapy for body image dissatisfaction: A practitioner's guide to using mindfulness, acceptance and values-based behavior change strategies.* Oakland, CA: New Harbinger.

Pinto-Gouveia, J., Carvalho, S. A., Palmeira, L., Castilho, P., Duarte, C., Ferreira, C., . . . Costa, J. (2016). Incorporating mindfulness and self-compassion in a new programme for binge eating (BEfree): Exploring processes of change. *Journal of Health Psychology.* Nov 1, 1359105316676628. Advance online publication. doi:10.1177/1359105316676628

Piran, N. (2016). Embodied possibilities and disruptions: The emergence of the Experience of Embodiment construct from qualitative studies with girls and women. *Body Image, 18*, 43–60. doi:10.1016/j.bodyim.2016.04.007

Piran, N. (2017). *Journeys of embodiment at the intersection of body and culture: The developmental theory of embodiment.* San Diego, CA: Elsevier. doi: 10.1016/c2015-0-04666-4.

Powers, M. B., Zum Vorde Sive Vording, M. B., & Emmelkamp, P. M. G. (2009). Acceptance and commitment therapy: A meta-analytic review. *Psychotherapy and Psychosomatics, 78*, 73–80. doi:10.1159/000190790

Sairanen, E., Tolvanen, A., Karhunen, L., Kolehmainen, M., Jarvela-Reijonen, E., Lindroos, S., . . . Lappalainen, R. (2017). Psychological flexibility mediates change in intuitive eating regulation in acceptance and commitment therapy interventions. *Public Health Nutrition, 78*, 1681–1691. doi:10.1017/S1368980017000441

Sandoz, E. K., & DuFrene, T. (2013). *Living with your body and other things you hate: How to let go of your struggle with body image using acceptance and commitment therapy*. Oakland, CA: New Harbinger.

Sandoz, E. K., Wilson, K. G., Merwin, R. M., & Kellum, K. K. (2013). Assessment of body image flexibility: The Body-Image Acceptance and Action Questionnaire. *Journal of Contextual Behavioral Science, 2*, 39–48. doi:10.1016/j.jcbs.2013.03.002

Tylka, T. L., Annunziato, R. A., Burgard, D., Daníelsdóttir, S., Shuman, E., Davis, C., & Calogero, R. M. (2014). The weight-inclusive versus weight-normative approach to health: Evaluating evidence for prioritizing well-being over weight loss. *Journal of Obesity, 2014*, 1–18. doi:10.1155/2014/983495

Tylka, T. L., & Kroon Van Diest, A. M. (2013). The Intuitive Eating Scale-2: Item refinement and psychometric evaluation with college women and men. *Journal of Counseling Psychology, 60*, 137–153. doi:10.1037/a0030893

Tylka, T. L., & Wood-Barcalow, N. L. (2015). What is and what is not positive body image? Conceptual foundations and construct definition. *Body Image, 14*, 118–129. doi:10.1016/j.bodyim.2015.04.001

Walloch, J. C., Cerezo, A., & Heide, F. (2012). Acceptance and commitment therapy to address eating disorder symptomatology in gay men. *Journal of LGBT Issues in Counseling, 6*, 257–273. doi:10.1080/15538605.2012.725648

Webb, J. B. (2015). Body image flexibility contributes to explaining the link between body dissatisfaction and body appreciation in white college-bound females. *Journal of Contextual Behavioral Science, 4*, 176–183. doi:10.1016/j.jcbs.2015.06.001

28

Health at Every Size

A Social Justice–Informed Approach to Positive Embodiment

ANDREA LAMARRE AND SIGRÚN DANÍELSDÓTTIR ■

Weight-neutral approaches to health emerged in the latter half of the twentieth century as a response to the dominant weight-centered paradigm, which holds body weight and its management as central determinants of health and well-being. Weight-neutral approaches focus on other aspects of health and well-being as important and celebrate the natural diversity of bodies. The roots of these approaches can be traced to diverse underpinnings, including feminist discourse on appearance and embodiment (Fallon, Katzman, & Wooley, 1994; Wolf, 1991); the formation of the fat liberation movement in the 1970s and 1980s (Schoenfielder & Wieser, 1983; Wann, 2009); and the antidieting movement in the 1990s (Fraser, 1998; Kratina, King, & Hayes, 2003). Weight-neutral approaches also found their base in the early yet mounting scientific evidence that revealed the failure of weight loss treatments and highlighted sociocultural risk factors for eating disorders, biological influences on body weight, health improvements in the absence of weight loss, and the injustice of weight stigma (Crandall, 1994; Garner, Garfinkel, Schwartz, & Thompson, 1980; Garner & Wooley, 1991; Leibel, Rosenbaum, & Hirsch, 1995; Miller, 1999; Striegel-Moore, Silberstein, & Rodin, 1986).

At first, this new approach was simply referred to as "the nondiet approach," as it emphasized turning away from weight management through restriction and instead focused on self-acceptance and reliance on internal cues as guides for eating (i.e., intuitive eating) (Robison & Kratina, 2003). The tenets of the nondiet approach were later adapted as the Tenets of Health at Every Size (see Robison & Kratina, 2003, for a review). As shown in Figure 28.1, this model addresses health policy, treatment settings, and individual self-care.

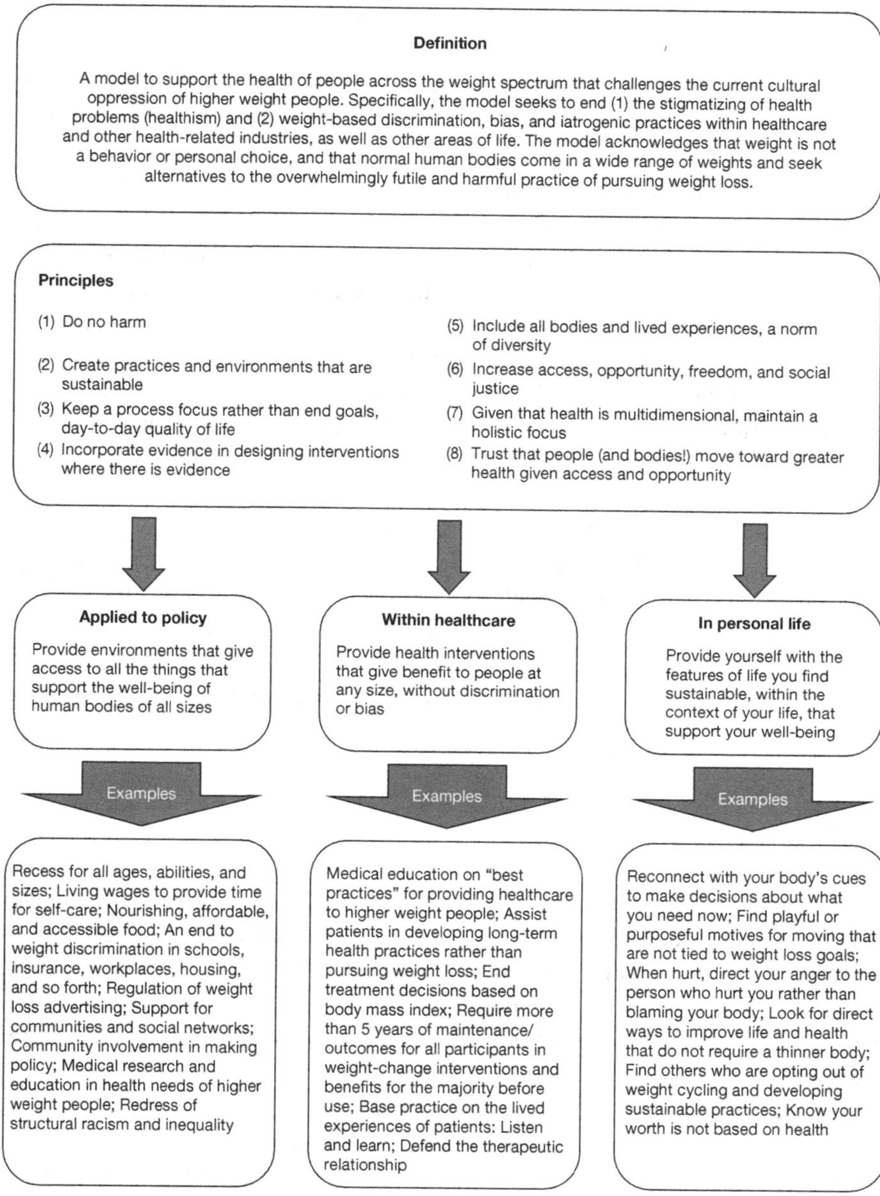

Figure 28.1 A Health at Every Size (HAES) model for health promotion (Tylka et al., 2014).
Tylka et al. (2014) is open access, published in the *Journal of Obesity.* All authors retain copyright to the published work.

PRINCIPLES OF HEALTH AT EVERY SIZE

Currently, Health at Every Size® (HAES®) is a registered trademark of the Association for Size Diversity and Health (n.d.), and its principles are as follows:

- **Weight Inclusivity:** Accept and respect the inherent diversity of body shapes and sizes and reject the idealizing or pathologizing of specific weights.
- **Health Enhancement:** Support health policies that improve and equalize access to information and services and personal practices that improve human well-being, including attention to individual physical, economic, social, spiritual, emotional, and other needs.
- **Respectful Care:** Acknowledge our biases, and work to end weight discrimination, weight stigma, and weight bias. Provide information and services from an understanding that socioeconomic status (SES), race, gender, sexual orientation, age, and other identities impact weight stigma; support environments that address these inequities.
- **Eating for Well-Being:** Promote flexible, individualized eating based on hunger, satiety, nutritional needs, and pleasure, rather than any externally regulated eating plan focused on weight control.
- **Life-Enhancing Movement:** Support physical activities that allow people of all sizes, abilities, and interests to engage in enjoyable movement to the degree that they choose.

SHOW ME THE DATA

Concerns about the harms of weight-centered approaches have been a major driving force behind the evolution of HAES and the call for a paradigm shift in weight-related research, prevention, and treatment. Proponents of this paradigm shift assert that weight science has been going through a prolonged Kuhnian dilemma where the premises that uphold a weight loss paradigm—that dietary restraint will yield sustained changes in weight and concomitant improved health outcomes—are not in sync with scientific results (e.g., Bacon & Aphramor, 2011; Cogan, 1999a, 1999b; Cogan & Ernsberger, 1999; Miller, 1999).

Twenty years ago, Kassirer and Angell (1998) stated, in a famed *New England Journal of Medicine* editorial:

> Given the enormous social pressure to lose weight, one might suppose there is clear and overwhelming evidence of the risks of obesity and the benefits of weight loss. Unfortunately, the data linking overweight and death, as well as the data showing the beneficial effects of weight loss, are limited, fragmentary, and often ambiguous. (p. 2)

In the years since, scientific evidence has only reaffirmed this conclusion. It is by now well established that the weight range currently defined as "overweight" (body mass index [BMI] 25.0–29.9) is associated with *lower* risk of mortality, and the range defined as "mild obesity" (BMI 30.0–34.9), where the majority of individuals classified as "obese" are situated, is unrelated to mortality (Flegal, Caroll, Kit, & Ogden, 2012; Flegal, Kit, Orpana, & Graubard, 2013). The correlation between higher BMI and mortality appears to be primarily due to increased risk at BMI levels greater than 35; however, correlation does not imply causation. As weight increases, so do a number of other factors—stigma is one example—that have their own health implications.

Many scholars have highlighted that the relationship between weight and health is not as clear or robust as one might assume based on mainstream scientific discourse (e.g., Bacon & Aphramor, 2011; Bombak, 2013; Cogan, 1999b; Cogan & Ernsberger, 1999; Mann, Tomiyama, & Ward, 2015; Tylka et al., 2014). Most weight science research to date has failed to control for central confounding variables known to impact both weight and health and the relationship between the two, including SES, weight stigma, lifestyle behaviors, weight loss practices, and metabolic fitness. This omission poses a serious threat to the validity of the knowledge produced by weight science, and the fact that it has not prompted more effective improvements in research design remains concerning.

Studies that do control for central confounding factors usually find that the association between health and BMI is substantially weakened and sometimes eliminated (e.g., Barry et al., 2014; Matheson, King, & Everett; 2012; Wei et al., 1999; Wessel et al., 2004). For example, a large population study from the National Health and Nutrition Examination Survey III (NHANES) found that when health-promoting behaviors (i.e., exercising regularly, eating five or more fruits and vegetables daily, not smoking, and consuming alcohol in moderation) were included in the analysis, the association between BMI and all-cause mortality disappeared (Matheson et al., 2012). Among participants who did not report any of these behaviors, however, mortality rates rose predictably alongside elevated BMI, with subjects in the obese category having many times the risk of those at lower BMI levels.

Studies also consistently report fitness to be a stronger predictor of mortality than weight. This was most recently evidenced by a meta-analysis showing similar mortality risks for individuals with high cardiorespiratory fitness irrespective of BMI category (Barry et al., 2014). Additionally, SES is strongly related to health and longevity (Marmot, 2003), and an inverse relationship exists between SES and weight in Western societies (Ernsberger, 2009). Despite this, some studies still do not control for SES in their analyses. Further, there is mounting evidence that weight stigma negatively impacts health, health behavior, and psychological well-being and thus may partly explain worse health outcomes among higher weight individuals (Hatzenbuehler, Phelan, & Link, 2013; Muennig, 2008; Puhl & Heuer, 2009). Regardless, it is extremely rare for weight research to control for weight stigma, and there are no studies to our knowledge that have adjusted for all major confounds (i.e., SES, health behavior, metabolic fitness, weight cycling, and weight stigma).

Another important consideration is that decades of research have depicted how weight loss interventions continuously fail to produce lasting and significant results. In their review and meta-analysis, Ross Middleton, Paditar, and Perri (2012) noted that weight regain is typical after obesity treatment, with participants gaining back "on average, one-third to one-half of lost weight within the first year following treatment and returning to baseline weight within 3–5 years after the end of treatment" (p. 509). Despite a growing call for extended care following weight loss, the researchers found that extended care for up to 18 months yielded only an additional reduction of 3.2 kg on average (Ross Middleton et al., 2012). Another meta-analysis of 18 randomized, controlled weight loss trials with a follow-up of up to 6 years reported an average of only 1.64 kg in sustained weight loss after 2 years (Wu, Gao, Chen, & Van Dam, 2009). A systematic review of weight loss interventions in primary healthcare further concluded that the interventions yielded only minor reductions in weight, which were unlikely to be clinically significant (Booth, Prevost, Wright, & Gulliford, 2014). In their analysis of primary health data from nearly 200,000 individuals classified as obese, Fildes and colleagues (2015) found that the odds of losing even 5% of body weight were very low for both men and women (10% and 8%, respectively) and moving from obese to normal BMI was extremely rare. For men with a BMI between 30 and 35, the odds of attaining a normal BMI were 1 in 210, and they were 1 in 124 for women. For individuals with a BMI over 40, the odds were 1 in 1,290 for men and 1 in 677 for women.

Importantly, these findings are not new. It has now been 60 years since Stunkard and Hume (1959) concluded that "of those who enter obesity treatment, most will drop out. Of those who stay in treatment, most will not lose weight. Of those who do lose weight, most will regain it" (as cited in Lyons, 2009, p. 77). Since then, these findings have been repeatedly confirmed. In fact, a decade ago Mann and colleagues (2007) concluded that additional studies on weight loss approaches were not needed as the literature clearly demonstrates their ineffectiveness. Instead, Mann et al. (2015) urged that "the enormous quantity of financial resources currently devoted toward discovering the ideal restrictive diet be redirected toward evidence-based, scientifically grounded strategies to promote health" (p. 706).

This is precisely the aim of HAES and other weight-neutral approaches (e.g., Aphramor & Gingras, 2011; Bacon, Stern, Van Loan, & Keim, 2005; Mansfield & Rich, 2013; Tylka et al., 2014). There is now considerable evidence that demonstrates how improvements in mental and physical health can be made without weight loss (e.g., Mensinger, Calogero, Stranges, & Tylka, 2016; Pedersen & Saltin, 2015; Tylka et al., 2014). Interventions using HAES principles consistently produce similar benefits—and for longer than weight loss interventions—in biomedical health markers, such as blood pressure and lipids despite little or no weight changes, and psychological indicators, such as self-esteem and depressive symptoms (for review, see Bacon & Aphramor, 2011, and Tylka et al., 2014). For example, Bacon et al. (2005) conducted a randomized controlled trial comparing a 6-month HAES intervention delivered to groups weekly to a weight loss program of the same length, group-based format, and delivery frequency. All participants achieved significant improvements in low-density lipoprotein (LDL) cholesterol, systolic blood pressure, disordered eating, body dissatisfaction, self-esteem, and physical activity. However, these improvements were only maintained for the HAES group at 24-month follow-up. Similarly, a recent randomized controlled trial found that a 6-month weight-neutral intervention delivered to groups weekly had larger reductions in LDL cholesterol and greater improvements in intuitive eating compared to a weight loss group of the same length, group-based format, and delivery frequency (Mensinger et al., 2016). Despite the absence of weight loss, the HAES group produced equal improvements in cholesterol, physical activity, fruit and vegetable intake, self-esteem, and quality of life.

A recent review of studies examining intuitive eating, a central component of HAES, found that relying on internal cues of hunger and satiety was linked to increased body satisfaction, self-esteem, engagement in physical activity, and quality of life, as well as less depression, anxiety, and disordered eating (e.g., binge eating) (Schaefer & Magnuson, 2014; see also Chapter 7). There is also strong literature showing the benefits of physical activity on a range of conditions, including cardiovascular risk factors, independent of weight loss (Pedersen & Saltin, 2015). Furthermore, public health messages are met with greater approval and intentions for behavior change when they focus on healthy behaviors (e.g., fruit and vegetable consumption) instead of body weight (Puhl, Luedicke, & Peterson, 2013; Puhl, Peterson, & Luedicke, 2013). For example, a population study where over 1,000 adults were asked to review a random selection of antiobesity campaigns from the United States, the United Kingdom, and Australia reported that the campaigns perceived as most positive and motivating made no reference to obesity (Puhl, Peterson, et al., 2013).

A CALL FOR SOCIAL JUSTICE

There is evidence that the HAES approach is more aligned with social justice than mainstream approaches to health and weight. In three experimental studies examining cultural frameworks around fatness, Frederick, Saguy, and Gruys (2016) asked participants to read news articles that presented higher body weight in terms of a public health crisis, personal responsibility, HAES, or fat rights. They found that participants who read articles that presented higher weight as a personal failing or public health crisis reported more antifat attitudes and more willingness to discriminate against higher weight people than participants who read articles that presented HAES or fat rights. However, the researchers also found that articles on fat rights had a stronger impact on respect for body diversity than a HAES framework. The authors concluded that while HAES clearly conforms to the principle of doing no harm, it may not suffice to increase respect for higher weight people. For that, fat rights as human rights need to be emphasized regardless of the health of the human in question (see Calogero, Tylka, Mensinger, Meadows, & Daníelsdóttir, 2018).

Furthermore, while the HAES approach has always aimed for social change, the centralization of *health* at every size has been criticized for potentially contributing to the oppression of marginalized populations. Several critical scholars have highlighted both (a) the healthism inherent to an approach that foregrounds health and (b) how health itself can become an imperative that people must perform in order to be accepted as valuable, productive citizens (LeBesco, 2010; Welsh, 2011). *Healthism* refers to a "preoccupation with personal health as a primary—often *the* primary—focus for the definition, and achievement of, well-being" (Crawford, 1980, p. 386, italics in original). Particularly in the context of the growing acceptance among health promotion experts of a more weight-neutral approach, those concerned with healthism have turned to a focus on how health itself—and the need for the achievement of health—can take on "an evangelical fervor" (Brady, Gingras, & Aphramor, 2013, p. 346). They argue that the prevailing medical model in science and healthcare is underscored by a moralization of certain bodies, not only because they are fat, but also because they are deemed to be failing to live up to those standards of self-management that promise a long life and a productive citizenry (Crawford, 2006).

In order to move beyond healthism, advocates suggest advancing the perspective that health cannot be painted with a single brush: It will necessarily differ based on individuals' social locations, including their spaces of privilege and marginalization (Aphramor, 2010; Brady et al., 2013; Burgard, 2009; McKibbin, 2009). As Brady et al. (2013) convincingly delineated in their article about understanding HAES as a relational–cultural endeavor, weight loss and HAES paradigms share a common focus on the importance of engaging in efforts to improve and maintain health, which may be regarded as oppressive in and of themselves. Building on LeBesco's (2010) critique of the primacy of scientific discourse within the HAES paradigm, they noted that HAES proponents "fight science with science" (Brady et al., 2013, p. 347) in a way that may reinforce a framing of weight as primarily a medical issue.

Recognizing the way that health intersects with other spaces of belonging speaks to a necessary acknowledgment of the social determinants of health and further exemplifies how, in order to promote health and well-being, it is necessary promote greater inclusivity and work against oppression, and the intersections of oppressions, at a societal level. Intersectionality is an approach to understanding people's social identities as a composite of their various and related spaces of belonging, including their race, class, gender, sexuality, ability, SES, and so on (Crenshaw, 1991). Beyond simply looking at the additive impact of social oppressions, taking an approach to HAES that is based in intersectionality would entail attending to how each person in a body in society will have a unique experience of the world.

CONCLUSION: THE FUTURE OF HAES

The HAES paradigm continues to be informed by evolving scientific debate and critical social justice discourse. Historically, like other identity-based social movements, HAES and fat rights have primarily centered on a single feature of diversity—body size—as opposed to being intersectional. In recent years, however, many within the HAES movement have attempted to more fully integrate social justice premises, regarding it insufficient to advocate for the acceptance of larger bodies if bodies continue to be marginalized along other lines, including ability, race, SES, gender, sexuality, and more. There is increased recognition within multiple sociopolitical arenas that systems of oppression do not call out and marginalize folks along a single axis but conflate diverse marginalized identities in a complex structure that needs to be understood in its entirety (Crenshaw, 1991).

Intersectionality is not a static theory, but rather an open project. As Carbado, Crenshaw, Mays, and Tomlinson (2013) explained, we might think about "what intersectionality does as a starting point for thinking about what else the framework might be mobilized to do . . . to see the theory in places in which it is already doing work and to imagine other kinds of work that agents might employ intersectionality to perform" (pp. 304–305). Thus, we might imagine the HAES movement, as it evolves, as one place where intersectionality might help to do additional work that welcomes more bodies into the social imagination of valuable humanity.

Although promoting individual resilience and self-love are admirable goals, and in their own way radical and revolutionary within a society that teaches people to hate their bodies, the gains made from individual changes may be fleeting without sustained systemic work to challenge the ways in which inequalities are perpetuated. Body acceptance advocates have long noted that body diversity is not only normal but also desirable and should be framed as a positive (Wann, 1998). However, people who do not fit the norm are constantly reminded of their nonbelonging in a world where our bodies are still used to define who we are, regardless of how much we identify with that idea. Body shame is pervasive and rooted in systemic structures, including mainstream weight science. Thus, in order to challenge bodily discontent, we need to simultaneously move toward body peace at individual and systemic levels. We might draw on social justice movements—including antiracist, antisexist, and antiableist movements—and integrate these and the lessons learned from them into our approaches to promoting health at all sizes.

A truly effective approach to promoting positive embodiment needs to be rooted in social justice; it must bring to attention how experiences of body acceptance or discontent are always rooted in social structures, including the privileges and exclusions contained within them. With this acknowledgment, we suggest that in addition to individual strategies for body acceptance, we need campaigns, platforms, lobbies, and push back against the broader social systems that leave us out of step with our bodies. We need to accompany strategies for self-compassion, self-acceptance, and self-care with efforts to challenge tenacious social injustices: hiring advisory boards of people with various lived experiences as paid advisors to large health organizations; providing insurance policies that benefit those in the most need; recognizing the various forms expertise can take (including lived, embodied experience); making public spaces more accessible;

minimizing attitudinal and environmental barriers to physical activity; addressing food insecurity through the provision of a wider variety of food-purchasing options; and so much more. Thus, we encourage readers to look systemically for solutions to problems that appear personal; only through this bird's-eye view can we begin to truly redefine and promote health and sustained well-being.

REFERENCES

Aphramor, L. (2010). Validity of claims made in weight management research: A narrative review of dietetic articles. *Nutrition Journal*, *9*, 30. doi:10.1186/1475-2891-9-30

Aphramor, L., & Gingras J. (2011). Helping people change: Promoting politicised practice in the healthcare professions. In E. Rich, L. Monaghan, & L. Aphramor (Eds.), *Debating obesity: Critical perspectives* (pp. 192–218). London, England: Palgrave/Macmillan.

Association for Size Diversity and Health. (n.d.). The Health at Every Size® Approach. Retrieved April 28, 2017, from https://www.sizediversityandhealth.org/images/uploaded/ASDAH%20HAES%20Principles.pdf

Bacon, L., & Aphramor, L. (2011). Weight science: Evaluating the evidence for a paradigm shift. *Nutrition Journal*, *10*, 1–13. doi:10.1186/1475-2891-10-9

Bacon, L., Stern, J. S., Van Loan, M. D., & Keim, N. L. (2005). Size acceptance and intuitive eating improve health for obese, female chronic dieters. *Journal of the American Dietetic Association*, *105*, 929–936. doi:10.1016/j.ada.2005.03.011

Barry, V. W., Baruth, M., Beets, M. W., Durstine, J. L., Liu, J., & Blair, S. N. (2014). Fitness vs. fatness on all-cause mortality: A meta-analysis. *Progress in Cardiovascular Diseases*, *56*, 382–390. doi:10.1016/j.pcad.2013.09.002

Bombak, A. (2013). Obesity, Health at Every Size and public health policy. *American Journal of Public Health*, *104*, e60–e67. doi:10.2105/AJPH.2013.301486

Booth, H. P., Prevost, T. A., Wright, A. J., & Gulliford, M. C. (2014). Effectiveness of behavioural weight loss interventions delivered in a primary care setting: A systematic review and meta-analysis. *Family Practice*, *31*, 643–653. doi:10.1093/fampra/cmu064

Brady, J., Gingras, J., & Aphramor, L. (2013). Theorizing Health at Every Size as a relational-cultural endeavor. *Critical Public Health*, *23*, 345–355. doi:10.1080/09581596.2013.797565

Burgard, D. (2009). What is "Health at Every Size"? In E. Rothblum & S. Solovay (Eds.), *The fat studies reader* (pp. 42–53). New York, NY: New York University Press.

Calogero, R. M., Tylka, T. L., Mensinger, J. L., Meadows, A., & Daníelsdóttir, S. (2018). *Recognizing the fundamental right to be fat: A weight-inclusive approach to size acceptance and healing from sizeism. Women & Therapy*. Advance online publication. doi:10.1080/02703149.2018.524067

Carbado, D. W., Crenshaw, K. W., Mays, V. M., & Tomlinson, B. (2013). Intersectionality: Mapping the movements of a theory. *Du Bois Review*, *10*, 303–312.

Cogan, J. C. (1999a). A new national health agenda: Providing the public with accurate information. *Journal of Social Issues*, *55*, 383–400. doi:10.1111/0022-4537.00122

Cogan, J. C. (1999b). Re-evaluating the weight-centered approach toward health: The need for a paradigm shift. In J. Sobal & D. Maurer (Eds.), *Interpreting weight: The social management of fatness and thinness* (pp. 229–253). New York, NY: Aldine de Gruyter.

Cogan, J. C., & Ernsberger, P. (1999). Dieting, weight, and health: Reconceptualizing research and policy. *Journal of Social Issues, 55*, 187–205. doi:10.1111/0022-4537.00112

Crandall, C. S. (1994). Prejudice against fat people: Ideology and self-interest. *Journal of Personality and Social Psychology, 66*, 882–894. doi:10.1037/0022-3514.66.5.882

Crawford, R. (1980). Healthism and the medicalisation of everyday life. *International Journal of Human Services, 10*(3), 365–388.

Crawford, R. (2006). Health as a meaningful social practice. *Health, 10*(4), 401–420.

Crenshaw, K. (1991). Mapping the margins: Intersectionality, identity politics, and violence against women of color. *Stanford Law Review, 43*, 1241–1299. doi:10.2307/1229039

Ernsberger, P. (2009). Does social class explain the connection between weight and health? In E. Rothblum & S. Solovay (Eds.), *The fat studies reader* (pp. 25–36). New York, NY: New York University Press.

Fallon, P., Katzman, M. A., & Wooley, S. C. (1994). *Feminist perspectives on eating disorders*. New York, NY: Guilford Press.

Fildes, A., Charlton, J., Rudisill, C., Littlejohns, P., Prevost, A. T., & Gulliford, M. C. (2015). Probability of an obese person attaining normal body weight: Cohort study using electronic health records. *American Journal of Public Health, 105*, e54–e59. doi:10.2105/AJPH.2015.302773

Flegal, K. M., Caroll, M. D., Kit, B. K., & Ogden, C. L. (2012). Prevalence of obesity and trends in the distribution of body mass index among US adults, 1999–2010. *Journal of the American Medical Association, 307*, 491–497. doi:10.1001/jama.2012.39

Flegal, K. M., Kit, B. K., Orpana, H., & Graubard, B. I. (2013). Association of all-cause mortality with overweight and obesity using standard body mass index categories: A systematic review and meta-analysis. *Journal of the American Medical Association, 309*, 71–82. doi:10.1001/jama.2012.113905

Fraser, L. (1998). *Losing it: False hopes and fat profits in the diet industry*. New York, NY: Plume.

Frederick, D. A., Saguy, A. C., & Gruys, K. (2016). Culture, health, and bigotry: How exposure to cultural accounts of fatness shape attitudes about health risk, health policies, and weight-based prejudice. *Social Science & Medicine, 165*, 271–279. doi:10.1016/j.socscimed.2015.12.031

Garner, D. M., Garfinkel, P. E., Schwartz, D., & Thompson, M. (1980). Cultural expectations of thinness in women. *Psychological Reports, 47*, 483–491. doi:10.2466/pr0.1980.47.2.483

Garner, D. M., & Wooley, S. C. (1991). Confronting the failure of behavioral and dietary treatments for obesity. *Clinical Psychology Review, 11*, 729–780. doi:10.1016/0272-7358(91)90128-H

Hatzenbuehler, M. L., Phelan, J. C., & Link, B. G. (2013). Stigma as a fundamental cause of population health inequalities. *American Journal of Public Health, 103*, 813–821. doi:10.2105/AJPH.2012.301069

Kassirer, J. P., & Angell, M. (1998). Losing weight—An ill-fated New Year's resolution. *New England Journal of Medicine, 338*, 52–54. doi:10.1056/NEJM199801013380109

Kratina, K., King, N., & Hayes, D. (2003). *Moving away from diets* (2nd ed.). Lake Dallas, TX: Helm.

LeBesco, K. (2010). Fat panic and the new morality. In J. J. Metzl & A. Kirkland (Eds.), *Against health: How health became the new morality* (pp. 72–82). New York, NY: New York University Press.

Leibel, R. L., Rosenbaum, M., & Hirsch, J. (1995). Changes in energy expenditure resulting from altered body weight. *New England Journal of Medicine, 332*, 621–628. doi:10.1056/NEJM199503093321001

Lyons, P. (2009). Prescription for harm: Diet industry influence, public health policy, and the "obesity epidemic." In E. Rothblum & S. Solovay (Eds.), *The fat studies reader* (pp. 75–87). New York, NY: New York University Press.

Mann, T., Tomiyama, A. J., & Ward, A. (2015). Promoting public health in the context of the "obesity epidemic": False starts and promising new directions. *Perspectives on Psychological Science, 10*, 706–710. doi:10.1177/1745691615586401

Mann, T., Tomiyama, A. J., Westling, E., Lew, A. M., Samuels, B., & Chatman, J. (2007). Medicare's search for effective obesity treatments: Diets are not the answer. *American Psychologist, 62*, 220–223. doi:10.1037/0003-066X.62.3.220

Mansfield, L., & Rich, E. (2013). Public health pedagogy, border crossings and physical activity at every size. *Critical Public Health, 23*, 356–370. doi:10.1080/09581596.2013.783685

Marmot, M. G. (2003). Understanding social inequalities in health. *Perspectives in Biology and Medicine, 46*, S9–S23. doi:10.1353/pbm.2003.0056

Matheson, E. M., King, D. E., & Everett, C. J. (2012). Healthy lifestyle habits and mortality in overweight and obese individuals. *Journal of the American Board of Family Medicine, 25*, 9–15. doi:103122/jabfm.2012.01.110164

McKibbin, L. (2009). "The Food for Thought Pyramid." Retrieved April 28, 2017, from http://www.food-for-thought-pyramid.com

Mensinger, J. L., Calogero, R. M., Stranges, S., & Tylka, T. L. (2016). A weight-neutral versus weight-loss approach for health promotion in women with high BMI: A randomized-controlled trial. *Appetite, 105*, 364–374. doi:10.1016/j.appet.2016.06.006

Miller, W. C. (1999). Fitness and fatness in relation to health: Implications for a paradigm shift. *Journal of Social Issues, 55*, 207–219. doi:10.1111/0022-4537.00113

Muennig, P. (2008). The body politic: The relationship between stigma and obesity-associated disease. *BMC Public Health, 8*, 128. doi:10.1186/1471-2458-8-128.

Pedersen, B. K., & Saltin, B. (2015). Exercise as medicine—Evidence for prescribing exercise as therapy in 26 different chronic diseases. *Scandinavian Journal of Medicine & Science in Sports, 25*, 1–72. doi:10.1111/sms.12581

Puhl, R. M., & Heuer, C. A. (2009). The stigma of obesity: A review and update. *Obesity, 17*, 941–964. doi:10.1038/oby.2008.636

Puhl, R., Peterson, J. L., & Luedicke, J. (2013). Fighting obesity or obese persons? Public perceptions of obesity-related health messages. *International Journal of Obesity, 37*, 774–782. doi:10.1038/ijo.2012.156

Puhl, R., Luedicke, J., & Peterson, J. L. (2013). Public reactions to obesity-related health campaigns: A randomized controlled trial. *American Journal of Preventive Medicine, 45*, 36–48. doi:10.1016/j.amepre.2013.02.010

Robison, J., & Kratina, K. (2003). Health at Every Size, health for *every* body. In K. Kratina, N. King, & D. Hayes (Eds.), *Moving away from diets* (2nd ed., pp. 27–47). Lake Dallas, TX: Helm.

Ross Middleton, K. M., Paditar, S. M., & Perri, M. G. (2012). The impact of extended care on the long-term maintenance of weight loss: A systematic review and meta-analysis. *Obesity Reviews, 13*, 509–517. doi:10.1111/j.1467-789X.2011.00972.x

Schaefer, J. T., & Magnuson, A. B. (2014). A review of interventions that promote eating by internal cues. *Journal of the Academy of Nutrition and Dietetics, 114*, 734–760. doi: 10.1016/j.jand.2013.12.024

Schoenfielder, L., & Wieser, B. (1983). *Shadow on a tightrope: Writings by women on fat oppression*. San Francisco, CA: Aunt Lute Books.

Striegel-Moore, R. H., Silberstein, L. R., & Rodin, J. (1986). Toward an understanding of risk factors for bulimia. *American Psychologist, 41*, 246–263. doi:10.1037//0003-066x.41.3.246

Stunkard, A., & Hume, M. (1959). The results of treatment for obesity: A review of the literature and report of a series. *Archives of Internal Medicine, 103*, 79–85.

Tylka, T. L., Annunziato, R., Burgard, D., Daníelsdóttir, S., Shuman, E., Davis, C., & Calogero, R. (2014). The weight-inclusive vs. weight-normative approach to health: Evaluating the evidence for prioritizing well-being over weight loss. *Journal of Obesity, 2014*, Art. 983495. doi.org/10.1155/2014/983495

Wann, M. (1998). *Fat! So?: Because you don't have to apologize for your size!* Ten Speed Press: Berkeley, CA.

Wann, M. (2009). Fat studies: An invitation to a revolution. In E. Rothblum & S. Solovay (Eds.), *The fat studies reader* (pp. ix–xxv). New York, NY: New York University Press.

Wei, M., Kampert, J. B., Barlow, C. E., Nichaman, M. Z., Gibbons, L. W., Paffenbarger, R. S. Jr, & Blair, S. N. (1999). Relationship between low cardiorespiratory fitness and mortality in normal-weight, overweight, and obese men. *JAMA, 282*(16), 1547–1553.

Welsh, T. A. (2011). Healthism and the Bodies of Women: Pleasure and Discipline in the War against Obesity. *Journal of Feminist Scholarship, 1*(1), 33–48.

Wessel, T. R., Arant, C. B., Olson, M. B., Johnson, B. D., Reis, S. E., Sharaf, B. L., ... Bairey Merz, C. N. (2004). Relationship of physical fitness vs. body mass index with coronary artery disease and cardiovascular events in women. *Journal of the American Medical Association, 292*, 1179–1187. doi:10.1001/jama.292.10.1188

Wolf, N. (1991). *The beauty myth: How images of female beauty are used against women*. New York, NY: Morrow.

Wu, T., Gao, X., Chen, M., & Van Dam, R. M. (2009). Long-term effectiveness of diet-plus-exercise interventions vs. diet-only interventions for weight loss: A meta-analysis. *Obesity Reviews, 10*, 313–323. doi:10.1111/j.1467-789X.2008.00547.x

29

Mindfulness Training to Facilitate Positive Body Image and Embodiment

MELISSA J. ATKINSON AND TRACEY D. WADE ■

Mindfulness is defined as "the awareness that emerges through paying attention on purpose, in the present moment, and non-judgmentally to the unfolding of experience moment by moment" (Kabat-Zinn, 2003, p. 145). Practicing mindfulness fosters a capacity to acknowledge and observe one's experiences (including thoughts, emotions, sensations, and urges) as they ebb and flow, without judgment and criticism or efforts to avoid, ruminate, problem-solve, or otherwise direct them. It is intended to facilitate a full appreciation and welcoming of one's experiences, both positive and negative, and encourage flexibility and nonreactivity in one's responses. Mindfulness can be conceptualized as a trait, state, or skill; can be cultivated through various formal and informal training and practice exercises; and is associated with a growing evidence base as a useful approach across multiple disorders (Keng, Smoski, & Robins, 2011).

Regarding the body more specifically, mindfulness represents a recent approach that has been applied to body image concerns and negative affect—two constructs that are associated with negative impacts on mental and physical health and are established risk factors in the development of eating disorders (Jacobi & Fittig, 2010). As a therapeutic technique, mindfulness is said to alter one's relationship with negative experience (Teasdale, Segal, & Williams, 1995) and has been conceptualized as an emotion regulation skill (Aldao, Nolen-Hoeksema, & Schweizer, 2010). Thus, in the context of body image, mindfulness aims to facilitate a more adaptive response to unpleasant, unwanted, and sometimes unavoidable negative experiences related to the body and appearance (e.g., sociocultural pressures to be thin, appearance-related teasing or criticism, unfavorable social comparisons, negative self-evaluations, body dissatisfaction, anxiety, urges to engage in weight control practices).

Mindfulness has the potential for a two-prong approach to building positive body image and embodiment. First, it aims to encourage an increased sense of appreciation and attunement (e.g., being aware and present in the body, perhaps noticing positive aspects previously avoided or neglected) and psychological flexibility (e.g., capacity to refrain from automatic negative reactions when confronted with socially prescribed appearance ideals and pressures). Second, mindfulness may help to reduce the intensity and impact of negative experiences that do occur (e.g., dissatisfaction, disgust, distress, shame, depression, anxiety).

This chapter reviews how mindfulness may be of benefit in promoting positive body image and embodiment (including theorized processes and mechanisms of action), outlines key components of existing mindfulness-based body image intervention approaches and evidence of their efficacy, and concludes with important considerations for current practice and future development. As a caveat, we note that our chapter predominantly describes work related to reducing negative body image experiences and disordered eating, as research exploring the capacity for mindfulness to specifically impact positive body image and embodiment is still in its infancy.

PROPOSED MECHANISMS OF ACTION REGARDING THE BODY

There have been various mechanisms proposed for how mindfulness may produce benefit generally, including processes of increased mindful awareness, attention regulation, meta-awareness and cognitive defusion/decentering, emotion regulation, exposure, and changing perspective of the self (for reviews, see Baer, 2003; Keng et al., 2011; Chapters 4 and 27). With specific regard to body image, mindfulness may work via three proposed pathways. First, mindfulness encourages a noncritical and compassionate view of the self and body via the practice of nonjudgmental awareness and acceptance, which is particularly salient for body image disturbances involving negative self-evaluation as a core component. Second, mindfulness enables an ability to detach or distance (decenter) oneself from distressing thoughts and feelings arising from body and eating related triggers, thereby promoting increased flexibility and decreasing unhelpful automatic responses (e.g., rumination, worry, depression, urges to engage in weight control practices). Third, rather than avoiding thoughts and emotions, mindfulness encourages their constant observation and therefore may reduce distress and subsequent maladaptive behaviors via exposure, extinction, and new learning related to previous fear-based conditioned responses. Nevertheless, research is required to substantiate these proposed mechanisms in the specific context of body image and disordered eating.

INTERVENTION CONCEPTS AND ACTIVITIES

Mindfulness-based interventions for body image aim to encourage the cultivation of: fuller awareness and engagement with the present, both mind and body; a decentered stance toward thoughts and feelings that might arise related to the body or eating in order to promote nonreactivity (i.e., observing one's thoughts and feelings as transient mental events); and an attitude of kindness, acceptance, nonjudgment, and self-compassion toward one's self and body. As in established mindfulness interventions, namely, mindfulness-based stress reduction (MBSR; Kabat-Zinn, 1990) and mindfulness-based cognitive therapy (MBCT; Segal, Williams, & Teasdale, 2012), these concepts are introduced via formal and informal breathing and meditational exercises. For example, the "raisin exercise" guides participants to focus their full attention on eating a single raisin while observing each aspect of their experience (touch, sight, sound, smell, taste, sensations, thoughts, feelings) as if it were their first encounter. Another introductory exercise, the "3-minute breathing space," is a short meditative observation containing three steps: observing and acknowledging one's current experience, then focusing attention specifically on the breath, and finally expanding attention to include the whole body. These exercises aim to highlight the power of present moment attention to change the quality or nature of our experience and offer a way to respond skillfully to difficult thoughts and feelings rather than react automatically.

Building on these foundational exercises, specific applications are then made to body image, including practicing mindful awareness and acceptance in the context of body-related activities (e.g., eating, walking, climbing stairs, exercising/sports, dancing, gardening, bathing); during guided visualization of a feared or unpleasant body image scenario (imaginal exposure); and when being exposed to appearance-idealized media images and mirror reflections (in vivo exposure). Participants are also encouraged to use the 3-minute breathing space both as a set meditation and as a coping strategy for when they notice negative thoughts or feelings about the body. Table 29.1 outlines the key themes and example activities of a brief three-session, mindfulness-based body image intervention conducted with small groups of young adult women with body image concerns (Atkinson & Wade, 2015).

RESEARCH ON MINDFULNESS FOR BODY IMAGE AND DISORDERED EATING

In the domain of body image and disordered eating, research on mindfulness has used experimental methodology and focused on prevention and treatment of eating disorders.

Table 29.1 Overview of Atkinson and Wade's (2015, 2016) Brief Three-Session, Group-Based Mindfulness Intervention for Body Image

Overview	Example Exercises
SESSION 1: INTRODUCTION TO MINDFULNESS AND PRESENT MOMENT AWARENESS	
Nonjudgment awareness and acceptance framed as an alternative way of coping with distressing or unwanted body-related thoughts and feelings, in contrast to common strategies of avoidance and rumination. Mindfulness defined and present moment awareness introduced and practiced in session.	- Pink elephant thought suppression and magnification exercises (to highlight unintended negative consequences of avoidance and rumination, respectively, and provide rationale for mindfulness as alternative) - Raisin exercise (mindful eating) as described in the text - Brief mindfulness of breathing (10 minutes) *Homework:* - Identify personal coping strategies and associated costs - The 3-minute breathing space (3MBS; as described in the text) - Mindfulness while undertaking a routine task
SESSION 2: A NEW WAY OF RELATING TO EXPERIENCE	
Introduction to the idea that thoughts and feelings are just mental events that can be acknowledged and allowed to pass by. Participants practice decentering from and observing thoughts in the context of negative self-evaluations, exposure to idealized magazine images, and while recalling and visualizing a recent personal negative body image experience.	- Decentering thought exercise (e.g., comparing the difference between "*I am having the thought that* I am fat" versus "I am fat") - Practicing mindfulness stance while viewing idealized media images - Role-play decentered and accepting attitude with example negative or critical comments *Homework:* - 3MBS, particularly in response to distress - Mindfulness while undertaking a useful or pleasant body experience - Read "The Guest House" poem by Jelaluddin Rumi
SESSION 3: CULTIVATING NONJUDGMENT AND SELF-COMPASSION	
Introduced to concept of being welcoming of all experiences, both negative and positive. The downsides to body-related judgment and self-criticism are discussed and nonjudgment and self-compassion practiced. Participants discuss future events likely to exacerbate body image concerns and how they could use what they had learned in the program effectively.	- Reading and reflecting on "The Guest House" poem - Brainstorming compassionate and accepting responses to self-critical body-related thoughts - Practicing mindfulness while visualizing a scenario in which they commonly experienced body-related concern *Homework:* - Continue practice of the 3MBS - Generate a Top 5 list of nonjudgmental statements to use when they observe self-critical thoughts - Mindfulness mirror exposure

Experimental Work Related to Body Image and Eating

Researchers, including our team, have conducted a range of experimental studies involving systematic manipulation of mindfulness processes in order to observe their effects on body- and eating-related thoughts, emotions, and behaviors in real time (Godfrey, Gallo, & Afari, 2015) in both nonclinical and clinical samples. With respect to nonclinical samples, we conducted two studies that showed that brief mindfulness-based training in present moment awareness and acceptance (5–10 minutes) produced an immediate improvement in state body satisfaction and negative mood (compared to a control) among female undergraduates who had been exposed to idealized magazine images (Atkinson & Wade, 2016; Wade, George, & Atkinson, 2009). A recent study among body-dissatisfied female university students also indicated that 15–20 minutes of mindfulness-based acceptance training was beneficial in protecting against a reduction in body satisfaction and related distress following later media exposure, compared to control (Margolis & Orsillo, 2016).

Further experimental research has evaluated practicing a state of mindfulness during mirror exposure, which involves deliberately and systematically viewing one's body reflected in the mirror. Delinsky and Wilson (2006) found improvements in weight and shape concerns, body satisfaction, and self-esteem after three 1-hour sessions of mindfulness-based mirror exposure among young adult women with weight and shape concerns. Interestingly, Luethcke, McDaniel, and Becker (2011) found that three sessions of mindfulness-based mirror exposure was effective in improving weight and shape concerns, eating pathology, and depression, but *not* body satisfaction, in a nonclinical sample of undergraduate females. This finding is perhaps consistent with the idea that mindfulness targets unhelpful *reactions* to internal experiences (e.g., overevaluation, negative mood, urge to binge/restrict), but does not necessarily change those experiences directly (e.g., negative body evaluation). Finally, studies related to food exposure have found mindfulness to be more effective than distraction in reducing negative affect in a nonclinical sample of women (Marek, Ben-Porath, Federici, Wisniewski, & Warren, 2013) and in reducing high-caloric food intake among undergraduate men and women, which was mediated by greater eating enjoyment (Arch et al., 2016).

Only a handful of experimental studies have investigated how mindfulness induction influences the response to stressor tasks related to body image and disordered eating in clinical samples. Two studies have assessed mindfulness in the context of eating. Among women with a history of anorexia nervosa and experiencing current eating disorder psychopathology, practicing mindfulness prior to a meal resulted in greater experiential self-focus (present moment awareness of the whole experience during eating, including the body, as opposed to an analytical or ruminative focus) in those who were partially weight restored, whereas other participants reported aversive experiences (Cowdrey, Stewart, Roberts, & Park, 2013). A second study showed that women with a diagnosed eating disorder who completed a brief mindful eating exercise reported increased negative affect after the intervention (Marek et al., 2013). For those with significant eating pathology, paying full attention may actually serve to exacerbate perceived negative sensations (e.g., feeling of fullness, bloating, anxiety) and unintentionally increase the difficulty associated with eating, at least initially. Other work has examined the impact of mindful acceptance practice after exposure to pictures of thin models in clinical samples. Such practice had no effect on women with binge eating disorder in one study (Svaldi & Naumann, 2014) and improved body dissatisfaction in women with bulimia nervosa, but not anorexia nervosa, in a follow-up study (Naumann, Tuschen-Caffier, Voderholzer, Schafer, & Svaldi, 2016). Overall, the pattern of findings suggests a differential effect depending on clinical status, with mindfulness having neutral or negative effects on outcome variables in clinical samples (Marek et al., 2013; Svaldi & Naumann, 2014) and a neutral or positive effect in nonclinical samples (Atkinson & Wade, 2012; Marek et al., 2013; Wade et al., 2009). Further research is required to elucidate which stage of concerns would be most appropriate to introduce mindfulness and which aspects of mindfulness may be most beneficial at each stage.

While the research mentioned shows the potential usefulness of mindfulness in targeting negative body image concerns and mood, relatively little experimental work has assessed the impact of mindfulness for promoting positive body image and embodiment specifically. An initial study that we conducted with a nonclinical sample of female undergraduates indicated that a brief mindfulness intervention (15-minute in-laboratory session plus practice over 1 week) significantly increased body appreciation compared to an educational control (video documentary) after 1 week (Atkinson & Diedrichs, 2017). This mindfulness intervention also buffered against the negative effects of later media exposure (i.e., higher state weight satisfaction and lower internalization of appearance ideals and perceived appearance pressures compared to control); however, there was no effect of the intervention on body-related psychological flexibility. These findings show preliminary support for mindfulness in specifically increasing body appreciation; however, more research is needed to validate these findings and to investigate the impact of mindfulness on additional aspects of positive body image (e.g., broad conceptualization of beauty, self-care, intuitive eating) and embodiment (e.g., attuned sexuality, attuned self-care), as well as to determine whether this operates in a different way compared to reducing negative concerns.

Prevention of Eating Disorders

In the context of prevention, mindfulness-based interventions are designed to provide training of a range of mindfulness skills in order to prevent the development of a broad range of clinical concerns and disorders, including poor body image and eating disorders, and, we argue here, also enhance positive body image and embodiment. The current state of mindfulness research with regard to prevention is a new field dominated by uncontrolled trials. Comparison of mindfulness interventions to control conditions in schools has yielded mixed results.

A recent meta-analysis of 76 studies of mindfulness-based interventions with youth indicated small effect sizes overall across a range of outcomes, with smaller effects found in more rigorously designed studies, although larger effects were observed at follow-up (Klingbeil et al., 2017).

Targeted mindfulness-based interventions (e.g., incorporating a range of key mindfulness concepts and activities with a specific application) have also been evaluated with respect to body image and eating disorder prevention (for an overview of concepts related to body image, see Stewart, 2004). We developed a three-session, mindfulness-based intervention specifically targeting risk factors for eating disorders ("the mindfulness mode," outlined in Table 29.1) and conducted a preliminary randomized controlled trial delivered in a face-to-face, small-group format with a high-risk sample of older adolescent and young adult women experiencing body image concerns (Atkinson & Wade, 2016). The intervention resulted in postintervention improvements in weight and shape concerns, dietary restraint, thin-ideal internalization, eating disorder symptoms, and related psychosocial impairment, with large effect sizes relative to control. However, these effects were not maintained at 6-month follow-up, reflecting the importance of continued mindfulness practices. In addition, we observed very limited voluntary interest and uptake into the study. This is an obstacle for broad dissemination, with a follow-up study indicating that, along with time and scheduling difficulty, discussing sensitive issues with others in a group setting was a significant deterrent to participation (Atkinson & Wade, 2013).

In a second study, we adapted the three-session, mindfulness-based intervention for classroom delivery as one approach to circumventing barriers to uptake, and evaluated its effectiveness among adolescent girls across all levels of risk and with a range of facilitators (Atkinson & Wade, 2015). No significant intervention effects were observed overall; however, under expert facilitation (several years of mindfulness experience and familiarity with the intervention), significant improvements were observed in weight and shape concerns, dietary restraint, thin-ideal internalization, eating disorder symptoms, and related psychosocial impairment relative to control, with medium effect sizes. Significant effects emerged only at 6-month follow-up, highlighting the potential for sleeper effects as a result of continued mindfulness practice. This finding is contrasted with evaluations of a general mindfulness-based program delivered in a school setting, which found no effects on weight and shape concerns at postintervention or follow-up under expert facilitation (Johnson, Burke, Brinkman, & Wade, 2016). Thus, the specific application to body image as part of the intervention content may be a crucial element in conferring benefit in the context of universal prevention with adolescents.

It still remains to be explored whether eating disorder prevention efforts based on mindfulness do in fact enhance positive body image as we might expect. While not framed as an eating disorder prevention approach, Albertson, Neff, and Dill-Shackleford (2015) evaluated a mindfulness-based, self-compassion intervention (3 weeks of daily meditations) among women with clinical levels of body image concerns. Participants showed an increase in body appreciation, alongside reductions in body dissatisfaction, body shame, and contingent self-worth based on appearance. These findings are encouraging, and underline the value in further investigating whether mindfulness-based interventions impact positive body image and embodiment and how this relates to any reductions in risk or symptomatology in the specific context of eating disorders. This could inform intervention optimization to include a greater focus on positive aspects for maximized impact.

Treatment of Eating Disorders

Robust evidence exists in adults for the benefits of specific mindfulness-based interventions, such as MBSR and MBCT, for the treatment of anxiety and depression (especially of a recurrent nature) with moderate effect sizes (Khoury et al., 2013). Mindfulness-based interventions are being increasingly utilized in the treatment of eating disorder symptoms in both clinical and nonclinical populations, and studies examining the use of mindfulness with disordered eating are increasing rapidly. In 2011, a systematic review of the area identified eight studies (Wanden-Berghe, Sanz-Valero, & Wanden-Berghe, 2011), and a systematic review of MBCT in 2013 identified 16 studies across all eating disorders (Masuda & Hill, 2013). In 2014, a systematic review identified 14 eligible studies across binge eating, emotional eating, and weight loss (Katterman, Kleinman, Hood, Nackers, & Corsica, 2014), and in 2015, a meta-analysis was conducted on 19 studies related to binge eating only (Godfrey et al., 2015).

Of the studies examined in the 2015 meta-analysis, 53% delivered mindfulness as one of several techniques within the broader therapeutic framework of acceptance and commitment therapy (ACT; $n = 4$) or dialectic behavior therapy (DBT; $n = 6$). Despite preliminary evidence for the effectiveness of these therapies, including reducing eating disorder symptomatology in patients with anorexia nervosa, bulimia nervosa, and binge eating disorder, research delineating the unique contribution of mindfulness is required to specifically inform our understanding of the usefulness of mindfulness for disordered eating.

While a number of studies ($n = 10$) have examined mindfulness-focused interventions for binge eating (including bulimia nervosa), only three of these studies compared the intervention to a control or comparison condition (Table 29.2). In a randomized controlled study, Kristeller, Wolever, and Sheets (2014) found comparable results between mindfulness-based eating awareness training (MB-EAT), designed specifically to treat eating disorders, and a psychoeducational/cognitive behavioral intervention (PECB) in changing binge eating frequency and severity. Both intervention groups showed significant improvements compared with a wait-list control group. Second, in a nonrandomized controlled study, Smith et al. (2008) found only an insignificant reduction in binge eating between an MBSR group as compared with a cognitive behavioral stress reduction group. Third, in a nonrandomized controlled study, Pinto-Gouveia et al. (2017) found large positive effect sizes on binge eating

Table 29.2 Studies Examining Comparisons of a Mindfulness-Only Treatment for Binge Eating to Another Condition

Authors (year)	Sample	Treatment and Group Size	Comparison Group and Size	Between Group Effect Sizes (Cohen's *d*) and 95% Confidence Intervals
Kristeller et al. (2014)	*N* = 150 men and women classified as overweight/obese; 111 met *DSM-IV* or *DSM-5* binge eating disorder (BED) criteria, mean age 46.6, mean BMI 40.3, 12% male, 13% minority ethnicity	MB-EAT (*n* = 53); group treatment, nine weekly sessions followed by three monthly booster sessions **PECB (*n* = 50); group treatment, nine weekly sessions followed by three monthly booster sessions**	Wait list (*n* = 47)	*OBE days post-treatment* 1.13 (0.69–1.57); **0.93 (0.51–1.35)** *OBE days follow-up* 1.03 (0.60--1.47); **0.70 (0.29–1.11)** *Binge Eating Scale post-treatment* 1.26 (0.81–1.70); **0.83 (0.41–1.24)** *Binge Eating Scale follow-up* 1.41 (0.96–1.87); **1.06 (0.64–1.49)**
Smith et al. (2008)	*N* = 50; community sample signing up for stress reduction (inclusion criteria did not include BMI or binge eating), mean age 47.8, mean BMI 27.9, 25% male	MBSR (*n* = 36); group treatment, eight weekly sessions and a 1-day retreat	CBSR (*n* = 14); group treatment, eight weekly sessions	*Binge Eating Scale post-treatment* 0.52 (-0.10 to 1.15)
Pinto-Gouveia et al. (2017)	*N* = 36; women with BED, mean age 42, mean BMI 35	BEfree (*n* = 19); group treatment, 12 sessions conducted by psychologists	Wait list (*n* = 17)	*Binge Eating Scale post-treatment* 1.73 (0.97–2.50)

Note: BMI = body mass index; CBSR = cognitive behavioral stress reduction; *DSM-IV* = *Diagnostic and Statistical Manual of Mental Disorders, Fourth Edition; DSM-5* = *Diagnostic and Statistical Manual of Mental Disorders, Fifth Edition*; MB-EAT = mindfulness-based eating awareness training; MBSR = mindfulness-based stress reduction; OBE = objective binge episodes; PECB = psychoeducational/cognitive behavioral.

BEfree is a cognitive behavior therapy approach incorporating psychoeducation, values clarification, acceptance, mindfulness, and committed action. PECB and the findings for this program are in **bold** to set them apart from MB-EAT and its findings.

between BEfree, a psychological program based on psychoeducation, mindfulness, and self-compassion, and a wait-list control group.

In summary, the main focus of outcome evaluation studies on mindfulness as a treatment approach has been on binge eating. Apart from the incorporation of mindfulness within larger interventions such as ACT or DBT, there is very little evidence to suggest that mindfulness per se can be used to treat disordered eating, or indeed binge eating, given the lack of controlled comparison trials. Those studies that do exist suggest that there may be promise in this approach for binge eating, but more comparisons to active conditions are required; further studies may also help identify who may benefit most from a mindfulness approach. Finally, as noted, it is also clear that there is a need to assess mindfulness-based eating disorder treatments with respect to improvements in positive body image more specifically, in addition to reducing negative body image and eating disorder symptoms.

CONCLUSION: CONSIDERATIONS FOR MINDFULNESS TRAINING AND FUTURE RESEARCH

Overall, initial evidence across experimental, prevention, and treatment studies of mindfulness indicates some potential for this approach in improving body image and disordered eating. However, we present a number of caveats that require careful consideration prior to implementation. In both clinical and nonclinical populations, the importance of an appropriate level of facilitator familiarity and experience with both mindfulness and intervention delivery cannot be understated. In addition, it is vital to emphasize the importance of time spent practicing and incorporating mindfulness into one's day-to-day experience, particularly ongoing use after intensive intervention periods (e.g., framed as a "lifestyle" skill), as this appears to be necessary for continued benefits.

With regard to nonclinical populations, targeted application of mindfulness skills to body image concerns and triggers, rather than general mindfulness skills training, may be required (e.g., when delivered to adolescents in the school classroom toward universal prevention). Regarding high-risk and clinical populations, practicing mindfulness may result in negative effects among those with more severe eating pathology, thereby affecting treatment outcome. Experienced therapists may be able to mitigate such adverse effects. Our studies also suggest that young women with negative body image may be uncomfortable with face-to-face group delivery, suggesting the potential usefulness of online delivery modes.

Based on our review, we outline a number of areas for future research regarding the implementation of mindfulness training aimed at enhancing positive body image and intuitive eating while reducing engagement in disordered eating patterns. Specifically, we need further work to determine (a) the specific impact of mindfulness training on positive body image and embodiment by including relevant measures in outcome trials; (b) the extent to which mindfulness can promote intuitive eating given that mindfulness may work by increasing awareness of internal cues specific to eating (i.e., hunger and satiety); (c) optimal delivery characteristics such as level of facilitator training, session duration, and dosage necessary for benefits; (d) effectiveness in younger adolescents and in males, as currently we only have evidence of efficacy in older adolescent and young adult females (>15 years); and (e) the feasibility of online delivery modes to facilitate broader access. Further work is also necessary to isolate and assess a broader range of mindfulness skills with clinical samples in order to provide recommendations regarding its use in these populations and guard against potential iatrogenic effects. In addition, despite finding initial positive effects, we still have limited understanding regarding the specific processes by which mindfulness exerts such benefits; research studies using meditational and dismantling designs could therefore help in refining mindfulness-based interventions for body image, intuitive eating, and disordered eating. Finally, as always, there is still a need for larger randomized controlled trials, including alternative comparison interventions and adequate long-term follow-up, to provide firmer evidence for the usefulness of mindfulness for body image and eating behaviors.

REFERENCES

Albertson, E. R., Neff, K. D., & Dill-Shackleford, K. E. (2015). Self-compassion and body dissatisfaction in women: A randomized controlled trial of a brief meditation intervention. *Mindfulness*, *6*, 444–454. doi:10.1007/s12671-014-0277-3

Aldao, A., Nolen-Hoeksema, S., & Schweizer, S. (2010). Emotion-regulation strategies across psychopathology: A meta-analytic review. *Clinical Psychology Review*, *30*, 217–237. doi:10.1016/j.cpr.2009.11.004

American Psychiatric Association. (1994). *Diagnostic and statistical manual of mental disorders* (4th ed.). Washington, DC: Author.

American Psychiatric Association. (2013). *Diagnostic and statistical manual of mental disorders* (5th ed.). Washington, DC: Author.

Arch, J. J., Brown, K. W., Goodman, R. J., Della Porta, M. D., Kiken, L. G., & Tillman, S. (2016). Enjoying food without caloric cost: The impact of brief mindfulness on laboratory eating outcomes. *Behaviour Research and Therapy*, *79*, 23–34. doi:10.1016/j.brat.2016.02.002

Atkinson, M. J., & Diedrichs, P. C. (2018). *Brief cognitive interventions for improving positive body image and resilience to media exposure in young adult females*. Manuscript in preparation.

Atkinson, M. J., & Wade, T. D. (2012). Impact of metacognitive acceptance on body dissatisfaction and negative affect: Engagement and efficacy. *Journal of Consulting and Clinical Psychology*, *80*, 416–425. doi:10.1037/a0028263

Atkinson, M. J., & Wade, T. D. (2013). Enhancing dissemination in selective eating disorders prevention: An investigation of voluntary participation among female university students. *Behaviour Research and Therapy*, *51*, 806–816. doi:10.1016/j.brat.2013.09.012

Atkinson, M. J., & Wade, T. D. (2015). Mindfulness-based prevention for eating disorders: A school-based cluster randomized controlled study. *International Journal of Eating Disorders*, *48*, 1024–1037. doi:10.1002/eat.22416

Atkinson, M. J., & Wade, T. D. (2016). Does mindfulness have potential in eating disorders prevention? A preliminary controlled trial with young adult women. *Early Intervention in Psychiatry, 10*, 234–245. doi:10.1111/eip.12160

Baer, R. A. (2003). Mindfulness training as a clinical intervention: A conceptual and empirical review. *Clinical Psychology: Science and Practice, 10*, 125–143. doi:10.1093/clipsy.bpg015

Cowdrey, F. A., Stewart, A., Roberts, J., & Park, R. J. (2013). Rumination and modes of processing around meal times in women with anorexia nervosa: Qualitative and quantitative results from a pilot study. *European Eating Disorders Review, 21*, 411–419.

Delinsky, S. S., & Wilson, G. T. (2006). Mirror exposure for the treatment of body image disturbance. *International Journal of Eating Disorders, 39*, 108–116. doi:10.1002/eat.20207

Godfrey, K. M., Gallo, L. C., & Afari, N. (2015). Mindfulness-based interventions for binge eating: A systematic review and meta-analysis. *Journal of Behavioral Medicine, 38*, 348–362. doi:10.1007/s10865-014-9610-5

Jacobi, C., & Fittig, E. (2010). Psychosocial risk factors for eating disorders. In W. S. Agras (Ed.), *The Oxford handbook of eating disorders* (pp. 123–136). London, England: Oxford University Press.

Johnson, C., Burke, C., Brinkman, S., & Wade, T. (2016). Effectiveness of a school-based mindfulness program for transdiagnostic prevention in young adolescents. *Behaviour Research and Therapy, 81*, 1–11. doi:10.1016/j.brat.2016.03.002

Kabat-Zinn, J. (1990). *Full catastrophe living: The program of the stress reduction clinic at the University of Massachusetts Medical Center*. New York, NY: Delta.

Kabat-Zinn, J. (2003). Mindfulness-based interventions in context: Past, present, and future. *Clinical Psychology: Science and Practice, 10*, 144–156. doi:10.1093/clipsy.bpg016

Katterman, S. N., Kleinman, B. M., Hood, M. M., Nackers, L. M., & Corsica, J. A. (2014). Mindful meditation as an intervention for binge eating, emotional eating, and weight loss: A systematic review. *Eating Behaviors, 15*, 197–204. doi:10.1016/j.eatbeh.2014.01.005

Keng, S.-L., Smoski, M. J., & Robins, C. J. (2011). Effects of mindfulness on psychological health: A review of empirical studies. *Clinical Psychology Review, 31*, 1041–1056. doi:10.1016/j.cpr.2011.04.006

Khoury, B., Lecomte, T., Fortin, G., Masse, M., Therien, P., Bouchard, V., . . . Hofmann, S. G. (2013). Mindfulness-based therapy: A comprehensive meta-analysis. *Clinical Psychology Review, 33*, 763–771. doi:10.1016/j.cpr.2013.05.005

Klingbeil, D. A., Renshaw, T. L., Willenbrink, J. B., Copek, R. A., Chan, K. T., . . . Clifton, J. (2017). Mindfulness-based interventions with youth: A comprehensive meta-analysis of group-design studies. *Journal of School Psychology, 63*, 77–103. doi:10.1016/j.jsp.2017.03.006

Kristeller, J., Wolever, R. Q., & Sheets, V. (2014). Mindfulness-based eating awareness training (MB-EAT) for binge eating: A randomized clinical trial. *Mindfulness, 5*, 282–297. doi:10.1007/s12671-012-0179-1

Luethcke, C. A., McDaniel, L., & Becker, C. B. (2011). A comparison of mindfulness, nonjudgmental, and cognitive dissonance-based approaches to mirror exposure. *Body Image, 8*, 251–258. doi:10.1016/j.bodyim.2011.03.006

Marek, R. J., Ben-Porath, D. D., Federici, A., Wisniewski, L., & Warren, M. (2013). Targeting premeal anxiety in eating disordered clients and normal controls: A preliminary investigation into the use of mindful eating vs. distraction during food exposure. *International Journal of Eating Disorders, 46*, 582–585. doi:10.1002/eat.22152

Margolis, S. E., & Orsillo, S. M. (2016). Acceptance and body dissatisfaction: Examining the efficacy of a brief acceptance based intervention for body dissatisfaction in college women. *Behavioural and Cognitive Psychotherapy*, *44*, 482–492. doi:10.1017/S1352465816000072

Masuda, A., & Hill, M. L. (2013). Mindfulness as therapy for disordered eating: A systematic review. *Neuropsychiatry*, *3*, 433–447. doi:10.2217/NPY.13.36

Naumann, E., Tuschen-Caffier, B., Voderholzer, U., Schafer, J., & Svaldi, J. (2016). Effects of emotional acceptance and rumination on media-induced body dissatisfaction in anorexia and bulimia nervosa. *Journal of Psychiatric Research*, *82*, 119–125. doi:10.1016/j.jpsychires.2016.07.021

Pinto-Gouveia, J., Carvalho, S. A., Palmeira, L., Castilho, P., Duarte, C., Ferreira, C., . . . Costa, J. (2017). BEfree: A new psychological program for binge eating that integrates psychoeducation, mindfulness, and compassion. *Clinical Psychology & Psychotherapy*, *24*, 1090–1098. doi:10.1002/cpp.2072

Segal, Z. V., Williams, J. M. G., & Teasdale, J. D. (2012). *Mindfulness-based cognitive therapy for depression* (2nd ed.). New York, NY: Guilford Press.

Smith, B. W., Shelley, B. M., Dalen, J., Wiggins, K., Tooley, E., & Bernard, J. (2008). A pilot study comparing the effects of mindfulness-based and cognitive-behavioral stress reduction. *Journal of Alternative Complementary Medicine*, *14*, 251–258. doi:10.1089/acm.2007.0641

Stewart, T. M. (2004). Light on body image treatment: Acceptance through mindfulness. *Behavior Modification*, *28*, 783–811. doi:10.1177/0145445503259862

Svaldi, J., & Naumann, E. (2014). Effects of rumination and acceptance on body dissatisfaction in binge eating disorder. *European Eating Disorders Review*, *22*, 338–345. doi:10.1002/erv.2312

Teasdale, J. D., Segal, Z. V., & Williams, M. G. (1995). How does cognitive therapy prevent depressive relapse and why should attentional control (mindfulness) training help? *Behaviour Research and Therapy*, *33*, 25–39. doi:10.1016/0005-7967(94)E0011-7

Wade, T., George, W. M., & Atkinson, M. (2009). A randomized controlled trial of brief interventions for body dissatisfaction. *Journal of Consulting and Clinical Psychology*, *77*, 845–854. doi:10.1037/a0016879

Wanden-Berghe, R. G., Sanz-Valero, J., & Wanden-Berghe, C. (2011). The application of mindfulness to eating disorders treatment: A systematic review. *Eating Disorders*, *19*, 34–48. doi:10.1080/10640266.2011.533604

30

The Practice of Yoga

Can It Help in Addressing Body Image Concerns and Eating Disorders?

DIANNE NEUMARK-SZTAINER ■

Body image concerns, disordered eating, and eating disorders are significant public health problems, given their high prevalence and adverse health consequences. New and innovative strategies that are accessible, acceptable, and effective are needed to address these problems. The practice of yoga has its ancient roots in the East but is increasingly popular in the West, suggesting its potential acceptability as an intervention strategy within societies in which body image concerns and disordered eating behaviors are highly prevalent. Yoga participation has dramatically increased in the United States. As of January 2016, approximately 15% of US adults were estimated to practice yoga, and 34% indicated that they planned to practice yoga in the next 12 months (*Yoga Journal* & Yoga Alliance, 2016). The popularity of yoga and its increasing accessibility, in conjunction with its theoretical underpinnings suggesting its potential relevance for the enhancement of body awareness and a positive body image, have led to an interest in yoga among both practitioners and researchers working in the areas of body image and eating disorders.

This chapter begins with my own personal journey throughout the world of yoga and insights that I have gathered along the way about the relevance of this practice for a greater sense of connection to one's body and the enhancement of a positive body image. The chapter continues with a description of the theoretical underpinnings of yoga, supporting the notion that yoga may be a valuable tool to enhance positive body image and embodiment. The potential for yoga to help in the prevention of disordered eating behaviors and clinical eating disorders is then discussed. Finally, potential harmful effects of yoga on body image are considered.

MY OWN JOURNEY

One of the underlying premises of yoga is that it can help in bridging the connection between our inner selves and the outer world for a greater sense of peace within us and within the world. Given that premise, it is perhaps somewhat ironic (or not) that my own yoga journey began approximately 35 years ago in a bomb shelter on a kibbutz where I was living in northern Israel. Fortunately, times were peaceful, and the shelters were used for purposes other than protection, such as learning yoga. I loved the practice of yoga, but set it aside for a few decades, as life got busy with graduate studies, work, and raising children.

Approximately a decade ago, I returned to practicing yoga, this time in a community center in Minnesota, a northern state in the United States, where I currently live. As appears to happen with many yoga practitioners, I took up yoga for physical reasons (i.e., lower back pain), but continued the practice for a combination of physical, energetic, mental, emotional, and spiritual reasons. For example, through practicing yoga I became more in touch with sensations in my body. I began to notice when I was breathing too quickly (e.g., if asked to take on just one too many things at work) and to respond in accordance (e.g., by taking the time to carefully consider if I should turn down some opportunities). Additionally, and of particular relevance to this chapter, yoga helped me experience a strong sense of embodiment. Piran has described the various aspects of embodiment (Piran, 2002, 2015, 2016; Piran & Teall, 2012); one important aspect is to experience the body from the "inside out" rather than the "outside in." My yoga practice helped me move from an intellectual understanding of the concept of embodiment to a lived experience within my body.

My yoga practice grew from participating in weekly classes at a community center to trying different classes at a local yoga studio, seeking extended yoga workshops and retreats, and developing a regular home practice. In addition to (or because of) the personal benefits I experienced, my curiosity grew with regard to the potential value of this practice for the fields of body image and eating disorders. As a researcher, I was curious about the statements made by yoga instructors about the multiple benefits of yoga, some of which I believed were supported by empirical evidence (e.g., stress reduction) more than others (e.g., twisting out toxins from internal organs). My bookshelves began to include more books more about yoga philosophy, anatomy, and practices. I participated in a 200-hour teacher-training program. I then dedicated a year-long sabbatical leave to completing a 500-hour advanced teacher training and reviewing the scientific literature on yoga and eating disorders (Neumark-Sztainer, 2014). I taught yoga to individuals with body image concerns at an eating disorders treatment program. And, I began to develop a line of research in this area.

I was fortunate to have the opportunity to teach yoga at an eating disorders treatment program (The Emily Program) for 3 years. Lisa Diers, who, like myself, is a dietitian and a yoga instructor, developed and directed an extensive yoga program for clients with severe body image concerns and eating disorders (Diers,

2016; The Emily Program Website, 2017). I taught in the Yoga and Body Image program that she developed; in this program, clients participate in a 90-minute group session with a yoga instructor and a psychologist. Clients first check in, then participate in a yoga practice, and then process how the practice felt in their bodies. Participants varied greatly in their eating disorders and body weights (i.e., within the same class, students had anorexia nervosa and binge eating disorder, and body weights ranged from 80 to 600 pounds), but all had severe body image concerns. While the yoga practice certainly did not totally alleviate these body image concerns, participants began to talk differently about their bodies as a result of engaging in yoga. For example, participants talked about noticing that they often held their breath; that is, they had been depriving themselves of breathing. Others talked about connecting to their bodies and recognizing sensations of hunger and satiety for the first time in years. Teaching yoga to these women and men was a highlight of the week for me, and I learned so much from them.

I am currently developing a line of research in the area of yoga and body image, eating disorders, and weight-related problems. The knowledge gained from my personal practice, the teacher-training programs, and the experience of working within an eating disorders treatment program has guided the research questions that we are exploring. The more I learn, the greater my interest becomes, and the more I realize how much more there is to learn. The personal and the professional have come together for me through my strong interest in yoga.

THEORETICAL UNDERPINNINGS OF YOGA

Yoga means "to yoke" or "to join," for example, to unite ourselves with our highest nature; to join the internal with the external; to link the mundane to the spiritual; and to link the body, mind, and emotions. One of the key purposes of yoga is to quiet the fluctuations of the mind. Another major purpose of yoga is to discover who we really are through deep listening during the practice. Thus, while Westernized researchers, like myself, are interested in examining the impact of yoga on various health outcomes, such as weight status, body image, or eating disorders, it is noteworthy that any of these positive impacts of yoga may be regarded as "mere" side effects of the practice.

The theoretical underpinnings of yoga certainly suggest its potential value as a tool for promoting a greater sense of connection to one's body and a positive body image. The practice of yoga involves both physical and mindfulness components. The physical aspect of yoga can be adapted to meet different needs, skill levels, and body sizes. If yoga is offered within a supportive environment, one can learn to move in a manner that suits one's body. The mindfulness component of yoga offers individuals an opportunity to connect with themselves and their bodies in a positive and compassionate manner, which is so important in the promotion of a positive body image and the prevention or reduction of disordered eating behaviors. When the physical practices are linked to breath work and other aspects of yoga such as positive affirmations, moving inward, and deep relaxation, the benefits can be great.

A central component of yoga involves physical poses (i.e., asanas). While these poses can be physically challenging, with the potential for helping the practitioner feel empowered and strong, there are also many gentle poses that can practiced by people of varied skill levels that allow for a true sense of relaxation. Both physically challenging and gentle poses help the journey inward, for greater connection to oneself. In yoga classes within Westernized societies, there is often a strong emphasis on the physical component of yoga. While there may be too much emphasis on the physical component of yoga within classes, and this focus could possibly have harmful implications for body image, the physical postures are important as they offer an avenue for working with the physical body in a gentle, compassionate, and positive manner.

Another central component of yoga is the breath work (i.e., pranayama). By focusing on the breath, the yoga practitioner can calm the mind and potentially still (or decrease) negative body image thoughts and rumination about eating behaviors. One can observe the breath as it is, change the breath in accordance with a count, or use the breath to bring in what one needs more of and breathe out what is no longer useful. For example, one can breathe in a sense of nourishment, self-confidence, gratitude for one's body, and calmness and breathe out self-deprivation, self-doubts, body negativity, and stress. The breath can be linked to movement for a moving meditation or be used on its own in a more traditional meditation.

Through a regular practice of asana and pranayama, one learns to take the practice "off the mat." Thus, one might become more aware of feelings of discomfort (e.g., quick heart palpitations) and more likely to modify one's behavior in accordance. This heightened sense of connection to one's body and enhanced attunement and trust are potentially of great relevance to the development of a stronger sense of embodiment and a positive body image.

There are many other aspects of yoga that are beyond the scope of this chapter but are of relevance to the development of a positive body image and the prevention of eating disorders. For example, an important principle (i.e., yama) of yoga is that of nonviolence to oneself and others (i.e., ahimsa) (Adele, 2009). Poor eating behaviors, cutting, starvation, and overexercising are some examples of ahimsa that a yogic lifestyle would discourage. In yoga, an important concept is the koshas, or the five layers of being, with the physical body as the outermost layer and, deeper within, other bodies related to one's energetic, mental, emotional, and spiritual well-being. In some yoga practices, particularly yoga nidra (or sleep of the yogis), yoga practitioners work their way inward from the outer layers to the inner layers. The practice of coming inward through the koshas may help individuals get in touch with themselves at a deeper level and recognize the importance of caring for their physical bodies. For a deeper understanding of yoga, the reader is referred to more in-depth sources (Cook-Cottone, 2015; Desikachar, 1999; Kraftsow, 1999, 2002; Saraswati, 2002).

YOGA IN THE TREATMENT AND PREVENTION OF DISORDERED EATING AND EATING DISORDERS

The underlying tenets of yoga and its growing popularity suggest yoga's potential for reaching individuals at risk for, or experiencing, body image concerns, disordered eating behaviors, or eating disorders. It is also promising that there appears to be a movement within the yoga community to make yoga more accessible to persons from diverse backgrounds and body sizes (Moore, 2016; Stanley, 2017). While findings from Project EAT-IV, a large, population-based study of young adults, found that yoga was practiced more often by young adults who are female, white, of higher socioeconomic status, and with lower body mass indexes, findings also indicated that young adults from all backgrounds and those living in larger bodies practice yoga (Neumark-Sztainer et al., 2017).

Findings from intervention studies with different types of populations suggest that yoga may have positive implications for reducing eating disorder symptoms, enhancing body awareness, decreasing self-objectification, and improving overall body satisfaction awareness (Carei, Fyfe-Johnson, Breuner, & Brown, 2010; Impett, Daubenmier, & Hirschman, 2006; Klein & Cook-Cottone, 2013; McIver, McGartland, & O'Halloran, 2009; McIver, O'Halloran, & McGartland, 2009; Neumark-Sztainer, 2014; Pacanowski, Diers, Crosby, & Neumark-Sztainer, 2017). While these findings are promising, they should be viewed with caution given the small number of published studies, inconsistencies within and across studies, and limitations in study designs.

Population-based studies on yoga and body image can provide valuable information on the potential impact of yoga, as practiced in the community, on body image. Few studies that have examined yoga use in the general population have included measures of body image, and where they have, directions of association have tended to be positive but have not always been consistent (Delaney & Anthis, 2010; Lauche et al., 2017; Neumark-Sztainer, Eisenberg, Wall, & Loth, 2011; Sharpe, Blanck, Williams, Ainsworth, & Conway, 2007). For example, Sharpe et al. (2007) examined the use of complementary and alternative medicine (CAM) therapies for weight control in a large sample of adults in the United States and found lower levels of body satisfaction among those using CAM therapies for weight control. While they did not specifically examine associations with yoga, they did find that yoga was, by far, the most commonly used CAM therapy in the population for weight control. In a large population-based study of women in Australia, yoga/meditation was found to be associated with higher body satisfaction in women classified as nonoverweight; however, no association was found in women classified as having obesity (Lauche et al., 2017). In a recent analysis using data from Project EAT-IV, we examined associations between yoga and body satisfaction. This study had an important advantage over these other cross-sectional, population-based studies in that we were able to statistically adjust for prior body satisfaction and body mass index, assessed 5 years earlier in a previous study wave. Findings indicated that yoga was associated with improvements in body satisfaction at a population-based level, particularly among those with low prior levels of body satisfaction (Neumark-Sztainer, MacLehose, Watts, Pacanowski, & Eisenberg, 2018).

An important question is whether yoga can be helpful in treating eating disorders, as yoga is increasingly being utilized within eating disorders treatment programs. The research supporting the use of yoga for eating disorders treatment is limited in terms of number of studies and quality of study designs, but initial findings are promising. Findings from three small randomized controlled trials suggest that yoga may have a positive impact on negative affect prior to eating (Pacanowski et al., 2017); binge eating behaviors (McIver, McGartland, et al., 2009; McIver, O'Halloran, et al., 2009); and eating disorder symptoms (Carei et al., 2010). Clearly, more research is needed to assess the effectiveness of yoga in the treatment of eating disorders, its impact on different populations and different eating disorders, and the impact of different types of yoga practices.

Yoga also offers potential as a tool for preventing risk factors for eating disorders; however, there is very little research in this area. Two strategies for utilizing yoga within the field of eating disorders prevention are (a) integrating yoga into eating disorder prevention programs and (b) integrating eating disorders prevention into ongoing yoga classes through the training of yoga teachers (Neumark-Sztainer, 2014).

An excellent example of how yoga can be integrated into eating disorder prevention programs is the 14-week curriculum for older elementary schoolchildren, *Girls Growing in Wellness and Balance: Yoga and Life Skills to Empower* (Cook-Cottone, Kane, Keddie, & Hauqli, 2013). Sessions address topics such as mindful and intuitive eating, feelings, negative thoughts, self-image, and media awareness. Each didactic session is followed by a yoga practice that ties in the content taught. For example, following the session on self-image, the yoga session includes relaxation with a guided imagery devoted to finding personal strength. There has been minimal work done to evaluate the effectiveness of yoga in the prevention of eating disorders. Scime and Cook-Cottone (2008) conducted an evaluation of an earlier version of the program described here and found a positive impact on body dissatisfaction, bulimia, and social support in a nonrandomized, controlled study. Mitchell, Mazzeo, Rausch, and Cooke (2007) compared a brief yoga program to a dissonance-based intervention in a randomized controlled study and did not see significant changes among participants in the yoga condition. The authors concluded that the yoga intervention, which included weekly 45-minute sessions over a 6-week period, may have been too short and not intense enough to have an impact. We are currently implementing a small randomized controlled trial of a body image–focused yoga intervention that meets a few times a week to assess its impact on body image among college students Principal Investigator: C. Pacanowski).

Another strategy for utilizing yoga to prevent body dissatisfaction, disordered eating behaviors, and eating disorders is to integrate principles of eating disorders prevention into ongoing yoga classes. For example, yoga instructors teaching at community centers or studios or those involved in providing guidance for home practices (e.g., via online teaching strategies) can utilize language aimed at helping students feel more connected to, and more positive toward, their bodies. This strategy is important given the large number of individuals participating in yoga, with a particularly high percentage of women who are at increased risk for body image concerns, disordered eating behaviors, and eating disorders. Furthermore, there is some research suggesting that individuals attending mind–body classes (i.e., yoga/Pilates) are at equal or greater risk for disordered eating behaviors than the general population (Neumark-Sztainer et al., 2011). Thus, yoga classes may provide a suitable venue for reaching a captive audience that includes individuals at risk for problematic outcomes. Additionally, as previously discussed, the underlying philosophy of yoga supports the promotion of greater connection to one's body and greater acceptance of oneself. Thus, yoga classes provide an excellent framework for integrating work related to improving body image. Participants are there to engage in a practice of coming inward; they are moving their bodies in link with their breath; and yoga teachers often use language to encourage calmness, gratitude, acceptance, and empowerment.

Studies could not be found that specifically examined the impact of incorporating eating disorder prevention activities (e.g., training yoga teachers to use body-friendly language and to identify and approach high-risk individuals) into yoga classes for the general public. However, studies have examined the impact of participating in yoga on risk and protective factors for eating disorders. Findings suggest that high levels of yoga practice may be helpful in promoting body awareness, responsiveness, and appreciation (Daubenmier, 2005; Impett et al., 2006), which are key elements of embodiment.

A high priority should be to train yoga instructors on (a) the prevalence and severity of body image concerns, disordered eating, and eating disorders; (b) tools that they can use to identify people at risk for eating disorders and strategies to work with these individuals (without engaging in diagnosis or treatment); and (c) strategies for implementing body-friendly yoga classes that encourage participants to appreciate their bodies, work with the "body of the day," and truly listen to what their bodies want and need. Similarly, it is important to help yoga studios provide an environment in which persons of all shapes, sizes, and abilities feel comfortable practicing yoga. Some suggestions include: (a) have teachers who are diverse in terms of their gender, age, ethnicity, and weight status; (b) avoid having mirrors in areas where yoga is being practiced (Frayeh, 2015); (c) have protocols in place to address situations in which there is concern about either students or teachers; and (d) arrange for appropriate training for instructors.

POTENTIAL HARMS OF YOGA OF RELEVANCE TO BODY IMAGE

In any discussion regarding yoga and body image, it is important to consider the potential harmful effects of yoga. As previously noted, a recent analysis of data from Project EAT suggests that yoga is associated with improvements in body satisfaction at a population-based level, particularly among those with low prior levels of body satisfaction (Neumark-Sztainer et al., 2018). While these findings are very encouraging, it is likely that anyone who has participated in a group yoga class has, at times, felt some discomfort in one's body or in one's ability to engage in certain aspects of the yoga being taught. This discomfort could be a result of the teacher's language; the presence of other students in the class who are thinner, curvier, more flexible, stronger, or younger; or one's own insecurity or frustration with one's body size or shape, level of flexibility, strength, or yoga abilities. As an experienced yogi and body image researcher, I have learned to avoid going to classes in which I feel uncomfortable. For example, I will not attend classes in which the teacher employs language that values a certain body shape (e.g., six-packs), where the teacher is overly rigid, or where there is an atmosphere of competitiveness. I participate in different types of classes ranging from totally relaxing to physically demanding, but only those in which there is an instructor that helps me to feel comfortable in my own skin, emphasizes sensing the poses from the inside rather than focusing on how the poses look from the outside, and verbally gives permission and encourages students to listen to their bodies and modify the practice as needed or desired. However, I have concerns about individuals who go to classes where they may end up feeling worse about their bodies. The result may be that their body image worsens, they stop practicing yoga, or they become injured.

It seems that participating in a yoga class that promotes a more positive body image may have implications for a safer practice that better meets students' physical abilities and needs, although I am unaware of any research on this topic. An important skill learned in a yoga practice is that of discernment. In deciding whether to engage in a specific yoga pose, how deeply to take the pose, what modifications to make, and how long to hold the pose, the practice of discernment is crucial. One must learn to listen to one's body to determine where the line exists between taking oneself outside of one's comfort zone to experience a sense of accomplishment and not becoming injured in the pose. The line may differ every time one practices yoga in accordance with one's mood, prior activity, existing injuries, time of day, or a variety of factors. Thus, the process of discernment involves paying attention to, and meeting the needs of, "the body of the day." This process of discernment can then be carried "off of the mat" into daily life. Through the process of listening to one's body (e.g., quick breathing, heart palpitations), one can learn the art of discernment and make healthier choices. I believe that in a yoga class, it is easier to engage in healthy discernment when one feels more confident with one's body. Thus, having a more positive body image while doing yoga may actually lead to a safer practice, more comfort in one's practice, and fewer injuries.

In summary, although the extant research on yoga and body image does not suggest a negative impact of yoga on body image, there may be situations in which this is the case. There may be individuals for whom yoga, or certain yoga practices, is harmful from a body image perspective. Additionally, certain practices, or just too much yoga, may be harmful for individuals with active eating disorders; for example, I would certainly not recommend vigorous yoga, hot yoga, or a rigid practice to individuals with anorexia nervosa. Thus, with the increase in popularity in yoga, people who do not feel comfortable with the practice should be encouraged to seek out alternate activities and not feel a need to engage in yoga.

CONCLUSION AND NEXT STEPS

The underlying tenets of yoga and initial empirical findings suggest that yoga may have positive benefits for positive body image and embodiment. It seems highly likely that the impact may vary by approaches taken by instructors and the atmosphere in which yoga is taught. Therefore, yoga instructors should receive training on the importance of a positive body image; how to teach in a manner that promotes a positive body image; how to identify individuals in their classes who may feel uncomfortable with their bodies during yoga or be at risk for an eating disorder; and how to decrease the risks of harmful effects on students' body image. Clearly, further research examining yoga and body image is needed. Some suggestions for next steps for research include: (a) evaluate the impact of training programs addressing body image and eating disorders on yoga instructors' teaching behaviors; (b) assess the impact of participation in yoga classes in which efforts have been made to incorporate eating disorder prevention language, activities, and settings; (c) determine whether yoga classes specially designed to address risk and protective factors for eating disorders are more effective than more globally focused classes; and (d) identify the mechanisms by which yoga may be leading to an improved body image and embodiment to further inform interventions. The increasing popularity and accessibility of yoga, along with a movement to make yoga available to individuals of different backgrounds, shapes, sizes, and abilities, suggest that yoga may be a useful tool for enhancing body image and embodiment in the public.

REFERENCES

Adele, D. (2009). *The yamas and niyamas: Exploring yoga's ethical practice.* Duluth, MN: On-Word Bound Books.

Carei, T. R., Fyfe-Johnson, A. L., Breuner, C. C., & Brown, M. A. (2010). Randomized controlled clinical trial of yoga in the treatment of eating disorders. *Journal of Adolescent Health, 46*, 346–351. doi:10.1016/j.jadohealth.2009.08.007

Cook-Cottone, C. (2015). *Mindfulness and yoga for self-regulation: A primer for mental health professionals.* New York, NY: Springer.

Cook-Cottone, C., Kane, L., Keddie, E., & Hauqli, S. (2013). *Girls growing in wellness and balance: Yoga and life skills to empower* [Curriculum]. Sparta, WI: Schoolhouse Educational Services.

Daubenmier, J. J. (2005). The relationship of yoga, body awareness, and body responsiveness to self-objectification and disordered eating. *Psychology of Women Quarterly, 29*, 207–219. doi:10.1111/J.1471-6402.2005.00183.X

Delaney, K., & Anthis, K. (2010). Is women's participation in different types of yoga classes associated with different levels of body awareness and body satisfaction? *International Journal of Yoga Therapy*, *20*, 62–71. doi:10.17761/IJYT.20.1.T44L6656H22735G6

Desikachar, T. K. V. (1999). *The heart of yoga: Developing a personal practice*. Rochester, VT: Inner Traditions International.

Diers, L. (2016). How yoga teachers can incorporate yoga into eating disorder treatment. In C. Costin & J. Kelly (Eds.), *Yoga and eating disorders: Ancient healing for modern illness* (pp. 184–194). New York, NY: Routledge, Taylor & Francis Group.

The Emily Program. (2017). Home page. Retrieved July 19, 2017, from https://www.emilyprogram.com/

Frayeh, A. (2015). *The effect of mirrors on women's body image and affective responses to yoga* (Doctoral dissertation, University of Minnesota). Retrieved July 19, 2017, from the University of Minnesota Digital Conservancy, http://hdl.handle.net/11299/181728

Impett, E. A., Daubenmier, J. J., & Hirschman, A. L. (2006). Minding the body: Yoga, embodiment, and well-being. *Sexuality Research and Social Policy*, *3*, 39–48.

Klein, J., & Cook-Cottone, C. (2013). The effects of yoga on eating disorder symptoms and correlates: A review. *International Journal of Yoga Therapy*, *23*, 41–50.

Kraftsow, G. (1999). *Yoga for wellness: Healing with the timeless teachings of Viniyoga*. New York, NY: Penguin Group.

Kraftsow, G. (2002). *Yoga for transformation: Ancient teachings and holistic practices for healing body, mind, and heart*. New York, NY: Penguin Compass.

Lauche, R., Sibbritt, D., Ostermann, T., Fuller, N. R., Adams, J., & Cramer, H. (2017). Associations between yoga/mediation use, body satisfaction, and weight management methods: Results of a national cross-sectional survey of 8,009 Australian women. *Nutrition*, *34*, 58–64. doi:10.1016/j.nut.2016.09.007

McIver, S., McGartland, M., & O'Halloran, P. (2009). "Overeating is not about the food": Women describe their experience of a yoga treatment program for binge eating. *Qualitative Health Research*, *19*, 1234–1245. doi:10.1177/1049732309343954

McIver, S., O'Halloran, P., & McGartland, M. (2009). Yoga as a treatment for binge eating disorder: A preliminary study. *Complementary Therapies in Medicine*, *17*, 196–202. doi:10.1016/J.Ctim.2009.05.002

Mitchell, K. S., Mazzeo, S. E., Rausch, S. M., & Cooke, K. L. (2007). Innovative interventions for disordered eating: Evaluating dissonance-based and yoga interventions. *International Journal of Eating Disorders*, *40*, 120–128. doi:10.1002/eat.20282

Moore M. (2016) Embody love: How yoga teachers help prevent and treat eating disorders and negative body image. In: C. Costin & J. Kelly (Eds.), *Yoga and eating disorders: Ancient healing for modern illness* (pp. 124–136). New York, NY: Routledge, Taylor & Francis Group; 2016.

Neumark-Sztainer, D. (2014). Yoga and eating disorders: Is there a place for yoga in the prevention and treatment of eating disorders and disordered eating behaviours? *Advances in Eating Disorders*, *2*, 136–145. doi:10.1080/21662630.2013.862369

Neumark-Sztainer, D., Eisenberg, M. E., Wall, M., & Loth, K. A. (2011). Yoga and Pilates: Associations with body image and disordered-eating behaviors in a population-based sample of young adults. *International Journal of Eating Disorders*, *44*, 276–280. doi:10.1002/eat.20858

Neumark-Sztainer, D., MacLehose, R. F., Watts, A. W., Eisenberg, M. E., Laska, M. N., & Larson, N. (2017). How is the practice of yoga related to weight status? Population-based findings from Project EAT-IV. *Journal of Physical Activity and Health, 14*, 905–912. doi:10.1123/jpah.2016-0608

Neumark-Sztainer, D., MacLehose, R. F., Watts, A. W., Pacanowski, C. R., & Eisenberg, M. (2018). Yoga and body image: Findings from a large population-based study of young adults. *Body Image, 24*, 69–75. doi:10.1016/j.bodyim.2017.12.003

Pacanowski, C. R., Diers, L., Crosby, R. D., & Neumark-Sztainer, D. (2017). Yoga in the treatment of eating disorders within a residential program: A randomized controlled trial. *Eating Disorders, 25*, 37–51. doi:10.1080/10640266.2016.1237810

Piran, N. (2002). Embodiment: A mosaic of inquiries in the area of body weight and shape preoccupation. In S. M. Abbey (Ed.), *Ways of knowing in and through the body: Diverse perspectives on embodiment* (pp. 211–214). Welland, ON, Canada: Soleil.

Piran, N. (2015). New possibilities in the prevention of eating disorders: The introduction of positive body image measures. *Body Image, 14*, 146–157. doi:10.1016/j.bodyim.2015.03.008

Piran, N. (2016). Embodied possibilities and disruptions: The emergence of the Experience of Embodiment construct from qualitative studies with girls and women. *Body Image, 18*, 43–60. doi:10.1016/j.bodyim.2016.04.007

Piran, N., & Teall, T. (2012). The developmental theory of embodiment. In G. L. McVey, M. P. Levine, N. Piran, & B. Ferguson (Eds.), *Preventing eating-related and weight-related disorders: Collaborative research, advocacy, and policy change* (pp. 171–199). Waterloo, ON, Canada: Wilfrid Laurier University Press.

Saraswati, S. (2002). *Yoga nidra* (6th ed.). Munger, India: Yoga Publications Trust.

Scime, M., & Cook-Cottone, C. (2008). Primary prevention of eating disorders: A constructivist integration of mind and body strategies. *International Journal of Eating Disorders, 41*, 134–142. doi:10.1002/eat.20480

Sharpe, P. A., Blanck, H. M., Williams, J. E., Ainsworth, B. E., & Conway, J. M. (2007). Use of complementary and alternative medicine for weight control in the United States. *Journal of Alternative and Complementary Medicine, 13*, 217–222. doi:10.1089/acm.2006.6129

Stanley, J. (2017). *Every body yoga: Let go of fear, get on the mat, love your body*. New York, NY: Workman Publishing.

Yoga Journal & Yoga Alliance. (2016). The 2016 Yoga in America Study. Retrieved July 19, 2017, from https://www.yogajournal.com/page/yogainamericastudy

31

Brain Integration, Embodied Mindfulness, and Movement-Based Approaches to Facilitate Positive Body Image and Embodiment

CATHERINE P. COOK-COTTONE ■

Embodiment refers to inhabiting the body as a source for emotions, cognitions, and actions (Cook-Cottone, 2015a; Cook-Cottone & Guyker, 2018; Khoury et al., 2017; Piran, 2016, 2017). Despite our overreliance and emphasis on cognitive experiences and processes, both in our lives and in clinical interventions, the brain primarily functions from and for the body (Cook-Cottone, 2015b; Ogden & Fisher, 2015). Neurologically speaking, the body is our sensing, experiencing, and acting system, our interface between our inner and outer worlds (Cook-Cottone, 2015b). Siegel (2016) used the term *embodied brain* to refer to the whole body system that gives rise to the experience of who we know as the self. Thus, how we experience the body, perceive it, identify with it, treat it, and move from it is an aggregation of both our internal and our external experiences (Cook-Cottone, 2015b). Awareness of and connection with the body is prerequisite to and part of embodiment and maintenance of well-being (Cook-Cottone, 2015a, 2015b; Ogden & Fisher, 2015; Piran, 2016).

It is from these embodied roots that the more practical aspects positive body image and positive embodiment are derived (Cook-Cottone, 2015a). Nevertheless, as Ogden, Minton, and Pain (2006) noted, "The body, for a host of reasons, has been left out of the 'talking cure'" (p. xxvii). Since the philosophical beginnings of psychology, there has been an understanding that consciousness is shaped by the body's sensory and perceptual experiences (see the works of Locke, Berkeley, and Hume in the sixteenth and seventeenth centuries). Recent models of embodiment, or grounded cognition (see Barsalou, 2008), argue that the brain and its systems for perception, bodily states, and situated action underlie all cognition. Our thoughts are grounded in our sensations, perceptions of those sensations, experiences of our body, actions we take, and the social and environmental contexts within which we take those actions. Accordingly, how we think about our body, about anything, is not "brain bound" (Siegel, 2016, p. 10).

Years ago, as a new assistant professor studying eating disorders, I read *Sensing the Self: Women's Recovery from Bulimia* by Sheila M. Reindl (2001). I still have the copy of the book with dog-eared pages, darkly underlined passages, and notes in the margins. Reindl laid out what she learned from intently listening to women's accounts of recovery from bulimia nervosa. She learned that in order to recover, these women had to make a substantial shift in terms of how they experienced themselves. That is, they had to shift from a judgment-based relationship to a sensing- and experiencing-based relationship with themselves and their physical, psychological, and social self-experiences. Reindl (2001) detailed the lived experiences and embodiment of women as they regained awareness of and connection with the sensing self through intention, embodiment, and attuned acts of self-care. For these women, change and healing did not occur through a shift in thinking. Instead, transformation came from a shift in being.

How can this kind of transformation translate into talking therapy? The theoretical and neurological rationale of embodied mindfulness and movement-based approaches asserts that change lies in the doing, being, and active practice of embodiment (Cook-Cottone, 2015b, 2016; Ogden & Fisher, 2015). Change is more than the cognitive: It must be lived (Cook-Cottone, 2015b; 2016; Ogden & Fisher). In this chapter, I review embodiment as it relates to brain integration, briefly review some of the related theory and research, and highlight interventions that facilitate embodiment and neurological integration.

EMBODIMENT AND BRAIN INTEGRATION

Embodiment-based approaches emphasize the lived experiences of the body, feelings, and physiological states (Piran, 2016). As we see it, embodiment can take both positive and negative forms (see Piran, 2016, 2017). Levels of embodiment can range from a full experience of inhabiting the body as manifested in the depth of a healing yoga practice (high) to a fragile linkage of presence within the body as experienced in dissociation (low). Girls' and women's narratives, as well as cross-sectional research, suggest that positive embodiment is inclusive of body connection and comfort, agency and functionality, experience and expression of desire, attuned self-care, and subjective being (see Piran, 2016, 2017). Gaete and Fuchs (2007) and Blood (2005) argued for a broader term than body image, suggesting that it references too heavily on the construct of body as object. Aligned with

Piran's (2016, 2017) notion of body connection, Gaete and Fuchs suggested the term *emotional body experience*.

Brain researchers highlight the importance of integration in brain functioning for optimal learning and adaptation. Such integration can relate to positive embodiment. Initial research on brain functioning, body image, and eating has focused on comparing brain activity and body dissatisfaction between women with current or past history of anorexia nervosa and women with no history of anorexia (McFadden, Tregellas, Shott, & Frank, 2014). McFadden et al. studied the salience network and the default mode network of the brain using functional magnetic resonance imaging (fMRI). The salience network is involved in the performance of specific tasks through assessing internal and external stimuli and linking them with behavioral choices; associated brain regions are the insula, which detects and responds to salient stimuli, and the anterior cingulate cortex, which is involved in the motor response and the assessment of reward systems. The default mode network involves intrinsic brain activity that is not associated with the performance of particular tasks and is linked to interoception and self-referential processing; associated brain regions include the posterior cingulate cortex, cuneus/precuneus, and the medial prefrontal, medial temporal, and inferior parietal cortices. McFadden et al. found reduced salience network activity among 20 women diagnosed with restrictive anorexia and 22 women who recovered from restrictive anorexia compared to controls. Reduced activity can relate to challenges in responding to stimuli, such as food or taste, reward processing, and learning new behaviors. McFadden et al. also found reduced default mode network activity among women diagnosed with restrictive anorexia, but not recovered anorexics, compared to controls. They suggested that this might relate to challenges in self-awareness, body image distortion, or recognition of starvation state among women actively dealing with anorexia nervosa. As the authors noted, alterations in the salience network and default mode network have been found in other psychiatric groups, such as those with autism, schizophrenia, depression, anxiety, and attention deficit disorder.

Studies of the impact of trauma on brain integration provide another source of information regarding possible links between brain functioning and the experience of the body. It is of relevance that the presence of sexual and physical abuse, as well as physical violations beyond childhood, among women with a range of disordered eating patterns is significantly higher than that of nonpsychiatric controls (e.g., Brewerton, 2007; Tagay, Schlottbohm, Reyes-Rodriguez, Repic, & Senf, 2014). Researchers of trauma and the brain describe multiple integrative challenges in trauma survivors (e.g., van der Kolk, McFarlane, & Weisaeth, 1996). These include, among others, disruptions to neurophysiological connections between cortical and subcortical regions of the brain, memory systems, and brain centers that process cognitions, emotions, bodily sensations, and actions. The brain processes associated with flashbacks or trauma memories are an example of such disruptions. The associated state of hyperarousal leads to the suppression of the transfer of sensory input from lower brain structures to some parts of the limbic systems (e.g., hippocampus) and the neocortex, such that higher level processing of cognitive, emotional, sensory, and bodily information cannot take place (e.g., Ogden & Fisher, 2015; van der Kolk et al., 1996). Brain research therefore suggests that positive embodiment, involving complex psychological processes, such as body connection, agency, and attuned self-care, therefore rely on the integrative functioning of the brain. However, further study of embodiment and the brain is needed.

EMBODYING INTERVENTIONS ENHANCING BRAIN INTEGRATION

Approaches have been developed to enhance neurological integration and embodied well-being, including embodied mindfulness and postural and mindful-action interventions.

Embodied Mindfulness

Mindfulness is a holistic, integrative process that shifts our relationship with our bodily sensations, emotions, and cognitions through repeated practice (Cook-Cottone 2015b; Khoury et al., 2017). The manner in which the body is conceptualized, referenced, and integrated into practice is critical (Cook-Cottone & Douglass, 2017). In these approaches, the body is not something to overcome or suppress, it is a resource for change and well-being. Using evidence from neurobiology, Khoury and colleagues (2017) explicated the concept of *embodied mindfulness* and argued for the utility of mindfulness as a mechanism of positive change. Emerging research agrees. Levine and Smolak (2016) highlighted embodiment via mindfulness as a potent future direction in the prevention of disordered eating and risk factors. Across interventions, the process generally occurs in three steps. First, during practice a client explores and differentiates the sensations and perceptions that may be linked to automatic thoughts and beliefs with a sense of curiosity, compassion, and kindness (Cook-Cottone, 2015b; Siegel, 2016). Second, based on what is noticed in mindful awareness, a client engages in mindful actions to better partner, or integrate, body and mind. This may include no action and simply allowing for experience and breath (Cook-Cottone, 2015b). Third, a client returns to simple awareness and being (Cook-Cottone, 2015b; Siegel, 2016).

Using the body as a key component of intervention, self-compassion protocols have been found to improve body image and reduce body dissatisfaction. In a systematic review, Rahimi-Ardabili, Reynolds, Vartanian, McLeod, and Zwar (2018) found that mindfulness practices such as self-compassion appear to be helpful for body image. For example, Albertson, Neff, and Dill-Shackleford (2015) conducted a randomized controlled trial using self-compassion meditation for body image among women; these women reported significantly greater improvement in body appreciation and a reduction in body dissatisfaction compared to the control group at post-test and 3-month follow-up. This study integrated body and sensation awareness into 3 weeks of meditation (i.e., compassionate body scan, affectionate breathing, and a self-compassion meditation). To illustrate technique, within the self-compassion meditation, the body is a central focal point as the practitioner is guided to recall a challenging or difficult experience and scan for where this is felt and experienced in the body, to notice aspects of the sensation of the feeling/experience, to practice allowing the sensation and softening the body around the sensation, and to acknowledge the challenge and effort involved in doing the difficult work of felt experience (Albertson et al., 2015).

Embodied mindfulness practices can also be helpful in identifying and responding to triggers (Brewer, Elwafi, & Davis, 2014). First, a client is guided to engage in mindful attention to triggers or what is identified by the brain as important (i.e., the salience network) and accompanying affective reactions. Mindful awareness of the trigger and reactions can help cut through the chain of contingencies that set us up for negative cognitions, ruminations, and cravings (Brewer et al., 2014). Rather than move quickly into problematic patterns of behavior, clients are mindful, aware, and carefully choose actions that help them stay present and engaged in the present moment (i.e., grounding breaths, focus on sensations, mindful movement; Cook-Cottone, 2015b). Mindfulness training and practice provide repeated opportunities to practice this shift toward engagement with the body and the present moment, supporting neurological change. In their review, Khoury et al. (2017) described the role of the bottom-up processes, such as the awareness of body signals (i.e., the body as a messenger, interoceptive awareness), as crucial in self-regulation due to the facilitation of awareness and identification of one's emotional state resulting in increased ability to self-regulate.

Brewer et al. (2014) detailed the key neurological mechanism that may be involved in this change. This includes alterations of the default mode network, given its dominance in mind-wandering and self-referential processing. According to Brewer et al. (2014), the default mode network has two primary nodes, the medial prefrontal cortex and the posterior cingulate cortex, known to be temporally linked to a number of peripheral nodes and not linked to brain regions involved in self-monitoring (i.e., the dorsal anterior cingulate cortex) and cognitive control (i.e., the dorsolateral prefrontal cortex).

Sensorimotor psychotherapy is an approach developed for the treatment of trauma. It emphasizes the importance of addressing bottom-up processes anchored in arousal and associated motor systems in the brainstem, and emotional and sensory perceptions processed in the middle brain (limbic system), toward enhancing the integrative and adaptive functioning of the brain (Ogden et al., 2006). The body in sensorimotor psychotherapy is a source of information, knowledge, and memories sometimes "knowing" what the individual does not know cognitively (Ogden et al., 2006). This work addresses symptom-bound cognitions. Symptom-bound cognitions are thoughts that are a manifestation of brain networks associated with symptoms such as catastrophic thoughts, related anxiety, or trauma memories (Hinton & Otto, 2006). Symptom-bound cognitions are viewed as representations of past somatic experiences (e.g., "I am never safe" or "I am worthless and unloveable"; Ogden et al., 2006, p. 3).

Awareness and management of the arousal threshold provide a way that this type of therapy integrates the body as a resource in interventions (Cook-Cottone, 2015b). Siegel (2016) and Ogden and Fisher (2015) described the window of tolerance as a band of arousal within which we function well. When we are feeling safe, we typically move through various arousal states depending on our experiences and stress, ranging from low arousal and calm (e.g., experienced while reading) and high arousal (e.g., alerted to the sound of a siren). Shifts in arousal occur through neuroception, the nervous system's ability to automatically assess the environment for safe and dangerous stimuli (Ogden & Fisher, 2015; Porges, 2011). When threatened, our salience network is activated. The autonomic nervous system engages, and we move into hyperarousal as the survival system prepares us to fight, flee, or call for help (Ogden & Fisher, 2015). If this does not work, the arousal system can drop to a state of hypoarousal: We may become immobilized, shut down, or freeze (Ogden & Fisher, 2015). Within the window of tolerance, we can stay positively and effectively embodied and regulate our arousal. However, in the more extreme states of hyperarousal (too much) and hypoarousal (too little), the window of tolerance is exceeded, and we experience dysregulated arousal (Ogden & Fisher, 2015; Siegel, 2016). Through embodied mindfulness practice, we can learn to recognize, as a felt sense, when we are functioning within our window of tolerance and to apply breath work and movement and body-based strategies to self-regulate (Cook-Cottone, 2015b; Ogden & Fisher, 2015). In self-regulation, the brain networks integrate and work together to facilitate awareness, regulation, and efficacy (Cook-Cottone, 2015b).

During sensorimotor therapy, clients are taught to observe the relationship between their physical experiences and how they have coded and organized and their emotional experiences (Ogden et al., 2006). Self-representations, such as "I am a bad person," are explored in how they might affect what is physically sensed or perceived, posture, autonomic arousal, and movement. Equally, clients explore how physical sensations, postures, and movement affect their emotional state and influence the content of their thoughts and the words that they use (Ogden et al., 2006). Through this process of mindful awareness of bodily sensations, movement and postural tendencies, sensory experiences, and associated cognitive narratives, a gradual shift in brain organization takes place. In particular, mindfulness activates the medial prefrontal cortex, which is associated with interoceptive awareness and internal awareness, as well as with deactivation of the amygdala—and, hence, supports emotion regulation (Creswell, Way, Eisenberger, & Lieberman, 2007). In outcome evaluation studies of sensorimotor therapy, positive effects have been observed in the areas of trauma symptoms, mood, overall health, and social dysfunction (Gene-Cos, Fisher, Ogden, & Cantrel, 2016).

Postural and Mindful-Action Interventions

Recent studies of postural work supported Ogden's work, which includes working with clients' postures. In a randomized controlled trial, Michalak, Mischnat, and

Tiesmann (2014) found that hospitalized patients with depression who were randomly assigned to an upright sitting position during a recall task showed unbiased recall of positive and negative words, while slumped patients showed a recall biased toward more negative words. Michalak et al. therefore suggested that relatively minor changes in the motoric system may affect the core cognitive bias in depression. These findings were supported by Wilkes, Kydd, Sagar, and Broadbendt (2017), who found in a randomized controlled trial among a community sample with mild-to-moderate symptoms of depression that a postural manipulation to sit upright, versus maintaining a usual posture, was associated with high-arousal positive affect. Further, upright shoulder angle was associated with lower negative affect and lower anxiety across both groups.

Yoga is another domain that emphasizes work on bodily postures, and its impact on well-being has become an important field of study. Yoga is a form of positive embodiment and a potential pathway to positive body image (Boudette, 2006; Douglass, 2011; see Chapter 30). Practitioners of yoga can move from an experience of thinking about the body to "embodying new ways of thinking" (Douglass, 2011, p. 85). Douglass also suggested that yoga can be a very powerful tool through which practitioners can encounter their inner lives and begin to notice and understand the effect of sensations, perceptions, and cognitions on embodied experience. Similar to the process of sensorimotor therapy (Ogden & Fisher, 2015; Ogden et al., 2006), the instructor provides support and physical cues to guide students inward through increasing interoceptive awareness and outward through proprioceptive and spatial awareness (Cook-Cottone & Douglass, 2017). As practitioners move through poses, hold them, and engage in breath work, they can experience body awareness, practice choices grounded in their physical sensations, and notice the effects of their choices and actions on the body (Cook-Cottone, 2015a).

There is a body of research that supports the use of yoga to enhance well-being, embodiment, and positive body image. In a comprehensive review and meta-analysis, Hendriks, de Jong, and Cramer (2017) found yoga to significantly influence four central indicators of positive mental health: psychological well-being, life satisfaction, social relationships, and mindfulness. In an extensive review, Schmalzl, Powers, and Blom (2015) detailed the neurophysiological and neuroanatomical centers that may underlie the particular tasks involved in yoga implicating key areas. They hypothesized that yoga-based practice promotes increased connectivity within, and dynamic shifting between, motor, cognitive, and emotional neurocircuitry, with potential beneficial effects for mind–body integration and self-regulation. Further, while highlighting the need for further study in this area due to methodological limitations in current research, Schmalzl et al.'s review of outcome studies of yoga interventions among nonclinical participants provided support for positive outcomes on measures of stress, body awareness, and cognitive functioning. Furthermore, Neumark-Sztainer, MacLehose, Watts, Pacanowski, and Eisenberg (2018) found that those who practiced yoga at least 30 minutes per week had higher body satisfaction than those who did not. Specific to positive body image and embodiment, there is a growing body of work suggesting that yoga practice may show benefits (see Chapter 30).

CONCLUSION

Building on the theoretical and empirical body of evidence and borrowing from what is known in fields such as trauma, embodied mindfulness and postural and mindful-action approaches appear to be associated with shifts toward greater integration of brain functioning, as well as of mind and body. These approaches contrast with interventions that rely primarily on emotional and cognitive change processes. Research is needed to explore if what works for trauma and depression works for those who struggle with negative body image and disembodiment. Further study of neurophysiological brain mechanisms associated with a range of experiences of embodiment, as well as of shifts in these mechanisms through engagement in a range of embodied mindfulness and movement-based (i.e., postural and mindful action) interventions, is needed as well. Studies that examine shifts in interoceptive and proprioceptive awareness, body connection, and the integration of bodily, emotional, and cognitive processing would be of particular interest. Perhaps if the evidence supports such valuable outcomes, the body and work with the body will be considered as important as the talking cure.

REFERENCES

Albertson, E. R., Neff, K. D., & Dill-Shackleford, K. E. (2015). Self-compassion and body dissatisfaction in women: A randomized controlled trial of a brief meditation intervention. *Mindfulness, 6*, 444–454. doi:10.1007/s12671-014-0277-3

Barsalou, L. W. (2008). Grounded cognition. *Annual Review of Psychology, 59*, 617–645. doi:10.1146/annurev.psych.59.103006.093639

Blood, S. K. (2005). *Body work: The social construction of women's body image*. Hove, England: Routledge. doi:10.4324/9780203495100

Boudette, R. (2006). Question and answer: Yoga in the treatment of disordered eating and body image disturbance: How can the practice of yoga be helpful in recovery from an eating disorder? *Eating Disorders, 14*, 167–170. doi.org/10.1080/10640260500536334

Brewer, J. A., Elwafi, H. M., & Davis, J. H. (2014). Craving to quit: Psychological models and neurobiological mechanisms of mindfulness training as treatment for addictions. *Psychology of Addictive Behaviors, 27*, 366–379. doi:10.1037/a0028490

Brewerton, T. D. (2007). Eating disorders, trauma, and comorbidity: Focus on PTSD. *Eating Disorders, 15*, 285–304. doi:10.1080/10640260701454311

Cook-Cottone, C. P. (2015a). Incorporating positive body image into the treatment of eating disorders: A model for attunement and mindful self-care. *Body Image, 14*, 158–167. doi:10.1016/j.bodyim.2015.03.004

Cook-Cottone, C. P. (2015b). *Mindfulness and yoga for self-regulation: A primer for mental health professionals*. New York, NY: Springer.

Cook-Cottone, C. (2016). Embodied self-regulation and mindful self-care in the prevention of eating disorders. *Eating Disorders, 24*, 98–105. doi:10.1080/10640266.2015.1118954

Cook-Cottone, C. P., & Douglass, L. L. (2017). Yoga communities and eating disorders: Creating safe space for positive embodiment. *International Journal of Yoga Therapy.* Advance online publication. doi:10.17761/IJYT2017_Methods_Cook-Cottone_Epub

Cook-Cottone, C. P., & Guyker, W. (2018). The development and validation of the Mindful Self-Care Scale (MSCS): An assessment of practices that support positive embodiment. *Mindfulness, 9*, 161–175. doi:10.1007/s12671-017-0759-1

Creswell, J. D., Way, B. M., Eisenberger, N. I., & Lieberman, M. D. (2007). Neural correlates of dispositional mindfulness during affect labeling. *Psychosomatic Medicine, 69*, 560–565. doi:10.1097/PSY.0b013e3180f6171f

Douglass, L. (2011). Thinking through the body: The conceptualization of yoga as therapy for individuals with eating disorders. *Eating Disorders, 19*, 83–96. doi:10.1080/10640266.2011.533607

Gaete, M. I., & Fuchs, T. (2007). From body image to emotional body experience in eating disorders. *Journal of Phenomenology, 47*, 17–40.

Gene-Cos, N., Fisher, J., Ogden, P., & Cantrel, A. (2016). Sensorimotor psychotherapy group therapy in the treatment of complex PTSD. *Annals of Psychiatry and Mental Health, 4*, 1080.

Hendriks, T., de Jong, J., & Cramer, H. (2017). The effects of yoga on positive mental health among healthy adults: A systematic review and meta-analysis. *Journal of Alternative and Complementary Medicine, 23*, 505–517. doi:10.1089/acm.2016.0334

Hinton, D. E., & Otto, M. W. (2006). Symptom presentation and symptom meaning among traumatized Cambodian refugees: Relevance to a somatically focused cognitive-behavior therapy. *Cognitive and Behavioral Practice, 13*, 249–260. doi:10.1016/j.cbpra.2006.04.006

Khoury, B., Knäuper, B., Pagnini, F., Trent, N., Chiesa, A., & Carrière, K. (2017). Embodied mindfulness. *Mindfulness, 8*, 1160–1171. doi:10.1007/s12671-017-0700-7

Levine, M. P., & Smolak, L. (2016). The role of protective factors in the prevention of negative body image and disordered eating. *Eating Disorders, 24*, 39–46. doi:10.1080/10640266.2015.1113826

McFadden, K. L., Tregellas, J. R., Shott, M. E., & Frank, G. K. (2014). Reduced salience and default mode network activity in women with anorexia nervosa. *Journal of Psychiatry & Neuroscience, 39*, 178–188. doi:10.1503/jpn.130046

Michalak, J., Mischnat, J., & Teismann, T. (2014). Sitting posture makes a difference—Embodiment effects on depressive memory bias. *Clinical Psychology & Psychotherapy, 21*, 519–524. doi:10.1002/cpp.1890

Neumark-Sztainer, D., MacLehose, R. F., Watts, A. W., Pacanowski, C. R., & Eisenberg, M. E. (2018). Yoga and body image: Findings from a large population-based study of young adults. *Body Image, 24*, 69–75. doi:10.1016/j.bodyim.2017.12.003

Ogden, P., & Fisher, J. (2015). *Sensorimotor psychotherapy: Intervention for trauma and attachment*. New York, NY: Norton.

Ogden, P., Minton, K., & Pain, C. (2006). *Trauma and the body: A sensorimotor approach to psychotherapy*. New York, NY: Norton.

Piran, N. (2016). Embodied possibilities and disruptions: The emergence of the Experience of Embodiment construct from qualitative studies with girls and women. *Body Image, 18*, 43–60. doi:10.1016/j.bodyim.2016.04.007

Piran, N. (2017). *Journeys of embodiment at the intersection of body and culture: The developmental theory of embodiment*. San Diego, CA: Elsevier. doi:10.1016/c2015-0-04666-4

Porges, S. W. (2011). *The polyvagal theory: Neurophysiological foundations of emotions, attachment, communication, and self-regulation*. New York, NY: Norton.

Rahimi-Ardabili, H., Reynolds, R., Vartanian, L. R., McLeod, L. V. D., & Zwar, N. (2018). A systematic review of the efficacy of interventions that aim to increase self-compassion on nutrition habits, eating behaviours, body weight and body image. *Mindfulness, 9*, 88–400. doi:10.1007/s12671-017-0804-0

Reindl, S. M. (2001). *Sensing the self: Women's recovery from bulimia*. Cambridge, MA: Harvard University Press.

Schmalzl, L., Powers, C., & Blom, E. H. (2015). Neurophysiological and neurocognitive mechanisms underlying the effects of yoga-based practices: Towards a comprehensive theoretical framework. *Frontiers in Human Neuroscience, 9*, 235. doi:10.3389/fnhum.2015.00235

Siegel, D. (2016). *Mind: A journey to the heart of being*. New York, NY: Norton.

Tagay, S., Schlottbohm, E., Reyes-Rodriguez, M. L., Repic, N., & Senf, W. (2014). Eating disorders, trauma, PTSD, and psychosocial resources. *Eating Disorders, 22*, 33–49. doi:10.1080/10640266.2014.857517

van der Kolk, B. A., McFarlane, A. C., & Weisaeth, L. (1996). *Traumatic stress*. New York, NY: Guilford Press.

Wilkes, C., Kydd, R., Sagar, M., & Broadbent, E. (2017). Upright posture improves affect and fatigue in people with depressive symptoms. *Journal of Behavior Therapy and Experimental Psychiatry, 54*, 143–149. doi:10.1016/j.jbtep.2016.07.015

32

Promoting Positive Body Image and Embodiment in Schools

Past, Present, and Future

ZALI YAGER ■

Schools and teachers have a unique opportunity to impact children's body image in a range of ways. Almost all youth are engaged in school settings where there are opportunities for formal and informal learning to take place. Body image is a common topic that is explored in middle and secondary schools, though the exact nature of learning about body image, who teaches it, and which subject area this comes under varies across states and countries. Whole-school approaches to the promotion of positive body image go beyond the classroom to incorporate training for teachers and school staff, involvement of parents and families, changes to the school physical and social environment, and partnerships with communities and other organizations (Cook-Cottone, Tribole, & Tylka, 2013; O'Dea & Maloney, 2000; Piran, 1999).

This chapter focuses first on determining where elements of positive body image and embodiment content may have been present in controlled prevention studies that were effective in improving body image among primary and secondary school settings and were published during the past 10 years. Potential future directions in promoting positive body image and embodiment among schoolchildren and for conducting research are discussed.

POSITIVE BODY IMAGE: A REVIEW OF PREVENTION PROGRAMS (2007–2017)

The aim of this review was to determine whether any of the elements of positive body image and embodiment have been featured in school-based prevention programs geared toward improving body image and whether measures of positive body image were used in outcome evaluations.

Method

Similar methods to those utilized in a previous evaluation of secondary school-based programs (Yager, Diedrichs, Ricciardelli, & Halliwell, 2013) were employed, and the review was extended to include programs conducted in junior and middle schools as well as primary school settings. The following inclusion criteria were adopted: (a) Programs were delivered during school hours in the classroom (not in physical education or sports); (b) interventions were aimed at universal-selective prevention (but not at indicated or targeted prevention); (c) outcome evaluations included a control group; (d) programs were effective in improving body image or body dissatisfaction from pre- to post-test on at least one outcome measure; and (e) outcome evaluation studies were published in peer-reviewed journals during the 10 years 2007–2017 inclusive. Effective programs were reviewed, as these interventions offer evidence-based paths for improving body image.

For this review, the program description sections of studies that fulfilled the inclusion criteria were examined to see whether the studied programs included components related to the definitions of positive body image and embodiment. Two tables were constructed to reflect the content included in the reviewed prevention programs, one for students 12 years and older (Table 32.1) and one for children under the age of 12 (Table 32.2). Overall, 10 content areas were included in the review according to existing definitions of positive body image (see Tylka & Wood-Barcalow, 2015b) and positive experiences of embodiment (see Piran, 2016).

An additional aim of the review was to identify whether specific positive body image measures have been used in studies to date. Articles were reviewed to determine whether the Body Appreciation Scale (BAS; Avalos, Tylka, & Wood-Barcalow, 2005) or its updated version, the BAS-2 (Tylka & Wood-Barcalow, 2015a), was used. The Body Esteem Scale (B. K. Mendelson, Mendelson, & White, 2001), which assesses positive body evaluation, was also included, with the caveat that positive body evaluation is a very narrow and incomplete conceptualization of positive body image (Tylka & Wood-Barcalow, 2015b).

Results for Programs with Adolescents

Table 32.1 presents the review of the eight programs that have been successful in improving body image among young people aged 12 years and over, published over the 10 years studied. The most common elements of positive body image that were identified included protective filtering (i.e., rejecting harmful body messages and body image threats and internalizing positive body messages), for example, through media literacy and critique of stereotyping by appearance (100%, eight

Table 32.1 Evidence of Features of Positive Body Image and Embodiment in Existing Effective Secondary School–Based Programs for Adolescents

	Includes Components of Positive Body Image (Tylka & Wood-Barcalow, 2015a)			
Program	**Appreciating the Unique Beauty and Functionality of Their Body**	**Body Acceptance and Broad Conceptualization of Beauty (Respecting Diversity in Others)**	**Feeling Confident and Comfortable in Their Own Body**	**Focusing on Their Body's Assets and Not Their Body's Imperfections**
Dove Confident Me: Five-Session Program (Diedrichs, Atkinson, & Garbett, in press)	✘	✓	✘	✘
Dove Confident Me: Single-Session Program (Diedrichs et al., 2015)	✘	✓	✘	✘
Succeed Body Image Program (Halliwell et al., 2015)	✘	✘	✘	✓
The Body Project (Halliwell & Diedrichs, 2014)	✘	✘	✘	✘
Me, You, and Us (Sharpe et al., 2013)	✘	✓	✘	✘
Happy Being Me (Richardson & Paxton, 2010)	✘	✘	✘	✘
Dove Body Think (Richardson, Paxton, & Thomson, 2009)	✘	✓	✘	✘
Media Smart (Wilksch & Wade, 2009)	✘	✘	✘	✘

Note: BAS = Body Appreciation Scale; BES = Body Esteem Scale.

	Includes Components of Positive Experience of Embodiment (Piran, 2016)					Outcome Measures	
Protective Filtering (e.g., Media Literacy, Critiques of Stereotypes or Historic Body Ideals)	Positive Body Connection and Comfort (Activities that Enhance a Positive Connection to One's Embodied Self)	Agency and Voice Through Activism and Projects that Invite Participants to Express Their Views with Others	Attuned Self-Care Through Attunement to One's Physical, Emotional, and Relational Needs	Resisting Objectification, Through Development of Media Literacy and Engagement in Meaningful Pursuits Not Focused on an Objectified Gaze on One's appearance	Connection and Expression of Desires	BAS	BES
✓	✘	✓	✘	✓	✘	No	Yes
✓	✘	✓	✘	✓	✘	No	Yes
✓	✘	✓	✘	✓	✘	Yes	No
✓	✘	✓	✘	✓	✘	No	No
✓	✓	✓	✓	✓	✘	No	Yes
✓	✘	✘	✘	✓	✘	No	No
✓	✘	✘	✘	✓	✘	No	No
✓	✘	✓	✘	✓	✘	No	No

Table 32.2 EVIDENCE OF FEATURES OF POSITIVE BODY IMAGE AND EMBODIMENT IN EXISTING EFFECTIVE SCHOOL-BASED PROGRAMS FOR CHILDREN

	Includes Components of Positive Body Image (Tylka & Wood-Barcalow, 2015b)				
Program	**Appreciating the Unique Beauty and Functionality of Their Body**	**Body Acceptance and Broad Conceptualization of Beauty (Respecting Diversity in Others)**	**Feeling Confident and Comfortable in Their Own Body**	**Focusing on Their Body's Assets and Not Their Body's Imperfections**	**Protective Filtering (e.g., Media Literacy, Critiques of Stereotypes or Historic Body Ideals)**
Happy Being Me (Bird, Halliwell, Diedrichs, & Harcourt, 2013)	✘	✘	✘	✘	✓
Taiwanese Program (Yeh, Liou, & Chien, 2012)	✘	✓	✘	✘	✓
Beautiful from the Inside Out (Norwood et al., 2011)	✘	✓	✘	✘	✓
PriMA (Wick et al., 2011)	✘	✘	✘	✘	✓
Shapesville (Dohnt & Tiggemann, 2008)	✓	✓	✘	✘	✓

Note: BAS = Body Appreciation Scale; BES = Body Esteem Scale; PriMA = Primary Prevention of Anorexia Nervosa in Preadolescent Girls (translated from German).

Includes Components of Positive Experience of Embodiment (Piran, 2016)					Outcome Measures	
Positive Body Connection and Comfort (Activities that Enhance a Positive Connection to One's Embodied Self)	Agency and Voice Through Activism and Projects that Invite Participants to Express Their Views with Others	Attuned Self-Care Through Attunement to One's Physical, Emotional, and Relational Needs	Resisting Objectification, Through Development of Media Literacy and Engagement in Meaningful Pursuits Not Focused on an Objectified Gaze on One's Appearance	Connection and Expression of Desires	BAS	BES
✘	✘	✘	✓	✘	No	No
✘	✘	✘	✓	✘	No	No
✘	✘	✓	✓	✘	No	Yes
✘	✘	✓	✓	✘	No	No
✘	✘	✘	✓	✘	No	No

programs); and having a broad acceptance and conceptualization of beauty (50%, four programs). The most common elements of the positive experience of embodiment that were included were resisting objectification (100%, eight programs) and agency and voice through activism (75%, six programs). Three programs used the Body Esteem Scale to capture body image, and one used the BAS.

Results for Programs with Children

Table 32.2 presents the review of the five programs that have been successful in improving body image among children, aged 12 years and under, published during the 10 years studied. The component of positive body image involving protective filtering, for example through media literacy and critiquing stereotypes, was again present in 100% of effective programs (five programs). Similar to the programs among adolescents, having a broad acceptance and conceptualization of beauty was also present in 60% of programs with children (three programs). Two elements that might support positive experiences of embodiment were found in programs with children: rejecting objectification (100%, five programs) and attuned self-care through a focus on physical and emotional needs (40%, two programs). In contrast to the results with adolescents, agency, voice, and activism did not seem to feature in programs with primary schoolchildren. None of the programs had been evaluated using the BAS, and one used the Body Esteem Scale.

Discussion

In this review, classroom-based programs that have been successful in improving body image in youth and included positive body image or embodiment content were identified. Some elements of positive body image and positive embodiment were present in these programs to varying degrees. All reviewed programs included rejecting objectification and building a protective filter, usually through media literacy or reducing fat talk and social comparisons. With adolescents, a focus on developing agency and voice through activism was popular, with many programs incorporating group projects to create schoolwide change or to communicate with advertisers and policymakers to advocate for change. Among children, a focus on a broad conceptualization of beauty was more common, with programs tending to focus on the positive impact of diversity. The programs that included the most components of positive body image and embodiment were Me, You, and Us (Sharpe, Schober, Treasure, & Schmidt, 2013) for adolescents and Beautiful from the Inside Out (Norwood, Murray, Nolan, & Bowker, 2011). In many cases, articles included in this review evaluated the same program, for example, the Dove Confident Me program (Atkinson et al., 2017; Diedrichs et al., 2015) was based on the Happy Being Me program (Richardson & Paxton, 2010), and the Succeed Body Image Program (Halliwell, Jarman, McNamara, Risdon, & Jankowski, 2015) was based on The Body Project (Halliwell & Diedrichs, 2014).

Some elements of positive body image and embodiment (e.g., feeling confident and comfortable in one's own body, positive connection to and expression of desires) were absent in effective body image programs.

Body image programs to date have largely been based on a pathological risk factor model, and many were focused on prevention of eating disorders rather than promoting positive body image. The more recent elaboration of the concepts of positive body image and positive embodiment could therefore offer a framework for future potential interventions that take a strengths-based, salutogenic approach alongside other developments in health promotion and health education (Becker, Glascoff, & Felts, 2010).

In terms of evaluation, very few programs utilized measures that might be able to capture improvements in positive body image. Measuring positive body image or other ways of inhabiting the body positively may enable researchers to capture the positive change that might be occurring in existing body image programs (Piran, 2015).

NEW POSSIBILITIES FOR SCHOOL-BASED PROGRAMS: PHYSICAL ACTIVITY, MINDFULNESS, AND EXPANDING FRAMEWORKS OF INTERVENTION

Given that only a few effective classroom-based body image programs have incorporated elements of positive body image and embodiment, it seems prudent to provide recommendations for future programming. Table 32.3 provides suggestions for potential content that is aligned with the elements of positive body image and embodiment.

One area that could be developed and explored further toward the development of positive body image and embodiment in schools is positive movement such as yoga and dance. Although this review captured only classroom-based interventions, it is suggested that programs that aim to promote positive body image in schools could take place outside of the formal class environment. In the developmental theory of embodiment, Piran and her colleagues (Piran, 2016; see also Chapter 10) described immersed engagement in joyful physical activities that are nonobjectifying or sexualizing as contributing to positive embodiment. Similarly, others have suggested that mindful movement can enhance positive body image by increasing the connectedness to the body and the reduction of objectification (Menzel & Levine, 2011).

Three studies with adolescent girls suggested a positive association between engagement in yoga and dance and positive body esteem. In a cross-sectional study in the United States with adolescent girls, participation in yoga and Pilates was associated with lower body dissatisfaction (Neumark-Sztainer, Eisenberg, Wall, & Loth, 2011). A study in the United Kingdom with 50 girls, ages 13–14, who reported high body dissatisfaction and low levels of physical activity found that a 6-week, twice-weekly, aerobic dance program enhanced feelings of attractiveness and physical self-worth compared to the regular physical education classes,

Table 32.3 Suggested School-Based Program Content for Developing Positive Body Image and Embodiment

Construct	Element	Recommendation
Positive body image	Appreciating the unique beauty and functionality of their body	- Engagement in yoga and positive physical activity experiences that emphasize body functionality - Individual reflection around positive physical qualities and beauty
	Body acceptance and broad conceptualization of beauty (respecting diversity in others)	- Read and discuss picture storybooks that emphasize the value of diversity, such as *My body Is Brilliant* (for children) - Critique and reconstruct conceptualizations of beauty at societal and personal levels
	Feeling confident and comfortable in their own body	-Guided mindful reflection in relation to positive movement experiences and how they feel
	Focusing on their body's assets and not their body's imperfections	- Engagement in positive physical activity experiences that emphasize body functionality - Brainstorm and focus on strengths and assets inside and out
	Protective filtering (e.g., media literacy, critiques of stereotypes or historic body ideals)	- Media literacy exercises as found in Dove Confident Me (Diedrichs et al., in press) or viewing the *Evolution* film clip (Halliwell, Easun, & Harcourt, 2010)
Embodiment	Positive body connection and comfort	- Mindfulness meditations including a "body scan" - Reflection on positive physical activity experiences
	Agency and voice through activism and projects that invite participants to express their views with others and physical agency	- Group projects that allow young people to identify their own issues and opportunities for activism, such as those included in the Succeed Body Image Program (Halliwell & Diedrichs, 2014) and Dove Confident Me (Diedrichs et al., in press); engagement in physical experiences that emphasize competence and functionality
	Attuned self-care through attunement to one's physical, emotional, and relational needs	- Motivational interviewing to support goal setting and planning for engagement in activities that keep us healthy, including food, physical activity, and mindfulness (for adolescents)

(*continued*)

Table 32.3 Continued

Construct	Element	Recommendation
	Refection of objectification and engagement in meaningful pursuits not focused on an objectified gaze on one's appearance	- Exploring and critiquing objectification of the female body in the media, for example, through a comparison of how men and women are portrayed in sports photography (for adolescents) and media literacy exercises to resist objectification
	Connection and expression of desires	- Listening to the body in relation to hunger and satiety

which involved swimming (Burgess, Grogan, & Burwitz, 2006). These gains were not maintained postintervention, suggesting that continuous participation in the program may be needed for body image benefits. A small qualitative study in the United Kingdom with 17-year-old women and men reported that participants felt more connected to, and less self-conscious about, their bodies following participation in "dance movement psychotherapy" (Grogan et al., 2014).

There is some evidence regarding the association between engagement in positive movement experiences and body esteem among children aged 5–12 years. A twice-weekly, 40-minute circuit training involving hopping, skipping, and jumping led to improvement in body esteem among UK girls and boys aged 10–11, compared to a no intervention control group; however, this improvement was not sustained at the 6-month follow-up (Duncan, Al-Nakeeb, & Nevill, 2009). A prevention program, called "Girls' Group," that included yoga as a major program component was found to reduce body dissatisfaction and drive for thinness among fifth-grade girls from the United States (Scime, Cook-Cottone, Kane, & Watson, 2006). Among older adolescent girls from the United States, the "New Moves" multicomponent program involved physical education classes and was found to improve intervention girls' body satisfaction at follow-up (Neumark-Sztainer et al., 2010).

A second area that could be developed and explored further toward the development of positive body image and embodiment among youth in schools is the impact of interventions that focus on mindfulness and self-compassion (see also Chapters 25 and 29). While these approaches have been found effective in enhancing body appreciation among adult women, little research has been done with youth. The strong evidence supporting the use of school-based mindfulness interventions for depression and anxiety (T. Mendelson et al., 2010) suggests that it would be prudent for researchers to evaluate the mindfulness programs that are currently available in order to determine their potential impact on other indicators of children's mental health, including positive body image.

A third area that could help move school-based interventions toward positive body image and embodiment is expanding the theoretical frameworks that inform the construction of prevention programs for youth. While for the past 20 years the majority of prevention work in the field of eating disorders has been informed by etiological models that focus exclusively on risk factors (Stice, Marti, & Durant, 2011), targeting protective factors that enhance the development of positive body image and embodiment can enrich prevention work (Smolak, 2013). The construction of integrated models that include protective as well as risk factors is recent and requires further prospective studies (see also Chapter 10). Similarly, prevention programs can be informed by salutogenesis, a health promotion approach focusing on the development of well-being rather than the prevention of disease (Becker et al., 2010), as reflected in positive psychology in health education (Steck, Abrams, & Phelps, 2004); positive education (Norrish, Williams, O'Connor, & Robinson, 2013); and a strengths-based approach to health education (Lopez & Louis, 2009). Whole-school approaches toward the enhancement of positive body image and the prevention of eating disorders, such as health-promoting schools (e.g., O'Dea & Maloney, 2000; Piran, 1999) or comprehensive school health (Haines, Neumark-Sztainer, Perry, Hannan, & Levine, 2006; McVey, Tweed, & Blackmore, 2007) can further continue to inform progress in this field.

CONCLUSION

This review highlights the ways that elements of positive body image and embodiment have been included in past programs and how scholars can develop programs including these elements in the future. There is sufficient evidence that future school-based programming could include positive movement experiences, self-compassion, and mindfulness, as well as be informed by salutogenic theories that integrate protective factors into etiological models.

It is critical that scholars begin to incorporate validated tools to measure positive body image and embodiment in their school-based programs. The BAS-2C (Body Appreciation Scale-2 for Children), revised specifically for children and validated on 9- to 11-year-old girls and boys, is one possibility (Halliwell, Jarman, Tylka, & Slater, 2017). In line with the work of Halliwell et al. (2015), it is argued that effective existing body image intervention programs should be replicated and include measures of positive body image and embodiment. It is also important that new programs aimed at enhancing positive body image and embodiment incorporate components of programs that have been found effective in controlled outcome studies (Halliwell et al., 2015).

REFERENCES

Atkinson, M. J., Diedrichs, P. C., & Garbett, K. M. (2017). Evaluating a School-Based Intervention for Body Image ('Dove Confident Me: 5-Part Body Confidence Workshops for Schools') Among Adolescent Girls and Boys: Results from a Cluster Randomized Controlled Effectiveness Trial. *Journal of Adolescent Health, 60*(2), S5.

Avalos, L., Tylka, T. L., & Wood-Barcalow, N. (2005). The Body Appreciation Scale: Development and psychometric evaluation. *Body Image, 2*, 285–297. doi:10.1016/j.bodyim.2005.06.002

Becker, C. M., Glascoff, M. A., & Felts, W. M. (2010). Salutogenesis 30 years later: Where do we go from here? *International Electronic Journal of Health Education, 13*, 25–32.

Bird, E., Halliwell, E., Diedrichs, P. C., & Harcourt, D. (2013). Happy Being Me in the UK: A controlled evaluation of a body image intervention with pre-adolescent children. *Body Image, 10*, 326–334. doi:10.1016/j.bodyim.2013.02.008

Burgess, G., Grogan, S., & Burwitz, L. (2006). Effects of a 6-week aerobic dance intervention on body image and physical self-perceptions in adolescent girls. *Body Image, 3*, 57–66. doi:10.1016/j.bodyim.2005.10.005

Cook-Cottone, C. P., Tribole, E., & Tylka, T. L. (2013). *Healthy eating in schools: Evidence-based interventions to help kids thrive.* Washington, DC: American Psychological Association.

Diedrichs, P. C., Atkinson, M. J., Steer, R. J., Garbett, K. M., Rumsey, N., & Halliwell, E. (2015). Effectiveness of a brief school-based body image intervention "Dove Confident Me: Single Session" when delivered by teachers and researchers: Results from a cluster randomised controlled trial. *Behaviour Research and Therapy, 74*, 94–104. doi:10.1016/j.brat.2015.09.004

Dohnt, H. K., & Tiggemann, M. (2008). Promoting positive body image in young girls: An evaluation of "Shapesville." *European Eating Disorder Review, 16*, 222–233. doi:10.1002/erv.814

Duncan, M. J., Al-Nakeeb, Y., & Nevill, A. M. (2009). Effects of a 6-week circuit training intervention on body esteem and body mass index in British primary school children *Body Image, 6*, 216–220. doi:10.1016/j.bodyim.2009.04.003

Grogan, S., Williams, A., Kilgariff, S., Bunce, J., Heyland, J. H., Padilla, T., . . . Davies, W. (2014). Dance and body image: Young people's experiences of a dance movement psychotherapy session. *Qualitative Research in Sport, Exercise, and Health, 6*, 261–277. doi:10.1080/2159676X.2013.796492

Haines, J., Neumark-Sztainer, D., Perry, C. L., Hannan, P. J., & Levine, M. P. (2006). VIK (Very Important Kids): A school-based program designed to reduce teasing and unhealthy weight-control behaviors. *Health Education Research, 21*, 884–895. doi:10.1093/her/cyl123

Halliwell, E., & Diedrichs, P. C. (2014). Testing a dissonance body image intervention among young girls. *Health Psychology, 33*, 201–204. doi:10.1037/a0032585

Halliwell, E., Easun, A., & Harcourt, D. (2010). Body dissatisfaction: Can a short media literacy message reduce negative media exposure effects among adolescent girls? *British Journal of Health Psychology, 16*, 396–403. doi:10.1348/135910710X515714

Halliwell, E., Jarman, H., McNamara, A., Risdon, H., & Jankowski, G. (2015). Dissemination of evidence-based body image interventions: A pilot study into the effectiveness of using undergraduate students as interventionists in secondary schools. *Body Image, 14*, 1–4. doi:10.1016/j.bodyim.2015.02.002

Halliwell, E., Jarman, H., Tylka, T., & Slater, A. (2017). Adapting the Body Appreciation Scale-2 for Children: A psychometric analysis of the BAS-2C. *Body Image, 21*, 97–102. doi:10.1016/j.bodyim.2017.03.005

Lopez, S. J., & Louis, M. C. (2009). The principles of strengths-based education. *Journal of College and Character, 10*, 4. doi:10.2202/1940-1639.1041

McVey, G. L., Tweed, S., & Blackmore, E. (2007). Healthy Schools-Healthy kids: A controlled evaluation of a comprehensive universal eating disorder prevention program. *Body Image, 4*, 115–136. doi:10.1016/j.bodyim.2007.01.004

Mendelson, B. K., Mendelson, M. J., & White, D. R. (2001). Body Esteem Scale for adolescents and adults. *Journal of Personality Assessment, 76*, 90–106. doi:10.1207/S15327752JPA7601_6

Mendelson, T., Greenberg, M. T., Dariotis, J. K., Gould, L. F., Rhoades, B. L., & Leaf, P. J. (2010). Feasibility and preliminary outcomes of a school-based mindfulness intervention for urban youth. *Journal of Abnormal Child Psychology, 38*, 985–994. doi:10.1007/s10802-010-9418-x

Menzel, J. E., & Levine, M. P. (2011). Embodying experiences and the promotion of positive body image: The example of competitive athletics. In R. M. Calogero, S. Tantleff-Dunn, & J. K. Thompson (Eds.), *Self-objectification in women: Causes, consequences, and counteractions* (pp. 163–186). Washington, DC: American Psychological Association.

Neumark-Sztainer, D., Eisenberg, M. E., Wall, M., & Loth, K. A. (2011). Yoga and Pilates: Associations with body image and disordered eating behaviors in a population-based sample of young adults. *International Journal of Eating Disorders, 44*, 276–280. doi:10.1002/eat.20858

Neumark-Sztainer, D., Friend, S. E., Flattum, C. F., Hannan, P. J., Story, M., Bauer, K. W., . . . Petrich, C. A. (2010). New Moves-Preventing weight-related problems in adolescent girls: A group-randomised study. *American Journal of Preventive Medicine, 39*, 421–432. doi:10.1016/j.amepre.2010.07.017

Norrish, J. M., Williams, P., O'Connor, M., & Robinson, J. (2013). An applied framework for positive education. *International Journal of Wellbeing, 3*, 147–161. doi:10.5502/ijw.v3i2.2

Norwood, S. J., Murray, M., Nolan, A., & Bowker, A. (2011). Beautiful from the Inside Out: A school-based programme designed to increase self esteem and positive body image among preadolescents. *Canadian Journal of School Psychology, 26*, 263–282. doi:10.1177/0829573511423632

O'Dea, J., & Maloney, D. (2000). Preventing eating and body image problems in children and adolescents using the Health Promoting Schools Framework. *The Journal of School Health, 70*, 18–22. doi: 10.1111/j.1746-1561.2000.tb06441.x

Piran, N. (1999). Eating disorders: A trial of prevention in a high risk school setting. *Journal of Primary Prevention, 20*, 75–90. doi:10.1023/A:1021358519832

Piran, N. (2015). New possibilities in the prevention of eating disorders: The introduction of positive body image measures. *Body Image, 14*, 146–157. doi:10.1016/j.bodyim.2015.03.008

Piran, N. (2016). Embodied possibilities and disruptions: The emergence of the Experience of Embodiment construct from qualitative studies with girls and women. *Body Image, 18*, 43–60. doi:10.1016/jbodyim2016.0.4.007.

Richardson, S. M., & Paxton, S. J. (2010). An evaluation of a body image intervention based on risk factors for body dissatisfaction: A controlled study with adolescent girls. *International Journal of Eating Disorders, 43*, 112–122. doi:10.1002/eat.20682

Richardson, S. M., Paxton, S. J., & Thomson, J. S. (2009). Is BodyThink an efficacious body image and self esteem program? A controlled evaluation with adolescents. *Body Image, 6*, 75–82. doi:10.1016/j.bodyim.2008.11.001

Scime, M., Cook-Cottone, C., Kane, L., & Watson, T. (2006). Group prevention of eating disorders with fifth-grade females: Impact on body dissatisfaction, drive for thinness and media influence. *Eating Disorders, 14*, 143–155. doi:10.1080/10640260500403881

Sharpe, H., Schober, I., Treasure, J., & Schmidt, U. (2013). Feasibility, acceptability and efficacy of a school-based prevention programme for eating disorders: Cluster randomised controlled trial. *British Journal of Psychiatry, 203*, 428–435. doi:10.1192/bjp.bp.113.128199

Smolak, L. (2013). Risk and protective factors in body image problems: Implications for prevention. In G. L. McVey, M. P. Levine, N. Piran, & H. B. Ferguson (Eds.), *Preventing eating-related and weight-related disorders* (pp. 147–167). Waterloo, ON, Canada: Wilfred Laurier University Press.

Steck, E. L., Abrams, L. M., & Phelps, L. (2004). Positive psychology in the prevention of eating disorders. *Psychology in the Schools, 41*, 111–118. doi:10.1002/pits.10143

Stice, E., Marti, C. N., & Durant, S. (2011). Risk factors for onset of eating disorders: Evidence of multiple risk pathways from an 8-year prospective study. *Behaviour Research and Therapy, 49*, 622–627. doi:10.1016/j.brat.2011.06.009

Tylka, T. L., & Wood-Barcalow, N. L. (2015a). The Body Appreciation Scale-2: Item refinement and psychometric evaluation. *Body Image, 12*, 53–67. doi:10.1016/j.bodyim.2014.09.006

Tylka, T. L., & Wood-Barcalow, N. L. (2015b). What is and what is not positive body image? Conceptual foundations and concept definition. *Body Image, 14*, 118–129. doi:10.1016/j.bodyim.2015.04.001

Wick, K., Brix, C., Bormann, B., Sowa, S., Strauss, B., & Berger, B. (2011). Real-world effectiveness of a German school-based intervention for primary prevention of anorexia nervosa in preadolescent girls. *Preventive Medicine, 52*, 152–158. doi:10.1016/j.ypmed.2010.11.022

Wilksch, S. M., & Wade, T. D. (2009). Reduction of shape and weight concern in young adolescents: A 30-month controlled evaluation of a media literacy program. *Journal of the American Academy of Child and Adolescent Psychiatry, 48*, 652–661. doi:10.1097/CHI.0b013e3181a1f559

Yager, Z., Diedrichs, P. C., Ricciardelli, L. A., & Halliwell, E. (2013). What works in secondary schools? A systematic review of classroom-based body image programs. *Body Image, 10*, 271–281. doi:10.1016/j.bodyim.2013.04.001

Yeh, M., Liou, Y., & Chien, L. (2012). Development and effectiveness of a school programme on improving body image among elementary school students in Taiwan. *Journal of Advanced Nursing, 68*, 434–443. doi:10.1111/j.1365-2648.2011.05735

33

Cognitive Dissonance–Based Interventions to Facilitate Positive Body Image and Embodiment

EMMA HALLIWELL AND PHILLIPPA C. DIEDRICHS ■

Prospective research indicated that positive body image, defined as body appreciation, predicts adaptive eating behaviors among adolescent girls over a 1-year period (Andrew, Tiggemann, & Clark, 2016). Experimental research indicated that women with high body appreciation do not experience body dissatisfaction after exposure to models who embody sociocultural appearance ideals, whereas those with low body appreciation experience body dissatisfaction after exposure (Andrew, Tiggemann, & Clark, 2015; Halliwell, 2013). In addition, several dimensions of positive body image are correlated with multiple indicators of well-being, such as self-esteem, proactive coping, optimism, positive affect, self-compassion, life satisfaction, and subjective happiness (see Chapters 2, 3, and 5). The combined evidence indicates that positive body image is protective against body image–related concerns and bolsters psychological and physical well-being (Halliwell, 2015).

Therefore, it is important to identify factors, and develop interventions, that promote positive body image. There are parallel processes that will support this endeavor. One is to draw on evidence and theory to directly target predictors of positive body image in new interventions. The second, an equally important undertaking, is to examine the efficacy of existing evidenced-based body image interventions in promoting positive body image. This will allow us to capitalize on current good practice, avoid duplication of efforts, learn from past mistakes, and more strategically and rapidly advance the field of body image interventions. Cognitive dissonance-based interventions (CDIs), commonly labeled as the *Body Project*, emerge in meta-analyses as the most effective selective eating disorder prevention and body acceptance programs for girls and women (Stice, Shaw, &

Marti, 2007; Watson et al., 2016). This chapter examines whether CDIs might also be used to promote aspects of positive body image.

COGNITIVE DISSONANCE–BASED INTERVENTIONS AND NEGATIVE BODY IMAGE

Theoretically, CDIs are underpinned by cognitive dissonance theory (Festinger, 1957) and the dual-pathway model for disordered eating (Stice, 2001). Cognitive dissonance theory posits that humans are motivated to avoid inconsistencies between their cognitions and behaviors. For example, a person who believes that thin women are more successful and attractive will act in accordance with this belief by restricting food intake to try to lose weight (concordant behavior), rather than listening and responding to her body's needs (discordant behavior). Experiencing inconsistencies, or dissonance, is associated with discomfort. Therefore, people will often change their cognitions or behavior to reduce dissonance. This theory is supported by over 60 years of research evidence and has been utilized in interventions to address diverse areas of health, such as safe sex, smoking, and substance misuse (Freijy & Kothe, 2013).

The dual-pathway model is based on prospective research predicting the development of eating pathology in women (Stice, 2001). The model posits that sociocultural pressures to be thin result in increased internalization of the thin ideal, which subsequently increases body dissatisfaction and negative affect, which are the dual paths leading to disordered eating behavior. Based on this model, CDIs are designed to engage participants in counterattitudinal activities that require them to verbally and behaviorally challenge the thin ideal. This putatively creates cognitive dissonance among girls and women who have internalized the thin ideal, as they are acting in a manner inconsistent with their attitudes. Theoretically, this dissonance then motivates them to change their beliefs (i.e., reduce internalization of the thin ideal) to correspond with their actions. Studies with adolescent girls and young women have supported the underlying theory of CDIs, and reductions in internalization of the thin ideal have been shown to mediate the effects of the intervention (Seidel, Presnell, & Rosenfield, 2009; Stice et al., 2007).

Initial evaluations of CDIs were conducted by Eric Stice and colleagues. They examined selective delivery, whereby adolescent girls and women with existing body image concerns self-selected into the intervention. Efficacy trials indicated that CDIs led to reductions in thin-ideal internalization, body dissatisfaction, negative affect, disordered eating, functional impairment, and eating disorder onset over a 3-year follow-up period compared to assessment-only control and alternative intervention groups (see Stice, Rohde, Butryn, Shaw, & Marti, 2015).

In a parallel program of research, Carolyn Becker and colleagues evaluated CDIs as a semimandatory program for university women. Becker was the first to utilize a peer-led intervention delivery approach where sorority members were trained to deliver the manualized program to their peers. Task-shifting delivery of the intervention to peer leaders was an important step in enhancing the scalability of the intervention. This program of research provided evidence that CDIs are also effective among lower risk populations, although with smaller effect sizes compared to higher risk populations (e.g., Becker, Smith & Ciao, 2006).

In the United Kingdom, we have evaluated a universal, semimandatory, peer-led CDI among university women on campus (Diedrichs, Halliwell, & Paraskeva, 2014; Halliwell & Diedrichs, 2014a), as well as universal (Halliwell & Diedrichs, 2014b) and selective (Halliwell et al., 2017; Jarman, Treneman-Evans, & Halliwell, 2017) versions of the program among adolescent girls in schools. Consistent with evidence from the United States, our research indicated that CDIs are associated with reductions in thin-ideal internalization, restrained eating, body dissatisfaction, and negative affect among university women and adolescent girls.

The CDIs have also been evaluated by independent research groups in Australia (Atkinson & Wade, 2015; Cruwys, Haslam, Fox, & McMahon, 2015) and Europe (Daníelsdóttir, Agustsdóttir, Thorsdóttir, & Jonsson, 2012). All studies but one (Atkinson & Wade, 2015) identified significant reductions in body dissatisfaction among female participants taking part in CDIs. In addition, a CDI called *Free Being Me* has been disseminated to over 3 million girls in 124 countries through the World Association for Girl Guides and Girl Scouts, with an implementation study showing good acceptability globally (Diedrichs, 2016; Diedrichs, Craddock, Gau, & Stice, 2017). Free Being Me is based on the Body Project, but was adapted to include activities and language appropriate for nonformal education settings and to suit the girl-guiding culture.

There has been some preliminary work adapting CDIs to address men's body image concerns. Two studies have evaluated versions of the Body Project specifically adapted to focus on men's body image. Body dissatisfaction was reduced immediately postintervention and at 1-month follow-up among gay undergraduate men (Brown & Keel, 2015) and 3-month follow-up among predominantly heterosexual undergraduate men (Jankowski et al., 2017) who completed the intervention compared to control groups. Both studies also found reductions in appearance-ideal internalization postintervention that were not sustained at follow-up. Brown and Keel (2015) found the intervention was associated with sustained reductions in romantic partner objectification, dietary restraint, and bulimic symptoms. In contrast, intervention participants in Jankowski et al.'s 2017 study did not report changes in bulimic pathology but did report reductions in muscularity-enhancing behaviors and appearance comparisons. Kilpela et al. (2016) adapted the Body Project to be delivered to a mixed-sex group. A pilot randomized controlled trial found improvements on negative affect, and multiple aspects of body dissatisfaction among undergraduate men and improvements on some aspects of body dissatisfaction were maintained at 2- and 6-month follow-ups. Interestingly, in the mixed-sex group, results for women were not promising. These studies provide some preliminary evidence that CDIs tailored to address men's concerns can improve body image among men. However, much more research is needed before we can be confident that adapted CDI is an effective body image intervention for men.

In summary, there is evidence from independent research groups across several countries that CDIs reduce body image concerns and other risk factors for the development of eating disorders among girls and women. There is also some preliminary evidence that CDIs can reduce body image concerns among men. Thus, it is important to consider whether this program extends beyond the reduction of negative outcomes to also promote positive body image (Halliwell, 2015; Piran, 2015).

Arguably, the primary psychological mechanism of CDIs is cognitive dissonance. However, the intervention is multifaceted, incorporating dissonance, psychoeducational content, media literacy, body acceptance, and behavioral components. The key intervention activities involve (a) defining and challenging the thin ideal; (b) considering the costs of pursuing the thin ideal; (c) writing letters and engaging in role plays to discourage others from pursuing the thin ideal; (d) identifying and discussing positive aspects of one's own appearance and character; (e) practicing ways to avoid fat talk; (f) engaging in behavioral challenges; (g) discussing and engaging in social activism to tackle appearance pressures; and (h) using a self-affirmation exercise. By considering these activities in relation to each of the components of positive body image, we can conceptually understand how the intervention may enhance positive body image.

COGNITIVE DISSONANCE INTERVENTIONS, POSITIVE BODY IMAGE, AND EMBODIMENT

To facilitate our discussion of theoretical links between CDIs and positive body image, it is important to briefly define positive body image and the related construct of embodiment. Based on early qualitative and quantitative work on positive body image (e.g., Avalos, Tylka, & Wood-Barcalow, 2005; Frisén & Holmqvist, 2010; Wood-Barcalow, Tylka, & Augustus-Horvath, 2010), Menzel and Levine (2011) described three central components of positive body image: (a) appreciating the body's appearance and function; (b) being aware of and attentive to the body's experiences and needs; and (c) possessing a positive cognitive style for processing body-related messages in a self-protective way. Tylka and colleagues have been pivotal in progressing the empirical investigation of positive body image through the development of the Body Appreciation Scale (BAS, Avalos et al., 2005; BAS-2, Tylka & Wood-Barcalow, 2015), which assesses all three components of positive body image described by Menzel and Levine.

Recently, there has also been a focus on the concept of embodiment (Piran, 2015, 2016). While there is overlap between the concepts of positive body image and embodiment, embodiment presents a broader view of optimal relationships with the body. Piran (2016) described embodiment as attunement with inner states and pleasurable engagement with a broad range of bodily experiences and discussed embodiment in relation to societal expectations and structures. Piran identified five dimensions of the experience of embodiment, which both support and extend definitions of positive body image. In Figure 33.1, we integrate

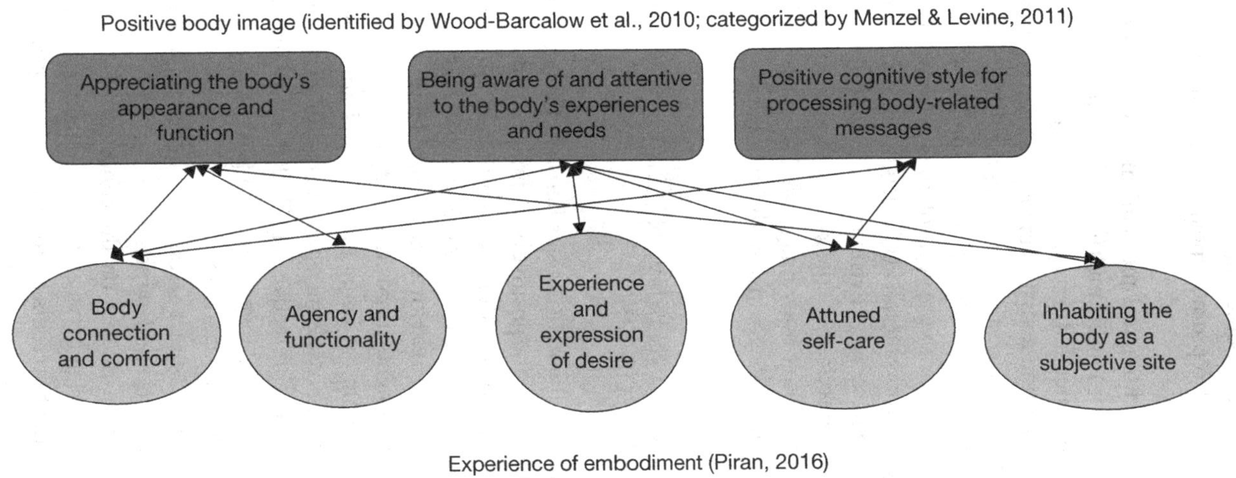

Figure 33.1 Integration of positive body image and embodiment theories.

components identified in models of positive body image and embodiment to facilitate our discussion of the likely impact of CDIs. Note that this figure is an oversimplification and, inevitably, loses some nuance of the dimensions. We recommend that readers consult the original references for more detail.

Three dimensions of embodiment are consistent with, and extend, the first component of positive body image: appreciating the appearance and function of the body. These are *body connection and comfort* (positive connection with the body and a range of positive feelings toward the body); *inhabiting the body as a subjective site versus as an objective site* (the extent to which girls and women value their subjective experiences of living in their body); and *agency and functionality* (the extent to which women experience physical and verbal agency in the world). Four embodiment dimensions link to the second component of positive body image: being aware of and attentive to the body's experiences and needs. These are *body connection and comfort, experience, and expression of desire* (the extent to which women can respond to desire in a self-caring way); *attuned self-care* (the extent to which girls and women attend positively to their bodily, emotional and relational needs); and *inhabiting the body as a subjective site versus as an objective site*. Finally, the third dimension of positive body image, self-protective cognitive processing style, can be associated with *body connection and comfort*, in that resistant self-talk is vital to maintaining a positive connection with the body in an adverse social environment, as well as *attuned self-care*. Theoretically, these aspects of positive body image and embodiment are supported to some extent via the content of CDI.

CDI and Appreciating the Body's Appearance and Function

Body connection and comfort, inhabiting the body as a subjective site versus an objective site, and agency and functionality, three of the five key dimensions of embodiment (Piran, 2016), are most directly supported by the mirror exercise within CDIs. This exercise invites participants to identify and verbalize positive aspects of their appearance and character, thereby combining body acceptance and dissonance. In this exercise, participants are instructed to stand in front of a mirror at home and write down 15 things they like about themselves, including physical, emotional, intellectual, and social qualities. They are required to include some physical attributes and are reminded that sometimes we like our bodies because of what they allow us to do, for example, our legs allow us to dance. In the next session, participants are invited to share aspects of their appearance and function that they like. This activity is clearly related to accepting and appreciating the body's appearance and function, a dimension of positive body image. It also relates to body connection and comfort, a dimension of positive embodiment. The activity also supports physical freedom (Piran, 2015) and agency and functionality (Piran, 2016) because it celebrates engaging with physical activities in the absence of appearance pressures.

Body connection and comfort as well as agency and functionality are also fostered through the letter-writing exercises, which involve writing a letter to persuade an adolescent girl or a younger self not to pursue the thin ideal. The content of these letters is read aloud to the group. Typically, the letters not only list the costs of pursuing the thin ideal but also appeals to the letter recipient to value her body as it is. The verbal elements of agency and functionality are supported through the very interactive nature of the intervention and through the role-play and quick comeback exercises. Participants prepare verbal responses to current and future appearance pressures and role-play giving these responses. They are guided to draw on the costs of pursuing thinness when preparing their responses. However, this activity can also provide opportunity to reinforce verbal agency around body acceptance, appreciate functionality, and prioritize subjective experiences of the body. We witness verbal responses such as "My thighs are chunky because they are all muscle, and they allow me to run fast" or "This body allowed me to have children—who cares if I have stretch marks?" In addition, agency and functionality as well as inhabiting the body as a subjective site are supported through the behavioral challenges (Piran, 2015). In these challenges, participants are asked to engage in valued activities that they have been avoiding because of appearance concerns, such as swimming or going to the beach.

There is also a social activism element to CDIs, and participants are encouraged to target broader changes among their immediate social group and the wider society. The ideas generated included actions like making posters to display around school, posting body-positive messages on toilet doors, engaging with staff to promote diversity in appearance, and, at a broader level, writing to magazine editors, posting on social media, and sticking disruptive Post-it notes on diet books in stores. This social activism should contribute to agency and functionality through supporting efficacy in the debate around body image.

CDIs and Attunement to the Body

Being aware of and attentive to the body's experiences and needs, or attuned self-care, is not a *direct* focus of CDI content. However, CDI draws a distinction between the "thin ideal" and the "healthy ideal." The healthy ideal is defined as "the way your unique body looks when you are doing the things necessary to appropriately and simultaneously maximize your physical health, mental health, and overall quality of life" (Becker & Stice, 2011, p. 20). Participants are encouraged to aspire to a healthy ideal rather than a thin ideal. However, it is important to note that the healthy ideal can be easily misconstrued by participants to include a focus on weight and body shape due to societal portrayals of what healthy bodies should "look" like; thus, it must be carefully and thoughtfully attended to by intervention group leaders. In addition, the dangers of neglecting bodily experiences and needs are central to discussions of the costs of pursuing the thin ideal and the role plays. Typically, in the role-play scenarios, participants highlight the damage that pursuing thinness can have on meaningful relationships in their lives or their health (e.g., restrictive eating leading to immune deficiencies and frail bones).

CDI and Cognitive Style for Processing Body-Related Messages

Developing a self-protective cognitive processing style is facilitated through a number of CDI activities, such as critiquing the thin ideal, discussions of photo editing, quick comebacks, and letter writing.

EMPIRICAL EVIDENCE LINKING CDI AND BODY APPRECIATION

For the last 7 years, we have delivered CDIs to undergraduate women as a semimandatory component of an undergraduate module. In recent cohorts, we have included a global measure of positive body image, the BAS-2 (Tylka & Wood-Barcalow, 2015), in our evaluation. To tease apart different elements of the positive body image construct, we included the Surveillance subscale of the Objectified Body Consciousness Scale (OBCS; McKinley & Hyde, 1996) to assess the extent to which women inhabit the body as a subjective site versus an objectified site. We also included a measure relating to attuned self-care, the Intuitive Eating Scale (Tylka, 2006), to assess the extent to which individuals are aware of their bodily cues for food and eat in response to these cues.

Data from 101 women in the United Kingdom revealed that participating in 4 hours of CDI increased body appreciation and intuitive eating and reduced surveillance across a 2-month follow-up compared to assessment-only controls (Halliwell & Diedrichs, 2014a). Our results are consistent with data from the United States (Becker, Hill, Greif, Han, & Stewart, 2013; Kroon Van Diest & Perez, 2013) showing reductions in surveillance among women who participated in CDIs. These reductions were sustained at 5 months (Kroon Van Diest & Perez, 2013) and 8 months (Becker et al., 2013) postintervention but were not evident after a 1-year period, despite changes on dual-pathway model variables being maintained (Kroon Van Diest & Perez, 2013). Therefore, it may be that the intervention does not have such a robust impact on inhabiting the body as a subjective site as it has on the dual-pathway model variables that it directly targets.

We have also examined the impact of CDIs on adolescent girls (Halliwell, Jarman, Risdon, McNamara, & Jankowski, 2015; Halliwell et al., 2017; Jarman et al., 2017). In a universal trial with 62 girls aged 14–15, a 1-hour version of a CDI led to a significant increase in body appreciation compared to controls (Halliwell et al., 2015). Moreover, the effect size for body appreciation was equivalent to that for body dissatisfaction in the same study. In a more recent study involving 240 girls aged 13–15, again intervention participants reported increased body appreciation at postintervention compared to a randomized control group. However, the effect size for body appreciation was smaller than for body dissatisfaction, and neither intervention effect was sustained at a 3-month follow-up (Halliwell et al., 2017).

In a selective trial with 99 girls aged 14–18, we examined specific components of positive body image. Four hours of CDI were associated with significant increases in both body appreciation and body connectedness (as assessed via the Body Connection subscale of the Experience of Embodiment Scale; Piran & Teall, 2012) that were maintained at a 3-month follow-up. The effect sizes were similar across both measures of positive body image and dual-pathway model variables.

Our universal trial with 104 girls aged 12–13 examined the impact of a CDI on self-protective cognitive style (Halliwell & Diedrichs, 2014b). One month after participants had received either four weekly 20-minute CDI sessions or attended lessons as usual, they took part in a study investigating attitudes to advertising. Participants were randomly allocated to view advertisements featuring ultrathin media models or control product-only advertisements. Participants who had not participated in the CDI reported negative effects of media exposure that are typically found in research (Grabe, Ward, & Hyde, 2008), reporting lower body satisfaction after viewing models compared to control advertisements. However, for girls who had received the CDI, there was no difference in body satisfaction in the model and control conditions. This finding suggests that the CDI enhanced resilience to model exposure, and CDI participants likely used self-protective cognitive processing when faced with these images. However, we did not directly measure processing of images, and media images are only one source of appearance-related pressure. Therefore, further research is needed before strong conclusions can be drawn about the impact of CDIs on cognitive processing styles.

One study has examined the impact of CDIs on positive body image among men. Jankowski et al. (2017) delivered the Body Project M, which is a two-session, 90-minute intervention in which the program content was tailored to men (e.g., discussing the "male appearance ideal" instead of the "thin ideal"), to a sample of undergraduate men from the United Kingdom and measured the outcome variables postintervention and at a 3-month follow-up. Jankowski et al. found sustained improvements (i.e., at both postintervention and follow-up) in body appreciation among these men who completed the intervention compared to an assessment-only control group.

These studies provide preliminary evidence that CDIs may help to improve overall levels of positive body image among young adults and adolescents, at least in the short term. However, further research with samples of women and men is needed to examine (a) the potential for these effects to be sustained over time; (b) the differential impact of CDIs on positive and negative body image; and (c) the impact of CDIs on separate components of positive body image.

Experimental research allows us to quantify the impact of CDIs on positive body image. However, we cannot tell from these data how participants experienced the intervention and whether the content has resonated with aspects of their embodiment beyond body dissatisfaction and disordered eating. In order to evaluate the acceptability of the semimandatory version of the CDI among women, we conducted a series of focus groups (Stewart & Halliwell, 2014). Eleven CDI participants and four peer leaders took part in one of three focus groups. One of the themes that emerged is particularly relevant here and related to intervention terminology. Terms such as *thin ideal* and *fat talk* were experienced as communicating a strong emphasis on weight throughout the intervention. Women reported "there is more to the ideal than just being thin," and one participant commented as follows:

> I think there's a lot of emphasis on being thin. . . . I think there was a girl. . . . She said that she'd been bullied for being too thin and she was really struggling to try and put on weight. . . . It gets . . . a bit too much like . . . "thin is bad" and obviously that isn't the point.

We also included open-ended questions in our studies, and this feedback echoed the focus group feedback. In response to the question, "What didn't you like about the sessions?" both adolescent girls (Halliwell et al., 2017) and university women (Halliwell & Diedrichs, 2014) reported that there was too much focus on thinness as an aspect of appearance dissatisfaction.

The CDI focus on thinness and the thin ideal is a result of the theoretical grounding in eating disorder prevention. It is important to remember that improvements on positive body image were found despite this emphasis on thinness. However, body fat dissatisfaction is only one area of body image, and positive body image and embodiment require a more global experience of the body. Therefore, relatively small changes to the terminology used may increase the acceptability of the intervention to a wider group of participants, may validate the discussion of other aspects of body concern and appreciation, and may strengthen and broaden the impact of CDI on positive body image. Indeed, the CDI designed for the World Association for Girl Guides and Girl Scouts changed the terminology in the intervention from "thin ideal" to "the image myth" to represent the broad-ranging attributes encompassed in societal appearance ideals. It is critical that any changes are carefully evaluated to ensure that they do not dampen the established effectiveness of the intervention on risk factors for eating disorders.

CONCLUSION AND FUTURE DIRECTIONS

In summary, preliminary findings suggest that CDI may be effective at targeting aspects of positive body image relating to (a) appreciating the body's appearance and function; (b) being aware of and attentive to the body's experiences and needs; and (c) possessing a positive cognitive style for processing body-related messages in a self-protective manner. In a similar way, it may be effective in addressing components of embodiment.

More specifically, a handful of studies suggested that CDIs can lead to increases in body appreciation, body connectedness, a subjective (vs. objectified) experience of the body, and intuitive eating among girls and women. In addition, adolescent girls who participated in CDIs were more resilient to exposure to thinness-related messages in the media, suggesting that they employed a protective cognitive processing style when viewing media images. It is encouraging that improvements on these aspects of positive body image were sustained 3 months postintervention in some studies. One study has also found that an adapted version of the CDI can increased body appreciation among men (Jankowski et al., 2017).

Of course, these findings need replication across other studies and by independent research groups. Also, the follow-up period needs to be extended to examine the robustness of improvements on positive body image. This is particularly important, as changes in the subjective experience of the body were not maintained a year later while changes in eating disorder risk factors were sustained (Kroon Van Diest & Perez, 2013). Also, in some studies, the effect sizes were smaller for positive body image than for dual-pathway model variables. This suggests that CDI scripts may need to be modified to adequately target aspects of positive body image. Relatively minor modification to CDI scripts could facilitate a focus on broader appearance ideals and increase the emphasis on body appreciation and functionality. However, it is critical that changes are evaluated in randomized controlled trials to ensure that the effectiveness of CDIs is not compromised by these adaptations.

There are components of positive body image and embodiment that have been neglected in this research. Specifically, there has been limited exploration examination of CDI effects on experience and expression of desire, attuned self-care, and agency. Numerous validated measures are available that could be utilized in future research in this area. In addition, the impact of CDIs on self-protective processing is well suited to evaluation using experimental outcome variables, such as our media exposure manipulation (Halliwell & Diedrichs, 2014b). There is an additional benefit of using experimental method here, as demand characteristics are reduced if participants are naïve to the hypotheses and, particularly, if the experimental element is presented as part of a separate study. Current evidence is based on a mainly white, middle-class, heterosexual, able-bodied, and young sample of women. It is critical that future research examines CDIs and positive body image among diverse groups. Further, qualitative research will also be important to explore participants' experience of a CDI in relation to positive body image and embodiment. This future research will inform further development of the intervention.

REFERENCES

Andrew, R., Tiggemann, M., & Clark, L. (2015). The protective role of body appreciation against media-induced body dissatisfaction. *Body Image*, *15*, 98–104. doi:10.10166/j.bodyim.2015.07.005

Andrew, R., Tiggemann, M., & Clark, L. (2016). Predictors and health-related outcomes of positive body image in adolescent girls: A prospective study. *Developmental Psychology*, *52*, 463–474. doi:10.1037/dev0000095

Atkinson, M. J., & Wade, T. D. (2015). Mindfulness-based prevention for eating disorders: A school-based cluster randomized controlled study. *International Journal of Eating Disorders, 48*, 1024–1037. doi:10.1002/eat.22416

Avalos, L., Tylka, T. L., & Wood-Barcalow, N. (2005). The Body Appreciation Scale: Development and psychometric evaluation. *Body Image, 2*, 285–297. doi:10.1016/j.bodyim.2005.06.002

Becker, C. B., Hill, K., Greif, R., Han, H., & Stewart, T. (2013). Reducing self-objectification: Are dissonance-based methods a possible approach? *Journal of Eating Disorders, 1*, 10. doi:10.1186/2050-2974-1-10.

Becker, C. B., Smith, L. M., & Ciao, A. C. (2006). Peer facilitated eating disorders prevention: A randomized effectiveness trial of cognitive dissonance and media advocacy. *Journal of Counseling Psychology, 53*, 550–555. doi:10.1037/0022-0167.53.4.550

Becker, C. B., & Stice, E. (2011). *Succeed body image programme manual.* Oxford, England: Oxford University Press.

Brown, T. A., & Keel, P. K. (2015). A randomized controlled trial of a peer co-led dissonance-based eating disorder prevention program for gay men. *Behaviour Research and Therapy, 74*, 1–10. https://doi.org/10.1016/j.brat.2015.08.008

Cruwys, T., Haslam, S. A., Fox, N. E., & McMahon, H. (2015). "That's not what we do." Evidence that normative change is a mechanism of action in group interventions. *Behaviour Research and Therapy, 65*, 11–17. doi:10.1016/j.brat.2014.12.003

Daníelsdóttir, S., Agustsdóttir, E. B., Thorsdóttir, F., & Jonsson, F. H. (2012,). *Eating disorder prevention in Iceland.* Nordic Eating Disorder Society Congress, Copenhagen, Denmark.

Diedrichs, P. C. (2016). Eating disorder prevention in the real-world. In T. Wade (Ed.), *Encyclopedia of feeding and eating disorders* (pp. 1–6). Singapore: Springer. doi:10.1007/978-981-287-087-2

Diedrichs, P. C., Craddock, N., Gau, J., & Stice, E. (2017). *Acceptability and feasibility of a dissonance-based body image intervention for Girl Guides and Girl Scouts: Results from a dissemination and implementation study across nineteen countries.* Manuscript in preparation.

Diedrichs, P. C., Halliwell, E., & Paraskeva, N. (2014). Extending the evidence base for eating disorders prevention: The impact of a dissonance-based intervention on positive body image, intuitive eating and self-objectification. *Journal of Eating Disorders, 2*, O38. doi:10.1186/2050-2974-2-S1-O38.

Festinger, L. (1957). *A theory of cognitive dissonance.* Stanford, CA: Stanford University Press.

Freijy, T., & Kothe, E. J. (2013). Dissonance-based interventions for health behaviour change: A systematic review. *British Journal of Health Psychology, 18*, 310–337. doi:10.1111/bjhp.12035

Frisén, A., & Holmqvist, K. (2010). What characterizes early adolescents with a positive body image? A qualitative investigation of Swedish girls and boys. *Body Image, 7*, 205–212. doi:10.1016/j.bodyim.2010.04.001

Grabe, S., Ward, L. M., & Hyde, J. S. (2008). The role of the media in body image concerns among women: A meta-analysis of experimental and correlational studies. *Psychological Bulletin, 134*, 460–476. doi:10.1037/0033-2909.134.3.460

Halliwell, E. (2013). The impact of thin idealized media images on body satisfaction: Does body appreciation protect women from negative effects? *Body Image, 10*, 509–514. doi:10.1016/j.bodyim.2013.07.004

Halliwell, E. (2015). Future directions for positive body image research. *Body Image, 14*, 177–189. doi:10.1016/j.bodyim.2015.03.003

Halliwell, E., & Diedrichs, P. C. (2014a, July). *Evaluating the effectiveness of a peer-led body image program on broad outcomes*. Paper presented at Appearance Matters 6, Bristol, England.

Halliwell, E., & Diedrichs, P. C. (2014b). Testing a dissonance body image intervention among young girls. *Healthy Psychology, 33*, 201–204. doi:10.1037/a0032585

Halliwell, E., Jarman, H., Risdon, H., McNamara, A., & Jankowski, G. (2015). Dissemination of evidence-based body image interventions: A pilot study into the effectiveness of using undergraduate students as interventionalists in secondary schools. *Body Image, 14*, 1–4. doi:10.1016/j.bodyim.2015.02.002

Halliwell, E., Jarman, H., Treneman-Evans, G., Smith-Clark, S., Smith-Clark, F., & Diedrichs, P. C. (2017). *Evaluating dissonance eating disorder prevention in UK secondary schools*. Manuscript in preparation.

Jankowski, G. S., Diedrichs, P. C., Atkinson, M. J., Fawkner, H., Gough, B., & Halliwell, E. (2017). A pilot controlled trial of a cognitive dissonance-based body dissatisfaction intervention with young British men. *Body Image, 23*, 93–102. doi:10.1016/j.bodyim.2017.08.006

Jarman, H., Treneman-Evans, G., & Halliwell, E. (2017). *The feasibility and acceptability of dissonance eating disorder prevention in UK schools*. Manuscript in preparation.

Kilpela, L. S., Blomquist, K., Verzijl, C., Wilfred, S., Beyl, R., & Becker, C. B. (2016). The Body Project 4 All: A pilot randomized controlled trial of a mixed-gender dissonance-based body image program. *International Journal of Eating Disorders, 49*, 591–602. https://doi.org/10.1002/eat.22562

Kroon Van Diest, A. M., & Perez, M. (2013). Exploring the integration of thin-ideal internalization and self-objectification in the prevention of eating disorders. *Body Image, 10*, 16–25. doi:10.1016/j.bodyim.2012.10.004

McKinley, N. M., & Hyde, J. (1996). The Objectified Body Consciousness Scale: Development and validation. *Psychology of Women Quarterly, 20*, 181–215. doi:10.1111/j.1471-6402.1996.tb00467.x

Menzel, J. E., & Levine, M. P. (2011). Embodying experiences and the promotion of positive body image: The example of competitive athletics. In R. M. Calogero, S. Tantleff-Dunn, & J. K. Thompson (Eds.), *Self-objectification in women: Causes, consequences, and counteractions* (pp. 163–186). Washington, DC: American Psychological Association.

Piran, N. (2015). New possibilities in the prevention of eating disorders: The introduction of positive body image measures. *Body Image, 14*, 146–157. doi:10.1016.j.bodyim.2015.03.008

Piran, N. (2016). Embodied possibilities and disruptions: The emergence of the experience of embodiment construct from qualitative studies with girls and women. *Body Image, 18*, 43–60. doi:10.1016.j.bodyim.2016.04.007

Piran, N., & Teall, T. L. (2012). *The Experience of Embodiment Scale*. Unpublished manual.

Seidel, A., Presnell, K., & Rosenfield, D. (2009). Mediators in the dissonance eating disorder prevention program. *Behaviour Research and Therapy, 47*, 645–653. doi:10.1016/j.brat.2009.04.007

Stewart, K., & Halliwell, E. (2014). *Extending the scope of CDI: Insights from focus group*. Unpublished manuscript.

Stice, E. (2001). A prospective test of the dual-pathway model of bulimic pathology: Mediating effects of dieting and negative affect. *Journal of Abnormal Psychology, 101*, 124–135. doi:10.1037//0021-843x.110.1.124

Stice, E., Rohde, P., Butryn, M. L., Shaw, H., & Marti, C. N. (2015). Effectiveness trial of a selective dissonance-based eating disorder prevention program with female college students: Effects at 2-and 3-year follow-up. *Behaviour Research and Therapy, 71*, 20–26. doi:10.1016/j.brat.2015.05.012

Stice, E., Shaw, H., & Marti, C. N. (2007). A meta-analytic review of eating disorder prevention programs: Encouraging findings. *Annual Review of Clinical Psychology, 3*, 233–257. doi:10.1146/annurev.clinpsy.3.022806.091447

Tylka, T. L. (2006). Development and psychometric evaluation of a measure of intuitive eating. *Journal of Counseling Psychology, 53*, 226–240. doi:10.1037/0022-0167.53.2.226

Tylka, T. L., & Wood-Barcalow, N. L. (2015). The Body Appreciation Scale-2: Item refinement and psychometric evaluation. *Body Image, 12*, 53–67. doi:10.1016/j.bodyim.2014.09.006

Watson, H. J., Joyce, T., French, E., Willan, V., Kane, R. T., Tanner-Smith, E. E., . . . Egan, S. J. (2016). Prevention of eating disorders: A systematic review of randomized, controlled trials. *International Journal of Eating Disorders, 49*, 833–862. doi:10.1002/eat.22577.

Wood-Barcalow, N. L., Tylka, T. L., & Augustus-Horvath, C. L. (2010). "But I like my body": Positive body image characteristics and a holistic model for young-adult women. *Body Image, 7*, 106–116. doi:10.1016/j.bodyim.2010.01.001

34

Media Literacy Interventions to Facilitate Positive Body Image and Embodiment

SIMON WILKSCH

Media literacy traditionally has been explored as an approach to reduce the risks of body image concerns and disordered eating via lowering participants' tendency to internalize media messages. When reviewing existing media literacy interventions and their evidence, it becomes very clear that such interventions have primarily been developed and evaluated from the framework of the reduction of "negative" symptoms (e.g., weight concerns) or risk factors. In this chapter, it is argued that it would also be beneficial to integrate and measure "positive" features and protective factors (e.g., social connectedness, positive embodiment) within media literacy interventions. An overview of one such media literacy program (Media Smart) is provided through a positive embodiment lens and recommendations are discussed.

MEDIA LITERACY PROGRAMS: TARGET VARIABLES AND FINDINGS

Media literacy seeks to empower participants to adopt a critical evaluation of media content so that they can identify, analyze, challenge, and propose alternatives to stereotypical and unhealthy messages presented in the mass media (Levine, Piran, & Stoddard, 1999). The approach targets *media internalization*, which refers to investment in societal ideals of appearance that become rigid principles: the thin ideal for girls and women and the muscular ideal for boys and men. Thin-ideal internalization is now a widely accepted prospectively identified risk factor for eating disorders (Stice, 2002) and body dissatisfaction (Stice &

Whitenton, 2002), and it has been supported as a risk factor for negative body image (Cafri, Yamamiya, Brannick, & Thompson, 2006) and disordered eating (e.g., Hausenblas et al., 2013) in meta-analytic reviews of prospective or experimental studies. While a number of studies have found support for muscular-ideal internalization as a risk factor for poor body image in males (Hausenblas et al., 2013), it has not been explored nearly as much as thin-ideal internalization. Overall, though, there is solid scientific justification for targeting media internalization and related variables (e.g., perceived appearance-related pressures) in prevention research (Stice, 2002).

The media literacy approach to eating disorder prevention has been used extensively as either the primary goal of a program (e.g., Wilksch & Wade, 2009a) or one facet of multifactorial programs (e.g., Diedrichs et al., 2015). A recent systematic review of 16 studies suggested that higher media literacy is indeed protective against the negative effects on body image from exposure to idealized images (e.g., McLean, Paxton, & Wertheim, 2016). Further, studies have found significant reductions in eating disorder risk factors and negative body image from media literacy program participation (e.g., Wilksch et al., 2015).

Within the universal eating disorder risk reduction field, media literacy holds the appeal of being a topic of broad interest to program participants, regardless of their level of eating disorder risk; this is important where so many risk factors are often personal and not easily shared in a group setting (Wilksch & Wade, 2009b). Media literacy provides a neat inroad to addressing overevaluation of shape and weight (Wilksch & Wade, 2010) without needing to have explicit discussions about unhelpful eating behaviors (Austin, 2000). Media literacy programs have a number of goals: (a) teach participants about how the media generates images; (b) support participants in questioning the pursuit of media-generated appearance ideals because they often involve alterations through different "airbrushing" techniques; and (c) engage participants in discussions of important areas in life other than appearance, such as personal qualities, abilities in nonappearance domains, and relationships.

While the focus of early media literacy efforts was on magazines, movies, and television, the media now also include the online world, where social media is now a significant aspect of young people's lives (McLean, Wertheim, Masters, & Paxton, 2017). Indeed, time spent online was significantly associated with increased media internalization in a sample of 1,087 young adolescent girls (Tiggemann, & Slater, 2013). Thus, media literacy remains a topical, relevant skill and includes features beyond body image (e.g., online safety, personal privacy, bullying; see also Chapter 23). Further, broadly defined media literacy is often included in school curricula (albeit rarely the body image area), and thus schools are usually happy to accommodate such programs. There are also indirect features of media literacy programs that likely further augment their benefit. The use of interactive learning strategies, where working in small groups on tasks that are then shared with the class, might lead to increased social connectedness and feelings of self-confidence. In one study that included a range of self-esteem domains, Wade, Davidson, and O'Dea (2003) found significantly higher levels of self-esteem related to friendships as a result of participating in a five-lesson interactive media literacy program relative to a control group. This interactive approach was also supported by a meta-analysis of 66 eating disorder prevention trials, which found that interactive programs were more effective than a psychoeducational, didactic approach (Stice, Shaw, & Marti, 2007).

Researchers advocating the use of media literacy interventions have, at times, been criticized for their implied emphasis on social experiences, especially the media, as risk factors for eating disorders ("Is It Time . . . ," 2007). However, addressing media internalization as a risk factor does not imply the exclusion of other biopsychosocial factors. Another criticism voiced at media literacy programs is that researchers have found a significant impact on a number of outcome measures (e.g., weight concerns, dieting), but have not yet documented a reduction in the incidence of clinical or subclinical eating disorders. Perhaps a better term to describe media literacy programs is "eating disorder risk reduction" rather than "eating disorder prevention" (Becker, 2015; Wilksch, 2014).

MEDIA LITERACY'S ROLE IN ENHANCED BODY ESTEEM AND REDUCED DISORDERED EATING

Wilksch and Wade (2015) recently reviewed 12 media literacy studies and found emerging evidence for two programs based on randomized controlled trials (RCTs) (e.g., Espinoza, Penelo, & Raich, 2013; González, Penelo, Gutiérrez, & Raich, 2011; Wilksch & Wade, 2009a; Wilksch et al., 2015). In particular, these programs, reviewed in the material that follows, have shown significant benefits to participants in more than one study, impacted participants over a minimum 12-month follow-up period, and provided no evidence of harm. In their review, Wilksch and Wade (2015) highlighted that, in general, the quality of media literacy trials has increased over the past 20 years. In particular, programs are now generally (a) multiple session rather than single session (i.e., sufficient intensity); (b) utilizing validated measures to assess risk factors (i.e., media internalization, perceived pressure to be thin/muscular, dieting, and shape and weight concerns); (c) using robust analyses that covary baseline scores; (d) allowing for missing data; and (e) including much larger sample sizes. It is of interest that the two programs found to have the strongest evidence target universal classes of young adolescent girls and boys.

First, a media literacy program from Spain (*Eating, Feminine Aesthetic Beauty Model and Mass Medias: How to Train Critical Students in Secondary School*) resulted in significantly lower scores on a measure of disordered eating attitudes and behaviors at 2.5-year follow-up in young adolescent girls and boys ($N = 443$; González et al., 2011). Results also showed that, following media literacy training, participants reported significantly higher body satisfaction than was reported in the control group at the 2.5-year follow-up (Espinoza et al., 2013). An effectiveness RCT was then conducted, with young adolescent girls experiencing significantly lower disordered eating attitudes and weight-related teasing at a 12-month follow-up compared to girls in the control group ($N = 565$; Sánchez-Carracedo et al., 2016).

Second, *Media Smart* (Australia) has been evaluated in two major RCTs, with over 2,000 participants. Girls in the first trial who received the program had significantly lower shape and weight concerns at a 2.5-year follow-up than girls in a control group ($N = 540$; Wilksch & Wade, 2009a). In the second trial, girls in Media Smart had half the onset rate of clinical concerns about shape and weight, as compared to girls in the control group at a 12-month follow-up ($N = 1{,}316$; Wilksch et al., 2015). Significant reductions in a range of other risk factors (e.g., negative affect, weight-related teasing) were also found, while supplementary moderator analyses found that higher risk young adolescent girls and boys experienced important immediate benefits from Media Smart, while low-risk participants experienced prevention in growth of risk over the follow-up period (Wilksch, 2010; Wilksch & Wade, 2014). Media Smart was developed through a pilot study ($N = 237$; Wilksch, Tiggemann, & Wade, 2006) and has also been piloted in small-scale trials testing effectiveness of teacher delivery (Wilksch, 2015) and efficacy in a sample of young adolescent girls with Type 1 diabetes (Wilksch, Starkey, Gannoni, Kelly, & Wade, 2013).

As evidenced, most media literacy trials have determined efficacy by reducing prospectively identified eating disorder or body image risk factors (or preventing growth in such risk factors) relative to controls. In contrast, research has not focused on assessing positive outcomes, such as positive body image, embodiment, and well-being. This focus may be at least partly explained by the following: (a) Some researchers in the prevention field are also clinicians providing treatment to patients with eating disorders; and (b) reductions in clinical outcomes are thought to be appealing to funding agencies (Becker, 2015; Wilksch, 2017).

EXAMINING MEDIA SMART THROUGH A POSITIVE BODY IMAGE AND EMBODIMENT LENS

Media Smart is considered one of the leading universal media literacy programs for young adolescent girls and boys (Levine & Smolak, 2015; Piran, 2015). The protective factor singled out by the Media Smart program is the enhanced critical examination of media messages and familiarity with the alterations of visual representations. Indeed, media literacy likely sculpts the positive body image component of protective filtering, whereby people filter information in a body-protective manner—that is, they accept information that is consistent with a positive view of their bodies while rejecting messages that could endanger it (Tylka & Wood-Barcalow, 2015). People with a protective filter are aware of the unrealistic and fabricated nature of media images, reject and challenge these sources of information, and interpret and internalize messages that are compassionate toward their bodies (Wood-Barcalow, Tylka, & Augustus-Horvath, 2010). Media literacy further expands people's conceptualizations of beauty from the narrow media standards (i.e., the thin ideal and the muscular ideal), and having a broad conceptualization of beauty is consistent with positive body image (Tylka & Iannantuono, 2016; Tylka & Wood-Barcalow, 2015).

Considering additional processes that may take place during Media Smart may widen the understanding of protective factors that could enhance the effectiveness of this program. The developmental theory of embodiment (DTE; Piran, 2016, 2017; see also Chapter 10) can provide a broader lens into such protective factors. We therefore discuss the Media Smart program through the lens of this theory, with the caveat that the involvement of additional protective processes will need to be studied empirically. According to the DTE, protective factors belong to three domains: physical, mental, and social power/relational connections domains.

Physical Domain

The DTE includes four protective factors in the physical domain: immersion in nonobjectifying and nonsexualizing joyful physical activities, safety in the body territory (safety from violations or from forced body alterations), attuned care of the body, and freedom in experiences of desire (Piran, 2017). Media Smart includes varied activities that highlight the artificial nature of idealized media images and encourage the questioning of pursuing media ideals; such questioning is reinforced by the program facilitator, who models body acceptance. Further, program participants are encouraged to consider what their own priorities are in terms of goals, values, personal qualities, and skills. These processes may enhance participants' abilities to practice attuned self-care, which is a component of physical freedom. It should be mentioned in this regard that a small trial of Media Smart with preadolescent girls with Type 1 diabetes found the program significantly increased self-efficacy related to diabetes management along with improvements in self-esteem and body esteem (Wilksch et al., 2013). Participants were also rated by their parents as assuming more responsibility for specific diabetes-related tasks at follow-up.

Interestingly, though physical activity is not explicitly discussed in Media Smart, the program has been found to increase helpful physical activity, such as playing outside and bike riding, relative to no-intervention controls and another body image intervention (Wilksch et al., 2015). Similarly, while the program does not explicitly encourage participants to consume less media, in the same study a main effect for group found that Media Smart participants reported significantly lower screen time compared with controls (mean scores across the postintervention to 12-month follow-up period). Thus, being critically informed about the media may promote reduced media consumption, whereby media consumption may then be replaced by other activities that are arguably more "helpful" (e.g., physical activity). Participants in the program may therefore benefit from a greater opportunity to engage in joyful physical activities, a protective factor of positive embodiment. Such engagement can be operating throughout the follow-up period to support the maintenance of gains.

Similarly, while eating is not discussed in the program, results indicated significant main effects for self-reported dieting, where Media Smart participants reported lower levels than control group participants (Wilksch & Wade, 2009a). Eating concerns have also been significantly lower in girls in Media Smart than those in a comparison program (Wilksch et al., 2015). Indeed, the freedom and comfort in experiencing and expressing desire, such as appetite, is a protective factor of positive embodiment. Finally, the fact that preadolescent girls with Type 1 diabetes assumed more responsibility for specific diabetes-related tasks at follow-up may be due to reduced weight concerns as a result of participating in Media Smart.

Safety and the respectful ownership of the body, the fourth protective factor in the physical domain of the DTE, include not only fewer physical violations, but also feeling less coerced to engage in body alterations. It is possible that related to the critical stance adopted by program participants, norms of expected body alterations attenuated among peers during the program, reducing peer pressures for such engagement.

Mental Domain

The DTE describes a critical stance toward (as contrasted with the internalization of) social expectations and discourses in the mental domain. These can be in relation to gender, ethnicity/race, weight, social class, and all other dimensions of social location (Piran, 2017). Media Smart begins by defining stereotypes, identifying and questioning stereotypical media presentations of men, women, and success. Participants are invited to prepare posters about these stereotypes to share with the class. An example of such a poster was of an image of a model wearing a bikini with a speech bubble where the group wrote, "Gee it's cold in here. Not sure why I'm wearing a bikini to advertise prescription glasses." Participants also examine and select advertisements that convey positive (i.e., inclusive, realistic message) or negative (i.e., portrayal of unrealistic, extreme idealized images) body image messages. Following that, they engage in a writing campaign to an advertising company expressing their support or concern for the positive (i.e., inclusive, realistic) or negative (i.e., unrealistic, narrow beauty ideal) message contained in the advertisement. These activities in Media Smart enhance a critical stance and resistance toward adverse social stereotypes and expectations. Moreover, the fact that girls who completed Media Smart had reduced concerns about shape and weight, body dissatisfaction, ineffectiveness, and depressive symptoms at various follow-ups compared to girls in control groups (Wilksch et al., 2015; Wilksch & Wade, 2009a), suggests that Media Smart helps protect certain additional aspects of mental well-being.

Social Power Domain

The DTE includes four protective factors in the social power and relational connections domain: freedom from harassment and prejudicial treatment, freedom from appearance-based social power, access to empowering relationships, and membership in equitable communities (Piran, 2017). There are different social/relational activities and features in Media Smart that may serve to build the protective factors of non–appearance-related social power, access to empowering relationships, and membership in equitable communities. Media Smart's activism project, as described previously, builds non–appearance-related social power. Media Smart participants engage in role plays in which they respond to unhelpful appearance-based comments (e.g., about clothing), where small groups act out three helpful ways to respond (e.g., walking away, peers intervening to assist, etc.), thus promoting freedom from appearance-based social power. Most learning activities in Media Smart are conducted through work in pairs, small groups, or sharing with the class, thus encouraging confidence in expressing voice, as well as the sharing of opinions and the respecting of others, which promote empowering relationships and equitable communities. Throughout the program, participants are given the message that one's opinions are to be valued and worthy of being communicated with peers and others and where diversity of such opinions is encouraged.

Of relevance to the social power domain of the DTE, Media Smart is somewhat unique among eating disorder risk reduction programs in its inclusion of both girls and boys. Both girls and boys have been found to benefit from the program, and though not yet measured quantitatively, qualitative feedback has suggested that boys' attitudes toward girls' appearance can shift away from stereotypical media presentations. In-class feedback also suggested that both girls and boys appreciated the "real-world" approach of having both genders in the room as this afforded the opportunity to hear what the other gender thinks on issues in an organic manner. Given the adverse impact of gender inequity, especially as it becomes accentuated during puberty (Piran, 2002, 2010, 2017), engaging equitably in Media Smart can have an important impact on cross-gender relationships and may, in particular, enhance the experience of effectiveness and voice among girls. Further, participants in earlier versions of Media Smart reported increased self-esteem related to close friendships relative to a control group (Wade et al., 2003), which helps to counter challenges girls experience in their relational patterns during early adolescence (Brown, 2003; Piran, 2017).

Last, participants in Media Smart reported a reduction in weight-based teasing and reduced appearance-related pressures (Wilksch et al., 2015), suggesting that peers in Media Smart may reduce the focus on appearance in their everyday interactions with one another. The pattern of results on the varied measures assessed in outcome evaluation studies of Media Smart suggest the value of examining empirically a range of protective social experiences that may be associated with this program and may act as mediators of observed positive changes.

CONCLUSION AND FUTURE DIRECTIONS

Over the last two decades, the media literacy field has grown strongly, with the emergence of prospective risk factor research supporting the targeting of media internalization and an increase in the number of methodologically rigorous media literacy prevention trials. It is now time for researchers to investigate protective factors within media literacy interventions. With this in mind, two future directions are recommended:

1. The impact of media literacy on positive body image and positive embodiment constructs should be investigated. Media literacy programs have sought to reduce eating disorder risk factors, including negative body image. It has been assumed that reducing such risk factors will help individuals move away from judging self-worth through unhelpful appearance-based domains and move toward more adaptive domains (e.g., personal qualities, character, skills). Yet, simply lowering negative body image (e.g., body dissatisfaction) will not automatically increase positive dimensions of body image (e.g., body appreciation, functionality appreciation, broadly conceptualizing beauty), as they are distinct constructs and positive body image is a more comprehensive construct than low levels of body dissatisfaction (Tylka & Wood-Barcalow, 2015). Moreover, body dissatisfaction is common given the omnipresence of sociocultural appearance ideals, and therefore it may be more reasonable to help individuals accept and appreciate the internal and external aspects of their bodies than like every aspect of their appearance. Therefore, in prevention programs, we should give more attention to increasing body appreciation, embodiment, and related constructs (e.g., body image flexibility). We can work toward this goal by incorporating measures of positive body image and embodiment (see Chapters 1–9) into media literacy programs. As a result, we will have outcome assessments that will help us determine (a) whether positive body image and embodiment are comprehensively addressed in these programs, (b) whether these programs build positive body image and embodiment while offsetting risk factors, and (c) whether program content needs to be tailored to more effectively address positive body image and embodiment.
2. The need for media literacy programs specifically targeted to children. Consistent with giving greater research attention to positive body image, it would also make sense to develop and evaluate media literacy programs with younger audiences. Media literacy, as well as other interventions, do need to focus further on children of various ages (both preschool and primary school age) to maximize the likelihood of positive embodiment and protective messages before they enter the adolescent years and concomitant period of increased risk. This suggestion is in line with previous calls for a stepped approach to eating disorder prevention, with age-appropriate interventions being delivered across the child, adolescent, and early adult years (Wilksch, 2014). Presumably, we have a better chance of creating or maintaining positive embodiment *before* the individual has been exposed for years to

unhelpful media messages without tools to challenge these messages. To illustrate, some great work has been conducted with parents of preschool children (Hart, Damiano, & Paxton, 2016), and work of this type needs to continue given recent evidence of body image concerns in very young children. Indeed, as parents of preschool age children will be aware, many messages containing weight stigma are presented in well-loved children's books and television programs and thus serve as evidence that early prevention work is imperative.

REFERENCES

Austin, S. B. (2000). Prevention research in eating disorders: Theory and new directions. *Psychological Medicine, 30*, 1249–1262. doi:10.1017/s0033291799002573

Becker, C. B. (2015). Our critics might have valid concerns: Reducing our propensity to conflate. *Eating Disorders, 24*, 79–89. doi:10.1080/10640266.2015.1113833

Brown, L. M. (2003). *Girlfighting: Betrayal and rejection among girls.* New York, NY: New York University Press.

Cafri, G., Yamamiya, Y., Brannick, M. T., & Thompson, J. K. (2006). The influence of sociocultural factors on body image: A meta-analysis. *Clinical Psychology Science and Practice, 12*, 421–433. doi:10.1093/clipsy.bpi053

Diedrichs, P. C., Atkinson, M. J., Steer, R. J., Garbett, K. M., Rumsey, N., & Halliwell, E. (2015). Effectiveness of a brief school-based body image intervention "Dove Confident Me: Single Session" when delivered by teachers and researchers: Results from a cluster randomised controlled trial. *Behaviour Research and Therapy, 74*, 94–104. doi:10.1016/j.brat.2015.09.004

Espinoza, P., Penelo, E., & Raich, R. M. (2013). Prevention programme for eating disturbances in adolescents. Is their effect on body image maintained at 30 months later? *Body Image, 10*, 175–181. doi:10.1016/j.bodyim.2012.11.004

González, M., Penelo, E., Gutiérrez, T., & Raich, R. M. (2011). Disordered eating prevention programme in schools: A 30-month follow-up. *European Eating Disorders Review, 19*, 349–356. doi:10.1002/erv.1102.

Hart, L. M., Damiano, S. R., & Paxton, S. J. (2016). Confident body, confident child: A randomized controlled trial evaluation of a parenting resource for promoting healthy body image and eating patterns in 2- to 6-year old children. *International Journal of Eating Disorders, 49*, 458–472. doi:10.1002/eat.22494

Hausenblas, H. A., Campbell, A., Menzel, J. E., Doughty, J., Levine, M., & Thompson, J. K. (2013). Media effects of experimental presentation of the ideal physique on eating disorder symptoms: A meta-analysis of laboratory studies. *Clinical Psychology Review, 33*, 168–181. doi:10.1016/j.cpr.2012.10.011

Is it time for a public health approach to eating disorders? [Editorial]. (2007). *The Lancet*, 369, 1142. doi.org/10.1016/S0140-6736(07)60537-6

Levine, M. P., & Smolak, L. (2015). The role of protective factors in the prevention of negative body image and disordered eating. *Eating Disorders*, 1–8.

Levine, M. P., Piran, N., & Stoddard, C. (1999). Mission more probable: Media literacy, activism, and advocacy as primary prevention. In N. Piran, M. P. Levine, &

C. Steiner-Adair (Eds.), *Preventing eating disorders: A handbook of interventions and special challenges* (pp. 3–25). Philadelphia, PA: Brunner/Mazel.

McLean, S. A., Paxton, S. J., & Wertheim, E. H. (2016). The role of media literacy in body dissatisfaction and disordered eating: A systematic review. *Body Image, 19*, 9–23. doi:10.1016/j.bodyim.2016.08.002

McLean, S. A., Wertheim, E. H., Masters, J., & Paxton, S. J. (2017). A pilot evaluation of a social media literacy intervention to reduce risk factors for eating disorders. *International Journal of Eating Disorders, 50*, 847–851. doi:10.1002/eat.22708

Piran, N. (2002). Embodiment: A mosaic of inquiries in the area of body weight and shape preoccupation. In S. Abbey (Ed.), *Ways of knowing in and through the body: Diverse perspectives on embodiment* (pp. 211–214). Welland, Ontario: Soleil.

Piran, N. (2010). A feminist perspective on risk factor research and on the prevention of eating disorders. *Eating Disorders, 18*, 183–198.

Piran, N. (2015). New possibilities in the prevention of eating disorders: The introduction of positive body image measures. *Body Image, 14*, 146–157. doi:10.1016/j.bodyim.2015.03.008

Piran, N. (2016). Embodied possibilities and disruptions: The emergence of the Experience of Embodiment construct from qualitative studies with girls and women. *Body Image, 18, 43–60*. doi:10.1016/j.bodyim.2016.04.007

Piran, N. (2017). *Journeys of embodiment at the intersection of body and culture: The developmental theory of embodiment*. San Diego, CA: Elsevier. doi: 10.1016/c2015-0-04666-4

Sánchez-Carracedo, D., Fauquet, J., López-Guimerà, G., Leiva, D., Puntí, J., Trepat, E., . . . Palao, D. (2016). The MABIC project: An effectiveness trial for reducing risk factors for eating disorders. *Behaviour Research and Therapy, 77*, 23–33. doi:10.1016/j.brat.2015.11.010

Stice, E. (2002). Risk and maintenance factors for eating pathology: A meta-analytic review. *Psychological Bulletin, 128*, 825–848. doi:10.1037//0033-2909.128.5.825

Stice, E., Shaw, H., & Marti, C. N. (2007). A meta-analytic review of eating disorder prevention programs: Encouraging findings. *Annual Review of Clinical Psychology, 3*, 207–231. doi:10.1146/annurev.clinpsy.3.022806.091447

Stice, E., & Whitenton, K. (2002). Risk factors for body dissatisfaction in adolescent girls: A longitudinal investigation. *Developmental Psychology, 38*, 669–678. doi:10.1037//0012-1649.38.5.669

Tiggemann, M., & Slater, A. (2013). NetGirls: The Internet, Facebook, and body image concern in adolescent girls. *International Journal of Eating Disorders, 46*, 630–633. doi:10.1002/eat.22141

Tylka, T. L., & Iannantuono, A. C. (2016). Perceiving beauty in all women: Psychometric evaluation of the Broad Conceptualization of Beauty Scale. *Body Image, 17*, 67–81. doi:10.1016/j.bodyim.2016.02.005

Tylka, T. L., & Wood-Barcalow, N. L. (2015). What is and what is not positive body image? Conceptual foundations and construct definition [Special series]. *Body Image, 14*, 118–129. doi:10.1016/j.bodyim.2015.04.001

Wade, T. D., Davidson, S., & O'Dea, J. A. (2003). A preliminary controlled evaluation of a school-based media literacy program and self-esteem program for reducing eating disorder risk factors. *International Journal of Eating Disorders, 33*, 371–383. doi:10.1002/eat.10136

Wilksch, S. M. (2010). Universal school-based eating disorder prevention: Benefits to both high- and low-risk participants on the core cognitive feature of eating disorders. *Clinical Psychologist, 14*, 62–69. doi:10.1080/13284207.2010.500310

Wilksch, S. M. (2014). Where did universal eating disorder prevention go? *Eating Disorders, 22*, 184–192. doi:10.1080/10640266.2013.864889

Wilksch, S. M. (2015). School-based eating disorder prevention: a pilot effectiveness trial of teacher-delivered Media Smart. *Early Intervention in Psychiatry, 9*, 21–28. doi:10.1111/eip.12070

Wilksch, S. M. (2017). How can we improve dissemination of universal eating disorder risk reduction programs? *Eating Behaviors, 25*, 58–61. doi:10.1016/j.eatbeh.2016.03.036

Wilksch, S. M., Paxton, S. J., Byrne, S. M., Austin, S. B., McLean, S. A., Thompson, J. K., . . . & Wade, T. D. (2015). Prevention across the spectrum: A randomized controlled trial of three programs to reduce risk factors for both eating disorders and obesity. *Psychological Medicine, 45*, 1811–1823. doi:10.1017/s003329171400289x

Wilksch, S. M., Starkey, K., Gannoni, A., Kelly, A., & Wade, T. D. (2013). An interactive program to enhance protective factors for eating disorders in girls with Type 1 diabetes. *Early Intervention in Psychiatry, 7*, 315–321. doi:10.1111/eip.12012

Wilksch, S. M., Tiggemann, M., & Wade, T. D. (2006). Impact of interactive school-based media literacy lessons for reducing internalization of media ideals in young adolescent girls and boys. *International Journal of Eating Disorders, 39*, 385–393. doi:10.1002/eat.20237

Wilksch, S. M., & Wade, T. D. (2009a). Reduction of shape and weight concern in young adolescents: A 30-month controlled evaluation of a media literacy program. *Journal of the American Academy of Child and Adolescent Psychiatry, 48*, 652–661. doi:10.1097/chi.0b013e3181a1f559

Wilksch, S. M., & Wade, T. D. (2009b). School-based eating disorder prevention. In S. J. Paxton & P. J. Hay (Eds.), *Treatment approaches for body dissatisfaction and eating disorders: Evidence and practice* (pp. 7–22). Melbourne, Australia: IP Communications.

Wilksch, S. M., & Wade, T. D. (2010). Risk factors for clinically significant importance of shape and weight in adolescent girls. *Journal of Abnormal Psychology, 119*, 206–215. doi:10.1037/a0017779

Wilksch, S. M., & Wade, T. D. (2014). Depression as a moderator of benefit from Media Smart: A school-based eating disorder prevention program. *Behaviour Research and Therapy, 52*, 64–71. doi:10.1016/j.brat.2013.11.004

Wilksch, S., & Wade, T. D. (2015). Media literacy in the prevention of eating disorders. In L. Smolak & M. P. Levine (Eds.), *The Wiley handbook of eating disorders* (pp. 610–624). Chichester, England: Wiley. doi:10.1002/9781118574089.ch45

Wood-Barcalow, N. L., Tylka, T. L., & Augustus-Horvath, C. L. (2010). "But I like my body": Positive body image characteristics and a holistic model for young-adult women. *Body Image, 7*, 106–116. doi:10.1016/j.bodyim.2010.01.001

35

Feminist and Social Justice–Informed Approaches Toward the Enhancement of Positive Embodiment

NIVA PIRAN ■

I am writing this chapter during the #MeToo campaign. Women in particular sectors are voicing publicly in larger numbers the sexual violations they experienced from men in power, with adverse consequences to their self and body experiences. Considering the high rates of sexual violations and harassment found in surveys around the world, most women, especially in less privileged positions, are still forced to maintain their silence about sexual violations. As a woman professional and researcher in the field of body image and eating disorders, I have called for implementing policies that will enhance the safety of girls in schools as a component of health promotion initiatives in the fields of body image and eating disorders, yet prevention programs commonly do not address the issue of violence against girls. We are therefore at a risk of perpetuating the silence about violence against women and the centrality of power and privilege to embodied distress. The chapter is written with this consciousness in mind.

This preamble brings to the fore issues of societal structures of power, body experiences, and social justice that have been central to social critical theory, including feminist scholarship. While not frequently incorporated into the field of body image and eating disorders, the socially critical lens offers unique implications to the conceptualizations of embodied well-being and distress and related health promotion strategies. The chapter starts by addressing social critical perspectives and their relationship to health promotion strategies. It then describes key components of perspectives informed by feminism and social justice (F/SJ) toward positive embodiment, as well as prevention programs and initiatives that have aimed to endorse such perspectives. The chapter ends with conclusions and suggestions for future work in the field.

SOCIAL CRITICAL PERSPECTIVES, THE BODY, AND HEALTH PROMOTION STRATEGIES

Socially critical theorists, including feminist scholars, have highlighted the inextricable connection between societal structures of power and privilege and individuals' experiences of inhabiting their bodies. Foucault (1995) described this connection in the following way, "The body is directly involved in a political field; power relations have an immediate hold upon it; they invest it, mark it, train it, torture it, force it to carry out tasks" (p. 25). Similarly, Merleau-Ponty (1962) emphasized the way in which individuals embody social norms, and Butler (1997) suggested that gender is produced through enacting socially constructed scripts.

While the maintenance of embodied practices that align with social norms and rules helps maintain existing structures of societal power, interrogating these norms and pursuing subversive shifts in embodied practices can, in turn, induce societal changes/transformations. Important social movements toward social justice started with interrogating and changing the embodied lives of individuals, such as Marxism, racism and slavery, the civil rights and Black Lives Matter movements in the United States, feminism, and the #MeToo campaign. The body, therefore, can inform and guide movements toward social justice and equity.

In terms of health promotion, the tight relationship between the quality of embodied lives and societal structures of power suggests that positive ways of inhabiting the body can be enhanced through social transformations that aim at social justice and the equitable distribution of power and resources. Such explication of the specific underlying ideology that guides F/SJ-informed health promotion interventions is important because, as Seedhouse (1997) described, "All health promotion—even the most routine and mundane—is based on one political philosophy or another" (p. 69). In the health promotion field, biomedical and lifestyle interventions that target the individual and deemphasize the shaping of health and related behaviors by structural issues are contrasted with approaches that target the community (e.g., community members' empowerment) and structural factors (e.g., policy, the distribution of resources) (Raphael, 2000). F/SJ-informed programs align with community and structural approaches to health promotion.

KEY ELEMENTS IN F/SJ-INFORMED APPROACHES TO ENHANCED POSITIVE EMBODIMENT

Key elements in F/SJ-informed health promotion approaches to positive embodiment relate to the (a) goals, (b) content, (c) process, and (d) assessment of health promotion interventions. In this section, the description of each of these four key dimensions of F/SJ-informed approaches starts with a general introduction, continues with addressing its relevance to interventions in the field of body image and embodiment, and ends with a description of specific examples of F/SJ-informed school-based prevention programs and their outcomes. F/SJ-informed approaches can target varied social domains and institutions, all the way from widely disseminated values and laws to schools and families.

Goals: Embodied Equity and Social Justice

The F/SJ-informed approaches to health promotion target transformations at all levels of the social environment toward enhanced social equity and justice. This involves countering adverse systemic factors that perpetuate inequities and disenfranchise particular bodies in varied social organizations, such as political institutions and the law, industry, the media, community-based organizations, schools, and families.

The law is a most powerful tool toward achieving social justice in the treatment of diverse bodies. Social activists, politicians, and professionals who advocate for, and sponsor, legal bills toward enhanced social justice are doing pivotal health promotion work. For example, toward acceptance of diverse body sizes, legal paths to prohibit weight discrimination at work, housing, and other domains of life, grounded in civil rights laws, are being pursued in the United States (see Chapters 36 and 37). Legal pursuits to enhance the occupational safety in the fashion industry, typically of girls and young women, have led so far to laws requiring a medical evaluation of models and a minimum body mass index of 18.5 in France and Israel, respectively (see Chapters 36, 37). An example of a law that has had a major positive impact on the way girls and women engage with the physical environment is Title IX in the United States, the Education Amendment Act, which has facilitated progress toward equalizing opportunities for girls and women in sports (Koller, 2010); engagement in recreational sports that do not require a lean or thin body shape is a protective factor to body dissatisfaction and eating problems (Smolak, Murnen, & Ruble, 2000). Sexual harassment, defined as a form of gender discrimination, is prohibited under Title VII of the federal Civil Rights Act 1964, as well as under different states' human rights and occupational laws; sexual harassment has been linked to negative body image, self-esteem, and disordered eating patterns (Harned & Fitzgerald, 2002; Piran & Thompson, 2008).

The F/SJ ideologies are needed to counter pervasive oppressive social ideologies in the body domain across all social systems. Without critical social education, disruptions to social justice in the body domain will continue to be enacted daily even when such acts contravene existing laws. For example, without public education, body-based harassment related to weightism, sexism, racism, classism, heterosexism, as well as to prejudice toward visible differences or physical disabilities will continue to exist, adversely affecting body and self-esteem and disrupting relational connections. Similarly, without F/SJ educational campaigns, the media will continue to objectify and sexualize women, including women athletes known for their physical competence (Daniels, 2016), and cast "white" and thin bodies in preferred movie roles (Piran, 2017).

At the other end of the spectrum, the family is also a social system that can be transformed toward greater equity and social justice. F/SJ perspectives suggest expanding current trends in the education of parents (see Hart, Damiano, Chittleborough, Paxton, & Jorm, 2014) to include treating children of different genders (and skin tones, weights, and physical abilities) similarly; encouraging their strengths, assertiveness, voice, and "taking space"; providing physical safety and comfortable (rather than "pretty") clothing; allocating similar resources to the pursuits of a range of interests (including sports); avoiding the use of oppressive labels such as "tomboy," "slut," or "PMS"; and modeling equitable relationships (Piran, 2017).

School-Based Programs Targeting Schoolwide Transformative Changes Toward Body Equity. School systems are important sites for social transformations guided by F/SJ perspectives. The health-promoting school model, developed by the WHO (World Health Organization; 2017), specifically highlights the centrality of transforming school environments toward greater equity and social justice in enhancing students' physical and mental well-being.

Within the body image field, the health-promoting school model has been utilized to transform a school environment toward greater equity in a high-risk residential dance school setting. The Dance School Ecological Prevention Program (DSEPP) (Piran, 1999a, 1999b, 2001) included educational sessions with school staff, as well as ongoing age- and gender-cohesive focus groups with students (ages 10–18) in which they examined together the varied ways the school affected their body experiences and made collective decisions about aspects of the school environment that they wanted to see changed. They then devised action plans to see these changes through. Consequently, the body became a site of critical knowledge and power, rather than a site of individual shame. These processes of reflection and action resulted in changes to the school curriculum, policies, physical setting, school staff and committees, and peer norms (Piran, 2001). Three whole-school surveys over a 10-year period suggested that the implementation of the program was associated with significant reductions in negative body image and disordered eating patterns and greater acceptance of body weight. A 15-year, cohort-based follow-up evaluation of the program suggested it might have provided long-term protection from ongoing pressures in the ballet world and in the society at large (Bar, Cassin, & Dionne, 2017). However, these outcome evaluations involved the comparisons of cohorts within the same dance school, without the availability of a similar dance school as a control group.

The Very Important Kids (VIK) program (Haines, Neumark-Sztainer, Perry, Hannan, & Levine, 2006) aimed to transform the school environment toward greater equity in the domain of weight. A participatory process of inquiry with all stakeholders of the school community identified teasing as a central issue affecting body image and self-image. Consequently, the authors implemented systemic interventions that included staff training regarding weightism and a student-conducted no-teasing campaign and theatre show. Compared to a matched control school, there was a reduction in the rate of teasing and in students' reported negative peer weight-related norms and an increase in self-efficacy to impact weight-teasing norms. No change was found in disordered eating patterns or body satisfaction. Transforming the school environment toward greater equity is a promising approach that needs further systematic study.

Content: Reliance on Critical Knowledge

The F/SJ-informed health promotion interventions rely on critical knowledge, namely, the understanding of the ways in which "societal structures and power relations play in promoting inequalities and disenabling people" (Raphael, 2000, p. 360). The focus in critical knowledge is on the shaping of individuals' social environments, and hence of their lived embodied experiences, by intersecting dimensions of social location, often involving both social privileges and disenfranchisements.

Regarding gender, two research-based theories examine issues of power, gender, and quality of embodied lives. In particular, these theories target social processes that create "feminine embodiment," described by Bordo (1989) as the "conviction of lack, insufficiency, subjugation, demoralization, debilitation, whereby energies are spent on self-modification" (p. 14). Objectification theory (Fredrickson & Roberts, 1997) highlights the ubiquitous presence of the objectifying lens of women's bodies in a patriarchal social world. This disempowering experience leaves women feeling shame about their bodies and disrupts their performance and agency in the world (Calogero, 2012). The developmental theory of embodiment (Piran, 2017; see Chapter 10) describes 10 adverse (and 10 facilitative) key social processes in relation to gender and other dimensions of social location that create disenfranchised bodies: "corseted" from equitable participation in the public sphere. In the physical domain, the theory highlights, for example, violations of the body and the constriction of engagement in immersed joyful activities. In the mental domain of internalized social discourses, the theory includes both appearance-related discourses (e.g., objectification) and comportment-related discourses (e.g., being submissive/demure). In the social power and relational connection domain, the theory includes, for example, discrimination and harassment. In particular, the theory highlights the importance of looking at *concurrent* social processes that disempower diverse girls and women.

Both objectification theory and the developmental theory of embodiment could inform prevention programs currently conducted with youth in schools. For example, both theories suggest the perpetuation of the gender power imbalance through the objectification of women and would therefore suggest minimizing the inclusion of sexualized and objectified images of girls and women in prevention programs, even with the intent of criticizing them. The developmental theory of embodiment would, further, suggest targeting a larger range of social factors that socialize girls and women into inequity, such as violence against girls and women, barriers to joyful physical engagement, nonappearance "femininity" discourses (e.g., being submissive/demure), and body-based harassment (Piran, 2015, 2017).

Critical knowledge regarding the impact of other dimensions of social location on embodied experiences can, similarly, guide F/SJ-informed health promotion programs. For example, a lifestyle program emphasizing exercise and a healthy diet would only serve to further disenfranchise youth living in financially strained homes, who face challenges related to engagement in physical activity, safety, body-based harassment, and choices regarding food consumption. According to a 16-year-old girl of a working class background who participated in a qualitative study on embodiment, "There is too much fat and crap in the food and you see more kids and they're getting fatter. And I wouldn't blame them because healthy food costs more than junk food! And they want us to be healthier, then lower down the cost of healthy food!" (Piran, 2017, p. 182). Instead, a social justice approach would focus on targeting body-based harassment and related social justice education at school, free school- and community-based programs of joyful physical activities, and increased access to affordable nutritious foods in schools and neighborhoods.

School-Based Programs Utilizing Critical Knowledge in the Body Image Domain. F/SJ-informed school programs incorporate critical knowledge in constructing the planned interventions. The Full of Ourselves program (Steiner-Adair et al., 2002), which advances power, health, and leadership for girls in general middle school settings, addresses a range of gender-based risk factors through participatory discussions, art projects, and role plays. For example, inviting girls to "dialogue" with their bodies aims to counteract the normative disruption of self-body connection and "bioenergetic" punching and assertive training aim to enhance girls' agency in the world. Weight prejudice is presented in the program as a social justice issue, similar to sexism, racism, and other societal prejudices, and trains participants to become activists at school and at home. In terms of outcome evaluation, a nonrandomized controlled study revealed that girls participating in Full of Ourselves improved body esteem but not eating behaviors relative to a control group. Consistent with F/SJ approaches, the authors suggested the need to incorporate changes to the school environment and to strengthen the activism component of the program.

While access to critical knowledge can inform the planning of prevention programs, participatory processes with students and other stakeholders of the school community can lead to the construction of new knowledge that, in turn, can inform an ongoing prevention program (e.g., Haines et al., 2006; Piran, 2001). There are therefore advantages to using emergent processes of critical knowledge construction as part of a health promotion initiative.

Process: Empowerment Through Community-Based Critical Knowledge Production, Equitable Relational Connections, and Activism

A central process of social transformations toward equity and justice in the body domain involves the empowerment of communities, groups, and individuals who have been disenfranchised and silenced and have faced embodied inequity (Piran, 2017). One aspect of such empowerment relates to knowledge construction. Thus, F/SJ-informed health promotion initiatives often invite community members or program participants to take part in processes of knowledge production and action strategies (Piran, 1999b, 2001; Raphael, 2000). Further, as different authors suggested (e.g., Hill Collins, 2000; Piran, 2001, 2017; Raphael, 2000), both empowerment and critical knowledge construction often occur in equitable relational communities and contexts. Grounded in collective support and validation, individuals can then engage in social activism (Hill Collins, 2000; Piran, 2001).

Within the body image field, both empowerment and the enhancement of relational connections have become increasingly common elements of prevention programs for youth through their engagement in participatory group processes, knowledge construction, and activism projects (see Chapters 34 and 35). As students engage in collective projects, their relational connections are enhanced (Wade, Davidson, & O'Dea, 2003).

Examining empowerment and activism on a broader scale, varied organizations have utilized virtual platforms and online communities to counter a range of issues related to social justice. Examples include the SPARK Movement, a girl-fueled organization working to ignite an antiracist gender injustice movement (http://www.sparkmovement.org), and change.org, an international platform for change via starting campaigns, mobilizing support, and working with decision-makers to drive solutions (https://www.change.org).

School-Based Programs Utilizing Empowerment Through Community-Based Critical Knowledge Production, Equitable Relational Connections, and Activism to Enhance Body Esteem. F/SJ-informed school programs (e.g., Piran, 1999b, 2001; Steiner-Adair et al., 2002) consider empowerment a key component of health promotion programs in the body domain. Further, the original media literacy program for the prevention of eating disorders, GO GIRLS! Media Literacy, Activism, and Advocacy Project (Piran, Levine, & Irving, 2000), was developed with a strong emphasis on F/SJ ideology and hence with a focus on empowerment and social transformations. The program also emphasized relational connections between participants and with women program facilitators. As the program was adapted to school-based and coeducational administration (Wade et al., 2003) and the media literacy component received greater emphasis, activism and advocacy remained important. Randomized controlled trials have found that media literacy programs delivered in schools are linked to reduced disordered eating and shape/weight concerns and higher body satisfaction among girls and boys (see Chapter 34).

The original cognitive dissonance eating disorder prevention program, aimed at countering the internalization of the thin ideal, has also undergone changes over time (see Chapter 33). However, all versions of the program include a number of empowering elements. Cognitive dissonance interventions were found in randomized controlled trials to reduce risk factors of eating disorders (see Chapter 33). Importantly, Halliwell and Diedrichs (2014) included measures of positive body image and embodiment in their studies and found increases in body appreciation (via Body Appreciation Scale-2; Tylka & Wood-Barcalow, 2015; see Chapter 2) and body comfort (via Body Connection subscale of the Experience of Embodiment Scale; Piran & Teall, 2012; see Chapter 1).

Two additional afterschool programs, developed with an emphasis on empowerment, have been studied. A randomized controlled trial of a 10-week empowerment program, Girls on the Go! (Tirlea, Truby, & Haines, 2016), conducted at a community health center with girls ages 10–16, who were identified as facing a range of body and self-esteem issues, found significant improvements on measures of self-esteem, self-efficacy to handle physical and mental challenges, and eating practices. The afterschool REbeL prevention program for high school students, who self-select to participate in the after-hours club (e.g., Breithaupt, Eickman, Byrne, & Fischer, 2017), combines empowerment principles with the cognitive dissonance approach to prevention. In its first uncontrolled study, there was a trend (although nonsignificant) toward higher self-esteem and empowerment at postintervention. In the second study, empowerment significantly increased, while internalization of the thin ideal significantly decreased at postintervention. There were no changes in body esteem or perceived pressures for thinness.

Assessment: Complexity in Assessing Health Promotion Activities Aimed at Social Justice

The F/SJ ideologies, and the corresponding interests in social change, critical knowledge production, and processes of empowerment and activism inherently present complexities to the assessment of outcome. In particular, Raphael (2000) suggested that the methods should be able to reflect the way in which "the observed phenomena reflect structural aspects of society, illuminate the role of power relations within society, and lead to means of moving towards a more just world" (p. 365). While the assessment of coping skills for dealing with adverse social conditions is in line with F/SJ-informed approaches and can be conducted through randomized controlled designs and the completion of standardized measures by individual participants, such methodology comprises only one component of assessing F/SJ approaches (e.g., Foster-Fishman, Nowell, & Yang, 2007; Piran, 2010; Raphael, 2000). In addition, the goal of social change involves an assessment of shifts in the *social conditions* that enhance well-being. Such assessment necessitates utilizing different system-level indicators, such as the introduction of new laws, policies, services, or stakeholder committees, as well as qualitative feedback about the lived experience of stakeholders through surveys, focus groups, or individual interviews. Further, critical knowledge production and processes of change through activism follow emergent, complex, and unique paths that cannot be standardized and therefore can be reflected only through systematic qualitative observations and interviews.

In the domain of body image, few school-based programs embraced social justice and equity as their stated ideology. To examine processes involved in enhancing social equity, Piran (2001) conducted an intensive qualitative case study (Tebes, Kaufman, & Connell, 2003) of the content and action themes that emerged through the implementation of the DSEPP, leading to a new theoretical understanding about oppressions in the body domain. While there have been no similar case study explorations of media literacy or cognitive dissonance prevention programs, Halliwell and colleagues, importantly, pursued qualitative feedback about the cognitive dissonance programs (see Chapter 33).

CONCLUSION AND DIRECTIONS FOR FUTURE RESEARCH

While F/SJ perspectives suggest that body-anchored experiences are centrally linked to social equity and disenfranchisement, this lens has not been widely embraced within the body image and eating disorders fields. Consequently, most interventions with families and schools have not been explicitly informed by F/SJ ideology. Nonetheless, components central to F/SJ-informed paradigms, most commonly empowerment and participatory approaches to the construction of knowledge, have been incorporated into school-based health promotion programs. Further, the fields of body image and eating disorders may be shifting into a growing emphasis on social justice, such as the emphasis on weight discrimination as a social justice issue (e.g., the Health at Every Size® special interest group within the Academy for Eating Disorders).

There are many ways in which F/SJ perspectives could continue to enrich the fields of body image and eating disorders. First, the alignment between F/SJ-informed etiological theories of embodied well-being and distress and health promotion initiatives can be examined, leading to possible revisions of current health promotion initiatives for parents, school-age children, and larger activism projects (Piran, 2015, 2017). Second, F/SJ perspectives would suggest broadening the conceptualization of putative mechanisms of change within body image and eating disorder prevention programs to include factors such as empowerment and greater equity in relationships. Third, a similar expansion should be considered in the evaluation of program outcome by including measures of positive ways of inhabiting the body (see constructs described in Section I; Piran, 2015) as well as utilizing a range of research methodologies.

REFERENCES

Bar, R. J., Cassin, S. E., & Dionne, M. M. (2017). The long-term impact of an eating disorder prevention program for professional ballet school students: A 15-year follow-up study. *Eating Disorders, 25*, 375–387.

Bordo, S. (1989). The body and the reproduction of femininity: A feminist appropriation of Foucault. In A. M. Jaggar & S. R. Bordo (Eds.), *Gender/body/knowledge* (pp. 13–33). New Brunswick, NJ: Rutgers University.

Breithaupt, L., Eickman, L., Byrne, C. E., & Fischer, S. (2017). Enhancing empowerment in eating disorder prevention: Another examination of the REbeL peer education model. *Eating Behaviors*, *25*, 38–41. doi:10.1016/j.eatbeh.2016.05.003

Butler, J. (1997). Performative acts and gender constitution: An essay in phenomenology and feminist theory. In K. Conboy, N. Medina, & S. Stanbury (Eds.), *Female embodiment and feminist theory* (pp. 401–417). New York, NY: Columbia University Press.

Calogero, R. M. (2012). Objectification theory, self-objectification, and body image. In T. Cash (Ed.), *Encyclopedia of body image and human appearance* (pp. 574–580). San Diego, CA: Elsevier. doi:10.1016/b978-0-12-384925-0.00091-2

Daniels, E. A. (2016). Replacing sexy and skinny with strong and powerful: How feminist research on media depictions of women can effect change. In T.-A. Roberts, N. Curtin, L. Cortina, & L. E. Duncan (Eds.), *Best perspectives on building a better psychological science of gender* (pp. 257–274). Basel, Switzerland: Springer.

Foster-Fishman, P. G., Nowell, B., & Yang, H. (2007). Putting the system back into systems change: A framework for understanding and changing organizational and community systems. *American Journal of Community Psychology*, *39*, 197–215. doi:10.1007/s10464-007-9109-0

Foucault, M. (1995). *Discipline and punish: The birth of the prison* (2nd ed.). New York, NY: Vintage.

Fredrickson, B. L., & Roberts, T-A. (1997). Objectification theory: Toward understanding women's lived experiences and mental health risks. *Psychology of Women Quarterly*, *21*, 173–206. doi:10.1111/j.1471-6402.1997.tb00108.x

Haines, J., Neumark-Sztainer, D., Perry, C. L., Hannan, P. J., & Levine, M. P. (2006). VIK (Very Important Kids): A school-based program designed to reduce teasing and unhealthy weight-control behaviors. *Health Education Research: Theory and Practice*, *21*, 884–895. doi:10.1093/her/cyl123

Halliwell, E., & Diedrichs, P. C. (2014). Testing a dissonance body image intervention among young girls. *Health Psychology*, *33*, 201–204. doi:10.1037/a0032585

Harned, M. S., & Fitzgerald, L. F. (2002). Understanding a link between sexual harassment and eating disorder symptoms: A mediational analysis. *Journal of Consulting and Clinical Psychology*, *70*, 1170–1181. doi:10.1037//0022-006x.70.5.1170

Hart, L. M., Damiano, S. R., Chittleborough, P., Paxton, S. J., & Jorm, A. F. (2014). Parenting to prevent body dissatisfaction and unhealthy eating patterns in preschool children: A Delphi consensus study. *Body Image*, *11*, 418–425. doi:10.1016/j.bodyim.2014.06.010

Hill Collins, P. (2000). *Black feminist thought: Knowledge, consciousness, and the politics of empowerment* (2nd ed.). New York, NY: Routledge.

Koller, D. L. (2010). Not just one of the boys: A post-feminist critique of Title IX's vision for gender equity in sports. *Connecticut Law Review*, *43*, 401–456. doi:10.2139/ssrn.2064794

Merleau-Ponty, M. (1962). *Phenomenology of perception*. New York, NY: Humanities Press.

Piran, N. (1999a). Eating disorders: A trial of prevention in a high risk school setting. *Journal of Primary Prevention, 20*, 75–90. doi:10.1023/a:1021358519832

Piran, N. (1999b). The reduction of preoccupation with body weight and shape in schools: A feminist approach. In N. Piran, M. P. Levine, & C. Steiner-Adair (Eds.), *Preventing eating disorders: A handbook of interventions and special challenges* (pp. 148–150). Philadelphia, PA: Brunner/Mazel.

Piran, N. (2001). Re-inhabiting the body from the inside out: Girls transform their school environment. In D. L. Tolman & M. Brydon-Miller (Eds.), *From subjects to subjectivities: A handbook of interpretive and participatory methods* (pp. 218–238). New York, NY: New York University Press.

Piran, N. (2010). A feminist perspective on risk factor research and on the prevention of eating disorders. *Eating Disorders, 18*, 183–198. doi:10.1080/10640261003719435

Piran, N. (2015). New possibilities in the prevention of eating disorders: The introduction of positive body image measures. *Body Image, 14*, 146–157. doi:10.1016/j.bodyim.2015.03.008

Piran, N. (2017). *Journeys of embodiment at the intersection of body and culture: The developmental theory of embodiment*. San Diego, CA: Elsevier. doi: 10.1016/c2015-0-04666-4

Piran, N., Levine, M. P., & Irvine, L. M. (2000). GO GIRLS! Media literacy, activism, and advocacy project. *Healthy Weight Journal, 14*, 89–90.

Piran, N., & Teall, T. L. (2012). The developmental theory of embodiment. In G. McVey, M. P. Levine, N. Piran, & H. B. Ferguson (Eds.), *Preventing eating-related and weight-related disorders: Collaborative research, advocacy, and policy change* (pp. 171–199). Waterloo, ON, Canada: Wilfred Laurier Press.

Piran, N., & Thompson, S. (2008). A study of the adverse social experiences model to the development of eating disorders. *International Journal of Health Promotion and Education, 46*, 65–71. doi:10.1080/14635240.2008.10708131

Raphael, D. (2000). The question of evidence in health promotion. *Health Promotion International, 15*, 355–367. doi:10.1093/heapro/15.4.355

Seedhouse, D. (1997). *Health promotion: Philosophy, prejudice and practice*. New York, NY: Wiley.

Smolak, L., Murnen, S. K., Ruble, A. E. (2000). Female athletes and eating problems: A meta-analysis. *International Journal of Eating Disorders, 27*, 371–380. doi:10.1002/(sici)1098-108x(200005)27:4<371::aid-eat1>3.0.co;2-y

Steiner-Adair, C., Sjostrom, L., Franko, D. L., Pai, S., Tucker, R., Becker, A., & Herzog, D. (2002). Primary prevention of risk factors for eating disorders in adolescent girls: Learning from practice. *International Journal of Eating Disorders, 32*, 401–411. doi:10.1002/eat.10089

Tebes, J. K., Kaufman, J. S., & Connell, C. M. (2003). The evaluation of prevention and health promotion programs. In T. P. Gullotta & M. Bloom (Eds.), *Encyclopedia of primary prevention and health promotion* (pp. 42–61). New York, NY: Kluwer Academic/Plenum.

Tirlea, L., Truby, H., & Haines, T. (2016). Pragmatic, randomized controlled trials of the Girls on the Go! program to improve self-esteem in girls. *American Journal of Health Promotion, 30*, 231–241. doi:10.1177/0890117116639572

Tylka, T. L., & Wood-Barcalow, N. L. (2015). The Body Appreciation Scale-2: Item refinement and psychometric evaluation. *Body Image, 12*, 53–67. doi:10.1016/j.bodyim.2014.09.006

Wade, T. D., Davidson, S., & O'Dea, J. A. (2003). A preliminary controlled evaluation of a school-based media literacy program and self-esteem program for reducing eating disorder risk factors. *International Journal of Eating Disorders*, *33*, 371–383. doi:10.1002/eat.10136

World Health Organization. (2017). *What is a health promoting school?* Retrieved from http://www.who.int/school_youth_health/gshi/hps/en/

36

Public Health Interventions to Facilitate Positive Embodiment

Implementation and Future Directions

RACHEL F. RODGERS, DEBRA L. FRANKO, AND ALICE S. LOWY ■

Positive embodiment reflects positive dimensions of the experience of individuals, primarily girls and women, as they engage with their bodies in the world. These experiences include those related to positive feelings and comfort with one's own body, embodied agency, connection and expression of desires, attunement to self-care, and inhabiting the body as a subjective site while resisting objectification (Piran, 2016, 2017). Importantly, positive embodiment is thought to be associated with physical and mental freedom as well as increased social power (Piran, 2015). Increasing positive embodiment may be possible through individual-level interventions that can successfully promote these protective factors across the life span. However, given that the sociocultural pressures and socializing forces in Western culture that promote the thin ideal and police and discipline the bodies of disempowered groups are detrimental to positive embodiment, additional universal prevention efforts aiming to modify these forces are warranted (Bell, Rodgers, & Paxton, 2017; Piran, 2017).

Public health approaches constitute one avenue for such universal prevention efforts (Taylor, Franko, Neumark-Sztainer, Paxton, & Shapiro, 2007). A small number of public health interventions have aimed, directly or indirectly, to increase these positive ways of inhabiting the body. The present chapter reviews public health interventions at the national and local levels, as well as industry-led efforts, that have the potential to positively impact embodiment, by first considering initiatives that have specifically targeted body image factors and second considering those that have targeted protective factors for positive embodiment. While few evaluative data are available, the strengths and limitations of existing programs will be considered.

PUBLIC HEALTH INTERVENTIONS: DEFINITION AND POTENTIAL FOR POSITIVE EMBODIMENT

Public health interventions are aimed at creating changes in the macro environment such that risk factors for detrimental outcomes are reduced and protective factors that promote well-being are enhanced. Aspects of the macro environment that may be targeted include the mass media, legislation and policy, or economic forces. Changes in the macro environment have an exceptional potential for prevention efforts due to their reach and impact (Austin, 2012).

To realize such changes, public health interventions may involve modifications in regulation or practices. In addition, however, they may rely on health communication and education, including persuasive communication to promote behavioral change and awareness raising. Increasingly, such campaigns may include a mix of health communication media that include both Internet content and social media approaches (Garnett et al., 2014).

Traditionally, public health interventions have been initiated by national or local authorities or associated institutions. However, initiatives may also be launched by organizations with public health interests, both within the nonprofit sector and by industry as social consciousness becomes an increasing area of focus for businesses.

PUBLIC HEALTH INTERVENTIONS AND POSITIVE EMBODIMENT

A number of existing public health efforts have the potential to increase positive embodiment. Some of these efforts target body image–related aspects; others may impact positive embodiment more indirectly by targeting dimensions related to its protective factors.

Body Image–Related Efforts

A number of public health initiatives have been launched with the aim of promoting positive body image, healthy eating patterns, and increased physical activity, which have the potential to increase positive embodiment. While this is not an exhaustive review, examples of such efforts are discussed next. In particular, we present examples of publicly funded efforts, legislation initiatives, and industry-initiated efforts.

Publicly Funded Efforts

Several recent publicly funded efforts are interesting to consider with respect to their capacity to enhance positive embodiment.

French Loi Santé

In early 2017, a French law aiming to decrease appearance pressures related to the fashion industry was implemented. The new law aimed first to decrease the well-documented detrimental effect of exposure to thin-ideal imagery on body image (Levine & Murnen, 2009) by requiring the inclusion of a disclaimer label on advertising images in which the shape and weight of models had been digitally modified. Second, the law aimed both to protect fashion models and to target the promotion of standards of extreme thinness through the inclusion of underweight models in fashion shows by requiring fashion models to obtain a medical certificate attesting to their good health, taking body mass index (BMI) into consideration. Consistent with the promotion of positive embodiment, the law aims to decrease social pressures toward thinness. However, recent studies suggested possible challenges regarding the impact and implementation of this law. For example, warning or disclaimer labels on advertising images may be unhelpful and even exacerbate the detrimental effects of exposure to these images among particularly vulnerable groups (Bury, Tiggemann, & Slater, 2016; Danthinne, Giorgianni, & Rodgers, 2018). Further, fashion models themselves considered regulations related to minimal BMI requirements for models either unfeasible or unlikely to be effective (Rodgers, Ziff, Lowy, Yu, & Austin, 2017). Evaluations of the impact of the French law are therefore warranted to ascertain whether it is successful in promoting positive body image and embodiment; however, to date none have been published.

The Québec Charter for a Healthy and Diverse Body Image

In 2009 in Québec, Canada, the Ministry of Culture, Communications, and the Status of Women spearheaded the development of a charter aiming to bring together professionals from the fashion, music, and advertising industry around a set of voluntary standards aiming to promote positive body image. The charter criticizes social standards of thinness, highlighting their role in the development of disordered eating behaviors, and invites professionals within these industries to contribute to diversifying representations of women's bodies in the media in weight, shape, and age. The charter was disseminated throughout the general population as well as the Quebec school system, and a number of cultural events were organized with the goal of supporting and promoting the creation of fashion and media products that were consistent with the aims of the charter. An examination of the reach, acceptability, and perceived usefulness of the charter was conducted in 2010 among a sample of just over 1,000 young women residing in Quebec, revealing that approximately one third of the young women reported recognizing the charter and perceiving it as having the potential for a positive impact (Gauvin & Steiger, 2012). While these rates are not high, the dissemination and promotion of the charter continued through 2015, by which time its reach had likely increased. However, its success in decreasing environmental pressures to conform to strict appearance ideals and thus promoting positive embodiment is unclear.

Girls Make Your Move

A national-level initiative spearheaded by the Australian Government Department of Health in 2016, Girls Make Your Move, aimed to increase levels of physical activity among girls, recognizing the associations between body image concerns to the gender gap in physical activity (Slater & Tiggemann, 2011). The campaign aimed to encourage and support adolescent girls to be more active through sport or other physical activity and was disseminated through materials primarily targeting young women aged 15–18, including in print, on TV, and on social media. The campaign presented a range of different physical activities in the hopes of highlighting some of the less common ones, including stereotypically male sports, by asking, "Have you thought about roller blading, boxing, rock climbing, or yoga?" A longitudinal evaluation of the campaign conducted among just over 1,000 girls aged 12–19 years highlighted its success in terms of reach and penetration, with up to 82% of the young women interviewed recognizing the campaign and identifying the aims of the campaign as the promotion of physical activities, inclusion, and empowerment (Tan & Miller, 2016). A large proportion of the girls included in the evaluation reported having made behavioral changes as a result of seeing the campaign, but most interestingly, they reported increases in the perception of the importance of physical activity for girls and young women, with endorsement increasing from 68% to 73%, as well as the perception of physical activity being fun, with an increase from 47% to 52%. This campaign provides one of the few examples of a public intervention that was independently evaluated, and the findings cautiously suggest the potential for positive effects on girls' feelings of pleasurable engagement in physical activity, one of the protective factors for positive embodiment (Piran, 2016, 2017).

New York Campaign for Self-Esteem in Girls

Aiming to target body image concerns, in 2013, Mayor Bloomberg launched a campaign in New York City that aimed to increase self-esteem, targeting girls aged 7–12 years . The campaign was disseminated mainly via messaging in public places, on buses and trains, and consisted of images of girls from diverse ethnic and racial backgrounds accompanied by statements regarding their positive attributes, such as "I'm a girl. I'm clever, adventurous, outgoing, unique, smart and strong," and ending with "I'm beautiful the way I am." While no formal evaluations of the campaign could be found, the initiative aimed to propose countermessages to those present in the environment that socialize girls to feel limited in their roles and capabilities. Yet, the campaign was also critiqued for its emphasis on physical appearance and its potential for reinforcing appearance as a central aspect of female identity. Thus, while the intention of the campaign aligned with the promotion of positive embodiment, evaluation data are necessary to determine the effects of the campaign.

Legislation Related to Appearance-Based Discrimination

Rates of weight- and appearance-based discrimination are high, including in the workplace (Rudolph, Wells, Weller, & Baltes, 2009). Recently, a new legal approach to prohibit weight discrimination in the workplace grounded in civil rights laws has been garnering support (see also Chapter 37). This approach has been successful in the state of Michigan in the United States, where it is now specifically prohibited to engage in discrimination on the basis of height and weight in employment. Currently, similar legislation is being campaigned for, supported by the Strategic Training Initiative for the Prevention of Eating Disorders (STRIPED) in the state of Massachusetts. In fall 2017, a bill was introduced to make it unlawful to discriminate on the basis of height and weight in employment, housing, or public accommodations in the state (STRIPED, 2017). Such efforts clearly align with the conceptual framework for increasing positive embodiment by aiming to increase equality and social power related to weight and shape.

Industry-Initiated Efforts

Recently, several large brands have launched initiatives framed as efforts to promote positive body image.

Dove

The Unilever brand *Dove* launched its Campaign for Real Beauty in 2004 in an effort to reduce appearance anxiety among women. One of the most widely disseminated pieces of the campaign was a short video, *Dove Evolution* (https://www.dove.com/uk/dove-self-esteem-project/help-for-parents/media-and-celebrities/the-evolution-video.html) illustrating the different processes that contribute to the modification of the appearance of a model when creating images for advertising campaigns. The video highlights the use of beauty procedures and makeup, as well as lighting and finally digital modification of the image, emphasizing the difference between the initial appearance of the model and the final image. To date, three independent evaluations of this video have been conducted among female adolescents and young women. Two of these suggested that viewing the video seemed to mitigate the detrimental effects of exposure to mainstream thin-ideal media images on body image in the very short term among female adolescents ages 10–13 (Halliwell, Easun, & Harcourt, 2011) and among female undergraduates (Quigg & Want, 2011). However, in contrast, the third evaluation among young women did not reveal any capacity for the video to mitigate the negative effects of media exposure on body image in either the short or medium term (Cragg, Mulgrew, & Kannis-Dymand, 2017). Thus, the usefulness of these early efforts for the promotion of positive embodiment is unclear.

More recently, Dove created a collaboration with the World Association of Girl Guides and Girl Scouts to disseminate Free Being Me, an adapted version of an evidence-based and successful program for the promotion of positive body image and prevention of eating disorders (Stice, Marti, Spoor, Presnell, & Shaw, 2008; see also Chapter 33). To date, Free Being Me has been disseminated in over 120 countries to 3 million young people. The evaluation data so far suggest that the program has been successfully delivered across the world, although challenges existed in terms of program fidelity and sustainability (Craddock, Diedrichs, Powe, & Stice, 2017). In addition, preliminary findings suggest that the scaled-up program was successful in improving body image (Diedrichs, Craddock, Powe, & Stice, 2017). These findings suggest that the Free Being Me project funded by Dove, and disseminated in collaboration with community partners, might have the capacity to promote positive embodiment.

In parallel, Dove has adapted Happy Being Me, a school-based intervention that has been successful in increasing positive body image (Richardson & Paxton, 2010; see also Chapter 32). The adapted program, Dove Confident Me, has been formatted into a single session to be delivered by teachers. Initial evaluations of the program have suggested short-term benefits for body image among adolescents ages 11–13 years, including on measures of positive body image (Diedrichs et al., 2015), suggesting that Dove Confident Me may have potential for promoting positive embodiment.

Aerie Real

Another campaign of interest is the Aerie Real effort initiated in January 2014 by the large US based underwear company *Aerie,* which decided to cease digitally modifying the bodies of the models used in their advertising. Importantly, this decision was accompanied by a broadening in the ethnic diversity of the models portrayed as well as the iconography, shifting toward a less sexualized depiction. An experimental investigation of the impact of the new Aerie Real images revealed that among a subgroup of the most vulnerable young women (i.e., those with high rates of appearance comparison), these images seemed less detrimental to body image relative to the previous, digitally modified, images produced by Aerie (Convertino, Rodgers, Franko, & Jodoin, 2016). In addition, findings from qualitative interviews with young women, who are the target group for the brand, revealed that these new images seemed to be judged favorably overall. Importantly, the young women interviewed spoke about how comfortable the models looked in their bodies and how this in turn made them feel comfortable and proud of their bodies (Rodgers, Lowy, et al., 2018). In addition, participants described feeling less pressure to conform to strict social appearance standards. These findings are promising in terms of the capacity for increasing diversity of multiple forms (or types) in media images to be an effective tool for promoting positive embodiment.

Efforts Targeting Protective Factors

While efforts targeting body image and related dimensions are an important pathway for promoting positive embodiment, it has been suggested that a number of other factors contribute to positive embodiment. Such factors are positive experiences of social power and equality, positive connection to one's social location, freedom from constraining gender roles and other social stereotypes, and physical freedom to engage in joyful physical experiences and experience a pleasurable connection to desires (Piran, 2015, 2017). Considering these mechanisms for impacting positive embodiment suggests the potential helpfulness of public health interventions targeting dimensions that are not directly related to body image. A few examples of these are reviewed next. It is important to note, however, that the public health efforts described have not been evaluated regarding their impact on body image or related aspects; therefore, their capacity to promote positive embodiment, while theoretically supported, is not evidence based at present.

Publicly Funded Efforts

Policy efforts across the globe have aimed to increase the social power of women, and other marginalized groups, by fighting for equality of rights and opportunity, as well as gender-specific rights in areas such as reproduction. They are numerous and include efforts to legalize pregnancy terminations and same-sex marriage, increase access to education and leadership positions for women and ethnic minorities, and so on. These efforts share common goals of increasing women and other minority groups' (a) rights to engage and participate in social and professional activities, including through mentoring and affirmative action as well as (b) freedom from constraining gender and cultural roles. These initiatives have the potential to shift culture and to promote positive embodiment at the individual level.

Industry-Initiated Efforts

In 2014, the Procter and Gamble feminine hygiene products brand Always launched its #LIKEAGIRL campaign, designed to boost confidence among girls by challenging stereotypes regarding the gender gap in capabilities, particularly physical competence. The campaign was mainly disseminated online through videos and social media–tailored content, such as the hashtag and emojis. The campaign had a wide reach, with over 76 million views of the online videos, and thus was estimated to have been viewed by 53% of girls and women ages 13–34 years old in the United States (Coscia, 2017). In the first 3 months, the campaign generated 35,000 comments on social media and 4,500 postings of user-generated content. Regarding cultural change, and the promotion of more equalitarian gender roles, evaluation data revealed that 76% of a mixed-gender sample of 1,500 individuals between 13 and 34 years old described the phase "like a girl" as not having negative connotations following exposure to the campaign (Coscia, 2017). In March 2015, the campaign received an award from the United Nations in recognition of its impact on female empowerment worldwide. Again, these findings do not directly speak to the capacity of the campaign to increase positive embodiment; however, the preliminary support for its success in targeting stereotypes associated with the physical capabilities of women is aligned with protective factors for positive embodiment.

THE IMPORTANCE OF DOING NO HARM

It is also important to consider how some public health initiatives, while well intentioned, may also have the potential to decrease positive embodiment or impede its development. Examples that may have such unintended negative effects include some campaigns aiming to promote weight control. Indeed, some of these campaigns have been criticized for their potential for increasing body shame, stigmatizing larger-bodied individuals, and generally decreasing attributes associated with positive embodiment (O'Dea, 2004; Rodgers, 2016). One such initiative was the introduction of weight or BMI report cards in a number of states in the United States. In Arkansas, for example, this was shown be associated with negative consequences, such as parental encouragement of dieting (Evans & Sonneville, 2009), which has been shown to be associated with poorer body image and disordered eating among adolescents (Rodgers & Chabrol, 2009). In addition, parents have been shown to report increases in unhealthy weight control behaviors in their children following the introduction of BMI report cards (Thompson & Madsen, 2017). Therefore, as highlighted by many authors in this area, ensuring that public health efforts do no harm is a critical concern (O'Dea, 2004; Saul & Rodgers, 2016).

GENDER AND OTHER SOCIAL IDENTITIES

The majority of our discussion thus far has focused on women, and indeed, they have been the center of much of the positive embodiment literature to date (Piran, 2016, 2017). However, as Piran emphasized, the experience of embodiment is shaped by social experiences at the intersection of multiple dimensions of social location: gender, ethnicity/race, social class, weight, physical health and ability, sexual orientation, sexual identity, immigration, and others. The experience of embodiment thus also affects men at the intersection of multiple dimensions of social location. These identities need to be considered in planning health promotion initiatives.

Mainstream culture places increasing pressures on men to adhere to stereotypical and hegemonic norms of masculinity, which includes a focus on muscularity (Franko et al., 2015). It has been suggested that socialization into hegemonic masculinity may increase barriers to accessing healthcare and promote the likelihood of engaging in a range of risky and unhealthy behaviors resulting from pressure to display and maintain power and status (Griffith, Gilbert, Bruce, & Thorpe, 2016). Moreover, perceived pressure to conform to traditional norms of masculinity has been shown to be associated with poorer body image and disordered eating patterns (Franko et al., 2015). Thus, men, regardless of their other intersecting identities, may also benefit from public health interventions aiming to promote positive embodiment. To date, however, very few efforts have targeted men, and those that did have sometimes been criticized for unintentionally promoting stereotypical masculinity and thus potentially backfiring in their attempt to do otherwise (Fleming, Lee, & Dworkin, 2014).

In contrast, programs that have aimed to challenge gender norms have shown some success in promoting positive health outcomes that may be related to positive embodiment. In this way, the Male Advocates for Responsible Sexuality (MARS) program, funded by the US Office of Population Affairs and targeting males ages 13 to 25, has been found to have positive effects in terms of promoting healthy attitudes and behaviors in the context of sexuality (Zukoski & Cupples, 2008), which may therefore translate to positive embodiment. Efforts to expand public health interventions promoting positive embodiment to a wider range of groups are warranted.

CONCLUSION AND FUTURE DIRECTIONS

While public health initiatives with the potential to positively impact embodiment exist, they are still few in number, and their impact is unclear. One of the notable gaps highlighted here is the lack of evaluation data to support most of the public health efforts described. One critical future direction in this area will be the evaluation of policy and regulatory initiatives aimed at changing practice standards and voluntary codes in both publically funded and industry-led initiatives (including some initiatives described in this chapter). The extension of these efforts to include a broader array of groups, including boys and men, is necessary. More organized, cohesive, and deliberate action to involve stakeholders in the creation and implementation of such efforts might contribute to increasing the number of public health initiatives capable of promoting positive embodiment and contributing to the prevention of related concerns.

REFERENCES

Austin, S. B. (2012). A public health approach to eating disorders prevention: It's time for public health professionals to take a seat at the table. *BMC Public Health, 12*, 854. doi:10.1186/1471-2458-12-854

Bell, M. J., Rodgers, R. F., & Paxton, S. J. (2017). Towards successful evidence-based universal eating disorders prevention: The importance of zooming out. *Eating Behaviors, 25*, 89–92. doi:10.1016/j.eatbeh.2016.10.012

Bury, B., Tiggemann, M., & Slater, A. (2016). The effect of digital alteration disclaimer labels on social comparison and body image: Instructions and individual differences. *Body Image, 17*, 136–142. doi: 10.1016/j.bodyim.2016.03.005

Convertino, A. D., Rodgers, R. F., Franko, D. L., & Jodoin, A. (2016). An evaluation of the Aerie Real campaign: Potential for promoting positive body image? *Journal of Health Psychology*. doi:10.1177/1359105316680022

Coscia, A. (2017). Always #LIKEAGIRL: Changing the meaning of words to make girls proud to be girls. Retrieved from https://www.marketingsociety.com/sites/default/files/thelibrary/P%26G%20Always%20like%20a%20girl_0.pdf

Craddock, N., Diedrichs, P. C., Powe, B., & Stice, E. (2017, June). *Acceptability and feasibility of a dissonance-based body image intervention for Girl Guides and Girl Scouts: Qualitative results from a dissemination and implementation study across nineteen countries.* Paper session presented at the International Conference on Eating Disorders, Prague, Czech Republic.

Cragg, D. N., Mulgrew, K. E., & Kannis-Dymand, L. (2017). Can disclaimer labels or Dove Evolution commercial mitigate negative effects of thin-ideal exposure? *Journal of Health Psychology*. doi:10.1177/1359105317690037

Danthinne, E., Giorgianni, F., & Rodgers, R. (2018). *The usefulness of labeling media images for the prevention of body image and eating concerns: A systematic review.* Manuscript in preparation.

Diedrichs, P. C., Atkinson, M. J., Steer, R. J., Garbett, K. M., Rumsey, N., & Halliwell, E. (2015). Effectiveness of a brief school-based body image intervention "Dove Confident Me: Single Session" when delivered by teachers and researchers: Results from a cluster randomised controlled trial. *Behaviour Research and Therapy, 74*, 94–104. doi:10.1016/j.brat.2015.09.004

Diedrichs, P. C., Craddock, N., Powe, B., & Stice, E. (2017, June). *Effectiveness of a dissonance-based intervention for Girl Guides and Girl Scouts on body image and disordered dating: Results from a global pragmatic controlled trial.* Paper session presented at the International Conference on Eating Disorders, Prague, Czech Republic.

Evans, E. W., & Sonneville, K. R. (2009). BMI report cards: Will they pass or fail in the fight against pediatric obesity? *Current Opinion in Pediatrics, 21*, 431–436. doi:10.1097/MOP.0b013e32832ce04c

Fleming, P. J., Lee, J. G. L., & Dworkin, S. L. (2014). "Real men don't": Constructions of masculinity and inadvertent harm in public health interventions. *American Journal of Public Health, 104*, 1029–1035. doi:10.2105/AJPH.2013.301820

Franko, D. L., Fuller-Tyszkiewicz, M., Rodgers, R. F., Gattario, K. H., Frisén, A., Diedrichs, P. C., . . . Thompson-Brenner, H. (2015). Internalization as a mediator of the relationship between conformity to masculine norms and body image attitudes and behaviors among young men in Sweden, US, UK, and Australia. *Body Image, 15*, 54–60. doi:10.1016/j.bodyim.2015.05.002

Garnett, B. R., Buelow, R., Franko, D. L., Becker, C., Rodgers, R. F., & Austin, S. B. (2014). The importance of campaign saliency as a predictor of attitude and behavior change: A pilot evaluation of social marketing campaign fat talk free week. *Health Communication, 29*, 984–995. doi:10.1080/10410236.2013.827613

Gauvin, L., & Steiger, H. (2012). Overcoming the unhealthy pursuit of thinness: Reaction to the Québec charter for a healthy and diverse body image. *American Journal of Public Health, 102*, 1600–1606. doi:10.2105/AJPH.2011.300479

Griffith, D. M., Gilbert, K. L., Bruce, M. A., & Thorpe, R. J., Jr. (2016). Masculinity in men's health: Barrier or portal to healthcare? In J. Heidelbaugh (Ed.), *Men's health in primary care* (pp. 19–31). Cham, Switzerland: Humana Press. doi:10.1007/978-3-319-26091-4_2

Halliwell, E., Easun, A., & Harcourt, D. (2011). Body dissatisfaction: Can a short media literacy message reduce negative media exposure effects amongst adolescent girls? *British Journal of Health Psychology, 16*, 396–403. doi:10.1348/135910710X515714

Levine, M. P., & Murnen, S. K. (2009). "Everybody knows that mass media are/are not [pick one] a cause of eating disorders": A critical review of evidence for a causal link between media, negative body image, and disordered eating in females. *Journal of Social and Clinical Psychology, 28*, 9–42. doi:10.1521/jscp.2009.28.1.9

O'Dea, J. A. (2004). Prevention of child obesity: "First, do no harm." *Health Education Research, 20*, 259–265. doi:10.1093/her/cyg116

Piran, N. (2015). New possibilities in the prevention of eating disorders: The introduction of positive body image measures. *Body Image, 14*, 146–157. doi:10.1016/j.bodyim.2015.03.008

Piran, N. (2016). Embodied possibilities and disruptions: The emergence of the Experience of Embodiment construct from qualitative studies with girls and women. *Body Image, 18*, 43–60. doi:10.1016/j.bodyim.2016.04.007

Piran, N. (2017). *Journeys of embodiment at the intersection of body and culture: The developmental theory of embodiment.* San Diego, CA: Elsevier. doi: 10.1016/c2015-0-04666-4

Quigg, S. L., & Want, S. C. (2011). Highlighting media modifications: Can a television commercial mitigate the effects of music videos on female appearance satisfaction? *Body Image, 8*, 135–142. doi:10.1016/j.bodyim.2010.11.008

Richardson, S. M., & Paxton, S. J. (2010). An evaluation of a body image intervention based on risk factors for body dissatisfaction: A controlled study with adolescent girls. *International Journal of Eating Disorders, 43*, 112–122. doi:10.1002/eat.20682

Rodgers, R. F., & Chabrol, H. (2009). Parental attitudes, body image disturbance and disordered eating amongst adolescents and young adults: A review. *European Eating Disorders Review, 17*, 137–151. doi:10.1002/erv.907

Rodgers, R. F. (2016). The role of the "Healthy Weight" discourse in body image and eating concerns: An extension of sociocultural theory. *Eating Behaviors, 22*, 194–198. doi:10.1016/j.eatbeh.2016.06.004

Rodgers, R. F., Lowy, A. S., Long, S., Yates, K., Collinson, D., Franko, D. L., & Kruger, L. (2018). *Is not photoshopping a viable universal prevention strategy? A qualitative study of the impact of unmodified advertisement images from Aerie.* Manuscript submitted.

Rodgers, R. F., Ziff, S., Lowy, A. S., Yu, K., & Austin, S. B. (2017). Results of a strategic science study to inform policies targeting extreme thinness standards in the fashion industry. *International Journal of Eating Disorders, 50*, 284–292. doi:10.1002/eat.22682

Rudolph, C. W., Wells, C. L., Weller, M. D., & Baltes, B. B. (2009). A meta-analysis of empirical studies of weight-based bias in the workplace. *Journal of Vocational Behavior, 74*, 1–10. doi:10.1016/j.jvb.2008.09.008

Saul, J., & Rodgers, R. F. (2016). Wellness, not weight: Changing the focus in children and adolescents. *Journal of the American Academy of Child & Adolescent Psychiatry, 55*, 7–9. doi:10.1016/j.jaac.2015.10.005

Slater, A., & Tiggemann, M. (2011). Gender differences in adolescent sport participation, teasing, self-objectification and body image concerns. *Journal of Adolescence, 34*, 455–463. doi:10.1016/j.adolescence.2010.06.007

Stice, E., Marti, C. N., Spoor, S., Presnell, K., & Shaw, H. (2008). Dissonance and healthy weight eating disorder prevention programs: Long-term effects from a randomized efficacy trial. *Journal of Consulting and Clinical Psychology*, *76*, 329–340. doi:10.1037/0022-006X.76.2.329

Strategic Training Initiative for the Prevention of Eating Disorders. (2017). *Policy brief: Fighting weight discrimination in Massachusetts.* Retrieved from https://cdn1.sph.harvard.edu/wp-content/uploads/sites/1267/2017/02/FINAL-H952_PolicyBrief_Sept-20-20171.pdf

Tan, B., & Miller, K. (2016). *Summary report of the evaluation of the 2016 "Girls Make Your Move" physical activity for young women campaign* [A GfK Australia Research Report]. Retrieved from https://campaigns.health.gov.au/girlsmove/campaign-evaluation/evaluation-research-report-phase-1

Taylor, C. B., Franko, D. L., Neumark-Sztainer, D., Paxton, S. J., & Shapiro, J. R. (2007). Public-health approach to eating disorders. *The Lancet*, *369*(9577), 1928. doi:10.1016/S0140-6736(07)60912-X

Thompson, H. R., & Madsen, K. A. (2017). The report card on BMI report cards. *Current Obesity Reports*, *6*, 163–167. doi:10.1007/s13679-017-0259-6

Zukoski, A., & Cupples J. B. (2008). *Male Advocates for Responsible Sexuality (MARS) program final report (2003–2008).* Corvallis, OR: Benton County Health Department.

37

Policy Initiatives to Promote Positive Embodiment and Reduce Weight Stigma

REBECCA M. PUHL AND MARY S. HIMMELSTEIN

In North America and many Westernized countries, weight-based stigma and discrimination exist toward people whose body size deviates from stringent societal ideals of thinness (Brewis, SturtzSreetharan, & Wutich, 2018; Puhl & Heuer, 2009). Weight-based discrimination is a prevalent form of discrimination among US adults, especially among women, and leads to unfair treatment, adverse health outcomes, and reduced quality of life for individuals who are targeted (Puhl, Andreyeva, & Brownell, 2008; Puhl & Heuer, 2009). These experiences not only affect adults but also are frequent occurrences for youth, who are vulnerable to victimization because of their body size. Indeed, youth, parents, and educators report weight-based bullying as a common and problematic form of bullying among youth (Bradshaw, Waasdorp, O'Brennan, & Gulemetova, 2013; Bucchianeri, Eisenberg, & Neumark-Sztainer, 2013; Puhl, Luedicke, & DePierre, 2013).

Growing concerns about the prevalence and damaging consequences of weight-based bullying, stigma, and discrimination have led to increasing calls for policy measures to help address these problems and protect people from weight-based prejudice on a broader scale. This chapter reviews policy efforts that have been proposed or implemented to facilitate positive embodiment for youth and adults, including evidence on public attitudes about policies and laws that aim to reduce weight-based inequities. We examine relevant policy initiatives and research evidence in North America, Europe, and other parts of the world, highlighting the strengths and limitations of these efforts. We also identify directions for future policy research that can improve on existing initiatives to promote equitable treatment of people of diverse body sizes.

POLICY EFFORTS TO ADDRESS WEIGHT DISCRIMINATION IN ADULTS

Currently, very few legal measures exist to protect people from weight-based discrimination. No countries have enacted federal laws that prohibit weight discrimination. While it remains legal to discriminate on the basis of weight under federal law in the United States, state-level legislative efforts have emerged as an alternative approach for implementing legislation, with initiatives aiming to include body weight in existing state-level civil rights statutes. In 1976, Michigan passed the Elliot–Larson Civil Rights Act, which included prohibiting weight discrimination, making it the first and only state in the United States with this legislation (Elliott–Larsen Civil Rights Act, 1976). Since passing this law, evidence from a statewide survey using a stratified random sample suggests there are lower rates of self-reported weight-related employment discrimination in Michigan (Roehling, Roehling, & Wagstaff, 2013). Yet, over 40 years later, no other states have successfully passed similar laws. In the meantime, an increasing number of cities, six in total so far, across the United States have begun implementing legislation at the local level. While these efforts are promising, the vast majority of Americans have no legal protections or recourse if they face weight discrimination.

Given the lack of success in policy efforts to add body weight as a protected class in state-level and federal civil rights statutes, some Americans have attempted to seek recourse for weight discrimination through the Americans with Disabilities Act (ADA). In 2009, the US Congress passed the ADA Amendments Act, which modified ADA definitions of disability to include "severe obesity" as an "impairment" (Pomeranz & Puhl, 2013). Under this amendment, several court cases have since ruled in favor of plaintiffs who have been discriminated because of their weight. However, addressing obesity as a disability may promote further stigma of people with higher body weight and may only apply to a few of the discrimination cases. Thus, broader policy and legal measures are needed to address weight discrimination.

Similar to the United States, many other countries have human rights laws in place that prohibit discrimination based on characteristics such as race, national or ethnic origin, sex, religion, or disability; however, body weight remains absent (Australian Government, 2015; Canadian Human Rights Act, 2015). As in the United States, initial efforts to ban weight discrimination in other countries may have more success on a smaller scale. For example, in 2016, the city of Reykjavik in Iceland added body weight as a protected category in its new human rights code, which prohibits weight stigma and discrimination in employment, public services, and public health communication (Reykjavík City Council, 2016). Given research evidence documenting weight stigma and discrimination in many countries (Brewis, Wutich, Falletta-Cowden, & Rodriguez-Soto, 2011; Crandall et al., 2001), similar policy initiatives may continue to emerge elsewhere.

A key component of successful policy efforts to enact legislation is public support. Without social approval, the incentive for political will to push for policy change is diminished. In recent years, research has increasingly examined public support for different policy and legal measures to address weight discrimination. To date, most of this evidence is within the United States. In a series of national studies beginning in 2010, research has documented public support for three types of laws to address weight discrimination: (a) adding body weight as a protected class in existing state-level civil rights laws; (b) providing people with a body mass index (BMI) in the "obese" range with the same legal protections as people with disabilities; and (c) prohibiting weight discrimination specifically in the workplace, including in hiring practices, wages, and job termination (Puhl & Heuer, 2011). Table 37.1 summarizes the extent of public support for each of these legal measures from 2010 through 2015. These findings show consistently high levels of public support for laws to address weight discrimination in employment and for adding body weight as a protected class to state-level civil rights statutes. Across these studies, women were more likely than men to support these legal measures, as were liberals compared to conservatives. However, the most recent evidence from 2015 found no differences in public support by gender or political orientation, suggesting that there could be increasing consensus on the need to address weight discrimination as a legitimate social injustice.

Less is known about public support for policy measures outside the United States. A recent multinational study (with the United States, Canada, Australia, and Iceland) found a similar pattern of support for the same three proposed legal measures mentioned previously (Puhl, Latner, et al., 2015). Across these countries, public support was strongest for laws that would prohibit employers from denying employment, assigning lower wages, and refusing promotion to people based on their body weight. A recent national study from Germany documented moderate public support for laws to address weight discrimination, with levels of support generally lower compared to the United States and Iceland (Hilbert et al., 2017). Still, patterns of public support were similar in Germany, with higher public support from women (vs. men) and people with higher body weight (vs. lower weight). While there is still much to learn about public attitudes toward different legal remedies to reduce social inequities based on body weight, this initial evidence suggests that public support to address this problem is present in multiple countries.

POLICY EFFORTS TO ADDRESS WEIGHT-BASED BULLYING IN YOUTH

For youth, weight stigma is experienced in the form of teasing, bullying, and victimization. With increasing evidence highlighting body weight to be one of the most prevalent reasons that youth are bullied (Bucchianeri et al., 2013; Puhl, Suh, & Li, 2017), it is important to ensure that vulnerable youth are protected from this form of bullying in existing antibullying policies and legislation. To date, attention in this area has focused on legislation in the United States, where there is currently no federal law that prohibits bullying in schools, but every state has its own

Table 37.1 NATIONAL US STUDIES OF PUBLIC SUPPORT FOR LAWS TO REDUCE WEIGHT DISCRIMINATION IN ADULTS

Proposed Laws to Reduce Weight Discrimination	**US National Study Samples**						
	2010[a] (*N* = 1,001)	**2010**[b] (*N* = 1,114)	**2011**[c] (*N* = 1,098)	**2012**[c] (*N* = 1,202)	**2013**[c] (*N* = 1,202)	**2014**[d] (*N* = 1,207)	**2015**[d] (*N* = 1,204)
% OF PARTICIPANTS SUPPORTING PROPOSED LAWS							
1. *It should be illegal for an employer to do all of the following:* (a) *Refuse to hire a qualified person because of his/her body weight.* (b) *Fire a qualified employee because of his/her body weight.* (c) *Deny a promotion or appropriate compensation to a qualified employee because of his/her body weight.*	73%	70%	81%	74.7%	78.9%	78.3%	79.4%
2. *My state should include body weight in their civil rights law in order to protect people from discrimination based on their body weight, similar to laws that protect against discrimination due to race, religion, and sex.*	54%	57%	70.1%	70%	76.3%	76.9%	80.9%
3. *Persons who have obesity should be subject to the same legal protection and benefits offered to people with physical disabilities.*	45%	40%	61.6%	60.7%	69%	71%	73.9%

[a] Puhl and Heuer, 2011.
[b] Puhl, Heuer, and Sarda, 2011.
[c] Suh, Puhl, Liu, and Fleming Milici, 2014b.
[d] Puhl, Suh, and Li, 2016.

antibullying law. The comprehensiveness of state antibullying laws varies considerably according to whether or not they enumerate characteristics that place youth at heightened risk for bullying and, if so, how many characteristics are included. Enumeration is important in comprehensive antibullying statutes because it provides concrete protections to vulnerable students, provides clear notification to students and teachers that bullying is not permitted, and encourages earlier reporting and teacher intervention with student-reported bullying incidents (Puhl, Luedicke, & King, 2015). Although research is needed to assess the impact and outcomes of policy changes involving enumeration of body weight in bullying statutes, research on other forms of youth victimization indicates that when characteristics are not enumerated, there is a risk of lack of enforcement and protection for students, less intervention, and cases where bullying incidents are not addressed (Puhl, Luedicke, et al., 2015). A number of state laws enumerate characteristics such as gender, race, ethnicity, disability, and sexual orientation that place youth at heightened risk for bullying. To date, however, only three state laws (New York, New Hampshire, and Maine) include body weight as a distinguishing characteristic that places youth at heightened risk of harassment (US Department of Health and Human Services, 2014). Given the high rates of weight-based bullying, this raises concerns that state laws may not be protecting vulnerable youth from victimization and points to an opportunity for advocacy efforts to strengthen existing state antibullying laws to include body weight as an enumerated characteristic.

At the school level, similar challenges are present. Although most school districts in the United States are required to have school-based antibullying policies, these also vary considerably according to the frequency of enumerated characteristics. A 2015 analysis of 9,296 school districts across the country found that characteristics of race, sex, religion, disability, and sexual orientation were enumerated in at least 60% of antibullying policies. However, "appearance" was only listed in 19.5% of policies, and body weight was absent (Kull, Kosciw, & Greytak, 2015). Evidence has found that students reported higher levels of bullying and poorer mental health outcomes in schools with policies that have only partly enumerated or not enumerated characteristics, compared to schools with comprehensive policies that enumerate characteristics where bullying percentages are lower (Hatzenbuehler, Keyes, & Hasin, 2009; Kosciw, Greytak, Bartkiewicz, Boesen, & Palmer, 2012). Thus, students who are teased or bullied because of their body weight may not be adequately protected with existing provisions in school-based policies.

The absence of body weight in both school-based policies and antibullying laws warrants targeted efforts to strengthen these measures to improve protections for vulnerable youth. Public support, and parental support in particular, is an important catalyst for motivating this policy change. National US studies have examined trends in parental and public support in this area, with clear and consistent findings. As depicted in Table 37.2, a high majority of American parents, the general public, and professionals from the eating disorders field support efforts to strengthen both school-based antibullying policies (83–96%) and antibullying laws (76–94%) to protect youth from weight-based bullying (Puhl & Luedicke,

Table 37.2 National US Studies of Parental and Public Support for Policies/Laws to Address Weight-Based Bullying in Youth

Proposed Policies and Legislation to Address Youth Weight Bullying	US National Study Samples				
	US Parents[a] (N = 919)	US Parents[b] (N = 2,185)	US Parents[c] (N = 1,804)	US General Public[d] (N = 944)	Professionals in the Eating Disorders Field[d] (N = 1,420)
% of participants supporting proposed policies/laws					
Schools should have antibullying policies that protect students from being bullied about their weight.	85–88%	86%	87.6%	83.4%	96.1%
Existing antibullying laws should be modified to include protections for youth who are bullied about their weight.	78–84%	N/A	86.2%	76.8%	94.6%

[a] Puhl and Luedicke, 2014.
[b] Suh et al., 2014a.
[c] Puhl et al., 2017.
[d] Puhl et al., 2014.

2014; Puhl, Neumark-Sztainer, Austin, Luedicke, & King, 2014; Puhl et al., 2017; Suh, Puhl, Liu, & Fleming Milici, 2014a).

Recent research suggests that attitudes of teachers and educators align with parental policy support. A study of 240 educators found strong support for addressing weight bullying through antibullying policies (92%), staff training (89%), and school curriculum (89%) (Puhl, Neumark-Sztainer, Austin, Suh, & Wakefield, 2016). Furthermore, a national US study found considerable public support (ranging from two thirds to three quarters of participants) for enacting state and federal antibullying laws that enumerate distinguishing characteristics, including characteristics of physical appearance and body weight (Puhl, Luedicke, et al., 2015). Research outside the United States on public support for policy measures to address weight-based bullying in youth remains scarce. However, a recent multinational study (comparing the United States, Canada, Australia, and Iceland) found high levels of public support (65–87%) across all countries for government augmentation of antibullying laws to include weight-based bullying, and at least 75% of participants across countries agreed that schools should promote awareness of weight-based bullying and implement policies to address this problem (Puhl, Latner, et al., 2016). Taken together, there appears to be substantial public and parental support for policy change to better protect youth from weight stigma in the school setting, where bullying is a prevalent problem.

OTHER POLICY INITIATIVES TO PROMOTE POSITIVE EMBODIMENT

Beyond policies to address weight-based inequities, discrimination, and bullying, there are other types of policy initiatives that could facilitate and promote positive embodiment. These policies generally fall into two broad categories: (a) policies targeting media depictions of body size and (b) policies aimed at addressing eating disorder prevention, which include funding for programs to promote positive body image.

Media-Focused Policies

In the last 10 years, there have been regular efforts in the US Congress to introduce policies targeting the media. The Healthy Media for Youth Act called for the US government to improve positive embodiment through (a) allocating federal funds to award nonprofit grants aimed at educating boys and girls in media literacy; (b) coordination from the Centers for Disease Control and Prevention and national health organizations to support research on the impact of media depictions of girls and women on child development; and (c) requiring the Federal Communications Commission (FCC) to convene a task force to develop steps for promoting positive depictions of girls and women in the media (Healthy Media for Youth Act, 2009, 2011). The Truth in Advertising Act called for the FCC to submit a report to Congress on the use of commercial products (e.g., Photoshop) to alter physical characteristics of faces and bodies in advertisements and recommendations for appropriate regulations for future use of these techniques in advertising (Truth in Advertising Act, 2014, 2016). To date, both of these bills have failed to move forward in Congress each time they were introduced.

Internationally, several countries and cities have created advertisement bans, required labeling for digitally altered images in advertising, and called for a greater depiction of diverse body types in advertising. Beginning in 2016, the mayor of London banned advertisements on London's transportation systems that could create pressure to achieve an unrealistic or unhealthy body shape or contribute to poor body esteem (London Mayor, 2016). Similarly, the Advertising Standards Authority in Britain banned several advertisements depicting excessively thin models (Bilefsky, 2016). Liberal Democrats in the United Kingdom called for bans of advertising using digitally altered images of faces or bodies or for such ads to include a warning label (Prince, 2009). Israel and France enacted legislation requiring advertisements that have been digitally altered to be clearly labeled; companies who fail to label altered images face a fine (Friedman, 2017; Nota, 2013). It should be noted, however, that such labeling may not produce the intended positive outcomes (Tiggemann, Slater, Bury, Hawkins, & Firth, 2013); thus, it may be more impactful for legislation to ban advertisements that use digitally altered images rather than allow the use of such advertisements with warning labels. In Spain, the government passed a law in 2010 to prohibit television advertising before 10:00 pm for body-altering cosmetic surgery because these advertisements could increase body dissatisfaction in youth (Paxton, 2012). Countries, including Australia, Canada, France, and Italy, have also called on the fashion and media industries to endorse voluntary codes of conduct that promote diverse body sizes in advertising and to stop digitally enhancing images of models (Bonawitz, 2006; Paxton, 2012).

Addressing Body Image in Policies Targeting Eating Disorders

Policies and legislation aimed at the prevention and treatment of eating disorders or obesity often include initiatives to develop programs to improve healthy body image or body image development. Within the United States, there are three notable examples of proposed national legislation. The Improved Nutrition and Physical Activity Act (IMPACT Act) proposed policy to increase training of health professionals to identify, treat, and prevent obesity and eating disorders. Specific to body image, this act aimed to allocate funding for research and programming to assess the influence of media literacy on body image and for interventions to address positive body image and self-esteem (IMPACT Act, 2009a, 2009b). The IMPACT Act initially passed in the US Senate in 2003; it has yet to be passed in both the House and Senate to become law.

The Federal Response to Eliminate Eating Disorders Act (FREED Act) proposed policies to (a) increase preventive health related to eating and health behavior in youth; (b) develop education and intervention programs to promote healthy eating and behavior in youth; and (c) disseminate interventions to promote healthy eating and behavior in youth (FREED Act, 2009, 2011, 2013). The second and third aims of this legislation included research on body image programming and interventions that included a positive embodiment component. Despite considerable bipartisan support, the FREED Act was not enacted into law. Most recently, the Anna Westin Act of 2015 called for policy to (a) direct the National Institute of Mental Health to create public service announcements about eating disorders, such as educating the public about discrimination based on body size and media effects on body image; and (b) require the Federal Trade Commission (FTC) to submit a report to Congress on strategies to reduce digitally altered images of faces and bodies in the media (Anna Westin Act, 2015a, 2015b). Key provisions from this act were passed into law in 2016, but there has not yet been formal assessment of the systematic impact of this legislation.

Several state-level policies related to body image have also been proposed, but few have passed. The California legislature introduced (but did not pass) a bill to require the Occupational Safety and Health Administration (OSHA) Standards Board to consult with eating disorder specialists to develop and implement a safety and health standard for models (AB-2539, 2016). Several states, including California, Massachusetts, and New York, have proposed or passed legislation on the sale of dietary supplements and weight loss products to minors. Massachusetts introduced a bill to move dietary supplements behind the counter and limit their sale to minors; it did not pass (H. 3471, 2015). New York moved ipecac from behind the counter, so individuals must ask the pharmacist in order to purchase the drug (Pomeranz, Taylor, & Austin, 2013). Also in New York, the Council of Fashion Designers of American (CFDA) recommended, but could not enforce, a policy for designers to implement an ID check to ensure that all models performing in fashion week were at least 16 years old and healthy (Krupnick, 2012). Finally, California made it a misdemeanor for a coach to give laxatives to a minor to encourage weight loss (Pomeranz et al., 2013).

Internationally, some of the strongest policies aimed at eating disorder prevention emerged from government regulations of actions by the fashion industry. France passed the Model Health Law in 2015 (Friedman, 2017). Under this law, models working in France must provide a medical certificate demonstrating they are healthy to work; the medical evaluation for models over the age of 16 includes evaluation of BMI (Friedman, 2017). The French government had previously banned websites that promoted excessive thinness (i.e., pro-anorexia websites) (Friedman, 2017). Several other countries, including Israel, Italy, and Spain, have similar policies. Italy directed the fashion industry to add larger sizes to collections and promote "full-bodied" women in their advertising campaigns and shows (Bonawitz, 2006). In Spain, fashion week in Madrid banned models who had a BMI of less than 18 (Bonawitz, 2006). Similarly, in Israel fashion models are required to have a BMI of at least 18.5 (Nota, 2013). Governments in Australia,

Canada, France, and Italy have called on media and fashion companies to endorse voluntary codes of conduct, to commit to displaying diverse bodies in advertising, and to avoid digital manipulation of images to create unrealistic body expectations (Puhl et al., 2014). In the meantime, policy research scholars in the United States continue to call for laws to regulate BMI of runway models in the fashion industry (Record & Austin, 2016).

SUPPORT FOR BODY-POSITIVE POLICIES

About 40% of Americans support the idea that the government should regulate the weight of fashion models, while over 70% of eating disorder specialists support this type of legislation (Puhl et al., 2014). Models themselves have reported that new policies could help improve their working conditions (Rodgers, Ziff, Lowy, Yu, & Austin, 2017), such as requiring a 30-minute break for lunch for modeling sessions lasting over 6 hours or prohibiting employers from terminating a model based on weight gain or a change in body shape or size. While models rated these types of policies to have high potential impact, they were less certain about the feasibility of implementing such measures and were not supportive of minimal BMI requirements.

Regarding the labeling of digitally altered images in advertising, about two thirds of the American public have expressed support for these policies, while over 90% of eating disorder specialists support government regulations for labeling digitally altered images in advertising (Puhl et al., 2014). Many Americans (~58%) also support government regulations for weight loss products and for limiting the sale of these products to minors (Puhl et al., 2014). Parents have also expressed support for a number of media-focused policies affecting children, including substantial support (77–82%) for laws that would require children's television programs to portray children with diverse body sizes and avoid weight stigma (Suh et al., 2014a).

CONCLUSION AND FUTURE DIRECTIONS FOR POLICY RESEARCH AND ADVOCACY EFFORTS

A key next step in policy research is assessing the potential feasibility and impact of implementing proposed policies and legislation. Some preliminary evidence from the United States suggests that policies requiring schools to strengthen antibullying policies to protect students from being bullied about their weight are viewed to be high in both feasibility and potential impact among the general public and professionals in the eating disorders field (Puhl et al., 2014). However, more research is needed to assess the potential impact of policy proposals on both structural and individual changes to promote positive embodiment and to seek opinions about feasibility directly from policymakers and other key decision-makers.

Clearly, there is also a need for more dialogue about policy, and policy research, across different countries to identify and compare potential policy strategies to promote positive embodiment and guide research in this area. Cross-cultural and multinational studies assessing viable policy initiatives and social approval for these efforts are needed, as are organized advocacy efforts to inform colleagues and activists in different countries of new policy proposals or progress with existing initiatives to reduce weight stigma and promote positive embodiment.

Finally, more can be done to elevate weight stigma and positive embodiment as policy priorities among advocacy groups and key organizations. There is a need to more actively engage people in diverse settings who can contribute to policy efforts. Too often, parents, educators, employers, researchers, and healthcare professionals are neglected as key voices in public policy discourse about body weight. Increasing public awareness of the importance of body acceptance and weight stigma is a first step, but we must go further to mobilize diverse groups to help motivate the political support that is necessary to champion policies and laws that can improve the lives of people across diverse body sizes.

REFERENCES

AB-2539. (2016). California State Legislature. Retrieved from http://www.leginfo.ca.gov/pub/15-16/bill/asm/ab_2501-2550/ab_2539_bill_20160219_introduced.html

Anna Westin Act. (2015a). S. 1865, 114 Cong. Retrieved from https://www.congress.gov/114/bills/s1865/BILLS-114s1865is.pdf

Anna Westin Act. (2015b). H.R. 2515, 114th Cong. Retrieved from https://www.congress.gov/114/bills/hr2515/BILLS-114hr2515ih.pdf

Australian Government. (2015). Sex Discrimination Act 1984 Amended 2015. Retrieved from https://www.legislation.gov.au/Details/C2016C00880

Bilefsky, D. (2016, April 7). British group says model for Gucci is "unhealthily thin." *New York Times*, p. A4. Retrieved from https://www.nytimes.com/2016/04/07/business/international/gucci-ad-unhealthily-thin-model.html

Bonawitz, A. (2006, December 16). Italy bans "too-thin" models. *CBS News*. Retrieved from http://www.cbsnews.com/news/italy-bans-too-thin-models/

Bradshaw, C. P., Waasdorp, T. E., O'Brennan, L. M., & Gulemetova, M. (2013). Teachers' and education support professionals' perspectives on bullying and prevention: Findings from a national education association study. *School Psychology Review*, *42*, 280–297.

Brewis, A., SturtzSreetharan, C., & Wutich, A. (2018). Obesity stigma as a globalizing health challenge. *Globalization and Health*, *14*, 20. https://doi.org/10.1186/s12992-018-0337-x

Brewis, A. A., Wutich, A., Falletta-Cowden, A., & Rodriguez-Soto, I. (2011). Body norms and fat stigma in global perspective reports body norms and fat stigma in global perspective CA2 Online-Only Material: Supplement A. *Current Anthropology*, *52*, 269–276. doi:10.1086/659309

Bucchianeri, M. M., Eisenberg, M. E., & Neumark-Sztainer, D. (2013). Weightism, racism, classism, and sexism: Shared forms of harassment in adolescents. *Journal of Adolescent Health*, *53*, 47–53. doi:10.1016/j.jadohealth.2013.01.006

Canadian Human Rights Act. (2015). R.S.C., 1985, c. H-6. Retrieved from http://laws-lois.justice.gc.ca/PDF/H-6.pdf

Crandall, C. S., D'Anello, S., Sakalli, N., Lazarus, E., Nejtardt, G. W., & Feather, N. T. (2001). An attribution-value model of prejudice: Anti-fat attitudes in six nations. *Personality and Social Psychology Bulletin, 27*, 30–37. doi:10.1177/0146167201271003

Elliott–Larsen Civil Rights Act. (1976). Act 453 of 1976. Retrieved from https://www.michigan.gov/documents/act_453_elliott_larsen_8772_7.pdf

Federal Response to Eliminate Eating Disorders Act. (2009). H.R. 1193, 111th Cong. Retrieved from https://www.congress.gov/111/bills/hr1193/BILLS-111hr1193ih.pdf

Federal Response to Eliminate Eating Disorders Act. (2011). H.R. 1148, 112th Cong. Retrieved from https://www.congress.gov/112/bills/hr1448/BILLS-112hr1448ih.pdf

Federal Response to Eliminate Eating Disorders Act. (2013). H.R. 2101, 113th Cong. Retrieved from https://www.congress.gov/113/bills/hr2101/BILLS-113hr2101ih.pdf

Friedman, V. (2017, May 8). A new age in French—modeling. *New York Times*. Retrieved from https://www.nytimes.com/2017/05/08/fashion/france-laws-thin-models.html

H. 3471. (2015). Massachusetts State Legislature, 189th. Retrieved from https://malegislature.gov/Bills/189/House/H3471

Hatzenbuehler, M. L., Keyes, K. M., & Hasin, D. S. (2009). Associations between perceived weight discrimination and the prevalence of psychiatric disorders in the general population. *Obesity, 17*, 2033–2039. http://doi.org/10.1038/oby.2009.131

Healthy Media for Youth Act. (2009). S. 3852, 111th Cong. Retrieved from https://www.congress.gov/bill/111th-congress/senate-bill/3852

Healthy Media for Youth Act. (2011). H.R. 2513, 112th Cong. Retrieved from https://www.congress.gov/bill/112th-congress/house-bill/2513

Hilbert, A., Hübner, C., Schmutzer, G., Daníelsdóttir, S., Brähler, E., & Puhl, R. (2017). Public support for weight-related antidiscrimination laws and policies. *Obesity Facts, 10*, 101–111. doi:10.1159/000456012

IMPACT Act. (2009a). H.R. 2276, 111th Cong. Retrieved from https://www.congress.gov/111/bills/hr2276/BILLS-111hr2276ih.pdf

IMPACT Act. (2009b). S. 1503, 111th Cong. Retrieved from https://www.congress.gov/111/bills/s1503/BILLS-111s1503is.pdf

Kosciw, J. G., Greytak, E. A., Bartkiewicz, M. J., Boesen, M. J., & Palmer, N. A. (2012). *The 2011 national school climate survey*. Retrieved from http://www.glsen.org/sites/default/files/2011 National School Climate Survey Full Report.pdf

Krupnick, E. (2012, January 27). CFDA health guidelines for models released, focus on age and eating disorders. *Huffington Post*. Retrieved from http://www.huffingtonpost.com/2012/01/27/cfda-health-guidelines-for-models_n_1236213.html

Kull, R. M., Kosciw, J. G., & Greytak, E. (2015). *From statehouse to schoolhouse: Anti-bullying policy efforts in US states and school districts*. Retrieved from http://www.glsen.org/sites/default/files/GLSEN - From Statehouse to Schoolhouse 2015_0.pdf

London Mayor. (2016, June 13). *Mayor in crackdown on body image advertisements on the TfL network*. Retrieved from https://www.london.gov.uk/press-releases/mayoral/mayor-in-crackdown-on-body-image-advertisements

Nota, B. (2013, January 3). Israeli law bans skinny, BMI-challenged models. *ABC News*. Retrieved from http://abcnews.go.com/International/israeli-law-bans-skinny-bmi-challenged-models/story?id=18116291

Paxton, S. J. (2012). Public health interventions for body dissatisfaction and eating disorders: Learning from Victoria. Preventing eating-related and weight-related disorders: Collaborative research, advocacy, and policy change, 71–84.

Pomeranz, J. L., & Puhl, R. M. (2013). New developments in the law for obesity discrimination protection. *Obesity, 21*, 469–471. http://doi.org/10.1002/oby.20094

Pomeranz, J. L., Taylor, L. M., & Austin, S. B. (2013). Over-the-counter and out-of-control: Legal strategies to protect youths from abusing products for weight control. *American Journal of Public Health, 103*, 220–225. doi:10.2105/AJPH.2012.300962

Prince, R. (2009, August 3). Airbrushing of photos should be banned, liberal democrats say. *The Telegraph*. Retrieved from http://www.telegraph.co.uk/news/politics/liberaldemocrats/5962358/Airbrushing-of-photos-should-be-banned-Liberal-Democrats-say.html

Puhl, R. M., Andreyeva, T., & Brownell, K. D. (2008). Perceptions of weight discrimination: Prevalence and comparison to race and gender discrimination in America. *International Journal of Obesity, 32*, 992–1000. doi:10.1038/ijo.2008.22

Puhl, R. M., & Heuer, C. A. (2009). The stigma of obesity: A review and update. *Obesity, 17*, 941–964. doi:10.1038/oby.2008.636

Puhl, R. M., & Heuer, C. A. (2011). Public opinion about laws to prohibit weight discrimination in the United States. *Obesity, 19*, 74–82. doi:10.1038/oby.2010.126

Puhl, R. M., Heuer, C. A., & Sarda, V. (2011). Framing messages about weight discrimination: Impact on public support for legislation. *International Journal of Obesity, 35*, 863–72. doi:10.1038/ijo.2010.194

Puhl, R. M., Latner, J. D., O'Brien, K. S., Luedicke, J., Daníelsdóttir, S., & Salas, X. R. (2015). Potential policies and laws to prohibit weight discrimination: Public views from 4 countries. *Milbank Quarterly, 93*, 691–731. doi:10.1111/1468-0009.12162

Puhl, R. M., Latner, J. D., O'Brien, K. S., Luedicke, J., Forhan, M., & Daníelsdóttir, S. (2016). Cross-national perspectives about weight-based bullying in youth: Nature, extent and remedies. *Pediatric Obesity, 11*, 241–250. doi:10.1111/ijpo.12051

Puhl, R. M., & Luedicke, J. (2014). Parental support for policy measures and school-based efforts to address weight-based victimization of overweight youth. *International Journal of Obesity, 38*, 531–538. doi:10.1038/ijo.2013.207

Puhl, R. M., Luedicke, J., & DePierre, J. A. (2013). Parental concerns about weight-based victimization in youth. *Childhood Obesity, 9*, 540–548. doi:10.1089/chi.2013.0064

Puhl, R. M., Luedicke, J., & King, K. M. (2015). Public attitudes about different types of anti-bullying laws: Results from a national survey. *Journal of Public Health Policy, 36*, 95–109. doi:10.1057/jphp.2014.46

Puhl, R. M., Neumark-Sztainer, D., Austin, S. B., Luedicke, J., & King, K. M. (2014). Setting policy priorities to address eating disorders and weight stigma: Views from the field of eating disorders and the US general public. *BMC Public Health, 14*, 524. http://doi.org/10.1186/1471-2458-14-524

Puhl, R. M., Neumark-Sztainer, D., Austin, S. B., Suh, Y., & Wakefield, D. B. (2016). Policy actions to address weight-based bullying and eating disorders in schools: Views of teachers and school administrators. *Journal of School Health, 86*, 507–515. doi:10.1111/josh.12401

Puhl, R. M., Suh, Y., & Li, X. (2016). Legislating for weight-based equality: National trends in public support for laws to prohibit weight discrimination. *International Journal of Obesity, 40*, 1320–1324. doi:10.1038/ijo.2016.49

Puhl, R. M., Suh, Y., & Li, X. (2017). Improving anti-bullying laws and policies to protect youth from weight-based victimization: Parental support for action. *Pediatric Obesity, 12*, e14–e19. doi:10.1111/ijpo.12129

Record, K. L., & Austin, S. B. (2016). "Paris thin": A call to regulate life-threatening starvation of runway models in the US fashion industry. *American Journal of Public Health, 106*, 205–206. doi:10.2105/AJPH.2015.302950

ReykjavíkCityCouncil.(2016).ThecityofReykjavík'sHumanRightsPolicyof2006,Revision 2016. Retrieved from http://reykjavik.is/en/city-of-reykjaviks-human-rights-policy

Rodgers, R. F., Ziff, S., Lowy, A. S., Yu, K., & Austin, S. B. (2017). Results of a strategic science study to inform policies targeting extreme thinness standards in the fashion industry. *International Journal of Eating Disorders, 50*, 284–292. doi:10.1002/eat.22682

Roehling, M. V., Roehling, P. V., & Wagstaff, M. F. (2013). Sex differences in perceived weight-based employment discrimination when weight discrimination is illegal. *Employee Responsibilities and Rights Journal, 25*, 159–176. doi:10.1007/s10672-013-9217-y

Suh, Y., Puhl, R., Liu, S., & Fleming Milici, F. (2014a). Parental support for policy actions to reduce weight stigma toward youth in schools and children's television programs: Trends from 2011 to 2013. *Childhood Obesity, 10*, 533–541. doi:10.1089/chi.2014.0050

Suh, Y., Puhl, R. M., Liu, S., & Fleming Milici, F. (2014b). Support for laws to prohibit weight discrimination in the United States: Public attitudes from 2011 to 2013. *Obesity, 22*, 1872–1879. http://doi.org/10.1002/oby.20750

Tiggemann, M., Slater, A., Bury, B., Hawkins, K., & Firth, B. (2013). Disclaimer labels on fashion magazine advertisements: Effects on social comparison and body dissatisfaction. *Body Image, 10*, 45–53. http://doi.org/10.1016/j.bodyim.2012.08.001

Truth in Advertising Act of 2014. (2014). H.R. 4341, 113rd Cong. Retrieved from https://www.congress.gov/113/bills/hr4341/BILLS-113hr4341ih.pdf

Truth in Advertising Act of 2016. (2016). H.R. 4445, 114th Cong. Retrieved from https://www.congress.gov/bill/114th-congress/house-bill/4445

US Department of Health and Human Services. (2014, June). State anti-bullying laws ancd policies. Retrieved from https://www.stopbullying.gov/laws

38

The *Handbook of Positive Body Image and Embodiment*

From the Present to the Future

NIVA PIRAN AND TRACY L. TYLKA ■

Two central goals guided the construction of this edited volume on positive body image and embodiment. One goal was to create a scholarly forum whereby knowledge about these important domains could be consolidated into a comprehensive resource for researchers and practitioners. A second goal was to facilitate further progress in the fields of positive body image and embodiment by capturing the breadth inherent in integrating these two fields and inviting scholars from around the world to go beyond current knowledge and draw pathways for future progress to research and practice. As co-editors, we hope and believe that the volume achieved its goals, to a large measure through the strong contributions of chapter authors.

The first section of the book reflects the richness of looking at positive ways of inhabiting the body. Constructs and related measures that address positive ways of inhabiting the body are both one dimensional and multidimensional; they assess positive connection to the body and body appreciation and to attunement to one's needs, desires, and movement. Further, several of the measures also highlight intraindividual strategies (e.g., the filtering out of adverse information, self-talk, emotional processing, and adopting a resistant stance toward negative social pressures) that support maintaining positive body connection even when the social environment is challenging. As the chapters in this section indicate, these measures are positively associated with body esteem and other indicators of well-being and negatively associated with body dissatisfaction and disordered eating patterns. Further, their conceptual articulation opens opportunities to broaden the range of factors included in etiological theories of body image and embodiment, especially the addition of protective factors. Moreover, the description of positive ways of inhabiting the body also establishes important goals to work toward when planning constructive social transformations, health promotion interventions, and therapy. This section suggests the value of incorporating measures of positive ways of inhabiting the body into etiological and intervention research; such practice could strengthen both our understanding of well-being and distress and the outcome of our interventions.

The inextricable connection between positive ways of inhabiting the body and protective factors is reflected in the second section of the book that, we hope, propels the further study of a broad range of protective factors and guides practitioners and activists in implementing constructive changes in the social environment of youth and adults. The description of protective factors in this section starts with the physical experiences of mindful movement, personal safety, and connection to desires. Resistance to social expectations that regulate the way individuals inhabit their bodies, in particular objectification and other gender-related molds, comprises another group of protective factors. The last group of factors addresses the role of resistance to prejudices that disenfranchise particular bodies and of membership in accepting and protective social environments in enhancing positive ways of living in the body. This organization of the second section reflects the structure of protective factors described by the developmental theory of embodiment (Piran, 2016, 2017), highlighting the value of studying integrated etiological models. Future study of protective factors requires, in particular, research utilizing prospective designs, the examination of integrated etiological models, and intervention studies that are guided by known protective factors and that utilize measures of positive ways of inhabiting the body as a component of a comprehensive outcome evaluation. Furthermore, scholars must become activists to create movements that work to eradicate body-based stigmas (e.g., size, race, age, physical ability, social class, gender identity) and objectification, as well as become advocates for those individuals who face these stigmas and objectification. Indeed, only in environments free of stigma and objectification can individuals experience personal safety, which is bedrock to and safeguard of positive embodiment.

The third section of the book clarifies the value of adding a positive lens in examining established therapy and prevention interventions that have focused to date on reducing negative body image. The chapters delineate ways in which particular components of therapy (e.g., compassion- and emotion-focused therapies, acceptance and commitment therapy) and prevention (e.g., media literacy, cognitive dissonance, and mindfulness) link to elements of the constructs of positive embodiment and positive body image. Such affinity can help explain observed changes to body esteem and disordered eating patterns, as well as to positive body image and embodiment. Treatment and prevention approaches that focus directly on individuals' positive connection to their bodies, such as yoga and other movement-based approaches, are specific examples of the link between components of interventions and the constructs of positive embodiment and body image. Further, as authors suggest, the correspondence between aspects of interventions and dimensions of positive body image and embodiment also point at possible revisions to existing programs, such as placing greater emphasis on attunement to bodily needs and desires and on agency. In a similar vein, scrutinizing existing prevention programs aimed at lowering negative body image suggests that these programs already include a number of protective factors that are not often considered explicitly, such as the deepening of relational connections. The consideration of protective factors also indicates the potential benefit of adding protective factors, such as engagement in joyful physical activities. The search for constructive social transformations through changes to existing laws, policies, and norms can also be informed by protective factors, highlighting, in particular, the centrality of social justice in providing a constructive social environment where all bodies could flourish. There is therefore productive cross-fertilization between the fields of positive body image and embodiment and approaches to treatment and prevention. Future research should amplify on these important connections.

Across the domains of positive ways of inhabiting the body, protective factors, and interventions, research needs to be enriched by the studies of diverse populations across all aspects of social locations, such as gender, ethnicity/race, size, sexual orientations, gender identities, physical abilities, and appearance differences. Taking this a step further, we also must investigate how these social locations interlock and intersect to shape embodiment for all individuals, rather than only those with privileged social locations.

As a whole, the edited volume suggests many promising paths in incorporating a positive lens to the study of the way people inhabit their bodies and related protective factors and in enriching health promotion and therapy interventions. We are looking forward with much anticipation to future progress in these fields.

REFERENCES

Piran, N. (2016). Embodied possibilities and disruptions: The emergence of the Experience of Embodiment construct from qualitative studies with girls and women. *Body Image*, *18*, 43–60. doi:10.1016/j.bodyim.2016.04.007

Piran, N. (2017). *Journeys of embodiment at the intersection of body and culture: The developmental theory of embodiment*. San Diego, CA: Elsevier. doi: 10.1016/c2015-0-04666-4

INDEX

Tables and figures are indicated by an italic *t* and *f* following the paragraph number

Printed in the USA/Agawam, MA
May 2, 2022
792472.002